CRIMINAL LAW AND PROCEDURE

The West Legal Studies Series

Your options keep growing with West Legal Studies
Each year our list continues to offer you more options for every area of the law to meet your course or on-the-job reference requirements. We now have over 140 titles from which to choose in the following areas:

Administrative Law	Family Law
Alternative Dispute Resolution	Federal Taxation
Bankruptcy	Intellectual Property
Business Organizations/Corporations	Introduction to Law
Civil Litigation and Procedure	Introduction to Paralegalism
CLA Exam Preparation	Law Office Management
Client Accounting	Law Office Procedures
Computer in the Law Office	Legal Research, Writing, and Analysis
Constitutional Law	Legal Terminology
Contract Law	Paralegal Employment
Criminal Law and Procedure	Real Estate Law
Document Preparation	Reference Materials
Environmental Law	Torts and Personal Injury Law
Ethics	Will, Trusts, and Estate Administration

You will find unparalleled, practical support
Each book is augmented by instructor and student supplements to ensure the best learning experience possible. We also offer custom publishing and other benefits such as West's Student Achievement Award. In addition, our sales representatives are ready to provide you with dependable service.

We want to hear from you
Our best contributions for improving the quality of our books and instructional materials is feedback from the people who use them. If you have a question, concern, or observation about any of our materials, or you have a product proposal or manuscript, we want to hear from you. Please contact your local representative or write us at the following address:

West Legal Studies, 3 Columbia Circle, P.O. Box 15015, Albany, NY 12212-5015

For additional information point your browser at
www.westlegalstudies.com

WEST
THOMSON LEARNING

CRIMINAL LAW AND PROCEDURE

AN INTRODUCTION

SECOND EDITION

Ronald J. Bacigal
University of Richmond, Virginia

WEST
THOMSON LEARNING

Australia Canada Mexico Singapore Spain United Kingdom United States

WEST LEGAL STUDIES

Criminal Law and Procedure: An Introduction, Second Edition
by Ronald J. Bacigal

Business Unit Director:
Susan L. Simpfenderfer

Editorial Assistant:
Lisa Flatley

Executive Marketing Manager:
Donna J. Lewis

Executive Editor:
Marlene McHugh Pratt

Executive Production Manager:
Wendy A. Troeger

Channel Manager:
Nigar Hale

Acquisitions Editor:
Joan M. Gill

Production Manager:
Carolyn Miller

Cover Image:
©1999 Comstock, Inc.

Developmental Editor:
Rhonda Dearborn

Printed in the United States
1 2 3 4 5 XXX 05 04 03 02 01

For more information contact Delmar,
3 Columbia Circle, PO Box 15015,
Albany, NY 12212-5015.

Or find us on the World Wide Web at
http://www.westlegalstudies.com

For permission to use material from this text or product, contact us by
Tel (800) 730-2214
Fax (800) 730-2215
www.thomsonrights.com

Library of Congress Cataloging-in-Publication Data

Bacigal, Ronald J.
   Criminal law and procedure: an introduction / Ronald J. Bacigal.—
   2nd ed.
     p. cm.
   Includes index.
   ISBN 0-7668-3083-7
    1. Criminal law—United States. 2. Criminal procedure
    — United States. I. Title

KF9219 .B23 2001
345.73—dc21

2001026520

NOTICE TO THE READER

To Patty, Billy, Audrey and C.T.

BRIEF CONTENTS

Contents

CHAPTER 2

ESSENTIAL ELEMENTS OF CRIMES   27

CHAPTER 3

PARTIES TO A CRIME AND INCHOATE OFFENSES   43

CHAPTER 4

DEFENSES 61

CHAPTER 5

CRIMES AGAINST A PERSON 81

C H A P T E R   11

GOVERNMENT MONITORING OF COMMUNICATIONS AND THE FOURTH AMENDMENT EXCLUSIONARY RULE   213

C H A P T E R   12

INTERROGATION AND SELF-INCRIMINATION   231

C H A P T E R   13

PRELIMINARY STAGES OF THE PROSECUTION   253

C H A P T E R   1 4

PRETRIAL MOTIONS   273

C H A P T E R   1 5

TRIAL   297

C H A P T E R   16

VERDICT, PUNISHMENT, AND JUDICIAL REVIEW   317

GLOSSARY

INDEX

TABLE OF CASES

The principal cases are in bold type. References are to pages. Cases cited in principal cases and within other quoted materials are not included.

PREFACE

The goal of this book is to provide an introduction to both the practice and the theory of Criminal Law. Thus, it may be used in a number of diverse educational programs such as undergraduate criminal law classes, associate-degree criminal justice programs, or paralegal courses. Depending on the needs of the students, sections of the book addressing either theory or practice can be emphasized, ignored, or given cursory coverage. For example, in a course emphasizing theoretical aspects of the criminal justice system, the contractual relationship between counsel and client (Chapter Eight) can be deleted in favor of focusing on Chapter Eleven's coverage of the fundamental conflict between individual privacy and the government's use of electronic surveillance. In contrast, a course stressing the pragmatic aspects of criminal practice might cover the contractual nature of the attorney client relationship, while omitting coverage of electronic surveillance, which is used in only a small number of actual cases. The first half of the book covers substantive criminal law, while the second half discusses both the constitutional dimensions of criminal procedure and practical aspects of the criminal justice process.

Because this text covers both substantive criminal law and criminal procedure, it is suitable for a single course designed to provide an overview of the entire criminal justice system, or it can be used in separate courses focusing on either substantive or procedural law. If this book is used in separate courses covering substantive and procedural law, the text can be augmented with materials or lecture references to the laws of a specific jurisdiction. Chapters One through Seven define criminal responsibility and address the major felonies recognized in most if not all jurisdictions. Although these chapters provide a textual foundation for a course on substantive criminal law, they can be tailored to a particular jurisdiction by supplementing the text with statutory and case law from a specific locality. For example, Chapter Six acquaints students with the elements of common law burglary, but students preparing for careers as paralegals will need to become familiar with specific forms of statutory burglary in their own states.

In a course limited to the procedural aspects of criminal law, Chapters Eight through Sixteen contain enough material to support a semester-long course. Because a great deal of criminal procedure is of constitutional dimension, these chapters have universal application. There remains, however, ample opportunity to supplement constitutional procedure with the rules of a particular locality. For example, Chapter Fourteen notes that each jurisdiction has rules governing the timing and content of motions for pretrial discovery.

Whatever the nature of the course in which this book is used, the text material constitutes a narrative account of the law. Abundant case summaries are interwoven with the text to bring the "real world" into the classroom. The use of these case excerpts can be varied to suit individual tastes. The cases enhance the textual discussion of law, but for the most part, any case may be eliminated without depriving the student of exposure to the relevant law.

NEW TO THE SECOND EDITION

- Many new cases have been included in this second edition to illustrate key concepts. Some of these cases include *Hill v. State* in Chapter Four, *City of Indianapolis v. Edmond* in Chapter Nine, and *United States v. McVeigh* in Chapter Fourteen.
- New information on "Guilty but Mentally Ill" in Chapter Four.
- Added information on "Civil Rights and Hate Crimes" in Chapter Five.
- New information on "Voice Identification" in Chapter Nine.
- New material addressing special prosecutor Ken Starr and the *Clinton* case in Chapter Thirteen.
- New information on the scope of discovery and Rule 16 of the Federal Rules of Civil Procedure as well as the Jencks Act in Chapter Fourteen.
- Added information on "Discovery Orders Against the Victims or Third Parties" as well as "Remedies for Violation of Discovery Orders" in Chapter Fourteen.
- New information on "The Right to Appeal" and "Prosecution Appeals" in Chapter Sixteen.

CHAPTER FORMAT

- Chapter outlines open each chapter to focus attention on the main elements the student will encounter.
- Key terms are set in boldface type and defined in the margin where they first appear within the chapter.
- Exhibits, such as jury instructions, sample documents, and forms, illustrate how theories discussed in the chapter appear in the "real world."
- A chapter summary provides a brief review of the main points covered.
- Concept summary charts at the end of many chapters depict and contrast the key points covered.
- Discussion questions and practice exercises are designed to stimulate deliberation and practical application of the chapter material.
- Web sites that are germane to chapter materials.

SUPPORT MATERIAL

This book is accompanied by a support package that will assist students in learning and aid instructors in teaching. The following supplements accompany this text:

- An instructor's manual and testbank includes suggestions on classroom coverage, descriptions of hypothetical situations to stimulate classroom discussion, suggested "answers" or approaches to the discussion questions, and a brief summary of the facts and holding of each case cited within the chapter. A comprehensive test bank provides objective test questions and answers.
- The test bank found in the *Instructor's Manual* is also available in a computerized format on CD-ROM. The platforms supported include Windows 3.1, Windows 95, Windows NT, and Macintosh. Features include:
  - Multiple methods of question selection
  - Multiple outputs—that is print, ASCII, RTF
  - Graphic support (black and white)
  - Random questioning output

- Special character support
- Come visit us at westlegalstudies.com where you will find valuable information specific to this book such as hot links and sample materials to download, as well as other West Legal Studies products.

Additional support is available in the form of

- West's online computerized legal-research system offers students "hands-on" experience with a system commonly used in law offices. Qualified adopters can receive ten free hours of Westlaw®. Westlaw® can be accessed with Macintosh and IBM PCs and compatibles. A modem is required.
- *Strategies and Tips for Paralegal Educators,* a pamphlet by Anita Tebbe of Johnson County Community College, provides teaching strategies specifically designed for paralegal educators. A copy of this pamphlet is available to each adopter. Quantities for distribution to adjunct instructors are available for purchase at a minimal price. A coupon in the pamphlet provides ordering information.
- *Survival Guide for Paralegal Students,* a pamphlet by Kathleen Mercer Reed and Bradene Moore, covers practical and basic information to help students make the most of their paralegal courses. Topics covered include choosing courses of study and note-taking skills.
- West's Paralegal Video Library includes the following videos, which are available at no charge to qualified adopters:
- *The Drama of the Law II:* Paralegal Issues Video
- *I Never Said I Was a Lawyer:* Paralegal Issues Video
- The Making of a Case Video
- Mock Trial Videos—*Anatomy of a Trial: A Contracts Case—Business Litigation*
- Mock Trial Videos—*Trial Techniques: A Products Liability Case*
- Arguments to the United States Supreme Court
- Court TV videos that are available for purchase include:
- *New York v. Ferguson—Murder on the 5:33: The Trial of Colin Ferguson*
- *Ohio v. Alfieri—Road Rage*
- *Flynn v. Goldman Sachs—Fired on Wall Street: A Case of Sex Discrimination?*
- *Dodd v. Dodd: Religion and Child Custody in Conflict*
- *Fentress v. Eli Lilly & Co., et al.—Prozac on Trial*
- *In RE Custody of Baby Girl Clausen—Child of Mine: The Fight for Baby Jessica*

ACKNOWLEDGMENTS

My appreciation goes to the reviewers of the text for their ideas and suggestions on how to improve the text.

Suzanne Bailey, Western Illinois University, Illinois
Sharon Halford, Community College of Aurora, Colorado
Edwards C. O'Boyle, Gwinnett College of Business, Georgia
Linda Potter, Michigan Delta College
Joy Smucker, Highline Community College, Washington

A special thanks goes to the editors at West Publishing including Joan Gill (Acquisitions Editor), Rhonda Dearborn (Developmental Editor), and Carolyn Miller (Production Manager).

INTRODUCTION

OUTLINE

Criminal law is an intricate and fascinating subject. The American Bar Association maintains that criminal law is the proper concern of all lawyers, and it also is of primary concern to the general public. Any skeptics may view a typical night of television programs and compare the number of "cop" shows with the number of shows that focus on contract law or property law.

People have an understandable curiosity and fascination with a branch of law that deals with thieves, rapists, robbers, and murderers—the seamy side of life. At the other end of the spectrum, however, criminal law, primarily constitutional procedure, addresses our highest aspirations: the right to privacy, liberty, freedom, and the need to limit government power over "we the people." Prosecutors often see themselves as protecting the community from dangerous lawbreakers, while defense counsel frequently characterize themselves as "Liberty's Last Champion," the motto of the National Association of Criminal Defense Lawyers.

These diametrically opposed views of criminal law have produced a criminal justice system that is like no other in the world. The United States leads the Western world in the number of persons incarcerated and condemned to death. At the same time, this country outstrips all nations in the constitutional and procedural protections given to those accused of crime. Similar paradoxes are manifested in the substantive law which defines criminal conduct. For example, the U.S. Supreme Court has elevated freedom of speech to unprecedented heights and guards against legislative attempts to criminalize the exercise of free speech (e.g., burning the American flag). The same court, however, has deferred to state legislatures that promulgate what some perceive to be puritanical laws against private sexual conduct (e.g., premarital or same gender sex). You may judge for yourself whether these contradictions are part of the strength or weakness of the American criminal justice system.

The first part of this book addresses substantive criminal law, which declares what conduct is criminal. Chapters One through Four discuss general principles of criminality that apply to most if not all crimes. Chapters Five, Six, and Seven address the definition of specific offenses like murder or larceny. The second part of the book (Chapters Eight through Sixteen) addresses the procedures through which the substantive law is enforced. However, considering the complexity of criminal procedure, an overview of the criminal justice process and the steps that carry an individual case from start to finish is a helpful place to start.

OVERVIEW OF A CRIMINAL CASE

The procedural stages in a criminal case are not the same in all states. This overview presents a "typical felony case" in a "typical" jurisdiction.

Pre-arrest Investigation

When an alleged crime is reported or discovered, the police must investigate to determine whether a crime was committed, and if so, by whom. The principal participants in this "cops and robbers" stage are the police and those whom they suspect of criminal activity. The courts, prosecutors, and defense counsel normally address the investigatory process in retrospect when determining whether the police acted in accordance with constitutional or statutory provisions governing police investigative practices. Chapters Nine, Ten, and Eleven address the most frequently litigated pre-arrest investigative procedures: temporary detentions, search and seizure, and electronic surveillance.

Arrest

An arrest generally occurs when the police investigation uncovers facts sufficient to constitute probable cause to arrest—in other words, a reasonable belief that the suspect committed a crime. Although a judicial officer, normally a magistrate, may determine the adequacy of the facts constituting probable cause and issue an arrest warrant, the majority of arrests are made by police officers acting without a judicially issued warrant.

An arrest, of course, does not mean the end of police investigation of the crime. Incident to arrest, the police officer usually will search the suspect's person and remove any weapons, contraband, or evidence relating to the crime. Following arrest, police investigation may continue in the form of interrogation of the suspect, further searches for additional evidence, or placing the suspect in a lineup or other identification procedure.

Booking Process

In a typical arrest, the arrestee is transported to the police station and subjected to what is known as a booking process. The process is primarily clerical in nature and consists of (1) completing the arrest report and preparing the arrestee's permanent police record, (2) fingerprinting and photographing the arrestee, and (3) entering on the police "blotter" the name of the arrestee, the personal effects found in that person's possession, and the date, time, and place of arrest.

First Appearance Before a Judicial Officer

A person held in police custody has a right to a judicial hearing on the grounds for detaining the person. If the suspect was arrested without an arrest warrant, a judicial officer (perhaps a lower court judge, often a magistrate) must determine whether the police had probable cause to arrest the accused. If probable cause is lacking, the suspect must be released from custody. If the arrest was lawful, the judicial officer must determine whether to hold the arrestee in pretrial custody, or set bail, in which case the accused will be released pending trial. Bail may consist of posting cash or a secured bond with the court, or the accused may be released into the custody of another or released on "personal recognizance," which is an unsecured promise to appear for trial.

Preliminary Hearing

Many jurisdictions have eliminated the preliminary hearing stage and allow the prosecutor to go forward with the case by filing an "information" stating the charges, or by taking the case directly to a grand jury, which may indict the accused for specific crimes. A preliminary hearing is a judicial proceeding to determine whether there are reasonable grounds to require the accused to stand trial. The prime distinction between a preliminary hearing and a first appearance is that the preliminary hearing is an adversary proceeding in which the accused is allowed to introduce evidence, whereas a first appearance is normally an *ex parte* proceeding in which the judge or magistrate hears only the evidence that constituted probable cause to arrest the accused.

If the preliminary hearing judge determines that reasonable grounds to try the accused have not been shown, the accused must be released from custody. This release, however, is not an acquittal; a grand jury may subsequently indict the accused for the crime and force the accused to stand trial on the indictment.

Grand Jury Indictment

Many jurisdictions require that all felony charges be submitted to a grand jury composed of citizens selected to review the evidence and determine whether the evidence is sufficient to justify a trial on the charge sought by the prosecution. A grand jury has significant power to investigate crime, primarily by subpoenaing witnesses and documentary evidence relevant to the charge. Generally, only the prosecution's evidence is presented to the grand jury; the accused is not heard, nor is defense counsel permitted to be present or offer any evidence.

1. Arraignment and Plea

Arraignment consists of bringing the accused before the court, informing that person of the charges, and asking the accused to enter a plea to the charges. In some jurisdictions, arraignment may take place weeks in advance of the actual trial, while other jurisdictions postpone arraignment until the trial is scheduled to begin.

In most jurisdictions, the accused may enter a plea of guilty, not guilty, or *nolo contendere*. A plea of nolo contendere has the same effect as a plea of guilty, except that the admission of guilt cannot be used as evidence in any other action. For example, former Vice President Spiro Agnew pled nolo contendere to bribery charges, but the plea was not admissible in subsequent civil litigation concerning whether taxes were due on the unreported bribes.

In the majority of cases, the defendant's guilt and the applicable range of sentences are determined by a plea agreement struck between the prosecutor and defense counsel. In most plea agreements, the defendant agrees to plead guilty to a charge in exchange for the prosecutor's promise to drop other charges or to recommend a reduced sentence.

2. Pretrial Motions

Pretrial motions are requests that the trial court take some action, such as dismissing a defective indictment, ruling on the admissibility of illegally obtained evidence, or ordering the parties to disclose certain information. In essence, these matters can or must be disposed of prior to the trial on the merits of the case. All jurisdictions have rules governing the time period within which pretrial motions must be filed with the trial court.

3. Trial

The American criminal justice system is an adversarial process that assigns each participant in the trial a defined role. The judge is not an advocate for either side, but is concerned with enforcing procedural rules. The prosecutor's primary task is to marshall the evidence against the defendant. The defendant has no obligation to present any evidence or play any part in the trial, because a defendant may rely on the presumption of innocence and remain passive during the trial. The defense attorney is an advocate for the accused, with the primary responsibility of winning the case without violating the law. The jury (or the judge alone in a bench trial) hears the evidence from both sides and must decide whether the defendant committed the charged offense.

4. Sentencing

Some states permit the jury to set the punishment, but most jurisdictions entrust sentencing to the trial judge. By statute, certain convictions require a mandatory sentence, in which case the judge has no discretion. In most cases, the judge exercises some discretion and may impose any sentence within statutory limitations, or the judge may determine the appropriate sentence according to sentencing guidelines enacted by the legislature. As part of the sentencing determination, the judge also may be empowered to suspend a portion of the sentence and place the defendant on probation. Parole and time off for "good behavior" are awarded by correctional authorities and are not part of the initial sentencing process.

Appeal and Habeas Corpus

A convicted defendant may appeal a conviction to an appellate court, which will review the trial proceedings and either reverse or affirm the trial court decision. If the conviction is "reversed and remanded," then the defendant's conviction is set aside, although the defendant may be required to stand trial again. A second trial may be precluded, however, if the appellate court reverses the conviction because of insufficient evidence to justify the conviction.

The excerpts of cases in this book are the written opinions of appellate courts, announcing and often explaining their decisions. Most opinions are signed by one judge, and when joined by a majority of the judges, this opinion constitutes the judgment of the court. Judges who agree with the decision but wish to address other considerations may write separate concurring opinions. Judges who disagree with the court's decision may write dissenting opinions.

If the attempt to obtain a reversal of the conviction on appeal fails, the defendant may file a collateral attack on the conviction, the most common form of collateral attack being a *habeas corpus* petition. A habeas corpus petition is a collateral attack because it is not a continuation of the criminal process, but a civil suit brought to challenge the legality of the restraint under which a person is held. (*Habeas corpus* is a Latin term meaning "you have the body.") Because the action is a civil suit, the petitioner (the confined person) has the burden to prove that the confinement is illegal.

CRIMINAL JUSTICE PROFESSIONALS

Like any organization, the operation of our criminal justice system is dependent on the people who administer the system. Because of the popularity of movies and television shows about criminal justice, most people are familiar with the roles played by police officers, prosecutors, defense attorneys, and judges. Less publicized, but no less important, is the vital role played by coroners, magistrates, court clerks, probation officers, and paralegals.

Law Enforcement Agencies

Law enforcement agencies are charged with enforcing criminal laws that range from traffic offenses to serious felonies. At the national level, the Federal Bureau of Investigation (FBI) is the largest agency empowered to deal with violations of federal criminal laws. In addition to the FBI, other federal agencies investigate specific types of violations of federal law: for example, the Drug Enforcement Administration; the Bureau of Alcohol, Tobacco, and Firearms; the Customs Service; the Secret Service; and the Immigration and Naturalization Service.

At the state level, the State Police are charged with prevention and investigation of all crimes covered by state law. At the local level, police departments or sheriff's offices exercise broad powers as the chief law enforcement officers of their communities. Their responsibilities include enforcing state law as well as local ordinances.

Prosecutorial Agencies

Prosecutorial agencies review the information gathered by law enforcement agencies and decide whether to proceed with formal charges. At the national level, the U.S. Department of Justice and U.S. Attorney's offices, distributed geographically throughout the country, initiate a prosecution for a federal offense. At the state level, the State Attorney General's office may initiate certain prosecutions, but such offices normally limit their function to handling appeals of convictions. Most state prosecutions are initiated by district attorneys geographically distributed throughout the state.

Defense Bar

Criminal defendants may hire attorneys to represent them in all criminal prosecutions, no matter how minor the offense. Indigents, who cannot afford to hire counsel, may have defense counsel appointed at public expense whenever the indigent faces possible imprisonment. Many states have established a public defender's office to represent indigents. As a supplement to, or in place of, a public defender's office, many states utilize a court-appointed list of attorneys who have volunteered or been recruited to represent indigents.

Courts

In the federal system, the principal trial court is the U.S. District Court, which presides over the prosecution of serious federal crimes. Trials of federal misdemeanors are often handled by federal magistrates, who are appointed by federal district judges. The U.S. Circuit Courts of Appeal hear appeals from convictions in the District Court. Thirteen judicial circuits cover the United States and its possessions. The U.S. Supreme Court reviews the decisions of the lower federal courts and many decisions of the state courts.

The structure of state court systems vary considerably, but every state has one or more levels of trial courts and at least one appellate court. A common arrangement of a state court system includes a lower court, often called police court, magistrate court, or a court-not-of-record, which tries minor or petty offenses; a higher trial court, often called a court-of-record, which tries more serious offenses; and an appellate court, which reviews the decisions of the lower courts.

Coroners

A coroner's inquest is peculiar to homicide cases, and its function is to determine the cause of death. Although this determination is merely advisory and can be either accepted or ignored by the prosecutor, the inquest may uncover evidence useful to both the prosecution and the defense. Many jurisdictions have replaced the coroner system (which sometimes required a finding by the coroner's jury made up of six laypersons) with a medical examiner system staffed by forensic pathologists.

Magistrates

In some jurisdictions, magistrates are judges who preside over lower courts (often called magistrate or police court) in which traffic violations and minor misdemeanors are tried. In other jurisdictions, magistrates have no trial jurisdiction. As their primary function, they determine whether there is probable cause to issue search or arrest warrants. They also determine the conditions of any pretrial release of an arrested suspect.

Court Clerks

Court clerks, who may be elected or appointed in a given jurisdiction, handle the vast amount of paperwork involved in bringing a case to trial. For example, the clerk's office may be responsible for issuing subpoenas for witnesses or documents; filing the formal charge upon which the accused will stand trial; summoning the jurors and administering requests to be excused from jury duty; scheduling the court's docket and use of multiple courtrooms; and receiving pretrial motions requesting the court to take some form of action.

Probation Officers

Convicted defendants are sometimes granted a suspended sentence and may avoid incarceration as long as they demonstrate good behavior and comply with the terms of the court's granting of probation. Probation officers supervise the conduct of the individual on probation by monitoring whether the individual is gainfully employed, has made restitution to any victim of the crime, and is avoiding further breaches of the law. Prior to conviction, probation officers may be ordered to investigate the background of the defendant and prepare a presentence report recommending an appropriate sentence.

Paralegals

Like court clerks, paralegals may be responsible for organizing the vast amount of paperwork often generated by a criminal case: for example, obtaining and filing police reports, coroner's finding, transcripts of a preliminary hearing, grand jury indictments, and requests for and responses to pretrial discovery motions. What may be unique to criminal justice paralegals is their involvement in the factual investigation and legal research surrounding the case.

As part of their tasks related to *factual* investigation, paralegals may be asked to interview victims, witnesses, and police officers; draft preliminary charges when assisting a prosecutor; draft motions to dismiss the complaint when assisting defense counsel; draft subpoenas and locate witnesses; and prepare trial notebooks that organize the presentation of evidence, particularly any documents or exhibits to be used at trial.

Criminal justice paralegals are also responsible for many *legal* tasks requiring them to research the substantive law governing the charged offense, draft pretrial motions or responses to such motions, draft legal memoranda and briefs on contested points of law, prepare presentence reports or responses to such reports, and draft posttrial motions.

Summary

Although the specific tasks of criminal justice professionals vary, a fundamental knowledge of the substantive criminal law and the essence of criminal procedure is crucial to the performance of a criminal justice professional. In simplified form, the foundation for this specialized knowledge of the criminal justice system is the subject matter of this book.

SUBSTANTIVE CRIMINAL LAW

Part I

DEFINING AND PROVING CRIMES

Chapter *1*

CHAPTER OUTLINE

THE PURPOSES OF CRIMINAL LAW

Theories of Punishment

In the broadest sense, both civil and criminal law are attempts to create and maintain "the good society." The law of torts, the law of contracts, and every other branch of civil law prohibit or require specific conduct within the social community. For example, tort law demands that citizens behave reasonably to avoid injuring others. Contract law commands citizens to honor the commitments pledged in contracts. Failure to live up to these requirements subjects the citizen to suit in the civil courts and to the imposition of civil sanctions, most commonly, paying money damages to an injured party. Thus, civil law governs the issues that arise between individual parties over private rights. In a typical civil case, suit is brought by the injured party for damage to that party's personal rights, person, or property. The injured party (the plaintiff) seeks some sort of compensation (usually monetary) for the injury to that party's person or property.

As civil law does, criminal law also prohibits or requires specified conduct. Some of the commands of the criminal law are expressed as affirmative requirements to "file your income tax return," or "take care of your children." But most criminal law commands are prohibitions of conduct—"Do not murder, rape, or rob." Criminal law thus encompasses principles of right and wrong as well as the principle that wrong will result in penalty. A criminal case is brought by the government for violation or injury to public rights, and an individual who violates criminal laws has damaged the rights of the public as a whole, regardless of the status of any individual victim.

Of course those individual victims may pursue civil suits because a single act may give rise to both criminal and civil cases. The most famous example is the litigation surrounding O. J. Simpson. In criminal proceedings, Simpson was initially tried and acquitted of two charges of murder. The families of the victims then brought and prevailed in a civil suit against Simpson for wrongful death. (The constitutional prohibition against double jeopardy precludes multiple criminal prosecutions for the same offense, but has no application to civil suits.)

Thus, the most fundamental difference between the two branches of law is that civil law normally focuses on compelling a person to compensate an individual victim for any harm suffered, whereas criminal law uses punishment as a means of controlling the behavior of citizens. (Conviction of a crime carries a penalty of imprisonment or a fine paid to the government rather than to a particular victim.)

The forms of punishment utilized by the criminal justice system are designed to control behavior in a variety of ways:

1. *Incapacitation/Restraint:* Executing a criminal is the most extreme form of rendering a person incapable of committing future crimes. Criminals restrained in prison cannot cause further harm to the general public during the length of their sentence.

2. *Specific deterrence:* By punishing the criminal for the crime, society demonstrates its ability and willingness to protect itself against those who commit crimes. After being exposed to society's power to punish, the criminal will be taught a lesson and will refrain from any future misconduct.

3. *General deterrence:* When the general public observes criminals being punished for their crimes the public is deterred from criminal conduct for fear of similar punishment. The effectiveness of this rationale depends on the degree of punishment and the degree of certainty that criminals will be caught, convicted, and punished.

4. *Rehabilitation:* Society may seek to prevent a criminal from committing other crimes by forcing that person to undergo training, psychological counseling, or some form of moral or social education as to the need for law-abiding patterns of behavior.

5. *Retribution:* Punishment may express the moral condemnation of the community and is a lawful means of avenging a wrong. In upholding the constitutionality of the death penalty, the U.S. Supreme Court noted that "capital punishment is an expression of society's moral outrage at particularly offensive conduct. This function may be unappealing to many, but it is essential in an ordered society that asks its citizens to rely on legal processes rather than self-help to vindicate wrongs."[1] Public retribution also lessens the desire for private retribution by the victim or others who might seek personal revenge for the criminal's wrongdoing. For example, if the law punishes a Hatfield for killing a McCoy, the McCoys have less need to avenge their kin's death.

To a greater or lesser extent, all penal systems rely on a mixture of incapacitation, deterrence, rehabilitation, and retribution.

THE SOURCES OF CRIMINAL LAW

Criminal offenses are defined by common law, statute, or administrative regulation. Except for the crime of treason, constitutions generally do not delineate crimes, but constitutions impose limitations on the government's power to define criminal conduct.

Common Law

A great deal of our modern-day criminal law has its roots in English common law. English criminal law in the seventeenth and eighteen centuries was **common law** because the definition of crimes and the rules of criminal responsibility were largely promulgated and shaped by judges based on custom and tradition. (When a legislative body enacts penal statutes, judges may be restricted to interpreting statutory law and thus have less freedom to apply custom and tradition.) Far from being a matter of common sense or common knowledge, however, the common law was an elaborate set of rules generally understood only by the legal profession. William Penn demonstrated this point by persistently challenging a disconcerted court recorder's understanding of common law.

Common law
judge-made law defining crimes and establishing the rules of criminal responsibility according to custom and tradition.

TRIAL OF WILLIAM PENN
6 How.St.Trials 951 (1670)

Penn: *I desire you would let me know by what law it is you prosecute me, and upon what law you ground my indictment.*

Rec: *Upon the common law.*

Penn: *Where is that common law?*

Rec: *You must not think that I am able to run up so many years, and over so many adjudged cases, which we call common law, to answer your curiosity.*

Penn: *This answer I am sure is very short of my question, for if it be common, it should not be so hard to produce.*

Rec: *The question is, whether you are Guilty of this Indictment?*

Penn: *The question is not, whether I am Guilty of this Indictment, but whether this Indictment be legal. It is too general and imperfect an answer, to say it is the common law, unless we knew both where and what it is. For where there is no law, there is no transgression; and that law which is not*

in being, is so far from being common, that it is no law at all.

Rec: *You are an impertinent fellow, will you teach the court what the law is? It is Lex non scripts, that which many have studied 30 or 40 years to know, and would you have me tell you in a moment?*

Penn: *Certainly, if the common law be so hard to understand it is far from being common.*

Judicial activism
interpretation of the law by judges to achieve broad social goals.

Judicial restraint
practiced by judges who view judicial power as strictly limited by the separation of powers doctrine and by earlier case decisions.

American criminal law in the twentieth century is largely governed by penal statutes (enacted by Congress or state legislatures) that supplement or replace the common law. When the legislature rather than the judiciary formulates rules of criminal responsibility, a controversy may arise as to whether the judiciary retains authority to enforce, create, or reshape common law offenses. In many ways, this controversy is one facet of the debate between **judicial activism** employed by judges who interpret law as a means to achieve social goals; and judges who practice **judicial restraint** by viewing judicial power as strictly limited by the separation of powers doctrine. The clash between judicial activism and judicial restraint lies at the heart of *Shaw v. Director of Public Prosecutions.*

SHAW v. DIRECTOR OF PUBLIC PROSECUTIONS
House of Lords (1961)
2 W.L.R. 897, 2 All E.R. 446

The defendant, Frederick C. Shaw, published "The Ladies Directory," a booklet of some 28 pages, most of which were taken up with the names and addresses of women who were prostitutes, together with a number of photographs of nude female figures; and the matter published left no doubt that the advertisers could be got in touch with at the telephone numbers given and were offering their services for sexual intercourse and, in some cases, for the practice of sexual perversions. Shaw was convicted of "conspiracy to corrupt public morals" and appealed to the House of Lords. [Shaw was not charged with conspiracy to commit prostitution, because prostitution was not a crime in England].

VISCOUNT SIMMONDS

My Lords . . . I do not insist that every immoral act is indictable, such as telling a lie, or the like; but if it is destructive of morality in general, if it does, or may, affect all the King's subjects, it then is an offense of a public nature. In the sphere of criminal law I entertain no doubt that there remains in the courts of law a residual power to enforce the supreme and fundamental purpose

of the law, to conserve not only the safety and order but also the moral welfare of the State, and that it is their duty to guard it against attacks which may be the more insidious because they are novel and unprepared for. That is the broad head (call it public policy if you wish) within which the present indictment falls.

In the past, when Lord Mansfield declared that the Court of King's Bench was the *custos morum* [the guardian of morals] of the people and had the superintendency of offenses *conta bonos mores* [contrary to good morals], he was asserting, as I now assert, that there is in that court a residual power, where no statute has yet intervened to supersede the common law, to superintend those offences which are prejudicial to the public welfare. Such occasions will be rare, for Parliament has not been slow to legislate when attention has been sufficiently aroused. But gaps remain and will always remain since no one can foresee every way in which the wickedness of man may disrupt the order of society. I say, my Lords, that if the common law is powerless in such an event, then we should no longer do her reverence. But I say that her hand is still powerful and that it is for Her Majesty's judges to play the part which Lord Mansfield pointed out to them.

LORD REED

In my opinion there is no such general offence known to the law as conspiracy to corrupt public morals. To superintend the wickedness of man would leave it to the judges to declare new crimes and enable them to hold anything which they considered prejudicial to the community to be a misdemeanor. However beneficial that might have been in days when Parliament met seldom, or at least only at long intervals it surely is now the province of the legislature and not the judiciary to create new criminal offences.

Finally I must advert to the consequences of holding that this very general offense exists. It has always been thought to be of primary importance that our law, and particularly our criminal law, should be certain: that a man should be able to know what conduct is and what conduct is not criminal, particularly when heavy penalties are involved.

In the United States, the issue in *Shaw* would not be presented in such dramatic fashion. Even the most "activist" U.S. judge would be reluctant to claim power to act as enforcer of good public morals. However, constitutional litigation often raises questions of the relationship between the judicial function and public morals, particularly when expressed by a democratically elected legislature. For example, may a state legislature prohibit "immoral" sex between adult members of the same gender? The U.S. Supreme Court said yes in *Bowers v. Hardwick*.[2] (Refer to Chapter Seven.)

Model Penal Code

The courts of a particular jurisdiction may or may not be free to apply the common law depending on whether the particular jurisdiction has abolished common law crimes or retained the portions of common law unaltered by statute. Even in jurisdictions where the common law has been abolished, the court may sometimes consult the common law for whatever persuasive effect it has in analyzing statutory language. A court may also look to the Model Penal Code as a nonbinding guide to interpreting criminal law.

The **Model Penal Code** is a suggested model to guide enactment and interpretation of criminal law. The Code was promulgated by the American Law Institute, an association of lawyers, judges, and legal scholars. The Code is not law unless adopted and enacted by a legislature. Nonetheless, courts frequently cite the Model Penal Code as a rational and helpful guide to understanding criminal law.

Model Penal Code
a suggested guide for enactment and interpretation of criminal law; the Code is not law unless adopted and enacted by a legislature.

Statutory Law

The common law evolved through judicial decisions that sometimes identified obscure general principles subject to elaborate exceptions or technical qualifications. For example, common law arson covered the burning of a home, but not the use of explosives to destroy a home, unless some portion of the structure remained standing and caught fire after the explosion. These seemingly arbitrary interpretations can sometimes be explained by a common law judge's desire to avoid imposing the death penalty on the defendant. (All but the most minor crimes mandated capital punishment.) The logic behind other common law doctrines, if such logic ever existed, has been lost to antiquity. Finally, in some cases it may be that Charles Dickens's caustic comment is true: "If the law say that; the law be an ass."

When legislatures take over the primary task of defining crimes by enacting criminal codes, they often attempt to state the law in a more straightforward fashion. But despite the legislature's best efforts, some ambiguity will always be present in criminal codes. At other times a statute may be kept deliberately vague as part of a compromise to ensure its passage. In either case, the common law may assist a

Legislative intent
the purpose for which the legislators enacted a particular statute.

court in interpreting criminal law statutes. The common law, however, must yield to the clear language of the statute and to the **legislative intent** underlying the statute. (The intent of particular legislators is often expressed during debate over passage of a proposed statute.) Courts also may be called on to resolve a conflict between the words actually used in a statute, and what the legislature intended the words to mean. The conflict between legislative intent and the plain meaning of a statute divided the U.S. Supreme Court in *Caminetti v. United States.*

CAMINETTI v. UNITED STATES
Supreme Court of the United States, 1917
242 U.S. 470, 37 S.Ct. 192

[The case consolidated three convictions for violation of the White Slave Traffic Act—transporting women in interstate commerce for purposes of debauchery and for an immoral purpose. Each of the three defendants had transported a woman across state lines for the purpose of having the woman serve as his mistress and concubine.]

JUSTICE DAY delivered the opinion of the Court:

It is contended that the act of Congress is intended to reach only "commercialized vice," or the traffic in women for gain, and that the conduct for which the several petitioners were indicted and convicted, however, reprehensible in morals, is not within the purview of the statute when properly construed in the light of its history and the purposes intended to be accomplished by its enactment. In none of the cases was it charged or proved that the transportation was for gain or for the purpose of furnishing women for prostitution for hire, and it is insisted that, such being the case, the acts charged and proved, upon which conviction was had, do not come within the statute.

It is elementary that the meaning of a statute must, in the first instance, be sought in the language in which the act is framed, and if that is plain, and if the law is within the constitutional authority of the law-making body which passed it, the sole function of the courts is to enforce it according to its terms. Although the legislative history surrounding the White Slave Traffic Act indicates that Congress was primarily concerned with

"commerce" and "pecuniary gain" arising from White Slavery, when the language of the statute itself is plain, and not leading to absurd or wholly impracticable consequences, it is the sole evidence of the ultimate legislative intent. [Convictions upheld.]

JUSTICE McKENNA, dissenting:

The drafter of the White Slavery Act stated to Congress that: "The legislation is not needed or intended as an aid to the states in the exercise of the police powers in the suppression or regulation of immorality in general. It does not attempt to regulate the practice of voluntary prostitution, but aims solely to prevent panderers and procurers from compelling thousands of women and girls against their will and desire to enter and continue in a life of prostitution."

In other words, it is vice as a business at which the law is directed, using interstate commerce as a facility to procure or distribute its victims. This being the purpose, the words of the statute should be construed to execute it, and they may be so construed even if their literal meaning be otherwise. The judicial function should not shut its eyes to the facts of the world and assume not to know what everybody else knows. And everybody knows that there is a difference between the occasional immoralities of men and women and that systematized and mercenary immorality epitomized in the statute's graphic phrase "white slave traffic." And it was such immorality that was in the legislative mind, and not the other.

As recent Supreme Court nominees have learned, judicial interpretation of law fuels the political debate regarding judicial restraint and judicial activism. On a more practical level, interpretation of statutes is what allows judges, lawyers, and paralegals to ply their trade. An old adage advises lawyers, "If the law is against you, argue the facts. If the facts are against you, argue the law." This type of advice may apply when choosing whether to argue in favor of legislative intent or in favor of giving a statute its literal meaning. Any judge, lawyer, or paralegal must be prepared to research and analyze alternative ways of reading criminal statutes.

Although there is almost always some ambiguity in statutes, too much uncertainty can render the statute unconstitutionally vague—subject to the **vagueness doctrine**—when "men of common intelligence must necessarily guess at its meaning and differ as to its application."[3] Statutes punishing vagrants or "street people" are prime examples of impermissibly vague legislation because such statutes often loosely define vagrants as "rogues and vagabond, or dissolute persons, common drunkards, and persons wandering or strolling around from place to place without any lawful purpose." Such overly nebulous vagrancy statutes invite police and prosecutors to harass or punish persons whose lifestyles are offensive to them. The *Morales* case demonstrates that the vagueness doctrine places restrictions upon even understandable attempts to "preserve the city's streets and other public places so that the public may use such places without fear."

vagueness doctrine
holds any statute unconstitutional when citizens "must necessarily guess at its meaning and differ as to its application."

CITY OF CHICAGO v. MORALES
527 U.S. 41, 119 S.Ct. 1849 (1999)

JUSTICE STEVENS announced the judgment of the Court:

In 1992, the Chicago City Council enacted the Gang Congregation Ordinance, which prohibits "criminal street gang members" from "loitering" with one another or with other persons in any public place. The council found that "loitering in public places by criminal street gang members creates a justifiable fear for the safety of persons and property in the area" and that "aggressive action is necessary to preserve the city's streets and other public places so that the public may use such places without fear." The ordinance creates a criminal offense punishable by a fine of up to $500, imprisonment for not more than six months, and a requirement to perform up to 120 hours of community service.

Commission of the offense involves four predicates. First, the police officer must reasonably believe that at least one of the two or more persons present in a "public place" is a "criminal street gang member." Second, the persons must be "loitering," which the ordinance defines as "remaining in any one place with no apparent purpose." Third, the officer must then order "all" of the persons to disperse and remove themselves "from the area." Fourth, the person must disobey the officer's order. If any person, whether a gang member or not, disobeys the officer's order, that person is guilty of violating the ordinance.

Vagueness may invalidate a criminal law for either of two independent reasons. First, it may fail to provide the kind of notice that will enable ordinary people to understand what conduct it prohibits; second, it may au-

thorize and even encourage arbitrary and discriminatory enforcement. Accordingly, we first consider whether the ordinance provides fair notice to the citizen and then discuss its potential for arbitrary enforcement.

It is established that a law fails to meet the requirements of the Due Process Clause if it is so vague and standardless that it leaves the public uncertain as to the conduct it prohibits. The term "loiter" may have a common and accepted meaning, but the definition of that term in this ordinance—"to remain in any one place with no apparent purpose"—does not. It is difficult to imagine how any citizen of the city of Chicago standing in a public place with a group of people would know if he or she had an "apparent purpose." If she were talking to another person, would she have an apparent purpose? If she were frequently checking her watch and looking expectantly down the street, would she have an apparent purpose?

Since the city cannot conceivably have meant to criminalize each instance a citizen stands in public with a gang member, the vagueness that dooms this ordinance is not the product of uncertainty about the normal meaning of "loitering," but rather about what loitering is covered by the ordinance and what is not. The broad sweep of the ordinance also violates the requirement that a legislature establish minimal guidelines to govern law enforcement. There are no such guidelines in the ordinance. In any public place in the city of Chicago, persons who stand or sit in the company of a gang member may be ordered to disperse unless their purpose is apparent. The mandatory language in the enactment directs the police to issue an order without first making any inquiry about their possible purposes. It matters not whether the reason that a gang member and his father, for example, might loiter near Wrigley Field is to rob an unsuspecting fan or just to get a glimpse of Sammy Sosa leaving the ballpark; in either event, if their purpose is not apparent to a nearby police officer, she may—indeed, she "shall"—order them to disperse.

Recognizing that the ordinance does reach a substantial amount of innocent conduct, we turn, then, to its language to determine if it "necessarily entrusts lawmaking to the moment-to-moment judgment of the policeman on his beat." As we discussed in the context of fair notice, the principal source of the vast discretion conferred on the police in this case is the definition of loitering as "to remain in any one place with no apparent purpose."

As the Illinois Supreme Court interprets that definition, it "provides absolute discretion to police officers to determine what activities constitute loitering." The "no apparent purpose" standard for making that decision is inherently subjective because its application depends on whether some purpose is "apparent" to the officer on the scene. It applies to everyone in the city who may remain in one place with one suspected gang member as long as their purpose is not apparent to an officer observing them. Friends, relatives, teachers, counselors, or even total strangers might unwittingly engage in forbidden loitering if they happen to engage in idle conversation with a gang member.

In our judgment, the ordinance does not provide sufficiently specific limits on the enforcement discretion of the police "to meet constitutional standards for definiteness and clarity." We recognize the serious and difficult problems testified to by the citizens of Chicago that led to the enactment of this ordinance. We are mindful that the preservation of liberty depends in part on the maintenance of social order. However, in this instance the city has enacted an ordinance that affords too much discretion to the police and too little notice to citizens who wish to use the public streets.

Accordingly, we conclude that the ordinance enacted by the city of Chicago is unconstitutionally vague.

Administrative Regulations

The vagueness doctrine applies to both statutes and administrative regulations because the U.S. Supreme Court has recognized that administrative agencies may define criminal violations in promulgated regulations if the legislature provides sufficiently detailed standards to guide the drafting of regulations.

Although most crimes are defined in statutes or court decisions, administrative regulations also may identify certain conduct as criminal in nature. For example, the Internal Revenue Service (IRS) and the Environmental Protection Agency (EPA) promulgate regulations that supplement the more general laws enacted by Congress. In such situations, the courts must determine whether the regulating agency has acted within its delegated authority, or whether the agency has usurped the legislative power to make laws.

UNITED STATES v. MITCHELL
United States Court of Appeals, Fourth Circuit, 1994
39 F.3d 465 (4th cir. 1994)

OPINION OF THE COURT:
Mitchell was employed by the Fish and Wildlife Service of the United States Department of the Interior (FWS). Outside his employment at the FWS, Mitchell booked big-game hunting trips to Asia and promoted sport-hunting programs of exotic wild animals.

An acquaintance of Mitchell, Don Cox, travelled to the Punjab province of Pakistan where he illegally hunted and killed two Punjab urials and a Chinkara gazelle. Because he could not obtain permits from Pakistani wildlife authorities to export the hides and horns, Cox arranged to have Mitchell smuggle them out of Pakistan and into the United States.

On September 25, 1987, Mitchell arrived with the contraband at Dulles International Airport. He completed a United States Customs Service Declaration Form, but did not complete a FWS Declaration for Importation or Exportation of Fish or Wildlife Form. And, Mitchell failed to disclose that he was importing untanned animal hides into the United States.

Mitchell was convicted of violating 18 U.S.C. § 545 by importing merchandise "contrary to law" in that he failed to: (1) declare the items as required by the Customs regulation; (2) file a form required by the FWS regulation; and (3) comply with the Agriculture regulation.

[Mitchell contended that the "contrary to law" provision of § 545 does not embrace administrative regulations.]

In determining the scope of the "contrary to law" provision of § 545, we first examine the language of the statute. Because the word "law" within the meaning of § 545 is not defined, we must give the word its ordinary meaning. "Law" is commonly defined to include administrative regulations.

For regulations to have the force and effect of law they must first be "substantive" or "legislative-type" rules, as opposed to "interpretive rules, general statements of policy, or rules of agency organization, procedure, or practice." An inherent characteristic of a "substantive rule" is that it is "one affecting individual rights and obligations." Second, the regulation must have been promulgated pursuant to a congressional grant of quasi-legislative authority. Third, the regulation must have been promulgated in conformity with congressionally imposed procedural requirements such as the notice and comment provision of the Administrative Procedure Act.

Because the regulations Mitchell was charged with violating affect individual rights and obligations, were authorized and contemplated by appropriate grants of quasi-legislative authority, and were promulgated in conformity with applicable procedural requirements, we conclude that those regulations have the force and effect of law and therefore are encompassed by the "contrary to law" provision of § 545.

DISSENTING OPINION:

Where, as here, a defendant does something unpleasant, and does it in an underhanded way, the inclination is to uphold his conviction. However, I do not believe that is the proper and acceptable course when the statute under which he was convicted does not reach him. Accordingly, I respectfully dissent, even though applying the law correctly would lead to a nonserendipitous result.

It is not irrational to require Congress, if it means something, to say it. The language of the statute under which defendant Richard M. Mitchell was convicted, 18 U.S.C. § 545, prohibits importation into the United States in a manner "contrary to law." The question here is whether law means only statutory law or whether it also extends to Customs Service, Fish and Wildlife Service, and Department of Agriculture regulations. Unlike the majority, I conclude that it is grievously ambiguous whether failure to comply with a regulation is included within the statutory phrase "contrary to law," and that the ambiguity should therefore be applied in favor of the defendant.

Constitutional Limitations

The vagueness doctrine does not challenge the legislature's power to define crimes, it only requires that a penal statute be drafted with precision. Certain provisions of the U.S. Constitution, however, limit the legislative power to create crimes. For example, Article 1, Section 9, of the Constitution prohibits bills of attainder and ex post facto laws. **Bills of attainder** bypass the courts and convict an individual by legislative pronouncement. **Ex post facto laws** retroactively make innocent conduct illegal. They also may increase the punishment for a criminal act or decrease the standard of proof required for a conviction.

Unlike the explicit prohibition of bills of attainder and ex post facto laws, most constitutional provisions guarantee procedural fairness to criminal defendants. For example, the right to counsel, the right to a public trial, and the right to an impartial jury, are included within the U. S. Constitution's Bill of Rights. A few constitutional mandates within the Bill of Rights, however, go beyond procedural considerations by limiting the government's power to prohibit and punish certain conduct. For example:

Bills of attainder
legislative acts convicting an individual of a crime.

Ex post facto laws
laws that retroactively make innocent conduct illegal; increase the punishment for a criminal act; or decrease the standard of proof required for a conviction.

The First Amendment provides that "Congress shall make no law . . . abridging the freedom of speech." Thus a statute criminalizing the burning of the American flag violates the First Amendment right to freedom of speech.[4]

The Fourth Amendment right of privacy limits the government's power to regulate certain aspects of our private lives. Thus the legislature may not make it a crime for married couples to possess birth control devices.[5] As another example, the legislature may not punish people for possessing pornography in the privacy of their own homes.[6]

The Eighth Amendment prohibition of "cruel and unusual punishment" limits legislative authority to make some conduct criminal. As *Robinson v. California* noted, even one day in prison would be a cruel and unusual punishment for the "crime" of having a common cold.

ROBINSON v. CALIFORNIA
Supreme Court of the United States, 1962
370 U.S. 660, 82 S.Ct. 1417

JUSTICE STEWART delivered the opinion of the Court:

A California statute makes it a criminal offense for a person to "be addicted to the use of narcotics." This appeal draws into question the constitutionality of that provision of the state law.

The broad power of a State to regulate the narcotic drugs traffic within its borders is not here in issue. There can be no question of the authority of the state in the exercise of its police power to regulate the administration, sale, prescription and use of dangerous and habit-forming drugs. The right to exercise this power is so manifest in the interest of the public health and welfare, that it is unnecessary to enter upon a discussion of it beyond saying that it is too firmly established to be successfully called in question.

This statute, however, is not one which punishes a person for the use of narcotics, for their purchase, sale or possession, or for antisocial or disorderly behavior resulting from their administration. It is not a law which even purports to provide or require medical treatment. Rather, we deal with a statute which makes the "status" of narcotic addiction a criminal offense, for which the offender may be prosecuted "at any time before he reforms." California has said that a person can be continuously guilty of this offense, whether or not he has ever used or possessed any narcotics within the State, and whether or not he has been guilty of any antisocial behavior there.

It is unlikely that any State at this moment in history would attempt to make it a criminal offense for a person to be mentally ill, or a leper, or to be afflicted with a venereal disease. A State might determine that the general health and welfare requires that the victims of these and other human afflictions be dealt with by compulsory treatment, involving quarantine, confinement, or sequestration. But in the light of contemporary human knowledge, a law which made a criminal offense of such a disease would doubtless be universally thought to be an infliction of cruel and unusual punishment in violation of the Eight and Fourteenth Amendments.

We cannot but consider the statute before us as of the same category. In this Court, counsel for the State recognized that narcotic addiction is an illness. Indeed, it is apparently an illness which may be contracted innocently or involuntarily. We hold that a state law which imprisons a person thus afflicted as a criminal, even though he has never touched any narcotic drug within the State or been guilty of any irregular behavior there, inflicts a cruel and unusual punishment in violation of the Fourteenth Amendment. To be sure, [this defendant's punishment by] imprisonment for ninety days is not, in the abstract, a punishment which is either cruel or unusual. But the question cannot be considered in the abstract. Even one day in prison would be a cruel and unusual punishment for the "crime" of having a common cold.

The *Robinson* decision drew a distinction between conduct (which the defendant can control) and the defendant's status (which may be beyond control). Although a state may not punish a defendant because of status, society is not powerless to protect itself against a condition or status that threatens the general welfare.

The state may impose treatment, quarantine, or even confinement, as long as these measures are civil, not penal, in nature. For example, in *Allen v. Illinois*, a "sexually dangerous person" was confined for treatment, an action that was deemed to be merely a civil deprivation of liberty.[7] Although general Due Process considerations apply to such restraints on liberty, a citizen subject to civil confinement is not entitled to the full range of constitutional rights accorded to a person facing conviction and punishment.

PROVING THE CRIME

After the prosecution has identified the source (common law, statute, or administrative regulation) that defines the crime, the prosecution must prove that the defined crime occurred. A criminal trial represents the "who done it" stage of criminal proceedings because most trials involve a dispute about the facts surrounding the alleged crime. In a typical trial the prosecution presents evidence that the defendant committed the crime; evidence that the defendant may contest. In turn, the defendant may present additional evidence that establishes a defense; evidence that the prosecution may contest. At the conclusion of the presentation of evidence, the factfinder—most often a jury but sometimes a judge—must decide whose presentation of facts is legally persuasive. In jury trials, the jury determines the facts while the judge determines the law. In bench trials before a judge alone, the judge determines both fact and law.

Burden of Proof

When the presentation of evidence is concluded, the judge instructs the jury (1) whether the prosecution or the defendant has the **burden of proof** on each legal issue raised, (2) the amount of evidence required to meet the burden, and (3) the verdict to be returned when the burden is not met. The jury uses the judge's instructions to weigh the evidence and to resolve the factual claims and legal issues raised by the parties to the case (see Exhibit 1–1).

Burden of proof
the task of presenting evidence to a factfinder, normally a jury, who then weighs the cumulative evidence and decides whether it "constitutes the crime charged."

EXHIBIT 1–1
Instruction on the Burden of Proof: Reasonable Doubt

> **(a)** The defendant is presumed to be innocent of the offense with which the defendant is charged and this presumption of innocence goes with the defendant through the entire case, applies at every stage thereof and is sufficient to require you to find the defendant not guilty unless and until the prosecution proves guilt beyond a reasonable doubt.
>
> **(b)** The burden is upon the prosecution to prove by the evidence beyond a reasonable doubt every material and necessary element of the offense charged against the defendant. It is not sufficient that the jury may believe the defendant's guilt probable, or more probable than innocence. Suspicion or probability of guilt, however strong, will not authorize a conviction, but the evidence must prove guilt beyond a reasonable doubt. Unless you believe, upon a consideration of all the evidence before you, that guilt of the defendant has been proved beyond a reasonable doubt as to every material and necessary element of the offense charged against the defendant, then you shall find the defendant not guilty.
>
> **(c)** The burden resting upon the prosecution to prove guilt of the defendant beyond a reasonable doubt does not require that such guilt be proven beyond every imaginable, conceivable or possible doubt, but only beyond a reasonable doubt. If, upon consideration of all the evidence you are satisfied of the guilt of the defendant beyond a reasonable doubt, then you shall find the defendant guilty.

Proof beyond a reasonable doubt
often defined as proof that excludes every reasonable hypothesis except guilt; proof that excludes every reasonable possibility of innocence; or proof to a moral certainty.

A criminal defendant is presumed to be innocent and the prosecution bears the burden of proving beyond a reasonable doubt "every fact necessary to constitute the crime charged."[8] **Proof beyond a reasonable doubt** has been defined as proof that excludes every reasonable hypothesis except guilt; proof that excludes every reasonable possibility of innocence; or proof to a moral certainty. Although this standard of proof is the highest known to the law, the burden may be met by wholly circumstantial evidence. As *Epperly v. Commonwealth* demonstrates, even murder can be proved without direct evidence of a killing.

EPPERLY v. COMMONWEALTH
Supreme Court of Virginia, 1982
224 Va. 214, 294 S.E.2d 882

The defendant, Stephen Epperly, was tried by a jury, convicted of the first degree murder of Gina Hall, and sentenced to life imprisonment. The victim's body was never found. The evidence was entirely circumstantial, both as to proof of the *corpus delicti* [the body of the crime—the fact of its having been committed] and as to the element of premeditation. The defendant's appeal raises questions concerning the sufficiency of the evidence to prove these elements. We affirm the conviction.

The trial court instructed the jury that the Commonwealth must first prove that Gina was dead and that her death was caused by criminal violence [the *corpus delicti* of murder]. The instruction told the jury that these elements might be proved "either by direct evidence or by proof so strong as to produce the full assurance of moral certainty." Defendant agrees that this instruction correctly states the law, but argues that the evidence was insufficient to warrant the jury's finding the existence of the *corpus delicti*.

[The distinguished English jurist] Sir Matthew Hale wrote, "I would never convict any person of murder or manslaughter, unless the fact were proven to be done, or at least the body found dead." Many later writers have misconstrued this dictum to mean that there can be no conviction unless the prosecution produce the body of the victim. This may account for the familiar layman's misconception which equates *corpus delicti* with the body of the victim. This is not the law of England today, and probably never was.

Conceding that the *corpus delicti* may be proved circumstantially, defendant argues that in the absence of

the body, such proof can only be held sufficient where: (1) there is an eyewitness to the killing, (2) some identifiable remains of the victim are found, or (3) the accused confesses the crime or makes admissions which corroborate the circumstantial proof of violent death.

We are not persuaded that any such limitations should be imposed. When the evidence is circumstantial, the standard of proof is stringent. Such a requirement of strictness sufficiently protects the defendant from guesswork and speculation. Because it is not subject to the human frailties of perception, memory, and truthful recital, circumstantial evidence is often more reliable than the accounts of eyewitnesses. When convincing, it is entitled to the same weight as direct testimony.

The restriction on proof which the defendant advocates would place a premium on stealthy murder and successful concealment of the victim's body. Among the numerous atrocities of which Charles Manson was convicted in California in the 1970s was the murder of Shea, whose body was never found. The California Court of Appeal remarked: "The fact that Shea's body was never recovered would justify an inference by the jury that death was caused by a criminal agency. It is highly unlikely that a person who dies from natural causes will successfully dispose of his own body. Although such a result may be a theoretical possibility, it is contrary to the normal course of human affairs. The fact that a murderer may successfully dispose of the body of the victim does not entitle him to an acquittal. That is one form of success for which society has no reward."

Corpus delicti
the body of the crime—the fact of its having been committed.

The *Epperly* case dispels a common misperception that corpus delicti means "the body of the victim." **Corpus delicti** literally means "the body of the crime"; in *Epperly,* that a criminal homicide took place. Although the body of the victim may be the most direct evidence of death, standing alone, death does not establish that a crime occurred. Death may be due to natural causes, accident, or may be the result of justifiable or excusable homicide, in which case no crime occurs. A prosecutor who produces a deceased's body, but no evidence that the death was caused by the criminal acts of another, has failed to prove the corpus delicti of criminal homicide. The distinction between the body of the crime and the body of the victim becomes obvious when considering the corpus delicti of crimes other than homicide. For example, in larceny, the corpus delicti is that someone took another's property; in burglary, the corpus delicti is that someone broke and entered another's home.

If the prosecution fails to prove the corpus delicti and each element of the crime beyond a reasonable doubt, the defendant must be acquitted. The acquittal may take the form of a jury verdict or a directed verdict by the judge. A **directed verdict of acquittal** removes the case from jury deliberation because the court enters a finding of not guilty. The trial judge may direct a verdict of not guilty whenever a rational jury could have reached only one conclusion, i.e., that proof beyond a reasonable doubt has not been shown. By directing an acquittal, the judge guards against irrational action by the jury, and also saves time and money by freeing the jury from deliberations over an issue with only one logical resolution. No matter how damming the evidence, however, the judge may never direct a verdict of guilty in a jury trial. A criminal defendant has an absolute right to have the jury determine whether guilt has been proved beyond a reasonable doubt.

In most cases the judge does not direct an acquittal because conflicting evidence lends itself to different interpretations. When reasonable people could differ as to guilt or innocence, the case must be submitted to the jury in order to find out how these reasonable people resolve it. If the jury has a reasonable doubt that one or more of the elements of the crime has been proved, they will acquit. If they are convinced beyond a reasonable doubt as to each element of the crime, the jury will convict the defendant.

Burden of Proof on Subordinate Issues

Although guilt or innocence is the **ultimate issue** in a criminal trial, that ultimate issue often turns upon subordinate legal issues, each of which may carry a separate burden of proof. As to each legal issue that arises in the course of a jury trial, the jury must be informed whether the prosecution or the defendant bears the burden of proof, and the amount of proof required to meet that burden. The most commonly occurring subordinate legal issues are **affirmative defenses**, which admit that the defendant did the acts charged, but offer additional facts that justify or excuse the defendant's conduct (see Chapter Four). For example, the defendant admits killing someone, but claims that the killing was justifiable self-defense. In some jurisdictions, the prosecution would be required to prove beyond a reasonable doubt that the defendant did not act in self-defense, but in other jurisdictions the defendant might be given the burden of persuading the jury that the defendant acted in legitimate self-defense. Thus, in a murder prosecution the judge would instruct the jury on two separate burdens of proof: (1) the prosecution must prove that the defendant did in fact kill the victim, and (2) whether the defendant must prove self-defense or whether the prosecution must disprove self-defense. In jury trials, one of the most important tasks for a trial judge is to specify the burden of proof on each distinct legal issue raised by the parties.

When defendants are given the burden of proof on a subordinate issue, the burden is usually much less than proof beyond a reasonable doubt. Most typically, the burden is proof by a **preponderance of the evidence**. This standard asks the jury to determine whether more likely than not (more than 50 percent likely) the facts support a subordinate issue like self-defense. The law recognizes other burdens of proof

Directed verdict of acquittal
a device used to remove the case from the jury's consideration. The trial judge may enter an acquittal whenever a rational jury must conclude that the prosecution failed to prove guilt beyond a reasonable doubt.

Ultimate issue
the question of whether the defendant is guilty or not guilty of the charge.

Affirmative defenses
the defendant admits committing the acts charged, but seeks to justify or excuse the defendant's conduct by establishing additional facts.

Preponderance of the evidence
the standard of proof often required to establish an affirmative defense; asks the jury to determine whether an accused has established the reasonable likelihood of the defense.

Prima facie evidence
requires that the defendant offer some plausible evidence of the defendant's claim.

Clear and convincing evidence
is a higher standard than preponderance but lower than beyond a reasonable doubt.

such as **prima facie evidence,** which is a relatively low standard merely requiring that the defendant offer some plausible evidence of the defendant's claim; or **clear and convincing evidence,** which is a higher standard than preponderance but lower than beyond a reasonable doubt. The level of proof required, and the allocation of that burden of proof between prosecution and defense often hinges on whether the law seeks to encourage or discourage defendants from raising issues like affirmative defenses. For example, at the time of John Hinckley's trial for the attempted assassination of President Reagan, federal law presumed a defendant to be sane, but once the defendant presented a *prima facie* case of insanity, the burden of proving sanity beyond a reasonable doubt shifted to the government. Largely in reaction to the *Hinckley* verdict, Congress enacted the Insanity Defense Reform Act of 1984 (18 U.S.C. § 20):

(a) *Affirmative Defense.* It is an affirmative defense to a prosecution under any Federal statute that, at the time of the commission of the acts constituting the offense, the defendant, as a result of severe mental disease or defect, was unable to appreciate the nature and quality of the wrongfulness of his acts. Mental disease or defect does not otherwise constitute a defense.

(b) *Burden of Proof.* The defendant has the burden of proving the defense of insanity by clear and convincing evidence.

Presumptions and Permissible Inferences

In *Francis v. Franklin,* the U.S. Supreme Court distinguished presumptions from inferences:

A mandatory presumption instructs the jury that it must infer the presumed fact if the State proves certain predicate facts. A permissive inference suggests to the jury a possible conclusion to be drawn if the State proves predicate facts, but does not require the jury to draw that conclusion.[9]

In criminal cases, the accused is presumed to be innocent, which is a "true presumption" because the trier of fact is *compelled* to return an acquittal unless the government can rebut the presumption by proving guilt beyond a reasonable doubt. The **presumption** of innocence and other presumptions in favor of the defendant are thus nothing more than alternative expressions of the prosecution's burden of proof. For example, one state court characterized the common law presumption that a fire is accidental, as merely another way of stating that the prosecution must prove arson beyond a reasonable doubt.[10]

Presumption
a fact that must be inferred (presumed) on the basis of certain predicate facts that have been proved.

Although the defendant may be given the benefit of certain true presumptions like the presumption of innocence, the prosecution cannot utilize presumptions as a substitute for proof beyond a reasonable doubt. For example, in *Connecticut v. Johnson,* the trial judge instructed the jury that every person is presumed to intend the natural and necessary consequences of an action.[11] The U.S. Supreme Court held that this instruction amounted to a directed verdict on the issue of the defendant's intent, and thus violated the defendant's right to force the prosecution to prove criminal intent beyond a reasonable doubt.

On occasion, statutes or case decisions erroneously refer to presumptions in favor of the prosecution. For example, unexplained possession of recently stolen goods gives rise to a presumption that the defendant stole the items; or possession of burglary tools gives rise to a presumption that the defendant planned to commit burglary. In reality, these are not presumptions at all, but merely **permissible inferences.** The distinction lies in whether the jury is told that they *must presume* the fact for which the prosecution offers the evidence (for example, that the defendant is a thief or burglar), or whether they are told that they *may infer* the fact. Thus the instruc-

Permissive inferences
a possible conclusion that may be drawn but is not exclusively required if certain predicate facts are proved.

not on test

tion in *Connecticut v. Johnson* would have been proper if the judge had instructed the jury that they might infer that a person normally intends the natural and necessary consequences of an action.

Courts or legislatures may create any number of permissible inferences as long as the inferred fact logically follows from the evidence presented. An "illogical" inference, however, is unconstitutional because it invites the jury to reach a factually irrational result.[12] For example, possession of a large quantity of drugs gives rise to a rational inference that the defendant intended to distribute those drugs. On the other hand, possession of a small amount of drugs associated with personal use does not logically support an inference that the defendant is a drug dealer.

SUMMARY

Although all laws can be viewed as regulations designed to benefit general society, criminal law is unique in its use of imprisonment to enforce the law. With few exceptions, the government is the sole entity that may use physical force to coerce behavior from unwilling persons. The desire to limit and regulate such power accounts for many of the strict rules and "legal technicalities" surrounding criminal law. Our society's willingness to employ corporal punishment is influenced by our view of the ways in which punishment might further societal goals. For example, the choice between punishment as retribution or rehabilitation affects society's willingness to criminalize certain behavior and impose different forms of punishment.

Violations of administrative regulations are sometimes classified as criminal offenses, but most crimes are created and defined either by legislative enactment or judicial decision. When a penal statute is clear, the courts must respect the legislature's pronouncements unless the statute violates a constitutional provision. When a statutory definition of a crime is ambiguous, the courts must interpret the meaning of the statute, including legislative intent. When no statute covers the alleged crime, the courts may or may not be free to apply the common law depending on whether the particular jurisdiction has abolished common law crimes or retained the portions of common law unaltered by statute. Even in those jurisdictions where the common law has been abolished, the court may sometimes consult the common law for whatever persuasive effect it has in analyzing statutory language. A court also may look to the Model Penal Code as a nonbinding guide to interpreting criminal law. How far a court goes in interpreting law gives rise to the debate between judicial activists who employ interpretation of law as a means to achieve social goals, and judges who practice judicial restraint by viewing judicial power as strictly limited by established precedent. These two views are eloquently set forth in the *Shaw* case.

Once the definition of a crime is agreed upon, the prosecution must prove the facts necessary to constitute the crime. The constitutional concept of due process requires that the prosecution meet a strict burden of proof, that is, every element of the crime must be proved beyond a reasonable doubt. Although the prosecution may use circumstantial evidence and logical inferences to meet this burden, the prosecution may not utilize illogical inferences or presumptions as a substitute for proof.

By state law, a defendant may be given the burden to prove an affirmative defense such as insanity or self-defense. The factfinder, most often a jury but sometimes a judge, must view the factual evidence and determine whether the burden of proof has been met. Even in a jury trial the judge may take the case from the jury by directing a verdict of acquittal when the prosecution has clearly failed to meet its burden of proof. In a jury trial, however, the judge is precluded from directing a verdict of guilty because the defendant has a constitutional right to have the jury decide guilt beyond a reasonable doubt.

DISCUSSION QUESTIONS

1. Of what use is the common law when every state has enacted comprehensive criminal codes?
2. If the constitutional right to privacy protects people's right to possess obscene material in their own home *(Stanley v. Georgia)*, why does the right not protect a person's choice of a sexual partner of the same gender *(Bowers v. Hardwick)*?
3. If a pregnant woman addicted to drugs takes drugs that harm her fetus, can the woman be punished for a criminal act? Would this be punishing her for her "status" as a drug addict?

PRACTICE EXERCISES

1. Has your state abolished the common law or merely supplemented it with statutes?
2. What provisions governing criminal cases are contained within your state constitution?
3. Does your state constitution go beyond the federal constitution in limiting the state's power to define crimes?

WEB SITE

United States Department of Justice: Office of Justice Programs
www.ojp.usdoj.gov/

KEY TERMS

Common law
Judicial activism
Judicial restraint
Model Penal Code
Legislative intent
Vagueness doctrine
Bills of attainder

Ex post facto laws
Burden of proof
Proof beyond a reasonable doubt
Corpus delicti
Directed verdict of acquittal
Ultimate issue

Affirmative defenses
Preponderance of the evidence
Prima facie evidence
Clear and convincing evidence
Presumption
Permissive inferences

NOTES

1. *Gregg v. Georgia*, 428 U.S. 153, 96 S.Ct. 2909 (1976).
2. *Bowers v. Hardwick*, 478 U.S. 186, 106 S.Ct. 2841 (1986).
3. *Connally v. General Constr. Co.*, 269 U.S. 385, 391, 46 S.Ct. 126, 127 (1926).
4. *Texas v. Johnson*, 491 U.S. 397, 109 S.Ct. 2533 (1989).
5. *Griswold v. Connecticut*, 381 U.S. 479, 85 S.Ct. 1678 (1965).
6. *Stanley v. Georgia*, 394 U.S. 557, 89 S.Ct. 1243 (1969).
7. *Allen v. Illinois*, 478 U.S. 364, 106 S.Ct. 2988 (1986). The U.S. Supreme Court upheld a Kansas law mandating civil detention of individuals who are both mentally ill and "sexually violent predators." *Kansas v. Hendricks*, 521 U.S. 346, 117 S.Ct. 2072 (1997).
8. *In re Winship*, 397 U.S. 358, 90 S.Ct. 1068 (1970).
9. *Francis v. Franklin*, 471 U.S. 307, 105 S.Ct. 1965 (1985).
10. *Cook v. Commonwealth*, 226 Va. 427, 309 S.E.2d 325 (1983).
11. *Connecticut v. Johnson*, 460 U.S. 73, 103 S.Ct. 969 (1983).
12. *County Court of Ulster County v. Allen*, 442 U.S. 140, 99 S.Ct. 2213 (1979).

ESSENTIAL ELEMENTS OF CRIMES

Chapter 2

CHAPTER OUTLINE

Although variations can be found between jurisdictions, criminal offenses are often categorized according to certain criteria:

1. Punishment
   - *Capital offenses* are those for which the death penalty may be imposed.
   - *Felonies* carry a sentence of one year or more of incarceration.
   - *Misdemeanors* warrant less than one year of incarceration.
2. Mental State (Mens Rea)
   Crimes mala in se are inherently evil without denouncement by a statute (e.g., rape).
   Crimes mala prohibita are crimes only because of the existence of a statute or regulation (e.g., traffic laws).
   Specific intent crimes focus on what the defendant intended at the time of the offense (e.g., premeditated murder).
   Scienter crimes are based on the defendant's subjective knowledge (e.g., receiving property known to be stolen).
   General intent crimes may encompass accidental harm caused by recklessness or negligence (e.g., involuntary manslaughter).
   Strict liability crimes focus on the defendant's physical act and do not require any form of mens rea (e.g., statutory rape).
3. Harm
   Crimes against property (e.g., larceny)
   Crimes against habitation (e.g., burglary)
   Crimes against people (e.g., assault and battery)
   Crimes against the public peace (e.g., disorderly conduct)

Other less precise classifications such as "victimless" crime, violent and nonviolent crime, white-collar crime, and traffic "infractions," describe acts that, in some instances, may not be crimes at all.

Subsequent chapters explore the distinct features of individual crimes, but this chapter temporarily ignores the differences among individual crimes in order to focus on a broad overview of the fundamental concepts of all criminal offenses. Within the context of a basic analytical framework, each particular crime (sometimes described in overly legalistic or arcane language) can be examined and broken down into more manageable components.

A DEFINITION OF CRIME

The most basic concept in criminal law is the defining of criminal conduct. Exactly what is a crime? Professor Jerome Hall offered a definition of crime that is frequently cited: "legally proscribed human conduct causative of a given harm which conduct coincides with a blameworthy frame of mind and which is subject to punishment by the state." Although this definition is theoretically sound and helpful in a study of jurisprudence, it is not easily applied to the multitude of cases that arise every day in our nation's busy courts.

Another common definition of crime focuses on two elements: mens rea and actus reus. **Mens rea** is a generic term that encompasses a variety of wrongful states of mind. **Actus reus** "requires proof of a voluntary act by the defendant [the *actus*] . . . that results in the harm to society prohibited by the offense in question [the *reus*]."[1] Although combining the actus and the reus can sometimes be helpful, at other times the combination obscures the distinction between harm and conduct. No one definition of crime applies to all situations; however, a simplistic "working definition" of crime considers three elements that occur in most crimes:

Mens rea
wrongful state of mind.

Actus rea
an act by the defendant, which results in a prohibited harm to society.

1. Mental state (mens rea)
2. Physical act (a component of actus reus)
3. Social harm (another component of actus reus)

This working definition can be utilized when examining the legal requirements for any crime. For example, common law burglary requires breaking and entering in the nighttime, the dwelling house of another, with the intent to commit a felony therein. By using the working definition of crime, the legal definition of burglary can be separated into its constituent parts, as shown in Exhibit 2–1.

In similar fashion, common law larceny can be broken down into its constituent components as shown in Exhibit 2–2.

Before considering the separate requirements for a social harm, physical act, and mental state, one should note the interrelationship of these three requirements. If one of the requirements is altered, the nature of the crime may change drastically. Consider a simple situation in which the mental state and physical act of the defendant can be determined: the defendant intended to, and did, throw a stone at **A**. What crime has occurred?

At this point a determination of what crime was committed cannot be made because the consequences or harm of the defendant's mental state and physical act are unknown. What happened after the stone left the defendant's hand affects what crime occurred. Consider these possible consequences of the defendant's actions:

Harm	Crime
1. The stone missed **A**	Assault
2. The stone struck **A**'s shoulder	Battery
3. The stone put out **A**'s eye	Mayhem
4. The stone killed **A**	Homicide

Physical act

Breaking and entering in the nighttime

Social harm

The dwelling house of another

Mental state

With the intent to commit a felony therein

EXHIBIT 2–1
Criminal Elements of Burglary

Physical act

Taking and carrying away

Social harm

Personal property of another

Mental state

With the intent to deprive permanently

EXHIBIT 2–2
Criminal Elements of Larceny

In the stated situations, the crime ranges from the relatively minor offense of assault to the serious offense of homicide. Yet in all four situations, the defendant's mental state and physical act remain the same; only the harm caused by the defendant has changed. The harm caused is important even though the defendant had no control over the consequences of the act once the stone left the defendant's hand. Whether the stone missed **A** or killed **A** may have been determined by many factors beyond the defendant's control. For example, a strong wind may have blown the stone off course; **A** may have seen the stone and ducked; or after being struck, **A** was able to find a skilled doctor who could save **A**'s life.

Legal scholars have debated whether the definition and possible punishment for a crime should be contingent upon factors beyond a defendant's control.[2] Some suggest that when the stone leaves the defendant's hand, *moral* fault is fixed and should not be altered by fortuitous circumstances such as the proximity of a skilled doctor who saved the victim's life. Although such moral arguments are relevant in a discussion of ethics, the arguments do not control legal analysis which often relates the gravity of the offense to the actual harm caused.

The criminal law is not designed merely to enforce moral judgments because conviction and punishment serve social purposes such as deterrence of wrongdoers and public control over private retribution such as "blood feuds." Suppose, for example, that a Hatfield kills a McCoy with a stone. Theologians may debate whether the Hatfield's moral fault turns upon good or bad luck in missing or killing the victim with a single stone. The McCoys, however, will react differently to a stone that misses rather than a stone that kills a family member. The actual harm brought about by a defendant's conduct is an important part of defining crimes, because as Justice Holmes wrote, the "aim of the law is not to punish sins, but is to prevent certain external results."

The interrelationship of mental state, physical act, and the consequences of the defendant's actions can be further illustrated by considering another situation in which the defendant killed **A** by throwing a stone. Although some form of homicide may have occurred, the exact crime cannot be identified until the defendant's mental state is known. Consider these possibilities:

Mental state	**Crime**
1. An intent to kill	First degree murder
2. An intent to inflict serious harm	Second degree murder
3. An intent to inflict a minor wound	Manslaughter

In these three situations the defendant's physical act and the consequence of the act are the same; only the defendant's mental state varies. Depending upon the actual mental state of the defendant, the consummated crime ranges from involuntary manslaughter to first degree murder.

The stone-throwing examples with varying mental states or the harm caused demonstrate how alteration of one of the three requirements for crime—social harm, physical act, mental state—can change the nature of the crime. Each of the three requirements is considered in greater detail in the following sections.

SOCIAL HARM

The concept of a social harm is the most nebulous of the three requirements for criminal offenses. Although identification of social harm is ultimately a legal determination, the underlying basis for defining social harm might be better understood by a study of sociology or politics. Lawyers and judges are not free to create new crimes based on their perception of what constitutes a social harm. They are primarily concerned with recognizing and applying what society has already classified as social harm.

Understanding the concept of social harm begins with the realization that every harm that occurs in society is not classified as "social harm" for purposes of the criminal law. When Ms. Smith breaks a contract with Ms. Jones, society classifies this action as a civil harm to Jones, but society does not become involved in this private dispute except to the extent of providing civil courts as forums for resolving the controversy. Similarly, when a negligent driver damages your automobile, society does not step in to relieve you of the consequences or to remedy the financial harm done to you. The dispute over who pays for the harm done is left for the parties and/or the automobile insurance companies to resolve.

The criminal law becomes relevant only when a harm is identified as a harm to all of society rather than a harm to just one member of society. Although a law suit involving an automobile accident might be titled *Smith v. Jones,* a criminal prosecution for theft of an automobile would be titled *State v. Jones,* or *United States v. Jones* if it is a federal offense. One characteristic of criminal cases is that they are brought in the name of the government on behalf of the community. The relevant concern at this point is why society regards theft of a person's property as a social harm, but not damage to a person's property caused by another's negligence. The answer to this question would require an analysis of the sociological and political forces at work in society; forces that reflect society's sensitivity to personal harm and a pragmatic evaluation of the most practical and efficient procedure for handling a situation in which some harm has been done.

Even a cursory look at various state penal codes demonstrates that societies differ as to what constitutes a social harm for purposes of criminal law. In our nation some states legalize sexual relations between consenting adults of any gender, while other states classify same-gender sex as criminal sodomy. Even within the same jurisdiction, attitudes change with the passage of time. Many modern-day crimes involving consumer protection laws or civil rights violations were formerly regarded as merely civil disputes between private parties. Today, they may be federal or state crimes. The definition of social harm varies from jurisdiction to jurisdiction and from one time period to another, thus reflecting the changing social and political forces at work in society.

Although the legal system contributes to shaping society's attitude toward social harm, the day-to-day work of most lawyers and judges centers around those social harms previously recognized by legislative enactment or judicial decision. For example, common law burglary sought to protect against the social harm created by nighttime intrusions into dwelling houses. Intrusions into structures other than dwelling houses were not regarded as equally serious harms, thus such intrusions were not within the definition of common law burglary. Modern statutes, however, protect against illegal intrusion into almost every conceivable structure, for example, offices, schools, barns, automobiles, and even Cable TV lines. When a defendant is charged with some form of breaking and entering, a significant issue at trial will be whether the defendant caused the precise harm identified by a particular statute. For example, breaking into a Cable TV line is factually and *legally* distinct from the breaking and entry of structures such as dwellings. However, no legal distinction is made between the various forms of dwellings, be they mansions or hovels.

In most criminal cases, the parties are not free to engage in an unstructured debate over what should or should not be regarded as a social harm. The trial judge will grow impatient with a lawyer who treats the law as a blank slate and urges the judge to recognize or "create" new forms of social harm. The judge will demand that the attorney invoke or at least draw analogies to existing statutory or judicial concepts of previously recognized harms. The concept of social harm, however, is not stagnant, but grows as existing definitions of harm are interpreted or expanded to cover some new form of analogous harm. For example, does intrusion into a cardboard box in which a homeless person sleeps constitute the crime of burglary, which was created to protect a person's dwelling, be it mansion or hovel?

THE PHYSICAL ACT

Deliberate bodily movement
an affirmative action consciously taken by the defendant, distinguished from an unconscious or reflexive act.

Omission
the failure to act when the law imposes a duty to act.

Two fundamental principles underlie the criminal law's requirement for a physical act:

1. The physical act required for a crime normally consists of a **deliberate bodily movement,** which is distinguished from an unconscious or reflexive act such as one performed by a sleepwalker or a person in an epileptic seizure.[3]
2. Although an affirmative action (bodily movement) is normally required, an **omission,** or failure to act, can constitute a crime in some situations. An example would be the failure to perform a duty imposed by law, such as parents neglecting to feed their newborn infant.

PEOPLE V. BEARDSLEY
113 N.W. 1128 (Mich. 1907)

The defendant, a married man, invited a woman friend to his apartment while his wife was out of town. They both got drunk and the woman overdosed on morphine tablets. The defendant took her to the basement and told the janitor to let her out when she woke up. The woman never regained consciousness and the defendant was convicted of manslaughter on a theory that he owed to the victim a duty which he had failed to perform. We reverse the conviction.

The law recognizes that under some circumstances the omission of a duty owed by one individual to another, where such omission results in the death of the one to whom the duty is owing, will make the other chargeable with manslaughter. This rule of law is always based on the proposition that the duty neglected must be a legal duty, and not a mere moral obligation. We must eliminate from the case all consideration of mere moral obligation, and discover whether defendant was under a legal duty which required him to make all reasonable and proper efforts to save her. It is urged by the prosecutor that the respondent stood towards this woman for the time being in the place of her natural guardian and protector, and as such owed her a clear legal duty which he completely failed to perform.

The fact that this woman was in his house created no such legal duty as exists in law and is due from a husband towards his wife. Such an inference would be very repugnant to our moral sense. Defendant had assumed either in fact or by implication no care or control over his companion. Had this been a case where two men had voluntarily gone on a debauch together, and one had attempted suicide, no one would claim that this doctrine of legal duty could be invoked to hold the other criminally responsible for omitting to make effort to rescue his companion. How can the fact that in this case one of the parties was a woman change the principle of law applicable to it?

Applying the law in this case from the principle of decided cases, we do not find any legal duty on the part of the defendant toward the deceased.

With the preceding principles in mind, the criminal law generally addresses affirmative physical acts that fit within one of the following categories:

Evil thought
Express thought
Request
Agreement
Attempt
Consummation

These categories represent the various mental and physical steps a criminal can take from the point of first contemplating commission of a crime, until the point of actually performing all the physical acts necessary for the consummated offense. An examination of a single hypothetical situation involving burglary demonstrates how each physical act affects the nature of the crime.

Evil Thought

Suppose that **X** decides to break and enter her neighbor's house tonight in order to steal the neighbor's expensive stereo. **X** tells no one of her decision, but makes a firm commitment in her own mind to take the stereo. Has a crime occurred at this point?

By applying the working definition of crime—mental state, physical act, social harm—one can deduce that an evil mental state is present; **X** certainly has a "criminal" frame of mind. The social harm of this mental state is less obvious. Given the ambiguity of social harm, a particular jurisdiction might decide that social harm occurs whenever a citizen decides to break the law. Even if the elements of social harm and mental state are present, however, no crime occurred because **X** has not committed any physical act.

Society does not punish people for what they think, society only punishes conduct. Although some Orwellian society might employ "thought police," U.S. citizens remain entirely free to contemplate evil or antisocial conduct. The U.S. Supreme Court recognized that a person's "fantasies are his own and beyond the reach of government."[4] The criminal law becomes applicable only when the individual leaves the realm of private thought and begins to act in an antisocial manner.

Express Thought

Suppose that **X** now informs **Y** that she intends to burglarize her neighbor's home. **X** does not attempt to involve **Y** in the burglary, **X** merely expresses her own intentions. Has a crime occurred at this point?

X has now taken her evil thought and verbalized it by means of a willed bodily movement. (Wagging one's tongue may not be much of a physical act, but it does meet the legal requirement for bodily movement.) Although **X** has performed a physical act by expressing her intent, this physical act is still not the type normally required for commission of a crime. To punish **X** for a crime at this point would be very close to punishing her for what she thinks. Punishment might also conflict with the recognition of a broad right to freedom of speech.

The criminal law focuses on conduct which is itself socially harmful, rather than mere expressions of an intent to engage in harmful conduct in the future. The reluctance to punish mere speech reflects the value placed on the First Amendment and free speech, but it also reveals a practical realization that "talk is cheap" and that a bluff is often called by challenging the speaker to "put your money where your mouth is." Human nature being what it is, people frequently express a wish to engage in conduct that will never actually occur. Consider the practical problems that arise if society were to prosecute every individual who confides to a co-worker: "If the boss bothers me one more time, I'll punch her in the nose." Not enough judges, lawyers, or paralegals are available in this country to handle the volume of cases that would arise from labeling such speech as a crime.

Although society generally protects free speech, the mere utterance of words can constitute a crime in certain circumstances. For example, obscene language in public, communicating a threat, and perjury are criminal acts. With such limited exceptions, the criminal law does not generally punish citizens for "speaking their minds." In most cases, a physical act beyond a verbal statement is required.

Request

Suppose that when **X** informs **Y** of her intent to burglarize her neighbor's home, **X** asks **Y** to join her in the plan. Has a crime occurred at this point?

X has now gone beyond a mere verbal expression of what is in her own mind and is attempting to influence another's willingness to commit a crime. Although **X**'s physical act is still exclusively verbal, the social harm of her act has escalated. The additional harm is that **X** has solicited a presumably law-abiding citizen to engage in criminal conduct. In the eyes of the law, sufficient social harm and a sufficient physical act has now occurred to punish **X** for the crime of solicitation (see Chapter Three).

Note that **X** committed the crime of solicitation by merely asking **Y** to commit the crime. **Y**'s response to **X**'s invitation will be relevant in the next hypothetical situation involving conspiracy. Unlike conspiracy, however, the crime of solicitation is complete when the request is made.

Agreement

Suppose that after **Y** agrees to participate in the burglary, **X** and **Y** drive by the neighbor's house in order to select the particular window through which they will break and enter the house. Has a crime occurred at this point?

Even before driving past the neighbor's house, **X** and **Y** have concluded an agreement that they will jointly commit a crime. Although the defendants' conduct is exclusively verbal, the common law treats verbal agreement as sufficient for the crime of conspiracy (see Chapter Three).

Although no further act beyond agreement was required at common law, modern statutes often require the commission of an overt act before the crime of conspiracy is complete. For purposes of conspiracy law, an **overt act for a conspiracy** is defined as an act in furtherance of the conspiracy. Thus when **X** and **Y** drove by to "case" the neighbor's house they committed an act in furtherance of the conspiracy. They cannot use as a defense that they were driving a car on a public street, which is itself an innocent act. When an innocent act is committed in furtherance of the criminal agreement, the crime of conspiracy occurs. Nor can **X** and **Y** use as a defense any subsequent abandonment of their plan before completion. Abandonment is relevant in the following situations involving attempt and consummation, but the crime of conspiracy is complete when the overt act is performed.

✓ **Overt act for a conspiracy**
an act committed in furtherance of a conspiracy.

Attempt

Suppose that when the long-awaited night finally arrives, **X** and **Y** place a crowbar in the trunk of their auto and drive to the neighbor's house. They walk across the neighbor's lawn and use the crowbar to pry open a bedroom window. Has a crime occurred at this point?

X and **Y** have committed attempted burglary when they perform the physical act of prying open the window, but the consummated offense of burglary has not occurred because they have not entered the house. Breaking *and* entering are required elements of common law burglary (see Chapter Six).

The crime of attempted burglary did not occur when **X** and **Y** began their drive to the neighbor's house. Although driving by the house was a sufficient physical act for conspiracy, it is not the type of act required for an attempt. The **overt act for an attempted crime** is a substantial step toward commission of the crime. **X** and **Y**'s drive to the house was considered part of the planning or preparation

✓ **Overt act for an attempted crime**
a substantial step toward commission of the intended offense.

stage. An attempt requires that the defendant go beyond **mere preparation** and actually perform a physical act, which amounts to commencement of the consummation of the crime.

Precisely when an act goes beyond mere preparation and becomes the commencement of consummation is a difficult determination. No hard and fast definition of the physical act required for an attempt exists, but the various approaches to defining a sufficient overt act for an attempt are discussed in Chapter Three. What is important at this point is recognition that the physical act required for an attempt is an act beyond the physical act required for conspiracy.

Mere preparation
attempted crimes require that the defendant move beyond preparation and begin consumation of the offense.

Consummation

Suppose that **X** and **Y** pry open the window and step into the neighbor's house. A waiting police officer apprehends them. Has a crime occurred at this point?

X and **Y** finally have committed all of the physical acts required to constitute the offense of burglary. They cannot use as a defense that they were prevented from accomplishing their goal of stealing the stereo. Common law burglary requires the acts of breaking and entering with the "intent" to commit a felony. The planned felony need not be accomplished for burglary to occur. In fact, if **X** and **Y** performed the additional physical acts of taking and carrying off the stereo, the additional crime of larceny would occur (see Chapter Six).

Summary

The preceding examples involving burglary illustrate the possible steps a criminal might take from the point of first contemplating a crime until the point of actually carrying out all the physical acts required to complete the crime. As the criminal conduct escalates and comes closer to consummation, the criminal law escalates its response by increasing the severity of the offense charged at each stage of the planned and executed crime.

MENTAL STATE (MENS REA)

Although the first part of this chapter suggested that criminal law is not designed merely to enforce moral judgments, the origin and evolution of criminal law owes much to concepts of morality. During its early development, criminal law borrowed heavily from Canon law and religious concepts relating sin to moral fault. As a general rule a defendant had to have a blameworthy frame of mind—a state of knowing or failure to recognize that certain conduct was wrong—in order to be guilty of committing a common law crime. As the U.S. Supreme Court noted; "The contention that an injury can amount to a crime only when inflicted by intention is . . . as instinctive as the child's familiar exculpatory 'But I didn't mean to.' "[5] The Court further noted that:

> The unanimity with which [courts] have adhered to the central thought that wrongdoing must be conscious to be criminal is emphasized by the variety, disparity and confusion of their definitions of the requisite but elusive mental element. However, courts of various jurisdictions, and for the purposes of different offenses, have devised working formulae, if not scientific ones, for the instruction of juries around such terms as "felonious intent," "criminal intent," "malice aforethought," "guilty knowledge," "fraudulent intent," "willfulness," "scienter," to denote guilty knowledge or "mens rea," to signify an evil purpose or mental culpability.

Although many of the preceding terms have technical definitions, the fine gradations between the various states of mind frequently blur when applied to factual situations. As with all aspects of law, the concept of mens rea presents many gray areas in which definitions become vague and difficult to comprehend. The U.S. Supreme Court has referred to mens rea as an inexact hierarchy of culpable states of mind ranging from a specific intent or desire to cause the harm, to mere negligence in bringing about the prohibited harm. Although distinctions within this "inexact hierarchy" are difficult to draw, the mental states identified by the criminal law are grounded in simple common sense. Without the benefit of formal legal training, the average lay person could approximate the formal law's efforts to identify and distinguish criminals who have varying degrees of blameworthy states of mind.

An Example of Assessing Mens Rea

The relationship between common sense and the legalistic concept of mens rea can be illustrated by asking you to identify the hierarchy of culpable states of mind arising in five factual situations involving a death. With your instructor's indulgence, temporarily discard all your accumulated legal knowledge and rank the following five hypothetical actors according to your instinctual assessment of which actor is the most/least blameworthy.

Situation 1. A is hunting for deer when she encounters her long-time enemy. A shoots and kills her enemy.

Situation 2. B is also hunting when he observes a farmer enter his barn. B decides to tease the farmer by firing a shot through the roof of the barn. B aims his shot high to frighten but not injure the farmer. B's aim is off, however, and in fact he shoots and kills the farmer.

Situation 3. While hunting, C climbs over a fence without putting the safety on her rifle. The gun catches on the fence and fires, killing C's hunting companion.

Situation 4. While hunting, D fails to use his rifle's safety catch. He trips over a fallen branch and drops the rifle. The gun fires and kills D's hunting companion.

Situation 5. E is hunting with a new rifle purchased that morning. Unknown to E, the rifle has a manufacturing defect. When E cocks the rifle, it explodes and a shell fragment kills a hunting companion.

In all five situations a physical act resulted in another's death. What distinguishes the five hypothetical actors is their mental state.

Most Blameworthy A is most blameworthy because she specifically intended to kill another human being. **Specific intent** is a subjective desire to bring about a result (harm), or virtual certainty in knowing that one will cause a harm prohibited by law. All of the other hypothetical situations involve an unintentional killing contrary to the wish of the actor, but in A's situation, A consciously intended, and perhaps planned and premeditated, to take her enemy's life. The criminal law would treat this situation as the most serious crime and would invoke terms like *premeditation* and *malice aforethought* to justify a charge of first degree murder in those jurisdictions that recognize degrees of criminal homicide.

Second-Most Blameworthy Unlike A, B did not specifically intend to kill another human being. B did, however, engage in a dangerous act conscious of the fact that he was subjecting another person to a great risk of being injured or killed. While not as blameworthy as the person who specifically intends to kill, the law regards B as having a wanton and/or willful disregard for the possible harm that resulted from his act. A **wanton state of mind** is an extremely reckless disregard of the safety of

✓ **Specific intent**
the defendant subjectively intends or desires to bring about the prohibited social harm.

✓ **Wanton state of mind**
extremely reckless disregard of the safety of others, or of other prohibited consequences.

others. A **willful state of mind** is a particularly ambiguous concept, but in this hypothetical situation it could be defined as actual knowledge of the threat to another's safety. Wanton or willful states of mind are forms of malice that justify convicting **B** of second degree murder; first degree murder normally requires a more blameworthy mens rea. As the U.S. Supreme Court recognized, "The statutory and common law of homicide often distinguishes, either in setting the 'degree' of the crime or in imposing punishment, between a person who knows that another person will be killed as the result of his conduct, and a person who acts with the specific purpose of taking another's life."[6]

In the situations involving **A** and **B**, the law looks to the defendant's actual state of mind. When a person consciously intends to kill, or consciously chooses to create a great risk of death, the most serious criminal charges are warranted. Of course, in the absence of a confession, the actual state of mind of the defendant is always difficult to establish. As discussed in Chapter One, the burden of proof rests on the prosecution, but circumstantial evidence may be adequate to infer beyond a reasonable doubt what the defendant was thinking at the time of the alleged offense.

Third-Most Blameworthy

Unlike **A**, **C** did not specifically intend to kill anyone; and unlike **B**, **C** did not consciously expose another to great danger. **C**'s fault lies in her failure to act in a reasonable manner. Regardless of her actual intentions, **C** should have realized that she was performing a dangerous act in climbing a fence with a loaded gun, and she *should* have exercised greater care.

When the criminal law focuses on what defendants **A** and **B** were actually thinking, the courts must determine the subjective state of mind of **A** and **B**. Thus, evidence of the particular defendant's intent or knowledge is needed. When the law focuses on what defendant **C** should have been thinking or doing—sometimes referred to as a "general intent" rather than a "specific intent" crime—the law invokes an objective standard to assess conduct. The objective concept of a **reasonably prudent person standard** runs throughout the law and asserts that every individual's conduct is measured against the conduct of a reasonably prudent person under the same or similar circumstances. In such cases, guilt does not depend on the defendant's subjective awareness that her conduct was risky; the test is whether a reasonable person would have perceived the risk. Although **C** meant no harm to anyone, society requires every individual to act prudently in order to avoid even accidental injury. **C** failed to act prudently since the reasonably prudent person *should* have put the safety on before crossing the fence, because the reasonably prudent person *should* have recognized the situation was dangerous with potential to injure someone. When a person fails to act in a reasonable manner, by definition she has acted unreasonably or in other words, has shown negligence.

In tort law, **simple negligence** may be adequate grounds for recovering damages from the negligent actor. But a civil finding of negligence and the resulting compensation of the victim is different from a criminal conviction and the resulting potential imprisonment of the defendant. Many jurisdictions recognize degrees of negligence by distinguishing between simple (noncriminal) negligence and recklessness (criminal negligence). **Recklessness (criminal negligence)** is a gross deviation from a law-abiding person's conduct, even though no harm was intended. The distinction between criminal and noncriminal negligence can be illustrated by considering the next situation.

Fourth-Most Blameworthy

D also failed to act as a reasonably prudent person by walking with the safety off and by failing to observe that he was about to trip on a fallen branch. But **D**'s deviation from prudent conduct may not be as great as **C**'s deviation. The reasonably prudent person should know to be careful when walking with a loaded gun, but even more careful when climbing a fence with a weapon. The difference between recklessness (criminal negligence) and simple negligence is a matter of degree. The law seeks to determine how far the defendant has strayed from the conduct expected of reasonable persons.

Willful state of mind
actual knowledge of the threat to another's safety, or of other prohibited consequences.

Reasonably prudent person standard
measures the defendant's actual conduct against that of a reasonably prudent person under the same or similar circumstances.

Simple or civil negligence
occurs when a person fails to act as a reasonably prudent person under the circumstances.

Recklessness (criminal negligence)
the defendant's deviation from reasonable conduct is excessive, or more than simple (noncriminal) negligence.

Both **C**'s and **D**'s conduct will be measured against the same standard of a reasonably prudent person. Any deviation from the conduct of a prudent person is negligence, but at some point the deviation becomes so great that it is no longer a case of simple negligence, instead it is regarded as recklessness or criminal negligence. The task of setting the standard of care for reasonably prudent persons and assessing whether the defendant met that standard rests with the judge or jury. For instance, a jury might conclude that **C**'s deviation from prudent conduct was so extreme as to amount to recklessness, thus warranting a conviction for involuntary manslaughter. In contrast, **D**'s deviation might be regarded as simple negligence—adequate grounds for compensation in tort law, but normally beyond the scope of criminal law.

Least Blameworthy

Least Blameworthy   **E** could not be convicted of most common law offenses because the common law reserved punishment for those who had been at least reckless. Measuring **E**'s conduct against that required of the reasonably prudent person discloses that **E** has not been at fault. Any negligence or fault appears to lie with the manufacturer of the defective gun.

By statute, however, the legislature may elect to punish individuals for simple negligence (for example, vehicular homicide) or a statute may impose punishment even when the individual has acted reasonably (strict liability crimes). **Strict liability crimes** occur when the defendant commits an act that causes a prohibited harm, regardless of the defendant's state of mind or reasonableness of actions. For example, a legislature may choose to impose strict accountability on anyone handling hazardous materials such as firearms. Under such statutes, a crime occurs when the defendant commits an act (handling the firearm) which produces harm. Thus, although **E** could not be convicted of a common law crime, if the jurisdiction has a statute imposing strict liability on anyone who harms another with a firearm, **E** might still face prosecution.

Strict liability crimes are often criticized as unfair or contrary to our sense of justice. The court in *Commonwealth v. Olshefski* defended strict liability crimes against such criticism.

> ✓ **Strict liability crimes**
> the defendant commits an act that causes a prohibited harm, regardless of the defendant's state of mind or reasonableness of actions.

COMMONWEALTH V. OLSHEFSKI
64 Pa. C. & C. 343 (Pa. 1946)

The defendant's employee purchased a load of coal and had it loaded on defendant's truck. The coal was weighed by a licensed weigh master and the weight was given at 15,200 pounds. The defendant's truck was licensed to carry a gross weight of 15,750 pounds. The next day the defendant's truck was stopped by the State Police who weighed the load and found it to be 16,015 pounds. The defendant was convicted of a violation of the vehicle code for overloading his truck by 265 pounds. The defendant contends that because of the previously issued weigh bill, he was of the belief that his load was a legal load, and therefore he is not guilty of the crime charged.

In criminal law we have two distinct types of crimes: The one type of crime being the common-law crimes, which are designated as crimes mala in se, which means

that they are crimes because the act is bad in and of itself. The other type of crime which did not exist at common law covers those acts which are made criminal by statute, and are termed crimes mala prohibita, and simply means that they are crimes not because they are bad in and of themselves, but merely because the legislative authority makes the act criminal and penal.

In crimes that are mala in se, two elements are necessary for the commission of the crime, viz., the mental element and the physical element. In this type of crime intent is a necessary element, but in statutory crimes, which are simply mala prohibita, the mental element is not necessary for the commission of the crime, and one who does an act in violation of the statute and is caught and prosecuted, is guilty of the crime irrespective of his intent or belief. The power of the legislature to punish an act as a crime, even though it is not bad in and of itself, is an absolute power of the legislature, the only restriction being the constitutional restrictions, and it is the duty of the court to enforce these enactments irrespective of what the court might personally think about the prosecution or the wisdom of the act.

It is true that this rule of law may seem harsh and unjustifiable, but the court is powerless to correct it, and, therefore under our duty as judges, we are obliged to hold that this defendant violated the Vehicle Code by having his truck overloaded, and that he is guilty as charged.

Strict liability crimes exist only when created by statute, and legislatures rarely impose serious punishment for such crimes. However, one common form of strict liability felony—statutory rape—may impose criminal liability regardless of the defendant's state of mind as to the victim's age.

Summary

In the absence of a statute creating a strict liability offense, a crime normally requires a state of mind identified as (1) specific intent to cause a harm, (2) wanton or willful disregard for possible harm, or (3) recklessness in bringing about the harm. The Model Penal Code, on the other hand, identifies four states of mind—"purposely, knowingly, recklessly, or negligently" causing the death of another human being. Both the common law terms and the Model Penal Code terminology reflect general concepts and are not intended as precise lines of demarcation. For example, there is some overlap in these concepts because under some conditions a reckless homicide is murder, while under other conditions it is manslaughter. Thus both the common law and the Model Penal Code would characterize Situation 3 (climbing over the fence) as recklessness and manslaughter. Both the common law and the code would treat Situation 2 (firing at the barn) as murder, but the common law would use terms like wanton and willful, whereas the code would use the term extreme recklessness. Some states use terminology different from both the common law and the Model Penal Code, but the essence of the possible states of mind are reflected in the hunting hypothetical. These states of mind and others are addressed in greater detail in Chapter Five's consideration of the various forms of criminal homicide. For example, killing another human being is the act required for homicide, but in the absence of an accompanying mens rea, it is not criminal homicide.

Causation

Mental state, physical act, and social harm are the basic elements of most crimes, but the additional component of causation links the elements of conduct and harm. When a court concludes that the defendant is guilty of a crime, murder for example, the court has found (1) that the defendant possessed a proscribed state of mind, (2) that the defendant performed a physical act, and (3) that the act resulted in the social harm of death.

The concept of causality in criminal law requires a determination of why something occurred and who, if anyone, is responsible for causing the occurrence. Unlike tort law in which morally innocent persons may be held vicariously responsible for inflicting unintended harms, in many cases the criminal law employs the principle of causation to ensure that criminal responsibility is limited to those who are morally at fault. Thus analysis of causation in criminal cases is generally divided into factual cause, which is unconcerned with moral fault, and legal cause, which focuses on a defendant's wrongful conduct.

Factual Cause

Factual cause
a prohibited harm would not have occurred when it did in the absence of the defendant's conduct.

A defendant's physical act is the **factual cause** of a result if the result would not have occurred when it did in the absence of the defendant's conduct. This principle is often referred to as the "but-for test of causation." In *Price Waterhouse v. Hopkins*, the U.S. Supreme Court explained:

> . . . but-for causation is a hypothetical construct. In determining whether a particular factor was a but-for cause of a given event, we begin by assuming that that factor was present at the time of the event, and then ask whether, even if that factor had been absent, the event nevertheless would have transpired in the same way.[7]

The but-for test of causation can be illustrated in a hypothetical situation in which a defendant shoots a person who has hemophilia who then bleeds to death. "But for" defendant's firing the gun, the victim's death would not have occurred when it did, thus the defendant's act is a factual cause of the death—a necessary but not sufficient condition for the result. The defendant's act is a necessary but not sufficient condition for the result because the complete factual cause of any result is the sum of the necessary antecedents. The defendant's firing of the gun would not have caused the victim's death but for (1) the additional fact that the victim was within firing range; but for (2) the additional fact that the bleeding could not be stopped; and indeed, but for (3) the fact that the victim's mother passed on a hereditary condition of hemophilia, the victim might not have bled to death. All of these "but for" facts were necessary to bring about the victim's death.

Factual causation is merely a starting point in identifying the necessary antecedents for a result because factual causation does not resolve the question of who is ultimately responsible for the result. For example, factual causation doesn't tell us whether to punish the person who fired the shot, the doctor who failed to stop the bleeding, or the mother who passed on the hereditary condition of hemophilia. The task of identifying the legally culpable person is reserved for the concept of legal causation.

Legal Cause

Legal causation
one of the factual causes identified as the legally significant act that warrants conviction and punishment.

Factual causation analysis provides a pool of candidates or antecedents from which a court can choose. The court must resolve the issue of **legal causation** by forming a judgment that, among the many antecedent causes, one particular cause will best serve the purposes for which the criminal law was adopted. Thus a court or jury does not scientifically "discover" the legal cause of a harm, it "selects" the legal cause. This selection process rests upon the purposes to be served by convicting and punishing criminals (i.e., deterrence, rehabilitation, and the other goals of punishment discussed in Chapter One).

Consider again the hypothetical in which the defendant shot a person suffering from hemophilia. The defendant's act in pulling the trigger was identified as a "but-for" factual cause of the death. However, taking "but-for" analysis to its logical extreme, it was just as true that by passing on the hereditary condition of hemophilia, the victim's mother was another but-for cause of the death. The mother's act of giving birth to a child with hemophilia, while a factual cause of the death, was not a wrongful act, thus the criminal law will not label her as a murderer. Even if the mother had conceived the victim during a prohibited act of adultery, her wrongful contribution to the victim's death is minor, if not absurd, when compared with the contribution made by the defendant who pulled the trigger. It would trivialize the criminal law and violate common sense to regard the defendant and the victim's mother as equally responsible for the death.

The hypothetical shooting of a person with hemophilia who had been conceived during an act of adultery illustrates two fundamental principles that govern causation in criminal cases: (1) Factual causation must be determined by applying objective scientific principles of cause and effect. After this often elementary analysis is completed, the more difficult task of determining legal causation remains. (2) Legal causation does not turn upon scientific analysis, but upon assessment of the social purposes to be served by the criminal law. For example, society seeks to deter murderers by punishing people who fire bullets at another person. Society, however, seeks to deter illegitimate births by punishing people for adultery or fornication. A mother who gives birth to an illegitimate child will not be punished for murder when someone else kills the illegitimate child. A court must resolve the issue of legal causation by forming a judgment that among the many contributing factual causes of the harm, punishment of one particular cause will best serve the purposes of the criminal law.

SUMMARY

Familiarity with legal terms like *mala in se, mala prohibita, malice, specific intent,* and *general intent* is obviously helpful and sometimes necessary. The most important concern, however, is the fundamental principles expressed within these legal terms. Ultimately, most legal principles are grounded in society's conceptions of mental state, physical act, and social harm, which together form a "working definition" of crime.

The simplicity of this working definition is both helpful and deceiving. It can be deceiving because the terms *mental state, physical act,* and *social harm,* are often replaced by more technical terminology. Nonetheless, a simplistic working definition of crime may be helpful when analyzing both the facts and the law of any criminal case. Whether reviewing a case, reading a statute, or analyzing a "real life" or hypothetical fact situation, ask the following questions:

1. What is the mental state required for the crime charged? What facts establish the defendant's state of mind at the time of the alleged crime?
2. What physical acts must take place, or fail to take place, for the crime to occur? What did the defendant actually do or fail to do?
3. What is the harm prohibited by the crime? What facts prove that the prohibited harm occurred?

The full complexities of social harm, physical act, mental state, and causation, and the difficulty of applying these concepts to all forms of crime will become apparent in subsequent chapters. However, the suggested working definition provides a foundation for organizing the incredibly intricate world of criminal law. Should the complexity of the subject matter seem overwhelming, return to fundamentals and utilize the suggested working definition to regain a grasp of the essential elements of crimes.

DISCUSSION QUESTIONS

1. What purpose of criminal law is served when the government punishes people for causing harms they did not intend? For example, recklessly causing an automobile accident in which someone is killed?
2. Provide examples to illustrate each of the states of mind discussed in this chapter.
3. Is a legislature's power to create strict liability crimes limited in any way? If someone reasonably but mistakenly believes he or she has a valid divorce, would a second marriage make that person guilty of bigamy?

PRACTICE EXERCISES

1. What, if any, forms of strict liability crimes exist in your jurisdiction?
2. Does your jurisdiction recognize any form of statutory rape? Does it require that the defendant know or have reason to know the victim's age?
3. What forms of omission does your state recognize as adequate to constitute a crime?

4. Has your state defined a voluntary act for purposes of the criminal law? Are any cases recorded in which an intoxicated motorist is charged with drunk driving after passing out behind the steering wheel of a parked vehicle? What about a person with epilepsy who has a seizure while driving? [See *People v. Decina*, 157 N.Y.S.2d 558 (1956).]

WEB SITE

The National Archive of Criminal Justice Data
www.icpsr.umich.edu/NACJD

KEY TERMS

Mens rea
Actus rea
Deliberate bodily movement
Omission
Overt act for a conspiracy
Overt act for an attempted crime

Mere preparation
Specific intent
Wanton state of mind
Willful state of mind
Reasonably prudent person
  standard

Simple or civil negligence
Recklessness (criminal negligence)
Strict liability crimes
Factual cause *not*
Legal causation

NOTES

1. J. Dressler, "Understanding Criminal Law" 63 (1987).
2. See Stephen Schulhofer, "Harm and Punishment: A Critique of Emphasis on the Results of Conduct in the Criminal Law," *122 U. Pennsylvania Law Review 1497* (1974); Smith, "The Element of Chance in Criminal Liability, " *1971 Criminal Law Review 63.*
3. See *People v. Decina*, 2 N.Y.2d 133, 157 N.Y.S.2d 558, 138 N.E.2d 799 (1956); dissent argued that a driver rendered unconscious by an epileptic seizure is not "operating" a motor vehicle.

4. *Paris Adult Theatre I v. Slaton*, 413 U.S. 49, 93 S.Ct. 2628 (1973); addresses the possession of obscene materials.
5. *Morissette v. United States*, 342 U.S. 246, 72 S.Ct. 240 (1952).
6. *United States v. Bailey*, 444 U.S. 394, 100 S.Ct. 624 (1980).
7. *Price Waterhouse v. Hopkins*, 490 U.S. 228, 109 S.Ct. 1775 (1989).

PARTIES TO A CRIME AND INCHOATE OFFENSES

Chapter 3

CHAPTER OUTLINE

This chapter is concerned with individuals who personally perform the physical acts constituting a crime, as well as the circumstances under which a person may be held accountable for the criminal conduct of another person. (Review Chapter Two, which discusses the manner in which a person may move from soliciting a crime, to conspiring to commit a crime, to assisting in the completion of a crime.) This chapter also addresses inchoate or incomplete crimes which most often arise when the defendant involves other parties in a joint effort to commit a crime.

PARTIES TO A CRIME

Except for the offense of treason against the crown, the common law recognized three categories of parties to felonies:

- Perpetrators (principals in the first degree)
- Aiders and abettors (principals in the second degree)
- Accessories before the fact (accessories after the fact were punished for a separate crime)

Perpetrators

Perpetrator (principal in the first degree)
one who performs the physical acts that constitute the offense or commits the offense by use of an instrumentality.

Instrumentality
use of an inanimate object, an animal, or an innocent human being to commit a crime.

Innocent human agent
one who commits the physical acts constituting a crime, but who is innocent of the crime because of a legitimate defense.

The **perpetrator** or **principal in the first degree** is the person who (1) performs the physical acts that constitute the offense, or (2) commits the offense by use of some instrumentality. In the simplest case, the perpetrator commits a crime through personal actions by shooting or stabbing the victim (homicide), taking and carrying away another's personal property (larceny), or performing whatever acts are proscribed by law.

A perpetrator who does not commit the crime with the perpetrator's own hands may be guilty of using an **instrumentality,** such as an inanimate object, an animal, or an innocent human being. In the case of an inanimate object, the defendant might use a crowbar to smash a bedroom window and then use the crowbar to reach into the house and remove valuables from the victim's nightstand. Although the defendant's body never entered the victim's dwelling, the defendant is guilty of burglary (breaking and entering) based on manipulation of the crowbar to achieve an entry of the dwelling for purposes of consummating a larceny. In cases involving animals, a defendant might command an attack dog to kill the victim, and thereby use the dog to accomplish the intent of the crime. Tools, weapons and other instrumentalities are frequently used to commit crimes, and the law has little difficulty in looking behind the instrument to identify the human being who put the instrument to use in committing the crime.

The perpetrator's use of an "innocent" human agent as an instrumentality to commit a crime is less common because most agents qualify as conspirators or accomplices. An **innocent human agent** commits the physical acts constituting a crime, but is innocent of the crime because of a legitimate defense such as self-defense, insanity, or duress. Cases involving the use of innocent agents usually arise in rather bizarre factual situations as in the case of *Bailey v. Commonwealth.*

BAILEY v. COMMONWEALTH
Supreme Court of Virginia, 1985
229 Va. 258, 329 S.E.2d 37

The death of the victim, Gordon E. Murdock, occurred during the late evening of May 21, 1983, in the aftermath of an extended and vituperative conversation between Bailey and Murdock over their citizen's band radios. During the conversation, which was to be the last in a series of such violent incidents, Bailey and Murdock cursed and threatened each other repeatedly.

Bailey knew that Murdock had a problem with vision and that he was intoxicated on the night in question. Bailey also knew that Murdock owned a handgun and had boasted about how he would use it and shoot it and scare people off with it. Bailey knew further that Murdock was easily agitated and that he became especially angry if anyone disparaged his war hero, General George S. Patton. During the conversation in question, Bailey implied that General Patton and Murdock himself were homosexuals.

Also during the conversation, Bailey persistently demanded that Murdock arm himself with his handgun and wait on his front porch for Bailey to come and injure or kill him. Murdock responded by saying he would be waiting on his front porch, and he told Bailey to "kiss his mother or his wife and children goodbye because he would never go back home."

Bailey made anonymous telephone calls to the Police Department reporting that Murdock had a gun on the porch, had threatened to shoot up the neighborhood, and was talking about shooting anything that moves. Bailey insisted that the police "come out here and straighten this man out." Bailey called Murdock back on the radio and told Murdock that he was going to come up there in a blue and white car. [The police vehicles were blue and white.]

When the police officers arrived on the scene, they observed Murdock come out of his house with "something shiny in his hand." The police told Murdock to leave the gun alone and walk down the stairs away from it. Murdock cursed, then reached for the gun, stood up, advanced in the officer's direction, and opened fire. Three officers returned fire, and Murdock was struck. Lying wounded on the porch, he said several times, "I didn't know you was the police." He died from the gunshot wounds. In the investigation that followed, Bailey stated that he was "the hoss that caused the loss."

We have adopted the rule in this Commonwealth that one who effects a criminal act through an innocent or unwitting agent is a principal in the first degree. The question is not whether Murdock was Bailey's innocent or unwitting agent but whether the police officers who responded to Bailey's calls occupied that status. And, in resolving this question, we believe it is irrelevant whether Bailey and the police shared a common scheme or goal. What is relevant is whether Bailey undertook to cause Murdock harm and used the police to accomplish that purpose, a question which we believe must be answered affirmatively.

From a factual standpoint, it is clear from the sum total of Bailey's actions that his purpose in calling the police was to induce them to go to Murdock's home and unwittingly create the appearance that Bailey himself had arrived to carry out the threats he had made over the radio. And, from a legal standpoint, it is clear that, for Bailey's mischievous purpose, the police officers who went to Murdock's home and confronted him were acting as Bailey's innocent or unwitting agents.

We affirm the conviction.

In situations where an innocent actor has a legitimate defense, the perpetrator of the offense is the person who manipulated or caused the innocent actor to perform the physical acts that consummate the crime.

Aiders and Abettors

✓**Aider and abettor (principal in the second degree)** person who assists the perpetrator in the commission of the crime while being actually or constructively present at the scene of the crime.

An **aider and abettor (principal in the second degree)** assists the perpetrator in the commission of the crime while being actually or constructively present at the scene of the crime. The most common example of an aider and abettor is the "lookout" or "getaway driver" who waits outside a bank being robbed by the perpetrator. The lookout cannot use the defense of remaining physically outside the building while the actual robbery took place inside the bank. A person is constructively present if situated in a position to assist the perpetrator at the time of the offense. Assistance may take the form of inciting, encouraging, advising, or aiding in the physical acts required for the crime. As *Murray* illustrates, courts may make fine distinctions between merely being present during the commission of a crime and assisting in that crime.

MURRAY v. COMMONWEALTH
170 S.E.2d 3 (Va. 1969)

On January 1, 1968 Thomas Grace accosted Adolphus Coltes, knocked him down and stole his wallet. Defendant John Murray, who was with Grace before, during and after that incident, stands convicted of robbing Coltes as a principal in the second degree. The only issue on this appeal is whether the evidence adduced at Murray's trial supports his conviction.

On the morning of January 1, 1968, Murray and Grace saw Coltes walking west on Grace Street. When they approached Coltes, Grace tapped him on the shoulder and asked for the loan of a dollar. A Commonwealth witness, who was standing on a porch across the street, saw Coltes remove his wallet from his pocket. He noticed that Grace was on Coltes's left and Murray on his right— 'they were real close.' Grace then struck Coltes, knocked him down and picked up his wallet. Grace put Coltes's wallet in his pocket, and he and Murray ran away.

A person cannot be convicted as a principal in the second degree—that is, as an aider or abettor—upon evidence that he was merely present during the commission of a crime and fled from the scene of the crime. But the trier of fact can consider flight of the accused from the scene of the crime as a circumstance tending to establish his guilt. A person can be convicted as a princi-

pal in the second degree, however, upon evidence that he not only was present, but also committed some overt act—such as inciting, encouraging, advising or assisting in the commission of the crime—or shared the prime actor's criminal intent.

Murray's counsel contends the evidence showed only that Murray was present when Grace committed the crime and Murray fled from the scene of the crime. The Attorney General contends the evidence supported findings that Murray encouraged and assisted Grace in the criminal act and that he shared Grace's criminal intent. We agree with the Attorney General and affirm the conviction.

The Commonwealth's evidence showed not only circumstances tending to establish Murray's guilt—such as Murray's attempts to open the doors of parked automobiles and his flight with Grace after the robbery. The evidence also showed at least one overt act toward Coltes: Murray's standing 'real close' to Coltes immediately before the robbery. From this evidence, the trier of fact could properly infer that Murray, in concert with Grace, intended to intimidate Coltes as a prelude to robbing him.

Affirmed.

Assistance at the time of the offense and constructive presence are the prime factors that distinguish aiders and abettors from accessories before the fact.

Accessories Before the Fact

An **accessory before the fact** solicits, counsels, or advises another on how to commit the crime at some later date. An accessory before the fact does not differ appreciably from an aider and abettor except that an accessory is not present either actually or constructively when the crime is committed. The classic example of an accessory before the fact is the "mastermind" who formulates a plan to rob the bank, and while others carry out the plan, the mastermind establishes an alibi by attending the opera.

Although accessories before the fact can be distinguished from aiders and abettors on the basis of their presence at the scene of the crime, both categories of accomplices are similar in the type of assistance furnished to the perpetrator. Assistance may take the form of physical conduct or psychological influence on the perpetrator. The assistance must be in the form of an affirmative act because, generally speaking, a person who merely fails to take action to prevent a crime is not an accomplice. For example, in a notorious incident in New York City, a group of onlookers watched the violent mugging of a defenseless woman, but took no action to assist the woman or call the police. Whatever one may conclude about the moral deficiencies of such callous onlookers, they committed no criminal offense because, in the absence of a statute, they had no legal duty to assist another person; in popular parlance, "You are not your brother's keeper." Exceptions occur, however, when omission (the failure to take action) renders the person liable as an accomplice. Had police officers stood by and witnessed the mugging of a helpless victim, their failure to meet their legal duty to protect citizens might make the officers responsible as accomplices. Some jurisdictions have enacted "Good Samaritan" statutes requiring citizens to render assistance in certain situations.

With the exception of those situations in which a legal duty to take action is present, the law normally punishes accomplices only when they perform an affirmative act which assists the perpetrator. Once the accomplice takes action to assist the perpetrator, however, the degree of assistance is immaterial. Any aid, no matter how trivial, is sufficient if it assists or encourages the perpetrator in committing the crime. For example, in *Wilcox v. Jeffery*, the defendant applauded the perpetrator's performance of an illegal concert at an airport.[1] The defendant was convicted as an accomplice because his applause encouraged the perpetrator to perform the illegal act. Note that an accomplice situation is one of the instances in which a person may be convicted of a crime solely because of verbal acts (see Chapter Two). For example, a defendant may be charged as an accessory before the fact to the crime of arson if the defendant encourages another to set fire to an abortion clinic.

Although a person may physically assist or verbally encourage a perpetrator, that person is not an accomplice unless shown to have the mental state required for the crime. For example, if someone gives a hitchhiker a ride to the bank, that person does not become an accomplice when the hitchhiker robs the bank. Although performing a physical act that assisted the bank robber, the person driving the car did not *intentionally* assist in the hitchhiker's criminal conduct. Suppose, however, that the hitchhiker informed the driver of the intent to rob the bank. Suppose the driver responded, "Look, I don't want to get involved. I'm giving you a ride and what you do when you leave my car is your business." In this situation the driver has "knowledge" (scienter) of the impending crime, but does not share the perpetrator's "intent" to commit the crime. The courts have had considerable difficulty distinguishing knowledge from intent in such situations (the issue is addressed later in this chapter in the section covering conspiracy). As *Foster* illustrates, although knowledge may not be an adequate mens rea for the crime, knowledge may be circumstantial evidence of the intent required for the crime.

Accessory before the fact although not present when the crime is committed, one who previously solicited, counseled, or advised another on how to commit the crime.

FOSTER v. COMMONWEALTH
18 S.E.2d 314 (Va. 1942)

The defendant was arrested on a warrant charging him with keeping a house of ill fame. The defendant, Delbert Foster, and his wife, Mabel, lived in West Virginia. About four weeks before the night of the raid, February 16, 1941, she came to Roanoke, entered this house of prostitution and was following her vocation up to the very moment when the police broke in upon her. Her husband followed her in about three weeks, went to the house where she was and lived there until the time of his arrest. He said that his purpose in coming was to persuade his wife to return with him to West Virginia.

In his room was found a drawer packed with shirts, at least eight or ten of them freshly laundered, together with the average wardrobe of a man permanently located. A jury might have believed that his stay was not temporary and that he did not come merely to take his wife away. In short, it might have believed that he misstated his purpose in coming.

A jury might have believed that he was a principal or one of them; it might have believed that he was an accessory, and it might have believed that he was an aider or an abettor. This is a matter of no importance, the punishment in each instance is the same. The status of the accused may be established both by circumstantial evidence and by direct evidence. Notwithstanding rules as to the nonliability of a passive spectator, it is certain that proof that a person is present at the commission of a crime without disapproving or opposing it, is evidence from which, in connection with other circumstances, it is competent for the jury to infer that he assented thereto, lent to it his countenance and approval, and was thereby aiding and abetting the same.

The maintenance of these houses is a continuing offense. The defendant knew what the character of the house was when he moved into it in circumstances which indicated he intended to stay for an indefinite time, itself a separate offense. He may have had an interest in it, growing out of the fact that his wife was one of its principal inmates. He must have known that the proceeds of her earnings went in part to the maintenance of the den at which he was anchored. If he was paying board and room rent, he was contributing to its maintenance, and if he was given these accommodations free of charge, it must have been under a contract, express or implied, that he would keep quiet as to the character of the establishment. Certainly he was interested and certainly these privileges would have been accorded to no complete stranger. Any of the circumstances indicated would support this conviction. Juries are supposed to carry into the jury box ordinary knowledge of men and affairs. Its members do not cease to be men because they are members. It is perfectly true that the Commonwealth must make out its case, but that case may be established both by direct evidence and by known and proven conditions.

Judgment affirmed.

In most jurisdictions accessories before the fact and aiders and abettors are charged, tried, convicted, and punished (except for the death penalty) as if they were perpetrators. Acting as a perpetrator, accessory, or aider and abettor is merely an alternative means of committing a crime. Just as a person may commit murder by using a gun, knife, or chainsaw, a person may also commit murder by being a perpetrator, accessory, or aider and abettor. Most often the indictment or charge against the accomplice will not even mention whether the person is or is not the actual perpetrator, but will merely state that the defendant did commit murder, rape, or robbery. Only in the Bill of Particulars or in pretrial discovery will the prosecution reveal whether the defendant is regarded as a perpetrator or an accomplice.

In addition to being responsible for the intended crime, an accomplice may be held responsible for unintended crimes. Suppose that **A** maintains a lookout outside the bank while **B** conducts the robbery. When a bank guard attempts to thwart the robbery, **B** shoots and kills the guard. Is **A** responsible for the killing? Accountability extends not only to the crime that the accomplice intentionally assisted but also for any other offense that is a natural and probable consequence of the intended offense. Although the killing of the bank guard was not planned, it is a foreseeable consequence of an armed robbery. In contrast, if **B** had killed a person for reasons unrelated to the robbery (e.g., an old enemy happened to be in the bank), **A** would not be held accountable for this unforeseeable homicide.

Accessories After the Fact

By acting in concert with the perpetrator before or during the commission of a crime, aiders and abettors and accessories before the fact help cause the crime and therefore are punishable for the crime. An accessory after the fact, however, does not contribute to the commission of the crime; such criminality is found in postcrime assistance. An **accessory after the fact** impedes the apprehension, trial, or punishment of a felon. The conduct of accessory after the fact is punished as a separate crime, which often carries comparatively minor punishment.

Accessory after the fact ✓
one who impedes the apprehension, trial, or punishment of a felon.

In order to convict the defendant of being an accessory after the fact the prosecution must prove:

1. A felony was committed. (At common law no one could be charged with accessory after the fact to misdemeanors. Some modern statutes, however, extend the crime of accessory after the fact to encompass misdemeanors.) Every trial of an accessory after the fact requires proof of two crimes: the underlying felony committed by another person; and the crime of assisting that person. Although the underlying felony must be proved at the accessory's trial, the felon usually need not have already been convicted of the felony. If the law required an actual conviction of the felon, the law would be rewarding an accessory after the fact who successfully assisted the felon in avoiding conviction.

2. The defendant charged with being an accessory after the fact knew that the underlying felony had been committed. The accessory's knowledge (scienter) of the commission of a felony can be proved by direct or circumstantial evidence. For example, when the jury is told that the defendant picked up a hitchhiker wearing a mask, carrying a weapon and a bag of bank money, the jury may infer that the defendant knew of the bank robbery.

3. The defendant charged with being an accessory after the fact intended to hinder apprehension, trial, or punishment. For example, if Dr. Mudd set the broken leg of John Wilkes Booth as a humanitarian act, Dr. Mudd was not an accessory after the fact to the assassination of President Lincoln. If Dr. Mudd's intent was to assist Booth in avoiding apprehension, Dr. Mudd might become an accessory after the fact.

4. The defendant charged with being an accessory after the fact assisted the felon to avoid apprehension, trial, or punishment. Assistance may take the form of hiding the felon, testifying to a false alibi, or aiding in a jailbreak. In the absence of a statute, mere failure to report a crime or volunteer helpful information to the police does not make the defendant an accessory after the fact.

Although they are not accessories after the fact to the committed offense, persons who conceal or fail to report a felony may be guilty of the separate crimes of misprison of a felony or compounding a felony. **Misprison of a felony** punishes the failure to report a known crime, while **compounding a felony** requires that the person accept a benefit in return for a promise to conceal a known crime. Many jurisdictions have eliminated these crimes or have replaced them with a statutory offense of obstructing justice.

Misprison of a felony
failure to report a known crime.

Compounding a felony ✓
accepting a benefit in return for concealing a known crime.

Exhibit 3–1 provides an example of a jury instruction explaining the definition of parties to a crime.

EXHIBIT 3–1
**Summary of Parties
to an Offense**

> - **Perpetrators** (principals in the first degree) are those who are the actual or immediate perpetrators of the crime.
> - **Aiders and abettors** (principals in the second degree) are those who did not with their own hands commit the act which constituted the crime, but who were present, aiding and abetting in its commission. The test for a principal in the second degree is whether that person was encouraging or inciting the commission of a crime by words, gestures, looks or signs, or in some manner offering aid or consent to its commission. Principals in the second degree are liable to the same extent as principals in the first degree.
> - An **accessory before the fact** is one not present at the time of commission of the offense, but who, in some way before its commission, contrives, instigates, or advises as to its commission.
> - An **accessory after the fact** is one not present at the time of commission of the offense, but who, knowing a felony to have been committed by another, thereafter receives, comforts, or assists the principal felon by way of personal help with a view to hindering apprehension or enabling the perpetrator to elude punishment.

INCHOATE CRIMES

Inchoate crime
an incomplete or imperfect
offense.

An **inchoate crime** is an incomplete or imperfect offense. Although the defendant fails to perform all of the acts required for a consummated offense, the law prohibits the endeavor to commit a crime in three instances: solicitation, conspiracy, and attempt. An attempted crime may be committed by the defendant acting alone, but the other two inchoate crimes occur only if the defendant brings a second person into the picture either to commit the offense for the defendant (solicitation), or to help the defendant in a joint effort (solicitation or conspiracy).

Solicitation

Solicitation
occurs when a person invites
or requests another to commit
a crime.

Solicitation occurs when a person invites or requests another to commit a crime. Chapter Two suggested a working definition of crime that focused on three components: mental state, physical act, and social harm. Analyzing solicitation according to this working definition discloses the three elements of the crime:

1. *Mental State:* The defendant charged with solicitation must specifically intend that another person commit an offense. A person is not guilty of solicitation unless *intentionally* inviting another to engage in a crime. Thus a defendant who jokingly suggests that a co-worker "punch-out" the boss is not guilty of solicitation, even if the co-worker takes the suggestion seriously and assaults the employer.
2. *Physical Act:* The defendant charged with solicitation must have requested or invited another to commit a crime. If the defendant possesses the requisite mental state, the crime of solicitation is complete when the defendant communicates the request to another. Solicitation rests "solely on communication without need for any resulting action."[2] Thus, no physical act in furtherance of the crime need be performed by either person.
3. *Social Harm:* By soliciting the commission of an offense, the defendant has tempted a presumably innocent person to commit a crime. The social harm occurs when the defendant asks another to commit a crime, even if the other person refuses the solicitation. An overt invitation to commit a crime must be distinguished from the covert use of an innocent human agent to commit

a crime (see the preceding section on perpetrators). For example, solicitation of a larceny occurs when the defendant suggests that **A** steal **B**'s television. If, however, the defendant induces **A** to take the television by fraudulently claiming that it belongs to the defendant, then the defendant has perpetrated the larceny through use of an innocent human agent.

Punishment for solicitation penalizes conduct at the earliest stage of preparation for committing a crime. It is the law's effort to nip criminal tendencies in the bud, and the charge is brought when the actors remain in this early stage of preparation. If the actors go beyond this preparatory stage to the next level of conspiracy, attempt, or consummation, the crime of solicitation is merged within these offenses. Legal **merger** is a concept wherein a previously distinct offense is subsumed within a greater offense, and the defendant can be convicted of either, but not both, offenses.

Merger
a previously distinct offense is subsumed within a greater offense; the defendant can be convicted of either, but not both, offenses.

When the actors complete the contemplated offense, solicitation ceases to be an independent crime, and becomes the basis for accomplice liability. In such situations solicitation is merely one way in which a person may assist another in the commission of a crime and thus be held accountable for the other's criminal acts. For example, if the police intervene as soon as **A** suggests that **B** murder **C**, **A** will be charged with solicitation of murder. If the police are unable to intervene until **C** is killed by **B**, **A** will be charged with being an accessory before the fact to murder.

Attempt

An **attempted crime** occurs when a person intends to commit a specific offense, and then performs an act that constitutes a substantial step toward consummating that offense. Although attempts do not bring about tangible harm, conduct that manifests criminal intent may disturb the public repose or cause apprehension, fear, or alarm in the community. Anyone who attempts to commit a crime may be dangerous, thus the community may incapacitate, deter, and punish such wrongdoers. Attempts, however, are generally punished less severely than the target offense, and if the target offense is consummated, the underlying attempt merges with the substantive offense.

Attempted crime
the defendant intends to commit a specific offense and performs an act that constitutes a substantial step toward completing that offense.

The mental state required for an attempted crime is the specific intent to commit a particular offense formed in the mind of the defendant. This requirement is true even when the intended offense could have been committed with some lesser mental state such as recklessness. The defendant in *Thacker* certainly acted recklessly, but he did not intend to kill anyone, and thus was not guilty of attempted murder.

THACKER v. COMMONWEALTH
Supreme Court of Virginia, 1922
134 Va. 767, 114 S.E. 504

Mrs. J. A. Ratrie, her husband, four children and a servant were camping for the summer. Upon retiring for the evening, Mrs. Ratrie placed a lighted lamp on a trunk by the head of her bed. After 11 o'clock she was awakened by the shots of a pistol and loud talking in the road nearby, and heard a man say, "I am going to shoot that God-dammed light out." The defendant fired three shots, two of which went through the tent, one just missing her head and the head of her baby, who was sleeping with her. The defendant did not know Mrs. Ratrie, and had never seen her before. He testified he did not know any of the parties in the tent, and had no ill will against either of them; that he simply shot at the light, without any intent to harm Mrs. Ratrie or any one else; that he would not have shot had he been sober, and regretted his action. The defendant was convicted of attempted murder and sentenced to two years in the penitentiary.

An attempt to commit a crime is composed of two elements: (1) The intent to commit it; and (2) a direct, ineffectual act done towards its commission. The law can presume the intention so far as realized in the act, but not an intention beyond what was so realized. The law does not presume, because an assault was made with a weapon likely to produce death, that it was an assault with the intent to murder. And where it takes a particular intent to constitute a crime, that particular intent must be proved either by direct or circumstantial evidence, which would warrant the inference of the intent with which the act was done.

When we say that a man attempted to do a given wrong, we mean that he intended to do specifically it, and proceeded a certain way in the doing. The intent in the mind covers the thing in full; the act covers it only in part. Thus to commit murder, one need not in-tend to take life, but to be guilty of an attempt to murder, he must so intend. It is not sufficient that his act, had it proved fatal, would have been murder. For example, if one from a housetop recklessly throws down a billet of wood upon the sidewalk where persons are constantly passing, and it falls upon a person passing by and kills him, this would be common-law murder, but if, instead of killing, it inflicts only a slight injury, the party could not be convicted of an assault with attempt to commit murder, since, in fact, the murder was not intended.

The application of the foregoing principles to the facts of the instant case shows clearly, as we think, that the judgment complained of is erroneous. While it might possibly be said that the firing of the shot into the head of Mrs. Ratrie's bed was an act done toward the commission of the offense charged, the evidence falls far short of proving that it was fired with the intent to murder her.

Mere preparation
portion of an attempted crime prior to the point at which consummation of the offense begins.

In *Thacker,* the defendant committed an act which came close to killing a person, but the defendant didn't intend to kill. *People v. Rizzo* raises the other possibility: is the defendant guilty of an attempt when the defendant intends to commit the crime but the act doesn't come close to success? **Mere preparation** to commit an offense is not yet an attempted crime. When a defendant is looking for an opportunity to commit a crime, is that person merely preparing for or actually attempting the crime? It's mere preparation according to *People v. Rizzo.*

PEOPLE v. RIZZO
Supreme Court of New York, 1929
246 N.Y. 334, 158 N.E. 888

The defendant and others planned to hold up a man carrying money for a payroll from the bank to a company. Armed with firearms, they started out in an automobile looking for the carrier of the money, whom Rizzo claimed to be able to identify. They drove from the bank to the company and back in an attempt to spot the carrier, but failed to find him. Meanwhile they were watched and followed by police officers who moved in and arrested the defendant and his cohorts. [In reversing the conviction of attempt to commit robbery, the court held that the acts of the defendant and his friends had not progressed to the point of nearness to commission of the act as is required for a conviction for attempt.]

In a word these defendants had planned to commit a crime, and were looking around the city for an opportunity to commit it, but the opportunity fortunately never came. Men would not be guilty of an attempt at burglary if they had planned to break into a building and were arrested while they were hunting about the streets for the building not knowing where it was. Neither would a man be guilty of an attempt to commit murder if he armed himself and started out to find the person whom he had planned to kill but could not find him.

One of the most difficult issues in the law of attempts is identifying the point at which the defendant's conduct has proceeded sufficiently far that it can be properly determined a criminal attempt. Would the defendants in *Rizzo* have been guilty of attempted robbery if they sighted the victim at a distance of thirty feet? Twenty feet? The courts have acknowledged that "the determination of when the preparation to commit an offense ceases and the perpetration of the offense begins, is a troublesome problem." One court explained, "The distinction between the preparation and the attempt is largely a matter of degree, and whether certain given conduct constitutes an actual attempt is a question unique to each particular case."[3] In an effort to balance how much has already been done against how much remains to be done, the courts have sought to distinguish preparatory conduct from a criminal attempt by applying the following tests:

1. *Last proximate act test.* The law generally deems the defendant to be guilty of an attempt after doing all that the defendant believes is necessary to complete the intended offense. For example, the defendant pulls the trigger of a gun aimed at the victim (attempted murder); the defendant picks up a television with the intent of stealing it (attempted larceny); or the defendant puts a crowbar to the window of the dwelling, intending to commit a felony (attempted burglary).
2. *Dangerous proximity test.* This test considers three factors: temporal and geographical nearness of the prohibited harm; seriousness of the harm; and the degree of apprehension created. For example, an attempt occurs when the defendant sights the intended victim and raises a gun with intent to fire, but is apprehended before pulling the trigger. In contrast, a defendant who goes to the store to purchase a rifle with intent to use it tomorrow is neither geographically nor temporally close to completion of the crime. This defendant is still in the preparatory stage.
3. *Probable desistance test.* This test focuses on how far the defendant has proceeded and the likelihood that the defendant will persist in the planned crime. The defendant has passed "the point of no return" when unlikely to voluntarily abandon the effort to commit the crime.

General defenses to crimes are addressed in Chapter Four, but the defenses of impossibility and abandonment are uniquely relevant to attempted crimes.

Impossibility

Perhaps no aspect of criminal law is more confusing than the law of impossible attempts. The fundamental question is whether a person should be convicted for conduct that cannot succeed in bringing about the intended offense. For example, is it attempted murder when the defendant pulls the trigger of a gun aimed at the intended victim, but unknown to the defendant, the gun is empty? If the answer to this question seems obvious, does the answer change if the defendant fires a loaded gun into an empty bed believed to be occupied by the intended victim? What if the defendant believes in voodoo and sticks pins into a replica of an intended victim in the expectation that such conduct will kill the victim? Should the defendant in any of these cases be acquitted because of a defense of impossibility?

The preceding situations are examples of **factual impossibility,** which is generally not accepted as a valid defense. Some courts have endeavored to treat situations like the "voodoo" killer as a valid defense because such attempts are inherently unrealistic ways to commit a crime. This classification is difficult to justify because an unloaded gun is also an inherently unrealistic way to kill someone. A person attempting to fire an unloaded gun is dangerous, in part because the person may move from an unloaded to a loaded gun. A person attempting to kill with voodoo may be equally dangerous if likely to move from an "unloaded" voodoo doll to a loaded

Factual impossibility a claim of defense because the defendant's conduct could not succeed in bringing about the intended offense.

gun. One cannot easily comprehend how a defendant who intends to kill can be convicted or acquitted of attempted murder based on the stupidity of choosing an ineffective method of killing.

Legal impossibility
a claim of defense because the defendant's state of mind precludes commission of a recognized crime.

Although factual impossibility is not widely accepted as a defense, **legal impossibility** is sometimes said to constitute a valid defense. However, most cases of legal impossibility seem indistinguishable from factual impossibility. For example, **X** and **Y** reside in a state where the age of consent for sexual intercourse is 16. **X** and **Y** each have intercourse with a 17-year-old female. **X** believed that the female was 15, so he thought he was committing statutory rape. **Y** knew that the female was 17, but he believed that the lawful age of consent was 18. Thus he also thought that he was committing statutory rape. Should either or both of these cases constitute attempted statutory rape? Should the cases be distinguished by categorizing **X**'s or **Y**'s mistaken beliefs as creating legal or factual impossibility?

The courts have never articulated a satisfactory rationale for handling the impossibility defense, and the modern trend is to abolish impossibility as a defense. For example, the Model Penal Code suggests that an attempt occurs when the defendant "purposely engages in conduct that would constitute the crime if the attendant circumstances were as he believes them to be."[4] Thus a defendant who truly believes in voodoo and acts upon that belief might be guilty of attempted murder under the Model Penal Code.

Abandonment

Abandonment
discontinuance of a plan to commit a crime; sometimes recognized as a valid defense to charges of attempting to commit the crime.

Although less paradoxical than the impossibility defense, the defense of **abandonment** is also surrounded by considerable ambiguity. Abandonment involves a defendant's discontinuance of a plan to commit a crime. For example, suppose the defendant puts poison in a friend's morning coffee. As the friend raises the coffee cup to drink, the defendant has a change of heart and snatches the cup from the friend's hand. Assume that the defendant crossed the line from mere preparation to a substantial act when the intended victim tried to drink the poison, thus an attempted murder occurred. Does the defendant's postattempt abandonment of the planned crime constitute a defense to attempted murder? Does the defendant's change of heart undo the harm of an attempt already committed? In those jurisdictions that recognize abandonment as a valid defense, the defendant must establish that abandonment was genuinely voluntary and not promoted by an increased danger of apprehension.[5] Abandonment because a police officer appeared on the scene is not a valid defense.

Conspiracy

Conspiracy
an agreement by two or more persons to commit an unlawful act. (An overt act in furtherance of a conspiracy is required in many jurisdictions.)

A **conspiracy** is an agreement by two or more persons to commit an unlawful act. The crime is "predominantly mental in composition because it consists primarily of a meeting of minds and an intent."[6] The working definition of crime separates conspiracy into its constituent parts:

1. *Mental State:* Conspiracy requires that two or more persons form a specific intent to accomplish an unlawful act. If an undercover police officer fakes an agreement with **D** to murder **V**, the police officer lacks the requisite intent that the murder be committed. Thus **D** is not guilty of conspiracy because he alone has the criminal intent, while conspiracy requires that at least two people share the criminal intent. Note, however, that the defendant may be guilty of solicitation or attempted conspiracy under the facts as he **believed** them to be.

   The specific intent required for conspiracy exists when the defendant "desires," "wants," or has as a "purpose" that the target offense be committed. A difficult question arises when the defendant performs an act knowing that it will help to accomplish the target offense, but the defendant may not care whether the crime is ever committed. For example, suppose that **Y** goes to **C**, a gun dealer, and announces that she is purchasing a gun to use in a bank robbery. If **C** sells the gun to **Y**, is **C** guilty of conspiracy to rob a bank? Case law is divided on this issue. Courts favoring conviction maintain that society must deter persons from furnishing items to people whom they know will use them unlawfully. Under this view, crime prevention must take priority over the freedom to sell one's wares to whomever one chooses.[7] The contra view favoring acquittal, maintains that conspiracy laws should not be used against those whose fault lies in failing to forego a normally lawful business activity because someone else plans to use the lawfully purchased item for an illegal purpose.[8]

2. *Physical Act:* At common law, conspiracy was complete upon formation of the agreement and no act in furtherance of the conspiracy was required. Today, most statutes require proof of the commission of an overt act in furtherance of the conspiracy. Unlike attempts, the overt act for conspiracy need not go beyond the preparatory stage by coming "close" to the consummation of the intended crime. Any act, no matter how trivial, may suffice for a conspiracy conviction so long as the act was performed in furtherance of the conspiracy. For example, if a lone arsonist purchases a pack of matches to start a fire in a dwelling, this action would not constitute attempted arson because it is mere preparation for the crime. But if two arsonists had agreed to burn the building, purchasing the matches may constitute an overt act for a conspiracy to commit arson. A single overt act by any party to a conspiracy completes the crime for all parties to the conspiracy, even those who join the conspiracy after the overt act was committed.

3. *Social Harm:* The law considers two or more people who unite to commit a crime a more dangerous situation because "the strength, opportunities and resources of many is obviously more dangerous and more difficult to police than the efforts of a lone wrongdoer."[9] At trial the prosecution must prove the existence of at least two guilty parties, which does not mean that two persons must be prosecuted and convicted of conspiracy. One conspirator may be convicted although the coconspirator died, fled the jurisdiction, or was given immunity. For example, former President Richard Nixon was named as an unindicted coconspirator for his role in the Watergate affair, but his prosecution was precluded by a presidential pardon.

The minimum requirement for a conspiracy is the existence of at least two persons who agree to commit a crime. Many conspiracies, however, involve additional people and even additional conspiracies. Thus, significant problems arise in determining whether the relationships that exist between a great number of individuals involve all of them in one single conspiracy, or whether there are distinct subgroups who formed separate conspiracies. Multiparty conspiracies can be conceptualized as resembling either a wheel or a chain as shown in Exhibit 3–2 and Exhibit 3–3.

Wheel Conspiracies   In the center of the wheel is one person (the hub) who had contact with other individuals (the spokes). For example, suppose that in planning a bank robbery, **X** recruits **A** as the lookout, **B** as the getaway driver, **C** as the expert safecracker, and **D** as the "muscle" who will handle firearms. Assume that **A, B, C,** and **D** have no contact with each other until the day of the robbery when they assemble, rob the bank, divide the proceeds, and disperse. Has one conspiracy between all the parties occurred, or four separate conspiracies between **X** (the hub) and each of the spokes: **A, B, C,** and **D**?

No simple rules govern legal analysis of wheel conspiracies. The law generally recognizes that no direct contact is necessary between every member of the conspiracy, but some community of interests must be shown. For example, each spoke must view contact with the hub as part of a plan broader than a one-on-one agreement. In the bank robbery hypothetical, each spoke must be aware that there are other parties besides the hub who will perform their role in the robbery. The individual spokes

EXHIBIT 3–2
A Wheel Conspiracy

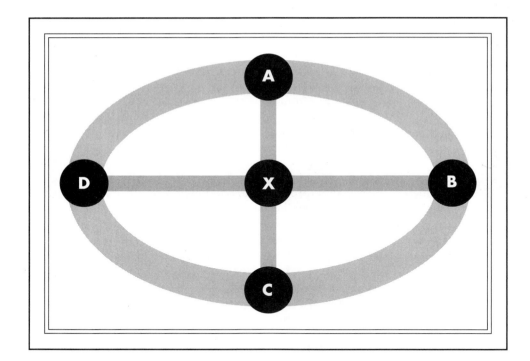

EXHIBIT 3–3
A Chain Conspiracy

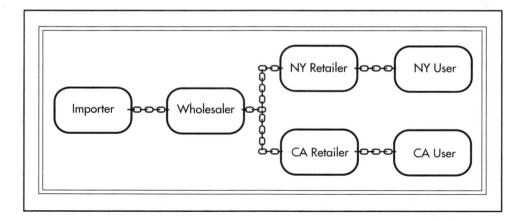

need not know the identity of the other spokes, but they must realize that they are joined together in a common enterprise to rob the bank. When these conditions are met, a wheel conspiracy is deemed to be but a single conspiracy formed by multiple parties.

Chain Conspiracies In chain conspiracies the parties are linked together in linear fashion, shown in Exhibit 3–3.

In this chain, narcotics are imported from abroad, distributed to national "wholesalers" who supply the drugs to "retailers" in California and New York, who then sell it to local users. Does this situation entail one conspiracy between the importer and all users, or are the California connection and the New York connection separate conspiracies? Again, no simple rule determines who is a party to what conspiracy. The court will consider the extent to which there was a community of interest among the parties, and the extent to which each link in the chain relied upon other links to successfully complete their tasks.[10] Thus, the situation presented in Exhibit 3–3 was held to be one giant conspiracy involving 88 defendants who conspired to import, sell, and possess narcotics.

The practical significance of separating criminal collaborations into one or multiple conspiracies affects not only the number of offenses to be charged, but also each conspirator's responsibility for acts performed by all other conspirators. If, for example, the New York and California retailers in Exhibit 3–3 are part of one conspiracy, then each could be liable for additional offenses committed thousands of miles away.

Liability of Coconspirators

In many circumstances conspirators are accomplices in the commission of a completed crime, and conversely, accomplices in the commission of a crime may be coconspirators. Normally each party who agreed to commit the crime has actively participated in the planning and commission of the offense. Some jurisdictions punish for both the completed crime and the conspiracy to commit the crime, while other jurisdictions merge conspiracy offenses into successfully completed crimes.

The liability of coconspirators for additional offenses beyond the planned crime is similar to the liability of accomplices. An earlier section of this chapter addressed the liability of a lookout (aider and abettor) for an unplanned murder committed inside the bank by the perpetrator. Under the rules governing accomplice liability, the lookout could be punished if the murder was a natural and probable consequence of the intended offense. The same result would be achieved under the **Pinkerton doctrine,** which provides that each member of a conspiracy is criminally responsible for any crime committed by another party to the agreement as long as the committed crime was the object of the conspiracy or a natural consequence of the unlawful agreement.

Pinkerton doctrine ✔
each member of a conspiracy is criminally responsible for any crime committed by another party to the agreement as long as the committed crime was the object of the conspiracy or a natural consequence of the unlawful agreement.

The only practical difference between accomplice liability and conspirator liability is that the Pinkerton doctrine, taken to the extreme, could result in greater liability than traditional accomplice liability. For example, suppose **A** and **B** purchase narcotics from **C**. If the parties have formed a conspiracy to use illegal drugs and if **A** dies from an overdose, is **B** responsible for a death that might be viewed as a natural consequence of the unlawful agreement? In theory, the Pinkerton doctrine could hold **B** responsible for the death, but in practice, the Pinkerton rule rarely has been invoked to justify such extensive liability. However, a number of states have enacted what is known as the "Len Bias" law. (Len Bias was a basketball star who died as a result of using cocaine.) Under these Len Bias statutes a person who conspires to manufacture or distribute illegal drugs is liable for a death resulting from use of such drugs.

Wharton's Rule   Wharton's rule, a defense unique to conspiracy charges, provides that no conspiracy has occurred if the agreement is made between only the parties necessary for the commission of a substantive offense. For example, common law adultery required an agreement by a man to have sexual intercourse with a married woman other than his wife. Thus, two people must cooperate in order to commit adultery. If only those two people agree to commit adultery, Wharton's rule prohibits a conviction for conspiracy to commit adultery. However, if more than the minimum number of persons agree to commit the crime, Wharton's rule does not apply. For example, a *ménage à trios* includes an extra person, thus all three of the participants may be convicted of conspiracy to commit adultery. Wharton's rule applies to only a few crimes (e.g., adultery, incest, bigamy, dueling), is not constitutionally mandated, and has fallen out of favor in many jurisdictions.[11]

Wharton's rule
states that no conspiracy has occurred in an agreement between only the parties necessary for the commission of a substantive offense.

SUMMARY

Perpetrators and those who assist them as aiders and abettors or accessories before the fact are punished for the resulting crime. Accessories after the fact are punished for a separate offense of rendering postcrime assistance to criminals. Conspirators may be accomplices to a crime that has been planned and successfully completed, but they also may be guilty of the separate offense of conspiracy to commit a felony. Both accomplices and conspirators are responsible for the acts of their cohorts when the cohorts act in furtherance of the planned crime, or when they commit an additional offense that is a natural and probable consequence of the intended offense.

Inchoate crimes like solicitation and attempt are crimes because the law may prohibit the endeavor to commit a crime. The crime of solicitation is conduct at the earliest stages of preparation for a crime, but attempted crimes require that the actor go beyond mere preparation and come close to consummation of the intended crime. The defenses of impossibility and abandonment are especially relevant to inchoate crimes. These defenses have proved to be troubling to courts and legal theorists, thus no universally accepted rules govern the application of these defenses to inchoate crimes. Determining the scope of a conspiracy, and in fact whether one or multiple conspiracies is the case, also has proven to be a matter on which courts frequently disagree.

Concept Summary

Parties to a Crime

Consult local law to determine what changes have been made in a particular jurisdiction.

Perpetrator (Principal in First Degree)	Commits the crime through the defendant's own hands or through some agent or instrumentality.
Aider and Abettor (Principal in Second Degree)	Physically or constructively present when the crime is committed; assists the perpetrator in the commission of the crime.
Accessory Before the Fact	Solicits, counsels, or advises another to commit the crime at some later date.
Accessory After the Fact	Knowingly impedes the apprehension, trial, or punishment of a felon.
Conspirators	Form an agreement to commit a crime. Statutes often require that at least one conspirator commit an overt act in furtherance of the agreement.
Solicitation	Intentionally request another to commit a crime. Solicitation merges with attempt, conspiracy, or the completed crime.
Attempt	Intent to complete a crime and performance of an overt act that goes beyond mere preparation. Attempt merges with the completed crime.
Misprison of a Felony	Although they are not parties to the felony, persons who conceal or fail to report a felony may be guilty of the separate crime of misprison of a felony or compounding a felony.

Discussion Questions

1. In the course of a botched bank robbery, the robber takes hostages and emerges from the bank to negotiate with the police. In order to show defiance of the police the robber raises a fist in the air and shouts: "Power to the people; death to the fascist pigs." A crowd of spectators raise their fists in a show of support and take up the chant started by the bank robber. Have the spectators become aiders and abettors to the bank robbery?

2. A friend, **A**, runs into **B**'s apartment and tells **B** that the police are chasing **A** for stealing a car—which is a lie because no car was stolen. **B** hides **A** in the bedroom and tells the police that **A** ran out the back door. The police leave but warn **B**: "Be careful, your friend just killed a police officer." Is **B** an accessory after the fact to the crime of auto theft (which did not occur)? Is **B** an accessory after the fact to a murder of which **B** were unaware? Is **B** an attempted accessory after the fact to auto theft (taking the facts as **B** believed them to be)?

3. Why does the law require different types of overt acts for attempted crimes and the crime of conspiracy? If buying matches to start a fire is insufficient for attempted arson, why is the same physical act adequate to complete the crime of conspiracy to commit arson?

4. When should an offense (e.g., solicitation, attempt) merge with a completed offense? When should an offense (e.g., conspiracy) remain a separate offense in addition to the completed crime?

5. Should accomplices receive the same punishment as perpetrators?

PRACTICE EXERCISES

1. What tests does your jurisdiction use to distinguish preparatory conduct from a criminal attempt?

2. How has your jurisdiction dealt with factual and legal impossibility as a defense to crimes?

3. Has your jurisdiction retained the traditional approach to perpetrators and accessories, or have the parties to a crime been redefined or reclassified?

4. Does your state exempt a relative from being charged as an accessory after the fact?

5. Does your state punish for misprision of a felony or compounding a felony?

WEB SITE

Federal Bureau of Investigation
www.FBI.gov

KEY TERMS

Perpetrator (principal in the first degree)
Instrumentality
Innocent human agent
Aider and abettor (principal in the second degree)
Accessory before the fact

Accessory after the fact
Misprison of a felony
Compounding a felony
Inchoate crime
Solicitation
Merger
Attempted crime

Mere preparation
Factual impossibility
Legal impossibility
Abandonment
Conspiracy
Pinkerton doctrine
Wharton's rule

NOTES

1. *Wilcox v. Jeffery,* All E.R. 464 (England 1951).
2. *People v. Lubow,* 29 N.Y.2d 58, 323 N.Y.S.2d 829, 272 N.E.2d 331 (1971).
3. *People v. Paluch,* 78 Ill.App.2d 356, 222 N.E.2d 508 (1966).
4. Model Penal Code § 5.01(1).
5. Model Penal Code § 5.01(4).
6. *Krulewitch v. United States,* 336 U.S. 440, 69 S.Ct. 716 (1949).
7. See *Direct Sales Co. v. United States,* 319 U.S. 703, 63 S.Ct. 1265 (1943); drug wholesaler guilty of conspiracy by furnishing drugs to physician known to be using the drugs for illegal purposes.

8. See *United States v. Falcone,* 109 F.2d 579 (2d Cir. 1940); sugar wholesaler not guilty of conspiracy by furnishing sugar knowing that it would be used to manufacture bootleg liquor.

9. *Krulewitch v. United States,* 336 U.S. 440, 69 S.Ct. 716 (1949).

10. See *United States v. Bruno,* 105 F. 2d 921 (2d Cir. 1939); the importer, wholesaler, and geographically disparate retailers were all part of a single conspiracy.

11. See *Iannelli v. United States,* 420 U.S. 770, 95 S.Ct. 1284 (1975).

DEFENSES

Chapter 4

T he term *defense* can be used in a generic sense to encompass anything that might preclude a finding of guilty. It is necessary, however, to distinguish among the common defenses, which are (1) procedural bars to conviction, (2) case-in-chief defenses, and (3) affirmative defenses.

Procedural bars to conviction resolve the case without a determination of factual guilt or innocence. The procedural bars most commonly invoked by defendants include claims that the court lacks jurisdiction or venue over the case; the statute of limitations has run; the appropriate time for a "speedy trial" has expired; or the prohibition of double jeopardy applies because the defendant has previously been tried for the same charge. If properly established, these claims decide the case prior to receiving any evidence of the defendant's guilt or innocence. For example, Federal Rule of Criminal Procedure 12(b) provides that "any defense . . . which is capable of determination without the trial of the general issue may be raised before trial by motion." (The specifics of these procedural bars are addressed in Chapter Fourteen.)

Once the trial court moves beyond procedural considerations to address the merits of the case, the defendant may enter a plea of not guilty, which is a defense in the most general sense of the word. The plea is a defense to the extent that it is an assertion of the presumption of innocence and places the burden on the prosecution to prove guilt beyond a reasonable doubt. The plea, however, does not raise a specific excuse or justification to which the prosecution must respond.

A defendant who pleads not guilty may take a more aggressive stance by offering a factual denial, such as alibi. An **alibi** is a claim that the defendant was not in a position to commit the crime charged. The alibi defense, however, is merely another way of calling upon the prosecution to prove its case. For example, the defendant may assert, "You can't prove that I robbed the bank in New York, because I was in Los Angles at the time." Although defendants are usually required to give the government pretrial notice of their alibi, the prosecution must prove the elements of the crime, such as presence at the scene of the crime. Thus, the defendant, who bears no burden of proof in an alibi defense, need not prove presence in Los Angles. Instead, the prosecution must prove that the defendant was in New York, which may necessitate disproving the defendant's presence in Los Angles.

A **case-in-chief defense**, like alibi, challenges the prosecution's version of the facts, but does not introduce an additional legal issue into the case. Case-in-chief defenses must be distinguished from affirmative defenses.

An **affirmative defense** admits that the defendant committed the acts charged, but seeks to justify or excuse the defendant's conduct by establishing some additional facts. For example, the defendant admits that she killed, but claims that the killing was in justifiable self-defense. This type of affirmative defense goes beyond a simple denial of guilt by raising a separate issue that may carry a separate burden of proof (see Chapter One).

In all jurisdictions, defendants must introduce some evidence in order to bring an affirmative defense to the attention of the jury. Jurisdictions differ, however, as to who bears the ultimate burden of proving or disproving affirmative defenses. Some jurisdictions place the burden on the defendant to prove the defense, while others require that the prosecution disprove the defense beyond a reasonable doubt. Except for constitutional considerations, local law distinguishes between case-in-chief and affirmative defenses. Local law also specifies who bears the burden of persuading the jury as to the validity of an affirmative defense. The remainder of this chapter addresses the most commonly raised affirmative and case-in-chief defenses.

COMPULSION, NECESSITY, AND DURESS

Necessity, duress, and the more general concept of compulsion are affirmative defenses because defendants claim that they were compelled to violate the law in order to accomplish some greater good or to avoid a greater evil. The Model Penal Code

Alibi
a claim that the defendant was not in a position to commit the crime charged.

Case-in-chief defense
challenges the prosecution's version of the facts, but does not introduce an independent legal claim into the case.

Affirmative defense
the defendant admits committing the acts charged, but seeks to justify or excuse the defendant's conduct by establishing additional facts.

specifically recognizes a choice-of-lesser-evils defense.[1] Under such a defense, a defendant may admit to stealing food to avoid starvation; to kidnapping a person in order to rescue the person from "brainwashing" by a religious cult; or to killing an innocent person in order to save several innocent lives.

Although the courts recognize necessity and duress as specific defenses in appropriate situations, the courts usually reject more general claims of compulsion, such as civil disobedience or obedience to superior orders. For example, protestors charged with breaching the peace by demonstrating at an abortion clinic may claim their actions were necessary in order to prevent women from obtaining abortions. Whatever the moral motivation of civil disobedience, it is not recognized as a valid application of the defense of necessity. Nor do the necessities of war justify blind obedience to patently illegal orders. It may be true that "war is hell," but the Nuremberg Trials following World War II and the trial of Lieutenant Calley for the massacre at My Lai, Vietnam, established that war is not beyond the reach of law.

UNITED STATES v. CALLEY
U.S. Court of Military Appeals, 1973
48 CMR 19

Lieutenant Calley was a platoon leader in C Company, a unit whose mission was to subdue and drive out the enemy in an area in the Republic of Vietnam which included the village of My Lai.

Captain Medina testified that he instructed his troops that they were to destroy My Lai by "burning the hootches, to kill the livestock, to close the wells and to destroy the food crops." Asked if women and children were to be killed, Medina said he replied in the negative, adding that, "You must use common sense. If they have a weapon and are trying to engage you, then you can shoot back, but you must use common sense." However, Lieutenant Calley testified that Captain Medina informed the troops they were to kill every living thing— men, women, children, and animals and under no circumstances were they to leave any Vietnamese behind them as they passed through the villages enroute to their final objective.

Entering the village, Calley's platoon encountered only unarmed, unresisting men, women, and children. On being told that a large number of villagers had been detained, Calley said Medina ordered him to "waste them." Calley further testified that he obeyed the orders because he had been taught the doctrine of obedience throughout his military career. Calley ordered his troops to kill the villagers, and Calley himself shot a number of women and children.

JUDGE QUINN delivered the opinion of the Court:

In the stress of combat, a member of the armed forces cannot reasonably be expected to make a refined legal judgment and be held criminally responsible if he guesses wrong on a question as to which there may be considerable disagreement. But there is no disagreement as to the illegality of the order to kill in this case. For 100 years, it has been a settled rule of American law that even in war the summary killing of an enemy, who has submitted to, and is under, effective physical control, is murder.

Whether Lieutenant Calley was the most ignorant person in the United States Army in Vietnam, or the most intelligent, he must be presumed to know that he could not kill the people involved here. An order to kill infants and unarmed civilians who were so demonstrably incapable of resistance to the armed might of a military force as were those killed by Lieutenant Calley is palpably illegal. We find no impediment to the trial court findings that Calley acted with murderous mens rea, including premeditation.

Although rejecting defenses based on a compulsion to obey superior orders or moral principles, the common law recognized specific forms of compulsion such as necessity and duress. Modern cases tend to blur the distinction between duress and necessity, but the U.S. Supreme Court noted that:

Common law historically distinguished between the defenses of duress and necessity. Duress was said to excuse criminal conduct where the actor was under an unlawful threat of imminent death or serious bodily injury, which threat caused the actor to engage in conduct violating the literal terms of the criminal law. While the defense of duress covered the situation where the coercion had its source in the actions of other human beings, the defense of necessity, or choice of evils, traditionally covered the situation where physical forces beyond the actor's control rendered illegal conduct the lesser of two evils. Thus, where **A** destroyed a dike because **B** threatened to kill him if he did not, **A** could argue that he acted under duress, whereas if **A** destroyed the dike in order to protect more valuable property from flooding, **A** could claim a defense of necessity.[2]

Necessity

Necessity excuses a violation of criminal law if (1) the defendant reasonably believes the threat of harm is imminent; (2) the only way to prevent the threatened harm is to violate the law; and (3) the harm that will be caused by violating the law is less serious than the harm the defendant seeks to avoid.

The defense of **necessity** or choice-of-lesser-evils recognizes that the defendant is justified in violating a criminal law if (1) the defendant reasonably believes that the threat of personal harm or harm to others is imminent; (2) the only way to prevent the threatened harm is to violate the law; and (3) the harm that will be caused by violating the law is less serious than the harm the defendant seeks to avoid.

The defense of necessity is a broad and amorphous concept that may arise in rather mundane cases involving minor violations of law. For example, a defendant exceeds the speed limit while rushing an injured person to the hospital. Prosecutors rarely bring such minor violations to trial, thus the reported cases raising the necessity defense often present dramatic situations that test the limits of criminal law. The most famous claims of necessity take place in an open lifeboat adrift on the high seas.

In *Regina v. Dudley*, three adult sailors and a 17-year-old youth were cast adrift in a small boat after their sailing vessel sank.[3] Weakened after twenty days with little food and water, two of the sailors killed the youth and fed upon his flesh in order to survive. Four days later, the survivors were rescued by a passing vessel. When prosecuted for murder, the survivors raised the defense of necessity, arguing that had they not killed the youth all four would have perished. The court refused to accept necessity as a justification for killing an innocent person. In a similar case, *United States v. Holmes*, crew members threw 14 passengers overboard after their lifeboat began to sink.[4] The court again rejected the defense of necessity, and convicted the sailors of manslaughter.

The debate over the decisions in the *Holmes* and *Dudley* cases and the limits of the necessity defense continues. In a classic publication, *The Case of the Speluncean Explorers*, Professor Lon Fuller posed a hypothetical case in which trapped cave explorers kill and eat one of their number in order to survive until rescue.[5] Professor Fuller advanced one view of necessity, which recognizes that "positive law is predicated on the possibility of men's coexistence in society. When a situation arises in which the coexistence of men becomes impossible, then the condition that underlies all of our precedents and statutes ceases to exist." Under such circumstances, therefore, endangered persons are in a "state of nature" beyond the reach of criminal law. Compare this reasoning with the view of Justice Cardozo:

There is no rule of human jettison. . . . Who shall choose in such an hour between the victims and the saved? Who shall know when masts and sails of rescue may emerge out of the fog?

Hill v. State presents a modern-day case in which the defendant sought to justify the necessity of killing in order to prevent the "moral wrong" of abortion.

HILL v. STATE
688 So.2d 901 (Fla. 1996)

Early on the morning of July 29, 1994, Hill went to the Ladies Center in Pensacola, Florida, where he had been protesting against abortion for six months, and waited outside. About one hour later, a pick-up truck driven by James Herman Barrett, also containing his wife June Griffith Barrett and Dr. John Bayard Britton, arrived at the Center. The Barretts volunteered at the Center on the last Friday of every month. On those days, they met Dr. Britton at the airport and escorted him to the Ladies Center, which he visited every Friday to perform legal abortions. As the truck entered the parking lot, Hill was standing in the middle of the driveway so that he was able to see the truck's occupants. As Barrett got out of the truck, Hill shot and killed him. Hill also shot and wounded June Barrett. He then moved closer to the truck before shooting and killing Dr. Britton. Hill was arrested shortly thereafter and stated that "at least there will be no more babies killed there today."

Hill was charged with two counts of first-degree premeditated murder, one count of attempted first-degree murder, and one count of shooting into an occupied vehicle. He pled not guilty to all counts. At trial, Hill sought to present the defense of justification or necessity, but the trial court did not permit it. He was subsequently convicted on all four counts.

The essential elements of the necessity defense are: Defendants must have reasonably believed that their action was necessary to avoid an imminent threatened harm, that there are no other adequate means except those which were employed to avoid the threatened harm, and that a direct causal relationship may be reasonably anticipated between the action taken and the avoidance of the harm.

We hold as a matter of law, that legal abortion is not a recognized harm and cannot be used to invoke the necessity defense. Permitting a defendant to vindicate his or her criminal activity in such a manner would be an invitation for lawlessness and tantamount to judicially sanctioning vigilantism. If every person were to act upon his or her personal beliefs in this manner, and we were to sanction the act, the result would be utter chaos. In a society of laws and not of individuals, we cannot allow each individual to determine, based upon his or her personal beliefs, whether another person may exercise her constitutional rights and then allow that individual to assert the defense of justification to escape criminal liability.

We recognize that, despite our proscription, some individuals, because of firmly held and honestly believed convictions, will feel compelled to break the law. If they choose to do so, however, they must be prepared to face the consequences. Thus, such private attempts to circumvent the law with the aim to deprive a pregnant woman of her right to obtain an abortion will not be tolerated by this Court.

Duress

In the classic situation involving duress, someone puts a gun to the defendant's head and threatens, "Either you rob that bank [or some other specified crime] or I'll kill you." **Duress** is sometimes treated as a subspecies of the necessity defense because the defendant is placed in a situation that requires choosing between the lesser of two evils. In other words, a defendant must necessarily commit a crime in order to avoid being killed or injured by the person threatening the defendant's life. Treating duress as a subspecies of the lesser-evils defense of necessity explains the general rule that duress may be a defense to any crime except homicide. When a defendant kills an innocent person in order to save her or his own life, one life has been taken in order to preserve one life. Thus the defendant has committed an equal evil, rather than a lesser evil. If a person is truly faced with a kill-or-be-killed situation, the law insists that person "ought rather to die than kill an innocent."

Other than homicide charges, duress is a defense if (1) someone threatens to kill or seriously injure the defendant or a member of the defendant's family unless the

Duress
an unlawful threat of imminent death or serious bodily injury, which induces a person to commit a crime; may be used as a defense (except in the case of murder).

defendant commits a crime; (2) the defendant believes that the threat is real and imminent; and (3) the defendant reasonably believes that committing the crime is the only way to prevent being killed or injured. If the defendant failed to take advantage of a reasonable opportunity to escape or to avoid doing the acts without being harmed, the defendant may not rely on duress as a defense.[6] If the elements of the duress defense are met, however, the defendant must be acquitted of the crime, while the coercing party may be convicted of the offense that the defendant committed. This situation is one in which a person may be convicted as a principal in the first degree for using an innocent person to carry out the crime (see Chapter Three).

MISTAKE AS A DEFENSE

Claims of mistake are not affirmative defenses because they do not alter the burden of proof. Claims of mistake are case-in-chief defenses that seek to negate an element of the charged offense, in most cases the mens rea of the crime.

As a general proposition, the common law stated that a mistake of fact may be a valid defense, but a mistake of law can never be a satisfactory defense because "ignorance of the law is no excuse." Like most generalities, this one obscures the variations and exceptions which recognize that some mistakes of fact are not a valid defense, while some mistakes of law are legitimate.

Mistake of Fact

Mistake of fact
a lack of knowledge of a particular piece of information, which may be a defense if it negates a material element of the offense.

The first step in analyzing a claim of mistake of fact is to identify the elements of the particular offense charged. If the **mistake of fact** negates a necessary element of the offense, the defendant has a valid defense. Suppose, for example, that upon exiting a restaurant the defendant, D, takes what she believes to be the umbrella of another customer, V. In fact, however, D mistakenly absconds with her own umbrella. Larceny requires that the defendant take and carry away the personal property of *another,* thus the defendant's mistake negates an essential element of larceny, for which she cannot be convicted. (In some jurisdictions the defendant may be convicted, however, of attempted larceny under the facts as she believed them to be. See Chapter Three.)

Now suppose that V picks up D's umbrella under the mistaken belief that it is V's own umbrella. V has carried away another's property but lacks the mental state required for common law larceny because V has shown no *intent* to deprive others of their personal property. V has a valid mistake of fact defense because her mistake negates an essential element of the charge—"accidental" larceny is not a common law crime.

Suppose, however, a statute created the offense of "negligent" larceny: for example, "no one may negligently deprive others of their personal property." Now, V's mistake may or may not be a valid defense depending upon whether the mistake is characterized as being reasonable or unreasonable. A reasonable mistake about the ownership of the property negates the required element of negligence, while an unreasonable mistake is, by definition, negligent (the mens rea required by the penal statute).

Alter the hypothetical umbrella-taking one last time by supposing that a strict liability statute provides, "Under no circumstances may a person take the personal property of another." The statute does not require any mental state for the crime, instead the statute prohibits the physical act of taking the personal property of another. Thus when V takes another's umbrella, it is irrelevant whether V does so intentionally or makes a reasonable or unreasonable mistake as to its ownership. V's mistake, if any, cannot rebut the mental state required for the crime because strict liability crimes do not require any mental state. In crimes in which the prosecution is not required to prove that the defendant acted with any particular mental state, the lack of criminal intent is immaterial so long as V performed the act that constitutes the crime.

The preceding hypothetical situations demonstrate that no general rule of law recognizes a certain type of mistake of fact as always or never a defense to a criminal charge. Each claim of mistake must be examined to determine whether it negates an element of the particular charge.

Mistake of Law

Although the law generally holds that "ignorance of the law is no excuse," a **mistake of law** may be a defense if it negates the mens rea required for the crime. In many cases, a mistake of fact is indistinguishable from a mistake of law. Suppose a defendant being prosecuted for bigamy claims that he believed he had obtained a legally valid divorce before remarrying. Is he mistaken about the *fact* of whether he is still married to his first spouse, or is he mistaken about his *legal* status as a married or single person? Does it matter whether the mistake is one of fact or law? According to the court decision in *Braun v. State*, the answer is no.

> **Mistake of law** ✓
> a lack of knowledge of a particular law, which may be a defense if it negates the mens rea required for the crime.

BRAUN v. STATE
Supreme Court of Maryland, 1962
230 Md. 82, 185 A.2d 905

The defendant was tried on a charge of bigamy, convicted and sentenced to five years' imprisonment. The defendant's main contention is that when he entered into the marriage with his second wife, he believed that his first wife had divorced him, that he, therefore, lacked any wrongful intent and hence was not guilty of bigamy.

Most American jurisdictions which have considered the question hold that the fact that the defendant may have believed in good faith that there had been a prior divorce or that a prior divorce was valid is no defense to a charge of bigamy if in fact there has been no divorce or it is invalid. Most American jurisdictions also follow a similar rule where the defendant in good faith, but mistakenly, believes his or her first spouse to be dead.

The problem of statutory construction is primarily whether or not a requirement of mens rea to establish guilt should be read into the statute. In light of the majority American rule and of the prior expressions of this Court, and in view of the fact that honest belief is not one of the exceptions from liability enumerated in the statute itself, we think that even if the defendant had entertained a bona fide belief that his first wife had divorced him before his second marriage, and even if this erroneous belief were to be regarded as a mistake of fact and not of law (which we do not decide), this would not constitute a defense to the charge of bigamy under our statute.

In *Braun,* the court did not feel compelled to characterize the defendant's mistake as one of fact or law because the court determined that the bigamy statute created a strict liability crime. Thus, no required mental state existed for the defendant's mistake to rebut. Suppose, however, that the bigamy statute provided, "No person shall enter into a second marriage while *knowingly* a party of an existing first marriage." Assuming that a defendant did not know that the first marriage was still in existence, would it matter whether her lack of knowledge was based on a mistake of fact or a mistake of law?

The Model Penal Code and many jurists suggest that mistakes of law and fact be treated in the same manner: a mistake of either type is a valid defense if it negates a material element of the offense.[7] Thus if knowledge is a necessary element of the crime of bigamy, the defendant has a valid defense regardless of whether the lack of knowledge was caused by a mistake of fact or law. Such an approach is an exception to the maxim that ignorance of the law is no excuse. The exception rests on distinguishing between mistakes of collateral law, (for example, the civil laws governing divorce), and mistakes as to the law defining a criminal offense. A claim that "I knew I had two husbands, but I didn't know there was a law against it," is not a defense to bigamy.

Although the courts' rejection of ignorance of the law defenses is sometimes based on the assertion that "every person is presumed to know the law," Justice Holmes suggested that

> The true explanation of the rule is the same as that which accounts for the law's indifference to a man's particular temperament, faculties, and so forth. Public policy sacrifices the individual to the general good . . . It is no doubt true that there are many cases in which the criminal could not have known that he was breaching the law, but to admit the excuse at all would be to encourage ignorance . . . and justice to the individual is rightly outweighed by the larger interests on the other side of the scales.[8]

INTOXICATION

Voluntary intoxication may be a defense if it produces clouded mental facilities that negate the mental state required for a particular crime.

A claim of **voluntary intoxication,** caused by either alcohol or drugs, is another case-in-chief defense whose validity may turn upon the mens rea required for the particular offense charged. Voluntary intoxication standing alone never excuses wrongdoing, but the condition that intoxication produces, for example, clouded mental faculties, may negate the mens rea required for a particular crime. For example, a defendant who takes drugs to build enough courage for a confrontation with a tormentor may be so intoxicated as to lack a specific intent to kill the tormentor, and thus may have a defense to premeditated murder. (The defendant's conduct, however, may be deemed to be wanton and willful, sufficient grounds for a conviction of second degree murder, which does not require a specific intent to kill.)

Some jurisdictions, however, refuse to recognize voluntary intoxication as a defense to any crime. In these jurisdictions, defendants who put themselves in positions to have no control over their actions are held to intend the consequences of their actions. Thus the defendants are deemed to have deliberately become intoxicated as a means of "psyching" up for the commission of an intended crime.

Involuntary intoxication may be a defense if the defendant did not know of the ingested substance's intoxicating effect or if someone forced or tricked the defendant into ingesting the intoxicating substance.

Although the claim is exceedingly rare, involuntary intoxication may constitute a defense to all crimes. **Involuntary intoxication** occurs if the defendant did not know of the ingested substance's intoxicating effect, or if someone forced or tricked the defendant into ingesting the intoxicating substance (for example, a "spiked" drink). A claim of involuntary intoxication may be a complete defense if the intoxication produced a mental condition comparable to insanity—albeit, "temporary" insanity—based on intoxication rather than mental disease.

INSANITY

Few aspects of criminal law have received as much attention and debate as the insanity defense. As a statistical matter, the defense is rarely raised, but when it is raised it is often in the context of particularly heinous and well-publicized cases: for example, John Hinckley's shooting of President Ronald Reagan, the murder of John Lennon, and serial killings, such as the Son-of-Sam case. Although the public seems fascinated by the "sick mind" that leads to such killings, the issue of insanity can arise at different stages of criminal proceedings: competency to stand trial, mental illness at the time of punishment, and insanity as a defense to conviction.

Competency to Stand Trial

A defendant who is insane at the time of trial cannot be subjected to prosecution.[9] The test for determining **competency to stand trial** is whether a defendant lacks the capacity to understand the proceedings or assist in her or his defense. In other words, the defendant must be rational, possess the ability to testify coherently, and be able to meaningfully discuss the case with legal representation. If the defendant is incompetent to stand trial, the proceedings must be suspended until such time as the defendant becomes competent. Thus incompetency is not a defense to a criminal charge; incompetency is one basis for a continuance or postponement of the trial.

An incompetent defendant may be committed to a mental institution for treatment designed to restore competency, but such confinement is only for purposes of treatment, not for purposes of punishment. The trial court must reevaluate the defendant's mental condition after a "reasonable period of time."[10] The court must then take appropriate action such as (1) try the defendant if competency to stand trial has been restored; (2) dismiss the charges if it appears that the defendant will never regain competency; and/or (3) commence *civil* proceedings to commit the defendant to a mental institution if the defendant is a threat to his or her own person or to others.

Competency to stand trial the defendant must be rational, possess the ability to testify coherently, and be able to meaningfully discuss the case with defense counsel.

Mental Illness at the Time of Punishment

The Eighth Amendment's cruel and unusual punishment clause prohibits the execution of a person who has become insane after being sentenced to death.[11] The execution must be postponed until such time as the condemned prisoner's sanity is regained. Convicted persons who become mentally ill while serving their sentences may be transferred to medical facilities within or outside the penitentiary, or may be forced to accept antipsychotic medication.[12]

Insanity as a Defense

Insanity at the time of the crime is the most frequently litigated aspect of insanity and may be a complete defense to all charges. Insanity excuses criminal liability because convicting and punishing insane people does not serve the objectives of criminal law (see Chapter One). For example, insane persons are not morally blameworthy, thus retribution is inappropriate. Mentally ill persons who cannot control their conduct cannot be deterred by threats of punishment. Incapacitation and rehabilitation of insane persons can be accomplished by civil commitment proceedings, which do not carry the moral stigma of criminal conviction.

Insanity is a legal concept, not a medical term, and jurisdictions apply some variation of the following legal tests for insanity: the *M'Naghten* "right-from-wrong" test, the irresistible impulse test, or the diminished capacity test.

M'NAGHTEN'S CASE
8 Eng. Rep. 718 (1843)

[Daniel M'Naghten suffered from delusions of persecution by government officials. He decided to kill Sir Robert Peel, the British Home Secretary. Lying in wait outside Peel's home, M'Naghten saw Peel's secretary, Edward Drummond, leave the house. Believing Drummond to be Peel, M'Naghten shot and killed him. The jury acquitted M'Naghten, and an irate Queen Victoria asked the House of Lords to reconsider the defense of insanity.]

LORD CHIEF JUSTICE TINDAL:

[Her majesty has inquired] what are the proper questions to be submitted to the jury, where a person alleged to be afflicted with insane delusion respecting one or more particular subjects or persons, is charged with the commission of a crime (murder, for example), and insanity is set up as a defence? And, in what terms ought the question to be left to the jury as to the prisoner's state of mind at the time when the act was committed?

And as these two questions appear to us to be more conveniently answered together, we have to submit our opinion to be, that the jurors ought to be told in all cases that every man is to be presumed to be sane, and to possess a sufficient degree of reason to be responsible for his crimes, until the contrary be proved to their satisfaction; and that to establish a defence on the ground of insanity, it must be clearly proved that, at the time of the committing of the act, the party accused was laboring under such a defect of reason, from disease of the mind, as not to know the nature and quality of the act he was doing; or, if he did know it, that he did not know he was doing what was wrong.

M'Naghten test for insanity determines whether the defendant is able to distinguish right from wrong.

Under the **M'Naghten test for insanity**, a defendant is insane if laboring under such a defect of reason that the person (1) did not know the nature and quality of the act committed (for example, the defendant believed it was a grape the defendant was squeezing instead of someone's throat); or (2) did not know that the act was wrong (for example, M'Naghten did not know it was wrong to kill a government official who he thought was oppressing him).

The *M'Naghten* rule was immediately criticized because it focused exclusively on the defendant's cognitive capacity while ignoring mental illnesses that may impair volitional capacity. Compulsive behavior, such as kleptomania and pyromania, occurs when the actor knows right from wrong, but nevertheless persists in the act because of an inner force the defendant is powerless to resist. If such behavior is to be exempted from responsibility, the irresistible impulse becomes a necessary adjunct to the *M'Naghten* test. Just one year after the *M'Naghten* decision, a Massachusetts case adopted and defined the **irresistible impulse test for insanity**.

Irresistible impulse test for insanity determines whether the defendant acted from an uncontrollable impulse.

If then it is proved, to the satisfaction of the jury, that the mind of the accused was in a diseased and unsound state, the question will be, whether the disease existed to so high a degree, that for the time being it overwhelmed the reason, conscience, and judgment, and whether the prisoner, in committing the homicide acted from an irresistible and uncontrollable impulse, if so, then the act was not the act of a voluntary agent, but the involuntary act of the body, without the concurrence of a mind directing it.[13]

In a much-publicized incident in 1994, Lorena Bobbitt sliced off her husband's penis with a kitchen knife while he was sleeping. She was acquitted of the charge of malicious wounding after arguing the irresistible impulse form of insanity.

Neither the irresistible impulse test nor the *M'Naghten* test recognizes degrees of insanity because they require that a person must wholly lack knowledge of wrongdoing, or wholly lack the capacity to control personal conduct. Thus legal insanity was seen as an all or nothing proposition, with no gray area. During the 1960s, different forms of a **diminished capacity test for insanity** recognized that defendants may lack "substantial," not total, mental capacity. For example, the Model Penal Code states that

Diminished capacity test for insanity recognizes that defendants may lack "substantial" but not total mental capacity.

A person is not responsible for criminal conduct if at the time of such conduct as a result of mental disease or defect he lacks substantial capacity either to appreciate the criminality [wrongfulness] of his conduct or to conform his conduct to the requirements of law.[14]

The diminished capacity test was used widely in federal courts until the acquittal on grounds of insanity of John Hinckley, Jr., for the attempted assassination of President Reagan. Much like the outcry that occurred in England when M'Naghten tried to shoot the Home Secretary and was then acquitted by reason of insanity, the aftermath of the attempted assassination of President Reagan, and the acquittal of Hinckley, stirred up emotions that fueled movements to reform the defense of insanity. Reacting to the well-publicized acquittal, Congress, for the first time, passed a statute establishing a uniform insanity test to be utilized in federal criminal trials. The **federal test for insanity** is set forth in the Insanity Defense Reform Act of 1984 which provides:

> § 20. Insanity Defense
> (a) Affirmative Defense. It is an affirmative defense to a prosecution under any Federal statute that, at the time of the commission of the acts constituting the offense, the defendant, as a result of severe mental disease or defect, was unable to appreciate the nature and quality of the wrongfulness of his acts. Mental disease or defect does not otherwise constitute a defense.
> (b) Burden of Proof. The defendant has the burden of proving the defense of insanity by clear and convincing evidence.[15]

The burden of proof placed on defendants in federal court is the highest burden that any jurisdiction imposes on a defendant who claims insanity. The states generally require either that the defendant prove insanity by a preponderance of the evidence, or the prosecution must disprove insanity beyond a reasonable doubt.

> **Federal test for insanity** uses the *M'Naghten* right-from-wrong standard, but requires that the defendant prove insanity by clear and convincing evidence.

Guilty but Mentally Ill

The new federal test for insanity was but one response to the Hinckley acquittal. A number of states have replaced the not guilty by reason of insanity verdict with a verdict of guilty but mentally ill. The prime distinction between the verdicts is the post-trial handling of the defendant. When a defendant (like Hinckley) is acquitted by reason of insanity, the state may not punish the defendant, but may seek in a *civil* court to have the defendant committed as a danger to himself or others. In such cases, the defendant must be reevaluated periodically, most typically every six months, in order to determine if the defendant is still a threat to himself or others. If the defendant ceases to be a threat, the defendant must be released from custody at once.

A defendant found **guilty but mentally ill** will be sentenced as any other defendant would be, then is immediately committed, without a separate civil proceeding, "in an appropriate facility for treatment, having regard for such conditions of security as the case may require." If the defendant ceases to be mentally ill, the defendant is released from the mental institution and will serve the remainder of the sentence in a penitentiary. Proponents of the guilty but mentally ill verdict maintain that it is an appropriate compromise between punishment and treatment. Critics of the verdict insist that guilty but mentally ill is an "oxymoronic term" and a mere charade for punishment of the mentally ill.

> **Guilty but mentally ill** confines the defendant for treatment until such time as the defendant is healthy and able to serve a sentence in a penitentiary.

Justifiable Use of Force

Use of defensive force is an affirmative defense (not a case-in-chief defense), because it does not dispute the prosecution's proof that the defendant used force. Instead the defendant raises an additional consideration as to whether the use of force was justified or excusable. Some jurisdictions require the defendant to prove by a preponderance of evidence that the use of force was permissible, while other jurisdictions require the prosecution to disprove the justification or excuse once it has been raised by the defendant.

Although the use of defensive force usually arises in cases involving a claim of self-defense to a homicide prosecution, the justifiable use of force may be a defense to any charges that the defendant killed, injured, or interfered with the liberty of another person. Justifiable force arises in a variety of situations involving defense of self, of others, of property, and of habitation.

Self-Defense

Self-defense
actions in a situation in which (1) the defendant was not the aggressor; (2) the defendant reasonably perceived an immediate threat of bodily harm; (3) the defendant reasonably believed that defensive force was necessary to avoid the harm; and (4) the amount of defensive force used was reasonable.

In order to establish **self-defense,** the defendant may be required to prove that (1) the defendant was not the aggressor; (2) the defendant reasonably perceived an immediate threat of bodily harm; (3) the defendant reasonably believed that defensive force was necessary to avoid the harm; and (4) the amount of defensive force used was reasonable.

Self-defense is not available to those who provoke an attack and then use force to repel it because "the law does not allow a man to create a bad or dangerous situation and then fight his way out." For example, **D** slaps **V** who responds by punching **D,** who then punches back. If **D** is charged with battery for punching **V,** **D** cannot claim self-defense because **D** was the aggressor who struck the first blow. If, however, **V** responded to the slap by pulling a gun, then **V** would become the aggressor by escalating a simple fistfight into a deadly battle. **D** could now use reasonable force to defend against **V** who becomes the "new" aggressor in this more serious attack.

After establishing status as a nonaggressor, the defendant may have to prove the threat of *immediate harm.* Threats of future harm do not justify the use of force because the defendant has other avenues for protection, such as reporting the threat to the police. An immediate threat means that unless the aggressor is combatted by defensive force, the defendant will suffer some injury.

The requirement for a threat of immediate harm has been challenged in recent times by the emergence of the "battered wife" or "battered child" syndrome. How does self-defense apply when the defendant kills a person who has physically and/or sexually abused the defendant over an extended period of time, but offers no immediate threat of violence at the time of the killing? The *Sands* case presents a tragic but all too familiar pattern of spousal abuse.

SANDS v. COMMONWEALTH
536 S.E.2d 461 (Va. 2000)

Victoria Shelton Sands was convicted in a jury trial for the first degree murder of her husband and use of a firearm during the commission of murder. On appeal, she contends the trial court erred by refusing to instruct the jury on the law of self-defense.

Two years after they were married, Thomas Sands began beating appellant. The beatings became progressively worse over time and, at the end they occurred on a daily basis. Appellant wanted to take her four-year-old son, leave Sands and get a divorce. Sands told her she could not leave and threatened repeatedly to kill her and her parents if she did. She said she believed Sands would

have found and killed her if she had gone to a shelter. Whenever she broached the subject of divorce, he beat her. When she broached the subject in late July 1998, Sands beat her and then held her hostage in their home for three weeks.

On August 17, 1998, Sands accompanied appellant to the hospital in North Carolina to visit her injured parents. Sands returned home that day while appellant remained with her parents. When appellant returned home on the evening of Saturday, August 22, 1998, Sands was angry because she had been gone and did not call to say she was coming home. Sands "went into a rage," beat appellant, and threatened to kill her, saying, "you will die, I promise you, you will die." Appellant did not flee the marital home because she was afraid Sands would come after her and kill her as he had threatened. Between Saturday night and Sunday morning, Sands hit appellant "hundreds and hundreds of times," and threatened her with a gun he always carried, which he repeatedly put up her nose.

At approximately 11:00 A.M. on Sunday, August 23, appellant tried to hide Sands' gun, and the couple got into another argument on the back porch of their home. Despite the fact that appellant held the firearm during this time, Sands pushed her into a sink and "threw" her down five or six concrete steps. Appellant found herself lying on the ground with Sands sitting on top of her holding the firearm. After Sands pinned appellant to the ground, he again told her he would kill her, and he fired two shots into the ground near her. Once back inside the house, Sands tried to goad appellant into shooting him. He picked up the gun, which he had previously placed on the counter, and cocked it. Sands then said, "If you want to shoot me here's the gun between us." The couple's four-year-old son entered the room, and the conflict came to a temporary end.

Shortly thereafter, appellant's aunt, Sallie Hodges, came to the house to get the couple's son so she could care for him while appellant returned to North Carolina to look after her parents. Sands told Hodges he would not allow appellant to leave. He then said to Hodges, "I'll kill you and your whole family . . . . I've knocked off a few [people] and I can knock off a few more too." Sands refused to allow Hodges to take the couple's son, and Hodges left.

Sands remained home all day, where he used cocaine and drank alcohol. Periodically, he lay down to watch television in the bedroom for five or ten minutes, but he always got up to beat appellant again and threaten her with the gun. He continued this pattern throughout the day. As the day progressed, Sands continued to tell appellant he was going to kill her, and appellant said she believed he was going to do it.

At about 10:00 P.M., appellant was able to use the telephone. She called Hodges to come get the couple's four-year-old son and take him to her house. While appellant was on the phone with Hodges, Donald Wright, the couple's neighbor, came to the couple's house and agreed to take the child to Hodges' house. Appellant said she wanted her son away from the house because she "sensed" Sands was going to kill her. After appellant called Hodges, she then called her sister-in-law, Angela Shelton, and asked Shelton to come to her house. Before Shelton arrived, Sands beat appellant again. During this beating, which appellant described as the "longest," Sands hit appellant's head with the butt of his gun and again put the barrel of the gun up her nose. He then returned to his position in the bedroom in front of the television.

When Shelton arrived, appellant was crying and upset. Shelton and appellant went into the bathroom where Shelton helped appellant undress so they could look at appellant's bruised and beaten body. After seeing the extent of her injuries, appellant started shaking and said, "the devil, look at what the devil's done to me. I've got to get this devil out of my house. He's evil." Appellant then "ran out of the bathroom, got the gun, went to the bedroom and shot [Sands]" five times while he was lying in bed, awake, watching television. After appellant shot Sands, she walked out of the bedroom, laid the gun down, and called the police.

An officer who saw appellant at the scene after the shooting testified that her bruises were readily apparent and that her nose was "twisted to the side." He thought her ribs and nose were broken. After the shooting, appellant was examined by an emergency room physician, who found that she had "multiple bruises and contusions throughout her body, most of which were extensive in the upper arms and in the flanks."

The trial court refused to instruct the jury on self-defense because "there is insufficient evidence [to support] a self-defense instruction."

Killing in self-defense may be either justifiable or excusable. "Justifiable homicide in self-defense occurs when a person, without any fault on his part in provoking or bringing on the difficulty, kills another under reasonable apprehension of death or great bodily harm to himself." In the case of justifiable homicide, the accused need not retreat, but is permitted to stand his [or her] ground and repel the attack by force, including deadly force, if it is necessary. Where the accused is to some degree at fault in the first instance in provoking or bringing on the difficulty but "retreats as far as possible, announces his desire for peace, and kills his adversary from a reasonably apparent necessity to preserve his own life or save himself from great bodily harm," the accused has committed excusable homicide and also is entitled to an acquittal.

Fear alone is not sufficient to justify a person's intentionally inflicting a mortal wound upon another; to justify taking the life of another, there must be an overt act indicating the victim's imminent intention to kill or seriously harm the accused. The term "imminent" has a connotation that is less than "immediate," yet still impending and present. Whether a threat of harm is imminent is ordinarily a question of fact to be decided based on all of the circumstances, which may include the defendant's ability to avoid the harm.

We hold the trial court erroneously refused to instruct the jury on self-defense. Under the facts of this case, the fact finder could reasonably have concluded that appellant was without fault in beginning the altercation, reasonably apprehended she was in imminent danger of death or serious bodily harm and, thus, was justified in shooting her husband to prevent him from killing her or further inflicting serious bodily harm upon her. "The law does not require a person to suffer the last lethal blow before being able to take up his weapon to defend his life." Appellant had suffered years of abuse at the hands of her husband, and she testified that, over time, the abuse had become more severe. The fact finder could have concluded that Sands' unrelenting physical abuse and persistent death threats, culminating in a series of threats and physical abuse lasting for more than twenty-four hours prior to the shooting, constituted an imminent threat of death or serious bodily harm. In a situation where her tormentor posed an ongoing threat to her life and physical well-being, appellant was entitled to have the fact finder determine whether she reasonably thought she was in imminent danger of serious bodily harm and had the right to defend herself. She had the right to have the jury decide whether she acted reasonably in seizing an opportune time to slay her tormentor rather than risk taking defensive action after her husband had a firearm in her face or was in the process of beating her again.

Because the evidence, viewed in the light most favorable to appellant, would support a finding that the homicide was justifiable, appellant had no duty under the law of self-defense to retreat in order to be entitled to the instruction. However, even assuming that a finding of "imminent harm" requires consideration of an accused's ability to flee to avoid the harm, the evidence, again viewed in the light most favorable to the appellant, supported a finding that appellant believed she could not flee because Sands would find and kill her and a finding that this belief was reasonable under the circumstances.

On these facts, the jury could have found appellant reasonably feared an imminent threat of death or serious bodily harm. Therefore, the trial court erroneously refused an instruction on self-defense. Accordingly, we reverse appellant's convictions and remand the case for a new trial.

The law's treatment of the battered wife or battered child remains controversial. Some courts have gone even further than *Sands* and hold that

> Where the battered woman syndrome is in issue, the proper standard to determine whether the accused's belief in asserting self-defense was reasonable is a subjective standard. The jury must determine, from the viewpoint of the defendant's mental state, whether the defendant's belief in the need to defend herself was reasonable.[16]

Compare, however, the view expressed in *Jahnke v. State:*

> Although many people, and the public media, seem to be prepared to espouse the notion that a victim of abuse is entitled to kill the abuser, that special justification defense is antithetical to the mores of modern civilized society. . . . To permit capital punishment to be imposed upon the subjective conclusion of the individual that prior acts and conduct of the deceased justified the killing would amount to a leap into the abyss of anarchy.[17]

Assuming that the defendant faces an immediate threat, the use of force to defend oneself must be necessary and it must reasonably correspond to the threat. Deadly force may be used to defend against an attack that threatens death or serious bodily injury, but deadly force may not be used to defend against less serious attacks. For example, it would be unreasonable to shoot a person who slapped your face, but reasonable to shoot someone about to shoot you. The question of whether defensive force is necessary raises the issue of the defendant's responsibility to retreat from the attack, rather than meet it with force.

Retreat
an avenue of safe escape; a prerequisite to self-defense in some jurisdictions.

The doctrine of **retreat** requires a defendant to forego the use of deadly force and take advantage of an avenue of completely safe escape. At common law and in a majority of the states, retreat is not required, and the defendant may use defensive force even when aware of a place to which the defendant can retreat in complete safety. This rule is often justified on grounds that retreat "smacks of cowardice." A significant minority of jurisdictions, however, require the defendant to retreat if aware of a completely safe avenue of escape. A "completely safe retreat" is rarely available in cases involving deadly threats, which commonly occur at the end of a firearm. Even those jurisdictions that require retreat recognize that defendants need not retreat when attacked in their own homes, which are every person's natural sanctuary from external aggression.

Defense of Others

At common law, a person was entitled to use reasonable force in defense of family members, but not in defense of strangers. Today, however, all jurisdictions recognize that a defendant may use reasonable force to defend any person. The jurisdictions are split, however, between two views defining the circumstances that justify the **defense of others.**

The **alter-ego theory** of self-defense applies when the defendant acts to protect a person who had a lawful right of self-defense. When the defendant rushes to the aid of a stranger, the defendant steps into the shoes of the stranger and may use any force that the stranger was entitled to use. For example, the defendant perceives that **X** is being mugged by **Y**. The defendant uses force to subdue **Y**, who turns out to be an undercover police officer making a lawful arrest of **X**. Because **X** would not be justified to use force against the police officer, the defendant, who stepped into **X**'s shoes, is not justified in using force. The alter-ego view places the burden on the defendant to choose the correct person to be rescued. Defendants act at their peril when they are ignorant of the true status of the victim and the attacker.

The counter theory to the alter-ego view is that the defendant may act upon reasonable perception of the facts, even when the perception is erroneous. If a reasonable person would believe that **Y** is a mugger, the defendant may use defensive force against **Y**, even when **Y** turns out to be an undercover police officer engaged in a lawful arrest. The Model Penal Code adopts the **reasonable perception theory** of defense of others.[18] However, a majority of the states apply the alter-ego theory to the defense of others.

Defense of Property and Habitation

The law places a higher value on life than on property, thus in most instances deadly force may not be used to protect property. For example, a citizen may not shoot a person who attempts to steal or damage the citizen's unoccupied automobile. The citizen, however, may protect property by using nondeadly force such as pushing the person away from the vehicle. Although protection of "mere" property does not justify deadly force, the law recognizes a distinction between dwellings and other property. Deadly force may be used, under some circumstances, to protect one's home. The rationale justifying deadly force to defend the home is that when a wrongdoer enters a person's dwelling, more than property is invaded. The invading wrongdoer has attacked the homeowner's primary source of safety and privacy, and as the common law recognized, "Where shall a person be safe if it be not in one's own house?"

As a practical matter, defense of habitation, defense of property, and self-defense often commingle in a single factual situation. For example, if a homeowner awakens to the sound of a nighttime intruder, does the homeowner perceive a threat to safety, home, or expensive stereo? Outside the home the defense of property also may be clouded by a claim of self-defense. For example, the defendant uses nondeadly force to defend against the theft of the defendant's automobile, but the thief responds by pulling a knife, thus threatening the defendant's life and thus justifying the defendant's use of deadly force. Defense of property or habitation rarely arises in contexts free from other claims of justifiable defensive force. But in situations that isolate the use of deadly force to protect property, (for example, the use of a spring gun to protect an unoccupied house), most jurisdictions prohibit the defendant from using deadly force to protect "mere" property.

Defense of others
the act of protecting another from harm, which may excuse or justify the defendant's use of force.

Alter-ego theory
a defendant acts to protect a person who has a lawful right of self-defense.

Reasonable perception theory
the defendant acts upon a perception that the aided person has a right to use defensive force, even when the perception is erroneous.

Forcible Arrest and Force Used to Resist Arrest

An arresting police officer may use only "reasonable" force to apprehend a suspect. The well-publicized Rodney King incident raised the issue of police officers exceeding their authority by using excessive force. At common law, deadly force could not be used for a misdemeanor arrest, but could be used to apprehend a felon. In *Tennessee v. Garner,* however, the U.S. Supreme Court held that deadly force may not be used to prevent the escape of an apparently unarmed suspected felon.[19] Deadly force is constitutionally permissible only when the arresting officer reasonably believes that a suspected felon poses a threat of serious physical harm, either to the officer or to others.

At common law a person could use nondeadly force to resist an unlawful arrest, but today, most jurisdictions prohibit any resistance to an arrest by a law enforcement officer. Any form of resistance to arrest exposes the officer and the arrestee to escalating violence, thus the citizen is required to forego resistance. The citizen must vindicate her right to be free of an unlawful arrest by litigating the propriety of the arrest at trial, or in a suit against the law enforcement official for violation of the citizen's civil rights. A citizen, however, may use defensive force against anyone, including police officers, who improperly threaten the citizen's life. At such point the defendant is not resisting arrest, but is using self-defense against an immediate threat of death or serious harm.

ENTRAPMENT

Entrapment is an affirmative defense because the defendant usually admits to committing the offense, but nonetheless seeks to avoid conviction and punishment. The entrapment defense focuses on whether the defendant was induced to commit the crime by a government agent (typically, an undercover police officer), and whether the defendant would have committed the offense without the inducement. Because entrapment is not a constitutional doctrine, the rules relating to it vary by jurisdiction and generally fall within either a "subjective" or "objective" concept of entrapment.

Subjective approach to entrapment
prohibits police officers from instigating criminal acts by people not predisposed to commit the crime.

The U.S. Supreme Court has explained that the **subjective approach to entrapment** is designed to:

> prohibit law enforcement officers from instigating criminal acts by persons otherwise innocent in order to lure them to its commission and to punish them. [This approach] focuses on the intent or predisposition of the defendant to commit the crime rather than on the government's conduct. . . . A line must be drawn between the trap for the unwary innocent and the trap for the unwary criminal.[20]

When a defendant is predisposed to commit the crime, the government may afford the defendant an opportunity to commit the crime or even encourage the commission of the crime. Thus an undercover police officer may approach a suspected drug dealer and ask if the dealer has any drugs for sale. A suspect who previously sold drugs to others is predisposed, hence not entrapped, to sell drugs on this occasion. If, on the other hand, the suspect was a wholly innocent person who had never sold drugs, the government may not approach the suspect and suggest the commission of a crime. If the suspect succumbed to such a suggestion and sold drugs, the suspect could legitimately invoke the defense of entrapment.

Objective approach to entrapment
focuses on whether the government's conduct in inducing the crime was beyond judicial toleration.

The **objective approach to entrapment** focuses, not on the defendant's propensity to commit the offense, but on the conduct of the government agents. "Whether the particular defendant was 'predisposed' or 'otherwise innocent' is irrelevant;

and the important question becomes whether the Government's conduct in inducing the crime was beyond judicial toleration."[21] For example, suppose you tell a friend (in reality an undercover police officer) that you would like to rob a bank but don't know how to do it. Suppose the friend/officer responds, "I'll make it easy for you. I'll get the gun, the get-away car, and I'll handle the actual robbery. All you have to do is wait outside in the car with the motor running." Your predisposition to commit the crime precludes the subjective concept of entrapment, but under the objective approach to entrapment the officer may have gone too far in participating in the crime.

As illustrated by *Jacobson v. United States,* the subjective and objectives tests are more separate and distinct in theory than in practice.

JACOBSON v. UNITED STATES
Supreme Court of the United States, 1992
503 U.S. 540, 112 S.Ct. 1535

In February 1984, defendant ordered two magazines and a brochure from a California adult bookstore. The magazines contained photographs of nude preteen and teenage boys. The young men depicted in the magazines were not engaged in sexual activity, and defendant's receipt of the magazines was legal under both federal and Nebraska law. Within three months, the law with respect to child pornography changed; Congress passed the act illegalizing the receipt through the mails of sexually explicit depictions of children. In the very month that the new provision became law, postal inspectors found defendant's name on the mailing list of the California bookstore that had mailed him the two magazines. There followed over the next two and a half years, repeated efforts by two Government agencies, through five fictitious organizations and a bogus pen pal, to explore petitioner's willingness to break the new law by ordering sexually explicit photographs of children through the mail.

Thirty-four months after the Government obtained defendant's name from the mailing list of the California bookstore, and twenty-six months after the Postal Service had commenced its mailings to defendant, he ordered a magazine depicting young boys engaged in various sexual activities. Although defendant claimed that the Government entrapped him into committing the crime, he was convicted for violating a provision of the Child Protection Act of 1984, which criminalizes the knowing receipt through the mails of a "visual depiction [that] involves the use of a minor engaging in sexually explicit conduct."

JUSTICE WHITE delivered the opinion of the Court:

In its zeal to enforce the law the Government may not originate a criminal design, implant in an innocent person's mind the disposition to commit a criminal act, and then induce commission of the crime so that the Government may prosecute. Where the Government has induced an individual to break the law and the defense of entrapment is at issue, the prosecution must prove beyond reasonable doubt that the defendant was disposed to commit the criminal act prior to first being approached by Government agents.

Had the agents in this case simply offered defendant the opportunity to order child pornography through the mails, and defendant had promptly availed himself of this criminal opportunity, it is unlikely that his entrapment defense would have warranted a jury instruction. But that is not what happened here. By the time defendant finally placed his order, he had already been the target of 26 months of repeated mailings and communications from Government agents and fictitious organizations. Therefore, although he had become predisposed to break the law by May 1987, it is our view that the Government did not prove that this predisposition was independent and not the product of the attention that the Government had directed at defendant since January 1985.

Law enforcement officials go too far when they "implant in the mind of an innocent person the *disposition* to commit the alleged offense and induce its commission in order that they may prosecute." When the Government's quest for convictions leads to the apprehension of an otherwise law-abiding citizen who, if left to his own devices, likely would have never run afoul of the law, the courts should intervene.

Summary

In the area of legal defenses, a distinction must be drawn between case-in-chief defenses and affirmative defenses. Case-in-chief defenses, such as alibi, merely deny some or all of the elements of the charged offense and call upon the prosecution to prove the essential elements beyond a reasonable doubt. In contrast, affirmative defenses, such as entrapment, introduce an additional element into the case and, depending on the jurisdiction, the defendant may be given the burden to prove the affirmative defense. The most commonly recognized affirmative defenses are necessity and/or duress, insanity (although some jurisdictions regard it as a case-in-chief defense), justifiable use of force, and entrapment. The entrapment defense generally focuses on the defendant's predisposition to commit the charged offense and the conduct of government agents who encouraged the commission of a crime.

Case-in-chief defenses, such as mistake and intoxication, focus on whether the mistake or intoxication negated some essential element of the charged offense, most often the required mental state for the crime. Although courts sometimes distinguish between mistakes of fact and mistakes of law, the distinction is elusive. Courts also distinguish between voluntary and involuntary intoxication, but cases of involuntary intoxication rarely arise.

The treatment of the insanity defense varies greatly, but most jurisdictions use some variation on or combination of the *M'Naghten* right-from-wrong test and the irresistible impulse test. The federal courts require that the defendant prove insanity by clear and convincing evidence, and a number of states have adopted a guilty but mentally ill verdict.

The use of force to defend one's self, another person, property, or habitation generally turns upon the nature of the threat posed and the reasonableness of the force used to meet the threat. The battered spouse or battered child syndrome, while not universally accepted, has altered traditional concepts of the use of force defense.

Concept summary

Defenses		

Consult local law to determine what changes have been made in a particular jurisdiction.

DEFENSE	TYPE OF DEFENSE	BURDEN OF PROOF
Alibi	Case-in-chief	Prosecution must prove beyond reasonable doubt that defendant was in position to commit the crime.
Necessity	Affirmative	Defendant must prove that the law was violated in order to avoid a greater evil.
Duress	Affirmative	Defendant must prove a threat of imminent and serious harm, and that committing the crime was necessary to avoid the harm.
Mistake	Case-in-chief	Prosecution must prove beyond a reasonable doubt that mistake did not negate an element of the offense.
Voluntary Intoxication	Case-in-chief	If recognized as a defense, the prosecution must prove beyond a reasonable doubt that intoxication did not negate the mens rea of the crime.
Involuntary Intoxication	Case-in-chief or affirmative	Requires proof that the defendant was not responsible for the acts that constituted the crime.

DEFENSE	TYPE OF DEFENSE	BURDEN OF PROOF
Insanity	Case-in-chief or affirmative	Prosecution may be required to prove sanity, or defendant may be given burden to prove insanity.
Self-Defense	Case-in-chief or affirmative	Defendant must offer proof of perceived immediate harm, which then prompted use of reasonable defensive force. (Reasonableness sometimes includes a duty to retreat.)
Defense of Others	Affirmative	Requires proof that the defendant reasonably or correctly perceived that force was necessary to protect another.
Defense of Property	Affirmative	Requires proof that the defendant used reasonable and nondeadly force to protect property.
Defense of Habitation	Affirmative	Requires proof that the defendant used reasonable, even though deadly, force to protect a dwelling.
Entrapment	Affirmative	Government agent instigates a criminal act by one not predisposed to commit the crime; or government agent's conduct in inducing crime is beyond judicial tolerance.

DISCUSSION QUESTIONS

1. What factors guide a court's or a legislature's decision to classify a defense as an affirmative defense or a case-in-chief defense? Who should bear the burden of proof for each of these defenses?
2. What factors guide a court's or a legislature's decision to adopt the alter-ego or reasonable perception test for defense of others?
3. What are your options if a police officer mistakes you for a fugitive and attempts to arrest you? What are your options if the officer begins to strike you with a billy stick?
4. Why should the government be permitted to suggest the commission of crimes to those who are predisposed to commit crimes? Are all "sting" operations entrapment?
5. How does the *M'Naghten* test of insanity—distinguishing right from wrong—differ from an ignorance of the law defense? Could you plead insanity if you were unaware that a statute made it a crime to protest within ten feet of an abortion clinic?

PRACTICE EXERCISES

1. What definition of insanity has your jurisdiction adopted? Who has the burden of proof on questions of insanity?
2. For which crimes does your jurisdiction recognize voluntary intoxication as a defense?
3. In your jurisdiction, who has the burden of proof when the defendant claims self-defense?
4. Does your jurisdiction recognize any form of the battered person syndrome?
5. What type of force may be used to protect property in your jurisdiction?
6. Does your jurisdiction permit a defendant to deny commission of the crime and simultaneously maintain entrapment? See *Mathews v. United States*, 487 U.S. 1240, 108 S.Ct. 2913 (1988).

WEB SITE

Office for Victims of Crime
www.ojp.usdoj.gov/ovc

KEY TERMS

Alibi
Case-in-chief defense
Affirmative defense
Necessity
Duress
Mistake of fact
Mistake of law
Voluntary intoxication
Involuntary intoxication

Competency to stand trial
M'Naghten test for insanity
Irresistible impulse test for insanity
Diminished capacity test for
 insanity
Federal test for insanity
Guilty but mentally ill
Self-defense

Retreat
Defense of others
Alter-ego theory
Reasonable perception theory
Subjective approach to entrapment
Objective approach to entrapment

NOTES

1. Model Penal Code § 3.02(1).
2. *United States v. Bailey,* 444 U.S. 394, 100 S.Ct. 624 (1980).
3. *Regina v. Dudley,* 14 Q.B.D. 273 (1884).
4. *United States v. Holmes,* 26 F. Cas. 360 (C.C.Pa. 1842).
5. Lon Fuller, "The Case of the Speluncean Explorers," 62 Harv. L. Rev. 616 (1949).
6. *United States v. Bailey,* 444 U.S. 394, 100 S.Ct. 624 (1980).
7. See Model Penal Code § 2.04(1)(a) Ordinarily, mistake of fact is a defense if it negates the mental state required to establish an element of the offense.
8. O. W. Holmes, Jr., The Common Law 48 (1881).
9. *Dusky v. United States,* 362 U.S. 402, 80 S.Ct. 788 (1960).
10. *Jackson v. Indiana,* 406 U.S. 715, 92 S.Ct. 1845 (1972).
11. *Ford v. Wainwright,* 477 U.S. 399, 106 S.Ct. 2595 (1986).
12. *Washington v. Harper,* 494 U.S. 210, 110 S.Ct. 1028 (1990).
13. *Commonwealth v. Rogers,* 48 Mass. (7 Metc.) 500 (1844).
14. Model Penal Code § 4.01(1).
15. 18 U.S.C.A. § 20.
16. *State v. Hodges,* 239 Kan. 63, 716 P.2d 563 (1986).
17. *Jahnke v. State,* 682 P.2d 991 (Wyo. 1984).
18. Model Penal Code § 3.05.
19. *Tennessee v. Garner,* 471 U.S. 1, 105 S.Ct. 1694 (1985).
20. *United States v. Russell,* 411 U.S. 423, 93 S.Ct. 1637 (1973).
21. *United States v. Russell,* 411 U.S. 423, 93 S.Ct. 1637 (1973). See also, *United States v. Coates,* 949 F.2d 104 (4th Cir. 1991). ("The government's conduct must be so outrageous as to shock the conscience of the court.")

CRIMES AGAINST A PERSON

Chapter 5

CHAPTER OUTLINE

This chapter addresses crimes somewhat arbitrarily classified as crimes against people. Ultimately all offenses are crimes against society (the collective people), but this chapter looks at offenses against individual victims. Although criminal homicide is obviously the most serious crime, other crimes against a person include assault and battery, rape or other nonconsensual sex offenses, and crimes against a person's liberty such as kidnapping or false imprisonment.

CRIMINAL HOMICIDE

Criminal homicide
taking another's life in a
manner proscribed by law;
a killing in the absence of
justification or excuse.

Homicide is the killing of a human being by another human being. Standing alone, homicide is not a crime because some killings are regarded as justifiable or excusable homicides: for example, executing a condemned prisoner, killing in self-defense, or shooting an enemy soldier during war time. **Criminal homicide** occurs when a person takes another's life in a manner proscribed by law. The common law divided criminal homicide into murder and manslaughter. Modern statutes often further subdivide murder into several degrees, distinguish voluntary manslaughter from involuntary manslaughter; and create additional forms of criminal homicide, such as negligent or vehicular homicide.

The various degrees of murder and manslaughter identify defendants on the basis of their mental states or their physical acts. Criminal homicide, however, comprises all forms of the same social harm of taking another's life. Even though the common law sometimes struggled with the legal definition of life and death, the criminal law's determination of when life begins and ends is greatly complicated by advances in medical science and the political and moral debates over abortion and euthanasia. Is abortion murder? Consider the following excerpt of Justice Blackmun's opinion in *Roe v. Wade* concluding that the definition of "person" does not include the unborn.

> In areas other than criminal abortion the law has been reluctant to endorse any theory that life, as we recognize it, begins before live birth or to accord legal rights to the unborn except in narrowly defined situations and except when the rights are contingent upon live birth. . . . In short, the unborn have never been recognized in the law as persons in the whole sense.[1]

What is a person "in the whole sense"? No one definition of a live person universally applies to all legal areas including constitutional law, contract law, tort law, and criminal homicide. Even the U.S. Supreme Court's abortion decisions have not provided a definition of a "person" for all purposes. In *Keeler v. Superior Court,* the California legislature defined homicide as the unlawful killing of a "human being," but did not define a human being. In other words, the California courts are left to their own discretion when interpreting the statutory term *human being* and must therefore determine whether they are bound by the U.S. Supreme Court's abortion decisions, by the common law definition of a human being, or by medical science. The difficulty in interpreting this critical concept provides the basis of the disagreement in *Keeler v. Superior Court.*

Today, many states have enacted feticide statutes that punish anyone who causes the death of a viable fetus. The question still remains, however, as to whether the mother herself can be prosecuted for illegally aborting a fetus. *State v. Ashley* held that aside from the "born alive" doctrine, the common law conferred immunity on a pregnant woman who intentionally injures her fetus.

If any controversy rivals the dispute surrounding abortion and the right to life, it is the debate over a right to die and the legal definition of death.[2] The common

KEELER v. SUPERIOR COURT
Supreme Court of California, 1970
2 Cal. 3d 619, 87 Cal.Rptr. 481, 470 P.2d 617

Mrs. Keeler was driving on a narrow mountain road after delivering her daughters to their home. The defendant, her ex-husband, blocked the road with his car, and she pulled over to the side. The defendant walked to her vehicle and said, "I hear you're pregnant. If you are you had better stay away from the girls and from here." Defendant helped her from the car, looked at her abdomen and became "extremely upset." He said, "You sure are. I'm going to stomp it out of you." He pushed her against the car, shoved his knee into her abdomen, and struck her in the face with several blows.

A Caesarian section was performed and the fetus was examined *in utero*. Its head was found to be severely fractured, and it was delivered stillborn. Both Mrs. Keeler and her obstetrician testified that fetal movements had been observed prior to the defendant's attack. Expert testimony concluded "with reasonable medical certainty" that the fetus had developed to the stage of viability, i.e., that in the event of premature birth on the date in question it would have had a 75 percent to 96 percent chance of survival.

JUSTICE MOSK delivered the opinion of the court:
We undertake a brief review of the origins and development of the common law of abortional homicide. . . . From that inquiry it appears that by the year 1850 an infant could not be the subject of homicide at common law *unless it had been born alive.* "The common law regarded abortion as murder only if the fetus is (1) quickened, (2) born alive, (3) lives for a brief interval, and (4) then dies. . . . We conclude that in declaring murder to be the unlawful and malicious killing of a "human being" the California Legislature intended that term to have the settled common law meaning.

The People urge, however, that the sciences of obstetrics and pediatrics have greatly progressed to the point where with proper medical care a normally developed fetus prematurely born at 28 weeks or more has an excellent chance of survival, i.e., is "viable"; that the common law requirement of live birth to prove the fetus had become a "human being" who may be the victim of murder is no longer in accord with scientific fact, since an unborn but viable fetus is now fully capable of independent life; and that one who unlawfully and maliciously terminates such a life should therefore be liable to prosecution for murder. We may grant the premises of this argument; indeed, we neither deny nor denigrate

the vast progress of medicine in the past century. But we cannot join in the conclusion sought to be deduced: we cannot hold this defendant to answer for murder by reason of his alleged act of killing an unborn—even though viable—fetus.

JUSTICE BURKE dissenting:
The majority suggest that we are confined to common law concepts, and to the common law definition of murder or manslaughter. However, the Legislature has defined those offenses for us: homicide is the unlawful killing of a "human being." Those words need not be frozen in place as of any particular time, but must be fairly and reasonably interpreted by this court to promote justice and to carry out the evident purposes of the Legislature in adopting a homicide statute.

We commonly conceive of human existence as a spectrum stretching from birth to death. However, if this court properly might expand the definition of "human being" at one end of that spectrum, we may do so at the other end. Consider the following example: All would agree that "Shooting or otherwise damaging a corpse is not homicide". . . . In other words, a corpse is not considered to be a "human being" and thus cannot be the subject of a "killing" as those terms are used in homicide statues. However, it is readily apparent that our concepts of what constitutes a "corpse" have been and are being continually modified by advances in the field of medicine, including new techniques for life revival, restoration and resuscitation such as artificial respiration, open heart massage, transfusions, transplants and a variety of life-restoring stimulants, drugs and new surgical methods. Would this court ignore these developments and exonerate the killer of an apparently "drowned" child merely because that child would have been pronounced dead in 1648 or 1850? Obviously not. Whether a homicide occurred in that case would be determined by medical testimony regarding the capability of the child to have survived prior to the defendant's act. And that is precisely the test which this court should adopt in the instant case.

Nothing should prevent this court from holding that "Baby Girl" Vogt, who, according to medical testimony, had reached the 35th week of development, had a 96 percent chance of survival, was "definitely" alive and viable, and thus a human being under California's homicide statutes.

law associated death with the cessation of heart and lung functions, but many jurisdictions now recognize a form of "brain death," or an absence of spontaneous brain functions. Because no universally accepted definitions circumscribe the concepts of birth and death, local statutes and state court decisions govern the issue.

STATE v. ASHLEY
701 So.2d 338 (Fla. 1997)

Although Kawana Ashley, an unwed teenager, was in the third trimester of pregnancy she had told no one. Her three-year-old son was being raised by her grandmother, Rosa, with whom Ashley lived, and Rosa had told Ashley that she would not care for another child if Ashley were to become pregnant again. On March 27, 1994, Ashley obtained a gun and shot herself. She was rushed to the hospital, underwent surgery, and survived. The fetus, which had been struck on the wrist by the bullet, was removed during surgery and died fifteen days later due to immaturity.

As a result of the death of the fetus, the State Attorney charged the teenager with alternative counts of murder and manslaughter, with the underlying felony for the murder charge being criminal abortion. The trial court dismissed the murder charge but allowed the manslaughter charge to stand.

The State argues that Ashley was properly charged with both murder and manslaughter, reasoning thusly: Ashley violated the criminal abortion statute, by performing a third-trimester abortion on herself with a .22 caliber firearm; because the fetus died as a result, the teenager committed third-degree murder; and further, because the fetus was born alive, Ashley committed manslaughter. We disagree.

At common law, while a third party could be held criminally liable for causing injury or death to a fetus, the pregnant woman could not be. The common law continues to be the law of Florida to the extent that it is consistent with the constitutions and statutory laws of the United States and Florida. In the present case, none of the statutes under which Ashley was charged "unequivocally" state that they alter the common law doctrine conferring immunity on the pregnant woman. In fact, none even hint at such a change. Nor are any of the statutes so repugnant to the common law that the two cannot coexist. Accordingly, we conclude that the legislature did not abrogate the common law doctrine of immunity for the pregnant woman. Every court to address the issue has rejected the use of the born alive doctrine to hold a pregnant woman criminally liable for her prenatal conduct whether the woman is charged under homicide statutes or other criminal statutes. We reached a similar result in *Johnson v. State,* 602 So.2d 1288 (Fla. 1992), wherein we held that a pregnant woman cannot be held criminally liable for passing cocaine in utero to her fetus. The relevant statutory section, we concluded, contained no indication of legislative intent to prosecute the woman.

Medical science prescribes rehabilitation, not imprisonment, for the offender.

Suicide

At common law successful suicide was a crime resulting in the forfeiture of all property owned by the one who committed suicide and ignominious burial, usually with a stake driven through the heart. Attempted suicide was treated as a misdemeanor and rarely prosecuted. Assisting suicide, however, is regarded as a serious crime, as evidenced by the publicity surrounding Dr. Jack Kevorkian. Dr. Kevorkian assisted twenty terminally ill persons in committing suicide, but was acquitted on three different occasions. In 1999, Dr. Kevorkian allowed the program *60 Minutes* to film him administering a lethal injection to a patient. This time, however, Dr. Kevorkian was convicted of murder and sentenced to ten to twenty-five years in prison. In 1997 Oregon enacted the Death With Dignity Act, decriminalizing physician-assisted suicide under certain circumstances. Two U.S. Supreme Court cases *Washington v. Glucksberg,*[3] and *Vacco v. Quill,*[4] held that terminally ill patients do not possess a U.S. constitutional privacy or due process right to physician-assisted suicide. The states remain free to recognize or reject such procedures.

Once the defendant's act of taking a human life is established, the courts look to the defendant's physical acts and mental state as the basis for distinguishing among the various degrees of murder and manslaughter.

Murder

The common law defined murder as a killing with malice aforethought. As was typical of many common law principles, malice aforethought was simply a comprehensive name for a number of different mental attitudes regarded as particularly heinous forms of homicide, and therefore murder. As one study of the common law put it, "When a particular state of mind came under their notice, the Judges called it malice or not according to their view of the propriety of hanging particular people." [5]

A defendant kills with **malice aforethought** when the defendant: (1) forms an intent to kill; (2) forms an intent to inflict grievous bodily harm on another; (3) displays a wanton or extremely reckless disregard for the risk to human life; or (4) commits a dangerous felony during the commission of which a death results.

The common law contained no degrees of murder. All defendants who killed with malice aforethought could be convicted of murder and sentenced to death. In the United States, the movement to lessen the number of crimes warranting capital punishment led many jurisdictions to enact statutory schemes establishing a sliding scale of punishment for capital murder, first degree murder, and second degree murder. Because degrees of murder are statutory creations, no universal rule governs the distinctions between capital, first degree, and second degree murder. The most commonly utilized approaches are discussed in the following sections.

Capital Murder
Capital murder often requires proof of a statutorily defined aggravating circumstance, in addition to the other requirements for murder. Prior to the 1970s many states authorized the death penalty for all forms of murder and for other dangerous felonies like rape and robbery. Capital punishment was temporarily abolished in the United States when the U.S. Supreme Court held the death penalty to be cruel and unusual punishment in violation of the Eighth and Fourteenth Amendments to the U.S. Constitution.[6] The severity of the punishment was not the issue that led the Court to this result; instead, the Court was concerned with the capricious manner in which individuals were sentenced to death. For instance, in many cases, juries exercised unfettered discretion to sentence a robber to the electric chair, or sentence a murderer to prison.

In response to the Supreme Court decision, and in an effort to reinstate the death penalty, many state legislatures enacted statutory provisions specifying the offenses and circumstances warranting capital punishment. When confronted with these new statutory standards for imposing the death penalty, the Supreme Court reversed itself and upheld the constitutionality of death sentences so long as the sentencing judge or jury is guided by statutory standards.

Most jurisdictions that utilize the death penalty limit its imposition to the most aggravated forms of murder: for example, the murder of multiple victims, one of the statutorily required circumstances existed and that the defendant met all of the other requirements for murder discussed in the next section. Exhibit 5–1 illustrates one state's statutory recognition of the most serious forms of murder.

First Degree Murder
The states that grade murder by degrees often treat premeditated killings as **first degree murder. Premeditation** is not easily defined, but the term suggests that the defendant acted in cold blood after careful deliberation. (In contrast, a killing in the heat of passion constitutes the lesser crime of voluntary

---

Marginal notes:

Malice aforethought distinguishes murder from manslaughter.

Capital murder killing characterized by the existence of a statutorily defined aggravating circumstance in addition to the other requirements for murder.

First degree murder killing characterized by premeditation.

Premeditation careful, prior deliberation of an act committed in cold blood.

EXHIBIT 5–1
Statutory Forms of Capital Murder in Virginia

Capital murder is the willful, deliberate, and premeditated killing of:

1. any person during the commission of abduction;
2. any person by another for hire;
3. any person by a prisoner confined in a state or local correctional facility;
4. any person during the commission of robbery or attempted robbery;
5. any person during the commission of, or subsequent to rape or attempted rape, forcible sodomy or attempted forcible sodomy or object sexual penetration;
6. a law-enforcement officer when such killing is for the purpose of interfering with the performance of his official duties;
7. more than one person as a part of the same act or transaction;
8. more than one person within a three-year period;
9. any person in the commission of or attempted commission of "drug" crimes when such killing is for the purpose of furthering the commission or attempted commission of such crimes;
10. any person by another pursuant to the direction or order of one who is engaged in a continuing criminal enterprise;
11. a pregnant woman by one who knows that the woman is pregnant and has the intent to cause the involuntary termination of the woman's pregnancy without a live birth;.
12. a person under the age of 14 by a person age 21 or older.

Instantaneous premeditation
a view of forethought to the crime that recognizes that "no time is too short for a wicked man to frame in his mind the scheme of murder."

Transferred intent
the act of killing a person while intending to kill someone else.

Felony-murder rule
applies a first degree murder charge to killing a person intentionally, recklessly, or even accidentally while committing a dangerous felony.

manslaughter.) The states are divided, however, as to how much deliberate thought is required for premeditation.

One view has been dubbed **instantaneous premeditation** because it recognizes that "no time is too short for a wicked man to frame in his mind the scheme of murder." This view states that the time required to premeditate is not days, hours, or even minutes, it may be no more than "a brief moment of thought."[7] Thus premeditation exists if the actor formed the intent "at the very moment" that the killing occurred. The doctrine of **transferred intent** also allows the law to punish a defendant who intends to kill one person, but actually kills another. For example, **X** fires at **Y,** but hits and kills **Z.** Although **Z** was an unintended victim, the law transfers **X**'s intent or premeditation to the actual victim. The *Scott* case applies the transferred intent doctrine to a drive-by shooting of unintended victims.

Jurisdictions rejecting the concept of instantaneous premeditation label it a "contradiction in terms," and require proof of some appreciable time to premeditate. No court requires a specific time period of deliberation, but the courts look to factors such as evidence of planning activity, preconceived motives to kill, or indications that the manner of killing (purchasing poison, for example) negates the likelihood of a sudden, rash decision to kill. Exhibit 5–2 (on the next page) presents a typical jury instruction in a case deciding guilt of first degree murder. A defendant who forms a nonpremeditated intent to kill may be guilty of second degree murder.

Defendants who do not premeditate a killing may still be guilty of first degree murder under the felony-murder rule. The **felony-murder rule** applies when a felon kills a person intentionally, recklessly, or even accidentally while the felon is committing a felony enumerated in the first degree murder statute. The rationale for the rule is that one who engages in inherently dangerous crimes should be aware of the high risk to human life created by the crime.

PEOPLE v. SCOTT
59 Cal.Rptr.2d 178 (1996)

A jury convicted defendants Damien Scott and Derrick Brown of various crimes for their part in a drive-by shooting where defendants fired an automatic weapon into a public park in an attempt to kill a certain individual, and fatally shot a bystander instead. The case presents the type of factual setting in which courts have uniformly approved reliance on the transferred intent doctrine as the basis of determining a defendant's criminal liability for the death of an unintended victim. We must decide in this case whether the doctrine of transferred intent may be used to assign criminal liability to a defendant who kills an unintended victim when the defendant is also prosecuted for the attempted murder of an intended victim.

Defendant Scott argues that when an accused is charged with attempted murder of the intended victim, and transferred intent is used to assign a defendant's liability for the killing of an unintended victim, the defendant is being prosecuted as if he intended to kill two people rather than one. Defendant asserts that, under these circumstances, transferred intent should not be applied.

The doctrine of transferred intent is typically invoked in the criminal law context when assigning criminal liability to a defendant who attempts to kill one person but accidentally kills another instead. Under such circumstances, the accused is deemed as culpable, and society is harmed as much, as if the defendant had accomplished what he had initially intended, and justice is achieved by punishing the defendant for a crime of the same seriousness as the one he tried to commit against his intended victim.

Application of the transferred intent doctrine is not foreclosed by the prosecutor having charged defendants with attempted murder of the intended victim. Contrary to what its name implies, the transferred intent doctrine does not refer to any actual intent that is capable of being "used up" once it is employed to convict a defendant of a specific intent crime against the intended victim. Rather, as applied here, it connotes a policy—that a defendant who shoots at an intended victim with intent to kill but misses and hits a bystander instead should be subject to the same criminal liability that would have been imposed had he hit his intended mark.

Conversely, reliance on a transferred intent theory of liability for the first degree murder of the unintended victim did not prevent the prosecutor from also charging defendants with attempted murder of the intended victim. In their attempt to kill the intended victim, defendants committed crimes against two persons. They may be held accountable for the death of the unintended victim on a theory of transferred intent. Their criminal liability for attempting to kill the intended victim is in accordance with the attempted murder statute.

Murder in the first degree is the deliberate, premeditated and malicious killing of a human being, and if you believe from the evidence, beyond a reasonable doubt, that the defendant deliberately, premeditatedly and maliciously killed the deceased, then you shall find the defendant guilty of murder in the first degree.

To constitute a deliberate, premeditated killing, it is not necessary that the intention to kill should exist for any particular length of time prior to the actual killing; it is only necessary that such intention should have come into existence for the first time at the time of such killing, or at any time previously.

EXHIBIT 5–2
Instruction on Premeditation

PEOPLE v. STAMP
Supreme Court of California, 1969
2 Cal. App.3d 203, 82 Cal. Rptr. 598

The defendants, armed with a gun and a blackjack, entered an office and ordered the employees to lie down on the floor while the robbers took the money and fled out the back door. Honeyman, who had been lying on the floor, was short of breath, sucking air, and pounding and rubbing his chest. About 15 minutes after the robbery had occurred, Honeyman collapsed on the floor. He was pronounced dead on arrival at the hospital. The coroner's report listed the immediate cause of death as heart attack.

Medical experts testified that although Honeyman had an advanced case of atherosclerosis, a progressive and ultimately fatal disease, there must have been some immediate upset to his system which precipitated the attack. It was their conclusion that but for the robbery there would have been no fatal seizure at that time. The fright induced by the robbery was too much of a shock to Honeyman's system.

JUSTICE COBEY delivered the opinion of the court:
Defendants' contention that the felony-murder rule is inapplicable to the facts of this case is without merit. Under the felony-murder rule, a killing committed in either the perpetration of or an attempt to perpetrate robbery is murder of the first degree. This is true whether the killing is willful, deliberate and premedi-tated, or merely accidental or unintentional, and whether or not the killing is planned as a part of the commission of the robbery.

The doctrine presumes malice aforethought on the basis of the commission of a felony inherently dangerous to human life. . . . Under this rule no intentional act is necessary other than the attempt to or the actual commission of the robbery itself. When a robber enters a place with a deadly weapon with the intent to commit robbery, malice is shown by the nature of the crime.

The doctrine is not limited to those deaths which are foreseeable. . . . Rather a felon is held strictly liable for *all* killings committed by him or his accomplices in the course of the felony. . . . As long as the homicide is the direct causal result of the robbery the felony-murder rule applies whether or not the death was a natural or probable consequence of the robbery. So long as a victim's predisposing physical condition, regardless of its cause, is not the *only* substantial factor bringing about his death, that condition, and the robber's ignorance of it, in no way destroys the robber's criminal responsibility for the death. . . . So long as life is shortened as a result of the felonious act, it does not matter that the victim might have died soon anyway. . . . In this respect, the robber takes his victim as he finds him.

Strict application of the felony-murder rule can lead to surprising results. *People v. Stamp* looks at the question of whether the defendants are responsible when a robbery victim experiences a heart attack.

The heart attack in the *Stamp* case is merely one example of the difficulties inherent in applying rules of causation to the felony-murder rule. To answer the question of whether the felons in *Stamp* "cause" the victim's death the court found that the robbers contributed to or helped cause the heart attack (at least in a "but-for" sense). As the court decision states, responsibility for a death that was largely unforeseeable comes from a strict liability "for *all* killings committed . . . in the course of the felony."

Another wrinkle to causation questions under the felony-murder rule arises when a nonfelon kills during the commission of the felony. Suppose that during the robbery in *Stamp,* Mr. Honeyman had shot and killed one of the robbers. Could the surviving robber be charged with felony-murder because he "caused" Mr. Honeyman to resist the felony with fatal force?

The strict liability approach of the *Stamp* case can extend the felony-murder rule to truly bizarre factual situations. For example, a robber pulls a gun and orders the victim into the alleyway where the victim is struck by a bolt of lightning. The robber can be guilty of first degree murder because "but for" the robbery the victim would not have been in position to be struck by lightning. The rationale for decisions, such as the *Stamp* decision, is that strict application of the felony-murder rule will make the felon proceed more carefully in the commission of the offense (e.g., "Mr. Victim, watch your step in that alley"), or will cause the felon to abandon the felony (e.g., "No robberies until those thunder clouds pass.")

Some jurisdictions reject the *Stamp* approach by exempting "freak" accidents like lightning bolts or heart attacks from the coverage of the felony-murder rule. In these jurisdictions, the felon is responsible only for deaths that were reasonably foreseeable. Other jurisdictions have abandoned the felony-murder rule entirely and have opted to deter dangerous situations by increasing the penalty for the underlying felony, rather than increase the punishment only when a death results from the felony. Jurisdictions that retain some form of the felony-murder rule normally limit the application of the rule to specified dangerous felonies, most commonly rape, robbery, arson, burglary, and kidnapping. If death results from the commission of any felony not specified as a form of first degree felony-murder, the defendant may be prosecuted for second degree murder.

Second Degree Murder

A person who forms a nonpremeditated intent to kill may be guilty of **second degree murder**. But an intent to kill is not required when the defendant possesses some other form of malice, such as an intent to inflict serious harm on another. For example, suppose the defendant does not intend to kill, but does intend to beat the victim "within an inch of the victim's life." If the defendant inadvertently goes the extra "inch" and actually kills the victim, the defendant has acted with malice and is guilty of second degree murder.

A defendant also may commit second degree murder if the killing is characterized by a **wanton state of mind** or extremely reckless disregard of the safety of others and the risk the defendant poses to human life. For example, the defendant does not intend to kill or injure the victim, but the defendant intends to frighten the victim by shooting in the victim's general direction. If an errant shot kills the victim, the defendant will be punished, not for actual intent, but for callous disregard for the value of human life. Courts have utilized a number of colorful terms to describe this form of malice: for example, "a depraved mind," "an abandoned and malignant heart," or "wickedness of disposition." These terms distinguish the defendant's mental state as one of "extreme" disregard for human life and different from a lesser form of recklessness that warrants a conviction of the lesser offense of involuntary manslaughter. Murder thus requires a more blameworthy level of risk-taking than does manslaughter.

Manslaughter

The critical distinction between murder and manslaughter is the presence or absence of malice: murder is a killing with malice aforethought; manslaughter is an unlawful killing without malice aforethought. The common law and most jurisdictions distinguish between voluntary and involuntary manslaughter.

Voluntary Manslaughter

A defendant who kills with malice aforethought is said to have made a cold-blooded decision to kill, to inflict serious injury, or to create a great risk of death. A person guilty of voluntary manslaughter also may have intended to kill, injure, or create a risk of death, but the intent arose, not from a cold-blooded decision, but from the heat of passion. For example, **B** walks into the bedroom and finds **C**, **B**'s spouse, committing adultery, whereupon **B**, enraged by the incident kills both **C** and **C**'s lover. A defendant is guilty of **voluntary manslaughter** when (1) killing while in a state of passion, (2) which was caused by adequate

Second degree murder killing with a state of mind characterized as a wanton or an extremely reckless disregard for the risk to human life.

Wanton state of mind extremely reckless disregard of the safety of others.

Voluntary manslaughter killing while in a state of passion, which was caused by adequate provocation and without a reasonable opportunity to cool off before killing.

provocation; and (3) the defendant did not have a reasonable opportunity to cool off before killing.

Whether the defendant was in the heat of passion is a factual question normally resolved by circumstantial evidence of the defendant's mental state. For example, the defense may offer proof that the defendant was crying, ranting, chewing on the rug, or whatever external manifestations indicate an internal state of extreme passion. The prosecution may counter with eyewitness accounts that the defendant appeared to be calm, or with such evidence as the defendant believed in free love but killed the lover of the defendant's spouse because the lover had cheated the defendant in a stock manipulation scheme. The jury, acting as fact-finder, must resolve the conflicting evidence and determine whether the defendant was truly in the heat of passion at the time of the killing.

Assuming that the defendant was in the heat of passion, the passion must have been prompted by adequate provocation. The law does not allow a hot-tempered person to initiate a bloodbath at the slightest provocation. For example, even if your favorite restaurant fails to specify—"Don't shoot the piano player"—you cannot vent your killing rage on a musician who defiles a beloved tune. **Adequate provocation** is a circumstance that "would naturally tend to arouse the passion of an ordinarily reasonable person." The most commonly recognized forms of adequate provocation are (1) discovery of a spouse engaged in adultery, (2) mutual combat or (3) a serious assault upon the defendant or the defendant's relatives. Words alone, no matter how insulting, do not

Adequate provocation
circumstances that "would naturally tend to arouse the passion of an ordinarily reasonable person."

PEOPLE v. PAGE
737 N.E.2d 264 (Ill. 2000)

Defendant has been convicted of three murders, the Goodman and Howell murders at issue in this case, as well as the murder of Dale Andrew Devine. Defendant argues that he was only guilty of voluntary manslaughter. At the time of the offense, the homicide statute provided that a person commits voluntary manslaughter if at the time of the killing he either had an actual but unreasonable belief regarding the need for self-defense, or was acting under a sudden and intense passion resulting from serious provocation.

Defendant contends that he and Goodman argued for 10 to 15 minutes over some photographs that Goodman refused to surrender. According to defendant, Goodman had taken photographs of defendant and Goodman having a homosexual relationship. Defendant said that he punched and stabbed Goodman when Goodman refused to move from the bathroom doorway, where the two were standing. In addition to this evidence, defendant said that he stabbed Goodman after Goodman began laughing at his request for the photographs.

Defendant's theory is that he killed Goodman while he was acting under a sudden and intense passion resulting from serious provocation. Defendant argues that the provocation here is that Goodman made sexual advances toward him. This is not one of the categories of provocation that this court has recognized. Serious provocation is conduct sufficient to excite an intense passion in a reasonable person. This court has recognized the following categories of provocation: substantial physical injury or substantial physical assault; mutual quarrel or combat; illegal arrest; and adultery with the offender's spouse.

Defendant cites additional cases which he contends "discuss what could be termed the 'homosexual panic' defense and demonstrate the accepted use of this 'defense' to obtain a manslaughter instruction." While these cases likewise involve fact scenarios where the victims made homosexual advances toward the defendants, the defendants' theories of voluntary manslaughter were based on the unreasonable belief in the need for self-defense, not on serious provocation, which is the theory advanced by defendant in this case.

For the foregoing reasons, we uphold the defendant's convictions for murder.

constitute adequate provocation in most jurisdictions. Although a minority of jurisdictions authorize the judge to decide what constitutes adequate provocation, the majority entrust this decision to the jury. *People v. Page* rejects an attempt to invoke "homosexual panic" as a killing in the heat of passion.

If a reasonable person would have been, and the defendant actually was, provoked to the heat of passion, such passion cannot continue indefinitely. When a reasonable person would have cooled off in the interim between the provocation and the killing, the defendant has not killed in the heat of passion. For example, after finding a spouse engaged in sexual intercourse with a lover, the betrayed spouse runs to get a gun while the adulterous lovers flee the house. The defendant finally catches up with them some ten hours later. Even if the particular defendant was a deeply passionate soul who remained in the heat of passion for ten hours, a jury is likely to conclude that a reasonable person would have cooled off in the time that elapsed between the provocation and the homicide. The defendant is thus guilty of cold-blooded murder rather than voluntary manslaughter.

The crime of voluntary manslaughter is best understood as a legal compromise—a partial concession to human emotions and passions. The law requires that people control their tempers, thus a passionate killing is not a complete defense that excuses the killing. But even "good" people are sometimes overcome by emotion, thus they are not as blameworthy as "bad" people who cold bloodedly act from a malignant heart. What would otherwise be the crime of murder is reduced to voluntary manslaughter because of the heat of passion, as noted in Exhibit 5–3.

EXHIBIT 5–3
Instruction on the Heat of Passion

(a) If at the time of the homicide the defendant's state of mind was caused by passion, anger, or rage, and was such that a reasonable doubt exists as to the defendant's having acted deliberately and with premeditation, you cannot find the defendant guilty of murder in the first degree.

(b) Even though you may believe from the evidence beyond a reasonable doubt that the defendant killed the deceased, if you further believe from the evidence that the killing was not from malice, but was done in the heat of passion, upon reasonable provocation, then you shall not find the defendant guilty of any higher offense than voluntary manslaughter.

(c) In order for the killing to amount to voluntary manslaughter, such killing must have resulted from an intentional act, without malice, either upon sudden heat of passion upon reasonable provocation, or in mutual combat, and if the prosecution has not proved such beyond a reasonable doubt, then the defendant cannot be guilty of that crime.

(d) If you believe from the evidence, beyond a reasonable doubt, that a sufficient time had elapsed for any passion and anger of the defendant, engendered by the conduct of the deceased, to have cooled and subsided, and that thereafter the defendant did with malice and premeditation kill the deceased, then you should find the defendant guilty of murder in the first degree.

(e) If you believe from the evidence that the conduct of the deceased was such as to reasonably provoke the passion and anger of the defendant and as a result, before a reasonable time had elapsed for the defendant's passion to subside and while still in the heat of said passion and anger and before reason returned, the defendant killed the deceased, you cannot find the defendant guilty of a higher grade of offense than voluntary manslaughter.

Involuntary manslaughter
a homicide that results from the defendant's reckless or criminally negligent conduct or the defendant's commission of an unlawful act.

Involuntary Manslaughter   Involuntary manslaughter is unrelated to voluntary manslaughter because it has nothing to do with the heat of passion. **Involuntary manslaughter** occurs when a homicide results from the defendant's reckless or criminally negligent conduct, or the defendant's commission of an unlawful act.

Reckless Conduct   The first form of involuntary manslaughter is a less serious form of recklessness than the extreme recklessness (malice) required for a conviction of second degree murder. Recklessness, however, is more serious than the simple negligence that may result in civil liability. The courts distinguish extreme recklessness (murder) from recklessness (manslaughter) by considering both the defendant's subjective state of mind and objective evidence of the extent to which the defendant's conduct endangered another. Consider the following hypothetical situation.

> **A** fires a rifle at some pigeons while **B** fires at the wheels of a passenger train. Both **A** and **B** intend to test the accuracy of their weapons, and neither intends to shoot a human being. Assume, however, that **A** and **B** each fire an errant bullet that kills a person. Assume further that scientific evidence indicates that given the direction of the bullets and the location of the victims, both **A** and **B** created a 40 percent chance that a person would be struck by a bullet.

An objective assessment of their conduct discloses that **A** and **B** posed an equal (40 percent) threat to human life. But an assessment of their subjective mental states reveals an important distinction. **B** was aware of the risk to human life because **B** knew that the passenger train, at which the gun was aimed, was occupied. **A**, however, was unaware that any person was in the vicinity. On the basis of their subjective states of mind, **B** might be guilty of second degree murder because of a "malignant heart." **A**, however, might be guilty of involuntary manslaughter because of nonmalignant but reckless conduct.

Now suppose that both **A** and **B** were firing at pigeons, but the scientific evidence indicates that from where **A** was standing there was a 40 percent chance that someone would be struck by a bullet. In contrast, from **B**'s position there was a 70 percent chance of hitting a person with a bullet. **A** and **B** no longer can be distinguished on the basis of their subjective states of mind because they both thought they were endangering pigeons, not human life. **A** and **B** can be distinguished, however, on the basis of the objective degree of risk that a person would be shot (40 percent for **A**; 70 percent for **B**). If the risk of death is great enough, **B** may be deemed extremely reckless and thus guilty of second degree murder. **A**, who was no less morally at fault than **B**, might be deemed "merely" reckless and thus guilty of involuntary manslaughter.

In actual cases the court will not have scientific evidence establishing the precise statistical likelihood that the defendant's conduct would cause death. When distinguishing recklessness from extreme recklessness, the courts make an inexact, but necessary, assessment of the degree of risk created, and the degree to which the defendant was subjectively at fault.

Misdemeanor-manslaughter rule
applies a manslaughter charge to a homicide that results from the defendant's commission of an unlawful act.

Misdemeanor-Manslaughter   The second form of involuntary manslaughter is often, but not necessarily, tied to reckless conduct. The **misdemeanor-manslaughter rule** recognizes that a homicide may result from the defendant's commission of an unlawful act, even though the act is not inherently dangerous to human life. The misdemeanor-manslaughter rule is a corollary of the felony-murder rule, and the controversy surrounding the felony-murder rule is equally applicable to the misdemeanor-manslaughter rule. For example, courts that limit the felony-murder rule to inherently dangerous felonies are likely to limit the misdemeanor-manslaughter rule to inherently dangerous misdemeanors. (Some courts distinguish between misdemeanors mala in se and misdemeanors mala prohibita, which are defined in Chapter One.) These courts limit the application of the misdemeanor-manslaughter rule to situations in which death is a reasonably foreseeable consequence, while other courts apply the "but-for" test that the *Stamp* case applied to the felony-murder rule.

Consider how various courts might deal with a situation where **D** committed the misdemeanor of driving a car without a valid driver's license. (**D**'s license expired and **D** simply failed to renew it.) While driving, **D**'s car skids on some unseen ice in the road and runs over and kills a pedestrian. Some courts would not invoke the misdemeanor-manslaughter rule in this case because the car's skid was an unavoidable accident unrelated to the validity of a driver's license. Other courts might invoke the "but-for" test of causation and hold that the death would not have occurred but for **D**'s crime of being on the highway when **D** had no right to be driving.

Other Forms of Homicide

At common law and in most jurisdictions, involuntary manslaughter is the lowest degree of criminal homicide. A defendant who killed another person through simple negligence might be liable in civil actions for wrongful death or some other form of tort, but simple negligence is usually beyond the reach of the criminal law. Some jurisdictions, however, have enacted statutes creating the crime of negligent homicide. Depending on the terms of the statute, a defendant might be criminally responsible for causing another's death through simple negligence, or the statute may recognize an interim degree of negligence that is lower than recklessness but higher than simple negligence. In effect, a jurisdiction may create or recognize as many degrees of negligence as it chooses. For example:

1. Wantonness or extreme recklessness = second degree murder.
2. Recklessness or gross negligence = involuntary manslaughter.
3. Criminal (nonreckless) negligence = negligent homicide.
4. Simple negligence = civil liability.

No clear or universally accepted definitions of these degrees of negligence have been established, thus judges and juries are entrusted to examine the particular facts of the case and discern what if any degree of negligence existed.

ASSAULT AND BATTERY

At common law, assault and battery were different crimes, but some jurisdictions have merged them into a single offense. All jurisdictions recognize various forms of aggravated assault and battery such as mayhem, malicious wounding, felonious assault, or assault with a deadly weapon.

Battery

Battery is defined as the wrongful application of force to the person of another (an unlawful touching). The "touching" element of battery does not require that the victim be injured in any way. For example, pinching a stranger's buttocks is an offensive and unlawful touching even if it does not cause physical harm. An unlawful touching may be of the person's body or anything attached to the body, for example, grabbing and pulling on a woman's shoulder bag or a man's necktie. A touching is unlawful if it occurs in the absence of justification, excuse, or consent. For example, law enforcement officials are legally justified in using reasonable force to arrest a criminal; a person who strikes another in self-defense has engaged in an excusable touching; and friends and lovers may consent to certain types of touching.

Battery
the unlawful application of force to the person of another.

Consensual touchings are regulated and restricted by law. Although you may consent to be hugged and kissed, or to a simple fistfight, you cannot consent to a duel or any type of conduct that involves serious injury. In certain situations, the law also mandates that a person consent to touchings the person might not wish to experience. For example, the law states that you must consent to the incidental touching that occurs in normal society, such as someone brushing against your shoulder in a crowded hallway. The law also implies consent from the particular facts in numerous situations. For example, the paramedic who administers emergency mouth-to-mouth resuscitation may not be someone you would choose to kiss. But whether the paramedic is physically attractive or ugly to you, the law will infer (actually, demand) that under the circumstances you consented to the touching.

The unlawful touching in a battery may involve direct body-to-body contact or an indirect touching by some instrumentality used by the defendant. The defendant causes a touching by launching any force in motion whether it be a thrown knife, a driven car, or a dog ordered to attack the victim. In a few situations, omission—the failure to act when faced with a duty to act—might cause a battery. Although most jurisdictions have specific statutes dealing with child neglect, a parent's failure to protect a child from an unlawful touching might make the parent criminally responsible for battery upon the child.

The mental state required for battery may be either an intent to strike another or a reckless act which results in a touching. For example, when you receive an A+ on your first examination in this course, you scream with joy and throw your textbook into the air. The book lands on your classmate's head and you now have begun, inadvertently, your life of crime. Although your classmate might accept an apology and excuse your exuberance, you have committed a battery at this point because you manifested a reckless disregard for the safety of others by throwing a heavy book in a crowded classroom.

Assault

Attempted battery form of assault
act in which the defendant specifically intends to, and comes close to, touching another.

Offer type of assault
places another in fear of an imminent battery.

Assault is categorized as one of two types: (1) an attempted battery or (2) placing another in fear or apprehension of an imminent battery. Like all attempts (see Chapter Three), the **attempted battery form of assault** requires that the defendant specifically intend to cause the harm (the unlawful touching), and that the defendant commit an overt act that comes close to achieving the harm. For example, someone intending to strike you throws a punch that misses the back of your head by an inch. An assault (attempted battery) has occurred even though you were unaware of the punch. This form of assault focuses on the defendant's mental state and physical act, while ignoring the victim's state of mind.

The other form of assault is referred to as an **offer type of assault** because it requires that the defendant commit an act which places the victim in reasonable apprehension of being struck. Apprehension in this case is simply an expectation of an unwanted touching; the victim need not be "fearful" of some serious injury. The apprehension, however, must be reasonable and it must be apprehension of an imminent touching. Someone who merely gives you the "evil eye" should not create reasonable apprehension of a battery; just as someone threatening to shoot you next week does not threaten imminent harm. Threats of future harm are not included within the crime of assault although they are often covered by statutes that criminalize the act of communicating a threat.

The modern movement toward "stalking laws" is another attempt to use statutes to prohibit threatening conduct that may not amount to an assault. Stalking laws and statutes prohibiting threats are thought to be necessary because an assault requires some physical act beyond mere communication of the defendant's hostility toward the victim. Stalking laws vary in their elements, but most prohibit following, harassing, threatening, lying in wait, or conducting surveillance of another person. The most difficult aspect of defining stalking is the mental state required for the crime. For example, in the case of a celebrity, how does the law distinguish a stalker from a devoted fan? The first stalking statutes required a specific intent to cause emotional distress or to invoke fear. Such statutes proved ineffective because many stalkers suffer from emotional or mental illness and may lack a specific intent to cause fear or harm. Later statutes have sought to punish whenever the stalker knew or should have known that the victim would suffer distress or fear.

Even a threat of immediate harm is not an assault if the defendant's conduct is confined to verbal threats. An assault occurs only if the defendant accompanies a threat with some additional physical conduct such as a menacing gesture. For example, the defendant simply glares at you and says, "I've never liked you and I think it's time to punch your lights out." This statement is a threat, and it may frighten you, but it is not yet an assault in the eyes of the law. It becomes an assault, however, if the defendant advances toward you, fists raised, while threatening to punch your lights out. Although the law sometimes makes verbal communications a crime, assault follows the more traditional rule that the defendant must engage in physical conduct beyond mere verbalization of state of mind.

The state of mind required for an offer type of assault is that the defendant either intend to frighten the victim or recklessly cause the victim to apprehend an imminent touching. A defendant who waives a gun in your face while threatening you, intends to frighten you. A defendant who fires a weapon into a house, believing it to be unoccupied, has no intent to frighten anyone; but if you are present, the defendant recklessly caused you to fear imminent harm.

By way of summary, consider whether the following situations constitute either form (attempted battery or offer type) of assault:

1. With intent to strike you, the defendant swings at, but misses the back of your head.
2. The defendant is demonstrating the latest karate kick in a crowded hallway, when a kick just misses your chin.
3. With intent to strike you, the defendant swings at but misses your chin.
4. The defendant's demonstration of a karate kick barely misses the back of your head.

Situation #1 is an attempted battery form of assault because of the defendant's intent. It is not an offer type of assault because you were not placed in fear. Situation #2 is an offer type of assault because you were fearful of an imminent touching. It is not attempted battery because the defendant did not intend to strike you. Situation #3 is both an attempted battery because of the defendant's intent, and an offer type of assault because of your fear. (Note, however, that most jurisdictions would permit only one charge of assault because attempt and offer are merely different methods of committing a single assault.) Situation #4 is not attempted battery because the defendant did not intend to strike you; and no offer type of assault occurred because you were not placed in fear. In this case, the defendant has not committed any form of recognized assault.

Aggravated Assault and Battery

Simple batteries require only an unlawful touching, not actual injury, and are usually classified as misdemeanors carrying relatively minor punishment. Aggravated assaults or batteries are attacks that actually result in more serious injuries or create the potential for serious injury because the attacker used a deadly weapon.

Mayhem was a common law form of aggravated battery where the victim was dismembered or disfigured in such a way that the victim was less able to engage in self-defense. For example, cutting off a person's hand hampered the ability to wield a sword. In a much-publicized incident in 1994, Lorena Bobbitt mutilated her

Mayhem
a common law crime in which the victim was dismembered or disfigured in such a way that the victim was less able to engage in self-defense.

Malicious wounding
the shooting, stabbing, cutting, or wounding of any person with the intent to maim, disfigure, disable, or kill.

husband by severing his penis. She was not charged with mayhem, instead she was charged with malicious wounding. (She was acquitted of the crime after arguing the irresistible impulse form of insanity.) The aggravated battery of **malicious wounding** does not depend on the victim's ability of self defense; it occurs when the defendant shoots, stabs, cuts or wounds any person with the intent to maim, disfigure, disable, or kill. Malicious wounding usually requires that the defendant utilize some weapon; many jurisdictions have statutes prohibiting any form of assault with a firearm or other dangerous weapon.

An aggravated assault and/or battery can also occur while the defendant is engaged in the commission of another crime. For example, if the defendant assaults a woman with the intent to rape, but is stopped before completing the crime, the defendant can be charged with "assault with intent to commit rape." Such aggravated assaults are felonies and often carry a severe penalty.

ROBBERY

Robbery
larceny from the victim's person or presence, by use of either force or threats of force.

Robbery is a type of assault against the person combined with a type of offense against property (larceny). **Robbery** is defined as larceny from the victim's person or presence by use of force or threat of force. A successful prosecution for robbery is contingent upon proving an underlying larceny, thus any defense to larceny is automatically a defense to robbery.[8] Once a larceny is established, the prosecution must prove the aggravating factors of forcibly taking from the victim's person. (The elements of larceny are discussed in the next chapter; the focus here is on the element that makes robbery an offense against the person rather than an offense against property.)

The requirement that the taking be from the victim's person encompasses anything taken from the victim's body or clothing. It also includes property taken from the victim's presence, but not attached to the victim's body. For example, as you are about to enter your car, a robber points a gun at you and orders you to stand aside while then driving off with your vehicle. Although you were not in physical contact with your vehicle, you were present and in a position to defend your property against theft but for the threat of violence. Robbery requires that your present ability to protect your property be overcome by force or threat. Thus if the thief had slipped into your car and driven off while your back was turned, the crime is still a theft from your presence but is a theft by stealth, not force or threat. Force or threat of force is the element that most distinguishes robbery from larceny.

Physical force utilized to move another's property is a necessary element of larceny, but robbery requires force directed at the person, not merely the person's property. For example, if a purse snatcher or pickpocket uses physical force to move property out of the owner's possession, the act is not considered robbery. Robbery may occur, however, if a pickpocket distracts you by bumping into you (i.e., applying force against your person) while picking your pocket, or if the purse snatcher knocks you down *before* taking your purse. Suppose, however, that the purse snatcher seizes your purse without touching you. You pursue the thief and a fight ensues. Various states have taken different approaches to the question of whether force used to prevent immediate recapture of the stolen property constitutes robbery or the separate offenses of larceny and a subsequent battery.[9]

If actual force is not used, a threat of force must produce a genuine fear by the victim that force will be used if the property is not surrendered. A gun-wielding robber who threatens, "Your money or your life," has committed robbery. The threat may also be to another person, for example, "Your money or your companion's life." The situations rarely arise and the law is uncertain as to whether threats to property can constitute robbery. For example, would the Wicked Witch of the West commit robbery if she threatened Dorothy, "Give me the ruby slippers or I'll kill your little dog"?

In most jurisdictions, a threat of immediate harm is required, because threats of future harm do not constitute robbery. Threats to inflict future harm, however, may constitute the crimes of extortion or blackmail. The type of threat required for **extortion** or **blackmail** goes beyond a threat of bodily harm and includes threats to injure a person's reputation or to expose a person to shame and ridicule. Unlike robbery, which must be committed in the presence of the victim, extortion or blackmail can be committed by telephone, mail, or any means of communication.

In *State v. Harrington* the court addressed the issue of whether the defendant made an unlawful threat or engaged in "hardball negotiations" on behalf of a client.

Extortion or blackmail
threats to injure a person's reputation or to expose a person to shame and ridicule.

STATE v. HARRINGTON
Supreme Court of Vermont, 1969
128 Vt. 242, 260 A.2d 692

The defendant was convicted of threatening to accuse Armand Morin of the crime of adultery. The indictment charges that the threat was maliciously made with the intent to extort $175,000 and to compel Morin to do an act against his will.

Mrs. Norma Morin retained the defendant attorney to obtain a divorce based upon Mr. Morin's numerous marital infidelities with women at the motel owned by the Morins. The defendant suggested that an effort should be made to procure corroborative evidence of Mr. Morin's marital misconduct. At this time a scheme was designed to procure the services of a woman who would visit the motel in an effort to obtain corroborative evidence of Morin's infidelity.

After some screening, a Mrs. Mazza was selected to carry out the assignment. Mrs. Mazza checked into the motel and attracted Mr. Morin's attention. The sequence of events that followed ultimately led Mr. Morin and Mrs. Mazza to her motel room. About midnight, the defendant and his associates entered the motel room and took several photographs of Morin and Mazza in bed and unclothed.

The defendant subsequently wrote to Mr. Morin and requested that Morin consent to a divorce on the catchall grounds of incompatibility and pay Mrs. Morin $175,000 to settle the divorce. In return for the settlement, the defendant offered to return to Mr. Morin "all tape recordings, all negatives, all photographs and copies of photographs that might in any way, bring discredit upon yourself. Finally, there would be an absolute undertaking on the part of your wife not to divulge any information of any kind or nature which might be em-

barrassing to you in your business life, your personal life, your financial life, or your life as it might be affected by the Internal Revenue Service, the United States Customs Service, or any other governmental agency." [The Court referred to these as "informer fees."]

The defendant wrote to advise Mr. Morin that should he refuse the settlement, Mrs. Morin would file for divorce and allege, in detail, all of the grounds for divorce, including adultery. The letter to Mr. Morin also stated: "to prove to you that we have all of the proof necessary to prove adultery beyond a reasonable doubt, we are enclosing a photograph taken by one of my investigators. The purpose of enclosing the photograph is simply to show you that cameras and equipment were in full operating order."

[The Vermont Supreme Court upheld the conviction because a demand for settlement of a civil action, accompanied by a malicious threat to expose the wrongdoer's criminal conduct, if made with intent to extort payment, against his will, constitutes the crime alleged in the indictment.]

The evidence at hand establishes beyond dispute the defendant's participation was done with preconceived design. The incriminating evidence which his letter threatens to expose was willfully contrived and procured by a temptress hired for that purpose. These factors in the proof are sufficient to sustain a finding that the defendant acted maliciously and without just cause, within the meaning of our criminal statutes. The sum of the evidence supports the further inference that the act was done with intent to extort a substantial contingent fee to the defendant's personal advantage.

VIOLENT SEX CRIMES

Some sex crimes, such as rape or sexual molestation, combine elements of assault and battery with some sexual component. Other sex offenses, such as incest or prostitution, isolate the sexual nature of the crime and do not require any form of assault. Sex crimes range from violent assaults to nonviolent private sexual conduct between consenting adults (see Chapter Seven).

Rape

Common law rape
sexual intercourse with a woman other than the defendant's wife by force and without the victim's consent.

Common law rape required that the defendant engaged in sexual intercourse with a woman other than his wife, and that the intercourse was by force and without the victim's consent. (Unless the victim was a minor or otherwise incapable of valid consent.) Penetration of the vagina by the penis was the only form of sexual intercourse that constituted common law rape, thus only women could be the victims of rape, while only males could be the perpetrators of rape. (Women could be charged as aiders and abettors, or accessories before the fact to a rape committed by a man. See Chapter Three.) Today, most statutes have made the crime of rape gender neutral by expanding the offense to encompass more than vaginal rape. For example, forcing the victim to engage in sodomy, oral sex, or inanimate sexual penetration of any body orifice may be a form of rape or some other statutory sexual offense.

The second element of common law rape—the marital rape exception—provided that a man could not be convicted of raping his wife. This exception was based on antiquated theories of the wife as chattel of the husband, or on strained theories of contract law, which suggested that by contracting a marriage the wife gave continuing consent to sex with her husband. (This consent could be withdrawn only by voiding the contract through divorce.) The Supreme Court of Georgia had little difficulty in responding to this theory of implied consent:

> "When a woman says I do, does she give up her right to say I won't?" This question does not pose the real question, because rape and aggravated sodomy are not sexual acts of an ardent husband performed upon an initially apathetic wife, they are acts of violence that are accomplished with physical and mental abuse and often leave the victim with physical and psychological damage that is almost always long lasting. Thus, we find the more appropriate question: When a woman says "I do" in Georgia, does she give up her right to State protection from the violent acts of rape and aggravated sodomy performed by her husband. The answer is no.[10]

Although theories of implied consent are no longer considered valid, a number of jurisdictions retain some form of the marital exception because of fears that charges of marital rape will be fabricated as part of a domestic dispute between married couples. However, even jurisdictions that retain the marital exception to rape recognize that a husband who physically forces his wife to have sex may be guilty of some aggravated form of assault and battery, or a separate statutory offense of marital rape.

Even more controversial than the marital exception to rape was the common law's requirement that the sexual intercourse occur without the victim's consent and through the use of force, which often turned upon whether the victim had resisted to the utmost. No jurisdictions currently require "utmost resistance," but many states still require that the victim demonstrate a lack of consent by offering reasonable resistance under the circumstances. For example, a woman need not offer any resistance to a firearm or knife, but in the absence of a show of force by the defendant, the woman might be required to offer at least a firm refusal to sexual overtures.

The current debate surrounding "date rape" and campus "codes of sexual conduct" challenges the requirement for any resistance, but also demonstrates the difficulty of determining just when persuasion ends and force begins. Are all forms of seduction rape? According to some scholars, seduction or sexual harassment may not involve physical force, but may instead entail the use of psychological power to subjugate a person. Consider one state's approach to sexual intercourse accomplished by threat or intimidation:

> There is a difference between threat and intimidation. As used in the statute, threat means expression of an intention to do bodily harm. Intimidation may occur without threats. Intimidation, as used in the statute, means putting a victim in fear of bodily harm by exercising such domination and control of her as to overcome her mind and overbear her will. Intimidation may be caused by the imposition of psychological pressure on one who, under the circumstances, is vulnerable and susceptible to such pressure.[11]

Now consider *State v. Rusk* and whether the incident is a crude seduction or a rape. Note the factors the court felt were significant in its conclusion that the defendant committed rape.

STATE v. RUSK
Supreme Court of Maryland, 1981
289 Md. 230, 424 A.2d 720

The complaining witness, Pat, a 21-year-old woman, met the defendant in a bar. They talked until midnight and Pat agreed to give the defendant a ride home. She parked the car in front of the defendant's apartment but refused his invitation to come into the apartment. The defendant reached over and turned off the ignition to her car and took her car keys. He got out of the car and said, "Now, will you come up?" Pat explained her subsequent actions:

"At that point, because I was scared, because he had my car keys. I didn't know what to do. I was someplace I didn't even know where I was. It was in the city. I didn't know whether to run. I really didn't think at that point, what to do." "Now, I know that I should have blown the horn. I should have run. There were a million things I could have done. I was scared, at that point, and I didn't do any of them."

She followed the defendant into his apartment where she sat in a chair beside the bed. The defendant left the room for about one to five minutes. Pat remained in the chair, made no noise and did not attempt to leave. When the defendant returned he turned off the light and sat down on the bed. Pat asked if she could leave, but the defendant said he wanted her to stay.

The defendant asked Pat to get on the bed with him. He pulled her by the arms to the bed and began to undress her, removing her blouse and bra. He unzipped her slacks and she took them off after he told her to do so. Pat removed the rest of her clothing, and removed the defendant's pants because "he asked me to do it." After they were both undressed the defendant started kissing Pat. She explained what happened next:

"I was still begging him to please let, you know, let me leave. I said, 'You can get a lot of other girls down there, for what you want,' and he just kept saying, 'no'; and then I was really scared because I can't describe, you know, what was said. It was more the look in his eyes; and I said, at that point—I didn't know what to say; and I said, 'If I do what you want, will you let me go without killing me?' Because I didn't know, at that point, what he was going to do; and I started to cry; and when I did, he put his hands on my throat, and started lightly to choke me; and I said, 'If I do what you want, will you let me go?' And he said, yes, and at that time, I proceeded to do what he wanted me to."

Pat testified that the defendant made her perform oral sex and then vaginal intercourse.

[The trial court convicted the defendant of rape, but the Court of Special Appeals reversed the conviction because] In all of the victim's testimony we have been unable to see any resistance on her part to the sex acts and certainly we can see no fear as would overcome her attempt to resist or escape. Possession of the keys by the accused may have deterred her vehicular escape but hardly a departure seeking help in the rooming house or in the street. We must say that 'the way he looked' fails utterly to support the fear required [for forcible rape].

[The (higher) court of appeals, however, reversed the Court of Special Appeals and reinstated the guilty verdict because] Considering all of the evidence in the case, with particular focus upon the actual force applied by the defendant to Pat's neck, we conclude that the jury could rationally find that the essential elements of [rape] had been established and that the defendant was guilty of that offense beyond a reasonable doubt.

Rape shield laws
prohibit use of evidence of a victim's prior sexual conduct, except for prior consensual sexual relations with the defendant.

In addition to expanding the definition of rape, most states have abolished two common law rules that were uniquely applicable to rape: first, that no person could be convicted of rape upon the uncorroborated testimony of the alleged victim; and second, the prior sexual experience of the alleged victim could be used to impeach her credibility at trial. (Impeachment is an attempt to discredit a witness's testimony.) The corroboration requirement was based on Lord Hale's observation that rape "is an accusation easily to be made and hard to be proved, and harder to be defended by the party accused, though never so innocent." Today, most jurisdictions have eliminated the corroboration requirement because they reject Lord Hale's assertion that conviction of an innocent person is more likely in a rape case than in any other crime.

Most jurisdictions also have enacted **rape shield laws** that prohibit evidence of the victim's prior sexual conduct, except for prior consensual sexual relations with the defendant. Any prior sexual relationship between the victim and the defendant may be helpful evidence as to whether consent was given on this particular occasion, but the victim's relations with other persons is irrelevant. A victim of rape need not be a previously "chaste person," and even a prostitute can be raped if no consent was given to the particular act in question.

Most states have statutes to protect children from sexual abuse, and every state has some form of Megan's Law. In New Jersey in 1994 Megan Kanka, a seven-year-old girl, was kidnapped, raped, and murdered by a recidivist sex offender who had been released from prison. In response, New Jersey enacted a statute requiring sex offenders to register with local law enforcement agencies who then make certain information available to different parties. In some states, the registration information is given only to law enforcement authorities, while in other states, depending on the level of danger perceived, the information is disseminated to the general public.

In addition to registration and notification laws, some statutes provide for commitment of sexual predators who are mentally abnormal. The U.S. Supreme Court upheld a Kansas law mandating civil detention of individuals who are both mentally ill and "sexually violent predators."[12] The statute defines a sexually violent predator as a person "who has been convicted of or charged with a sexually violent offense and who suffers from a mental abnormality or personality disorder which makes the person likely to engage in predatory acts of sexual violence."

Sex crimes range from violent assaults like rape to nonviolent private sexual conduct between consenting adults. Chapter Seven addresses sexual conduct that is not a crime against a specific person but may be classified as an offense against public order or decorum: for example, public indecency, pornography, and public profanity.

KIDNAPPING AND FALSE IMPRISONMENT

Both kidnapping and false imprisonment are offenses against a person's liberty or freedom of movement. **False imprisonment** consists of confining a person against the person's will, while **kidnapping** requires seizing and carrying away (asporting) a person by force, threat of force, fraud, or deception. The prime distinction between the two offenses is the requirement that the victim be physically moved in the course of a kidnapping. Thus all kidnappings are false imprisonments because they interfere with the victim's liberty (freedom of movement), but not all false imprisonments are kidnapping if the victim is confined in one spot rather than moved to another location. For example, if a storeowner detains a suspected shoplifter, confinement but not movement occurs. In contrast, a robber who escapes by taking the store owner as a hostage has kidnapped the victim. Kidnapping may be viewed as an aggravated form of false imprisonment.

At common law, false imprisonment was a misdemeanor and in modern times is rarely charged. For example, a suspected shoplifter wrongly detained against his or her will is often less interested in criminal prosecution of the storeowner, and more interested in filing a civil suit seeking damages for the tort of false imprisonment.

Kidnapping was also a misdemeanor at common law, but is now regarded as a serious crime. The famous kidnapping of Charles Lindbergh's son in the 1930s generated public outrage and led to sweeping changes in state and federal laws on kidnapping. The Federal Kidnapping Act, commonly known as the Lindbergh Law, provides

> Whoever unlawfully seizes, confines, inveigles, decoys, kidnaps, abducts, or carries away and holds for ransom or reward or otherwise any person, except in the case of a minor by a parent thereof . . . shall be punished by imprisonment.[13]

False imprisonment
confining a person against the person's will.

Kidnapping
seizing and carrying away another person by force, threat of force, fraud, or deception.

UNITED STATES v. WILLS
F.3d (4th Cir. 2000)

A grand jury sitting in the Eastern District of Virginia returned an indictment charging Wills with one count of kidnapping under 18 U.S.C. § 1201(a)(1) and one count of interstate stalking under 18 U.S.C. § 2261A. The indictment includes several factual allegations pertinent to this appeal. Count I of the indictment charges that [Wills] did knowingly and unlawfully inveigle and decoy and hold Zabiuflah Alam for the purpose of preventing him from testifying as a witness, and did unlawfully transport and cause Alam to be transported in interstate commerce from Virginia to Washington, D.C. resulting in the death of the victim.

On or around June 17, 1998, the government alleges that Wills left a flyer at Alam's Virginia residence advertising a job opportunity. A Washington, D.C. telephone number was listed as the contact number. That contact number was a cell phone number acquired by Wills. Between June 20, 1998 and June 25, 1998, Alam called the cell phone number listed on the flier to inquire about the job. On June 24, 1998, Wills phoned his brother and indicated that he was "getting ready to hurt him. . . ." allegedly referring to Alam. On or about June 25, 1998, during a phone conversation, Alam agreed to meet an unknown person at Union Station in Washington, D.C. on that date for a job interview. On June 25, 1998, Alam drove from Virginia to Union Station in Washington, D.C. for the job interview. On or about June 26, 1998, Wills told his brother on the phone that his business was "takin' care of." Alam's car was found and Alam has not been seen alive since June 25, 1998.

This case presents the question of whether jurisdiction is established under the Federal Kidnapping Act when a victim, acting because of false pretenses initiated at the instance of the defendant, transports himself across state lines without accompaniment by the alleged perpetrator or an accomplice.

The Federal Kidnapping Act currently addresses "Whoever unlawfully seizes, confines, inveigles, decoys, kidnaps, abducts, or carries away and holds for ransom or reward or otherwise any person when the person is willfully transported in interstate or foreign commerce." By its terms, the statute criminalizes kidnappings accomplished through physical, forcible means and also by nonphysical, nonforcible means. This case involves the scope of jurisdiction for kidnappings accomplished through deceit. Kidnappings by inveiglement and decoy are expressly prohibited by the Act.

The plain language of the Act does not require that the defendant accompany, physically transport, or pro-vide for the physical transportation of the victim. Rather, the Act only requires that the victim "is willfully transported." If Congress wished to make accompaniment by the defendant over state lines a requirement under the Act, it could easily have written the Act to provide for it. Nothing in the policy behind the passage of the Act justifies "rewarding the kidnapper simply because he is ingenious enough to conceal his true motives from his victim." Wills' actions in securing the cell phone in Washington, D.C., arranging the interview in Washington, D.C., and placing the flier at Alam's home in Virginia, support a finding that Alam was "willfully transported" within the meaning of the statute. The fact that Alam could have seen through the plan or could have decided not to explore the job option has no significance. Thus, the fact that Wills willfully caused unaccompanied travel over state lines is sufficient to confer jurisdiction.

The statute also provides that if the victim is not returned within twenty-four hours after the taking, the victim is presumed to have been transported across state lines, thus making the kidnapping a federal offense and authorizing Federal Bureau of Investigation involvement in the case. In recent years, a number of jurisdictions have enacted statutes covering a specific form of kidnapping known as "carjacking." In these cases, the victim may be locked in the trunk of a stolen vehicle and transported to another location.

The carrying away of the victim in a kidnapping requires that the forced movement be more than the movement incidental to the commission of another crime. For example, when a robber orders the victim into the alleyway, this movement is minor and incidental to the robbery. If, however, the robber locked the victim in the trunk of a vehicle and drove a substantial distance, a kidnapping has occurred. One of the most commonly litigated issues in kidnapping prosecutions is the extent of movement of the victim required to meet the carrying-away element.[14]

Parental kidnapping raises special problems. The Lindbergh Law specifically exempts from its coverage a taking "in the case of a minor by a parent." In recent years "childnapping" of one's own child in violation of a custody order has been dealt with by specific statutes. The federal Parental Kidnapping Prevention Act does not criminalize such conduct at the federal level, but it does require that all states respect child custody orders of other states.[15] Thus a person cannot defy a court order concerning custody of a child by kidnapping the child and fleeing to another jurisdiction. Most states have created the crime of childnapping but punish such crimes less severely than kidnapping by strangers.

CIVIL RIGHTS AND HATE CRIMES

Civil Rights Statutes

A number of federal and state statutes make it a criminal offense to deprive a person of that person's constitutional rights. Foremost are the following two federal enactments.

Section 241 of Title 18 of the U.S. Code provides:

> If two or more persons conspire to injure, oppress, threaten, or intimidate any citizen in the free exercise or enjoyment of any right or privilege secure to him by the Constitution or laws of the United States, or because of his having so exercised the same; or
>
> If two or more persons go in disguise on the highway, or on the premises of another, with intent to prevent or hinder his free exercise or enjoyment of any right or privilege so secure—
>
> They shall be fined not more than $10,000 or imprisoned not more than ten years, or both; and if death results, they shall be subject to imprisonment for any term of years or for life.

A companion provision, Section 242, reads:

> Whoever, under color of any law, statute, ordinance, regulation, or custom, willfully subjects any inhabitant of State, . . . to the deprivation of any rights, privileges, or immunities secured or protected by the Constitution or laws of the United States, or to different punishments, pains, or penalties, on account of such inhabitant being an alien, or by reason of his color, or race, than are prescribed for the punishment of citizens, shall be fined not more than $10,000 or imprisoned not more than ten years, or both; and if death results, they shall be subject to imprisonment for any term of years or for life.

These federal statutes were invoked in the notorious Rodney King case. Rodney King was the Black motorist whose beating by four White Los Angeles police officers was captured on videotape for all the world to see. The officers' first acquittal in state court sparked three days of rioting, resulting in 60 deaths, more than 16,000 arrests, and nearly $1 billion in property damage in Los Angeles. The four officers were subsequently tried in federal court under the preceding statutes, resulting in convictions of some of the officers. In addition to criminal remedies, there is also the Federal Civil Rights Act of 1871 (42 U.S.C. § 1983) under which a civil action may be brought by any person who has been deprived of his constitutional rights by a person who acts "under color of law." Mr. King is reported to have negotiated a substantial monetary settlement of his civil claim.

Hate Crimes

Public support for hate crime legislation has been fueled by recent and well-publicized crimes such as the brutal beating and killing of Matthew Shepard, a twenty-one-year-old homosexual in Laramie, Wyoming, and the dragging death of James Byrd behind a pickup truck in Jasper, Texas. At the federal level, Congress enacted the Church Arson Prevention Act in response to increases in the number of fires in places of worship made up of predominantly African American congregations; and the Violence Against Women Act of 1994 sought to recognize that "all persons within the United States shall have the right to be free from crimes of violence motivated by gender."

The courts have dealt with hate crimes by distinguishing between hate speech and acts of violence motivated by animus against persons because of race, ethnicity, religion, national origin, gender, sexual orientation, disability, and age. In *R.A.V. v. City of St. Paul*,[16] the U.S. Supreme Court struck down a city ordinance that made it a misdemeanor to place on public property a "symbol, object, appellation, characterization, or graffiti . . . which one knows or has reasonable grounds to know arouses anger, alarm or resentment in others on the basis of race, color, creed, religion, or gender." In this case, teenagers allegedly burned a cross inside the fenced yard of an African American family. In striking down the ordinance, the Court found that it was impermissible infringement on free speech. The very next year, however, the Court upheld a Wisconsin statute enhancing the penalties for a crime when the perpetrator intentionally selects the victim because of the victim's race.[17] Essentially, the Court has recognized that mere expressions of hatred are protected by the First Amendment, but violent expressions of prejudice may be punished by the states and the federal government.

SUMMARY

All criminal homicides focus on the same social harm of killing a human being. Although the felony-murder doctrine centers on the defendant's conduct in committing a dangerous felony, the forms or degrees of homicide are largely dependent on the defendant's mental state. A cold-blooded intent to kill is murder, often premeditated first degree murder. A nonpremeditated intent to kill, an intent to inflict serious harm, or a wanton or extremely reckless disregard for the risk of death or serious harm is generally regarded as second degree murder. Any of the preceeding mental states, if formed in the heat of passion, reduce murder to voluntary manslaughter. Involuntary manslaughter occurs when a killing results from the defendant's criminally negligent conduct or from the defendant's commission of an unlawful act (the misdemeanor-manslaughter rule).

The crimes of assault and battery punish less serious bodily harm to a person. Battery is an unlawful touching regardless of the presence or absence of actual injury, while assault encompasses an attempted battery or placing another in fear of an imminent battery. Mayhem and malicious wounding are aggravated assaults and batteries involving some harm or threat beyond an unlawful touching.

Robbery combines an assault or battery against a person with larceny of the person's property. Force or the threat of force is the element that most distinguishes robbery from mere larceny. The force must be directed at the person, not the person's property, thus purse snatchers commit larceny, not robbery, when they direct their physical force at the property taken. The crimes of blackmail and extortion punish for threats that do not involve bodily injury to the victim.

Rape is the most serious sex crime, and at common law only women could be victims of rape while only men could be perpetrators of rape. Most jurisdictions have altered the definition of rape to make it gender neutral. Rape shield laws usually eliminate the common law requirements that the victim must resist the rape to the utmost, that the victim's complaint of rape must be corroborated by other evidence, and that the victim's prior sexual experience is admissible evidence to impeach her credibility at trial.

Kidnapping and false imprisonment are offenses against a victim's liberty or freedom of movement. False imprisonment consists of confining a person against that person's will, while kidnapping requires forcibly moving the victim to another location. The prime distinction between the two offenses is the requirement that the victim be physically moved in the course of a kidnapping.

Concept Summary

Consult local law to determine what changes have been made in a particular jurisdiction.

	MENTAL STATE	ADDITIONAL FACTORS
Capital Murder	Intent to kill	Presence of specified aggravating factors
First Degree Murder	Premeditated intent to kill	Depending on the jurisdiction, premeditation may be instantaneous or require some opportunity for deliberation
Felony Murder	Intent to commit a dangerous felony	Kill a person intentionally, recklessly, or even accidentally while committing a dangerous felony
Second Degree Murder	Malice	A nonpremeditated intent to kill, the intent to inflict grievous harm, or wanton disregard for safety of others
Voluntary Manslaughter	Killing while in the heat of passion	Preceded by adequate provocation without time for the passion to cool
Involuntary Manslaughter	Recklessness or criminal negligence; or commission of an unlawful act	Less than wanton conduct, but more than simple negligence; Misdemeanor-manslaughter rule

Other Offenses Against a Person

CRIME	MENTAL STATE	PHYSICAL ACT	HARM
Battery	Intent to touch; or recklessness	Touch by any means	Another's person touched without consent or justification
Assault (Attempted Battery)	Intent to touch	Come close to touching	
Assault (Offer)	Intent to touch; or recklessness	Menacing gesture	Victim apprehends an immediate touching
Mayhem	Intent to maim, disfigure, disable, or kill	Strike or otherwise cause the victim to be struck	Victim is dismembered or disfigured
Malicious Wounding	Wanton disregard for risk of serious injury	Shoot, stab, cut, or wound	Victim suffers a serious injury
Communicating a Threat	Intent to intimidate or harass another	Threaten an injury	Victim is placed in fear
Robbery	Intent to take another's property	Use force or threats	Victim is deprived of property
Extortion Blackmail	Intent to obtain something of value	Threaten injury to reputation	Victim surrenders something of value
Common Law Rape	Intent to have sexual intercourse	Use force or threats to overcome the lack of consent	Penetration of the vagina by the penis
False Imprisonment	Without legal justification or excuse	Confine or detain a person against that person's will	Victim deprived of liberty
Kidnapping	Without legal justification or excuse	Seize and carry away a person against that person's will	Victim deprived of liberty

DISCUSSION QUESTIONS

1. If the dissent in the *Keeler* case became the law, a viable fetus could be the victim of homicide. Under such an approach, could a defendant plead justifiable defense of another when the defendant killed a doctor who was about to perform an abortion?
2. Since voluntary manslaughter is viewed as a crime of passion, why should any limitations be imposed on the type of provocation that moves the defendant to the heat of passion? Although few people would sympathize with a bad-tempered restaurant patron who flies into a killing rage because of an overcooked steak, isn't this "hot-blooded" killer still distinct from a "cold-blooded" killer?
3. When a fight breaks out in the course of a professional hockey game, one player uses a hockey stick to bludgeon an opposing player. By consenting to participate in a contact sport, has the victim consented to this touching, or has a battery occurred?
4. Has a rape occurred when an employee has sexual intercourse with the boss who said: "Have sex with me or I'll fire you"?
5. Have you committed any offense if you threaten your instructor, "Give me an A in the course or I'll tell everyone you are a bad instructor"? Are you depriving your instructor of any property?

PRACTICE EXERCISES

1. What definitions of the beginning and end of life has your jurisdiction used in homicide cases?
2. List grades of criminal homicide that are recognized in your jurisdiction. Does your jurisdiction have the felony-murder rule, and if so, to what felonies does it apply?
3. How has your jurisdiction dealt with sexual assault/rape between married couples?
4. Summarize your state's rape shield statute.
5. What crimes would you charge in these two situations:
   a. X fires at Y, but the bullet ricochets and kills Z.
   b. X fires at a rabbit but the bullet ricochets and kills Y.

WEB SITE

Hate Crime Report
www.FBI.gov/ucr/hatecm.htm

KEY TERMS

Criminal homicide	Wanton state of mind	Malicious wounding
Malice aforethought	Voluntary manslaughter	Robbery
Capital murder	Adequate provocation	Extortion
First degree murder	Involuntary manslaughter	Blackmail
Premeditation	Misdemeanor-manslaughter rule	Common law rape
Instantaneous premeditation	Battery	Rape shield laws
Transferred intent	Attempted battery form of assault	False imprisonment
Felony-murder rule	Offer type of assault	Kidnapping
Second degree murder	Mayhem	

NOTES

1. *Roe v. Wade,* 410 U.S. 113, 93 S.Ct. 705 (1973).
2. *Cruzan v. Director, Missouri Dept. of Health,* 497 U.S. 261, 110 S.Ct. 2841, (1990).
3. *Washington v. Glucksberg,* 521 U.S. 702, 117 S.Ct. 2258 (1997).
4. *Vacco v. Quill,* 521 U.S. 793, 117 S.Ct. 2293 (1997).
5. Report of the Royal Commission on Capital Punishment, 26–28 (1953).
6. *Furman v. Georgia,* 408 U.S. 238, 92 S.Ct. 2726 (1972).
7. *Government of Virgin Islands v. Lake,* 362 F.2d 770 (3d Cir. 1966).
8. *Mitchell v. Commonwealth,* 213 Va. 149, 191 S.E.2d 261 (1972). The victim testified that he had a sum of money and was beaten. No testimony showed that anything happened to the money. Thus, the robbery conviction was reversed because of failure to prove a taking.
9. In *People v. Jones,* 290 Ill. 603, 125 N.E. 256 (1919), the evidence was held insufficient to support a robbery conviction where the defendant had stealthily removed a pocketbook from his intoxicated victim's pocket and transferred it to his own. When the victim said, "You have my pocketbook," the defendant hit him over the eye and knocked him out. The court concluded no evidence showed a struggle to retain possession, but only an accusation after the theft occurred, and an assault in response to the accusation.
10. *Warren v. State,* 255 Ga. 151, 336 S.E.2d 221 (1985).
11. *Sutton v. Commonwealth,* 228 Va. 654, 324 S.E.2d 665, 669–70 (1985).
12. *Kansas v. Hendricks,* 521 U.S. 346, 117 S.Ct. 2072 (1997).
13. 18 U.S.C.A. § 1201.
14. *Commonwealth v. Hughes,* 264 Pa.Super. 118, 399 A.2d 694 (1979). "Although the victim was removed only a distance of two miles, the wooded area to which she was brought was in an isolated area, seemingly beyond the aid of her friends and police. Under the circumstances, two miles is a substantial enough distance to place the victim in a completely different environmental setting removed from the security of familiar surroundings." Compare *People v. Levy,* 15 N.Y.2d 159, 256 N.Y.S.2d 793, 204 N.E.2d 842 (1965) which reversed the conviction of kidnapping by defendants who abducted the victims in their own car, drove them a distance of 27 blocks for approximately 20 minutes while robbing them.
15. 28 U.S.C.A. § 1738A.
16. *R.A.V. v. City of St. Paul,* 505 U.S. 377, 112 S.Ct. 2538 (1992).
17. *Wisconsin v. Mitchell,* 508 U.S. 476, 113 S.Ct. 2194 (1993).

CRIMES AGAINST PROPERTY AND HABITATION

Chapter *6*

CHAPTER OUTLINE

Understanding theft crimes depends more on history than on logic. Common law judges created and refined theft offenses in response to two competing social forces: (1) the economic community's desire to expand the criminal law to deter new forms of dishonesty; and (2) resistance to expanding criminal law because it would increase the number of cases in which the death penalty would be imposed. (Capital punishment was the penalty for all but the most petit larcenies.) The resulting common law of theft was riddled with inconsistencies and "gaps," which permitted forms of dishonesty that did not amount to larceny. Statutes enacted to fill these gaps ultimately focused on three major forms of theft: larceny, embezzlement, and false pretenses. Although a number of jurisdictions have consolidated these three crimes under the general heading of theft, many jurisdictions retain the distinctions between larceny, embezzlement, and false pretenses.

THEFT OF PRIVATE PROPERTY

Larceny

At common law the elements of **larceny** were (1) the trespassory taking and (2) carrying away (3) of the personal property (4) of another (5) with intent to deprive the other of possession permanently.

Trespassory Taking
The most complicated aspect of larceny is the requirement that a trespassory taking of possession occur. A **trespass** is the action of a defendant who takes possession of another's personal property without consent or without legal justification. The concept of trespass was originally limited to secret takings because in the absence of physical force the owner of the property could refuse to consent to and thus prevent an attempted taking. No trespass was committed as long as the owner agreed to the taking, even if consent was obtained by fraud.

Voluntary, though fraudulent, transfers of property were beyond the scope of common law larceny because the courts recognized the economic doctrines of *laissez faire* and *caveat emptor* (let the buyer beware). When Jack, of "Jack and the Beanstalk," visited the village market to trade the family cow for a handful of beans, he was stuck with the bargain regardless of the magic quality of the beans. As an early English case stated, "making a fool of another" is not a crime. Although one who obtained property by deceit might be viewed as a clever person or a scoundrel, in neither case was the deceitful person thought to be deserving of execution by law. The crime of obtaining property by false pretenses (not punishable by death), was later created to punish clever persons who obtain property by making fraudulent representations.

The common law of larceny recognized only one form of fraud as constituting a trespassory taking. In *Pear's* case, the defendant rented the victim's horse for a day with the fraudulent intent to take it and sell it immediately.[1] Outwardly, the victim consented to the temporary taking of his horse, thus no trespassory taking for purposes of larceny was committed. But the court held that the defendant's fraud negated the victim's consent, thus lawful possession never passed to the defendant. Because the defendant merely received physical custody of the horse, he committed a special form of trespassory taking known as larceny by trick. Larceny by trick occurs when the victim intends to give up temporary control of the property, but the defendant intends to take the property permanently.

As *Pear's* case demonstrates, common law judges were able to expand the scope of larceny by distinguishing a trespassory taking of possession from a consensual passing of mere physical custody. A person has **custody** of property if the person exercises physical control over it, however, the right to use it is restricted by another's

Larceny
at common law, the trespassory taking and carrying away of the personal property of another with intent to deprive the other of permanent possession.

Trespass
taking possession of another's personal property without consent or legal justification.

Custody
physical control of property, but the use of the property is limited by another's lawful possession of the property.

Possession
the right to use property in a reasonably unrestricted manner.

lawful possession of the property. A person has **possession** of property when the person may use it in a reasonably unrestricted manner. For example, before going out of town, a friend hands you a set of car keys and asks you to start the car every few days to keep the battery from dying. You have mere custody of the vehicle because your use of it is restricted to the limited task of starting the engine. If, however, your friend had said, "Here are the car keys, use the car as you like while I am out of town," then you have been given relatively unrestricted use of the car and have it in your possession. In either case, if you sell the car you have deprived your friend of her property, but only in the first situation have you done so by a trespassory taking from your friend's possession. (Your friend remained in constructive possession of the car even though you had physical custody.) In the latter situation in which you had possession of the vehicle, your sale of the vehicle does not constitute common law larceny. It might, however, constitute embezzlement, which involves the misappropriation of property after obtaining possession of it in a nontrespassory manner. The courts have not established a precise point at which the degree of control over property changes from custody to possession, thus they must assess the particular facts of a case and decide who has custody and who has possession.

Asportation
any physical movement of property taken from another's possession.

Carrying Away (Asportation and Dominion)
Asportation is any physical movement of property taken from another's possession. For example, even a shoplifter who is caught before leaving the premises may commit larceny by moving the property from one area of the store to another area. *People v. Olivo* considers how far the shoplifter must go, and exactly what type of conduct amounts to asportation.

PEOPLE v. OLIVO
Supreme Court of New York, 1981
52 N.Y.2d 309, 438 N.Y.S.2d 242, 420 N.E.2d 40

These consolidated cases present a recurring question in this era of the self-service store which has never been resolved by this court: may a person be convicted of larceny for shoplifting if the person is caught with goods while still inside the store?

Although this court has not addressed the issue, case law from other jurisdictions seems unanimous in holding that a shoplifter need not leave the store to be guilty of larceny. This is because a shopper may treat merchandise in a manner inconsistent with the owner's continued rights—and in a manner not in accord with that of a prospective purchaser—without actually walking out of the store. Indeed, depending upon the circumstances of each case, a variety of conduct may be sufficient to allow the trier of fact to find a taking.

In many cases, it will be particularly relevant that defendant concealed the goods under clothing or in a container. Such conduct is not generally expected in a self-service store and may in a proper case be deemed an exercise of dominion and control inconsistent with the store's continued rights. Other furtive or unusual behavior on the part of the defendant should also be

weighed. Thus, if the defendant surveys the area while secreting the merchandise or abandons his or her own property in exchange for the concealed goods, this may evince larcenous rather than innocent behavior. Relevant too is the customer's proximity to or movement toward one of the store's exits. Certainly it is highly probative of guilt that the customer was in possession of secreted goods just a few short steps from the door or moving in that direction. Finally, possession of a known shoplifting device actually used to conceal merchandise, such as a specially designed outer garment or false bottomed carrying case, would be all but decisive.

Under these principles, there was ample evidence in each case to raise a factual question as to the defendant's guilt. In *People v. Olivo*, defendant not only concealed goods in his clothing, but he did so in a particularly suspicious manner. And, when defendant was stopped, he was moving toward the door, just three feet short of exiting the store.

In *People v. Gasparik*, defendant removed the price tag and sensor device from a jacket, abandoned his own garment, put the jacket on and ultimately headed for the main floor of the store. Removal of the price tag and sensor device, and careful concealment of those items, is highly unusual and suspicious conduct for a shopper. Coupled with defendant's abandonment of his own coat and his attempt to leave the floor, those factors were sufficient to make out a prima facie case of a taking.

In *People v. Spatzier,* defendant concealed a book in an attache case. Unaware that he was being observed in an overhead mirror, defendant looked furtively up and down an aisle before secreting the book. In these circumstances, given the manner in which defendant concealed the book and his suspicious behavior, the evidence was not insufficient as a matter of law.

In sum, in view of the modern definition of the crime of larceny, and its purpose of protecting individual property rights, a taking of property in the self-service context can be established by evidence that a customer exercised control over merchandise wholly inconsistent with the store's continued rights.

The defendant in *People v. Gasparik* (one of the consolidated cases in *People v. Olivo*) committed larceny when he donned a leather jacket, removed the price tag and sensor device, and attempted to leave the store. Suppose, however, that when the defendant attempted to leave, he discovered that the jacket was chained to the floor. Asportation has occurred because the shoplifter physically moved the property, but the element of **dominion** requires a carrying away from another's possession into the defendant's control. The defendant exercised some control by removing the price tag, but so long as the jacket remained chained to the store floor, the jacket remained under the control of the retailer. Such a situation is certainly attempted larceny, but a consummated larceny does not occur until the defendant acquires dominion over the item. This situation becomes a completed larceny if the shoplifter cuts the chain, thereby severing the merchant's control and carrying away the jacket into the defendant's control. Asportation and dominion are the external manifestations of the carrying-away element of larceny.

Dominion
carrying away from another's possession into the defendant's control.

Personal Property   The common law of larceny only protected personal property, not real estate. Once taken, items of personal property might be moved far away and lost forever, thus the law sought to deter the initial taking by threatening the thief with capital punishment for larceny. But real estate is immovable and the owner can invoke civil actions to regain the use of real estate. Thus criminal law (and the drastic punishment of death) was not needed to protect real property. Real property such as trees, shrubs, and crops become personal property, and subject to larceny, when severed from the land and carried off.

The common law of larceny also excluded intangible property from its coverage. In a court of law, Shakespeare would have had it backwards: "He who steals my purse steals everything; he who steals my good name steals trash." Today most jurisdictions have enacted statutes that prohibit the theft of intangibles such as computer time. The common law's focus on tangible personal property also precluded prosecution for theft of personal services. Suppose for example, that your barber cuts your hair and requests payment. If you refuse to pay you have deprived the barber of personal services but have not taken any personal property, and therefore cannot be convicted of common law larceny. This "gap" in larceny law has been closed by modern statutes that make the theft of services a form of criminal theft.

The personal property taken must have some value, but everything tangible has some value even if it is minute. The value of the taken property becomes significant because all jurisdictions distinguish between grand and petit larceny. The dollar value that separates **grand larceny** from petit larceny varies greatly among jurisdictions, thus local statutes must be consulted. All jurisdictions agree, however, that the value of any stolen item is based on the item's current market value. (The values of several items stolen from one person in a single transaction can be aggregated to make a case of grand larceny.) Value is computed according to the loss of market value suffered by the victim, not according to any gain achieved by the thief. Thus

$500

✓**Grand larceny**
distinguished from petit larceny by the value of the stolen property.

Robin Hood was guilty of larceny even though he derived no financial gain by "stealing from the rich to give to the poor." In modern times the issue of loss to the victim without gain to the defendant arises when a computer "hacker" distributes a virus that brings no benefit to the hacker, but causes great financial loss to others.

Property of Another Although logic would dictate that one cannot steal one's own property, one must remember that common law larceny focused on possession as distinct from mere custody or legal title. Thus one can steal property to which one holds title, if the property is taken from another who has possessory rights in the property. For example, when you pawn an item you retain legal title to the property but have surrendered possession to the pawnbroker. Should you subsequently take the item back without the pawnbroker's permission, you have violated the possessory rights "of another" and have committed larceny. In contrast, you cannot steal property in which you hold a joint right of possession. Thus, in community property states husbands and wives may have equal rights to possession of marital property and cannot be guilty of larceny of this jointly held property. The same is true of partners who steal assets held jointly by a business partnership.

Intent to Deprive Permanently To be guilty of larceny a defendant must take and carry away the personal property of another with the specific intent to deprive another of the property permanently. For example, if you take another's automobile with the intent to keep it or sell it, you have committed larceny. You are not guilty of larceny, however, if you intend to use the vehicle temporarily and then return it to the owner. In the case of automobiles, many states have statutes that penalize "joyriding" in which the defendant has no intent to deprive the owner of the vehicle permanently.

As is true of all specific intent crimes, the prosecution may rely on circumstantial evidence to establish the defendant's intent to deprive others of their property. For example, if you are apprehended while returning a "stolen" automobile to the owner's garage, the reasonable inference is that you had no intent to keep the vehicle forever. On the other hand, should you be apprehended with the vehicle hundreds of miles from the scene of the taking, or while you are attempting to sell the vehicle, the inference is strong that you intended to deprive the owner of the automobile permanently.

A defendant who takes another's property under the belief that the defendant has a legal right to possession of the property is not guilty of larceny. For example, you believe that your final examination paper is your property and take it from the professor's office without permission. Even though you may be wrong because the exam belongs to the professor or the school, your mistake is a defense (see Chapter Four) to larceny because the mistake negates the specific intent to steal another's property.

Embezzlement

The discussion of larceny illustrates the numerous "gaps" in common law larceny, the largest stemming from the requirement of trespassory taking. With the exception of larceny by trick, no amount of dishonesty or fraud constituted larceny so long as the defendant obtained the owner's permission to take possession of the property. This gap in the law was eliminated in England in the eighteenth century when Parliament created the crime of embezzlement. The embezzlement statute provided

> If any servant or clerk, or any person employed . . . by virtue of such employment receive or take into his possession any money, goods, bond, bill, note, banker's draft, or other valuable security, or effects, for or in the name or on the account of his master or masters, or employer or employers, and shall fraudulently embezzle, secrete, or make away with the same, or any part thereof . . . he shall be deemed to have feloniously stolen the same.[2]

Because embezzlement is a statutory offense, no single definition of the crime exists. Most definitions of **embezzlement** require two elements: (1) the defendant was entrusted with or came into possession of the property of another in a lawful manner; and (2) the defendant fraudulently converted the property with the intent to deprive another of the property permanently.

Entrustment of the Property

The most significant distinction between larceny and embezzlement is the manner by which the defendant initially acquires the property. If the defendant takes the property without the owner's consent—a trespassory taking—then larceny occurs if the other elements of the crime are satisfied. Embezzlers, however, do not "take" property because they already have been entrusted with possession of the property. The essence of embezzlement is a subsequent breach of trust by one who has been given lawful possession.

Consider again the example where your friend gives you the keys to her automobile. When your friend limited your use of the automobile to starting the engine, you were given only custody because possession constructively remained with your friend. If you subsequently sell the vehicle, you have performed a trespassory taking of the property away from the constructive possession of your friend. In contrast, when your friend authorized you to use the car in her absence, she entrusted you with possession which eliminates the possibility of trespass. Now your sale of the automobile is a breach of trust, and you have committed embezzlement. Embezzlement normally involves employees who receive funds on behalf of their employers, but embezzlement may apply to anyone who had property entrusted to them.

Conversion with Intent to Deprive Permanently

Conversion occurs when the defendant uses the property in a way that is inconsistent with another's right of possession. For example, selling the car that your friend loaned to you is inconsistent with her right to possession and is evidence of your intent to deprive her of her property permanently. On the other hand, it is not embezzlement if you use the vehicle in an unauthorized manner, but without the intent to deprive permanently. For example, a friend loans you her car because of your sad tale that you must get to the drugstore to buy medicine. If in fact you go to a tavern, you have breached your friend's trust and temporarily converted the car to your own use, but without the intent to deprive her of the car permanently.

The classic case of embezzlement often involves a defendant who took money with the intent to repay it, and thus claims that the theft was not "permanent." An intent to repay in the future, however, is not a defense to embezzlement. The law views the embezzler's intent as an intent to deprive permanently until or unless some future condition comes about: for example, "When my financial status improves I'll return the money I embezzled from the bank." The embezzler's financial status may never improve, and the victim cannot be forced to assume the risk of future contingencies.

False Pretenses

The prime distinction between the crime of false pretenses and the crimes of larceny or embezzlement is that false pretenses is an offense against title, whereas larceny and embezzlement concentrate on possessory rights. The criminal law normally focuses on a defendant's mental state, but with theft offenses it is also necessary to identify the victim's state of mind. In larceny, the victim intends either to pass nothing or to pass mere custody of the property. In embezzlement, the victim intends to pass temporary possession, not permanent possession. In false pretenses, however, the victim intends to pass permanent possession and title to the defendant.

The elements of **false pretenses** are (1) a false representation of a material fact (2) made with knowledge that the fact is false (3) with the intent to defraud the victim (4) thereby causing the victim to pass title to property.

Embezzlement
the defendant was entrusted with possession of the property of another, and then fraudulently converted the property with the intent to deprive another of the property permanently.

Conversion
use of another's property in a way that is inconsistent with the other's right of possession.

False pretenses
a false representation of a material fact made with knowledge that the fact is false and with the intent to defraud the victim, thereby causing the victim to pass title to property.

False Representation of Fact A false representation may be written, oral, or presented in the form of misleading conduct. In *Rex v. Barnard,* the defendant wore the cap and gown associated with Oxford students and obtained property from a merchant who extended credit to all students at the university.[3] The common law punished situations in which the defendant actively created a false impression, such as donning the cap and gown of an Oxford student. The crime of false pretenses, however, did not extend to situations where the defendant remained silent in the face of a victim's erroneous assumption about some material fact. Had the defendant in *Rex v. Barnard* not worn a cap and gown he would not have been required to disclose voluntarily his nonstudent status to a merchant who assumed that all young men of the town were Oxford students. Many modern statutes, however, punish such silence as a form of false pretenses.

A false representation must relate to an existing fact, not to mere opinion or promises to do something in the future. The criminal law seeks to protect people from cheats and con artists, but the law does not protect against all bad bargains made in the open market. Consumers may rely upon the accuracy of a merchant's factual representations ("This used car had one previous owner"). But consumers must recognize salespersons' "hype" ("This is the best car in the world for the money") as merely an expression of opinion. Of course, the line between fact and opinion is not always clear. Suppose that a used car salesperson falsely informs a prospective customer, "I just heard an economic expert say that inflation will reach double digits and the price of automobiles will skyrocket." This misstatement of fact about someone's opinion falls within the gray area of false representation because it mixes fact with opinion.

Representations of existing facts also must be distinguished from promises of future conduct. For example, "Loan me $100 and I'll pay you back next week," establishes a debtor–creditor relationship. The debtor's failure to live up to the promise of repayment is characterized as a civil default of a contractual obligation, not as criminal conduct. (The days of debtors' prison have long since passed.) Some jurisdictions, however, bring the debtor within the scope of false pretenses if the debtor had no intent to repay when promising future payment. In such situations the debtor's existing state of mind at the time the property was obtained is regarded as a "fact" that can be misrepresented within the meaning of false pretenses.

In most situations, passing a bad check with knowledge that an account carries insufficient funds to cover the check is a misrepresentation of fact, not a breach of promise. The prime exception to this rule involves post-dated checks. If a defendant offers a post-dated check and the victim agrees to accept it, the victim is extending credit in return for a promise of future payment, thus no false representation occurs. In the absence of such disclosure and agreement, the act of tendering a check is a representation of adequate funds. Although the crime of false pretenses encompasses knowingly passing bad checks, most jurisdictions have statutes creating separate crimes covering this form of fraud. Statutes also regulate forgery, another form of fraud which may or may not involve the passing of personal property.

Knowledge That the Represented Fact Is False All jurisdictions punish defendants who make false statements with actual subjective knowledge that the statement is false. Many jurisdictions also punish defendants who assert facts with a reckless disregard for truth. For example, you tell a salesperson that you are only interested in one-previous-owner used cars. Without checking the records the salesperson responds, "Sure, sure, all of our cars have had only one previous owner." You then purchase the car and discover it was previously owned by five other people. In this case, reckless disregard for the truth may make the salesperson guilty of obtaining your property (the money paid) by false pretenses.

Intent to Defraud the Victim Once the defendant is shown to have knowingly made a false representation, the defendant's intent to defraud the victim is apparent. The intent to defraud the victim and thereby permanently deprive the victim of property approximates the intent-to-steal element required in larceny prosecutions. The intent-to-defraud element of false pretenses normally arises in connection with the final element discussed in the next section.

Causing Victims to Pass Title to Their Property   The defendant must not only make the false representation with an intent to defraud, the defendant must succeed in causing the victim to part with the title to property because of the false representation. For example, a salesperson falsely assures you that the radio in a used car is in working order. If a working radio is a material fact that is important to your decision to purchase the car, the false representation played a part in causing you to part with your money.[4] If, however, the operation of the radio is of no importance to you, the salesperson's false representation did not induce you to purchase the automobile. Thus no crime of false pretenses has been committed although the defendant may be guilty of attempting to obtain property by false pretenses.

Incidently, even though "Fools and their money are soon parted," may be a well-proven axiom, the stupidity of the victim is no defense to a charge of false pretenses. If you represent that you own the Brooklyn bridge and find a "sucker" who buys it from you for $100, you have committed the crime of false pretenses.

Receiving Stolen Property

Receiving property with knowledge that it is stolen and with the intent to keep the property is just as criminal as taking, converting, or acquiring property by deception. In jurisdictions that regard larceny as a continuing trespass, one who assists in placing stolen goods farther from the victim's control may be guilty of larceny or may be an accessory after the fact to theft. The separate crime of **receiving stolen property** may be charged when the following elements are met: (1) receipt of property that has been stolen (2) with knowledge of its stolen nature, and (3) with intent to deprive the owner of the property.

Receipt of Stolen Property   Stolen property includes property acquired by larceny, embezzlement, false pretenses, or any other form of theft recognized by the particular jurisdiction. Receipt of stolen property may be by actual or constructive possession because a defendant who exercises control over the property has received it, even if the defendant never physically touches the property. For example, a "fence" instructs the thief to deliver the property directly to a customer who will pay the fence for the property. The fence, while never touching or even seeing the stolen property, has controlled (constructively possessed) it by arranging for its sale. On the other hand, a person may come in contact with stolen property but not control or receive it. For example, *Moehring* holds that a hitchhiker may accept a ride in a stolen vehicle and not be guilty of receiving stolen property.[5]

Receiving stolen property exercising control over property that has been stolen with knowledge of its stolen nature and with intent to deprive the owner of the property.

MOEHRING v. COMMONWEALTH
290 S.E.2d 891 (Va. 1982)

The Commonwealth's evidence and the reasonable inferences deducible from that evidence do not establish that Moehring aided Faison in the theft or that he shared Faison's intent to deprive Keeling of his truck. All that the prosecution proved was that two men were observed walking south along Route 17 in the early morning hours of March 23, 1980; that each was attempting to "thumb" a ride from passing motorists; that one of the men, Faison, apparently despaired of success, left his fellow hitchhiker and went across the highway and stole a truck; that the other man, Moehring, continued walking and "thumbing", and that some minutes later Moehring was given a ride in the stolen truck.

When Faison committed his larceny of the truck, Moehring was across a double-lane highway some distance from the scene. Under such circumstances, it is difficult to regard him as a "lookout," or an accessory before the fact. And the mere acceptance by Moehring of a ride in the stolen vehicle did not in any way aid Faison.

Because larceny is a continuing offense, anyone who knows that personal property is stolen and assists in its transportation or disposition is guilty of larceny. However, in the instant case there is no evidence that Moehring assisted in any way in the transportation or disposition of the truck he knew to be stolen.

The presumption of fact arising from the unexplained possession of recently stolen property requires, a showing of exclusive possession of the stolen property by the accused, though such possession may be joint. There is no evidence in the record which demonstrates that Moehring exercised any degree of dominion or control over the stolen truck, or from which the court could have inferred that defendant possessed the truck jointly with Faison. Neither do we find evidence that established beyond a reasonable doubt that Moehring countenanced or approved the theft of the truck by Faison, or wished the venture to succeed. The most that can be said with reasonable certainty is that this defendant-hitchhiker accepted a ride from the first person who stopped and that he knew that person was driving a stolen vehicle. This conduct does raise a suspicion of guilt. However, it is not sufficient to establish beyond a reasonable doubt that the defendant committed grand larceny.

The judgment of the trial court is reversed and the case dismissed.

EXHIBIT 6–1
Instruction on Knowledge

> The element of knowledge may be satisfied by inferences drawn from proof that a defendant deliberately ignored what would otherwise have been obvious. A finding beyond a reasonable doubt of a conscious purpose to avoid enlightenment would result in an inference of knowledge. Stated another way, a defendant's knowledge of a fact may be inferred from willful blindness to the existence of a fact. Actual knowledge and deliberate or conscious avoidance of knowledge are the same thing. However, an honest mistake or error in judgment does not rise to the level of knowledge, intent or willfulness required under the law.

Knowledge That the Property Is Stolen　All jurisdictions recognize that actual subjective knowledge (scienter) that the property is stolen is a sufficient mens rea for the crime (see Exhibit 6–1). Some statutes reduce the mens rea to recklessness or even negligence. In either case, the defendant's knowledge that the acquired property is stolen may be established by circumstantial evidence such as purchasing the property for a fraction of its real value. For example, a stranger stops you on the street and offers you a $500 watch for $50. Will you assume that you have stumbled upon a special sale, or will you suspect that the watch is "hot"?

Another form of circumstantial evidence of a defendant's intent is the failure to explain possession of recently stolen property. In the absence of a plausible explanation, the jury may infer that the defendant knew the property was stolen. This situation raises the question of whether the defendant is being punished for failing to offer an explanation. Note how *Barnes v. United States* resolves the apparent conflict between the privilege against self-incrimination and using a defendant's silence to establish guilt.

Intent to Deprive the Owner of the Property　Stolen property is normally received for the benefit of the person receiving the property, and in most cases the defendant intends to use the property personally or sell it for a profit. However, the defendant need not benefit from receiving stolen property to be guilty, because guilt arises from the defendant's intent to deprive the owner of the use of the prop-

BARNES v. UNITED STATES
Supreme Court of the United States, 1973
412 U.S. 837, 93 S.Ct. 2357

JUSTICE POWELL delivered the opinion of the Court: Defendant Barnes was convicted in United States District Court on two counts of possessing United States Treasury checks stolen from the mails, knowing them to be stolen. The trial court instructed the jury that ordinarily it would be justified in inferring from unexplained possession of recently stolen mail that the defendant possessed the mail with knowledge that it was stolen. We granted certiorari to consider whether this instruction comports with due process.

In the present case we deal with a traditional common-law inference deeply rooted in our law. For centuries courts have instructed juries that an inference of guilty knowledge may be drawn from the fact of unexplained possession of stolen goods. This longstanding and consistent judicial approval of the instruction, reflecting accumulated common experience, provides strong

indication that the instruction comports with due process.

Defendant argues that the permissive inference in question infringes his privilege against self-incrimination. The trial court specifically instructed the jury that defendant had a constitutional right not to take the witness stand and that possession could be satisfactorily explained by evidence independent of defendant's testimony. Introduction of any evidence, direct or circumstantial, tending to implicate the defendant in the alleged crime increases the pressure on him to testify. The mere massing of evidence against a defendant cannot be regarded as a violation of his privilege against self-incrimination.

We find that the trial court's instructions on the inference to be drawn from unexplained possession of stolen property were fully consistent with defendant's constitutional rights.

erty. For example, a classmate gives you a course outline stolen from another student, whereupon you destroy the outline in order to prevent the student from using it to prepare for an examination. The mental state required for the offense of receiving stolen property is an intent to receive the property for a dishonest purpose, that is, anything other than an intent to return the property to the owner.

Consolidation of Theft Offenses   The common law distinctions between larceny, embezzlement, and false pretenses are often difficult to draw and even more difficult to justify in terms of logic. Accordingly, some jurisdictions have replaced the common law crimes with a single statutory offense called "theft." Although some statutes create entirely new definitions of theft, most consolidation statutes merely bring the common law offenses under a single statutory umbrella that retains many of the complicated rules that applied at common law. Consolidation statutes also typically address aggravated forms of theft such as robbery, extortion, or blackmail, which are discussed in Chapter Five.

CRIMES AGAINST HABITATION

Burglary

Common law burglary was a crime against property and also a crime against habitation. Crimes against habitation developed because of the importance of people's homes—a sanctuary that is entitled to special protection beyond that given to other forms of property. Common law **burglary** required (1) breaking and entering (2) another's dwelling (3) at night (4) with intent to commit a felony once inside.

Burglary
breaking and entering another's dwelling at night with intent to commit a felony once inside.

Breaking
setting aside some portion
of the structure that would
prevent intrusion.

Entry
an intrusion by any portion of
the burglar's body or an
instrumentality for purposes
of consummating a felony
within the dwelling.

Dwelling
a structure in which people
normally slept at night.

Curtilage
the area within which lie
structures closely associated
with the dwelling.

Breaking and Entering

Breaking was defined as setting aside (moving) some portion of the structure which, if unmoved, would prevent intrusion. An intruder who opens a closed but unlocked door has broken into the dwelling because she moved a portion of the structure that would prevent her entry. An intruder who enters a dwelling through an open door is an uninvited trespasser, but has not broken into the dwelling. The burglar must do more than take advantage of an existing opening; a burglar must "break" by creating the opening. Breaking thus requires more than crossing the plane of an open door by trespassing, but it requires less than some physical breaking or damage of the structure.

As was true of the technicalities surrounding trespassory taking for common law larceny, the legal complexities of a breaking may produce bizarre results when applied to difficult factual situations. For example, suppose you leave your front door partially open to take advantage of a cool summer breeze. A "skinny" intruder who can slip through the existing opening has not committed a breaking. But a "fat" intruder who must open the door wider to gain entry has committed a breaking.[6]

A burglar also could gain entry by a constructive breaking involving the use of fraud or threats of force. A burglar who gains entry by posing as an encyclopedia salesperson, and a burglar who threatens to shoot the homeowner unless the door is opened, have both committed a constructive breaking. Many modern statutes completely eliminate the requirement for a breaking or expand the concept of constructive breaking to encompass any form of unlawful entry, including the trespass of an uninvited intruder.

The common law required both a breaking and an entry of the dwelling, and also recognized special rules distinguishing between entry by the burglar or by some instrument employed by the burglar. An **entry** consisted of any intrusion, no matter how slight, of a portion of the burglar's body. A burglar who smashes a window and reaches a hand in to grab an item has entered the house even though most of the burglar's body remains outside the window. An instrumentality, however, does not "enter" the dwelling if the instrument is used merely to achieve the breaking. Throwing a rock through a window is a breaking but not an entry for purposes of burglary. Shooting through a window to kill the homeowner, however, is both a breaking and an entry because the instrumentality (the bullet) is being used to consummate a felony (murder) inside the dwelling. The common law recognized an entry when an instrumentality was used not merely to achieve the breaking, but to complete the intended felony.

Another's Dwelling

At common law the structure broken and entered had to be a **dwelling,** which was defined as a structure in which people normally slept at night. The word *normally* is significant because catching a catnap one night at your office does not convert the office into a dwelling house. The structure must be one in which people normally sleep because it is only homes, not offices, that are entitled to special protection. Thus a newly constructed house ready for occupancy is not a dwelling until someone moves in and begins to live in the house.[7] As long as a person normally sleeps in the structure it remains a dwelling even if the occupant is away on vacation when the burglar breaks and enters.[8] Hotel rooms which may or may not be occupied at the time are considered the dwelling of the landlord, even if the landlord does not live in the building.

The common law included within the definition of a dwelling those structures within the curtilage of the dwelling. **Curtilage** is defined as the area within which lie structures closely associated with the dwelling even if they are not physically attached to the dwelling: for example, structures in reasonable proximity to the dwelling, nearby barns, unattached garages, and tool sheds in the backyard. The rationale for including curtilage within the definition of a dwelling is the likelihood that a dweller who hears a nighttime prowler will go forth to protect both family and property. Despite the common law's precision in defining a dwelling, most jurisdictions have created statutory forms of burglary, which cover all buildings or structures regardless of their use as places of habitation.

People cannot burglarize their own homes because they are not intruding upon the habitation rights of another. Habitation rights, however, are distinct from ownership. A landlord may hold legal title to your rented apartment, but it is your dwelling because you have the right to possess and inhabit the apartment. A landlord who has reserved a right of unlimited entry (most commonly to check for damages) cannot burglarize your apartment. However, a landlord who has no right of entry can burglarize your apartment (dwelling) even though the landlord holds legal title to the apartment.

Although you held no title and paid no rent, your parents' home was your dwelling during your childhood. But as the juvenile defendants in *State v. Howe* learned, you can be "thrown out of your own home."

STATE v. HOWE
Supreme Court of Washington, 1991
116 Wash. 2d 466, 805 P.2d 806

The juvenile defendants in these three consolidated cases were each convicted of burglarizing their parents' homes. Each case raises the same central issue: When is a parental order to a juvenile to stay away from the parental home sufficient to establish the lack of privilege element of a burglary charge? If a person is privileged to enter the building, then he cannot be convicted of burglary. The juveniles in each of these cases assert that they were privileged to enter their parents' homes by virtue of their parents' obligation to provide for their dependent children.

The statutory parental obligation to provide for a dependent child is limited. The "necessary" care mandated by statute is the minimum standard of the quality and quantity of food, clothing, shelter and medical care that a parent is required by law to furnish. The parent does not have to provide that care directly, as long as he or she assures that such care is provided to the child. Thus, a parent fulfills her statutory duty when she provides alternative means for taking care of her child's necessities. Since the child's privilege to enter the parental home rises out of the parent's duty to provide for the child, once the parent fulfills that duty in some manner that does not require the child to have access to the home, the parent may revoke the child's privilege to enter. This revocation does not require a formal court proceeding, but it must be clearly and unequivocally conveyed to the child. The revocation can only be effective if the parent has first met his or her statutory duty to provide the necessary care for the child.

In conclusion, we hold that a juvenile can only be convicted of burglary of his family home if his privilege to enter the home is revoked. A juvenile's parents can only revoke his or her privilege to enter if they (1) do so expressly and unequivocally, and (2) provide some alternative means of assuring that the parents' statutory duty of care is met.

If a parent can evict a child from the home, can one spouse revoke the other's right to enter the dwelling? The definition of the dwelling of another and the question of who is privileged to enter the dwelling often arise in cases involving separated spouses. When one spouse moves out of the house and clearly no longer resides there, the house may become the exclusive dwelling of the spouse who remains behind. Thus an absentee spouse who has relinquished the privilege to enter without permission may be guilty of burglarizing the dwelling of another, even if the absentee spouse holds title to the home and continues to make the mortgage payments. Burglary is an offense against the right of habitation, not the right of ownership.

At Night At common law a burglary must occur at night, which was technically defined as that period between sunset and sunrise when not enough natural light was present to allow discernment of the countenance of a person's face. The common law placed special emphasis on the particular threat posed by nighttime intruders because of the additional alarm in hearing an intruder at night when homeowners are resting and not actively defending their "castles." The cover of darkness also facilitates the commission of the crime and hampers the identification of suspects. Although many jurisdictions have redefined burglary to encompass daylight entries, they often treat breaking and entry at night as an aggravating circumstance which justifies greater punishment.

Intent to Commit a Felony Inside An intruder who does not intend to commit a felony inside the dwelling is not a burglar. For example, a homeless person who breaks in to sleep in your warm basement has broken and entered (and may be guilty of trespass) but lacks the mental state required for burglary. Proving a person's subjective intent is always difficult, thus the prosecution will normally rely on circumstantial evidence to infer the intruder's intent. Most jurisdictions recognize that "a jury may infer an intent to steal from a breaking and entering of an occupied dwelling place in the nighttime, where the defendant can offer no other explanation for his presence."[9]

Burglary does not require that the burglar succeed in consummating an intended felony (theft of property, for example). As long as the burglar intends to commit the theft at the moment of breaking and entry, burglary is complete even if the burglar is scared off before taking any property. A thief who actually takes a homeowner's personal property commits the additional crime of larceny. Completing the larceny is also strong evidence of the intent to steal at the time of the breaking and entry.

Although most jurisdictions continue to recognize common law burglary as the most serious form of burglary, the crime has been expanded to cover many different forms of breaking and entry. Exhibit 6–2 illustrates one state's recognition of many forms of statutory burglary.

Arson

Arson
malicious burning of
another's dwelling house.

Arson was the other principal common law offense against habitation. The elements of **arson** include (1) malicious (2) burning of a (3) dwelling house of (4) another. Common law arson like common law burglary protected only the dwelling house of another, thus the previous discussion of dwellings in regard to burglary applies equally to arson. Burning structures other than dwellings was not common law arson, and defendants who burned their own dwellings with an intent to defraud an insurance company were not guilty of common law arson. As is true of burglary, modern statutes greatly expand the definition of arson; "commercial" arson for the purpose of insurance fraud is the most common form of modern-day arson.

The mental state required for arson is malice (see Chapter Two). Malice includes a specific intent to burn a dwelling or a wanton or willful disregard for the likelihood that a dwelling will be burned. "So long as defendant has actual subjective intention to do the act he does and does it in disregard of a conscious awareness that such conduct involves highly substantial risks that a structure . . . will be set afire, burned or caused to be burned . . . defendant acts willfully and maliciously."[10]

The most technical aspect of common law arson was the requirement that the dwelling house be "burned," which did not mean that the dwelling had to burn to the ground. It did, however, require that the dwelling sustain damage greater than being scorched by nearby heat or discolored by smoke. The distinction between scorching the structure, which was not arson, and charring the structure, which was

EXHIBIT 6–2
Statutory Forms of Burglary
in Virginia

1. *Dwelling houses:*
   (A) Break and enter in nighttime with intent to commit
       (1) a felony.
       (2) a larceny.
   (B) Enter without breaking in the nighttime
       (1) with intent to commit murder, rape, or robbery.
       (2) with intent to commit larceny or any felony other than murder, rape, or robbery.
   (C) Break and enter in the daytime
       (1) with intent to commit murder, rape, or robbery.
       (2) with intent to commit larceny or any felony other than murder, rape, or robbery.
   (D) Enter and conceal [at anytime]
       (1) with intent to commit murder, rape, or robbery.
       (2) with intent to commit larceny or any felony other than murder, rape, or robbery.
2. *Occupied dwelling house:*
   Break and enter day or night with intent to commit any misdemeanor except assault or trespass.
3. *Office, shop, manufactured home, storehouse, warehouse, banking house, or other house, or vehicle of habitation:*
   (A) Enter without breaking in nighttime
       (1) with intent to commit murder, rape, or robbery.
       (2) with intent to commit larceny or any felony other than murder, rape, or robbery.
   (B) Break and enter at anytime
       (1) with intent to commit murder, rape, or robbery.
       (2) with intent to commit larceny or any felony other than murder, rape, or robbery.
   (C) Enter and conceal at anytime
       (1) with intent to commit murder, rape, or robbery.
       (2) with intent to commit larceny or any felony other than murder, rape, or robbery.
4. *Banking house:*
   Enter in day or night armed with deadly weapon with intent to commit larceny of money, bonds, notes, or other evidence of debt.

arson, is elusive at best. In *Lynch v. State,* the court attempted to distinguish between burning and setting fire to a building.

> To set fire to a structure is to "place fire upon," or "against" or to "put fire in connection with" it. It is possible to set fire to a structure which, by reason of the sudden extinction of the fire, will fail to change the characteristics of the structure. [Although the structure has not been burned] nevertheless, it has been set fire to.[11]

If the distinction between charring and scorching seems bizarre or overly technical, the common law also had a strange view of the use of explosives. An explosion that destroyed a building was not arson unless some of the remaining building was subsequently burned by a fire caused by the explosion. Most modern statutes include explosions within the definition of arson, and these statutes also eliminate the requirement that the dwelling be charred or actually ignited. Contemporary definitions of arson often encompass endangering a structure by a nearby fire started for the purpose of burning the building.

SUMMARY

An important clue to distinguishing among larceny, embezzlement, and false pretenses, is the victim's state of mind regarding the property. In larceny cases, the victim intends either to pass nothing or to pass mere physical custody of the property. In embezzlement cases, the victim intends to entrust temporary possession of the property to another (most often an employee). In situations involving false pretenses, the victim intends to give up all rights to the property by passing title and possession to another.

In all three forms of theft, the defendants must have an intent to deprive another of the property permanently. The defendants, however, can be distinguished by their conduct when initially acquiring the property. Those who commit larceny must perform a trespassory taking; those who commit embezzlement must convert property

CONCEPT SUMMARY

Theft Offenses

Consult local law to determine what changes have been made in a particular jurisdiction.

CRIME	MENTAL STATE	PHYSICAL ACT	HARM	VICTIM'S INTENT
Larceny	Intent to deprive permanently	Trespassory taking	Interference with personal property rights	To pass no more than custody
Embezzlement	Intent to deprive permanently	Wrongful conversion	Interference with personal property rights	Trust another with possession
False Pretenses	Intent to deprive permanently	False representation	Interference with personal property rights	To pass title
Receiving Stolen Property	Knowing the property is stolen; no intent to return to owner	Exercise actual or constructive control over property	Interference with personal property rights	

Offenses Against Habitation

CRIME	MENTAL STATE	PHYSICAL ACT	HARM
Burglary	Intent to commit a felony inside a dwelling	Breaking and entering in the nighttime	Intrusion into another's dwelling
Arson	Intent to or wanton/ willful disregard for likelihood of burning	Burning	Dwelling is burned or charred

originally entrusted to them for a limited purpose; those who commit false pretenses must make a false representation of fact which causes the victim to pass title to property. The crime of receiving stolen property encompasses any form of conduct whereby the defendant takes control of stolen property for the purpose of depriving the owner of the item.

Burglary and arson are offenses against habitation, which explains at least to some extent, the technicalities surrounding the definition of a dwelling. Modern statutes often eliminate these technicalities and protect all structures, although dwellings may be given increased protection by enhancing the punishment of one who intrudes upon or burns a dwelling. Burglary focuses upon breaking and entering regardless of any damage to the structure. Common law arson, however, required that the structure be "burned." Arson requires a mental state of maliciously burning a dwelling; burglary requires a specific intent to commit a felony in the dwelling.

DISCUSSION QUESTIONS

1. When you steal your friend's lottery ticket, for which she paid $1, you have committed petit larceny. Do you become guilty of grand larceny if the ticket turns out to be a winning ticket worth $1 million?
2. You hand a bank teller a $200 check which the teller misreads as a check for $2,000. If you say nothing and accept the $2,000 in cash, are you guilty of obtaining money by false pretenses?

3. When you and your spouse separate, you obtain a court order prohibiting your spouse from entering your home. You return one night and find that your spouse used his key to enter and that he took his golf clubs. Is your spouse guilty of burglary? Larceny? Does your spouse have any defense if he believed that the golf clubs were exclusively his property?

PRACTICE EXERCISES

1. How does your jurisdiction deal with theft of intangibles such as computer time?
2. What types of structures are protected against breaking and entering by the burglary statutes of your jurisdiction?
3. How does your jurisdiction define the crime of arson? Does it distinguish between arson of a dwelling and "commercial" arson?
4. What charge would you bring in the following situation: S enters a supermarket and picks up a tube of glue and a large box of potato chips. S ducks behind

an aisle, empties the potato chips, places five T-bone steaks (value: $40) in the box, and reseals the box with glue. S takes the box to the cashier and offers the price ($1.69) marked on the box. The cashier notes the weight of the box and opens it to reveal the steaks.
5. What crime would you charge when B relates the following facts: For five days in a row B noted that the odometer on B's new car showed an increase of 30 miles every morning. Last night B hid near the garage and saw D get in the car and drive off.

WEB SITE

Crimes involving computers, intellectual property, and the Internet
www.cybercrime.gov

KEY TERMS

Larceny	Possession	Grand larceny
Trespass	Asportation	Embezzlement
Custody	Dominion	Conversion

False pretenses   Breaking   Curtilage
Receiving stolen property   Entry   Arson
Burglary   Dwelling

Notes

1. *King v. Pear,* 168 Eng. Rep. 208 (1779).
2. 39 Geo. III, c. 85 (1799).
3. *Rex v. Barnard,* 173 Eng. Rep. 342 (1837).
4. "The false pretense or representation must have materially influenced the owner to part with his property, but the false pretense need not be the sole inducing cause." *People v. Ashley,* 42 Cal. 2d 246, 267 P.2d 271 (1954).
5. *Moehring v. Commonwealth,* 223, Va. 564, 290 S.E.2d 891 (1982).
6. See cases collected at Annotation, 70 A.L.R.3d 881.
7. *Woods v. State,* 186 Miss. 463, 191 So. 283 (1939).
8. *State v. Bair,* 112 W.Va. 655, 166 S.E. 369 (1932). A summer home qualifies as a dwelling house even during the period when it is not occupied.
9. *United States v. Melton,* 491 F.2d 45 (D.C. Cir. 1973).
10. *State v. O'Farrell,* 355 A.2d 396, 398 (Me. 1976).
11. *Lynch v. State,* 175 Ind. App. III, 370 N.E.2d 401 (1977).

CRIMES AGAINST PUBLIC ORDER AND PUBLIC MORALITY

Chapter 7

CHAPTER OUTLINE

This chapter concludes the discussion of substantive crimes, and in some ways comes full cycle to the fundamental issues initially raised in the first two chapters. Chapter One identified a variety of sources of our criminal law and ways society uses punishment to control criminal behavior. Chapter Two suggested a working definition of crime that focused on three elements: mental state, physical act, and social harm. This chapter addresses what is often referred to as "victimless crime." For example, what is the harm in driving while intoxicated as long as no one is hurt? What is the harm in pulling the wings off a butterfly or other forms of cruelty to animals? These types of activities injure intangibles such as emotional security, morality, and the public peace. Criminal law not only protects people and their property from direct injury, it also protects against social harm. Defining social harm in broad terms justifies the category of crimes against the public, even when no individual victim of the crime can be named.

Crimes against public order also resurrect the issue raised in *Shaw v. Director of Public Prosecutions* (presented in Chapter One), in which the House of Lords debated the government's power to regulate and punish for violation of public morals. In such situations the government exercises a general **police power** to advance public health, safety, morality, and welfare. *Shaw* addressed whether courts have such inherent power. However, most crimes against public order or morality are regulated by statute. Thus, the issue is no longer whether courts may regulate morality, but whether a democratically elected legislature may enforce public morals. The U.S. Supreme Court suggested that "whatever differences of opinion may exist as to the extent and boundaries of the police power, and however difficult it may be to render a satisfactory definition of it, there seems to be no doubt that it does extend to . . . the preservation of good order and the public morals."[1]

Police power
the government's broad authority to advance public health, safety, morality, and welfare.

DISORDERLY CONDUCT

Disorderly conduct; breach of the peace; common nuisance
acts that disturb the tranquility or order of the community.

Sometimes lumped together as a single crime and sometimes covered by separate statutes, the crimes of **disorderly conduct, breach of the peace,** or creating a **common nuisance,** are all rather vaguely defined as acts that disturb the tranquility or order of the community. Public disturbances come in an infinite variety of forms: for example, loud parties or barking dogs may be a public nuisance; urinating in public may be disorderly conduct; and abusive language may lead to a breach of the peace. These broadly defined crimes against public order often conflict with the due process prohibition against statutes that are void for vagueness (see Chapter One). Was the defendant in *Thompson v. City of Louisville* engaging in eccentric but harmless behavior, or was he committing a breach of the peace?

THOMPSON v. CITY OF LOUISVILLE
Supreme Court of the United States, 1960
362 U.S. 199, 80 S.Ct. 624

The facts . . . are short and simple. Petitioner, a long-time resident of the Louisville area, went into the Liberty End Cafe about 6:20 on Saturday evening, January 24, 1959. In addition to selling food the cafe was licensed to sell beer to the public and some 12 to 30 patrons were present during the time petitioner was there.

When petitioner had been in the cafe about half an hour, two Louisville police officers came in on a "routine check." Upon seeing petitioner "out there on the floor dancing by himself," one of the officers, according to his testimony, went up to the manager who was sitting on a stool nearby and asked him how long petitioner had been in there and if he had bought anything. The officer testified that upon being told by the manager that petitioner had been there "a little over a half-hour and that he had not bought anything," he accosted Thompson and "asked him what was his reason for being in there and he said he was waiting on a bus." The officer then informed petitioner that he was under arrest and took him outside. This was the arrest for loitering. After going outside, the officer testified, petitioner "was very argumentative—he argued back and forth and so then we placed a disorderly conduct charge on him." Admittedly the disorderly conduct conviction rests solely on this one sentence description of petitioner's conduct after he left the cafe.

JUSTICE BLACK delivered the opinion of the Court: Petitioner's conviction for disorderly conduct was under a city ordinance which, without definition, provides that "whoever shall be found guilty of disorderly conduct in the City of Louisville shall be fined" etc. The only evidence of "disorderly conduct" was the single statement of the policeman that after petitioner was arrested and taken out of the cafe he was very argumentative. There is no testimony that petitioner raised his voice, used offensive language, resisted the officers or engaged in any conduct of any kind likely in any way to adversely affect the good order and tranquility of the City of Louisville. The only information the record contains on what the petitioner was "argumentative" about is his statement that he asked the officers "what they arrested me for." We assume, . . . that merely arguing with a policeman is not, because it could not be, "disorderly conduct" as a matter of the substantive law of Kentucky.

Thus we find no evidence whatever in the record to support these convictions. The judgments are reversed.

The Court noted that the defendant in *Thompson* did not use offensive language. One form of offensive language, and a common form of disorderly conduct, is the use of fighting words. The U.S. Supreme Court defined **fighting words** as words that (1) inflict injury, (2) tend to create a breach of the peace, and (3) are not primarily an expression of ideas protected by free speech.[2] For example, "You're ugly and your mother dresses you funny," is abusive language likely to result in retaliation and a breach of the peace. It is often difficult, but constitutionally necessary, to distinguish fighting words from language that may be offensive because the speaker is aggressively asserting his rights. The defendant in *City of Houston v. Hill* was a paralegal who used his familiarity with the law to become an advocate of gay rights, particularly when he perceived police harassment of homosexuals. Was he exercising his right to free speech, or did he cross the line to disorderly conduct?

Fighting words
words that inflict injury, tend to create a breach of the peace, and are not primarily an expression of ideas protected by free speech.

CITY OF HOUSTON v. HILL
Supreme Court of the United States, 1987
482 U. S. 451, 107 S.Ct. 2502

[The defendant worked as a paralegal and as executive director of the Houston Human Rights League. He was also a founder of the Gay Political Caucus. When he observed two police officers approach a friend, he shouted: "Why don't you pick on somebody your own size?" A police officer responded: "Are you interrupting me in my official capacity as a Houston police officer?" The defendant then shouted: "Yes, why don't you pick on someone your own size?" The defendant was arrested under an ordinance which provided that it "shall be unlawful for any person to assault, strike, or in any manner oppose, molest, abuse or interrupt any policeman in the execution of his duty." The Court found the ordinance to be an unconstitutional infringement on free speech].

JUSTICE BRENNAN delivered the opinion of the Court:
The ordinance is not limited to fighting words nor even to obscene or opprobrious language, but prohibits speech that "in any manner . . . interrupts" an officer. The Constitution does not allow such speech to be made a crime. The freedom of individuals to verbally oppose or challenge police action without thereby risking arrest

is one of the principal characteristics by which we distinguish a free nation from a police state. . . .

Although we appreciate the difficulties in drafting precise laws, we have repeatedly invalidated laws that provide the police with unfettered discretion to arrest individuals for words or conduct that annoy or offend them.

We are mindful that the preservation of liberty depends in part upon the maintenance of public order. But the first amendment recognizes, wisely we think, that a certain amount of expressive disorder not only is inevitable in a society committed to individual freedom, but must itself be protected if that freedom would survive.

Communication of a threat words conveying the intent to inflict harm; unlike the crime of assault, it does not require a menacing gesture.

Going beyond abusive language and actually threatening another person is often covered by separate statutes punishing the **communication of a threat.** By focusing on words alone, such statutes supplement the crime of simple assault, which often requires that the defendant engage in threatening conduct, such as a menacing gesture (see Chapter Five).

Although the law prohibits and punishes explicit threats, considerable controversy surrounds the issue of "street people" and "aggressive panhandling" as an implicit threat or menace that constitutes a breach of the peace. As *Robinson v. California* recognized (presented in Chapter One), a citizen cannot be punished simply on the basis of status: homelessness is not a crime. Homeless people, however, sometimes engage in conduct that is offensive to much of society. They frequently panhandle for money, which can be done in a friendly nonaggressive manner or in a menacing threatening way. The notorious incident in a New York subway involving Bernhard Goetz raised the issue of whether overly aggressive panhandlers might be perceived as muggers.[3] Partially in response to the Goetz incident, New York City banned begging and panhandling in its subway system. This ban was upheld against a challenge that claimed "begging is pure speech fully protected by the First Amendment." A federal court of appeals held that "most individuals who beg are not doing so to convey any social or political message. Rather, they beg to collect money." The court concluded that this is not speech protected by the First Amendment, but rather is conduct that may be regulated by the State.[4] New York, San Francisco, and many other large cities have taken steps to discourage aggressive panhandling.

In addition to threatening conduct or fighting words, indecent or obscene words may constitute disorderly conduct if they offend public sensibilities. (Many communities have separate statutes making it a crime to use loud and profane language in public.) Although both categories are sometimes included within a single statute, the law distinguishes between what is obscene and what is indecent. Obscenity requires a prurient interest in sex (a shameful or morbid concern with nudity or sex), but indecency merely refers to "nonconformance with accepted standards of morality."[5] Punishing for obscene language may violate either the constitutional prohibition against vagueness or the First Amendment right to free speech. The definition of obscenity has been particularly troubling to the courts (see the section of this chapter on Nonviolent Sex Offenses). One of the most famous quotes from the U.S. Supreme Court was Justice Stewart's admission that he could not define obscenity, "[B]ut I know it when I see it."[6]

Whatever the definition of obscenity may be, only the public aspects of obscenity may be punished as disorderly conduct or a breach of the peace. In *Stanley v. Georgia,* the U.S. Supreme Court held that possession of obscene material in the home is protected by the constitutional right to privacy.[7] The Court suggested that obscene material itself is not protected by the First Amendment, and the states are free to regulate or even ban obscenity, but "that power does not extend to mere possession by the individual in the privacy of his own home."

Punishing for indecent but not obscene language can violate the prohibition against vagueness, or may violate the First Amendment right to free speech. For example, motorists have been prosecuted for displaying bumper stickers that proclaim,

"Shit happens." Are these words descriptive of a philosophy of life protected by the First Amendment, or are they unnecessarily vulgar, offensive to at least some members of society, and thus subject to punishment? Criminalizing profane language has been a perplexing issue for the courts because profanity can range from the very offensive, to playful barbs at society's pet phobias. For an example of the latter, read the U.S. Supreme Court's ruling on whether a radio station could air the comedian George Carlin's monologue, "Seven Words You Can't Say on Television."[8]

UNLAWFUL ASSEMBLY AND RIOT

Disorderly conduct becomes more serious when it involves groups of people who threaten the public peace. At common law, an **unlawful assembly** was a gathering of three or more persons for any unlawful purpose or under circumstances endangering the public peace. A **riot** occurred when at least one member of the assembled group threatened or committed an act of violence.[9]

Once again, the government's efforts to maintain order and preserve the public peace can conflict with First Amendment rights, this time the right of the people "peaceably to assemble." Civil rights demonstrators, anti-abortion pickets, and other groups advancing a political cause may appear to police as threats to public order. If police act too quickly in breaking up all demonstrations, they may violate the demonstrators' First Amendment rights. But if police wait too long before taking action, the situation may erupt into a riot. Consider one of the bloodiest incidents in the history of the civil rights movement, described in Exhibit 7–1.

When a citizen fails to obey a police order to "move on," many localities consider that act a crime, but such an order cannot be used to prevent peaceful political protest. In *Brown v. Louisiana,* the U.S. Supreme Court reversed the convictions of five members of the Congress of Racial Equality who refused to obey a sheriff's

Unlawful assembly
a gathering of a designated number of persons (three at common law) for any unlawful purpose or under circumstances endangering the public peace.

Riot
at least one member of an unlawful assembly threatens or commits an act of violence.

EXHIBIT 7–1
88 Seconds in Greensboro

On November 3, 1979, an ideological clash between political extremists erupted into armed confrontation in Greensboro, North Carolina. The violence was triggered by a "Death to the Klan" rally, which pitted the Communists Workers Party against the Ku Klux Klan and a small group of American Nazis.

The rally began peacefully as demonstrators dressed in hardhats, jeans and blue workshirts led a group in protest songs—"People, people, have you heard, revolution is our word." The tranquility of the demonstration was shattered when a line of vehicles approached the demonstrators. The caravan of Klansmen and Nazis was led by a car with a Confederate flag on its license plate. As the vehicle approached the demonstrators, a passenger called out: "You asked for the Klan, now you've got them." The demonstrators returned the verbal taunt with cries of: "Ku Klux Klan, scum of the land," as they began beating on the car with a stick. Klan members exited from their vehicles and initiated a scuffle. At some point a single shot rang out. Within 88 seconds of their meeting, these volatile groups fired 39 shots and left five participants dead on the streets of Greensboro.

Federal and state law enforcement agencies had advance notice of the demonstration. They concluded, however, that a show of police force might result in unifying all groups against the police. They therefore made a tactical decision to keep a low profile. Officers were assigned to monitor the demonstration, but were told to keep out of sight. When word came over the police radio that the Klan was approaching the demonstration, the police were ordered to their pre-assigned positions. But the message came too late to avoid tragedy.[10]

order to "move on" and leave a segregated reading room of a public library.[11] Demonstrations, picketing, or "just hanging out on a street corner" do not constitute unlawful assembly or riot until a person or group threatens to break an existing law. The clash between First Amendment rights and unlawful assembly was manifest in *American Life League v. United States,* the first challenge to the Freedom of Access to Clinic Entrances Act (FACE).

AMERICAN LIFE LEAGUE v. UNITED STATES
United States District Court, Eastern District of Virginia, 1994
855 F.Supp. 137

The plaintiffs brought suit seeking to declare FACE an unconstitutional infringement on their First Amendment right to free speech, lawful assembly, and free exercise of religion.

The opinion of the court:
The essential elements of a violation of FACE are conduct and specific intent. The statute prohibits three kinds of conduct: (1) the use of force, (2) the threat of force, and (3) physical obstruction. The specific intent necessary to run afoul of FACE is intent to injure, intimidate, or interfere with a person who is obtaining or has obtained, or is providing or has provided, reproductive health services. The plaintiffs' non-violent activities fall within the statute because they allege that they will cause a physical obstruction of clinics that provide abortion services, with the requisite intent to financially injure the abortion providers and to "interfere with" the women who may be entering a facility to procure an abortion.

The plaintiffs argue that FACE is overbroad because it imposes penalties for forms of expression, such as praying and sidewalk counseling, covered by the First Amendment. FACE avoids infringing on legitimate First Amendment rights. Nothing in the statute prohibits pure speech; rather the statute criminalizes the use of force, threat of force, and physical obstruction. These acts have

long been outside the scope of First Amendment protection. Conduct does not become "speech" entitled to the protection of the First Amendment whenever the actor intends to express an idea through conduct. FACE is crafted to prohibit and penalize only those "potentially expressive" acts that Congress found were producing and would continue to produce "special harms distinct from their communicative impact." The First Amendment protects the plaintiffs' right to hold and express beliefs opposing abortion; it does not give them unfettered license to express those beliefs in conduct.

Finally, the plaintiffs assert that FACE violates the Free Exercise Clause as well as the Restoration of Religious Freedom Act, which provides that the government cannot "substantially burden a person's right to exercise of religion" unless it shows that such burden is the least restrictive means of furthering a compelling governmental interest. The plaintiffs have not alleged that physical obstruction of abortion clinics is a sacrament or important ritual necessary to their observance of their faith. Nothing in the statute impinges upon the plaintiffs' ability to pray for the souls of women who are obtaining abortions and for the souls of their unborn children. What is limited by the statute is what else they may do while praying and counselling. They may not pray and counsel so as to physically obstruct access to reproductive health service facilities.

PUBLIC INTOXICATION

Public intoxication
presence in a public place in a drunken state, which may be a form of disorderly conduct or covered by a specific statute.

Public intoxication may take the form of disorderly conduct or it may fall under a specific statute prohibiting drunkenness in public. Punishing for public drunkenness is not a status offense, even if the defendant is an alcoholic. In *Powell v. Texas,* the U.S. Supreme Court explained that the defendant was not punished for his status as an alcoholic, but rather for his presence in a public place in an inebriated condition.[12] Many of these offenses are never prosecuted; the intoxicated person is simply held until sober and then released. When prosecution is pursued, the charge is usually classified as a minor misdemeanor.

Driving Under the Influence

A more serious crime occurs when the defendant operates a motor vehicle while under the influence of alcohol or drugs. These crimes are often referred to as **DUI** (driving under the influence), or **DWI** (driving while intoxicated). Intoxication can be proved by circumstantial evidence: most commonly, **field sobriety tests** such as touching finger to nose, walking a straight line, and similar physical coordination and mental clarity tests. Intoxication also can be established from scientific testing of the alcoholic content of blood, breath, or urine samples furnished by the motorist. Most states have **implied consent** laws, which mandate that motorists, lawfully stopped for suspected DUI, must consent to chemical testing of their blood, breath, or urine. Failure to consent to such testing results in a suspension of the defendant's driver's license.

Driving under the influence is a factual condition that may be established with or without a blood or breath sample from the motorist. In the absence of any chemical tests the arresting officer can testify to the motorist's condition: for example, the motorist reeked of alcohol, was falling down drunk, or other descriptive statements. If a blood or breath sample was obtained, the prosecution may use this evidence to buttress the officer's testimony. The test results are not conclusive, however, because the motorist may still argue that he or she was not intoxicated despite a high blood-alcohol level. When the charge is driving while intoxicated, the quantity of alcohol in the defendant's system is not the determinative factor; the motorist's ability to operate the vehicle safely is the crucial issue. Thus the prosecution must prove both that the driver was under the influence of alcohol *and* that the motorist's driving ability was thereby impaired.

Most jurisdictions, however, classify as a separate crime the operation of a motor vehicle by a person with a blood-alcohol level above a certain amount (most commonly .08 percent). Under such statutes, the driver with a blood-alcohol level above the maximum allowed is not permitted to argue that safe operation of the motor vehicle was possible. If a defendant's blood-alcohol level exceeded the statutory maximum, the prosecution need not offer any evidence concerning actual driver performance. The nature and history of the distinction between these two forms of DUI was considered in *Davis v. Commonwealth*.

> **DUI (driving under the influence); DWI (driving while intoxicated)** the illegal operation of a motor vehicle while under the influence of alcohol or other drugs.
>
> **Field sobriety tests** physical coordination or mental clarity tasks administered by a police officer to determine whether a person is drunk; includes such tests as touching finger to nose or walking a straight line.
>
> **Implied consent laws** possession of a driver's license mandates voluntary submission to blood, breath, or urine tests; refusal to submit results in a suspension of the defendant's driver's license.

DAVIS v. COMMONWEALTH
Court of Appeals of Virginia, 1989
8 Va. App. 291, 381 S.E.2d 11

[Following an automobile accident, a State Trooper administered a field sobriety test. Subsequently, a blood test was administered. The test results were reported as 0.10 percent by weight by volume. Davis contends that regardless of the blood test results, he was not under the influence of alcohol. The accident, he claims, resulted from faulty brakes on his truck.]

The opinion of the court:
It is a matter of common knowledge based on human experience that outward manifestations of intoxication will vary from individual to individual. While one highly intoxicated individual may exhibit few, if any, outward manifestations of intoxication, another individual may appear to be very intoxicated after consuming a small quantity of alcohol.

Undoubtedly, in part because of these difficulties but primarily in response to the public safety concerns over driving while intoxicated, in the 1980s state legislatures enacted legislation to strengthen the current laws against driving while under the influence of alcohol. Central to that legislation was the use of chemical tests to prescribe a maximum blood alcohol level beyond which driving would be unlawful. In theory, such tests eliminated the difficulties inherent in a subjective determination whether a person was "under the influence of alcohol." The use of a chemical test is appealing because of its objectivity and certainty.

[Consistent with the national trend, our legislature prohibited] drinking and driving under either of two separate and distinct circumstances. Code § 18.2-266 (ii) prohibits driving "while under the influence of alcohol." In order to facilitate that determination, when chemical tests are performed, Code § 18.2-269 continues to provide for certain presumptions for and against

the conclusion that a driver was "under the influence of alcohol" at the time of the alleged offense, that is, when he was driving.

In contrast, Code § 18.2-266(i) prohibits *driving* while the driver has a blood alcohol concentration of .10 percent or more as measured by a chemical test. The inquiry under Code § 18.2-266(i) is not whether a driver was in fact "under the influence of alcohol" to a degree that his ability to drive safely was affected; rather, the issue is whether *at the time he was driving* his blood alcohol concentration was a least .10 percent as measured by a subsequently administered chemical test.

Habitual offender

a person who has been adjudged guilty of drunk driving on a specified number of occasions (more than one).

First-time DUI offenders are often assigned to some form of driver-safety training program. **Habitual offenders,** those who have been adjudged guilty of drunk driving on a specified number of occasions, may have their driver's license revoked. Habitual offender determinations are normally regarded as civil proceedings, but driving after having been adjudged a habitual offender constitutes a criminal offense.

DRUG CRIMES

The possession or use of drugs is frequently cited as an example of a victimless crime on grounds that no one is victimized when an adult makes a voluntary choice to ingest narcotics. Of course that assessment changes if drugs are given to children or forced on a defenseless fetus. For example, if a pregnant woman ingests drugs, one can argue that she is victimizing the fetus. In recent years, a growing number of cases in which women who exposed their fetus to cocaine or other illegal drugs have been prosecuted. The charges brought in such cases range from criminal child abuse to assault with a deadly weapon. Such charges remain controversial and some courts have held that the crime of supplying drugs to minors was never intended to apply "in the context of criminally prosecuting mothers for delivery of a controlled substance to a minor by the way of the umbilical cord."[13]

The claim that drug use is victimless arises from the U.S. Supreme Court's recognition of the constitutional right to privacy. For example, in *Stanley v. Georgia,* the Court invoked the right of privacy to prohibit a state from punishing a person for possessing obscene materials in the privacy of that individual's home. Does the right of privacy grant the freedom to do whatever a person wishes with her or his own body? The Alaska Supreme Court cited the right of privacy to protect possession of marijuana by an adult for personal use in the home.[14]

Many people take issue with the claim that use of drugs is a victimless crime. Public opinion polls generally identify "street crime" and the "drug problem" as primary concerns of American voters. Law enforcement officials point out that a great deal of violent crime is committed by drug users or drug dealers. Additional crimes occur when rich and powerful drug lords use their wealth and intimidation to corrupt law enforcement officials. On the economic side, the incapacitation brought on by drugs and/or AIDS contracted by drug users drains the financial resources of the United States, particularly the large metropolitan areas.

Although debate continues over decriminalizing drugs, the federal government has launched a "War on Drugs" to be fought on both the supply side and the demand side. Most hard drugs like cocaine, heroin, and crack, are grown or produced outside the United States. Stronger efforts are being made to attack the supply side by preventing illegal drugs from entering the country. On the demand side, the United States is the biggest market in the world for illegal drugs. Shrinking the market by prosecuting drug users reduces the financial incentive for drug lords to use escalating violence to control the market.

The federal government is primarily responsible for controlling the flow of drugs into the country, but many states have joined the War on Drugs by adopting the Uniform Controlled Substances Act. This act has five schedules of controlled substances, ranking the less harmful narcotics or marijuana as misdemeanors or less serious felonies. The most serious felonies are reserved for the most harmful drugs, defined according to their potential for abuse, legitimate medical use, and physical danger to the user. Although all states address the supply side by prohibiting the manufacture or actual sale of controlled substances, most states focus on the demand side by addressing the crimes of (1) actual possession of a controlled drug, (2) constructive possession, and (3) possession with intent to distribute.

1. **Actual possession** of a controlled substance requires physical contact with or control over the drug, and a mens rea of knowing that the substance is an illegal drug. Thus a mistaken belief that the substance in a person's possession is a medically prescribed drug constitutes that person's defense against a possession charge because the mistake negates the mens rea required for the crime (see Chapter Four). The clearest cases of actual possession occur when the illegal drug is found on the defendant's person or in an area exclusively controlled by the defendant; such as the defendant's automobile or residence.

2. **Constructive possession** may occur when the controlled substance is in a place accessible to the defendant and subject to the defendant's control, even if he or she has no physical contact with the illegal drug. Difficult cases arise when a defendant is one of several persons who had access to the drug. For example, the police raid a party and find narcotics on the coffee table. Was the defendant actually using the narcotics, or was the defendant merely present in a location where others used the illegal drug? In some states presence in a location with knowledge that others possess or use illegal drugs has been made a separate crime, but all states permit the judge or jury to infer constructive possession from the circumstantial evidence in the case. Was there sufficient circumstantial evidence that the defendant in *Tucker v. Commonwealth* had constructive possession of cocaine?

Actual possession
physical contact with or control over the drug, and knowledge that the substance is an illegal drug.

Constructive possession
occurs when a controlled substance is in a place accessible to the defendant and subject to the defendant's control.

TUCKER v. COMMONWEALTH
Court of Appeals of Virginia, 1994
18 Va. App. 141, 442 S.E.2d 419

At about 1:15 A.M., Officer Alder stopped the vehicle in which appellant and his cousin, James W. Neal, Jr., were riding. Appellant and Neal consented to patdowns, and to a search of the car. No evidence of cocaine was found in the car. During the automobile search, Neal sat in one of the police cars. Immediately after sitting down, Neal asked if he could get out to urinate. After Neal got out, the police officer felt his car rock, and he observed Neal bent over and leaning against the right rear passenger portion of the car. Upon re-entering the car, Neal "made a big production" about having to tie his shoe. After releasing the pair, the officers found a plastic baggie of cocaine three feet from the right rear passenger door of the police car. The officers also were unable to find a wet spot to indicate that Neal had urinated near the car. An officer hid in the woods near the site and, fifteen minutes later, spotted appellant and Neal returning to the scene on foot. They "walked up and down that side of the street" where the police car had been parked. The police officer emerged from the woods and identified himself as a police officer. Neal remained at the scene, but appellant fled. [The appellant appealed his conviction for possession of cocaine.]

The opinion of the court:

In order to justify appellant's conviction, the Commonwealth had to prove beyond a reasonable doubt that he possessed the cocaine, either actually or constructively, with an awareness of its presence and character. Although appellant's mere proximity to the cocaine is insufficient to support his conviction, possession may be shown by other evidence, including his conduct and statements prior to arrest. Finally, "possession need not always be exclusive. The defendant may share it with one or more."

The evidence in this case clearly supports a finding that Neal possessed the cocaine while in appellant's car,

discarded it beside the police car, and returned to the scene to retrieve it. Despite appellant's denials, the evidence also supports a finding that appellant knew about the drugs when he returned with Neal to the scene of the automobile stop.

Despite this conclusion, the evidence is insufficient to support a finding that appellant had constructive possession of the drugs contemporaneous with Neal's actual possession. Occupancy of the premises on which drugs are found does not give rise to a presumption of possession; instead, it is only one factor to be considered along with other evidence in determining whether a defendant constructively possessed drugs. In this case, there was no other evidence to show that appellant had knowledge of the nature and presence of the substance *at the time Neal had actual possession.* The evidence, therefore, creates a mere suspicion of guilt which is insufficient to sustain a criminal conviction. [Appellant's conviction is reversed.]

Possession with intent to distribute
a purposeful plan to sell or provide illegal drugs to others.

Accommodation defense
the defendant intended to provide the illegal drug to others without making a profit.

3. **Possession with intent to distribute** is generally regarded as a much more serious crime and carries a more severe punishment than actual or constructive possession. By punishing drug dealers, the criminal justice system strikes at the supply side of illegal drug use. In a typical case, the defendant may claim that the drugs were possessed for personal use, but this argument can be rebutted by circumstantial evidence. For example, possession of a few marijuana cigarettes may indicate strictly personal use; but possession of several kilograms, a scale, numerous small plastic bags, and other paraphernalia associated with drug dealing infers an intent to distribute drugs. Although the defendant may have an intent to distribute, many jurisdictions recognize an **accommodation defense.** In such cases the defendant intends to supply the illegal drug to others but makes no profit from the sale of the drugs. This action is still a crime, but less serious than the crime of selling drugs for profit.

All drug offenses require that the defendant commit some act, that is, possess, use, or distribute the controlled substance. As *Robinson v. California* established, a person cannot be convicted of a crime because of his status as a drug addict (see Chapter One).

NONVIOLENT SEX OFFENSES

No area of victimless crime causes as much controversy as offenses against public morality. The least, although still considerable, amount of controversy surrounds sexual conduct that has some public aspect. Public sex acts, nudity in public, and prostitution (when solicitation occurs in public places) are commonly condemned by statute. As *Hart v. Commonwealth* demonstrates, the courts continue to struggle with concepts of mere nudity, indecent exposure, and obscene displays.

HART v. COMMONWEALTH
Court of Appeals of Virginia, 1994
18 Va. App. 77, 441 S.E.2d 706.

On June 10, 1992, the defendant entered the office supply store where Bonnie Faulk worked and asked her for help locating a refill for his pen. While Faulk was assisting him, she looked up and saw that "he had dropped his pants," which were "real short running shorts," and that he was then "wearing [only] a real skimpy G-string." Although the G-string covered his penis, "it was very form fitting," such that Faulk could see the outline of his penis. She also testified that his buttocks and remaining pubic area were exposed and that she could see his pubic hair. Defendant picked up his shorts and said, "These darn things just keep falling off." He then modeled for her, slowly turned around, and asked her what she "[thought] of the whole picture." He told her "he had searched all over town for this particular swim suit" and that he liked to wear it, or nothing at all, when he went out on his boat. He also said that the shorts "were great" because they attached with velcro, which "gave easy access to women who wanted him." After being in the store for ten or fifteen minutes, defendant put his shorts back on and left, but returned six day later at almost the same time wearing the same shorts. When Faulk's manager came out of the back room, defendant "started to look around, dart his eyes. He got real nervous, real shaken up, . . . grabbed a pen, . . . immediately went to pay for it," and then left.

The defendant appeals his conviction for indecent exposure under a statute that provides that "every person who intentionally makes an obscene display or exposure of his person, or the private parts thereof, in any public place . . . shall be guilty of a Class 1 misdemeanor."

The opinion of the court:
As defined in relevant part in the statute, "obscene" means

that which, considered as a whole, has as its dominant theme or purpose an appeal to the prurient interest in sex, that is, a shameful or morbid interest in nudity, sexual conduct, or sexual excitement . . . and which goes substantially beyond customary limits of candor in description or representation of such matters.

Under this definition, the evidence was clearly sufficient to support the trial court's conclusion that defendant's exposure of his "private parts" was obscene. The trial court was entitled to conclude that defendant's statements, in conjunction with his actions, clearly established that his actions had as their dominant purpose an appeal to the prurient interest in sex as defined in the Code.

Dissenting Opinion:
Although the defendant's conduct was indecent, vulgar, and bizarre, the evidence did not prove either that his conduct was proscribed by Code § 18.2-387 or that his conduct was obscene.

Although the statute is styled "Indecent exposure," a conviction under Code § 18.2-387 may not be sustained unless the proof establishes that the "display or exposure" was "obscene." Mere nudity is insufficient basis to declare conduct obscene. Indecency is different than obscenity. Moreover, proof that conduct was indecent is insufficient to prove that it was obscene. To establish that an act is obscene the proof must establish a "prurient interest in sex," and not just sexual desires.

Defendant's comments, as was his conduct, were vulgar and indecent, but his comments and his conduct did not rise to the level of an obscenity. Though his comments were certainly offensive to the woman to whom he spoke, even in conjunction with his conduct, they did not satisfy the test of prurience.

When sexual conduct occurs in the privacy of one's bedroom, the clash between public morality and individual freedom of choice becomes intense. Although common law rape was limited to penile-vulva contact between a man and a woman, the common law also punished sodomy and incest. **Incest** is sex between closely related family members, but most statutes prohibiting incest focus on sexual relations with children. In such cases, child abuse laws also apply. **Sodomy** is sometimes defined as "a crime against nature"; or "any sexual intercourse held to be abnormal, especially bestiality or anal intercourse." Some states continue to treat anal intercourse or oral sex,

Incest
sex between closely related family members.

Sodomy
"a crime against nature"; "any sexual intercourse held to be abnormal, especially bestiality or anal intercourse."

even between married couples, as a form of criminal sodomy. Other states allow this type of activity between consenting adults. In *Bowers v. Hardwick*, the U.S. Supreme Court indicated that regulation of sexual conduct would be left to the individual states.

BOWERS v. HARDWICK
Supreme Court of the United States, 1986
478 U. S. 186, 106 S.Ct. 2841

[In August 1982, respondent was charged with violating the Georgia statute criminalizing sodomy by committing that act with another adult male in the bedroom of respondent's home. Respondent brought suit in the federal courts challenging the constitutionality of the statute. He asserted that he was a practicing homosexual, that the Georgia sodomy statute, as administered by the defendants placed him in imminent danger of arrest].

JUSTICE WHITE delivered the opinion of the Court:
This case does not require a judgment on whether laws against sodomy between consenting adults in general, or between homosexuals in particular, are wise or desirable. It raises no question about the right or propriety of state legislative decisions to repeal their laws that criminalize homosexual sodomy, or of state court decisions invalidating those laws on state constitutional grounds. The issue presented is whether the Federal Constitution confers a fundamental right upon homosexuals to engage in sodomy and hence invalidates the laws of the many States that still make such conduct illegal and have done so for a very long time. This case also calls for some judgment about the limits of the Court's role in carrying out its constitutional mandate.

* * *

The law is constantly based on notions of morality, and if all laws representing essentially moral choices are to be invalidated under the Due Process Clause, the courts will be very busy indeed. Even respondent makes no such claim, but insists that majority sentiments about the morality of homosexuality should be declared inadequate. We do not agree, and are unpersuaded that the sodomy laws of some 25 States should be invalidated on this basis.

CHIEF JUSTICE BURGER concurring:
I join the Court's opinion, but I write separately to underscore my view that in constitutional terms there is no such thing as a fundamental right to commit homosexual sodomy.... This is essentially not a question of personal "preferences" but rather of the legislative author-

ity of the State. I find nothing in the Constitution depriving a State of the power to enact the statute challenged here.

JUSTICE BLACKMUN dissenting:
This case is [not] about "a fundamental right to engage in homosexual sodomy...." Rather, this case is about "the most comprehensive of rights and the right most valued by civilized men," namely, "the right to be let alone."

The Court's almost obsessive focus on homosexual activity is particularly hard to justify in light of the broad language Georgia has used. Unlike the Court, the Georgia Legislature has not proceeded on the assumption that homosexuals are so different from other citizens that their lives may be controlled in a way that would not be tolerated if it limited the choices of those other citizens.... The sex or status of the persons who engage in the act is irrelevant as a matter of state law.

In a variety of circumstances we have recognized that a necessary corollary of giving individuals freedom to choose how to conduct their lives is acceptance of the fact that different individuals will make different choices.... The Court claims that its decision today merely refuses to recognize a fundamental right to engage in homosexual sodomy; what the Court really has refused to recognize is the fundamental interest all individuals have in controlling the nature of their intimate associations with others.

JUSTICE STEVENS dissenting:
Although the meaning of the principle that "all men are created equal" is not always clear, it surely must mean that every free citizen has the same interest in "liberty" that the members of the majority share. From the standpoint of the individual, the homosexual and the heterosexual have the same interest in deciding how he will live his own life, and more narrowly, how he will conduct himself in his personal and voluntary associations with his companions. State intrusion into the private conduct of either is equally burdensome.

Bowers deferred to the legislature's decision to either criminalize or tolerate (if not approve) private sexual relations. But in *Griswold v. Connecticut,* the U.S. Supreme Court held that the State legislature could not make it a crime for married couples to possess birth control devices.[15] More recently, however, the Fourth Circuit Federal Court of Appeals refused to consider a challenge to a state law prohibiting unmarried adults from engaging in fornication and cohabitation.[16] Such challenges invoke the right to privacy, a controversial right because it is not explicitly recognized in the text of the U.S. Constitution.

The courts have been more willing to act when state regulation of personal relations violates an explicit command of the constitution. For example, before the Civil Rights movement of the 1960s, sixteen states prohibited marriage between members of different races. In *Loving v. Virginia,* a white man and a black woman were lawfully married in another state, then moved to Virginia which forbade interracial marriages.[17] The Lovings were convicted and sentenced to one year in jail, suspended on condition that they leave Virginia and not return for twenty-five years. The U.S. Supreme Court invoked the Equal Protection clause and reversed the conviction because "under our Constitution, the freedom to marry or not marry, a person of another race resides with the individual and cannot be infringed by the state."

SUMMARY

Creating crimes against public order or public morality is said to be justified by the government's inherent power to promulgate laws protecting security, morality, and the public peace. The crimes of disorderly conduct, breach of the peace, or creating a common nuisance, focus on acts that disturb the tranquility or order of the community. The definition of these crimes must be tested against the constitutional prohibition against vagueness and against the First Amendment's protection of free speech.

Disorderly conduct by groups may constitute the crimes of unlawful assembly or riot. The First Amendment, however, specifically grants the people the right "peaceably to assemble." Thus a fine line must be drawn between assemblies advocating a political cause and groups that threaten the public order. Historically, the most difficult cases concerning unlawful assembly arose during the civil rights movement. Today, the issue is most often raised by militant proponents of the Right to Life, or by gay rights advocates.

Public intoxication is a form of disorderly conduct; however, it is often covered by a separate statute prohibiting being drunk in public. The public nature of the intoxication rather than the status of being an alcoholic is punishable under these statutes. Driving a motor vehicle while intoxicated (by alcohol or drugs) is treated as a serious crime in most jurisdictions. States have dealt with the drunk driving problem by creating separate crimes: (1) driving while impaired, regardless of the blood-alcohol level; (2) driving with a blood-alcohol level above a designated amount; and (3) implied consent laws, which punish those who wrongfully refuse to consent to chemical testing of their blood, breath, or urine.

Drug crimes today focus on both the supply side and the demand side of drug use. Statutes punish for (1) actual possession of a controlled substance, (2) constructive possession of the substance and (3) possession with intent to distribute the substance.

Nonviolent sex offenses are the most controversial aspects of crimes against public morality. Although statutes prohibiting sodomy or deviate sexual conduct are rarely enforced, the U.S. Supreme Court has granted the individual states broad discretion to decide whether to, and how to, regulate such conduct.

CONCEPT SUMMARY

Crimes Against Public Order/Morality

Consult local law to determine what changes have been made in a particular jurisdiction.

CRIME	MENTAL STATE	PHYSICAL ACT	HARM
Disorderly Conduct	Reckless or strict liability	Conduct in a public place	Disturbs the tranquility or order of the community
Unlawful Assembly	Any unlawful purpose	Three or more people gather	Endangers the public peace
Riot	Any unlawful purpose	Three or more people gather and threaten or commit an act of violence	Endangers the public peace
Drunk Driving		Operate a vehicle while intoxicated Operate a vehicle with a blood-alcohol level above a certain amount	
Possession of Drugs	Knowledge that the substance is an illegal drug	Actual or constructive possession	
Intent to Distribute	Intent to supply an illegal drug	Actual or constructive possession	

DISCUSSION QUESTIONS

1. Is "hate speech" directed against a racial group the type of fighting words that constitute disorderly conduct, or are such words primarily an expression of ideas protected by free speech?
2. If the First Amendment protects the burning of the American flag, does the amendment protect the burning of a cross on someone's lawn?
3. If you are hanging out on a street corner with your friends, when do you have to obey a police officer's command to "Break it up and move along"?
4. What possible charges does a motorist face if apprehended while driving a vehicle under the influence of intoxicants?
5. What level of knowledge of the contents of a videotape constitutes possession of obscene material?

PRACTICE EXERCISES

1. How does your jurisdiction deal with a defendant who rides in an automobile with a driver the defendant knows to be intoxicated? Is the defendant an accessory to drunk driving?
2. How has your jurisdiction addressed situations in which a person is found in a location where illegal drugs are present?
3. Does your jurisdiction recognize the accommodation defense to a charge of illegal distribution of drugs?
4. What consensual sexual acts are prohibited in your jurisdiction? Have any of these statutes been challenged recently?

WEB SITE

National Criminal Justice Reference Service
virlib.ncjrs.org/drugsandcrime.asp

KEY TERMS

Police power	Riot	Actual possession
Disorderly conduct	Public intoxication	Constructive possession
Breach of the peace	DUI	Possession with intent to distribute
Common nuisance	DWI	Accommodation defense
Fighting words	Field sobriety tests	Incest
Communication of a threat	Implied consent laws	Sodomy
Unlawful assembly	Habitual offenders	

NOTES

1. *Boston Beer Co. v. Massachusetts*, 97 U.S. (7 Otto) 25 (1878).
2. *Chaplinsky v. New Hampshire*, 315 U.S. 568, 62 S.Ct. 766 (1942).
3. *People v. Goetz*, 68 N.Y.2d 96, 506 N.Y.S.2d 18 (1986).
4. *Young v. New York City Transit Authority*, 903 F.2d 146 (2d Cir. 1990).
5. *F.C.C. v. Pacifica Foundation*, 438 U.S. 726, 98 S.Ct. 3026 (1978).
6. *Jacobellis v. Ohio*, 378 U.S. 184, 84 S.Ct. 1676 (1964) (J. Stewart, concurring).
7. *Stanley v. Georgia*, 394 U.S. 557 89 S.Ct. 1243 (1969).
8. *F.C.C. v. Pacifica Foundation*, 438 U.S. 726, 98 S.Ct. 3026 (1978).
9. See Federal Riot Control Statute, 18 U.S. Code § 2102.
10. See Bacigal, "When Racists and Radical Meet," 38 Emory Law Journal 1145 (1989).
11. *Brown v. Louisiana*, 383 U.S. 131, 86 S.Ct. 719 (1966).
12. *Powell v. Texas*, 392 U.S. 514, 88 S.Ct. 2145 (1968).
13. *Johnson v. State*, 602 So.2d 1288 (Fla. 1992).
14. *Ravin v. State*, 537 P.2d 494 (Alaska 1975).
15. *Griswold v. Connecticut*, 381 U.S. 479, 85 S.Ct. 1678 (1965).
16. *Doe v. Duling*, 782 F.2d 1202 (4th Cir. 1986).
17. *Loving v. Virginia*, 388 U.S. 1, 87 S.Ct. 1817 (1967).

CRIMINAL PROCEDURE

Part II

INTRODUCTION TO PROCEDURE AND THE RIGHT TO COUNSEL

Chapter 8

CHAPTER OUTLINE

Many people malign procedure as the domain of nit-picking lawyers or bureaucrats who are so caught up in red tape that they overlook the substance of the matter. No one can deny, however, that criminal procedure has great practical importance because many cases are won or lost on procedural grounds. Since the 1960s and the heyday of the "Warren Court," the constitutional aspects of criminal procedure have taken on increased importance.

In addition to its practical affect on the outcome of individual cases, criminal procedure has served as a battleground for conflicting political theories on the purpose of the criminal justice system. One theory maintains that the criminal justice system's primary task is to identify and punish those who have violated the law; thus procedural rules must assist, not frustrate, the police and courts in their efforts to combat crime. A counter theory, however, suggests that procedural rules may override consideration of a particular defendant's guilt or innocence. Under this view, the criminal justice system may employ procedure to serve broader purposes such as the regulation of police misconduct. These conflicting theories of procedure often precipitate the formulation of specialized rules and procedures by the courts.

THE PURPOSE OF PROCEDURE

In a classic publication, "Two Models of the Criminal Process," Professor Vance Packer identified a Crime Control Model and a Due Process Model that isolate and contrast the conflicting goals of the criminal justice system.[1]

The Crime Control Model

Crime Control Model
focuses on determining factual guilt or innocence; favors only those procedures that help ensure the accuracy of the fact-finding process.

In the **Crime Control Model,** the criminal justice system operates to screen suspects, determine guilt, and secure appropriate dispositions of persons convicted of crimes. The high crime rate in the United States coupled with limited resources for combating crime suggest that the criminal justice system "must not be cluttered with ceremonious rituals"—the infamous legal technicalities—that fail to address the question of the defendant's actual guilt or innocence. Under the Crime Control Model, only those procedures that help ensure the accuracy of the fact-finding process are to be favored. For example, cross-examination of witnesses is proper and beneficial because it serves to reveal whether the witnesses are testifying truthfully. On the other hand, *Miranda* warnings prior to police interrogation are disfavored because they hamper efforts to obtain truthful confessions.

Factual guilt
a showing that in all probability the defendant committed the alleged crime.

Legal guilt
a factual determination of guilt made in a procedurally correct fashion.

The Crime Control Model focuses on **factual guilt**—a showing that in all probability the defendant committed the alleged crime. Some procedural rules, however, have nothing to do with the factual question of whether the defendant engaged in prohibited conduct. (In popular parlance, a guilty defendant may "get off on a technicality.") The justification for these procedures rests upon the concept of **legal guilt,** which requires that the factual determination be made in a procedurally correct fashion. For example, even though the factual determination is adverse to the defendant, the accused person is not legally guilty if:

- The tribunal that convicted the defendant lacked the power to deal with the case (jurisdiction).
- The tribunal was not geographically appropriate (venue).
- Too long a time elapsed between commission of the offense and the commencement of prosecution (statutes of limitations or lack of speedy trial).
- The defendant was previously convicted or acquitted of the same offense (double jeopardy).
- The crime was created after the defendant's conduct occurred (ex post facto).

These types of procedural requirements cannot be justified as furthering the accuracy of the fact-finding process. Their justification rests upon other grounds identified by the Due Process Model of the criminal justice system.

The Due Process Model

The **Due Process Model** derives its name from, and is based on, the Due Process clause of the Fourteenth Amendment: "nor shall any state deprive any person of life, liberty, or property, without due process of law." In the case of *Rochin v. California,* Justice Frankfurter stated, "Due process of law, as a historic and generative principle, precludes defining, and thereby confining these standards of conduct more precisely than to say that convictions cannot be brought about by methods that offend 'a sense of justice.'"

Due Process Model recognizes that determination of factual guilt may be subordinated to other goals, such as controlling and correcting misconduct by government officials.

ROCHIN v. CALIFORNIA
Supreme Court of the United States, 1952
342 U.S. 165, 72 S.Ct. 205

Having some information that the defendant was selling narcotics, three deputy sheriffs of the County of Los Angeles . . . made for the two-story dwelling house in which Rochin lived with his mother, common-law wife, brothers and sisters. Finding the outside door open, they entered and then forced open the door to Rochin's room on the second floor. Inside they found Rochin sitting partly dressed on the side of the bed, upon which his wife was lying. On a night stand beside the bed the deputies spied two capsules. When asked "Whose stuff is this?" Rochin seized the capsules and put them in his mouth. A struggle ensued, in the course of which the three officers "jumped upon him" and (unsuccessfully) attempted to extract the capsules. Rochin was handcuffed and taken to a hospital. At the direction of one of the officers a doctor forced an emetic solution through a tube into Rochin's stomach against his will. This "stomach pumping" produced vomiting. In the vomited matter were found two capsules which proved to contain morphine. . . . Rochin was convicted of possessing morphine and sentenced to sixty days' imprisonment. The chief evidence against him was the two capsules.

JUSTICE FRANKFURTER delivered the opinion of the Court:
The proceedings by which this conviction was obtained do more than offend some fastidious squeamishness or private sentimentalism about combatting crime too ener-

getically. This is conduct that shocks the conscience. . . . This course of proceeding by agents of government to obtain evidence is bound to offend even hardened sensibilities. They are methods too close to the rack and the screw to permit constitutional differentiation.

It has long since ceased to be true that due process of law is heedless of the means by which otherwise relevant and credible evidence is obtained. [The Court's confession] decisions are only instances of the general requirement that States in their prosecutions respect certain decencies of civilized conduct. Due process of law, as a historic and generative principle, precludes defining, and thereby confining, these standards of conduct more precisely than to say that convictions cannot be brought about by methods that offend a sense of justice. It would be stultification of the responsibility which the course of constitutional history has cast upon this Court to hold that in order to convict a man the police cannot extract by force what is in his mind but can extract what is in his stomach. . . .

[E]ven though statements contained in them may be independently established as true, coerced confessions offend the community's sense of fair play and decency. So here, to sanction the brutal conduct which naturally enough was condemned by the court whose judgment is before us, would be to afford brutality the cloak of law. Nothing would be more calculated to discredit law and thereby to brutalize the temper of a society.

The *Rochin* case demonstrates that the Crime Control Model does not encompass all of the goals of the U.S. criminal justice system. If the sole purpose of the system is to ensure an accurate fact-finding process, then who could name a more effective method of meeting that goal than by "pumping out" the contents of a defendant's stomach for government inspection? The Due Process Model recognizes that the goal of convicting criminals may be sacrificed (and the factually guilty may go free) in order to serve the goal of controlling and correcting misconduct by government officials. This concept of due process and the exclusion of illegally obtained evidence are controversial concepts further addressed in Chapter Eleven.

The conflicting goals of the Crime Control and Due Process models provide an important key to the study of criminal procedure. When examining any particular procedural rule, consider whether the rule is designed to aid the truth-seeking function of the criminal justice system, or whether the rule seeks to accomplish some other goal such as deterrence of police misconduct.

SOURCES OF PROCEDURAL LAW

The Supremacy Clause, Article VI of the U.S. Constitution, states that the federal constitution is "the supreme law of the land," and the important constitutional provisions applicable to the criminal justice system are found in the Bill of Rights (see Exhibit 8–1). For the first century of our nation's existence, however, the Bill of Rights was intended solely as a limitation on the exercise of power by the federal government and was not applicable to the states. When the Due Process Clause of the Fourteenth Amendment was adopted, the U.S. Supreme Court embarked upon a still ongoing "incorporation" debate as to which if any provisions of the Bill of Rights were incorporated within the concept of Due Process and thus binding upon the states. In many ways, the Supreme Court's incorporation debate is a continuation of the clash between Federalists and Anti-Federalists at the time of the Constitution's adoption. Like the original Anti-Federalists, modern-day proponents of states' rights argue that the states are free to operate their criminal justice system without federal oversight. Like their Federalist ancestors, however, current proponents of a strong federal government maintain that states cannot always be trusted to safeguard the liberty of its citizens. For example, the institution of slavery cast state government as a threat to, not a protector of, individual rights. Thus the Due Process clause, as interpreted by the federal judiciary, was adopted as a powerful brake on runaway state government.

The incorporation debate is one arena in which judicial power has swung like a pendulum between "liberal" and "conservative" Justices of the U.S. Supreme Court. The "liberal" Warren Court of the 1960s positioned the federal judiciary as a bulwark standing between citizens and state incursions upon their liberties. The current Rehnquist Court, however, has cut back on federal oversight of the states' criminal justice systems, and has encouraged the states to experiment with diverse approaches to criminal justice. Although some observers are impatient with the Supreme Court's shifting approach to constitutional procedures, others see great benefit in having the Justices continually participate in a de facto constitutional convention redefining the structure and relationship of our federal and state governments.

The federal constitutional rights applicable through the Due Process clause establish the minimum individual rights that must be recognized by all states. Although a state may not reduce individual rights below the federal constitutional level, each state is free to adopt procedures that create additional rights for its citizens. Through state constitutional provisions, statutory enactments, or Rules of Court promulgated by the state supreme court, every state has formulated detailed procedural rules that govern the operation of its criminal justice system. Although

EXHIBIT 8–1
Constitutional Provisions Relevant to
Criminal Proceedings

Amendment IV

The right of the people to be secure in their persons, houses, papers, and effects, against unreasonable searches and seizures, shall not be violated, and no warrants shall issue, but upon probable cause, supported by oath or affirmation, and particularly describing the place to be searched, and the persons or things to be seized.

Amendment V

No person shall be held to answer for a capital, or otherwise infamous crime, unless on a presentment or indictment of a grand jury, except in cases arising in the land or naval forces, or in the militia, when in actual service in time of war or public danger; nor shall any person be subject for the same offense to be twice put in jeopardy of life or limb, nor shall be compelled in any criminal case to be a witness against himself, nor be deprived of life, liberty, or property, without due process of law; nor shall private property be taken for public use, without just compensation.

Amendment VI

In all criminal prosecutions, the accused shall enjoy the right to a speedy and public trial, by an impartial jury of the state and district wherein the crime shall have been committed, which district shall have been previously ascertained by law, and to be informed of the nature and cause of the accusation; to be confronted with the witnesses against him; to have compulsory process for obtaining witnesses in his favor, and to have the assistance of counsel for his defense.

Amendment VIII

Excessive bail shall not be required, nor excessive fines imposed, nor cruel and unusual punishments inflicted.

Amendment XIV

. . . No state shall make or enforce any law which shall abridge the privileges or immunities of citizens of the United States; nor shall any state deprive any person of life, liberty, or property, without due process of law; nor deny to any person within its jurisdiction the equal protection of the laws.

the federal courts have the final word when interpreting the U.S. Constitution, the state courts make the final decision on the increased protections afforded its citizens by state law.[2]

Stages of a Criminal Prosecution

The operation of the criminal justice system can be divided into the investigatory and the adjudicatory stages.

Investigatory Stage

Most often the police conduct the **investigatory process** without prior judicial approval, and prior to intervention by lawyers. The principal participants at this stage are the police and those whom they suspect of criminal activity (the cops-and-robbers stage). The courts, prosecutors, and defense counsel normally address the investigatory process in retrospect when determining whether the police acted in accordance with constitutional or statutory provisions governing police investigative practices.

Investigatory process includes temporary detentions, arrests, searches and seizures, interrogation, and identification procedures as conducted by law enforcement officials.

The following four chapters address the most frequently litigated investigative procedures.

- Arrests and temporary detentions
- Search and seizure and identification procedures
- Eavesdropping
- Interrogation and self-incrimination

Adjudicatory Stage

Adjudicatory stage
formal judicial proceedings such as bail hearings, pretrial hearings, and trial itself.

In the **adjudicatory stage,** formal judicial proceedings normally begin after the police have completed their investigation and arrested the suspect. The last four chapters of the text present a sequential examination of the adjudicatory stages from bail hearings to judicial review of the trial. Although variations exist in many jurisdictions, the typical criminal prosecution follows a sequence of stages.

- First appearance before a judicial officer (bail)
- Preliminary Hearing
- Charging Process (grand jury indictment, information)
- Pretrial motions
- Entry of plea
- Trial
- Verdict
- Sentence
- Judicial review (appeal and habeas corpus)

THE RIGHT TO COUNSEL

Because of the complexities of criminal procedure, the courts identify the various stages of investigation or adjudication in which the accused is entitled to the expert assistance of a lawyer trained in the intricacies of the criminal justice system. The right to employ defense counsel is recognized in the Sixth Amendment to the U.S. Constitution. Because the right to counsel is deemed a fundamental right within the meaning of the Fourteenth Amendment's Due Process clause, the accused in a state prosecution has a similar right to retain an attorney. The right to employ counsel, however, is a qualified right limited to those with legitimate assets to hire private counsel. An important tool of the "War on Drugs" is the government's power to confiscate assets derived from illegal drug trafficking. Neither the Due Process clause nor the Sixth Amendment right to counsel is violated when a defendant is required to forfeit illegally acquired assets—assets being used to employ counsel.[3]

If the defendant for any reason lacks funds to retain an attorney, the defendant is treated as an indigent and may have counsel provided at government expense. A criminal defendant has the right to waive counsel and a right to self-representation, but such a waiver must be knowingly and intelligently made.

The Right to Counsel at Critical Stages

Adversary judicial proceedings
signal that the government has committed itself to prosecution of the defendant and that the adverse positions of government and defendant have solidified.

The purpose of the Sixth Amendment right to counsel is to protect an accused during critical confrontations with the government. The right to counsel attaches at the commencement of **adversary judicial proceedings,** which signal that the government has committed itself to prosecution of the defendant, and that the adverse positions of government and defendant have solidified. "It is then that a defendant finds himself faced with the prosecutorial forces of organized society, and immersed in the intricacies of substantive and procedural criminal law."[4]

A criminal trial in which the defendant faces a possible sentence of incarceration is obviously an adversary judicial proceeding. In the absence of a knowing and intelligent waiver, no person may be imprisoned for any offense unless represented by counsel.[5] The rule applies to both felonies and misdemeanors; the possibility of incarceration, not the nature of the offense, dictates the need for counsel. In misdemeanor cases, however, counsel need not be appointed if the court stipulates prior to trial that no confinement will be imposed. Such a stipulation may be entered upon the request of the prosecutor or upon the court's own motion. In either case, once the stipulation is entered no jail sentence may subsequently be imposed upon a defendant who requests counsel.

The right to counsel also applies to certain pretrial proceedings deemed to be critical stages of the criminal justice system because the defendant might be prejudiced by the absence of counsel.[6] The right to counsel at pretrial proceedings involving lineups and confessions is considered in subsequent chapters. The right to counsel at other pretrial proceedings depends upon whether the proceedings occur after the commencement of the adversarial judicial process. The initiation of adversary judicial proceedings has not been precisely defined for constitutional purposes, but the U.S. Supreme Court suggested that judicial proceedings may commence "by way of formal charge, preliminary hearing, indictment, information, or arraignment."[7] In contrast to such judicial proceedings, the Court has "never held that the right to counsel attaches at the time of arrest."[8]

INDIGENTS' RIGHT TO COUNSEL

An **indigent** is anyone who lacks funds to hire a defense lawyer. Indigents must be informed of their right to have defense counsel appointed at public expense whenever they face potential imprisonment upon conviction.

The U.S. Supreme Court ruled in 1938 that the Sixth Amendment "withholds from *federal* courts, in all criminal proceedings, . . . the power and authority to deprive an accused of his life or liberty unless he has or waives the assistance of counsel."[9] The Court, however, did not construe the Constitution to require the states to appoint counsel for indigents until the 1963 landmark decision in *Gideon v. Wainwright*.

Indigent
an accused facing prosecution who lacks funds to employ a defense attorney.

GIDEON v. WAINWRIGHT
Supreme Court of the United States, 1963
372 U.S. 335, 83 S.Ct. 792

[Petitioner was charged in a Florida state court with a felony under Florida law. Appearing in court without funds and without a lawyer, petitioner asked the court to appoint counsel for him, whereupon the following dialogue took place:

The Court: "Mr. Gideon, I am sorry, but I cannot appoint Counsel to represent you in this case. Under the laws of the State of Florida, the only time the Court can appoint Counsel to represent a Defendant is when that person is charged with a capital offense."

The Defendant: "The United States Supreme Court says I am entitled to be represented by Counsel".]

JUSTICE BLACK delivered the opinion of the Court:
Put to trial before a jury, Gideon conducted his defense about as well as could be expected from a layman. He made an opening statement to the jury, cross-examined the State's witnesses, presented witnesses in his own defense, declined to testify himself, and made a short argument "emphasizing his innocence to the charge

contained in the Information filed in this case." The jury returned a verdict of guilty, and petitioner was sentenced to serve five years in the state prison. Since 1942, the problem of a defendant's federal constitutional right to counsel in a state court has been a continuing source of controversy and litigation in both state and federal courts. To give this problem another review here, we granted certiorari and appointed counsel to represent petitioner.

[R]eason and reflection require us to recognize that in our adversary system of criminal justice, any person hauled into court, who is too poor to hire a lawyer, cannot be assured a fair trial unless counsel is provided for him. This seems to us to be an obvious truth. Governments, both state and federal, quite properly spend vast sums of money to establish machinery to try defendants accused of crime. Lawyers are everywhere deemed essential to protect the public's interest in an orderly society. Similarly, there are few defendants charged with crime, few indeed, who fail to hire the best lawyers they can get to prepare and present their defenses. That government hires lawyers to prosecute and defendants who have the money hire lawyers to defend are the strongest indications of the widespread belief that lawyers in criminal courts are necessities, not luxuries. The right of one charged with crime to counsel may not be deemed fundamental and essential to fair trials in some countries, but it is in ours. From the very beginning, our state and national constitutions and laws have laid great emphasis on procedural and substantive safeguards designed to assure fair trials before impartial tribunals in which every defendant stands equal before the law. This noble ideal cannot be realized if the poor man charged with crime has to face his accusers without a lawyer to assist him.

The government's obligation to provide counsel to those financially unable to employ counsel applies only when the defendant is truly indigent. If an accused claims indigency, the trial court must investigate whether the claim is valid. Many states set forth detailed criteria to guide the trial court's determination of indigency (see Exhibit 8–2).

After receiving the accused's claim of indigency, the trial court conducts a thorough examination of the financial resources of the defendant, giving consideration to (1) the net income of the accused, (2) all assets of the accused that are convertible into cash within a reasonable period of time, and (3) any exceptional expenses of the defendant or the defendant's family that would prohibit the hiring of private counsel.

If the court deems the claim of indigency to be valid, the accused must execute an affidavit that certifies the defendant is without means to employ counsel. Penalties are provided for false swearing, and the court advises the accused of potential punishment for any false statements submitted to the court or other government agencies investigating the claim of indigency. Any changes in the accused's financial condition must be reported to the court; if a defendant is no longer indigent, the court must then grant a reasonable continuance to allow the defendant to retain private counsel.

Upon conviction, the government may recover the compensation paid to court-appointed counsel and other expenses or court costs incurred in prosecuting the defendant if the defendant has the ability to reimburse the government. This expense is a civil liability, however, and not part of the defendant's punishment for the crime. Thus an indigent cannot be confined for failure to pay costs unless refusal to pay is willful.[10]

Statutes generally authorize a trial court to direct the government to pay reasonable expenses incurred by a court-appointed attorney as long as the expenses were appropriate, given the circumstances of the case. Such statutes have been utilized to provide for government funding of services necessary for an adequate defense, for example, expert witnesses and private investigators.[11] The U.S. Supreme Court has expressed doubts as to whether an indigent has a constitutional right to such services. In *Ake v. Oklahoma*, however, the Court recognized that when an indigent's sanity is a significant factor at trial, the government must ensure the defendant access to a competent psychiatrist who will assist in evaluation, preparation, and presentation of the defense.[12] *Ake* went on to state: "A criminal trial is fundamentally unfair if the State proceeds against an indigent defendant without making certain that he has access to the raw materials integral to the building of an effective

FINANCIAL STATEMENT—   Case No. ....
ELIGIBILITY DETERMINATION FOR INDIGENT DEFENSE SERVICES
Presumptive Eligibility:
☐ I currently receive the following type(s) of public assistance in _____
                                                                        City/County

  ☐ AFDC $_____   ☐ Food Stamps $_____   ☐ Medicaid ☐ Supplemental Security Income $_____
  ☐ Other (specify type and amount) _____
☐ I currently do not receive public assistance.
Names and addresses of employer(s) for defendant and spouse:
Self _____

Spouse _____

NET INCOME: **Self**   **Spouse**
Pay period (weekly, every second week, twice monthly, monthly) ....   _____   _____
Net take home pay (salary/wages, minus deductions required by law) .... $_____   _____
Other income sources (please specify)—see reverse

                                            .... $_____   _____   ┌─────────────┐
                          TOTAL INCOME $————+————= │   │ A
                                                                        └─────────────┘ COURT USE ONLY
ASSETS:
Cash on hand .... $_____   _____
Bank Accounts at: .... $_____   _____

Any other assets: (please specify)
                                                with a
_____   value of .... $_____   _____
Real estate – $_____ $_____   _____
                    Net Value   with net
_____ value of .... $_____   _____
Motor {   Year and Make
Vehicles {   with net
_____ value of .... $_____   _____
                    Year and Make

Other Personal Property: (describe)
_____   .... $_____   _____   ┌─────────────┐
                          TOTAL ASSETS $————+————= │   │ B
                                                                        └─────────────┘ COURT USE ONLY

┌──┐
│ Number in household _____   │
│ Number of dependents (spouse/children)   │
│ whom you support: _____   │
└──┘

EXCEPTIONAL EXPENSES (Total Exceptional Expenses of Family)
Medical Expenses (list only unusual and continuing expenses) .... $_____
Court-ordered support payments/alimony... $_____
Child-care payments (e.g. day care) .... $_____
Other (describe): _____
_____ } $_____   ┌─────────────┐ COURT USE ONLY
                          TOTAL EXPENSES $_____ = │   │ C
                COLUMN "A" plus COLUMN "B" minus COLUMN "C" equals available funds   = ┌─────────────┐
                                                                                        │   │
                                                                                        └─────────────┘

THIS STATEMENT IS MADE UNDER OATH: ANY FALSE STATEMENT OF A MATERIAL FACT TO ANY QUESTION CONTAINED
HEREIN SHALL CONSTITUTE PERJURY UNDER THE PROVISIONS OF § 19.2-161 OF THE CODE OF VIRGINIA. THE MAXIMUM
PENALTY FOR PERJURY IS CONFINEMENT IN THE PENITENTIARY FOR A PERIOD OF TEN YEARS.

I hereby state that the above information is correct to the best of my knowledge.

Name of defendant (type or print) _____

_____   _____
        Date   Signature
Sworn/affirmed and signed before me this day.

_____   _____   _____
        Date   Signature   Title
                    FINANCIAL STATEMENT—ELIGIBILITY DETERMINATION
FORM DC-333 4/93 (114:3-021 5/94)   **FOR INDIGENT DEFENSE SERVICES**

EXHIBIT 8–2
Statement of Indigency

defense." The broad language of *Ake* has led some lower courts to conclude that an
indigent may be entitled to "other services" at government expense whenever the attorney's failure to obtain such services would amount to inadequate representation
of counsel.[13]

WAIVER OF COUNSEL AND THE RIGHT OF SELF-REPRESENTATION

Any waiver of the right to counsel must be made "knowingly and intelligently," thus the prosecution carries a heavy burden to prove by clear, precise, and unequivocal evidence that an effective waiver has occurred. Although a court could possibly imply a waiver of counsel, most jurisdictions require the accused to execute a waiver in written form (see Exhibit 8–3).

TRIAL WITHOUT A LAWYER

Va. Code § 19.2-160

CASE NO. . . . .

. . . .

☐ General District Court
☐ Juvenile and Domestic Relations District Court
☐ Circuit Court

. . . . v. . . . .

WAIVER OF RIGHT TO BE REPRESENTED BY A LAWYER (CRIMINAL CASE)

I have been advised by a judge of this court of the nature of the charges in the cases pending against me and the potential punishment for the offenses, which includes imprisonment in the penitentiary or confinement in jail. I understand the nature of these charges and the potential punishment for them if I am found to be guilty.

I have been further advised by a judge of this court that I have the following rights to be represented by a lawyer in these cases:

a. I have a right to be represented by a lawyer.

b. If I choose to hire my own lawyer, I will be given a reasonable opportunity to hire, at my expense, a lawyer selected by me. The judge will decide what is a reasonable opportunity to hire a lawyer. If I have not hired a lawyer after such reasonable opportunity, the judge may try the case even though I do not have a lawyer to represent me.

c. If I ask the judge for a lawyer to represent me and the judge decides, after reviewing my sworn financial statement that I am indigent, the judge will select and appoint a lawyer to represent me. However, if I am found to be guilty of an offense, the lawyer's fee as set by the judge within statutory limits will be assessed against me as court costs and I will be required to pay it.

I understand these rights to be represented by a lawyer. I understand the manner in which a lawyer can be of assistance and I understand that, in proceeding without a lawyer, I may be confronted with complicated legal issues. I also understand that I may waive (give up) my rights to be represented by a lawyer.

Understanding my rights to be represented by a lawyer as described above and further understanding the nature of the case and the potential punishment if I am found to be guilty, I waive all of my rights to be represented by a lawyer in these cases, with the further understanding that the cases will be tried without a lawyer either being hired by me or being appointed by the judge for me. I waive these rights of my own choice, voluntarily, of my own free will, without any threats, promises, force or coercion.

_____
ADULT

Upon oral examination, the undersigned judge of this Court finds that the Adult, having been advised of the rights and matters stated above and having understood these rights and matters, thereafter has knowingly, voluntarily and intelligently waived his rights to be represented by a lawyer.

. . . .   _____
DATE   JUDGE

CASE NO. . . . .

TRIAL WITHOUT A LAWYER

EXHIBIT 8–3
Waiver of Counsel

The Sixth Amendment right to counsel does not permit representation by a third-party non-attorney.[14] (No matter how close a person is to his or her family, no one but a lawyer has the right to defend that person in a criminal court.) But after knowingly and intelligently waiving the right to counsel, a defendant must be allowed self-representation (**proceed pro se**).[15] Although not invoking the maxim, "He who represents himself has a fool for a client," the U.S. Supreme Court stated that a defendant "should be made aware of the dangers and disadvantages of self-representation, so that the record will establish that 'he knows what he is doing and his choice is made with eyes open.'"

Proceed pro se
a criminal defendant waives counsel and chooses self-representation.

When choosing a course of self-representation, a defendant must respect all rules of procedural and substantive law. For example, the defendant may not relate a personal version of the facts in closing argument unless previous testimony to those facts has been given. As one court noted, a defendant may not use self-representation as "a ploy . . . to testify without the safeguard of an oath or the risk of cross-examination or impeachment."[16] Perhaps belaboring the obvious, the courts also have held that a defendant who chooses self-representation cannot later assert that ineffective assistance of counsel was rendered.

Standby Counsel

When the defendant invokes the right of self-representation, the trial court may appoint standby counsel to aid an accused who later desires assistance in conducting a defense. The defendant, however, cannot be forced to cooperate with standby counsel. In *McKaskle v. Wiggins*, the U.S. Supreme Court addressed the participation of standby counsel and distinguished between the pro se defendant's control of the case before the jury and before the judge.[17]

1. *Proceedings before the jury:* The *McKaskle* court held that participation by standby counsel without the defendant's consent should not be allowed to destroy the jury's perception that the defendant is conducting self-representation. Standby counsel may not make or substantially interfere with any significant tactical decisions, or control the questioning of witnesses, or speak on any matter of importance without the consent of the defendant.
2. *Proceedings before the judge:* *McKaskle* also recognized that standby counsel may differ with the pro se defendant's arguments to the court, as long as the defendant is allowed to address the court freely. Any disagreements between standby counsel and the pro se defendant must be resolved in the defendant's favor whenever the matter is one that would normally be left to the discretion of counsel.

In essence, the U.S. Supreme Court recognized that standby counsel serves to steer a defendant through the basic procedures of trial, thereby relieving the trial judge of the need to explain and enforce basic rules of courtroom protocol. Standby counsel is also expected to assist the defendant in overcoming routine procedural obstacles. But the pro se defendant must be allowed to control the major aspects of the defense, such as the organization and content of any defense offered; making motions to the court; arguing points of law; participating in jury selection; questioning witnesses; and addressing the court and jury at appropriate points in the trial.

WITHDRAWAL OF COUNSEL

Once appointed, counsel must continue to represent the defendant until replaced by other counsel. A defendant or the attorney may request that counsel be relieved for good cause, but the mere fact that the accused is displeased or incompatible with a particular attorney does not necessitate appointment of new counsel.[18] In ruling upon a defendant's motion for substitution of counsel, the trial court considers the timeliness of the motion, the reasons for the defendant's complaint, and whether the attorney–client conflict is so great that it creates a total lack of communication, which prevents an adequate defense. A refusal without good cause to proceed with appointed counsel will be deemed a voluntary waiver of the right to counsel.

The accused has a right to competent counsel, but does not have a right to be represented by a particular attorney. Initially, a defendant may employ any attorney desired, but the right to counsel of choice is limited by a countervailing state interest in proceeding with prosecutions on an orderly and expeditious basis. Thus the defendant cannot require the court to postpone trial for years while the selected attorney tries to fit the case into a busy schedule. In the case of indigent defendants, the trial court has discretion to consider the defendant's request for a particular attorney. However, appointment of specific counsel may in practice be made by a Public Defenders Office—if one exists in the jurisdiction—or by the trial court's use of a system of rotation among members of the Bar who have volunteered or been recruited to list themselves on the court-appointed counsel register.

Generally, defense counsel must continue to represent the defendant throughout any appeals from the trial court. However, a continuing concern in the U.S. criminal justice system is the number of frivolous appeals filed by indigent prisoners, and the extent to which defense counsel may withdraw from participation in such appeals. The temptation to file such appeals stems from the indigent prisoner's realization of "nothing to lose," because the government bears the expense of litigating appeals. For example, one infamous "jailhouse lawyer" filed twenty suits in his own behalf and assisted fellow inmates in approximately 2,000 other appeals. When an attorney appointed to represent an indigent defendant believes the defendant's appeal to be wholly frivolous, the attorney may (1) advise the court that the appeal is frivolous and request permission to withdraw from the case; (2) submit a brief referring to anything in the record that might arguably support the appeal; (3) furnish the defendant with a copy of the brief in time to allow the defendant to raise any specific points; and (4) request the court to conduct an examination and decide whether the case is wholly frivolous.[19]

EFFECTIVE ASSISTANCE OF COUNSEL

The right to the assistance of counsel guarantees the defendant reasonable opportunity to consult with counsel before and during trial. *Geders v. United States* held that the Sixth Amendment right to counsel was violated when the trial court prevented defense counsel from consulting with the defendant during an overnight recess between defendant's direct and cross-examination.[20] The opportunity to consult with counsel prior to trial also influences the effective assistance of counsel. However, the U.S. Supreme Court has refused to adopt a per se rule that late appointment of counsel, even on the day of trial, automatically establishes inadequate representation.[21] The defendant carries the burden of proving ineffective assistance of counsel prejudiced the outcome of the trial or negated the reliability of the verdict.

The determination of effective assistance of counsel rests within the "good sense and discretion" of trial courts, and depends upon the facts and circumstances of each case. The courts have been most receptive to claims of ineffective assistance of counsel when defense counsel failed to advise the defendant of fundamental rights, such as the right to a jury trial. The courts are less willing to second-guess counsel's tactical decisions about what evidence or defense to offer. In order to prevail upon a claim of **ineffective assistance of counsel,** the defendant must meet two requirements:

Ineffective assistance of counsel
deficiency of counsel's performance was so serious as to deprive the defendant of a trial with a reliable result.

First, the defendant has the burden to show that counsel's performance was deficient. "This requires showing that counsel made errors so serious that counsel was not functioning as the 'counsel' guaranteed the defendant by the Sixth Amendment."[22]

Second, the defendant must show that the deficient performance prejudiced the defense. "This requires showing that counsel's errors were so serious as to deprive the defendant of a fair trial, a trial whose result is reliable."[23]

Among the more unpleasant realities of modern-day criminal practice is the realization that disgruntled clients may subsequently allege that counsel rendered inadequate representation. In order to defend against such allegations, counsel or legal staff normally maintain extensive files documenting the services rendered to the client.

REPRESENTATION OF MULTIPLE CLIENTS

Simultaneous representation of two or more defendants by a single attorney is not a per se violation of the accused's right to effective assistance of counsel. Serious problems arise, however, when the interests of the various defendants conflict. **Conflict of interests** problems can arise: (1) during pretrial plea negotiations—when the prosecution's offer to dismiss or reduce charges against one defendant in return for testimony against another defendant places a single defense counsel in a difficult if not untenable position; (2) during trial—when a conflict may prevent the attorney from challenging the admission of evidence prejudicial to one client but favorable to another; and (3) at the sentencing stage—when counsel may be unable to minimize the culpability of one client by emphasizing that of another. Potential conflict of interests problems also arise when two law partners are appointed to represent codefendants.[24]

Conflict of interests occurs when representation of one client jeopardizes the adequate representation of another; may prevent a single attorney from representing multiple clients.

Absent an objection from counsel, the trial court may assume either that multiple representation entails no conflict of interests, or that the lawyer and clients knowingly accept such risk of conflict.[25] When an attorney informs the trial court of a conflict of interests, the judge may explore the basis of counsel's assertion.[26] Failure of the trial court to either appoint separate counsel upon request or to determine that the risk of conflict is too remote to warrant separate counsel requires automatic reversal of any conviction. The harmless error doctrine (see Chapter Sixteen) does not apply, and the defendant need not prove actual prejudice.

An attorney who chooses to represent two or more defendants is ethically required to disclose to those clients the possibility of a conflict of interests. Counsel generally insists upon receiving a signed statement from each defendant stating that (1) the client fully understands the right to employ or request the appointment of individual counsel; (2) the client recognizes the possibility of a conflict of interest developing at some later point in time; (3) counsel has adequately explained the situation; (4) the client knowingly and voluntarily waives the right to individual counsel; and (5) the client requests counsel to represent him or her and the other defendants named in the statement.

ATTORNEY–CLIENT COMMUNICATIONS

Much of the contact between the defendant and defense counsel is beyond the realm of formal law. The American Bar Association's Code of Professional Responsibility governs certain behaviors in this area, but much of the attorney's relationship with a client is guided by practical considerations that have evolved from day-to-day practice.

The initial communication between counsel and client normally focuses on whether the lawyer agrees to represent the defendant. When counsel is appointed by the court, the attorney still seeks early communication with the defendant for the purpose of determining any reasons for not representing the accused, as in a potential conflict of interests. If any such reason exists, the judge is asked to appoint substitute counsel.

If the attorney accepts the case, a thorough and detailed interview with the defendant is conducted as soon as possible, because defendants, like other witnesses, forget facts that may be crucial in the defense of the case. Counsel normally explores all aspects of the charged offense while the facts are fresh in the accused's mind. At the same time, counsel investigates the background of the defendant, including any prior criminal record. Counsel may also contact the defendant's family and friends or any persons willing to help with investigation, or with the cost of bail and the attorney's fee.

Attorney–Client Privilege

Privilege for attorney–client communications protects the confidentiality of counsel's discussions with a defendant.

The **privilege for attorney–client communications** protects the confidentiality of counsel's interview with the defendant. The privilege also applies to the attorney's staff (e.g., paralegals and investigators) who are present during the confidential communications between attorney and client or who communicate with the client on behalf of the attorney. Unless the privilege is waived, the communications cannot be revealed in court. The privilege, however, does not extend to communications that enable the client to commit a crime or an act of fraud in destroying evidence or intimidating prospective witnesses.[27] If the prosecution claims that the attorney and client engaged in the planning of a crime or some form of fraud, the trial court may review the attorney–client communication in camera (a closed hearing) in order to determine whether the communication is privileged.

After speaking with the defendant, counsel normally interviews the investigating and arresting officers to determine their version of the facts. The attorney can then assess the complexity of the case and be in a position to talk intelligently about attorney's fees and investigative expenses.

CONTRACT TO RETAIN COUNSEL

Many experienced criminal defense lawyers feel that they should be paid in full in advance because convicted defendants sometimes feel no obligation to pay counsel for a losing effort. Although setting a fee in advance might seem prudent, attorneys sometimes experience difficulty in determining the appropriate fee prior to actual preparation of the case. If the fee is set too high, the client may go elsewhere for counsel. If the fee is set too low, the attorney may invest a great deal of time and work without adequate compensation.

When the defendant appears unable to raise sufficient funds to adequately compensate counsel for time and expense, counsel must decline to accept the case, lower the fee, or advise the defendant to contact another attorney who might be able to handle the matter for a smaller amount. Responsible attorneys do not take shortcuts by doing a less than professional job because of an inadequate fee. In some situations, counsel can accept a case for a smaller amount if the defendant wishes to enter a plea of guilty; however, the attorney must not use financial considerations to pressure a defendant into admitting guilt.

If a family member or a friend provides payment for retaining counsel, the attorney must establish clearly at the outset that the duty and loyalty of counsel is to the defendant and not to the person paying for the defendant's representation. If a conflict of interests exists between the defendant and the person who has offered to pay, counsel may refuse to accept payment from the third party. Whatever financial agreement is made, the contractual agreement to employ counsel normally specifies that counsel has not promised to obtain any particular disposition of the case and that all the attorney can do is to represent the client to the best of the attorney's ability.

SUMMARY

A key to understanding criminal procedure is the judiciary's use of procedure to accomplish two purposes identified by the Crime Control Model and the Due Process Model of our criminal justice system. The Crime Control Model is primarily concerned with factual guilt, thus it focuses on procedures that enhance the accuracy of the fact-finding process. The Due Process Model, however, sometimes sacrifices conviction of those who are factually guilty in order to limit and regulate the government's power to investigate and prosecute suspected criminals.

Federal courts, particularly the U.S. Supreme Court, interpret the federal constitutional provisions that govern both the investigatory and adjudicatory stages of the criminal justice system. States courts must follow the decisions of the federal courts when interpreting the U.S. Constitution, but state courts have the final word when interpreting state provisions that increase individual rights.

The right to counsel attaches to those stages of criminal prosecution or investigation at which the accused is entitled to the expert assistance of a lawyer trained in the intricacies of the criminal justice system. Indigents who lack funds to employ counsel must be provided with representation at government expense whenever possible imprisonment is a factor. All defendants, however, may make a knowing and intelligent waiver of counsel and choose to represent themselves.

Communications between counsel and the defendant are confidential and protected by the privilege for attorney–client communications. The privilege, however, does not extend to communications made to aid the client in committing a crime or performing an act of fraud such as destroying evidence or intimidating prospective witnesses. The financial nature of the attorney–client relationship is normally governed by local practice or Canons of Ethics.

CONCEPT SUMMARY

The Right to Counsel	
Consult local law to determine what changes have been made in a particular jurisdiction.	
Employment of Counsel	The defendant has the right to employ counsel of choice in any adversarial judicial proceeding.
Court-Appointed Counsel	The defendant must be indigent and faced with possible imprisonment.
Self-Representation	A defendant who "knowingly and intelligently" waives the right to counsel is entitled to self-representation (proceed pro se).
Standby Counsel	The court may appoint standby counsel to assist a pro se defendant, but the defendant must be permitted to retain control of the case.
Withdrawal of Counsel	Permission to withdraw rests within the discretion of the trial court, which must consider the timeliness of the request to withdraw, the reasons for the request, and any conflict between the defendant and counsel.

Effective Assistance of Counsel	Counsel's performance is defective if counsel made serious errors that deprived the defendant of a fair trial or undermined the reliability of the verdict.
Representation of Multiple Defendants	Simultaneous representation of two or more defendants by a single attorney is permissible if no serious conflict of interests exists between the defendants.
Attorney–Client Communications	Such communications are confidential and may not be disclosed without the consent of the client unless the communications involved the planning of a crime or some form of fraud.

DISCUSSION QUESTIONS

1. Suppose a condemned prisoner is placed in the electric chair, the switch is thrown, but the chair malfunctions. After the electric chair is repaired, may the prisoner be required to endure a second "execution"? Consider this question in light of a general sense of justice; Due Process; or the Eighth Amendment's prohibition of cruel and unusual punishment. See *Louisiana ex rel. Francis v. Resweber,* 329 U.S. 459, 67 S.Ct. 374 (1947).

2. What alternative methods can be used to achieve the benefits of the Due Process Model—that is, controlling official misconduct—without the "costs" of freeing those who are factually guilty of a crime?

3. Should indigent defendants be given matching funds to balance whatever resources the government devotes to prosecuting the indigent defendant?

4. Why are attorneys ethically prohibited from contingent fee contracts in criminal cases? Explain the objectionable nature of an attorney and client agreement such as "If you are convicted, my fee is $X; but if you are acquitted, the fee is $X+.."

5. Why is the federal constitutional right to counsel determined by a vague concept of the commencement of judicial proceedings? Why has the Supreme Court not declared that the right to counsel attaches at arrest, at defendant's first appearance in court, or at some clearly identified point?

PRACTICE EXERCISES

1. What is the test for determining indigency in your jurisdiction? What types of financial information are considered?

2. What action should an attorney take in handling a situation in which a conflict of interests arises between the clients the attorney represents?

3. What guidelines covering the contractual relationship between lawyer and client are provided by the local jurisdiction or Bar Association?

4. What steps can an attorney take to guard against claims of ineffective assistance of counsel?

5. Has the local jurisdiction addressed how an attorney deals with a client who plans to commit perjury at trial?

6. As part of a "confidential communication," may a client surrender the murder weapon to his or her lawyer?

WEB SITE

American Civil Liberties Union Criminal Justice
ACLU.orp./issues/criminal/hmcj.html

KEY TERMS

Crime Control Model
Factual guilt
Legal guilt
Due Process Model
Investigatory process

Adjudicatory stage
Adversary judicial proceedings
Indigent
Proceed pro se

Ineffective assistance of counsel
Conflict of interests
Privilege for attorney–client
  communications

NOTES

1. 113 U. Pennsylvania Law Review 1 (1964).
2. See *Michigan v. Long*, 463 U.S. 1032, 103 S.Ct. 3469 (1983).
3. *Caplin & Drysdale Chartered v. United States*, 491 U.S. 617, 109 S.Ct. 2646 (1989).
4. *United States v. Gouveia*, 467 U.S. 180, 104 S.Ct. 2292 (1984).
5. *Argersinger v. Hamlin*, 407 U.S. 25, 92 S.Ct. 2006 (1972).
6. *Coleman v. Alabama*, 399 U.S. 1, 90 S.Ct. 1999 (1970).
7. *Brewer v. Williams*, 430 U.S. 387, 97 S.Ct. 1232 (1977).
8. *United States v. Gouveia*, 467 U.S. 180, 104 S.Ct. 2292 (1984).
9. *Johnson v. Zerbst*, 304 U.S. 458, 58 S.Ct. 1019 (1938).
10. *Bearden v. Georgia*, 461 U.S. 660, 103 S.Ct. 2064 (1983).
11. 18 U.S.C.A. § 3006A(e).
12. *Ake v. Oklahoma*, 470 U.S. 68, 105 S.Ct. 1087 (1985).
13. *United States v. Sheppard*, 559 F.Supp. 571 (E.D.Va. 1983).
14. *Wheat v. United States*, 486 U.S. 153, 108 S.Ct. 1692 (1988).
15. *Faretta v. California*, 422 U.S. 806, 95 S.Ct. 2525 (1975).
16. *Townes v. Commonwealth*, 234 Va. 307, 362 S.E.2d 650 (1987).
17. *McKaskle v. Wiggins*, 465 U.S. 168, 104 S.Ct. 944 (1984).
18. *Morris v. Slappy*, 461 U.S. 1, 103 S.Ct. 1610 (1983).
19. *Anders v. California*, 386 U.S. 738, 87 S.Ct. 1396 (1967).
20. *Geders v. United States*, 425 U.S. 80, 96 S.Ct. 1330 (1976).
21. *Chambers v. Maroney*, 399 U.S. 42, 90 S.Ct. 1975 (1970).
22. *Strickland v. Washington*, 466 U.S. 668, 104 S.Ct. 2052 (1984).
23. *Hill v. Lockhart*, 474 U.S. 52, 106 S.Ct. 366 (1985).
24. *Burger v. Kemp*, 483 U.S. 776, 107 S.Ct. 3114 (1987).
25. *Cuyler v. Sullivan*, 446 U.S. 335, 100 S.Ct. 1708 (1980).
26. *Holloway v. Arkansas*, 435 U.S. 475, 98 S.Ct. 1173 (1978).
27. *United States v. Zolin*, 491 U.S. 554, 109 S.Ct. 2619 (1989).

SEIZURES OF A PERSON AND IDENTIFICATION PROCEDURES

Chapter 9

The Fourth Amendment to the U.S. Constitution states: The right of the people to be secure in their persons, houses, papers, and effects, against unreasonable searches and seizures, shall not be violated, and no Warrants shall issue, but upon probable cause, supported by Oath or affirmation, and particularly describing the place to be searched, and the persons or things to be seized.

The Fourth Amendment is the prime source of constitutional law governing arrests and temporary detentions of a person, which are discussed in this chapter. Search and seizure of property and government monitoring of private conversations are covered in the following two chapters. An arrest often leads to identification procedures that may trigger the Sixth Amendment right to counsel and the Fourteenth Amendment Due Process clause. The constitutional considerations governing identification procedures are addressed later in this chapter.

ARRESTS

In the course of a typical arrest the suspect is taken into custody, searched, transported to the police station, and subjected to a booking process. The suspect then faces a bail hearing. The **booking process** is primarily clerical in nature and consists of (1) completing the arrest report and preparing the arrestee's permanent police record, (2) fingerprinting and photographing the accused, and (3) entering on the police "blotter" the name of the arrestee, the personal effects found in the arrestee's possession, and the date, time, and place of arrest.

A full custodial arrest, followed by a booking procedure and a bail hearing, is costly in terms of time, money, and personnel. It also may cause the accused public embarrassment and financial or emotional hardship. Accordingly, many jurisdictions substitute a summons for an arrest warrant when the suspect is accused of minor offenses, including most misdemeanors. A **summons** commands the accused to appear at a stated time and place before a court of appropriate jurisdiction. Rather than being taken into custody, the accused gives a written promise to appear at the time and place stated in the summons. Willful violation of this promise to appear may be punished as contempt of court or as a separate crime under local law.

Arrest Warrants

Arrest warrants may be issued by a judge, magistrate, or in some jurisdictions, a clerk of court. An arrest warrant (see Exhibit 9–1) must be based upon **probable cause:** facts leading a person of reasonable caution to believe that the person to be apprehended has committed a specific offense. The facts constituting probable cause must be set forth in a **complaint** (shown in Exhibit 9–2) sworn to by a police officer or any other person familiar with the facts.

The only difference between the facts needed to establish probable cause and those needed to convict is the degree or quantum of proof, that is, reasonable belief rather than proof beyond a reasonable doubt. "Probable cause is determined by objective facts, not the subjective opinion of a police officer."[1] For example, in *Golden v. Commonwealth,*[2] an arrest for attempted prostitution lacked probable cause because although the defendant had verbally offered sexual intercourse, the defendant committed no overt act that would constitute an attempt. The court stated, however, that there was objective probable cause to arrest for solicitation to commit prostitution. Thus the officer had achieved the right result—arrest—for the wrong crime. The court then upheld the arrest because "the absence of probable cause to believe that a person committed a particular crime for which a person was arrested does not create an invalid arrest if, at the time of the arrest, the police had sufficient [objective] information to support an arrest of the person on a different charge."

Booking process
the primarily clerical function of recording information relating to the arrestee's identity.

Summons
commands the accused to appear at a stated time and place before a court of appropriate jurisdiction.

Probable cause
a reasonable belief that the suspect has committed a crime.

Complaint
sworn statement of facts establishing probable cause that a person committed a crime.

WARRANT OF ARREST – FELONY

VA. CODE §§ 19.2-71,-72

General District Court ☐ Criminal ☐ Traffic

☐ Juvenile and Domestic Relations District Court

CITY OR COUNTY

TO ANY AUTHORIZED OFFICER:

You are hereby commanded in the name of the Commonwealth of Virginia forthwith to arrest and bring the Accused before this Court to answer the charge that the Accused, within this city or county, on or about ...., did unlawfully and feloniously in violation of Section ...., Code of Virginia:

I, the undersigned, have found probable cause to believe that the Accused committed the offense charged, based on the sworn statements of ...., Complainant.

....   ☐ CLERK ☐ MAGISTRATE ☐ JUDGE
DATE AND TIME ISSUED

FORM DC-312 9/94 PC (114:3-021 4/95)

CASE NO. ....

HEARING DATE AND TIME

ACCUSED: ....

LAST NAME, FIRST NAME, MIDDLE NAME

ADDRESS/LOCATION

COMPLETE DATA BELOW IF KNOWN

RACE	SEX	BORN MO. DAY YR.	HT. FT. IN.	WGT.	EYES	HAIR

SSN

Commonwealth of Virginia
WARRANT OF ARREST
FELONY

☐ EXECUTED by delivering a copy to the Accused named above on this day:

....
DATE AND TIME OF SERVICE

............................, ARRESTING OFFICER

....
BADGE NO., AGENCY AND JURISDICTION

for ....
SHERIFF

Attorney for the Accused:

EXHIBIT 9–1
Arrest Warrant

CRIMINAL COMPLAINT

RULES 3A:3 and 7C:3

☐ General District Court

☐ Juvenile and Domestic Relations District Court

Under penalty of perjury, I, the undersigned Complainant swear or affirm that I have reason to believe that the Accused committed a criminal offense, on or about

_____ in the ☐ City ☐ County ☐ Town
DATE

of _____

I base my belief on the following facts:

The statements above are true and accurate to the best of my knowledge and belief.

In making this complaint, I have read and fully understand the following:
• By swearing to these facts, I agree to appear in court and testify if a warrant or summons is issued.
• The charge in this warrant cannot be dismissed except by the court, even at my request.

_____
SIGNATURE OF COMPLAINANT

_____
NAME OF COMPLAINANT

Subscribed and sworn to before me this day.

_____
DATE AND TIME

☐ CLERK ☐ MAGISTRATE ☐ JUDGE

FORM DC-311 9/94 PC (114:3-021 11/94)

CASE NO.

CRIMINAL COMPLAINT

ACCUSED: Name, Description, Address/Location

LAST NAME, FIRST NAME, MIDDLE NAME

COMPLETE DATA BELOW IF KNOWN

RACE	SEX	BORN MO.	DAY	YR.	HT. FT.	IN.	WGT.	EYES	HAIR

SSN

other identification or location information

EXHIBIT 9–2
Complaint

When issued, the arrest warrant must (1) be directed to a law enforcement official, (2) name the accused or set forth a description by which the accused can be identified with reasonable certainty, (3) describe the offense charged, (4) command that the accused be arrested and brought before a court of appropriate jurisdiction in the city, county, or town in which the alleged offense was committed, and (5) be signed by the issuing officer.

Generally, the execution of an arrest warrant carries no time limitation. The accused has no right to a "speedy arrest," thus delays in executing an arrest warrant do not affect the legality of the arrest.[3] When executing an arrest warrant, a police officer must endorse the date of execution and return the warrant to a judicial official having authority to grant bail. An arresting officer may use reasonable force to apprehend any suspect, but deadly force is constitutionally permissible only when an officer has probable cause to believe that a suspected felon poses a threat of serious physical harm, either to the arresting officer or to others.[4]

Most of the cases dealing with excessive force occur in the context of civil or criminal proceedings against the officers alleged to have used excessive force. The most recent and notorious example involved Amadou Diallo, a West African immigrant killed by New York City police officers in 1999. When four police officers approached Diallo, they mistakenly believed that he was reaching for a weapon (in fact he was unarmed and reaching for his wallet). The officers fired 41 shots, 19 of which struck and killed Diallo. The use of so much firepower led to charges of murder against the officers, but all four were acquitted by a jury.

Citizens are legally entitled to resist a police officer's use of excessive force, but jurisdictions differ as to whether citizens may resist an arrest solely because it is unlawful. (For example, the arresting officers do not use excessive force, but they lack probable cause for the arrest.) At common law, a citizen could use reasonable force to resist any unlawful arrest. Under principles of self-defense, the police officer was deemed to be an aggressor when attempting the unlawful arrest. Today, however, most jurisdictions forbid the use of physical force by citizens. Instead, the citizen must submit to the arrest and subsequently litigate the propriety of the arrest in court.

Warrantless Arrests

In theory, an arrest warrant should be obtained prior to taking an accused into custody. In practice, however, police officers often must respond to an evolving situation that does not allow time to obtain a warrant. For example, no court would require an officer to walk away from a bank robbery and return only when the officer has a warrant to arrest the robbers. In the absence of an emergency, however, the U.S. Supreme Court has recognized a constitutional distinction between warrantless arrests in public, and arrests in a suspect's dwelling.

Warrantless Arrests in Public In *United States v. Watson,* the U.S. Supreme Court upheld a **warrantless felony arrest** in a public place.[5] Even though the police officer failed to obtain an arrest warrant in a nonemergency situation in *Watson,* the Court upheld the warrantless arrest based on two factors: (1) the common law's approval of warrantless arrests and (2) the potential danger of allowing suspected felons to remain at liberty in the community. As long as the police have probable cause to arrest, they need not obtain a warrant before arresting a suspected felon in a public place.

The *Watson* case dealt only with arrests for felonies, but many states follow the common law distinction between warrantless arrests for felonies and misdemeanors. At common law, a warrantless misdemeanor arrest was invalid unless it was a **misdemeanor committed in the arresting officer's presence.** An offense is committed in the arresting officer's presence when the officer has direct personal knowledge—through sight, hearing, or other senses—that a misdemeanor is then

Warrantless felony arrest taking a suspected felon into custody, which may take place in a public place even though the police had adequate opportunity to procure an arrest warrant.

and there taking place. The officer's conclusion that a misdemeanor has occurred in the past does not justify a warrantless arrest.

United States v. Watson permitted a warrantless arrest based on a police officer's determination that there was probable cause to believe that the suspect committed a felony. *Gerstein v. Pugh*, however, required that the arrestee be taken before a judicial officer who must make an independent determination as to whether police officers had probable cause to arrest the suspect.

Warrantless Arrests in a Dwelling   In *Payton v. New York,* the U.S. Supreme Court drew "a firm line at the entrance to the house. Absent exigent circumstances, that

> **Misdemeanor committed in the arresting officer's presence** the officer has direct personal knowledge, through sight, hearing, or other senses, that a misdemeanor is then and there being committed.

GERSTEIN v. PUGH
Supreme Court of the United States, 1975
420 U.S. 103, 95 S.Ct. 854

JUSTICE POWELL delivered the opinion of the Court: A policeman's on-the-scene assessment of probable cause provides legal justification for arresting a person suspected of crime, and for a brief period of detention to take the administrative steps incident to arrest. Once the suspect is in custody, however, the reasons that justify dispensing with the magistrate's neutral judgment evaporate. There no longer is any danger that the suspect will escape or commit further crimes while the police submit their evidence to a magistrate. And, while the State's reasons for taking summary action subside, the suspect's need for a neutral determination of probable cause increases significantly. The consequences of prolonged detention may be more serious than the interference occasioned by arrest. Pretrial confinement may imperil the suspect's job, interrupt his source of income, and impair his family relationships. Even pretrial release may be accompanied by burdensome conditions that effect a significant restraint on liberty. When the stakes are this high, the detached judgment of a neutral magistrate is essential if the Fourth Amendment is to furnish meaningful protection from unfounded interference with liberty.

[The State] must provide a fair and reliable determination of probable cause as a condition for any significant pretrial restraint on liberty, and this determination must be made by a judicial officer whether before or promptly after arrest.

threshold may not reasonably be crossed without a warrant."[6] In order to enter the suspect's dwelling and arrest the suspect, the police must either possess an arrest warrant or be able to point to exigent circumstances that permit a warrantless entry and subsequently, an **arrest in a suspect's dwelling.**

The types of exigent circumstances recognized by the courts include (1) danger to police officers or others, (2) the officer's reasonable belief that contraband is about to be destroyed or removed from the dwelling, (3) information that the possessors of contraband are aware that the police may be on their trail, and (4) the likelihood of escape if the suspects are not swiftly apprehended. The U.S. Supreme Court also recognized that when an arrest begins in a public place, the police may continue their "hot pursuit" into the suspect's dwelling.[7]

Watson established one rule for warrantless arrests in public; *Payton* established a second rule for warrantless arrests in the suspect's dwelling. *Steagald v. United States* established a third rule, which requires the police to obtain a search warrant before entering a third-party dwelling to search for a suspect.

> **Arrest in a suspect's dwelling** taking a suspect into custody that requires either an arrest warrant or exigent circumstances that permit a warrantless entry.

STEAGALD v. UNITED STATES
Supreme Court of the United States, 1981
451 U.S. 204, 101 S.Ct. 1642

[The police entered Steagald's home in an effort to find one Lyons, for whom they had an arrest warrant. They did not find Lyons, but did find drugs in plain view, resulting in Steagald's prosecution and conviction.]

JUSTICE MARSHALL delivered the opinion of the Court: Whether the arrest warrant issued in this case adequately safeguarded the interests protected by the Fourth Amendment depends upon what the warrant authorized the agents to do. To be sure, the warrant embodied a judicial finding that there was probable cause to believe that Ricky Lyons had committed a felony, and the warrant therefore authorized the officers to seize Lyons. However, the agents sought to do more than use the warrant to arrest Lyons in a public place or in his home; instead, they relied on the warrant as legal authority to enter the home of a third person based on their belief that Ricky Lyons might be a guest there.

Regardless of how reasonable this belief might have been, it was never subjected to the detached scrutiny of a judicial officer. Thus, while the warrant in this case may have protected Lyons from an unreasonable seizure, it did absolutely nothing to protect [Steagald's] privacy interest in being free from an unreasonable invasion and search of his home. Instead, [Steagald's] only protection from an illegal entry and search was the agent's personal determination of probable cause. In the absence of exigent circumstances, we have consistently held that such judicially untested determinations are not reliable enough to justify an entry into a person's home to arrest him without a warrant, or a search of a home for objects in the absence of a search warrant. We see no reason to depart from this settled course when the search of a home is for a person rather than an object.

Consequences of an Illegal Arrest

Because an upcoming chapter addresses the Fourth Amendment exclusionary rule—which bars a trial court from considering evidence obtained in violation of the Fourth Amendment—the present section merely highlights those aspects of the exclusionary rule that apply directly to illegal arrests.

An illegal arrest does not deprive the trial court of jurisdiction to convict the defendant.[8] Even police misconduct, such as the use of excessive force or an illegal abduction of the defendant from another jurisdiction, does not eliminate the government's right to bring the defendant to trial. Although an illegal arrest does not affect the court's jurisdiction over the defendant, the illegal arrest does bear upon the evidence obtained from the defendant. (Permissible searches incident to arrest are addressed in Chapter ten.)

Derivative evidence
evidentiary items obtained as a result of an illegal arrest.

The Fourth Amendment exclusionary rule prohibits the introduction of **derivative evidence**: evidence derived from or obtained as a result of an illegal arrest. (The U.S. Supreme Court's metaphor is that such derivative evidence is the fruit of the poisonous tree.) If the arrest itself is illegal, all evidence seized in the course of the arrest and all evidence closely connected with the arrest may be inadmissible at trial. The types of evidence that may be suppressed include (1) tangible items seized during the arrest, (2) physical evidence such as fingerprints taken from the arrestee, (3) confessions obtained from the arrestee, and (4) eyewitness identifications contaminated by the illegal arrest.

TEMPORARY DETENTION

Prior to the decision in *Terry v. Ohio*, the terms *arrest* and *seizure* of a person were synonymous for purposes of the Fourth Amendment. *Terry*, however, recognized that limited seizures (**temporary detentions**) falling short of arrest are also covered by the Amendment. In *Terry v. Ohio,* a police officer observed three suspects apparently "casing" a store for a robbery. An officer who observes this type of suspicious activity must decide whether to arrest, to do nothing, or to take action that falls somewhere between these two extremes. The court, in *Terry v. Ohio* approved of a police officer's decision to stop and frisk suspects who threaten another's safety.

Confronted with a choice between ordering the police officer to do nothing or holding the Fourth Amendment inapplicable to anything short of a "full-blown" arrest, the *Terry* Court created a subcategory of Fourth Amendment seizures. In contrast to an arrestee, a detainee is not subjected to a full search nor is the person transported to the police station. In the course of a typical temporary detention, the

Temporary detentions
the suspect is briefly detained, at which time an officer may pat down the suspect's clothing to determine whether the suspect possesses a weapon.

TERRY v. OHIO
Supreme Court of the United States, 1968
392 U.S. 1, 88 S.Ct. 1868

CHIEF JUSTICE WARREN delivered the opinion of the Court:

Street encounters between citizens and police officers are incredibly rich in diversity. They range from wholly friendly exchanges of pleasantries or mutually useful information to hostile confrontations of armed men involving arrests, or injuries, or loss of life.

On the one hand, it is frequently argued that in dealing with the rapidly unfolding and often dangerous situations on city streets the police are in need of an escalating set of flexible responses, graduated in relation to the amount of information they possess. For this purpose it is urged that distinctions should be made between a "stop" and an "arrest" (or a "seizure" of a person), and between a "frisk" and a "search." Thus, it is argued the police should be allowed to "stop" a person and detain him briefly for questioning upon suspicion that he may be connected with criminal activity. Upon suspicion that the person may be armed, the police should have the power to "frisk" him for weapons.

On the other side the argument is made that the authority of the police must be strictly circumscribed by the law of arrest and search as it has developed to date in the traditional jurisprudence of the Fourth Amendment. It is contended with some force that there is not—and cannot be—a variety of police activity which does not depend solely upon the voluntary cooperation of the citizen and yet which stops short of an arrest based upon probable cause to make such an arrest.

* * *

It is quite plain that the Fourth Amendment governs "seizures" of the person which do not eventuate in a trip to the station house and prosecution for crime—"arrests" in traditional terminology. It must be recognized that whenever a police officer accosts an individual and restrains his freedom to walk away, he has "seized" that person. And it is nothing less than sheer torture of the English language to suggest that a careful exploration of the outer surface of a person's clothing all over his or her body in an attempt to find weapons is not a "search." Moreover, it is simply fantastic to urge that such a procedure performed in public by a policeman while the citizen stands helpless, perhaps facing a wall with his hands raised, is a "petty indignity." It is a serious intrusion upon the sanctity of the person, which may inflict great indignity and arouse strong resentment, and it is not to be undertaken lightly. We therefore reject the notions that the Fourth Amendment does not come into play at all as a limitation upon police conduct if the officers stop short of something called a "technical arrest" or a "full-blown search."

Each case of this sort will, of course, have to be decided on its own facts. We merely hold today that where a police officer observes unusual conduct which leads him reasonably to conclude in light of his experience that criminal activity may be afoot and that the persons with whom he is dealing may be armed and presently dangerous; where in the course of investigating this behavior he identifies himself as a policeman and makes reasonable inquires; and where nothing in the initial stages of the encounter serves to dispel his reasonable fear for his own or others' safety, he is entitled for the protection of himself and others in the area to conduct a carefully limited search of the outer clothing of such persons in an attempt to discover weapons which might be used to assault him. Such a search is a reasonable search under the Fourth Amendment, and any weapons seized may properly be introduced in evidence against the person from whom they were taken.

suspect is briefly detained on the street. To determine whether the suspect possesses a weapon, an officer may pat down the outer clothing. Because *Terry* extended the Fourth Amendment to temporary detentions, the applicability of the amendment no longer turns upon whether the seizure of a person is classified as an arrest under federal or state law.

Although the Fourth Amendment now applies to both arrests and temporary detentions, the two forms of seizures of a person are distinguished for purposes of determining whether they are "reasonable" seizures within the meaning of the amendment. In *Terry* the Court acknowledged that "full-blown" arrests and full searches of the person incident to arrest require full probable cause (a reasonable belief) that the suspect has committed a crime. In contrast, temporary detentions and a limited search incident to detention require only a lower standard of **reasonable suspicion** that the suspect has committed or is committing a crime. Following the decision in *Terry*, the U.S. Supreme Court developed additional rules governing the definition of a temporary detention, the grounds for a detention, the justification for a frisk or other investigation, and the scope of the investigation.

Reasonable suspicion
the required basis for a temporary detention; the suspect has committed or is committing a crime.

Definition of a Temporary Detention

The *Terry* Court recognized that: "Street encounters between citizens and police officers are incredibly rich in diversity. They range from wholly friendly exchanges of pleasantries or mutually useful information to hostile confrontations of armed men involving arrests, or injuries, or loss of life." Faced with an almost unlimited variety of contacts between citizens and police officers, the Supreme Court has attempted to distinguish between wholly voluntary encounters, which are not covered by the Fourth Amendment, and encounters that lose their voluntary nature and become seizures of the person. The Court has employed three tests to determine when a person has been seized for purposes of the Fourth Amendment:

1. **The *Brower* intentional means test.** In *Brower v. Inyo County*[9] the Supreme Court stated that "a seizure occurs only when there is a governmental termination of freedom of movement through means intentionally applied." Under the facts of *Brower,* a seizure occurred when the police erected a roadblock that stopped and killed a fleeing motorist. The Court explained that the crash into the roadblock was a seizure because the roadblock was *intended* to forcibly stop a motorist who refused to voluntarily comply with a police request to stop. *Brower* was subsequently distinguished in *Sacramento v. Lewis,*[10] which held that "no Fourth Amendment seizure would take place where a pursuing police car sought to stop the suspect only by the show of authority represented by flashing lights and continuing pursuit, but *accidentally* stopped the suspect by crashing into him."

2. **The *Mendenhall* reasonable person act.** *United States v. Mendenhall,*[11] employed an objective standard to define a seizure: whether a reasonable person under the circumstances would have believed that he was not free to leave. The Court explained that it is not a violation of the Fourth Amendment for police to approach an individual and ask if he is willing to stop and answer questions. Nor does a police officer's merely identifying himself as a police officer convert the encounter into a seizure of the person, so long as the citizen may decline the officer's invitation and walk away without interference from the officer. But when the circumstances indicate that the citizen would not be permitted to leave, a seizure has occurred and the police must comply with the Fourth Amendment. Thus the person approached "may not be detained even momentarily without reasonable, objective grounds for doing so; and his refusal to listen or answer does not, without more, furnish those grounds."[12] The relevant circumstances indicating that a person is not free to leave include the threatening presence of several officers, the display

of a weapon by an officer, some physical touching of the person of the citizen or the use of language or tone of voice indicating that compliance with the officer's request might be compelled.

3. **The *Hodari* submission or touching test.** In *California v. Hodari D.*, the U.S. Supreme Court held that a seizure occurs (1) when the officer touches the body of the accused, or (2) when the accused submits to a show of authority. Unlike the *Mendenhall* reasonable person test, the issue in *Hodari D.* was not what a reasonable person would have assumed under the circumstances, but what the accused actually did in response to the police officer's show of authority.

CALIFORNIA v. HODARI D.
499 U.S. 621, 111 S.Ct. 1547 (1991)

[A chase began when a group of inner city youths fled at the approach of an unmarked police car. Hodari fled down an alley where he was pursued by one of the police officers. In the course of the pursuit, Hodari discarded a small item. As Hodari eluded the pursuing officer, another officer circled around, cut off Hodari's escape route and tackled him to the ground. The officers then retrieved the item that Hodari discarded, which proved to be crack cocaine. The California Court suppressed the cocaine as the fruit of an illegal seizure after finding that the defendant "had been seized when he saw the officer running towards him, and that this seizure was unreasonable under the Fourth Amendment" because the State conceded that the officer did not have the reasonable suspicion required to justify stopping the defendant].

JUSTICE SCALIA delivered the Court's opinion:
The common law recognized that an arrest occurs when a police officer applies physical force to the defendant. The present case does not involve the application of any physical force; Hodari was untouched by the police officers at the time he discarded the cocaine. His defense relies instead upon the proposition that a seizure occurs when the officer, by means of physical force or *show of authority*, has in some way restrained the liberty of a citizen. Hodari contends that the officer's pursuit qualified as a show of authority calling upon Hodari to halt. The narrow question before us is whether a seizure occurs even though the subject does not yield. We hold that it does not.

The Fourth Amendment does not remotely apply to the prospect of a policeman yelling 'Stop, in the name of the law!' at a fleeing form that continues to flee. That is no seizure. An arrest requires *either* physical force *or*, where that is absent, *submission* to the assertion of authority.

JUSTICE STEVENS dissenting
The deterrent purposes of the exclusionary rule focus on the conduct of law enforcement officers, and on discouraging improper behavior on their part, and not on the reaction of the citizen to the show of force. In the present case, if the police officer had succeeded in tackling Hodari before he dropped the rock of cocaine, the rock unquestionably would have been excluded as the fruit of the officer's unlawful seizure. Instead, under the Court's logic-chopping analysis, the exclusionary rule has no application because an attempt to make an unconstitutional seizure is beyond the coverage of the Fourth Amendment, no matter how outrageous or unreasonable the officer's conduct may be.

The Supreme Court's three tests for a seizure of a person focus on different factors: *Brower* focuses on the arresting officer's state of mind; *Mendenhall* examines the perception of an objectively reasonable person; and *Hodari D.* considers the actual suspect's conduct when confronted with a show of authority. All three tests, however, serve the same purpose—distinguishing a voluntary police–citizen encounter from a seizure within the meaning of the Fourth Amendment. As long as the encounter between citizen and police officer remains voluntary and the citizen is free to terminate the encounter, it is not a Fourth Amendment seizure. In such situations, the police need not justify their decision to approach the citizen. However, the citizen who is not free to leave has been seized; therefore the police must establish appropriate constitutional grounds for having detained the citizen without that person's consent.

Grounds for a Detention

In *Terry*, the Supreme Court permitted a temporary detention "where a police officer observes unusual conduct which leads him reasonably to conclude in light of his experience that criminal activity may be afoot." This language is obviously vague, but two clear principles have emerged from *Terry* and subsequent cases:

1. Reasonable suspicion for a temporary detention is a lesser standard than the requirement of probable cause (reasonable belief) for an arrest.
2. Reasonable suspicion must, in most cases, be based on specific, objective facts.

The distinction between reasonable suspicion based on specific facts and an "inchoate and unparticularized suspicion or hunch" turns upon the factual situations of particular cases.[13] The types of specific facts that the courts have held to justify a temporary detention include:

1. Police observation of suspicious conduct such as the suspect's apparent "casing" of a robbery site in *Terry*
2. The suspect's location near the scene of a recent crime
3. Specific information from a reliable informer that the suspect is committing a crime
4. The suspect's match with a drug courier profile
5. A "wanted flyer" for the detained person
6. "Unprovoked flight" from the police is suggestive of wrongdoing, and therefore "is a pertinent factor in determining reasonable suspicion"[14]
7. Refusal to leave an area secured by police officers

The types of specific facts deemed not adequate to justify a temporary detention include:

1. An anonymous tip does not justify a stop and frisk merely because it alleges the illegal possession of a firearm[15]
2. Physical presence in a "high-crime" area
3. A police officer's "inchoate and unparticularized suspicion or hunch"
4. A defendant's "nervousness and refusal to make eye contact with a police officer"
5. "Criminal street gang members loitering" with one another or with other persons in a public place[16]

Although a temporary detention normally requires specific facts indicating the likelihood of criminal activity, in a few situations the U.S. Supreme Court has upheld a temporary seizure based on a statistical likelihood that sought-after evidence will be obtained. For example, *Michigan Dept. of State Police v. Sitz* upheld highway sobriety checkpoints on the basis of a statistical likelihood that intoxicated motorists would be encountered.[17] See also *National Treasury Employees Union v. Von Raab*, which upholds mandatory drug testing of Customs Service employees.[18] Another case to review is *Skinner v. Railway Labor Executives' Ass'n*, which upholds mandatory drug testing of railroad employees following major train accidents.[19] The use of statistical likelihoods has surfaced most often with respect to roadblocks and drug courier profiles.

Roadblocks Motorists stopped for any purpose at roadblocks or checkpoints set up by government officials on public highways and streets have been seized for Fourth Amendment purposes. Sobriety checkpoints and roadblocks to monitor compliance with motor vehicle licensing laws are constitutional when operated pursuant to a practice embodying neutral criteria. For example, when the officers at the checkpoint have no discretion regarding which vehicles to stop; instead they impartially stop every southbound vehicle, or every fifth vehicle, or the like. Even if the initial stop is lawful, police may not detain the vehicle beyond the brief period necessary to perform a quick and cursory check for alcohol or licensing violations, unless the police observe facts giving rise to a reasonable suspicion that some violation has occurred.

Although the courts have upheld sobriety and licensing checkpoints, the Supreme Court recently condemned the use of motorist checkpoints designed to uncover illegal drugs.

CITY OF INDIANAPOLIS v. EDMOND
531 U.S. 32, 121 S.Ct. 447 (2000)

JUSTICE O'CONNOR delivered the opinion of the Court:

In August 1998, the city of Indianapolis began to operate vehicle checkpoints on Indianapolis roads in an effort to interdict unlawful drugs. The city conducted six such roadblocks between August and November that year, stopping 1,161 vehicles and arresting 104 motorists. Fifty-five arrests were for drug-related crimes, while 49 were for offenses unrelated to drugs. The overall "hit rate" of the program was thus approximately nine percent. At each checkpoint location, the police stop a predetermined number of vehicles. Approximately 30 officers are stationed at the checkpoint. At least one officer approaches the vehicle, advises the driver that he or she is being stopped briefly at a drug checkpoint, and asks the driver to produce a license and registration. The officer also looks for signs of impairment and conducts an open-view examination of the vehicle from the outside. A narcotics-detection dog walks around the outside of each stopped vehicle.

Respondents were each stopped at a narcotics checkpoint, and then filed a lawsuit on behalf of themselves and the class of all motorists who had been stopped or were subject to being stopped in the future at the Indianapolis drug checkpoints. Respondents claimed that the roadblocks violated the Fourth Amendment of the United States Constitution. Respondents requested declaratory and injunctive relief for the class, as well as damages and attorney's fees for themselves.

A search or seizure is ordinarily unreasonable in the absence of individualized suspicion of wrongdoing. We have recognized only limited circumstances in which the usual rule does not apply. For example, we have upheld brief, suspicionless seizures of motorists at a fixed Border Patrol checkpoint designed to intercept illegal aliens, and at a sobriety checkpoint aimed at removing drunk drivers from the road. In none of these cases, however, did we indicate approval of a checkpoint program whose primary purpose was to detect evidence of ordinary criminal wrongdoing. Each of the checkpoint programs that we have approved was designed primarily to serve purposes closely related to the problems of policing the border or the necessity of ensuring roadway safety. Because the primary purpose of the Indianapolis narcotics checkpoint program is to uncover evidence of ordinary criminal wrongdoing, the program contravenes the Fourth Amendment.

Petitioners emphasize the severe and intractable nature of the drug problem as justification for the checkpoint program. There is no doubt that traffic in illegal narcotics creates social harms of the first magnitude. The same can be said of various other illegal activities, if only to a lesser degree. But the gravity of the threat alone cannot be dispositive of questions concerning what means law enforcement officers may employ to pursue a given purpose. We cannot sanction stops justified only by the generalized and ever-present possibility that interrogation and inspection may reveal that any given motorist has committed some crime. [Were we to hold otherwise] there would be little check on the ability of the authorities to construct roadblocks for almost any conceivable law enforcement purpose. Without drawing the line at roadblocks designed primarily to serve the general interest in crime control, the Fourth Amendment would do little to prevent such intrusions from becoming a routine part of American life.

Because the primary purpose of the Indianapolis checkpoint program is ultimately indistinguishable from the general interest in crime control, the checkpoints violate the Fourth Amendment.

Although the police may not establish a roadblock for the primary purpose of discovering drugs, there is no legal prohibition against police officers being alert to the possible presence of drugs while conducting a lawful checkpoint for alcohol or licensing violations. The U.S. Supreme Court has held that "subjective intentions play no role in ordinary, probable-cause Fourth Amendment analysis," and traffic-violation stops are often used as a pretext for a narcotics search.[20]

Drug Courier Profiles In combination with roadblocks or standing alone, drug courier profiles have been used to justify seizures of suspicious persons, particularly at airports, train and bus stations, or interstate highways. The use of a drug courier profile has received mixed results in the courts, partially because there are so many different profiles currently being used by many state and federal agencies. Most courts have held that a drug courier profile, without more, does not create reasonable suspicion justifying the seizure of a citizen. The U.S. Supreme Court has indicated that its analysis of the underlying facts constituting reasonable suspicion is not affected by whether some government agency labels those facts as all or part of a drug courier profile.[21]

Grounds for an Investigation

The initial detention of the suspect is permissible if based on adequate grounds, but separate grounds are required for further intrusions upon the suspect's right to privacy. *Terry* recognized that police officers may frisk or pat down the suspect in order to discover weapons that might be used to harm the officer or others nearby. A frisk consists of a patdown of the suspect's outer clothing, although this patdown may be extensive. *Terry* described a typical frisk: "the officer must feel with sensitive fingers every portion of the prisoner's body. A thorough search must be made of the prisoner's arms and armpits, waistline and back, the groin and area about the testicles, and entire surface of the legs down to the feet."

A frisk, however, does not automatically follow every valid detention. The police officer must have a reasonable basis for concluding that the detainee is an armed and dangerous person. The circumstances to be considered in evaluating the officer's belief include: (1) the area where the detention occurs (e.g., a high-crime neighborhood); (2) the time of the detention (e.g., daylight or late at night); (3) any suspicious conduct of the person accosted (e.g., nervousness at the approach of the officer); (4) the character of the offense the individual is suspected of committing (e.g., a crime of violence); and (5) the presence of drugs. More than one court has stated that "where there are drugs, there are almost always guns."[22]

In contrast to the frisk that may accompany a stop for a potentially violent crime, the courts have limited what police may do when conducting a routine traffic stop.

The officer may request a driver's license and vehicle registration, run a computer check, and issue a citation. When the driver has produced a valid license and proof that he is entitled to operate the car, he must be allowed to proceed on his way, without being subject to further delay by police for additional questioning. Any further detention for questioning is beyond the scope of the *Terry* stop and therefore illegal unless the officer has a reasonable suspicion of a serious crime.[23]

Although "stop and frisk" law was initially based on the need to protect police officers, subsequent cases have justified intrusions upon privacy designed to serve other substantial governmental interests, such as "effective crime prevention and detection." For example, *United States v. Place* approved a temporary seizure of personal luggage "for the purpose of pursuing a limited course of investigation, short of opening the luggage, that would quickly confirm or dispel the authorities' suspicion."[24] The limited investigation in the case consisted of subjecting the luggage to sniffing for illegal drugs by a specially trained police dog.

Scope of the Investigation

A frisk of the suspect may not be initiated for the purpose of seizing evidence; the sole purpose of a frisk is to discover weapons. The officer may intrude beneath the surface of a suspect's clothing only if the officer feels a hard object, which could be a weapon, or if the officer recognizes the object as seizable evidence. *Minnesota v. Dickerson* recognized this "plain feel" doctrine.

MINNESOTA v. DICKERSON
Supreme Court of the United States, 1993
508 U.S. 366 , 113 S.Ct. 2130

The defendant exited a notorious "crack house" and began walking toward the police. Upon spotting the squad car and making eye contact with one of the officers, the defendant abruptly halted and began walking in the opposite direction. His suspicion aroused, the officer ordered defendant to stop and submit to a patdown search. The search revealed no weapons, but the officer testified that: "As I pat-searched the front of his body, I felt a lump, a small lump, in the front pocket. I examined it with my fingers and it slid and it felt to be a lump of crack cocaine in cellophane." The officer then reached into defendant's pocket and retrieved a small plastic bag containing one fifth of one gram of crack cocaine.

JUSTICE WHITE delivered the opinion of the Court:
The purpose of a *Terry* search is not to discover evidence of crime, but to allow the officer to pursue his investigation without fear of violence. If the protective search goes beyond what is necessary to determine if the suspect is armed, it is no longer valid under *Terry* and its fruits will be suppressed.

We have already held that police officers, at least under certain circumstances, may seize contraband de-

tected during the lawful execution of a *Terry* search. If a police officer lawfully pats down a suspect's outer clothing and feels an object whose contour or mass makes its identity immediately apparent, there has been no invasion of the suspect's privacy beyond that already authorized by the officer's search for weapons; if the object is contraband, its warrantless seizure would be justified by the same practical considerations that inhere in the plain view context.

It remains to apply these principles to the facts of this case. Although the officer was lawfully in a position to feel the lump in defendant's pocket, because *Terry* entitled him to place his hands upon defendant's jacket, the court below determined that the incriminating character of the object was not immediately apparent to him. Rather, the officer determined that the item was contraband only after conducting a further search, one not authorized by *Terry* or by any other exception to the warrant requirement. Because this further search of defendant's pocket was constitutionally invalid, the seizure of the cocaine that followed is likewise unconstitutional.

Protective sweep
a cursory and limited search for weapons within the area under a suspect's immediate control.

Although *Terry* dealt only with a frisk of the person, *Michigan v. Long* extended a *Terry* search for weapons into those areas where the suspect might reach for weapons, for example, the passenger compartment of the suspect's vehicle.[25] The Court referred to this type of police action as a **protective sweep**: a cursory and limited search for weapons (not a search for evidence). The police are thus entitled to protect themselves against potential attack by frisking the person for weapons and by conducting a protective sweep of the area within the suspect's immediate control.

A frisk of a person is a limited intrusion upon privacy, which is less intrusive than a full search. The temporary detention and investigation of property must likewise be less intrusive than a full search. *Florida v. Royer* held that opening the defendant's luggage to search for illegal drugs was an improper invasion of privacy because the police failed to utilize the less intrusive alternative of subjecting the luggage to a "sniff test" by a specially trained canine. The U.S. Supreme Court held that "the investigative methods should be the least intrusive means reasonably available to verify or dispel the officer's suspicion in a short period of time."

The Court's reference to an appropriately "short period of time" is not subject to rigid time limitations. *United States v. Place*, condemned a ninety-minute detention of the defendant's luggage, but *United States v. Montoya de Hernandez* upheld a sixteen-hour incommunicado detention of a suspected drug smuggler at the border.[26] The constitutionality of investigative detentions turns upon a multitude of factors including (1) the length of the detention, (2) the purposes to be served by the detention (3) the time reasonably needed to accomplish those proposes, and (4) the officer's diligence and choice of investigative means.[27]

IDENTIFICATION PROCEDURES

Most identification procedures take place after the suspect is arrested. On occasion, however, the police may utilize identification procedures as a device to screen possible suspects and select the one who is to be arrested. In *Davis v. Mississippi*, however, the U.S. Supreme Court condemned a police "dragnet" which rounded up all suspects for fingerprinting.

DAVIS v. MISSISSIPPI
Supreme Court of the United States, 1969
394 U.S. 721, 89 S.Ct. 1394

[Defendant and 24 other black youths were detained for questioning and fingerprinting in connection with a rape for which the only leads were a general description given by the victim and a set of fingerprints around the window through which the assailant entered. Defendant's prints were found to match those at the scene of the crime, and this evidence was admitted at his trial.]

JUSTICE BRENNAN delivered the opinion of the Court:
At the outset, we find no merit in the suggestion that fingerprint evidence, because of its trustworthiness, is not subject to the proscriptions of the Fourth and Four-

teenth Amendments. Our decisions recognize no exception to the rule that illegally seized evidence is inadmissible at trial, however relevant and trustworthy the seized evidence may be as an item of proof.

The second and related argument is that, at the least, detention for the sole purpose of obtaining fingerprints does not require probable cause. It is true that at the time of the defendant's detention the police had no intention of charging defendant with the crime and were far from making him the primary focus of their investigation. But to argue that the Fourth Amendment does not apply to the investigatory stage is fundamentally to misconceive the purposes of the Fourth Amendment. Investigatory seizures would subject unlimited numbers of innocent persons to the harassment and ignominy incident to involuntary detention. Nothing is more clear than that the Fourth Amendment was meant to prevent wholesale intrusions upon the personal security of our citizenry, whether these intrusions be termed "arrests" or "investigatory detentions."

Detentions for the sole purpose of obtaining fingerprints are no less subject to the constraints of the Fourth Amendment. . . . It is clear that no attempt was made here to employ procedures which might comply with the requirements of the Fourth Amendment: the detention at police headquarters of defendant and the other young Negroes was not authorized by a judicial officer; defendant was unnecessarily required to undergo two fingerprinting sessions; and defendant was not merely fingerprinted during the December 3 detention, but also subjected to interrogation. The judgment of the lower court admitting the fingerprint evidence is therefore REVERSED.

Following arrest, the most commonly used identification procedures are lineups, showups, photographic arrays, fingerprinting, DNA, and blood tests. Pretrial identifications by eyewitnesses may be accomplished through **lineups** or **photographic arrays** in which a witness identifies the suspect from among several people or photographs. In a **showup** or **photographic showup,** a witness confirms whether a single person or photograph is the suspect. The eyewitness identifications are subject to the Due Process standard for impermissible suggestiveness, which applies to all pretrial identifications, while the right to counsel has limited application to lineups and showups.

Lineups
a suspect is exhibited to a witness in the company of others similar in appearance to the suspect.
Photographic arrays
photographs of several potential suspects are shown to a witness.
Showup
a single suspect is exhibited to a witness.
Photographic showup
a picture of a single suspect is shown to a witness.

Lineups and Showups

Few things short of a smoking pistol carry as much weight with a jury as an eyewitness who points to the defendant and says, "That's the one." Eyewitness identifications, however, are notoriously unreliable and probably account "for more miscarriages of justice than any other single factor."[28] A witness cannot always easily observe the height, weight, age, and other features of a suspect at the time of the crime because the encounter between the witness and the criminal is often brief, frequently in poorly lit conditions, and under stressful circumstances. Police identification processes can further aggravate the inherent unreliability of human perception and memory. For example, lineups often resemble a multiple-choice recognition test in which the eyewitness feels compelled to pick the "most correct answer" rather than choose "none of the above." Further problems are created if the police inadvertently or deliberately suggest the "right" choice to the witness.

Suspects who are placed in a lineup or showup are not witnesses against themselves. Violation of the Fifth Amendment privilege against compulsory self-incrimination occurs only when a suspect is "compelled to testify against himself, or otherwise provide the State with evidence of a testimonial or communicative nature."[29] Compulsory display of a suspect's physical characteristics in a lineup or showup is not testimonial or communicative in nature because it does not require the suspect to disclose any personal knowledge. Thus a defendant has no Fifth Amendment privilege against participating in a lineup or showup. The defendant's refusal to participate in a lineup or showup may be introduced as evidence of a consciousness of guilt. Courts also have used criminal or civil contempt to coerce or punish a suspect who refuses to comply with a court order to participate in some identification procedure. On other occasions, the police have forcibly conducted the identification proceeding over the accused's objection. Forcing the accused to furnish some form of identification evidence requires the police to control or "seize" the accused, which places the action within the Fourth Amendment requirement that such seizures be reasonable.

Schmerber v. California addresses both Fourth and Fifth Amendment problems that arise when police forcibly take identification evidence from a defendant.

SCHMERBER v. CALIFORNIA
Supreme Court of the United States, 1966
384 U.S. 757, 86 S.Ct. 1826

JUSTICE BRENNAN delivered the opinion of the Court:

[Defendant was convicted of the criminal offense of driving an automobile while under the influence of intoxicating liquor. At the direction of a police officer, a blood sample was withdrawn from the unconscious defendant's body by a physician at the hospital.]

THE PRIVILEGE AGAINST SELF-INCRIMINATION CLAIM

The critical question is whether defendant was compelled "to be a witness against himself." The prohibition of compelling a man in a criminal court to be witness against himself is a prohibition of the use of physical or moral compulsion to extort communications from him, not an exclusion of his body as evidence when it may be material. The defendant's objection in principle would forbid a jury to look at a prisoner and compare his features with a photograph in proof.

[B]oth federal and state courts have usually held that the [privilege against self-incrimination] offers no protection against compulsion to submit to fingerprinting, photographing, or measurements, to write or speak for identification, to appear in court, to stand, to assume a stance, to walk, or to make a particular gesture. The distinction which has emerged, is that the privilege is a bar against compelling "communications" or "testimony," but that compulsion which makes a suspect or accused the source of "real or physical evidence" does not violate the privilege.

Not even a shadow of testimonial compulsion upon or enforced communication by the accused was involved either in the extraction or in the chemical analysis. Since the blood test evidence, although an incriminating product of compulsion, was neither defendant's testimony nor evidence relating to some communicative act or writing by the defendant, it was not inadmissible on privilege grounds.

THE SEARCH AND SEIZURE CLAIM

The Fourth Amendment's proper function is to constrain, not against all intrusions as such, but against intrusions which are not justified by the circumstances, or which are made in an improper manner. In other words, the questions we must decide in this case are whether the police were justified in requiring defendant to submit to the blood test, and whether the means and procedures employed in taking his blood respected relevant Fourth Amendment standards of reasonableness.

We are told that the percentage of alcohol in the blood begins to diminish shortly after drinking stops, as the body functions to eliminate it from the system. Particularly in a case such as this, where time had to be taken to bring the accused to a hospital and to investigate the scene of the accident, there was no time to seek out a magistrate and secure a warrant. Given these special facts, we conclude that the attempt to secure evidence of blood-alcohol content in this case was an appropriate incident to defendant's arrest.

Finally, the record shows that the test was performed in a reasonable manner. Defendant's blood was taken by a physician in a hospital environment according to accepted medical practices. We are thus not presented with the serious questions which would arise if a search involving use of medical technique, even of the most rudimentary sort, were made by other than medical personnel or in other than a medical environment—for example, if it were administered by police in the privacy of the stationhouse. To tolerate searches under these conditions might be to invite an unjustified element of personal risk of infection and pain.

We thus conclude that the present record shows no violation of defendant's right under the Fourth Amendment to be free of unreasonable searches and seizures. It bears repeating, however, that we reach this judgment only on the facts of the present record. The integrity of an individual's person is a cherished value of our society. That we today hold that the Constitution does not forbid the States minor intrusions into an individual's body under stringently limited conditions in no way indicates that it permits more substantial intrusions, or intrusions under other conditions.

Impermissibly suggestive a situation in which the identification procedure gives rise to a substantial likelihood of irreparable misidentification.

Due Process and Impermissible Suggestiveness

The Fourteenth Amendment concept of Due Process is violated if a pretrial identification procedure is "so **impermissibly suggestive** as to give rise to a very substantial likelihood of irreparable misidentification."[30] Perhaps the best example of an impermissibly suggestive lineup is Richard Pryor's fictional account of being placed in a lineup with a pumpkin and a refrigerator. One could hardly imagine a lineup that more clearly suggests who the police regard as the likely criminal.

Impermissible suggestiveness is not determined by whether the police acted improperly in selecting identification procedures that are less than scientifically neutral. Unlike the U.S. Supreme Court's Due Process approach in *Rochin v. California*, a Due Process inquiry into pretrial identification procedures does not focus on the misconduct or failings of the police in choosing suggestive identification methods.[31] The relevant consideration in pretrial identification procedures is the ultimate reliability of the resulting identification, regardless of any deficiencies in the identification procedures actually utilized.

Manson v. Brathwaite presented the U.S. Supreme Court with a choice between the Crime Control Model's emphasis on reliable factual determinations and the Due Process Model's emphasis on police misconduct.

MANSON v. BRATHWAITE
Supreme Court of the United States, 1977
432 U.S. 98, 97 S.Ct. 2243

Several minutes before sunset, Glover, a black undercover police officer, purchased heroin from a seller through the open doorway of an apartment while standing for two or three minutes within two feet of the seller in a hallway illuminated by natural light. A few minutes later, Glover described the seller to a backup officer, D'Onofrio, as being "a colored man, approximately five feet eleven inches tall, dark complexion, black hair, short Afro style, and having high cheek-bones, and of heavy build. He was wearing at the time blue pants and a plaid shirt."

On the basis of the description, D'Onofrio thought that defendant might be the heroin seller. He obtained a single photograph of defendant from police files and left it at Glover's office. Two days later, while alone, Glover viewed the photograph, and identified it as that of the seller. At defendant's trial, Glover testified that there was "no doubt whatsoever" that the person shown in the photograph was the defendant. Glover also made a positive in-court identification. No explanation was offered by the prosecution for the failure to utilize a photographic array or to conduct a lineup.

JUSTICE BLACKMUN delivered the opinion of the Court:

The Courts of Appeals appear to have developed at least two approaches to such evidence. The first, or *per se* approach, focuses on the procedures employed and requires exclusion of the out-of-court identification evidence, without regard to reliability, whenever it has been obtained through unnecessarily suggestive confrontation procedures. The justifications advanced are

the elimination of evidence of uncertain reliability, deterrence of the police and prosecutors, and the stated "fair assurance against the awful risks of misidentification."

The second, or more lenient, approach is one that continues to rely on the totality of the circumstances. It permits the admission of the confrontation evidence if, despite the suggestive aspect, the out-of-court identification possess certain features of reliability. This second approach, in contrast to the other, is *ad hoc* and serves to limit the societal costs imposed by a sanction that excludes relevant evidence from consideration and evaluation by the trier of fact.

There are, of course, several interests to be considered and taken into account. The driving force has been the Court's concern with the problems of eyewitness identification. Usually the witness must testify about an encounter with a total stranger under circumstances of emergency or emotional stress. The witness' recollection of the stranger can be distorted easily by the circumstances or by later actions of the police. Thus [our prior decisions] reflect the concern that the jury not hear eyewitness testimony unless that evidence has aspects of reliability. It must be observed that both approaches before us are responsive to this concern. The *per se* rule, however, goes too far since its application automatically and peremptorily, and without consideration of alleviating factors, keeps evidence from the jury that is reliable and relevant.

The second factor is deterrence. Although the *per se* approach has the more significant deterrent effect, the totality approach also has an influence on police behavior. The police will guard against unnecessarily suggestive procedures under the totality rule, as well as the *per se* rule, for fear that their actions will lead to the exclusion of identifications as unreliable.

The third factor is the effect on the administration of justice. Here the *per se* approach suffers serious drawbacks. Since it denies the trier reliable evidence, it may result, on occasion, in the guilty going free. Also, because of its rigidity, the *per se* approach may make error by the trial judge more likely than the totality approach. And in those cases in which the admission of identification evidence is error under the *per se* approach but not under the totality approach—cases in which the identification is reliable despite an unnecessarily suggestive identification procedure—reversal is a Draconian sanction.

We therefore conclude that reliability is the linchpin in determining the admissibility of identification testimony.

According to *Manson v. Brathwaite,* the government may introduce evidence of a pretrial identification if the prosecution shows that the identification was reliable, even though partially induced by some suggestiveness. The reliability of a pretrial identification is determined by assessing the totality of the circumstances, summarized as follows in *Neil v. Biggers.*[32]

1. The opportunity of the witness to view the perpetrator at the time of the crime
2. The witness' degree of attention
3. The accuracy of the witness' prior description of the perpetrator
4. The level of certainty demonstrated by the witness at the confrontation with the suspect
5. The length of time between the crime and the confrontation between the witness and the suspect

Most often, the trial court will consider the preceding factors pursuant to defense counsel's pretrial motion to suppress the identification. However, the defense has no constitutional right to litigate the admissibility of identification testimony in a pretrial hearing outside the jury's presence.[33] Thus defense counsel may be required to challenge the pretrial identification by cross-examining the eyewitness in front of the jury.

Right to Counsel at Lineups

The effectiveness of any challenge to a suggestive lineup is largely dependent on defense counsel's knowledge of what took place at the lineup. In order to diminish the use of suggestive lineups and to provide counsel with a basis for challenging such lineups, *United States v. Wade* extended the Sixth Amendment right to counsel to certain identification procedures.

UNITED STATES v. WADE
Supreme Court of the United States, 1967
388 U.S. 218, 87 S.Ct. 1926

JUSTICE BRENNAN delivered the opinion of the Court: The question here is whether courtroom identifications of an accused at trial are to be excluded from evidence because the accused was exhibited to the witnesses before trial at a post-indictment lineup conducted for identification purposes without notice to and in the absence of the accused's appointed counsel.

The Government characterizes the lineup as a mere preparatory step in the gathering of the prosecution's evidence, not different—for Sixth Amendment purposes—

from various other preparatory steps, such as systematized or scientific analyzing of the accused's fingerprints, blood sample, clothing, hair, and the like. We think there are differences which preclude such stages being characterized as critical stages at which the accused has the right to the presence of counsel. Knowledge of the techniques of science and technology is sufficiently available, and the variables in techniques few enough, that the accused has the opportunity for a meaningful confrontation of the Government's case at trial through the ordinary processes of cross-examination of the Government's expert witnesses and the presentation of the evidence of his own experts. The denial of right to have his counsel present at such analyses does not therefore violate the Sixth Amendment; they are not critical stages since there is minimal risk that his counsel's absence at such stages might derogate from his right to a fair trial.

But the confrontation compelled by the State between the accused and the victim or witnesses to a crime to elicit identification evidence is peculiarly riddled with innumerable dangers and variable factors which might seriously, even crucially, derogate from a fair trial. The vagaries of eyewitness identification are well-known; the annals of criminal law are rife with instances of mistaken identification.

Since it appears that there is a grave potential for prejudice, intentional or not, in the pretrial lineup, which may not be capable of reconstruction at trial, and since presence of counsel itself can often avert prejudice and assure a meaningful confrontation at trial, there can be little doubt that for the defendant the post-indictment lineup was a critical stage of the prosecution at which he was "as much entitled to such aid [of counsel as] at the trial itself." Thus both the defendant and his counsel should have been notified of the impending lineup, and counsel's presence should have been a requisite to conduct of the lineup, absent an intelligent waiver.

United States v. Wade, and the companion case of *Gilbert v. California,* noted the dangers of misidentification, and recognized that the presence of counsel at identification proceedings would reduce any suggestive atmosphere and provide a better opportunity for the effective assistance of counsel at trial.[34] The U.S. Supreme Court did not elaborate on the role of counsel at the identification proceeding, thus it appears that counsel is to act primarily as an observer collecting information with which to reconstruct the events and cross-examine the eyewitness at trial. Just as the *Miranda* warnings act as a device to prevent coercive interrogation tactics, *Wade* and *Gilbert* allow a defendant to invoke the right to counsel as a device for preventing suggestive pretrial identification procedures. (At a minimum, they provide defense counsel with a basis for challenging the eyewitness's courtroom identification of the defendant.)

The U.S. Supreme Court's subsequent decisions in *Kirby v. Illinois* and *United States v. Ash* represent a dramatic retreat from *Wade*'s focus on how pretrial identification procedures may affect the fairness of the trial itself.[35] In *Kirby,* the Court did not view the right to counsel as a means of protecting the defendant's right to a fair trial. Instead, *Kirby* held that the right to counsel does not attach until the commencement of adversary judicial criminal proceedings. Such proceedings include indictment and preliminary hearing but do not include an arrest.[36] Thus the right to counsel does not attach to lineups or showups that take place in the interim between arrest and the commencement of adversary judicial proceedings.

United States v. Ash further limited the right to counsel by holding that a suspect has no right to counsel at photographic arrays or photographic showups. The Supreme Court held that neither the defendant nor defense counsel had a right to be physically present at photographic identification procedures, which does not present a trial-like confrontation at which the accused has the right to the assistance of counsel. Any suggestiveness that occurs at a photographic display must be considered under the Due Process standard for impermissible suggestiveness.

The *Wade-Gilbert* right to counsel has continuing vitality only when a physical confrontation between the defendant and a witness occurs after the initiation of judicial proceedings. Photographic displays at any stage, and physical confrontation before the commencement of judicial proceeding can be challenged only in terms of the Due Process standard for suggestiveness and reliability.

Excluding Identification Evidence at Trial

Failure to afford the defendant the right to counsel under the *Wade-Gilbert* rule, or an identification which violates Due Process, results in the exclusion of the pretrial identification. Thus a witness testifying at trial may not refer to any identification made pretrial. The witness, however, may be permitted to make an in-court identification from the witness stand if the in-court identification is not contaminated by the improper pretrial identification—that is, it is not the fruit of the poisonous tree. In order to utilize an in-court identification, the government must prove by clear and convincing evidence that the in-court identification has an origin independent of any improper pretrial identification. Application of this standard

> requires consideration of various factors; for example, the prior opportunity to observe the alleged criminal act, the existence of any discrepancy between any pre-lineup description and the defendant's actual description, any identification prior to lineup of another person, the identification by picture of the defendant prior to the lineup, failure to identify the defendant on a prior occasion, and the lapse of time between the alleged act and the lineup identification.[37]

If the trial court is not satisfied that the in-court identification originated independently of the out-of-court identification, the in-court identification is tainted evidence ("the fruit of the poisonous tree") and is not admissible.

In-court identifications are usually made by asking witnesses if they see the robber, rapist, murderer, and so forth in the courtroom, at which point the witness may point to the defendant sitting at the defense table. There is no right to test a witness's identification of the defendant by conducting an in-court lineup. Trial judges, however, have permitted either formal lineups or more subtle tactics of permitting several people to sit at the defense table so that witnesses cannot assume that the only persons at the table are the defense counsel and the defendant. On the other hand, a court recently refused to allow the accused's twin brother to sit in the courtroom, although the accused "was free to call his twin brother or any other person to show misidentification by a witness."[38] Another recent case held that in the absence of evidence that the witnesses or the jury will be confused, there is no *per se* rule entitling identical twins to separate trials.[39]

Voice Identification

Like visual identifications, a voice identification made in an unreliably suggestive atmosphere may constitute a violation of Due Process. Aside from constitutional issues, evidence law governs the admissibility of verbal statements made by the defendant. Any witness familiar with the defendant's voice may testify that he recognized the defendant's voice on a particular occasion. Conversations overheard on a telephone are admissible as substantive evidence when the identities of the parties to the conversation are established. However, a mere statement of identity by the party calling is not in itself sufficient proof of such identity. For example, when Lynda Tripp testified before the grand jury as to telephone conversations with Monica Lewinsky, Ms. Tripp had to establish that she was familiar with and recognized the caller's voice as that of Ms. Lewinsky. The identity of the caller would not be established by the caller stating: "Hi, this is Monica." If "caller ID" or some other form of computerized call-tracking system is used, the reliability of the device must be established.

A voice exemplar offered merely to establish the physical characteristics or a person's speech patterns is not testimonial in nature. A defendant may demonstrate his speech patterns to the jury without being sworn in as a witness and without being subject to cross-examination. For example, when a witness, testifies that he recognized the defendant's voice because of the defendant's distinctive accent, the defendant may speak in court in order to demonstrate that he does or does not have such an accent. The court retains discretion to exclude such statements if the judge concludes that the defendant might alter or attempt to disguise his voice when speaking in court.

The authentication of tape recordings is determined by the following type of proof: the recording device was capable of taking the conversation now offered in evidence; the operator of the device was competent to operate the device; the recording is authentic and correct; changes, additions, or deletions have not been made in the recording; the recording has been preserved in a manner that is shown to the court; and the speakers are identified.

Scientific Identifications

In addition to witness identification, certain identification procedures are conducted through scientific and medical testing. For example, Exhibit 9–3 shows the order for identification testing of a suspect in Virginia.

Fingerprint Evidence   Fingerprint evidence is perhaps the most universally accepted scientific evidence at trial, although such evidence is not conclusive unless coupled with other evidence indicating that the fingerprint was impressed at the time of the crime. As one court suggested, "Only if the circumstances regarding the fingerprint show that the accused was at the scene of the crime at the time the crime was committed, may one rationally infer that the accused committed the crime."[40]

Law enforcement officials routinely fingerprint suspects arrested for a felony or a serious misdemeanor. But when a suspect is not subject to arrest, *Hayes v. Florida* condemned the involuntary removal of a suspect from his home to a police station, and detention there for fingerprinting and interrogation.[41] The U.S. Supreme Court held that "transportation to and investigative detention at the stationhouse without probable cause or judicial authorization together violate the Fourth Amendment." The Court indicated, however, that the Fourth Amendment would permit seizures for the purpose of fingerprinting if police have reasonable suspicion and if the fingerprinting procedure is "carried out with dispatch." Although a stop and frisk is a commonplace police procedure, police departments have not rushed to follow the Court's suggestion to utilize brief "stop and fingerprint" encounters with suspects.

DNA Profiles   Deoxyribonucleic acid (DNA) is a complex molecule found in the nucleus of each human cell. It carries a person's genetic information. The components of the DNA molecule are arranged differently for every individual except between identical twins. A scientific process for analyzing DNA produces a print or profile that contains a pattern of bands believed to be unique to a particular person's DNA.

Utilizing DNA testing in court involves three steps: (1) creating a DNA profile of a sample; (2) determining whether the profiles of different samples match; and (3) if the samples match, computing the probability of a random match. Expert witnesses are required to offer statistical analysis of population frequencies and to assess the significance of a particular test result.

Many jurisdictions have statutes requiring convicted felons to furnish a blood sample for DNA printing; such prints are then stored in a data bank for future law enforcement purposes. The courts have generally upheld the admission of a DNA profile comparison to prove or disprove identity.

HLA Blood Tests   The results of a Human Leukocyte Antigen (HLA) blood test are often introduced in rape and incest prosecutions. Although such evidence does not by itself establish identity or guilt beyond a reasonable doubt, evidence of population percentages of certain combinations of blood characteristics is relevant evidence tending to establish the identity of the perpetrator of the crime.

_____ , □ Circuit Court   □ General District Court   Case No(s).: ....

_____   □ Juvenile and Domestic Relations District Court

□ Commonwealth of Virginia   ....

□ _____   v. _____

                                                    (FULL NAME)

Complete line below only if ordered to report and not remanded into custody

                                                                                        M   F
_____
          D.O.B.   SOCIAL SECURITY NUMBER   RACE   GENDER

ORDER FOR WITHDRAWAL OF BLOOD SAMPLES AND/OR FOR PREPARATION
OF REPORTS TO CENTRAL CRIMINAL RECORDS EXCHANGE

The defendant is

□ ordered to report to _____

                                    (AGENCY FACILITY)

on _____ at _____ (AM) (PM) with the following proof of identity:

   □ Virginia driver's license □ _____

□ remanded to the custody of _____

for the purposes checked below:

□ withdrawal of blood sample(s) for
   □ DNA (deoxyribonucleic acid) analysis to be sent to Bureau of Forensic Science within 15 days after withdrawal, §§19.2-310.2 and 19.2-310.3
   □ Testing for infection with HIV (human immunodeficiency virus), §§18.2-62 or 18.2-346.1
□ fingerprinting and obtaining data for the preparation of a report to the Central Criminal Records Exchange, §19.2-390

The defendant is Ordered to cooperate fully and promptly in providing information and permitting fingerprinting and/or withdrawal of blood samples as required by this Order. Upon completion of these procedure(s), the defendant shall be released but shall be subject to the terms and conditions of any other order(s) governing the defendant's release/incarceration.

Complete only if remanded into custody:

After completion of the above-described requirements, the defendant shall:

□ remain in custody to serve time.
□ be released but required to return to custody on _____ for deferred execution of sentence.
□ be released on probation or on suspended execution of sentence.
□ be released

_____   _____
          DATE ENTERED   JUDGE

To Agency/Facility:
Complete and return to the above-named court.
□ Fingerprinting/Blood Withdrawal completed as ordered.
□ Defendant failed to appear as ordered.
□ Defendant failed to provide required proof of identity.

I acknowledge receipt of this Order.

_____   _____   _____
      DATE   SIGNATURE AND TITLE   DEFENDANT

FORM CC-1390 7/92 (114:2-016 2/95)

EXHIBIT 9–3
Order for Identification Evidence

SUMMARY

Distinguishing between arrests and temporary detentions has important consequences for citizens and law enforcement. An arrest must be based on a reasonable belief that the person has committed a crime, while a temporary detention can be justified by reasonable suspicion. An arrest automatically authorizes a search of the suspect, but a "frisk" of the suspect must be based on some indication that the suspect is armed and dangerous. A search incident to arrest may encompass the suspect's entire body. A frisk, on the other hand, is initially confined to a patdown of the suspect's outer clothing. An arrest warrant is normally required before officers may arrest a suspect at home. Temporary detentions generally take place on the street or in other public places.

Most jurisdictions have statutes regulating the use of identification procedures involving DNA or other blood tests. However, constitutional dimensions determine the identification procedures involving lineups, showups, and photographic arrays. The Fourth Amendment controls the circumstances under which the government may seize a person and subject that person to identification procedures. The Fourteenth Amendment Due Process clause governs the suggestiveness of all pretrial identification procedures, but the Sixth Amendment right to counsel is limited to lineups or showups conducted after the commencement of adversary judicial criminal proceedings.

CONCEPT SUMMARY

Seizures of a Person

Consult local law to determine what changes have been made in a particular jurisdiction.

TYPE OF SEIZURE	JUSTIFICATION	WARRANT	ACCOMPANYING ACTIVITY
Arrest	Probable cause	Not required for felony arrest in public; required for arrest in a dwelling	Search of arrestee and area under the arrestee's control
Stop and Frisk	Reasonable suspicion	Not required	Frisk of the person; protective sweep of the area
Identification Procedure	Lawful seizure of the person	Not required	Lineup, showup, or material for scientific examination

DISCUSSION QUESTIONS

1. As the police approach a group of youths standing on a street corner, one youth bolts and runs away. The police pursue, shouting, "Stop in the name of the law." The youth continues to run and while running discards a bag of crack cocaine. The police finally tackle the youth to the ground, then return to retrieve the cocaine. At what point was the youth seized? At what point did the police have probable cause or reasonable suspicion to seize the youth? See *California v. Hodari D.*, 499 U.S. 621, 111 S.Ct. 1547 (1991).

2. At the local airport, you set off the alarm on the magnetometer. If you announce, "Never mind, I don't want to fly today," Can the security officials still detain you and search you for weapons?

3. What should (may) a defense counsel do if a client is about to be placed in a lineup with a pumpkin and a refrigerator?

4. What, if any, options does a suspect have if the police request a voice and handwriting sample? What may the police do if the suspect refuses to furnish the samples?

5. Does the situation in which a male police officer frisks a female suspect pose any constitutional problems? What steps could the officer substitute for the frisk?

PRACTICE EXERCISES

1. In your jurisdiction, when is a summons issued in lieu of an arrest warrant?

2. How does your jurisdiction distinguish between arrests for a felony or a misdemeanor?

3. If you were observing a lineup in which your client was placed, what factors might indicate to you that the lineup was suggestive?

4. If you were working as a police paralegal, what guidelines would you give to police concerning when and how to conduct a lineup?

5. Does your jurisdiction admit evidence of DNA tests? What other scientific evidence is admissible (e.g., drug sniffing dogs, tracking by bloodhounds, polygraph examinations)?

KEY TERMS

Booking process
Summons
Probable cause
Complaint
Warrantless felony arrest
Misdemeanor committed in the
    arresting officer's presence

Arrest in a suspect's dwelling
Derivative evidence
Temporary detentions
Reasonable suspicion
Protective sweep

Lineups
Photographic arrays
Showup
Photographic showup
Impermissibly suggestive

WEB SITE

National Commission on the Future of DNA Evidence
Ojp.usdoj.gov/nij/dna

NOTES

1. *Whren v. United States,* 517 U.S. 806, 116 S.Ct. 1769 (1996).
2. *Golden v. Commonwealth,* 519 S.E.2d 378 (Va. 1999).
3. See *Hoffa v. United States,* 385 U.S. 293, 87 S.Ct. 408 (1966).
4. *Tennessee v. Garner,* 471 U.S. 1, 105 S.Ct. 1694 (1985).
5. *United States v. Watson,* 423 U.S. 411, 96 S.Ct. 820 (1976).
6. *Payton v. New York,* 445 U.S. 573, 100 S.Ct. 1371 (1980).
7. *United States v. Santana,* 427 U.S. 38, 96 S.Ct. 2406 (1976).
8. *United States v. Crews,* 445 U.S. 463, 100 S.Ct. 1244 (1980).
9. *Brower v. County of Inyo,* 489 U.S. 593, 109 S.Ct 1378 (1989).
10. *Sacramento v. Lewis,* 523 U.S. 833, 118 S.Ct. 1708 (1998).
11. *United States v. Mendenhall,* 446 U.S. 544, 100 S.Ct. 1870 (1980).
12. *Florida v. Royer,* 460 U.S. 491, 103 S.Ct. 1319 (1983).
13. See *Reid v. Georgia,* 448 U.S. 438, 100 S.Ct. 2752 (1980).

14. *Illinois v. Wardlow,* 528 U.S. 119, 120 S.Ct. 673 (2000).

15. *Florida v. J.L.,* 529 U.S. 266, 120 S.Ct. 1375 (2000).

16. *Chicago v. Morales,* 527 U.S. 41, 119 S.Ct. 1849 (1999). The statute prohibiting such loitering violated the Due Process clause because it was unconstitutionally vague: (1) "it failed to provide the kind of notice that will enable ordinary people to understand what conduct it prohibits; (2) it may authorize and even encourage arbitrary and discriminatory enforcement."

17. *Michigan Dept. of State Police v. Sitz,* 496 U.S. 444, 110 S.Ct. 2481 (1990).

18. *National Treasury Employees Union v. Von Raab,* 489 U.S. 656, 109 S.Ct. 1384 (1989).

19. *Skinner v. Railway Labor Executives' Ass'n,* 489 U.S. 602, 109 S.Ct. 1402 (1989).

20. *Whren v. United States,* 517 U.S. 806, 116 S.Ct. 1769 (1996).

21. *United States v. Sokolaw,* 490 U.S. 1, 109 S.Ct. 1581 (1989).

22. *United States v. Sakyi,* 160 F.3d 164 (4th Cir. 1998).

23. *United States v. Rusher,* 966 F.2d 868 (4th Cir. 1992).

24. *United States v. Place,* 462 U.S. 696, 103 S.Ct. 2637 (1983).

25. *Michigan v. Long,* 463 U.S. 1032, 103 S.Ct. 3469 (1983).

26. *United States v. Montoya de Hernandez,* 473 U.S. 531, 105 S.Ct. 3304 (1985).

27. See *United States v. Sharpe,* 470 U.S. 675, 105 S.Ct. 1568 (1985).

28. *United States v. Wade,* 388 U.S. 218, 87 S.Ct. 1926 (1967).

29. *Schmerber v. California,* 384 U.S. 757, 86 S.Ct. 1826 (1966).

30. *Simmons v. United States,* 390 U.S. 377, 88 S.Ct. 967 (1968).

31. *Rochin v. California,* 342 U.S. 165, 72 S.Ct. 205 (1952).

32. *Neil v. Biggers,* 409 U.S. 188, 93 S.Ct. 375 (1972).

33. *Watkins v. Sowders,* 449 U.S. 341, 101 S.Ct. 654 (1981).

34. *Gilbert v. California,* 388 U.S. 263, 87 S.Ct. 1951 (1967).

35. *Kirby v. Illinois,* 406 U.S. 682, 92 S.Ct. 1877 (1972); *United States v. Ash,* 413 U.S. 300, 93 S.Ct. 2568 (1973).

36. *Moore v. Illinois,* 434 U.S. 220, 98 S.Ct. 458 (1977).

37. *United States v. Wade,* 388 U.S. 218, 87 S.Ct. 1926 (1967).

38. *Bond v. Commonwealth,* 529 S.E.2d 827 (Va. 2000).

39. *United States v. Johnson,* 219 F.3d 349 (4th Cir. 2000).

40. *Varker v. Commonwealth,* 14 Va.App. 445, 417 S.E.2d 7 (1992).

41. *Hayes v. Florida,* 470 U.S. 811, 105 S.Ct. 1643 (1985).

SEARCH AND SEIZURE OF PROPERTY

Chapter 10

CHAPTER OUTLINE

REASONABLE SEARCHES AND SEIZURES

The law of search and seizure is probably the most complicated, confusing, and yet fascinating aspect of criminal procedure. At times, each search and seizure case seems unique and the Supreme Court's decisions appear to rest on factual determinations rather than legal principles. At other times, the particular facts of a case seem far less important than the Court's reading of the Fourth Amendment as a vehicle for resolving the clash between the Crime Control and Due Process models of the criminal justice system.

The Fourth Amendment serves two fundamental purposes: It protects the privacy interests of individual citizens; and it regulates police investigatory activities. These purposes are at times complementary but can also conflict, thus a court's choice between the two purposes can lead to opposite results. For example, in a case involving compulsory surgery to remove a bullet for a ballistics test, defense counsel emphasized the extreme invasion of privacy inherent in governmental intrusions into a person's body. The prosecution, however, maintained that any intrusion upon privacy is constitutionally reasonable as long as the police comply with the Fourth Amendment's procedural requirements for a search warrant based on probable cause. Despite the police having followed proper procedures, and in fact obtaining lower court approval for the proposed surgery, *Winston v. Lee* held that such intrusive surgery would be an unreasonable search and seizure.[1]

In contrast to their positions in *Winston,* the prosecution and defense reversed the focus of their arguments in *Delaware v. Prouse.*[2] This case involved a random stop (seizure) of an automobile for purposes of inspecting the motorist's license and registration papers. The prosecution attempted to justify the stop of the vehicle by emphasizing the minimal invasion of privacy caused by a brief stop of the automobile. (A motorist who produces the proper papers would be delayed for only minutes before being permitted to proceed.) The defendant, however, focused on the absence of any probable cause or reasonable suspicion for stopping the vehicle. The U.S. Supreme Court adopted the defendant's position and found such random stops to be unreasonable within the meaning of the Fourth Amendment. Even though the Court conceded that the police made only a minimal intrusion upon privacy, the *Delaware v. Prouse* decision recognized that the probable cause requirement was a necessary limitation on the police power to select and stop motorists in an arbitrary or capricious manner.

In addition to reconciling the fundamental, yet sometimes conflicting purposes of the Fourth Amendment, the U.S. Supreme Court also must reconcile the relationship between the Amendment's two conjunctive clauses. The first clause of the Amendment, known as the **reasonableness clause,** establishes "the right of the people to be secure in their persons, houses, papers, and effects, against unreasonable searches and seizures." The second clause, the **warrant clause,** provides that "no warrant shall issue, but upon probable cause, supported by oath or affirmation, and particularly describing the place to be searched, and the person or things to be seized." At times the U.S. Supreme Court adopts the reasonableness approach of the first clause by holding that the absence of a warrant in a particular case is not a determinative factor in assessing a search's constitutionality. At other times the Court favors the warrant clause by holding that warrantless searches are "per se unreasonable," subject to a few "well-delineated exceptions." The recognized exceptions are discussed in later sections of this chapter, but the list of exceptions cannot be regarded as definitive; a search falling outside these exceptions might still be deemed constitutional under the general rubric of reasonableness.

Reasonableness clause
"the right of the people to be secure in their persons, houses, papers, and effects, against unreasonable searches and seizures."

Warrant clause
"no warrant shall issue, but upon probable cause, supported by oath or affirmation, and particularly describing the place to be searched, and the person or things to be seized."

Definition of a Search

The Fourth Amendment addresses only a specific type of activity: *governmental action* that is defined as a search or seizure. The amendment limits the search and seizure powers of the federal government, and through the Fourteenth Amendment's Due Process clause, defines the search and seizure powers of state governments. Searches and seizures conducted by private citizens or foreign police are beyond the coverage of the Fourth Amendment. The amendment is applicable, however, if a U.S. government official solicits or participates in a search conducted by private individuals or foreign governments. For example, a security officer at a private university may initiate a search of a dormitory room and pass on any seized items to public law enforcement officials who may then use them as evidence at the defendant's trial. The Fourth Amendment, however, would bar the use of the evidence if the campus security officer had conducted the search at the request of federal or state law enforcement officers. "Whether a private party should be deemed an agent or instrumentality of the Government for Fourth Amendment purposes necessarily turns on the degree of the Government's participation in the private party's activities."[3]

Even if federal or state officials participate in an investigation, the Fourth Amendment remains inapplicable unless the investigation is classified as a search or seizure. As one judge noted, if the government's quest for information or evidence is classified as a nonsearch, "the law doesn't give a constitutional damn" about whether the police complied with the Fourth Amendment. The U.S. Supreme Court's initial definition of a search focused upon property law concepts and emphasized three requirements:

1. Physical trespass upon the defendant's private property (most commonly an entry of a citizen's dwelling)
2. Seizure of the defendant's tangible property (for example, drugs, weapons, stolen goods)
3. The trespass and seizure were pursuant to criminal investigation by law enforcement agencies (investigations by fire marshals or public health inspectors initially fell beyond the scope of the Amendment.)

The preceding requirements defining search and seizure, although no longer constitutionally adequate, accurately describe the vast majority of searches and seizures that occur as part of law enforcement activity in this country. In *Katz v. United States*, however, the Court discarded the traditional definition of search and seizure because the definition overemphasized property law concepts. *Katz* chose to emphasize the right to privacy, which Justice Brandeis had earlier referred to as "the right to be let alone—the most comprehensive of rights and the right most valued by civilized men."[4]

KATZ v. UNITED STATES
Supreme Court of the United States, 1967
389 U.S. 347, 88 S.Ct. 507

[The petitioner was convicted of transmitting wagering information by telephone in violation of a federal statute. At trial the prosecution was permitted to introduce evidence of the petitioner's end of telephone conversations, overheard by FBI agents who had attached an electronic listening and recording device to the outside of the public telephone booth from which the petitioner had placed his calls. In affirming his conviction, the Court of Appeals rejected the contention that the recordings had been obtained in violation of the Fourth Amendment because "there was no physical entrance into the area occupied by the petitioner."]

JUSTICE STEWART delivered the opinion of the Court:
The petitioner has strenuously argued that the booth was a "constitutionally protected area." The Government has maintained with equal vigor that it was not. But this effort to decide whether or not a given "area,"

viewed in the abstract, is "constitutionally protected" deflects attention from the problem presented by this case. For the Fourth Amendment protects people, not places. What a person knowingly exposes to the public, even in his own home or office, is not a subject of Fourth Amendment protection. . . . But what he seeks to preserve as private, even in an area accessible to the public, may be constitutionally protected.

The Government stresses the fact that the telephone booth from which the petitioner made his calls was constructed partly of glass, so that he was as visible after he entered it as he would have been if he had remained outside. But what he sought to exclude when he entered the booth was not the intruding eye—it was the uninvited ear. He did not shed his right to do so simply because he made his calls from a place where he might be seen. No less than an individual in a business office,

in a friend's apartment, or in a taxicab, a person in a telephone booth may rely upon the protection of the Fourth Amendment. One who occupies it, shuts the door behind him, and pays the toll that permits him to place a call, is surely entitled to assume that the words he utters into the mouthpiece will not be broadcast to the world.

JUSTICE HARLAN, concurring:
As the Court's opinion states, "The Fourth Amendment protects people, not places." The question, however, is what protection it affords to those people. My understanding of the rule . . . is that there is a twofold requirement, first that a person have exhibited an actual (subjective) expectation of privacy and second, that the expectation be one that society is prepared to recognize as "reasonable."

Justice Harlan's twofold requirement for a subjective and reasonable expectation of privacy has become the dominant approach to defining a Fourth Amendment **search.** The issue of the defendant's actual or subjective desire for privacy often turns upon whether the defendant took normal precautions to protect privacy. Thus a failure to curtain one's windows or lower one's speaking voice may remove one's activity from Fourth Amendment protection. If evidence of the defendant's actual desire for privacy is present, *Katz* establishes a second requirement that the desire for privacy must be one that society is prepared to recognize as a reasonable expectation of privacy. *Katz* recognized that U.S. citizens reasonably expect that telephone conversations are not subject to warrantless eavesdropping by the government. In contrast, the Court subsequently held that a citizen's supposedly private conversations can be revealed by government undercover agents who participate in the conversation with the defendant's knowledge.[5] In the post-*Katz* era, the right to privacy has replaced property rights as the dominant consideration in defining Fourth Amendment searches.

The courts have found, however, that determining society's reasonable privacy expectations is an elusive process. *Oliver v. United States,* in which the police trespassed upon private property to view a suspect's backyard, addresses the question of a citizen's reasonable expectation of privacy and considers whether the police invaded a citizen's privacy or merely intruded upon **open fields.**

Search
a government official's intrusion upon a defendant's subjective expectation of privacy; and the expectation is one that society is prepared to recognize as reasonable.

Open fields
not protected by the Fourth Amendment because a person has no reasonable expectation of privacy in areas open to public view.

OLIVER v. UNITED STATES
Supreme Court of the United States, 1984
466 U.S. 170, 104 S.Ct. 1735

[Defendant Oliver complained that two state police officers went to his farm to investigate reports that he was growing marijuana. They drove past his house to a locked gate with a "No Trespassing" sign on it. The officers walked around the gate and followed a footpath for several hundred yards, passing a barn and a parked camper. Further investigation of the farm revealed a field of marijuana about a mile from Oliver's house.]

JUSTICE POWELL delivered the opinion of the Court: The special protection accorded by the Fourth Amendment to the people in their "persons, houses, papers, and effects," is not extended to the open fields. The distinction between the latter and the house is as old as the common law.

The historical underpinnings of the "open fields" doctrine also demonstrate that the doctrine is consistent with respect for "reasonable expectations of privacy." As Justice Holmes observed, the common law distinguished "open fields" from the curtilage, the land immediately surrounding and associated with the home. At common law, the curtilage is the area to which extends the intimate activity associated with the "sanctity of a man's home and the privacies of life," and therefore has been considered part of the home itself for Fourth Amendment purposes. Thus courts have extended Fourth Amendment protection to the curtilage; and they have defined the curtilage, as did the common law, by reference to the factors that determine whether an individual reasonably may expect that an area immediately adjacent to the home will remain private. Conversely, the common law implies, as we reaffirm today, that no expectation of privacy legitimately attaches to open fields.

The test of legitimacy is not whether the individual chooses to conceal assertedly "private" activity. Rather, the correct inquiry is whether the government's intrusion infringes upon the personal and societal values protected by the Fourth Amendment. As we have explained, we find no basis for concluding that a police inspection of open fields accomplishes such an infringement.

The open fields doctrine of *Oliver* has been applied to aerial surveillance of commercial properties and the backyard of a dwelling.[6] The Supreme Court also ruled that citizens have no expectation of privacy in garbage left for collection outside the curtilage of a home.[7] In contrast, however, the Court recently held that law enforcement officials violate an expectation of privacy by feeling in an exploratory manner, luggage placed in the overhead compartments of buses, airlines, or other means of public transportation,[8] and by allowing members of the news media to accompany officers during the search of a residence.[9]

Seizures Distinguished From Searches In most situations a search and a seizure are part of the same police investigation, and the search and seizure merge into each other. The U.S. Supreme Court has noted, however, that in certain cases, the search must necessarily be separate from the seizure. A search threatens privacy interests that are afforded "heightened protection," while a seizure may affect only the defendant's property rights.[10] *Soldal v. Cook County, Illinois,* however, indicates that *Katz*'s focus on privacy does not eliminate the Fourth Amendment's protection of property.

SOLDAL v. COOK COUNTY, ILLINOIS
Supreme Court of the United States, 1992
506 U.S. 56, 113 S.Ct. 538 (1992)

Edward Soldal and his family resided in their trailer home, which was located on a rented lot. The owners of the trailer park filed an eviction proceeding against the Soldals. Rather than await judgment in their favor, the owners of the trailer park chose to forcibly evict the Soldals and requested the presence of sheriff deputies to forestall any possible resistance. The owners proceeded to wrench the sewer and water connections off the side of the trailer home, disconnect the phone, tear off the trailer's canopy and skirting, and hook the home to a tractor.

The Soldals brought a civil suit alleging a violation of their rights under the Fourth Amendment. They claimed that the trailer park owners had conspired with Cook County deputy sheriffs to unreasonably seize and remove the Soldals' trailer home.

The Court of Appeals acknowledged that what had occurred was a "seizure" in the literal sense of the word, but concluded that in the absence of an interference with privacy or liberty, a "pure deprivation of property" is not cognizable under the Fourth Amendment.

JUSTICE WHITE delivered the opinion of the Court:
As a result of the state action in this case, the Soldals' domicile was not only seized, it literally was carried away, giving new meaning to the term "mobile home." We fail to see how being unceremoniously disposed of one's home in the manner alleged to have occurred here can be viewed as anything but a seizure invoking the protection of the Fourth Amendment.

The Fourth Amendment protects two types of expectations, one involving "searches," the other "seizures." A "search" occurs when an expectation of privacy that society is prepared to consider reasonable is infringed. A "seizure" of property occurs where there is some meaningful interference with an individual's possessory interests in that property.

Probable Cause for a Search

If the government's investigatory activity is classified as a search or seizure, in most cases it must be justified by some form of probable cause. The requirement of probable cause applies to searches pursuant to a warrant, to searches conducted without a warrant, and to arrests (seizures of the person).

Before the decisions in *Terry v. Ohio* and *Camara v. Municipal Court,* which involved an administrative inspection by public health officials, one type of search or seizure and one type of probable cause were generally at issue.[11] The U.S. Supreme Court has since recognized that a lower standard of probable cause may justify certain lesser intrusions upon privacy, such as administrative inspections or temporary detentions short of arrest. The Court's current approach to search and seizure does not treat probable cause as a uniform standard that must be met whenever the Fourth Amendment applies. Instead, the Court has formulated two distinct definitions of **probable cause.**

Probable cause
a reasonable belief that seizable items will be found in a particular place at the time that the search is to be conducted; a flexible standard identified by balancing the degree of intrusion upon individual privacy against the importance of the government purpose to be served by the intrusion.

1. Probable cause is sometimes viewed as a flexible standard derived from balancing private and governmental interest. Under this approach, the Court measures the degree of intrusion upon individual privacy against the importance of the government purpose to be served by the intrusion. For example, the need to search for evidence of murder might outweigh some minor privacy interest, but that same minor privacy interest might outweigh the government's need to prevent illegal parking. This balancing of private and governmental interests approach to the Fourth Amendment is sometimes referred to as a general standard of reasonableness. At other times it is referred to as a sliding scale of probable cause. Whatever the appropriate terminology, the balancing approach is most often applied to searches and arrests involving less serious intrusions upon privacy.

2. Probable cause is sometimes defined as information sufficient to justify a person of reasonable caution in the belief that seizable items are located in the place to be searched. The information establishing probable cause must be set out in an affidavit for a search warrant, shown in Exhibit 10–1. (In cases of a warrantless search, the police officer "steps into the shoes" of a magistrate and must assess the adequacy of the available information.)

When an affidavit for a search warrant is presented, a magistrate must determine probable cause by examining the factual information to answer three fundamental questions:

1. *What* am I sure of? (the nature and location of seizable items)
2. *How* sure am I? (the degree of probability as to the nature and location of the items)
3. *Why* am I sure? (the reliability of the factual information)

AFFIDAVIT FOR SEARCH WARRANT

VA. CODE ANN. §19.2- 54
RULE 3A-27

The undersigned Applicant states under oath:

1. A search is requested in relation to an offense substantially described as follows:

....

....

....

[☐ CONTINUED ON ATTACHED SHEET]

2. The place, person, or thing to be searched is described as follows:

....

....

....

[☐ CONTINUED ON ATTACHED SHEET]

3. The things or persons to be searched for are described as follows:

....

....

....

[☐ CONTINUED ON ATTACHED SHEET]

FORM DC-338 11/88 (114-3-021 2/95)

(OVER)

CASE NO.

AFFIDAVIT FOR SEARCH WARRANT

APPLICANT:

....
NAME

....
TITLE (IF ANY)

....
ADDRESS

Certified to Clerk of .... Circuit Court on

....
TITLE

....
SIGNATURE

Delivered to Clerk of .... Circuit Court on .... by the undersigned

....
TITLE

....
SIGNATURE

EXHIBIT 10–1
Affidavit for a Search Warrant

4. The material facts constituting probable cause that the search should be made are:

☐ CONTINUED ON ATTACHED SHEET

5. The object, thing or person searched for constitutes evidence of the commission of such offense.

6. ☐ I have personal knowledge of the facts set forth in this affidavit OR

☐ I was advised of the facts set forth in this affidavit, in whole or in part, by an informer. This informer's credibility or the reliability of the information may be determined from the following facts:

The statements above are true and accurate to the best of my knowledge and belief.

_____
APPLICANT

Subscribed and sworn to before me this day.

_____
TITLE OF APPLICANT (IF ANY)

_____ _____ _____
CLERK   MAGISTRATE   JUDGE

DATE AND TIME
FORM DC-338-(REVERSE) 1/81

EXHIBIT 10–1
Affidavit for a Search Warrant—
Continued

The Nature and Location of Seizable Items

Seizable items fall into four categories: (1) contraband, such as illegal drugs, (2) weapons and instrumentalities used in the commission of crime, (3) stolen property and, (4) evidence of the commission of crime.

The government's power to search for and seize such items is limited by the Fourth Amendment's requirement that warrants "particularly describe" the items to be seized. Generic descriptions such as stolen goods or weapons used in the robbery do not satisfy the particularity requirement of the Fourth Amendment. For example, rather than refer to weapons, a proper search warrant must particularly describe the weapon as a revolver, a cross-bow, a bazooka, or the like. Armed with this specific description, the searching officers may seize the identified item, but they are not authorized to seize anything and everything they suspect may be connected with a crime. "As to what is to be taken, nothing is left to the discretion of the officer executing the warrant."[12] Except for the operation of the plain view doctrine discussed subsequently, the searching officer may not search for or seize any item not listed in the search warrant.

Both the items to be seized and the place to be searched must be described with particularity. A search warrant directed against a multiple occupancy structure such as an apartment house, must specify a particular apartment to be searched. However, search warrants may refer to the defendant's entire premises and no mention need be made of individual rooms or floors within the residence. Although the entire premises may be searched, the police may look only in those portions of the premises where the described seizable items could be located. For example, a search for a small quantity of drugs justifies searching any small containers found on the premises, but a search for a fugitive would not justify searching in spaces too small to hide a person.

Unlike an arrest warrant, a search warrant does not require probable cause to believe that a crime has been committed by the person whose premises are to be searched. If police have probable cause to believe that seizable items are located on the premises, they may search an innocent person's home. For example, in *Zurcher v. Stanford Daily,* the police searched a newspaper office for photographs incriminating campus demonstrators.

ZURCHER v. STANFORD DAILY
Supreme Court of the United States, 1978
436 U.S. 547, 98 S.Ct. 1970

[Nine policemen were injured by demonstrators at Stanford University Hospital. Two days later the *Stanford Daily* carried articles and photos devoted to the demonstration and attack; the photos by a staff member indicated he had been located where he could have photographed the assailants. A warrant was obtained to search the *Daily's* offices for negatives, film, and pictures relevant to identification of the assailants. The lower court held that the Fourth Amendment forbade the issuance of a warrant to search for materials in the possession of one not suspected of crime.]

JUSTICE WHITE delivered the opinion of the Court:
Under existing law, valid warrants may be issued to search any property, whether or not occupied by a third party, at which there is probable cause to believe that fruits, instrumentalities, or evidence of a crime will be found. Nothing on the face of the Amendment suggests that a third-party search warrant should not normally issue. Against this background, it is untenable to conclude that property may not be searched unless its occupant is reasonably suspected of crime and is subject to arrest.

Whether the third party is suspect or not, the State's interest in enforcing the criminal law and recovering the evidence remains the same; and it is the seeming innocence of the property owner that the District Court relied on to foreclose the warrant to search. But as respondents themselves now concede, if the third party knows that contraband or other illegal materials are on his property, he is sufficiently culpable to justify the issuance of a search warrant.

Search warrants are often employed early in an investigation, perhaps before the identity of any likely criminal and certainly before all the perpetrators are or could be known. The seemingly blameless third party in possession of the fruits or evidence may not be innocent at all; and if he is, he may nevertheless be so related to or so sympathetic with the culpable that he cannot be relied upon to retain and preserve the articles that may implicate his friends, or at least not to notify those who would be damaged by the evidence that the authorities are aware of its location.

The Court's decision in *Zurcher* triggered an outcry from the communications media and led to statutory limitations on the applicability of the decision. In the Privacy Protection Act of 1980, Congress provided that law enforcement officials could not search for the work product of those engaged in public communication unless (1) there was probable cause to believe that the person possessing the materials was involved in a crime to which the materials related or (2) the immediate seizure of the work product was necessary to prevent death or serious bodily injury.[13]

The Degree of Probability That Seizable Items Will Be Found

The law is clear as to what is not probable cause. It requires less than proof beyond a reasonable doubt; it requires more than a bare suspicion. The law is less clear about what *is* probable cause. As the name implies, probable cause deals with probabilities, but the courts have not held that it means more probable than not. In *New York v. P.J. Video,* the Court stated that probable cause requires only "a fair probability" or "substantial chance" of criminal activity.[14]

This aspect of probable cause may seem surprisingly vague for a legal standard, but the Supreme Court has kept the standard somewhat ambiguous because in many jurisdictions the official issuing a search warrant (normally a magistrate) is a nonlawyer. The Court apparently feels that a vague standard based on "the practical consideration of day-to-day life" is preferable to a formalist legal standard that cannot be easily applied by the average magistrate. Courts thus encourage magistrates to avoid legalistic formulations of the burden of proof and to use common sense to determine whether a reasonable probability exists that seizable items are located in the place to be searched.

Because of the Supreme Court's strong preference for search warrants, "the scrutiny applied to a magistrate's probable cause determination to issue a warrant is less than that for warrantless searches."[15] Thus appellate review of a magistrate's probable cause determination is deferential in nature, and the reviewing court determines whether the evidence, viewed as a whole, provided the magistrate with a substantial basis for concluding that probable cause existed to issue the warrant. In the case of a warrantless search, however, the court gives no deference to the police officer's determination of probable cause.

The Reliability of the Facts Constituting Probable Cause

Perhaps no point of Fourth Amendment law is as clear as the courts' insistence that the magistrate who determines probable cause must remain "neutral and detached" when assessing a police officer's request for a search warrant.[16] A police officer filing an affidavit for a search warrant must offer concrete facts, not a mere affirmation that the officer believes that seizable items will be found. If the officer's mere belief were adequate grounds for the issuance of a search warrant, the magistrate would be reduced to simply "rubber stamping" the police officer's belief. Therefore, the affidavit for a search warrant must set forth more than the police officer's belief, no matter how sincere. The affidavit must contain detailed factual information so that the neutral and detached magistrate may "judge for himself the persuasiveness of the facts relied on to show probable cause."[17]

If the magistrate is satisfied that the affidavit sets forth facts establishing a reasonable belief that seizable items are located in the place to be searched, the magistrate must then further determine that the facts giving rise to this belief are reliable facts. The facts set forth in the affidavit for a search warrant must have one of two sources: (1) the officer filing the affidavit personally observed the facts or (2) someone (an informant) notified the officer of the facts. An **informant** is anyone who does not personally appear before the magistrate to swear to the facts in the affidavit for a search warrant.

The first situation, in which the police officer filing the affidavit personally observed the facts, involves no informant. Therefore, the magistrate need only determine the reliability of the police officer. In the second situation, the officer goes beyond personal observations and relays information from an informant. At this point the magistrate must be given additional facts that establish that the informant is a truthful person. The courts have recognized a number of factual circumstances sufficient to establish the reliability of an informant:

1. The informant is a victim, eyewitness, or responsible citizen.
2. The informant is a law enforcement official.
3. The informant previously furnished reliable information to the police.
4. The informant made a declaration against the informant's own penal interest.
5. The informant's statements have been corroborated.

For a number of years the requirement that affidavits contain separate sets of facts—facts establishing a reasonable likelihood of the presence of seizable items and facts establishing the reliability of informants—was referred to as the two prongs of *Aguilar*. This two-pronged test originated in *Aguilar v. Texas*.[18] It was further refined in *Spinelli v. United States*.[19] However, in *Illinois v. Gates*, the Supreme Court merged the two prongs of *Aguilar* into the **totality of circumstances** test. This test requires the magistrate to consider whether the total facts, including facts as to the veracity of informants, establish "a fair probability that contraband or evidence of crime will be found in a particular place."

Consider whether the lengthy facts in *Illinois v. Gates* precisely satisfy the two prongs of *Aguilar*, or whether the facts, in their totality, nonetheless establish probable cause to search.

Informant
a person who does not appear before a magistrate, but who provides information for the issuance of a search warrant.

Totality of circumstances
facts that establish a fair probability that seizable items will be found in a particular place.

ILLINOIS v. GATES
Supreme Court of the United States, 1983
462 U.S. 213, 103 S.Ct. 2317

On May 3, 1978, the Bloomingdale Police Department received by mail an anonymous handwritten letter which read as follows:

This letter is to inform you that you have a couple in your town who strictly make their living on selling drugs. They are Sue and Lance Gates, they live on Greenway, off Bloomingdale Rd. in the condominiums. Most of their buys are done in Florida. Sue his wife drives their car to Florida, where she leaves it to be loaded up with drugs, then Lance flies down and drives it back. Sue flies back after she drops the car off in

Florida. May 3 she is driving down there again and Lance will be flying down in a few days to drive it back. At the time Lance drives the car back he has the trunk loaded with over $100,000.00 in drugs. Presently they have over $100,000.00 worth of drugs in their basement.

They brag about the fact they never have to work, and are living on pushers. I guarantee if you watch them carefully you will make a big catch. They are friends with some big drug dealers, who visit their house often.

The letter was referred by the Chief of Police of the Bloomingdale Police Department to Detective Mader, who decided to pursue the tip. Mader learned, from the office of the Illinois Secretary of State, that an Illinois driver's license had been issued to one Lance Gates, residing at a stated address in Bloomingdale. He contacted a confidential informant, whose examination of certain financial records revealed a more recent address for the Gates, and he also learned from a police officer assigned to O'Hare Airport that "L. Gates" had made a reservation on eastern Airlines flight 245 to West Palm Beach, Fla., scheduled to depart from Chicago on May 5 at 4:51 P.M.

Mader then made arrangements with an agent of the Drug Enforcement Administration for surveillance of the May 5 Eastern Airlines flight. The agent later reported to Mader that Gates had boarded the flight, and that federal agents in Florida had observed him arrive in West Palm Beach and take a taxi to the nearby Holiday Inn. They also reported that Gates went to a room registered to one Susan Gates and that, at 7:00 A.M. the next morning, Gates and an unidentified woman left the motel in a Mercury bearing Illinois license plates and drove northbound on an interstate frequently used by travelers to the Chicago area. In addition, the DEA agent informed Mader that the license plate number on the Mercury was registered to a Hornet station wagon owned by Gates.

Mader signed an affidavit setting forth the foregoing facts, and submitted it to a judge of the Circuit Court of DuPage County, together with a copy of the anonymous letter. The judge of that court thereupon issued a search warrant for the Gates' residence and for their automobile.

At 5:15 A.M. on March 7th, only 36 hours after he had flown out of Chicago, Lance Gates, and his wife, returned to their home in Bloomingdale, driving the car in which they had left West Palm Beach some 22 hours earlier. The Bloomingdale police were awaiting them, searched the trunk of the Mercury, and uncovered approximately 350 pounds of marijuana. A search of the Gates' home revealed marijuana, weapons, and other contraband.

JUSTICE REHNQUIST delivered the opinion of the Court:

The Illinois court, alluding to an elaborate set of legal rules that have developed among various lower courts to enforce the "two-pronged test," found that the test had not been satisfied. First, the "veracity" prong was not satisfied because, "there was simply no basis [for] . . . conclud[ing] that the anonymous person [who wrote the letter to the Bloomingdale Police Department] was credible." The court indicated that corroboration by police of details contained in the letter might never satisfy the "veracity" prong, and in any event, could not

do so if, as in the present case, only "innocent" details are corroborated. In addition, the letter gave no indication of the basis of its writer's knowledge of the Gates' activities.

We agree with the Illinois Supreme Court that an informant's "veracity," "reliability" and "basis of knowledge" are all highly relevant in determining the value of his report. We do not agree, however, that these elements should be understood as entirely separate and independent requirements to be rigidly exacted in every case, which the opinion of the Supreme Court of Illinois would imply.

Perhaps the central teaching of our decisions bearing on the probable cause standard is that it is a "practical, nontechnical conception." "In dealing with probable cause, . . . as the very name implies, we deal with probabilities. These are not technical; they are the factual and practical considerations of everyday life on which reasonable and prudent men, not legal technicians, act."

Moreover, the "two-pronged test" directs analysis into two largely independent channels—the informant's "veracity" or "reliability" and his "basis of knowledge." There are persuasive arguments against according these two elements such independent status. Instead, they are better understood as relevant considerations in the totality of circumstances analysis that traditionally has guided probable cause determinations: a deficiency in one may be compensated for, in determining the overall reliability of a tip, by a strong showing as to the other, or by some other indicia of reliability.

The traditional standard for review of an issuing magistrate's probable cause determination has been that so long as the magistrate had a "substantial basis for . . . conclud[ing]" that a search would uncover evidence of wrongdoing, the Fourth Amendment requires no more. We think reaffirmation of this standard better serves the purpose of encouraging recourse to the warrant procedure and is more consistent with our traditional deference to the probable cause determinations of magistrates than is the "two-pronged test."

Ordinary citizens, like ordinary witnesses, generally do not provide extensive recitations of the basis of their everyday observations. Likewise, as the Illinois Supreme Court observed in this case, the veracity of persons supplying anonymous tips is by hypothesis largely unknown, and unknowable. As a result, anonymous tips seldom could survive a rigorous application of either of the *Spinelli* prongs. Yet, such tips, particularly when supplemented by independent police investigation, frequently contribute to the solution of otherwise "perfect crimes." While a conscientious assessment of the basis for crediting such tips is required by the Fourth Amendment, a standard that leaves virtually no place for anonymous citizen informants is not.

For all these reasons, we conclude that it is wiser to abandon the "two-pronged test" established by our decisions in *Aguilar* and *Spinelli*. In its place we reaffirm the totality of the circumstances analysis that traditionally has informed probable cause determinations.

[P]robable cause does not demand the certainty we associate with formal trials. It is enough that there was a fair probability that the writer of the anonymous letter had obtained his entire story either from the Gates or someone they trusted. And corroboration of major portions of the letter's predictions provides just this probability. It is apparent, therefore, that the judge issuing the warrant had a "substantial basis for . . . conclud[ing]" that probable cause to search the Gates' home and car existed. The judgment of the Supreme Court of Illinois, therefore, must be reversed.

Execution of a Search Warrant

If a search warrant (shown in Exhibit 10–2) is proper at the time it is issued, the search itself may become unconstitutional because of the manner in which it is carried out. When assessing the constitutionality of a search the courts have considered (1) the time at which the search is conducted, (2) the manner of entering the defendant's premises, and (3) the scope of the search conducted by the police officers.

The Time Factor   All jurisdictions have statutes or court rules that limit the time in which a search warrant may be executed. For example, federal search warrants must be executed within ten days of their issuance. Although the U.S. Supreme Court has not ruled on the issue, most courts recognize that a search warrant executed beyond the statutory period is an illegal search. Some jurisdictions also have statutory provisions regulating whether a search warrant may be executed during the daytime or nighttime. The Supreme Court, however, has never addressed this issue.[20]

The Manner of Entering the Defendant's Premises   In most situations, police officers must seek admittance by announcing their presence, identifying themselves as police officers, and stating their purpose.[21] This procedure is commonly referred to as the **knock and notice** requirement. Some states specifically provide for the issuance of no knock warrants in certain cases, most commonly, drug offenses.

In the absence of a "no knock" warrant, a number of exceptions allow the officers to dispense with the notice requirement and force entry into the defendant's premises. These exceptions apply when (1) announcing their presence would create a danger to the officers' safety, (2) announcing their presence would allow suspects to escape, or (3) giving notice would be likely to result in the destruction of the evidence sought to be seized. In *Richards v. Wisconsin*,[22] the Supreme Court refused to approve of no knock entries simply because the police were searching for drugs which might easily be destroyed. Lower courts, however, have distinguished between mere possession and sale or distribution of drugs. As one court recognized, "The connection between illegal drug operations and guns in our society is a tight one, . . . thus the police could reasonably suspect from the continuous use of the home as a drug stash house that guns would be present and that knocking and announcing their presence would be dangerous."[23]

Failure to comply with the knock and notice requirement, or to establish a recognized exception, renders the search unconstitutional.

The Scope of the Search   Because "nothing is left to the discretion of the officer executing the warrant," police may only search the premises described in the warrant and may only search for the items listed in the warrant.[24] The scope of the search is thus controlled by the nature and size of the items enumerated in the warrant. For example, a search for a small quantity of drugs may extend to the opening of small containers, but a search for a stolen automobile tire must be limited to those areas large enough to contain the item.

Knock and notice
police must announce their presence, identify themselves, and state their purpose (no knock warrants dispense with this requirement).

The conduct of the search is also governed by the **plain view doctrine,** which applies when the police are properly searching for items listed in the warrant, but come upon other seizable items not mentioned in the warrant.[25] The application of the plain view doctrine is one of the situations in which the courts distinguish between a search and a seizure. Although the search warrant controls and limits the scope of the "search," the propriety of a "seizure" may turn upon the operation of the plain view doctrine. For example, suppose the police open the defendant's closet to look for a stolen automobile tire described in the search warrant, but they spot narcotics in the closet. The police may seize the narcotics under the plain view doctrine because they were lawfully searching only for an item listed in the warrant, and because they recognized the narcotics as seizable items as soon as they appeared in plain view. On the other hand, if the police looked for the stolen automobile tire in a small desk drawer, they exceeded the proper scope of the warrant. Any items found in the drawer were uncovered only by an "improper view" (an illegal search) of the drawer.

Plain view doctrine
the police may seize items not specified in a search warrant if they discover such items while conducting a valid search.

WARRANTLESS SEARCHES

Although the U.S. Supreme Court often insists that warrantless searches must fall within a "few well-delineated exceptions," numerous exceptions to the general rule that searches must be conducted pursuant to a warrant permit warrantless searches. The remainder of this chapter addresses the exceptions that occur most often in criminal law practice: search incident to arrest, automobile searches, consent searches, and searches under exigent circumstances.

Search Incident to Arrest

A **search incident to arrest** is proper only if the arrest itself is lawful. An illegal arrest contaminates all items seized pursuant to that arrest, such as physical items taken from the person arrested, the defendant's fingerprints, or the defendant's subsequent confession. All items derived from an illegal arrest are subject to exclusion from evidence at the defendant's trial. If the arrest itself is lawful, the search must be incident to or substantially contemporaneous with the lawful arrest. The search may actually precede the arrest if the search and arrest are nearly simultaneous. Thus the "hot pursuit" doctrine permits the police to conduct a limited search while in pursuit of a fleeing defendant.[26]

The justification for a search incident to arrest is threefold: (1) an arrested defendant retains no significant expectation of privacy; (2) police must take immediate action to guard against the defendant's use of weapons to resist arrest or effect an escape; and (3) the police must act to prevent the defendant from destroying evidence. This threefold basis for the search incident exception requires that a distinction be drawn between searches of the arrestee's person, and searches of the areas under the control of the arrestee.

Search incident to arrest
must be substantially contemporaneous with a lawful arrest.

Search of the Arrestee
By arresting a suspect, the police have seized the entire person, including any items found on the suspect's body. The defendant may be fully searched at the place of arrest or during administrative processing at the police station. Items on the defendant's person, such as a shoulder bag, may be searched at the time of the arrest or "inventoried" at the police station.[27] Although the Supreme Court stated that an arrested person retains no significant expectation of privacy in the arrestee's person, many states have enacted statutes governing the conduct of strip searches and body cavity searches.[28] For example, one statute provides that strip searches (examination of genitalia, buttocks, or female breasts) must be conducted by persons of the same sex as the person arrested and out of the sight of all

other persons.[29] Body cavity searches (examination of or intrusion into body orifices) must be conducted under the supervision of medically trained personnel.

Search of the Area Under the Control of the Arrestee   The search of areas under the control of the arrestee is justified by the practical need to remove weapons and evidence from the defendant's control. A search may be made only in the area into which the arrestee might reach or lunge in order to grab a weapon or evidentiary items. Identifying the area or items within "lunging distance" of the arrestee turns upon the specific facts of the particular case. In addition to searching the areas under the control of the arrestee, the police may conduct a protective sweep of other areas in order to guard against other dangerous persons who might attack the police. This protective sweep is not designed to uncover evidence, but merely to discover if other persons are present on the premises. Thus the police in *Maryland v. Buie* could inspect the basement of the defendant's house because they suspected that a confederate was hiding there.

MARYLAND v. BUIE
Supreme Court of the United States, 1990
494 U.S. 325, 110 S.Ct. 1093

JUSTICE WHITE delivered the opinion of the Court:
A "protective sweep" is a quick and limited search of a premises, incident to an arrest and conducted to protect the safety of police officers or others. It is narrowly confined to a cursory visual inspection of those places in which a person might be hiding. In this case we must decide what level of justification is required by the Fourth and Fourteenth Amendments before police officers, while effecting the arrest of a suspect in his home pursuant to an arrest warrant, may conduct a warrantless protective sweep of all or part of the premises.

On February 3, 1986, two men committed an armed robbery of a Godfather's Pizza restaurant in Prince George's County, Maryland. One of the robbers was wearing a red running suit. The same day, police obtained arrest warrants for Jerome Edward Buie and his suspected accomplice in the robbery.

On February 5, the police executed an arrest warrant for Buie. Once inside, the officers fanned out through the first and second floors. Corporal Hames Rozar announced that he would "freeze" the basement so that no one could come up and surprise the officers. With his service revolver drawn, Rozar twice shouted into the basement, ordering anyone down there to come out. When a voice asked who was calling, Rozar announced three times: "This is the police, show me your hands." Eventually, a pair of hands appeared around the bottom of the stairwell and Buie emerged from the basement. He was arrested, searched, and handcuffed by Rozar. Thereafter, another officer entered the basement "in case there was someone else" down there. He noticed a

red running suit lying in plain view on a stack of clothing and seized it. (The lower court denied Buie's motion to suppress the running suit.)

The ingredients to apply the balance struck in *Terry* are present in this case. Possessing an arrest warrant and probable cause to believe Buie was in his home, the officers were entitled to enter and to search anywhere in the house in which Buie might be found. Once he was found, however, the search for him was over, and there was no longer that particular justification for entering any rooms that had not yet been searched.

That Buie had an expectation of privacy in those remaining areas of his house, however, does not mean such rooms were immune from entry. In *Terry* we were concerned with the immediate interest of the police officers in taking steps to assure themselves that the persons with whom they were dealing were not armed with or able to gain immediate control of a weapon that could unexpectedly and fatally be used against them. In the instant case, there is an analogous interest of the officers in taking steps to assure themselves that the house in which the suspect is being or has just been arrested is not harboring other persons who are dangerous and who could unexpectedly launch an attack. The risk of danger in the context of an arrest in the home is as great as, if not greater than, it is in the on-the-street or roadside investigatory encounter.

We should emphasize that such a protective sweep aimed at protecting the arresting officers, if justified by the circumstances, is nevertheless not a full search of the premises, but may extend only to a cursory inspection those spaces where a person may be found. The sweep lasts no longer than is necessary to dispel the reasonable suspicion of danger and in any event no longer than it takes to complete the arrest and depart from the premises.

The Fourth Amendment permits a properly limited protective sweep in conjunction with an in-home arrest when the searching officer possesses a reasonable belief based on specific and articulable facts that the area to be swept harbors an individual posing a danger to those on the arrest scene.

Automobile Searches

Contrary to popular rhetoric, the Fourth Amendment requirement for a search warrant contains no single "automobile" exception. A warrantless search of an automobile may occur under three distinct rationales: (1) the automobile may be an area under the control of an arrestee; (2) an automobile may be searched in emergency situations; and (3) an impounded automobile may be "inventoried" pursuant to police department regulations.

Vehicles Under the Control of the Arrestee
Following a lawful arrest of a motorist, the police may search the areas of the vehicle that are under the arrestee's control. For example, the front seat, back seat, and glove compartment. In order to avoid endless litigation over which particular area of an automobile was actually within reach of the arrestee, the U.S. Supreme Court announced a "straightforward" rule: "when a policeman has made a lawful custodial arrest of the occupant of an automobile, he may, as a contemporaneous incident of that arrest, search the passenger compartment of that automobile."[30] While legitimately searching the vehicle's interior, the police often encounter containers such as suitcases, packages, or clothing. The U.S. Supreme Court recognized that "if the passenger compartment is within the reach of the arrestee, so also will containers in it be within his reach." Thus the police may open such containers within the course of their search of the automobile's interior.

Although the interior of the automobile may be searched incident to arrest, the same is not necessarily true of the vehicle's trunk. If the police arrest a motorist who is standing at the rear of the car with the trunk open, the trunk can be searched because it is within lunging distance. In most cases, however, a motorist is inside the vehicle, and the trunk cannot be searched incident to arrest. Of course, a given case may include both probable cause to arrest the driver and probable cause to search the entire car. (See the next section dealing with emergency searches of automobiles.) The two types of searches are distinct, however, and should not be confused. Each type of search requires a separate justification and imposes separate limitations on the scope of the search.

In *Michigan v. Long,* the Supreme Court held that a protective sweep for weapons could extend to areas of a vehicle under the control of a person detained, but not arrested.[31] Unlike a search incident to arrest, the protective sweep in *Michigan v. Long* was limited to a search for weapons. The Court also stressed that it was not authorizing protective sweeps every time a motorist is stopped for investigation or for a traffic violation. A protective sweep is permissible only when the circumstances reasonably warrant the officer's belief that the suspect is dangerous and may gain immediate control of weapons.

Current law is unsettled as to the search of passengers and their property found in an automobile when the driver is arrested. The law is clear that police may order the driver and all passengers to exit the automobile. In addition, the police may "pat down" a passenger for weapons if there is reasonable suspicion that the passenger is armed and dangerous. The unsettled aspect of the law arose in *Wyoming v. Houghton*[32] when the police searched the purse of a passenger. The Court upheld the search in this case because the search was based on probable cause to search the car (see the next section), not on the fact that the driver of the car had been arrested. The Court stated that it was not prepared to rule on whether police could search a passenger's purse merely because the purse was found in an automobile whose driver had been arrested.

In recent years, considerable controversy has arisen as to whether law enforcement officials stop and arrest drivers for some minor traffic violation as a pretext for searching the automobile. Such claims are particularly troubling when the police target drivers because of race, a phenomenon often referred to as DWB—driving while Black. In *Whren v. United States*,[33] however, the Court held that so long as there are objective facts establishing a traffic violation, the trial courts may not inquire into a police officer's subjective basis for stopping and searching the vehicle. The Court stated that: "The constitutional basis for objecting to intentionally discriminatory application of laws is the Equal Protection Clause, not the Fourth Amendment. Subjective intentions play no role in ordinary, probable-cause Fourth Amendment analysis."

A somewhat related police practice was challenged in *Ohio v. Robinette*,[34] where a police officer on "drug interdiction patrol" stopped the defendant for speeding. While issuing the traffic ticket, the officer asked to search the car for drugs. It was the officer's standard practice to ask all motorists for consent to search, and the officer had conducted 786 consensual searches in one year. The Court held that the officer's practice was permissible and that citizens are not entitled to be told that they are free to decline an officer's request to search their vehicle or that they would be free to leave even if they did not consent to a search.

Search of Vehicles Based Upon Exigent Circumstances

In *Carroll v. United States,* the Court held that automobiles may be searched without a search warrant when officers have probable cause to believe that seizable items are within the vehicle and the vehicle could be moved before the police obtain a warrant from a magistrate.[35]

Carroll recognized the inherent mobility of automobiles as one of the first forms of exigent circumstances. Subsequent cases, however, have made it clear that ready mobility is not the only basis for this exception. *California v. Carney* recognized that vehicles, even mobile homes, are not as "private" as dwellings, and thus are entitled to less protection under the Fourth Amendment.

CALIFORNIA v. CARNEY
Supreme Court of the United States, 1985
471 U.S. 386, 105 S.Ct. 2066

[Drug Enforcement Agents searched the defendant's Dodge Mini Motor Home while it was parked in a public parking lot.]

CHIEF JUSTICE BURGER delivered the opinion of the Court:
The reasons for the vehicle exception are twofold. Besides the element of mobility, less rigorous warrant requirements govern because the expectation of privacy with respect to one's automobile is significantly less than that relating to one's home or office. These reduced expectations of privacy derive from the pervasive regulation of vehicles capable of traveling on the public highways.

Automobiles, unlike homes, are subjected to pervasive and continuing governmental regulation and controls, including periodic inspection and licensing requirements. As an everyday occurrence, police stop and examine vehicles when license plates or inspection stickers have expired, or if other violations, such as exhaust fumes or excessive noise, are noted, or if headlights or other safety equipment are not in proper working order.

The public is fully aware that it is accorded less privacy in its automobiles because of this compelling governmental need for regulation. In short, the pervasive schemes of regulation, which necessarily lead to reduced expectations of privacy, and the exigencies attendant to ready mobility justify searches without prior recourse to the authority of a magistrate so long as the overriding standard of probable cause is met.

While it is true that respondent's vehicle possessed some, if not many of the attributes of a home, it is equally clear that the vehicle falls clearly within the scope of the exception laid down in *Carroll* and applied in succeeding cases. Like the automobile in *Carroll,* respondent's motor home was readily mobile. Absent the prompt search and seizure, it could readily have been moved beyond the reach of the police. Furthermore, the vehicle was licensed to "operate on public streets; [was] serviced in public places; . . . and [was] subject to extensive regulation and inspection." And the vehicle was so situated that an objective observer would conclude that it was being used not as a residence, but as a vehicle.

As was true of searches of vehicles incident to arrest, searches of vehicles based on exigent circumstances often bring the police into contact with containers such as luggage, packages, or clothing. *United States v. Ross* held that a lawful search extends to "the entire area in which the object of the search may be found and is not limited by the possibility that separate acts of entry or opening may be required to complete the search."[36] The U.S. Supreme Court refused to recognize any "nice distinctions" between glove compartments, trunks, and wrapped packages. When police have probable cause to believe a seizable item is located somewhere in the vehicle, they may search any container or any part of the vehicle where the item could be located. If there is probable cause to believe seizable items are located within the automobile, the Fourth Amendment does not recognize "a distinction among packages or containers based on ownership. . . . A passenger's personal belongings, just like the driver's belongings or containers attached to the car like a glove compartment, are 'in' the car, and the officer has probable cause to search for contraband *in* the car."[37]

Inventory of Impounded Automobiles   In a number of situations the police may find themselves in control of an automobile, but without probable cause to search the vehicle. For example, the vehicle may have been towed for illegal parking, or as in *Colorado v. Bertine,* the police arrest the driver and then must take steps to protect the vehicle from theft or vandalism. The police may merely lock the vehicle and place it in an impoundment lot, or they may inventory the property contained within the vehicle. An inventory of the contents of the vehicle is an intrusion upon privacy and thus covered by the Fourth Amendment. This intrusion, however, does not require probable cause to believe that the vehicle contains evidence of a crime.

COLORADO v. BERTINE
Supreme Court of the United States, 1987
479 U.S. 367, 107 S.Ct. 738

[A Boulder, Colorado, police officer arrested respondent for driving his van while under the influence of alcohol. After respondent was taken into custody and before a tow truck arrived to take the van to an impoundment lot, another officer, acting in accordance with local police procedures, inventoried the van's contents, opening a closed backpack in which he found various containers holding controlled substances, cocaine paraphernalia, and a large amount of cash.]

CHIEF JUSTICE REHNQUIST delivered the opinion of the Court:
An inventory search may be "reasonable" under the Fourth Amendment even though it is not conducted

pursuant to warrant based upon probable cause. In *South Dakota v. Opperman*, 428 U.S. 364 (1976), this Court assessed the reasonableness of an inventory search of the glove compartment in an abandoned automobile impounded by the police. We found that inventory procedures serve to protect an owner's property while it is in the custody of the police, to insure against claims of lost, stolen, or vandalized property, and to guard the police from danger. In light of these strong governmental interests and the diminished expectation of privacy in an automobile, we upheld the search.

The Supreme Court of Colorado expressed the view that the search in this case was unreasonable because Bertine's van was towed to a secure, lighted facility and because Bertine himself could have been offered the opportunity to make other arrangements for the safekeeping of his property. But the security of the storage facility does not completely eliminate the need for inventorying; the police may still wish to protect themselves or the owners of the lot against false claims of theft or dangerous instrumentalities. And while giving Bertine an opportunity to make alternate arrangements would undoubtedly have been possible, the real question is not what "could have been achieved," but whether the Fourth Amendment *requires* such steps. . . . The reasonableness of any particular governmental activity does not necessarily or invariably turn on the existence of alternative "less intrusive" means.

We conclude that reasonable police regulations relating to inventory procedures administered in good faith satisfy the Fourth Amendment, even though courts might as a matter of hindsight be able to devise equally reasonable rules requiring a different procedure.

The police need not obtain a search warrant before inventorying the contents of an automobile, but they must be acting pursuant to departmental policy for handling seized or impounded vehicles. For example, police department policy may specify that all vehicles will be inventoried when the driver has been arrested, but vehicles will not be subject to inventory when the vehicles were towed for a parking violation. Should the police wish to depart from standard procedure by inventorying a vehicle towed for illegal parking, they must obtain a search warrant.

Consent Searches

Consensual search
the defendant's permission to search must be freely and voluntarily given.

The Fourth Amendment protects a citizen's right to privacy and liberty, but like any constitutional right, this right can be waived and the citizen may consent to a search. A valid **consensual search** eliminates the need to obtain a search warrant and the need for probable cause. In place of a warrant or probable cause, the police need only prove that the defendant's consent to search was freely and voluntarily given.

Consent searches raise two questions: (1) On a practical level, why would anyone consent to a search knowing it will reveal seizable items? (2) As a constitutional question, is consent given by a defendant who is unaware of the right to withhold consent voluntarily? The short answer to the first question is that people often consent to a search, perhaps in hope that the police won't find a cleverly hidden item. The constitutional question is answered in *Schneckloth v. Bustamonte.*

SCHNECKLOTH v. BUSTAMONTE
Supreme Court of the United States, 1973
412 U.S. 218, 193 S.Ct. 2041

While on routine patrol at 2:40 A.M., a police officer stopped an automobile when he observed that one headlight and its license plate light were burned out. Six men were in the vehicle. When the driver could not produce a driver's license, the officer asked if any of the five had any evidence of identification. Only Alcala produced a license, and he explained that the car was his brother's. The officer asked Alcala if he could search the car.

Alcala replied, "Sure, go ahead," and actually helped in the search of the car, by opening the trunk and glove compartment. Three checks that had previously been stolen from a car wash were found wadded up under the left rear seat. The checks in question were admitted in evidence at Bustamonte's trial.

JUSTICE STEWART delivered the opinion of the Court:
The precise question in this case is what must the state prove to demonstrate that a consent was "voluntarily" given.

In this case there is no evidence of any inherently coercive tactics—either from the nature of the police questioning or the environment in which it took place. Indeed, since consent searches will normally occur on a person's own familiar territory, the specter of incommunicado police interrogation in some remote station house is simply inapposite. There is no reason to believe, under circumstances such as are present here, that the response to a policeman's question is presumptively coerced; and there is, therefore, no reason to reject the traditional test for determining the voluntariness of a person's response.

Our decision today is a narrow one. We hold only that when the subject of a search is not in custody and the State attempts to justify a search on the basis of his consent, the Fourth and Fourteenth Amendments require that it demonstrate that the consent was in fact voluntarily given, and not the result of duress or coercion, express or implied. Voluntariness is a question of fact to be determined from all the circumstances, and while the subject's knowledge of a right to refuse is a factor to be taken into account, the prosecution is not required to demonstrate such knowledge as a prerequisite to establishing a voluntary consent.

The voluntariness of consent to search is governed by the totality of the surrounding circumstances. For example, the youth of the defendant; the defendant's lack of formal education or prior experience with the police; the circumstances of custody; and the psychological impact of these factors on the defendant. No single factor is controlling, and the police officer's failure to inform the defendant of the right to refuse consent does not render the consent involuntary. Where consent is obtained through coercion, however, it will not be deemed voluntary. In *Bumper v. North Carolina,* consent to the search of a house was involuntary because the officer claimed to have a search warrant, thus the occupant merely bowed to the inevitable in permitting the search.[38]

When conducting a consent search the police have no more authority than they have been given by the consent. The terms of the defendant's consent establish the permissible scope of the search in regard to time, duration, area, and intensity. Thus a defendant might consent to a search of her living room and kitchen, but withhold consent to search the bedroom. According to *Florida v. Jimeno,* the defendant must clearly state what he does and does not consent to have searched.

FLORIDA v. JIMENO
Supreme Court of the United States, 1991
500 U.S. 248, 111 S.Ct. 1801

[After stopping the defendant's car for a traffic violation, the police officer declared that he had reason to believe that the defendant was carrying narcotics in the car, and asked permission to search it. The defendant consented and the officer found cocaine inside a folded paper bag on the car's floorboard. The trial court granted defendant's motion to suppress the cocaine on the ground that his consent to search the car did not carry with it specific consent to open the bag and examine its contents.]

CHIEF JUSTICE REHNQUIST delivered the opinion of the Court:
The standard for measuring the scope of a suspect's consent under the Fourth Amendment is that of "objective" reasonableness—what would the typical reasonable person have

understood by the exchange between the officer and the suspect? The question before us, then, is whether it is reasonable for an officer to consider a suspect's general consent to a search of his car to include consent to examine a paper bag lying on the floor of the car. We think that it is.

The scope of a search is generally defined by its expressed object. In this case the terms of the search's authorization were simple. Defendant granted the police officer permission to search his car, and did not place any explicit limitation on the scope of the search. The officer informed defendant that he believed the defendant was carrying narcotics, and that he would be looking for narcotics in the car. A reasonable person may be expected to know that narcotics are generally carried in some form of a container. "Contraband goods rarely are strewn across the trunk or floor of a car." The authori-

zation to search in this case, therefore, extended beyond the surfaces of the car's interior to the paper bag lying on the car's floor.

Defendant argues, and the Florida trial court agreed with him that if the police wish to search closed containers within a car they must separately request permission to search each container. But we see no basis for adding this sort of superstructure to the Fourth Amendment's basic test of objective reasonableness. A suspect may of course delimit as he chooses the scope of the search to which he consents. But if his consent would reasonably be understood to extend to a particular container, the Fourth Amendment provides no grounds for requiring a more explicit authorization.

The judgment of the Supreme Court of Florida is accordingly reversed.

The *Jimeno* opinion added that the "scope of a search may be further defined during the course of the search by the passive acquiescence of the person whose property is being searched." The defendant's failure to object when the police officer began to open the paper bag was regarded as an indication that the defendant had consented to a search of the bag.

Third-Party Consent One of the difficult concepts in the area of consent searches is the realization that one person may consent to a governmental intrusion upon the privacy rights of another person. *United States v. Matlock* held that **third-party consent** may be given by one who shares use, access, or control of the property or premises.[39] For example, roommates who share unrestricted use of joint premises share authority to admit others, including police officers. Whatever a defendant's subjective expectation of privacy might be; by sharing use, access, or control with a third party, the defendant "assumes the risk" that the third party will consent to a search.

Although third-party consent searches arise most often in situations involving spouses and parent-child relationships, the legal status of the parties is not the controlling factor. When determining whether a third party has the right to consent to a search, legal considerations give way to the practical day-to-day living arrangement between the parties. For example, a parent cannot consent to the search of a footlocker set aside for a child's exclusive use.[40] Thus the consent of a third party cannot extend to areas or materials used exclusively by the defendant, *unless* the police act in good faith. *Illinois v. Rodriguez* condoned a police officer's mistaken belief that he has been given authority to search.

Third-party consent
permission to search given by
one who shares use, access, or
control of the defendant's
property or premises.

ILLINOIS v. RODRIGUEZ
Supreme Court of the United States, 1990
497 U.S. 177, 110 S.Ct. 2793

JUSTICE SCALIA delivered the opinion of the Court:
On July 26, 1985, police were summoned to the residence of Dorothy Jackson. They were met by Ms. Jackson's daughter, Gail Fischer, who showed signs of a se-

vere beating. She told the officers that she had been assaulted by defendant Edward Rodriguez earlier that day in an apartment on South California. Fischer stated that Rodriguez was then asleep in the apartment, and she consented to travel there with the police in order to unlock the door with her key so that the officers could enter and arrest him. During this conversation, Fischer several times referred to the apartment on South California as "our" apartment, and said that she had clothes and furniture there. It is unclear whether she indicated that she currently lived at the apartment, or only that she used to live there.

The police officers drove to the apartment on South California, accompanied by Fischer. They did not obtain an arrest warrant for Rodriguez, nor did they seek a search warrant for the apartment. At the apartment, Fischer unlocked the door with her key and gave the officers permission to enter. They moved through the door into the living room, where they observed in plain view drug paraphernalia and containers filled with white powder that they believed (correctly, as later analysis showed) to be cocaine.

At trial, the evidence showed that although Fischer, with her two small children, had lived with Rodriguez beginning in December 1984, she had moved out on July 1, 1985, almost a month before the search at issue here, and had gone to live with her mother. She took her children's clothing with her, though leaving behind some furniture and household effects. During the period after July 1 she sometimes spent the night at Rodriguez's apartment, but never invited her friends there, and never went there herself when he was not home. Her name was not on the lease nor did she contribute to the rent. She had a key to the apartment, which she said at trial she had taken without Rodriguez's knowledge. On these

facts the State has not established that, with respect to the South California apartment, Fischer had "joint access or control for most purposes." To the contrary, the Appellate Court's determination of no common authority over the apartment was obviously correct.

What the defendant is assured by the Fourth Amendment is not that no government search of his house will occur unless he consents; but that no such search will occur that is "unreasonable." There are various elements, of course, that can make a search of a person's house "reasonable"—one of which is the consent of the person or his co-tenant. The essence of defendant's argument is that we should impose upon this element a requirement that we have not imposed upon other elements that regularly compel government officers to exercise judgment regarding the fact: namely, the requirement that their judgment be not only responsible but correct.

In order to satisfy the "reasonableness" requirement of the Fourth Amendment, what is generally demanded of the many factual determinations that must regularly be made by agents of the government—whether the magistrate issuing a warrant, the police officer executing a warrant, or the police officer conducting a search or seizure under one of the exceptions to the warrant requirement—is not that they always be correct, but that they always be reasonable.

We see no reason to depart from this general rule with respect to facts bearing upon the authority to consent to a search.

Searches Under Exigent Circumstances

Many of the "well-delineated exceptions" to the warrant clause requirement are merely specific types of exigent circumstances. Search incident to arrest, hot pursuit, and temporary detentions are particular types of emergencies that occur often enough to be treated as separate exceptions to the warrant clause. This section addresses the basic rationale used to identify exigent circumstances that may not fit within the other well-established categories.

An **exigent circumstance** is a situation in which a law enforcement officer confronts "an immediate major crisis in the performance of duty [which] affords neither time nor opportunity to apply to a magistrate."[41] In *Camera v. Municipal Court*, the Court spoke of dispensing with the warrant requirement whenever "the burden of obtaining a warrant is likely to frustrate the governmental purpose behind the search."[42] In determining whether the delay to obtain a warrant will frustrate the purpose of the search, the courts consider three factors: (1) the time required to obtain a warrant, (2) the time required to frustrate the search by destroying or altering the object of the search, and (3) the likelihood that the destruction or alteration will take place.

Exigent circumstance
a situation in which a law enforcement officer confronts "an immediate major crisis in the performance of duty which affords neither time nor opportunity to apply to a magistrate."

Obtaining a Warrant   The time factor for exigent circumstances requires the court to examine the particular facts and assess the difficulty or ease with which a warrant could have been obtained. The time required to obtain a warrant varies according to the physical setting involved. For example, in urban communities magistrates may be available twenty-four hours a day at a central and convenient location. But in rural areas, particularly at night, police officers may have difficulty locating an available magistrate or judge who can quickly review the affidavit for a search warrant.

Destroying the Evidence The second factor in defining exigent circumstances requires the court to assess the difficulty or ease with which the purpose of the search could be frustrated, most typically by the defendant's destruction of the sought-after evidence. This determination also requires close examination of the particular facts. For example, the time required to dismantle an apparatus for manufacturing illegal drugs differs from the time required to flush a small quantity of drugs down a nearby commode.

Likelihood of Destruction The third factor, determining the likelihood that destruction of evidence will occur, is perhaps the most difficult determination when identifying exigent circumstances. Except in rare cases, the sought-after evidence will not self-destruct.[43] An affirmative act is normally required to destroy or alter the evidence, therefore the courts must assess the probability that someone will act to destroy the evidence. If the defendant has the power to destroy the evidence, the courts assume that the defendant would likely take advantage of such an opportunity. The likelihood that third parties will destroy evidence, however, is much less clear. In *Vale v. Louisiana*, the U.S. Supreme Court was unimpressed by the possibility that the defendant's mother and brother could destroy evidence.[44] The Court indicated that an emergency exists only when the actual destruction of evidence is imminent. The lower courts, however, often recognize the threat of third-party destruction of evidence as an exigent circumstance.

A warrantless search is one possible response to an emergency situation. An alternative response is for the police to **freeze the status quo** (act to prevent the destruction of evidence) until a warrant can be obtained. In *Segura v. United States*, police officers entered Segura's apartment, secured the premises by preventing anyone from entering, and remained there for nineteen hours until other officers arrived with a search warrant.[45] According to the U.S. Supreme Court, securing the premises did not intrude upon privacy, although it did interfere with the defendant's property rights to the premises. The Court suggested that seizures which freeze the status quo could be justified on grounds that would not justify a search because

> society's interest in the discovery and protection of incriminating evidence from removal or destruction can supersede, at least for a limited period, a person's possessory interest in property, provided that there is probable cause to believe that that property is associated with criminal activity.

Administrative Searches

Prior to *Katz v. United States*, the criminal justice system was not concerned with inspections by administrative agencies other than law enforcement agencies. For example, in *Frank v. Maryland*, the U.S. Supreme Court held that "inspections" by health department officials were not searches within the meaning of the Fourth Amendment because the amendment was primarily concerned with searches for evidence of criminal activity, and only peripherally concerned with the right of privacy.[46] The *Frank* case was overturned in *Camara v. Municipal Court*, when the U. S. Supreme Court stated that it was "anomalous to say that the individual and his private property are fully protected . . . only when the individual is suspected of criminal behavior."

Camara and *Katz* together defined a search as any government action that intrudes upon a legitimate expectation of privacy. The underlying motivation for the search,

Freeze the status quo an act to prevent the destruction of evidence until a warrant can be obtained, which is permitted when the police encounter exigent circumstances.

whether it be criminal investigation or benign purposes of public health and safety, is no longer relevant in defining the scope of Fourth Amendment protections. Thus in *New Jersey v. T.L.O.*, the Fourth Amendment was applied to a public school official's search for cigarettes that violated the school's no smoking policy.[47] When the vice-principal found marijuana in a student's purse, the subsequent criminal prosecution demonstrated that administrative inspections are relevant to the criminal justice system when evidence of criminal activity is discovered in the course of an inspection conducted by a civil agency.

Absent consent or exigent circumstances, a search warrant is required before administrative inspections can take place. *Camara*, however, recognized that most citizens allow inspection of their property without a warrant and consequently "warrants should normally be sought only after entry is refused." The courts also have recognized a form of "implied" consent that is uniquely applicable to inspections of certain heavily regulated businesses: for example, liquor distributors, firearm dealers, operations under the Mine Safety and Health Act, and automobile junkyards.[48] A defendant's decision to enter into a business subject to heavy government regulation amounts to implied consent to the warrantless inspections authorized by existing statutes or administrative regulations. However, the implied consent doctrine was limited to closely regulated industries in *Marshall v. Barlow's, Inc.*, where the U.S. Supreme Court refused to approve warrantless inspections under the broadly applicable Occupational Safety and Health Act (OSHA).[49]

In the absence of consent, the courts have recognized only limited grounds for an emergency that excuses the failure to obtain a warrant authorizing an inspection. The emergency exception to the administrative warrant requirement rarely arises in the context of routine inspections for violations of the building code or violations of health and safety regulations. The major cases applying the emergency exception arose from a fire marshal's inspection of a fire scene. In *Michigan v. Tyler*, and *Michigan v. Clifford*, the U.S. Supreme Court recognized that firefighters need no warrant to enter a blazing building, nor to remain on the scene to investigate the cause of a blaze after it has been extinguished.[50] After the emergency has passed, however, a subsequent post-fire search can be conducted only pursuant to a warrant, consent, or the identification of some new exigency.

SUMMARY

The Fourth Amendment protects certain forms of privacy, and sets forth the procedural requirements that the government must follow when intruding upon protected privacy interests. The scope or coverage of the amendment turns upon the definition of a search, which is in turn determined by identifying the forms of privacy that are entitled to constitutional protection. The *Katz* decision rests the definition of a search on a two-pronged test: the citizen must manifest a subjective desire for privacy; and the desire must be one that society is prepared to recognize as reasonable or legitimate.

When a search occurs, the government must establish that the search was constitutionally "reasonable." The definition of reasonableness hinges upon the basis for conducting the search: (1) Did police have probable cause? (2) Was a search warrant obtained? (3) Did an exception which excuses the absence of a search warrant occur? (4) Was the search carried out in a proper manner?

At times, however, the U.S. Supreme Court abandons the above matrix for determining reasonableness and substitutes a reasonable balancing of governmental and individual interests as presented in the totality of the circumstances. Familiarity with the most commonly occurring exceptions to the warrant requirement is helpful, but the general rubric of reasonableness might encompass searches that do not fall within one of the traditional exceptions authorizing warrantless searches.

CONCEPT SUMMARY

Checklist for Lawful Searches

Consult local law to determine what changes have been made in a particular jurisdiction.

Probable Cause	Reliable facts indicating that seizable items are likely to be found at the place and time of the search
Warrant	Required in the absence of an emergency or consent
Knock and Notice	Requirement that police knock and announce their presence and purpose unless an emergency justifies their unannounced entry
Scope of the Search	Any area that could contain the items listed in the search warrant
Duration of the Search	Lasts until all items listed in the warrant are found (when all items are located, the search must end)
Plain View	Any additional seizable items that come into the plain view of police while they are searching for the items enumerated in a warrant

Warrantless Searches

TYPE OF SEIZURE	JUSTIFICATION	SCOPE OF SEARCH
Incident to Arrest	Lawful arrest, contemporaneous search	Arrestee's person and areas under arrestee's control
Exigent Circumstances	Probable cause to search; an emergency precludes obtaining a search warrant	Anywhere the seizable item could be located
Freeze the Status Quo	Probable cause to search; an emergency precludes obtaining a search warrant	Prevention of the potential destruction of evidence until a search warrant is obtained
Consent of Suspect	Free and voluntary consent	Areas authorized to be searched by the suspect
Consent of Third Party	Party exercises use, access, or control over the area to be searched	Areas authorized to be searched by the third party
Inventory of Automobile	Inventory conducted pursuant to police department regulations	Whatever areas of the automobile are specified in the regulations
Administrative Inspection	Implied consent because of heavily regulated industry; or an emergency situation exists	Areas subject to government inspection

DISCUSSION QUESTIONS

1. What is the ultimate test for the constitutionality of a warrantless search: whether the search was reasonable under the totality of the circumstances, or whether it was reasonable for the police to act without a warrant?

2. Does a person's reasonable expectation of privacy include that a police helicopter will not fly over the person's house and look through a broken window? See *Florida v. Riley*, 488 U.S. 445 (1989).

3. While the police are executing a warrant to search a house for a stolen television, they open the bedroom closet and find the television. They then open a second closet and find cocaine. May they seize the cocaine under the plain view doctrine?

4. If the police are searching for narcotics, does the possibility of destruction always justify a no knock entry?

5. If a suspect is arrested inside the suspect's home, may the entire home be searched incident to arrest?

PRACTICE EXERCISES

1. When are police permitted to search the trunk of an automobile?

2. Does your jurisdiction have rules governing strip searches and/or body cavity searches?

3. Under what circumstances may a roommate consent to a search of a person's apartment? Has your jurisdiction evolved any special rules governing consent by parents, children, or spouses?

4. What is the procedure in your jurisdiction for obtaining an administrative search warrant?

5. Has your jurisdiction dealt with "anticipatory" search warrants? For example, may the police obtain a search warrant because they anticipate that drugs will be delivered to the suspect's dwelling tomorrow?

WEB SITE

Legal Information Institute, Law.cornell.edu

KEY TERMS

Reasonableness clause	Informant	Consensual search
Warrant clause	Totality of circumstances	Third-party consent
Search	Knock and notice	Exigent circumstance
Open fields	Plain view doctrine	Freeze the status quo
Probable cause	Search incident to arrest	

NOTES

1. *Winston v. Lee*, 470 U.S. 753, 105 S.Ct. 1611 (1985).
2. *Delaware v. Prouse*, 440 U.S. 648, 99 S.Ct. 1391 (1979).
3. *Skinner v. Railway Labor Executives' Assoc.*, 489 U.S. 602, 109 S.Ct. 1402 (1989).
4. See *Olmstead v. United States*, 277 U.S. 438, 48 S.Ct. 564 (1928).
5. See *Hoffa v. United States*, 385 U.S. 293, 87 S.Ct. 408 (1966) (Chapter 11).
6. *Dow Chemical v. United States*, 476 U.S. 227, 106 S.Ct. 1819 (1986); *Florida v. Riley*, 488 U.S. 445, 109 S.Ct. 693 (1989).
7. *California v. Greenwood*, 486 U.S. 35, 108 S.Ct. 1625 (1988).
8. *Bond v. United States*, 529 U.S. 334, 120 S.Ct. 1462 (2000).
9. *Wilson v. Layne*, 526 U.S. 603, 119 S.Ct. 960 (1999).
10. See *Segura v. United States*, 468 U.S. 796, 104 S.Ct. 3380 (1984).
11. *Terry v. Ohio*, 392 U.S. 1, 88 S.Ct. 1868 (1968); *Camara v. Municipal Court*, 387 U.S. 523, 87 S.Ct. 1727 (1967).
12. *Stanford v. Texas*, 379 U.S. 476, 85 S.Ct. 506 (1965).
13. 42 U.S.C.A. § 2000aa (1982).
14. *New York v. P.J. Video*, 475 U.S. 868, 106 S.Ct. 1610 (1986).
15. *Ornelas v. United States*, 517 U.S. 690, 116 S.Ct. 1657 (1996).
16. See *Lo-Ji Sales, Inc. v. New York*, 442 U.S. 319, 99 S.Ct. 2319 (1979).
17. See *Berger v. Commonwealth*, 213 Va. 54, 189 S.E.2d 360 (1972).
18. *Aguilar v. Texas*, 378 U.S. 108, 84 S.Ct. 1509 (1964).
19. *Spinelli v. United States*, 393 U.S. 410, 89 S.Ct. 584 (1969).

20. See *Gooding v. United States,* 416 U.S. 430, 94 S.Ct. 1780 (1974).
21. See *Ker v. California,* 374 U.S. 23, 83 S.Ct. 1623 (1963).
22. *Richards v. Wisconsin,* 520 U.S. 385, 117 S.Ct. 1416 (1997).
23. *United States v. Grogins,* 163 F.3d 795 (4th Cir. 1998).
24. See *Stanford v. Texas,* 379 U.S. 476, 85 S.Ct. 506 (1965).
25. See *Horton v. California,* 496 U.S. 128, 110 S.Ct. 2301 (1990).
26. See *Warden v. Hayden,* 387 U.S. 294, 87 S.Ct. 1642 (1967).
27. See *Illinois v. Lafayette,* 462 U.S. 640, 103 S.Ct. 2605 (1983).
28. See *United States v. Robinson,* 414 U.S. 218, 94 S.Ct. 467 (1973).
29. Va. Code § 19.2-59.1.
30. *New York v. Belton,* 453 U.S. 454, 101 S.Ct. 2860 (1981).
31. *Michigan v. Long,* 463 U.S. 1032, 103 S.Ct. 3469 (1983).
32. *Wyoming v. Houghton,* 526 U.S. 295, 119 S.Ct. 1297 (1999).
33. *Whren v. United States,* 517 U.S. 806, 116 S.Ct. 1769 (1996).
34. *Ohio v. Robinette,* 519 U.S. 33, 117 S.Ct. 417 (1996).
35. *Carroll v. United States,* 267 U.S. 132, 45 S.Ct. 280 (1925).
36. *United States v. Ross,* 456 U.S. 798, 102 S.Ct. 2157 (1982).
37. *Wyoming v. Houghton,* 526 U.S. 295, 119 S.Ct. 1297 (1999).
38. *Bumper v. North Carolina,* 391 U.S. 543, 88 S.Ct. 1788 (1968).
39. *United States v. Matlock,* 415 U.S. 164, 94 S.Ct. 988 (1974).
40. *United States v. Block,* 590 F.2d 535 (4th Cir. 1978).
41. *District of Columbia v. Little,* 178 F.2d 13 (D.C. Cir. 1949).
42. *Camera v. Municipal Court,* 387 U.S. 523, 87 S.Ct. 1727 (1967).
43. But see, *Schmerber v. California,* 384 U.S. 757, 86 S.Ct. 1826 (1966). Chapter 8, section I.
44. *Vale v. Louisiana,* 399 U.S. 30, 90 S.Ct. 1969 (1970).
45. *Segura v. United States,* 468 U.S. 796, 104 S.Ct. 3380 (1984).
46. *Frank v. Maryland,* 359 U.S. 360, 79 S.Ct. 804 (1959).
47. *New Jersey v. T.L.O.,* 469 U.S. 325, 105 S.Ct. 733 (1985).
48. *Colonnade Catering Corp. v. United States,* 397 U.S. 72, 90 S.Ct. 774 (1970); *United States v. Biswell,* 406 U.S. 311, 92 S.Ct. 1593 (1972); *Donovan v. Dewey,* 452 U.S. 594, 101 S.Ct. 2534 (1981); *New York v. Burger,* 482 U.S. 691, 107 S.Ct. 2636 (1987).
49. *Marshall v. Barlow's, Inc.,* 436 U.S. 307, 98 S.Ct. 1816 (1978).
50. *Michigan v. Tyler,* 436 U.S. 499, 98 S.Ct. 1942 (1978); *Michigan v. Clifford,* 464 U.S. 287, 104 S.Ct. 641 (1984).

GOVERNMENT MONITORING OF COMMUNICATIONS AND THE FOURTH AMENDMENT EXCLUSIONARY RULE

Chapter **11**

CHAPTER OUTLINE

This chapter concludes a three-chapter consideration of the Fourth Amendment by addressing two areas: (1) the legal standards governing use of informers and eavesdropping, and (2) the Fourth Amendment's exclusionary rule, which applies to certain forms of government monitoring of communications and to searches and seizures.

GOVERNMENT EAVESDROPPING

Prior to the U. S. Supreme Court's focus on privacy rights in *Katz v. United States*, the Fourth Amendment did not apply to the seizure of communications.[1] *Olmstead v. United States* is the most famous example of the Court's pre-*Katz* insistence that the amendment only protected against a physical trespass upon real property or a physical seizure of personal property.[2] In *Olmstead*, federal officers monitored a defendant's telephone conversations by installing listening devices on the telephone lines *outside* the defendant's house. The Court held that conversations were intangibles and not included within the Fourth Amendment's prohibition against unreasonable searches and seizures of "persons, houses, papers, or effects." According to *Olmstead*, eyes and ears cannot "search" as neither can trespass; nor can eyes and ears "seize" tangible property.

In a famous dissent, Justice Brandeis laid the groundwork for the protection of privacy rights ultimately endorsed when *Katz* overturned the *Olmstead* decision:

> The makers of our Constitution undertook to secure conditions favorable to the pursuit of happiness. They recognized the significance of man's spiritual nature, of his feelings and of his intellect. They knew that only a part of the pain, pleasure and satisfactions of life are to be found in material things. They sought to protect Americans in their beliefs, their thoughts, their emotions and their sensations. They conferred, as against the Government, the right to be let alone—the most comprehensive of rights, and the right most valued by civilized men. To protect that right, every unjustifiable intrusion by the Government upon the privacy of the individual, whatever the means employed, must be deemed a violation of the Fourth Amendment.

Katz's adoption of the expectation of privacy rationale extended the reach of the Fourth Amendment to certain forms of electronic eavesdropping. Congress and many state legislatures have enacted specific statutes further regulating the government's use of electronic eavesdropping.

Warrantless Eavesdropping

In the absence of electronic devices, the Fourth Amendment does not apply to governmental action that deceives individuals into revealing information. The U.S. Supreme Court promulgated this rule in *Hoffa v. United States*.

HOFFA v. UNITED STATES
Supreme Court of the United States, 1966
385 U.S. 293, 87 S.Ct. 408

[James Hoffa was convicted for endeavoring to bribe members of a jury during the so-called Test Fleet trial, which ended in a hung jury. A substantial part of the government's case came from the testimony of one Partin, a local union official. After being released from jail where he had been held pending state and federal charges, Partin made frequent visits to the Hoffa hotel suite, on which occasions he was continually in the company of Hoffa and his associates. The Court assumed that Partin was a government informer and had been compensated for his services.]

JUSTICE STEWART delivered the opinion of the Court: The argument is that Partin's failure to disclose his role as a government informer vitiated the consent that the petitioner gave to Partin's repeated entries into (Hoffa's hotel) suite, and that by listening to the petitioner's statements Partin conducted an illegal "search" for verbal evidence. Where this argument fails is in its misapprehension of the fundamental nature and scope of Fourth Amendment protection. What the Fourth Amendment protects is the security a man relies upon when he places himself or his property within a constitutionally protected area, be it his home or his office, his hotel room or his automobile.

In the present case, however, it is evident that no interest legitimately protected by the Fourth Amendment is involved. Partin was in the suite by invitation, and every conversation which he heard was either directed to him or knowingly carried on in his presence. [Hoffa], in a word, was not relying on the security of the hotel room; he was relying upon his misplaced confidence that Partin would not reveal his wrongdoing.

Neither this Court nor any member of it has ever expressed the view that the Fourth Amendment protects a wrongdoer's misplaced belief that a person to whom he voluntarily confides his wrongdoing will not reveal it.

The *Hoffa* case predated the *Katz* decision, thus the *Hoffa* Court focused on the security of Hoffa's hotel room as a constitutionally protected "area." After *Katz*'s recognition that the Fourth Amendment protects "people, not places," the discussion of the security of a hotel room becomes less relevant. Although the Court's language has changed in the post-*Katz* era, the Court has not altered its approach to undercover agents. A speaker who converses with another assumes the risk that the listener will not honor the speaker's expectation of confidentiality. According to *Hoffa,* "the risk of being overheard by an eavesdropper or betrayed by an informer or deceived as to the identity of one with whom one deals is probably inherent in the conditions of human society. It is the kind of risk we necessarily assume whenever we speak."

Warrantless Electronic Eavesdropping

Hoffa was affirmed and extended in *United States v. White* in which the U.S. Supreme Court held that a listener's use of recording or transmitting devices does not bring Fourth Amendment protections into play.[3] The Court rejected the argument that the amendment should distinguish between "naked ear" listeners and those listeners who carry electronic recording or transmitting devices. The *Hoffa* and *White* cases permit the government to monitor communications whenever one party to the conversation agrees to repeat, record, or transmit the conversation to the government.

Justice Harlan filed an eloquent dissent in *United States v. White,* and it remains to be seen if his dissent will someday have the effect of Justice Brandeis' dissent in *Olmstead.*

Authority is hardly required to support the proposition that words would be measured a good deal more carefully and communication inhibited if one suspected his conversations were being transmitted and transcribed. Were third-party bugging a prevalent practice, it might well smother that spontaneity—reflected in frivolous, impetuous, sacrilegious, and defiant discourse—that liberates daily life. Much offhand exchange is easily forgotten and one may count on the obscurity of his remarks, protected by the very fact of a limited audience, and the likelihood that the listener will either overlook or forget what is said, as well as the listener's inability to reformulate a conversation without having to contend with a documented record. All these values are sacrificed by a rule that

Electronic tracking devices
often some form of "beeper" that emits an electronic signal indicating the position of the beeper placed on a moving person or object.

Pen register
records the numbers dialed on a telephone by monitoring electrical impulses, but does not overhear conversations.

permits official monitoring of private discourse limited only by the need to locate a willing assistant.

The rationale of *United States v. White* has been extended to **electronic tracking devices,** which are normally some form of "beeper" emitting an electronic signal indicating the position of the beeper. In *United States v. Knotts,* the police placed an electronic beeper in a five-gallon drum and tracked the movements of the drum when it was placed in an automobile and driven to the defendant's property.[4] The Supreme Court held that a defendant "has no reasonable expectation of privacy in his movements from one place to another," thus the Fourth Amendment did not apply to monitoring while the drum and vehicle were on public streets. As to monitoring while the vehicle was on private property, but outside the defendant's dwelling, the Court applied the open fields doctrine. Because visual view in open fields is permissible, so too is technological enhancement of sensory faculties. In *United States v. Karo,* however, the monitoring continued when a beeper was taken into the defendant's dwelling.[5] The U.S. Supreme Court recognized that monitoring the inside of a defendant's dwelling "violates the Fourth Amendment rights of those who have a justifiable interest in the privacy of the residence."

In most situations the police must obtain a warrant before using a tracking beeper because they have no way of knowing in advance whether the beeper will be transmitting its signals from inside private premises. The Electronic Communications Privacy Act of 1986 also added a provision, Section 3117, dealing with court authorization of mobile tracking devices.

In *Smith v. Maryland,* the U.S. Supreme Court held that the installation and use of a pen register is not a search within the meaning of the Fourth Amendment.[6] A **pen register** records the numbers dialed on a telephone by monitoring electrical impulses, but it does not overhear conversations and does not indicate whether calls were actually completed. The Court distinguished the *Katz* decision and excluded pen registers from Fourth Amendment coverage because wiretaps and electronic bugs permit the police to acquire the contents of communications, whereas pen registers do not. The substance of a communications is protected by the Fourth Amendment, but the Court refused to recognize any legitimate expectation of privacy in dialing phone numbers that may or may not initiate a conversation.

Congress subsequently enacted a statute, 18 U.S.C. 3121 et seq., governing the use of pen registers. The statute allows the FBI to obtain an parte order from a court by submitting an affidavit that "the information likely to be obtained is relevant to an ongoing criminal investigation." Unlike the wiretap statute discussed in the following section, when utilizing a pen register the FBI need not make a showing of probable cause, and the court does not have discretion to refuse to issue the order.

Court-Ordered Electronic Eavesdropping

If the government does not obtain the consent of at least one party to a conversation, the government must acquire a warrant before listening to a communication that the defendant intends to be private. Electronic listening devices, particularly wiretaps, are by their very nature indiscriminate seizures. Thus warrants authorizing electronic listening devices may violate the Fourth Amendment's requirement for "particularly describing the place to be searched, and the . . . thing to be seized." For example, a wiretap placed on the defendant's telephone for thirty days may pick up the particularly described and sought-after incriminating conversation, but it might likewise seize a great number of wholly innocent conversations. The danger of indiscriminate wiretaps was an important consideration which led the Supreme Court to strike down a New York wiretap statute in *Berger v. New York.*[7]

In response to the decisions in *Berger* and *Katz,* Congress enacted **Title III of the Omnibus Crime Control and Safe Streets Act,** a regulatory scheme aimed at wiretapping and eavesdropping. (Many states have enacted modified versions of Title III.) Because unregulated electronic surveillance poses a threat to the privacy rights of all citizens, the Omnibus Crime Control and Safe Streets Act requires electronic surveillance warrants to meet higher standards than are required for search warrants to seize tangible property. For example, search warrants for tangible property may be applied for by any law enforcement officer and may be issued by a magistrate. But in the federal system, an application to authorize electronic surveillance under Title III must be submitted by the U.S. Attorney General, or a designee of the Attorney General, and approved by a federal judge. In addition to the normal type of information contained in an affidavit for a traditional search warrant, the application for electronic surveillance must include:

Title III of the Omnibus Crime Control and Safe Streets Act
a regulatory scheme governing wiretapping and eavesdropping.

1. Information establishing that normal investigative procedures have failed, are likely to fail, or are dangerous. (For example, placing an undercover police officer within the inner circles of organized crime may endanger the officer's life.)
2. Information establishing that the communication to be seized relates to one of the offenses enumerated in Title III. (The offenses include most serious felonies.)
3. The name, if known, of the person committing the offense and whose communications are to be intercepted.
4. A statement of all known previous applications involving any of the same persons or places specified in the current application. (This provision is designed to alert the judge to any continuing harassment of a particular citizen. For example, J. Edgar Hoover's monitoring of the political activities of Martin Luther King, Jr.)
5. A statement of the period of time for which the interception is required to be maintained.

A federal court may authorize electronic surveillance for a period of up to thirty days, thereafter an extension of an additional thirty days may be granted. The court may require progress reports in order to determine whether to terminate or extend an electronic wiretap. Every court order and extension requires that the electronic surveillance be conducted in a manner that minimizes eavesdropping on communications not otherwise subject to interception. For example, the FBI must stop listening to and/or recording a conversation when it becomes apparent that the conversation is a wholly innocent communication.[8] The court order, however, need not specify the precise procedures to be followed by the executing officers. A covert entry (e.g., breaking into a defendant's residence) to install a listening device is not a *per se* violation of either the Omnibus Crime Control and Safe Streets Act, or the Fourth Amendment.[9]

The Omnibus Crime Control and Safe Streets Act applies to the federal government, but 42 states, the District of Columbia, and the Virgin Islands have similar statutes empowering the courts to issue orders allowing wire, oral, or electronic surveillance as an investigative tool. In 1999, the courts granted 1,350 applications for wire, oral, or electronic surveillance (601 by federal judges; 749 by state judges). Seventy-two percent of all applications for intercepts cited narcotics as the most serious offense under investigation, followed by racketeering and gambling. Single-family dwellings were the most common placement for wiretaps. Other locations included mobile telephones, electronic pagers, and cellular telephones. These types of figures are compiled and reported annually by the Administrative Office of the U.S. Courts.

Some of the provisions of the Omnibus Crime Control and Safe Streets Act of 1968 were rendered obsolete by ensuing technological innovations. Congress has recognized that law enforcement agencies must be empowered to use advanced technology in order to keep up with the latest maneuvering of computer hackers and techno-savvy criminals. At the same time, Congress acknowledged that innocent people must be given protections that will not be quickly outmoded by technological advances. The legislative scheme was updated in the Stored Communications Act, 18 U.S.C. § 2701-10 and the Electronic Communications Privacy Act, 18 U.S.C.A. § 2510(12). These Acts expand coverage to include electronic communications defined as "any transfer of signs, signals, writings, images, sounds, data, or intelligence of any nature transmitted in whole or in part by a wire, radio, electromagnetic, photo electronic or photo optical system that affects interstate or foreign commerce."

In the summer of 2000, the House Judiciary Committee's subcommittee on the Constitution held hearings on the FBI's use of special software and hardware (called Carnivore) to collect information from e-mail messages traveling through an Internet service provider's e-mail server. The FBI conceded that it must comply with the wiretap law when it seeks access to the content of e-mail messages. However, *Smith v. Maryland,* supra, established that a telephone user has no legitimate expectation of privacy in telephone numbers dialed, thus the FBI takes the same view of e-mail. The FBI likens Carnivore operations to the results obtained by a combination of telephone trap-and-trace and pen register devices, which produce a list of telephone calls to and from a particular number. However, this collection of "to" and "from" information occurs only after Carnivore initially scans information from incoming and outgoing e-mail messages, reads the messages, and then filters them according to the "to" and "from" protocols. The ACLU opposed the government's use of Carivore on grounds that filtering (i.e., looking for) one person's mail requires inspection of every single e-mail message traveling through a server. Although a wiretap on a public telephone, permissible under current law, would expose many innocent conversations, the volume of calls on a single public phone would not approach the millions of e-mail messages carried by a server like Pegasus. The ACLU maintained that Congress never intended this type of wide-scale intrusion when passing the pen register and wiretap laws.

Following the congressional hearings, the Clinton administration announced plans to draft a bill to update wiretap laws. The bill regulated under what circumstances law enforcement could view, listen to, and trace e-mails, cellular phone calls, and transmissions over cable networks. The bill sought to correct outmoded language and to be technologically neutral, that is, apply equal standards to both hardware and software surveillance. The bill has not yet been enacted into law.

Title III of the Omnibus Crime Control Act also contains an exclusionary provision that is broader than the Fourth Amendment exclusionary rule (see the next section). Any communication overheard in violation of Title III is inadmissible in all government proceedings such as grand jury proceedings, preliminary hearings, and other stages of prosecution where the Fourth Amendment exclusionary rule may not apply.

THE EXCLUSIONARY RULE

The Purpose of the Exclusionary Rule

For the first 150 years of its existence, the Fourth Amendment was dubbed "the right without a remedy." Although a defendant might establish that the police violated his right to be free of unreasonable searches and seizures, a court was powerless to do anything about an illegal search or seizure that had already taken place.

In 1914 in *Weeks v. United States,* the U. S. Supreme Court adopted an **exclusionary rule** which barred the prosecution from introducing evidence seized by federal law enforcement officers who had conducted an illegal search.[10]

Exclusionary rule bars the prosecution from introducing evidence seized in the course of an illegal search.

The exclusionary rule created in *Weeks* was applicable only to federal cases because the guarantees of the Fourth Amendment were not yet applicable to the states under the Due Process clause of the Fourteenth Amendment. In 1949, however, *Wolf v. Colorado,* recognized that "security of one's privacy against arbitrary intrusion by the police—which is at the core of the Fourth Amendment—is basic to a free society."[11] Thus the states were made subject to the substantive provisions of the Fourth Amendment.

Although *Wolf* held that the substantive right to be free from unreasonable searches and seizures was binding upon the states, at the same time, the Supreme Court indicated that "the ways of enforcing such a basic right raise questions of a different order." The Court explained that the exclusionary rule adopted in *Weeks* "was not derived from the explicit requirements of the Fourth Amendment"; instead, the rule was regarded as a judicially created (not constitutionally mandated) device for enforcing the amendment. In *Wolf,* the Court paid homage to the diversity inherent in a federal system and encouraged the states to formulate their own exclusionary rule or to experiment with other methods of enforcing the Fourth Amendment.

The period of experimentation, however, lasted only twelve years. *Mapp v. Ohio* overruled *Wolf* and concluded that the exclusionary rule was constitutionally mandated in both federal and state prosecutions.

MAPP v. OHIO
Supreme Court of the United States, 1961
367 U.S. 643, 81 S.Ct. 1684

JUSTICE CLARK delivered the opinion of the Court: Today we once again examine *Wolf*'s constitutional documentation of the right to privacy free from unreasonable state intrusion, and, after its dozen years on our books, are led by it to close the only courtroom door remaining open to evidence secured by official lawlessness in flagrant abuse of that basic right, reserved to all persons as a specific guarantee against that very same unlawful conduct. We hold that all evidence obtained by searches and seizures in violation of the Constitution is, by that same authority, inadmissible in a state court.

[O]ur holding is not only the logical dictate of prior cases, but it also makes very good sense. There is no war between the Constitution and common sense. Presently, a federal prosecutor may make no use of evidence illegally seized, but a State's attorney across the street may, although he supposedly is operating under the enforceable prohibitions of the same Amendment. Thus the State, by admitting evidence unlawfully seized, serves to encourage disobedience to the Federal Constitution which it is bound to uphold.

There are those who say, as did Justice (then judge) Cardozo, that under our constitutional exclusionary doctrine "the criminal is to go free because the constable has blundered." In some cases this will undoubtedly be the result. But, "there is another consideration—the imperative of judicial integrity." The criminal goes free, if he must, but it is the law that sets him free. Nothing can destroy a government more quickly than its failure to observe its own laws, or worse, its disregard of the charter of its own existence. As Justice Brandeis, dissenting, said in *Olmstead v. United States:* "Our government is the potent, the omnipresent teacher. For good or for ill, it teaches the whole people by its example. . . . If the government becomes a lawbreaker, it breeds contempt for law; it invites every man to become a law unto himself; it invites anarchy." Nor can it lightly be assumed that, as a practical matter, adoption of the exclusionary rule fetters law enforcement. Only last year this Court expressly considered that contention and found that "pragmatic evidence of a sort" to the contrary was not wanting.

The federal courts themselves have operated under the exclusionary rule of *Weeks* for almost half a century; yet it has not been suggested either that the Federal Bureau of Investigation has thereby been rendered ineffective, or that the administration of criminal justice in the federal courts has thereby been disrupted. Moreover, the experience of the states is impressive . . . The movement toward the rule of exclusion has been halting but seemingly inexorable.

The ignoble shortcut to conviction left open to the State tends to destroy the entire system of constitutional restraints on which the liberties of the people rest. Having once recognized that the right to privacy embodied in the Fourth Amendment is enforceable against the States, and that the right to be secure against rude invasions of privacy by state officers is, therefore, constitutional in origin, we can no longer permit that right to remain an empty promise. . . . Our decision, founded on reason and truth, gives to the individual no more than that which the Constitution guarantees him, to the police officer no less than that to which honest law enforcement is entitled, and, to the courts, that judicial integrity so necessary in the true administration of justice.

The *Mapp* Court pointed to three justifications for the constitutional nature of the exclusionary rule.

1. Judicial integrity requires that courts refuse to become accomplices in the willful disobedience of the constitutional prohibition against unreasonable searches and seizures.
2. The intimate relationship between the Fourth and Fifth Amendment (which contains its own exclusionary rule) establishes the constitutional nature of an exclusionary rule.
3. Deterrence of unreasonable searches and seizures can only be achieved by denying law enforcement officials the fruits of their illegality.

Since *Mapp* was decided, the U.S. Supreme Court has disregarded the first two justifications for the exclusionary rule and emphasized that "the 'prime purpose' of the rule, if not the sole one, is to deter unlawful police conduct."[12] The Court's emphasis on deterrence ultimately led to adoption of the good faith exception to the exclusionary rule.

Government Participation in Illegal Searches

As *Mapp* and *Weeks* point out, the Fourth Amendment is a limitation upon the search and seizure powers of the federal and state governments. The amendment applies to all federal and state officials and is not limited to law enforcement personnel. Thus, the amendment applies to searches conducted by *public* school officials and to *public* employer searches for work-related purposes.[13] The amendment and its exclusionary rule, however, are "wholly inapplicable 'to a search or seizure, even an unreasonable one, effected by a private individual not acting as an agent of the Government or with the participation of any government official.'"[14]

Whether a private party should be deemed an agent of the government for Fourth Amendment purposes turns on the degree of the government's participation in the private party's activities. For example, a private security guard, acting alone, may search an employee's locker and turn the fruits of the search over to public law enforcement officials who may use the evidence at trial. The exclusionary rule, however, would bar the use of the evidence if the private security guard had conducted the search at the behest of federal or state law enforcement officers. Not only may the police accept the fruits of a private search, they also may reexamine the seized property as long as the police "do no more than the private parties have already done."[15] For example, the police may reopen a package previously opened and then resealed by a private courier.

Foreign law enforcement officials also are exempt from the restraints of the Fourth Amendment. Unless circumstances "shock the judicial conscience," the exclusionary rule does not apply to searches conducted by a foreign sovereign in its own territory. Nor is the Fourth Amendment extraterritorial in its coverage; thus U.S. agents may search and seize property owned by a nonresident alien and located in a foreign country.

UNITED STATES v. VERDUGO-URQUIDEZ
Supreme Court of the United States, 1990
494 U.S. 259, 110 S.Ct. 1056

Respondent is a citizen and resident of Mexico. He is believed by the United States Drug Enforcement Agency to be one of the leaders of a large and violent organization in Mexico that smuggles narcotics into the United States. Based on a complaint charging respondent with various narcotics-related offenses, the Government obtained a warrant for his arrest on August 3, 1985. In January 1986, Mexican police officers, after discussions with United States Marshals, apprehended [the respondent] in Mexico and transported him to the United States Border Patrol station in Calexico, California. There, United States Marshals arrested respondent and eventually moved him to a correctional center in San Diego, California.

Following respondent's arrest, a DEA agent arranged for searches of respondent's Mexican residences. The agent did not seek a search warrant from a United States magistrate or judge, but instead obtained authorization from the Director General of the Mexican Federal Judicial Police. Thereafter, DEA agents working in concert with officers of the MFJP searched respondent's properties in Mexico and seized certain documents.

JUSTICE REHNQUIST delivered the opinion of the Court:

"The people" protected by the Fourth Amendment, and by the First and Second Amendments, and to who

rights and powers are reserved in the Ninth and Tenth Amendments, refers to a class of persons who are part of a national community or who have otherwise developed sufficient connection with this country to be considered part of that community. . . . The purpose of the Fourth Amendment was to protect the people of the United States against arbitrary action by their own Government; it was never suggested that the provision was intended to restrain the actions of the Federal Government against aliens outside of the United States territory.

For better or for worse, we live in a world of nation-states in which our Government must be able to "function effectively in the company of sovereign nations." Some who violate our laws may live outside our borders under a regime quite different from that which obtains in this country. Situations threatening to important American interests may arise half-way around the globe, situations which in the view of the political branches of our Government require an American response with armed force. If there are to be restrictions on searches and seizures which occur incident to such American actions, they must be imposed by the political branches through diplomatic understanding, treaty, or legislation.

Standing to Invoke the Exclusionary Rule

Nearly all claims to enforce constitutional rights may be raised only by those who have standing to assert them. The Fourth Amendment is no exception to this general rule. A motion to exclude evidence seized as a result of an illegal search may be raised only by a person who has **standing** before the court—that is, "a victim of the search or seizure . . . as distinguished from one who claims prejudice only through the use of evidence gathered as a consequence of a search or seizure directed at someone else."[16] Only defendants whose "personal" Fourth Amendment rights have been violated may invoke the exclusionary rule because defendants cannot vicariously assert the Fourth Amendment rights of some third party who was subjected to an illegal search or seizure. This principle is true, according to *United States v. Payner,* even when the government deliberately violates the rights of a subordinate in order to obtain evidence against the "ring leader."

Standing
the defendant must be "a victim of the search or seizure"; the defendant's personal right to privacy was violated.

UNITED STATES v. PAYNER
Supreme Court of the United States, 1980
447 U.S. 727, 100 S.Ct. 2439

An IRS investigation into the financial activities of American citizens in the Bahamas focused on a certain Bahamian bank. When an official [Wolstencroft] of that bank visited the United States, IRS agents stole his briefcase for a time, removed hundreds of documents from the briefcase and photographed them. As a result, defendant Payner was convicted of federal income tax violations. The District Court invoked its supervisory power to exclude the tainted evidence after finding that "the Government counsels its agents that the Fourth Amendment standing limitations permits them to purposefully conduct an unconstitutional search and seizure of one individual in order to obtain evidence against third parties who are the real targets of the government intrusion" and that IRS agents "transacted the 'briefcase caper' with a purposeful, bad faith hostility toward the Fourth Amendment rights of the bank official [Wolstencroft] in order to obtain evidence against persons like Payner."

JUSTICE POWELL delivered the opinion of the Court: [Our prior decisions make it clear that] the defendant's Fourth Amendment rights are violated only when the challenged conduct invaded *his* legitimate expectation of privacy rather than that of a third party. The District Court recognized that Payner lacks standing under the Fourth Amendment to suppress the documents illegally seized from Wolstencroft. The Court of Appeals did not disturb the District Court's conclusion that "Jack Payner possessed no privacy interest in the Castle Bank documents that were seized from Wolstencroft."

The District Court and the Court of Appeals believed, however, that a federal court should use its supervisory power to suppress evidence tainted by gross illegalities that did not infringe the defendant's constitutional rights. . . . We certainly can understand the District Court's commendable desire to deter deliberate intrusions into the privacy of persons who are unlikely to become defendants in a criminal prosecution. No court should condone the unconstitutional and possible criminal behavior of those who planned and executed this "briefcase caper."

[Our prior decisions, however, also demonstrate that] the suppression of probative but tainted evidence exacts a costly toll upon the ability of courts to ascertain the truth in a criminal case. Our cases have consistently recognized that unbending application of the exclusionary sanction to enforce ideals of governmental rectitude would impede unacceptably the truth-finding functions of judge and jury. After all, it is the defendant, and not the constable, who stands trial.

Our Fourth Amendment decisions have established beyond any doubt that the interest in deterring illegal searches does not justify the exclusion of tainted evidence at the instance of a party who was not the victim of the challenged practices.

The District Court erred, therefore, when it concluded that "society's interest in deterring bad faith conduct by exclusion outweighs society's interest in furnishing the trier of fact with all relevant evidence."

Derivative Evidence: "The Fruit of the Poisonous Tree"

Derivative evidence (the fruit of the poisonous tree) all secondary evidence obtained by the police as the result of an illegal search.

The exclusionary rule applies to evidence that is the direct result of an illegal search and seizure. For example, in *Mapp v. Ohio*, the government sought to introduce obscene materials seized during an illegal search of the defendant's house. Quite often, however, an illegal search may lead to a confession, a subsequent arrest, another search, or to identification of a witness who will testify against the defendant. In such situations, the Court must determine if such derivative evidence is tainted by the prior illegal search. Exhibit 11–1 provides an example of a legal motion to suppress evidence obtained illegally. **Derivative evidence** includes all secondary evidence obtained by the police because of an illegal search. (To use the Supreme Court's metaphor, the evidence is "the fruit of the poisonous tree.")

The defendant moves this Court to suppress the following evidence seized as a result of a search of the defendant and premises located at _____ in the city of _____ :

(a) (description of seized items) ;
(b) any other items obtained as a result of the search;
(c) any statements or admissions made by the defendant at the time of the defendant's arrest.

As grounds for the above motion, defendant states that the search of the defendant's premises and person, and the seizure of the above specified articles of evidence was had and done pursuant to an illegal search warrant, attached hereto as "Exhibit A" and incorporated into this motion by reference.

1. The defendant was arrested and premises were searched without an arrest warrant, without a valid search warrant, and without probable cause in violation of the Fourth Amendment of the United States Constitution.

2. The issuance of the search warrant was based upon an affidavit which states that the informant was a reliable source of information when in fact said informant was not a reliable source of information. The following, among other things, are deficiencies in the affidavit which was the basis upon which the search warrant was issued:

(a) Said affidavit omits to state when and where the informant allegedly overheard the defendant state that the defendant was going to pick up illegal drugs and bring them back to defendant's residence.

(b) Said affidavit omits to state that the informant overheard the defendant say that the defendant was going to use the defendant's car for the alleged purpose of transporting the illegal drugs, or how the drugs were to be transported, thus negating any probable cause for the issuance of a search warrant for the defendant's car.

(c) Said affidavit omits to state that the informant ever saw illegal drugs in the defendant's possession, or that said informant has ever heard that the defendant was involved in any use of illegal drugs, in order to distinguish what the informant thought was a reliable statement from mere idle gossip or jesting.

3. That the affidavit presented to the issuing magistrate by the affiant, based upon alleged reliable information by an unnamed informant, was insufficient to enable said magistrate to form an unbiased and impartial decision without further information concerning the informant's reliability and the alleged facts reported by said informer.

4. The search of the defendant's person incident to the unlawful arrest was therefore illegal and all fruits of the search must be suppressed.

WHEREUPON this petitioner prays:

(a) That a hearing be held in order to determine whether probable cause existed to authorize the issuance of said search warrant;

(b) That all of the evidence seized pursuant to said search warrant (listed above) be suppressed and excluded from his trial; and

(c) That all non-contraband evidence seized during said search be returned to the petitioner.

EXHIBIT 11–1
Motion to Suppress Illegally Obtained Evidence

Once the defendant establishes that an illegal search occurred, the prosecution must prove that the evidence offered at trial has no causal connection to the illegal search. In *Wong Sun v. United States*, the U.S. Supreme Court refused to adopt a "but-for" test of causation which would define tainted evidence as all evidence that "would not have come to light but for the illegal actions of the police."[17] In place of a "but-for" test of causation, the courts have recognized that evidence is not tainted when the prosecution establishes (1) the connection between the illegal search and the tainted evidence has been weakened by the passage of time or the occurrence of intervening circumstances; (2) the evidence was obtained from a source independent of the illegal search; or (3) the discovery of the evidence was inevitable.

Dissipating the Taint   The passage of time between the illegal search and the discovery of secondary evidence is a material element in determining causation. Generally, the longer the interval between illegal conduct and the obtaining of evidence, the less likely is a court to find any meaningful connection between the illegality and the procuring of the evidence. Thus in *Taylor v. Alabama,* a six-hour gap between the illegal arrest and the defendant's confession was held insufficient to break the causal connection between the arrest and the confession.[18] But in *United States v. Ceccolini,* a four-month gap between an illegal search and the discovery of a witness helped break the causal connection between the two.[19]

Regardless of the time period involved, a change in circumstances may break the connection between a constitutional violation and subsequently obtained evidence. For example, *Wong Sun v. United States* recognized that releasing the defendant from illegal custody dissipated the connection between the first illegal arrest and a confession obtained after the defendant was lawfully rearrested. In *Brown v. Illinois,* however, the Supreme Court refused to hold that giving the *Miranda* warnings would always break the causal connection between an illegal arrest and a subsequent confession.[20]

Perhaps the clearest example of dissipating the taint occurs when the defendant commits an additional crime. In *United States v. Sprinkle,*[21] the defendant resisted an illegal arrest by fleeing and shooting at the police officers. When the defendant was apprehended he was charged with unlawful possession of a firearm. Because of the illegal arrest, the trial court initially suppressed evidence that the defendant possessed a weapon (i.e., but for the illegal arrest, the police would never have learned that the defendant had a firearm). The appellate court, however, held that "there is a strong policy reason for holding that a new and distinct crime, even if triggered by an illegal stop, is a sufficient intervening event to provide independent grounds for arrest," and thus constitutes an exception to the fruit of the poisonous tree exclusionary rule doctrine.

Independent Discovery   Violations of the defendant's Fourth Amendment rights do not necessitate suppression of evidence discovered "by means sufficiently distinguishable to be purged of the primary taint."[22] Suppose for example, that a narcotics squad is searching the defendant's apartment pursuant to a lawful warrant, while a homicide squad illegally arrests and searches the defendant. Suppose further, that the illegal search of the defendant uncovers a list of deliveries of heroin to the defendant's apartment. An officer of the homicide squad then telephones the defendant's apartment and tells the searching officers to look for heroin. The searching officer responds, "We already found the drugs." In such a situation, the officers made an **independant discovery** of the heroin (through a lawful search of the apartment); therefore, the evidence was not tainted by the illegal arrest and search of the defendant.

Independent discovery
the exclusionary rule does not bar evidence obtained by means unrelated to any illegal search.

Inevitable discovery
the exclusionary rule does not bar evidence that "ultimately or inevitably would have been discovered by lawful means."

Inevitable Discovery   The doctrine of **inevitable discovery** differs from independent discovery because in the case of inevitable discovery the court must determine what would have happened even without an illegal search. The seized evidence will not be suppressed if "the prosecution can establish by a preponderance of the evidence that the information ultimately or inevitably would have been discovered by lawful means."[23] In the previous example involving the narcotics and homicide squads, suppose that when the homicide detective telephones advice to search for heroin, the narcotics agent replies, "I know how to do my job. We planned to look everywhere that heroin could be hidden." Although the discovery of heroin in the apartment occurs after the illegal arrest and search of the defendant, normal police search procedures would have uncovered the heroin even in the absence of the defendant's arrest. Because the discovery of the heroin was inevitable, the illegal arrest did not play a part in uncovering this evidence, thus the evidence will not be suppressed under the exclusionary rule.

Collateral Use of Illegally Seized Evidence

In a criminal trial the exclusionary rule prohibits the prosecution from using illegally seized evidence to prove the defendant's guilt. However, the exclusionary rule is generally not applicable to collateral stages of a criminal prosecution. A **collateral stage** is one that does not directly relate to the defendant's ultimate guilt or innocence. For example, the exclusionary rule is normally inapplicable in grand jury proceedings,[24] preliminary hearings,[25] bail hearings,[26] sentencing determinations,[27] and probation revocation hearings.

In the criminal trial itself, the collateral use of illegally seized evidence arises when the government seeks to impeach the credibility of a defendant's testimony as to innocence. For example, in *Walder v. United States* a defendant charged with possession of illegal drugs testified that he had never possessed any narcotics.[28] The prosecution rebutted this assertion by introducing evidence that heroin had been seized (illegally) from the defendant's home some two years prior to the time of the present charge. The trial judge instructed the jury that evidence derived from the two-year-old illegal search and seizure could not be considered as proof of the defendant's guilt. The evidence was admissible, however, for the limited purpose of impeaching the defendant's truthfulness as a witness. For example, if he lied about whether he possessed narcotics two years ago, maybe he has lied about whether he possessed them at the time of the present charge.

The holding in *Walder* was based on the rationale that "sufficient deterrence flows when the evidence in question is made available to the prosecution in its *case in chief*." The U.S. Supreme Court stated that no further deterrence value would be accomplished by denying the prosecution the use of illegally obtained evidence for the limited purpose of impeachment. However, evidence obtained in violation of the Fourth Amendment cannot be used to impeach the testimony of defense witnesses other than the defendant.[29]

Collateral stages proceedings that do not directly relate to the defendant's ultimate guilt or innocence in which the exclusionary rule is normally inapplicable.

Good Faith Exception to the Exclusionary Rule

Under current law, the sole purpose of the exclusionary rule is to deter police misconduct. When the police mistakenly, but reasonably, believe that they are searching pursuant to a warrant properly issued by a magistrate or judge, are they guilty of misconduct? Can the police reasonably conduct an unreasonable search? The Supreme Court answered these questions in *United States v. Leon,* which articulates the **good faith exception.**

Good faith exception the prosecution may introduce the results of an illegal search, if the police relied in good faith upon a search warrant.

UNITED STATES v. LEON
Supreme Court of the United States, 1984
468 U.S. 897, 104 S.Ct. 3405

JUSTICE WHITE delivered the opinion of the Court: This case presents the question whether the Fourth Amendment exclusionary rule should be modified so as

not to bar the use in the prosecution's case-in-chief of evidence obtained by officers acting in reasonable reliance on a search warrant issued by a detached and neutral magistrate but ultimately found to be unsupported by probable cause.

The wrong condemned by the Amendment is "fully accomplished" by the unlawful search or seizure itself, and the exclusionary rule is neither intended nor able to "cure the invasion of the defendant's rights which he has already suffered." The rule thus operates as "a judicially created remedy designed to safeguard Fourth Amendment rights generally through its deterrent effect, rather than a personal constitutional right of the person aggrieved."

[The remedy of exclusion] must be resolved by weighing the costs and benefits of preventing the use in the prosecution's case-in-chief of inherently trustworthy tangible evidence obtained in reliance on a search warrant issued by a detached and neutral magistrate that ultimately is found to be defective.

To the extent that proponents of exclusion rely on its behavioral effects on judges and magistrates in these areas, their reliance is misplaced. First, the exclusionary rule is designed to deter police misconduct rather than to punish the errors of judges and magistrates. Second, there exists no evidence suggesting that judges and magistrates are inclined to ignore or subvert the Fourth Amendment or that lawlessness among these actors requires application of the extreme sanction of exclusion.

Third, and most important, we discern no basis, and are offered none, for believing that exclusion of evidence seized pursuant to a warrant will have a significant deterrent effect on the issuing judge or magistrate.

[With respect to deterring police misconduct] when an officer acting with objective good faith has obtained a search warrant from a judge or magistrate and acted within its scope, in most such cases, there is no police illegality to deter. . . . "Once the warrant issues, there is literally nothing more the policeman can do in seeking to comply with the law." Penalizing the officer for the magistrate's error, rather than his own, cannot logically contribute to the deterrence of Fourth Amendment violations.

We conclude that the marginal or non-existent benefits produced by suppressing evidence obtained in objectively reasonable reliance on a subsequently invalidated search warrant cannot justify the substantial costs of exclusion.

The decision in *Leon* left only three situations in which the exclusionary rule can be applied to searches conducted pursuant to a warrant:

1. The magistrate abandoned the prescribed detached and neutral role in issuing the warrant.[30]
2. The officers were dishonest or reckless in preparing their affidavit for the search warrant.[31]
3. The officers could not have harbored an objectively reasonable belief in the existence of probable cause.

To date, *Leon* is limited to searches pursuant to a warrant, but *Leon*'s rationale and its emphasis on deterrence could be extended to warrantless good faith searches. For example, in *Illinois v. Rodriguez,* the U.S. Supreme Court upheld a warrantless search based on the police officer's reasonable, though mistaken, belief that a third party had actual authority to consent to the search.[32]

Disposition of Seized Property

Any property taken from an accused by an unlawful search and seizure shall be returned if the accused is lawfully entitled to have possession of such property. Stolen goods will be returned to the rightful owner, while contraband (the possession of which is unlawful) will be destroyed or otherwise disposed of by court order. When the police seize property for a criminal investigation, they must give the owner notice that they have taken the property because the owner has no other reasonable means of ascertaining who is responsible for his loss. However, Due Process does not require the police to provide the owner with notice of state law remedies for recovering the property. (Such remedies are established by published, generally available state statutes and case law.)[33]

In addition to seizing actual contraband, the government may seek forfeiture of property used in criminal activity. Historically, Colonial American courts exercised jurisdiction to seize smuggled goods, and during America's experiment with Prohibition, statutes authorized the seizure and forfeiture of property used to manufacture or sell alcoholic beverages. The current emphasis on the "War on Drugs" led Congress to enact the Comprehensive Forfeiture Act of 1984, which calls for forfeiture of property when "a substantial connection between the property and the underlying criminal activity" is shown. Everything of value furnished or intended to be furnished in exchange for drugs, and all moneys or other property traceable to such an exchange are forfeited to the government. Such forfeiture provisions are civil in nature, and thus not a part of the criminal justice system. The constitutional protections embodied in the Due Process Clause, the Sixth Amendment right to counsel, and the Fifth Amendment Double Jeopardy Clause are generally inapplicable to forfeiture proceedings.[34]

Many states have their own forfeiture statutes and have also enacted so-called "Son of Sam" laws that provide for forfeiture of the proceeds received from a depiction of the defendant's felony in a movie, book, magazine, or television production. In *Simon & Schuster, Inc. v. New York Crime Victim Board,* however, the Supreme Court found New York's "Son of Sam" law to be unconstitutional because it infringed upon free speech.[35]

SUMMARY

The monitoring of private conversations by undercover agents, spies, or turncoat friends is not prohibited by either the Fourth Amendment or the Omnibus Crime Control and Safe Streets Act as long as the government obtains the consent of one party to the conversation. In the absence of consent, the government must obtain court approval to monitor private conversations. The Omnibus Crime Control and Safe Streets Act details the procedures that must be followed when a court authorizes electronic surveillance. These procedures exceed the requirements for a search warrant to seize tangible property. The statute also creates an exclusionary rule that is broader that the Fourth Amendment's exclusionary rule.

The Fourth Amendment exclusionary rule is a limitation on federal and state power, thus it is inapplicable when private parties or foreign governments conduct searches and seizures of U.S. citizens. The protections of the exclusionary rule are also limited to those who have standing to invoke the rule. Only defendants whose personal constitutional rights have been invaded may seek to exclude the fruits of an illegal search or seizure.

The fruits of an illegal search or seizure include evidentiary items taken in the course of the search and all secondary evidence derived from the illegal search. The doctrines of independent or inevitable discovery identify items that are not derived from the illegal search, and thus are not subject to the exclusionary rule. The exclusionary rule may be invoked in the course of a trial on the merits of the defendant's guilt or innocence, but the rule is generally not applied to pretrial stages of the criminal justice system.

The good faith exception to the exclusionary rule permits the introduction of evidentiary items seized by police officers who, in good faith, relied upon the issuance of a search warrant. The U.S. Supreme Court indicated that when police officers act in good faith reliance on a search warrant, no police misconduct has occurred that must be deterred by applying the exclusionary rule.

CONCEPT SUMMARY

Requirements for a Motion To Supress

Consult local law to determine what changes have been made in a particular jurisdiction.

Government Action	The exclusionary rule is applicable against government officials. It has no application to the activities of private persons or foreign officials.
Search	Only those governmental activities defined as a search are subject to the exclusionary rule. (I.e., did the government intrude upon a citizen's reasonable expectation of privacy?)
Standing	The defendant's personal Fourth Amendment rights must have been violated. The defendant may not vicariously assert another's constitutional rights.
Derivative Evidence	The items must have been seized during or as a result of an illegal search.
Independent Discovery	Items seized independent of an illegal search are not subject to the exclusionary rule.
Inevitable Discovery	Items that inevitably would have been discovered by lawful means are not subject to exclusion.
Good Faith Exception	The results of an illegal search will not be suppressed if the police relied in good faith upon a search warrant.
Collateral Use	The results of an illegal search may be introduced in collateral proceedings and at stages of the trial unrelated to the merits of the case.

DISCUSSION QUESTIONS

1. Has the Fourth Amendment been violated when a police officer, disguised as a priest, slips into the confessional and listens to your confession?
2. If the risk of betrayal by a confidant is inherent in our society, is there any difference between a confidant who is a turncoat friend and a confident who is an undercover agent sent by the government to gain your confidence and elicit your statement? See Justice Douglas's dissent in *Hoffa*.
3. Should the good faith exception be extended to warrantless searches? When a police officer mistakenly but reasonably believes that the search is based on probable cause and that it falls within an exception to the requirement for a search warrant, is the officer guilty of misconduct?
4. More so than any other aspect of criminal procedure, the exclusionary rule dramatizes the conflict between the Crime Control and Due Process models of the U.S. criminal justice system. Which is the appropriate question: Is the criminal to go free merely because "the constable blundered"? If the government becomes a lawbreaker, does it invite anarchy?
5. Is the standing requirement inconsistent with the rationale for the exclusionary rule (to deter police misconduct)?

PRACTICE EXERCISES

1. Does your jurisdiction have statutes regulating electronic surveillance? Do the statutes differ from the federal statutes?
2. Does your jurisdiction recognize the good faith exception to the Fourth Amendment exclusionary rule? On what basis can a state refuse to follow the U.S. Supreme Court's recognition of the good faith exception?
3. Has your jurisdiction recognized the inevitable discovery exception to the exclusionary rule? If so, how does a court determine what would have been discovered? What is the burden of proof?
4. Consider the following hypothetical situation: Smith comes to Brown's apartment and gives Brown counterfeit money in exchange for heroin. Smith and Brown depart, leaving the money and drugs on a

coffee table in the living room. The police illegally break into the apartment and seize the items on the coffee table. Brown has standing to object to the seizure of which items? Smith has standing to object to the seizure of which items?

5. Does your state have a comprehensive forfeiture statute? What is subject to forfeiture and under what circumstances?

WEB SITE

Report of the administrative offices of the U.S. courts
US courts.gov/wiretap99/contents.html

KEY TERMS

Electronic tracking devices
Pen register
Title III of the Omnibus Crime
   Control and Safe Streets Act

Exclusionary rule
Standing
Derivative evidence
Independent discovery

Inevitable discovery
Collateral stages
Good faith exception

NOTES

1. *Katz v. United States,* 389 U.S. 347, 88 S.Ct. 507 (1967).
2. *Olmstead v. United States,* 277 U.S. 438, 48 S.Ct. 564 (1928).
3. *United States v. White,* 401 U.S. 745, 91 S.Ct. 1122 (1971).
4. *United States v. Knotts,* 460 U.S. 276, 103 S.Ct. 1081 (1983).
5. *United States v. Karo,* 468 U.S. 705, 104 S.Ct. 3296 (1984).
6. *Smith v. Maryland,* 442 U.S. 735, 99 S.Ct. 2577 (1979).
7. *Berger v. New York,* 388 U.S. 41, 87 S.Ct. 1873 (1967).
8. See, *Scott v. United States,* 436 U.S. 128, 98 S.Ct. 1717 (1978).
9. *Dalia v. United States,* 441 U.S. 238, 99 S.Ct. 1682 (1979).
10. *Weeks v. United States,* 232 U.S. 383, 34 S.Ct. 341 (1914).
11. *Wolf v. Colorado,* 338 U.S. 25, 69 S.Ct. 1359 (1949).
12. *United States v. Janis,* 428 U.S. 433, 96 S.Ct. 3021 (1976).
13. *New Jersey v. T.L.O.,* 469 U.S. 325, 105 S.Ct. 733 (1985); *O'Connor v. Ortega,* 480 U.S. 709, 107 S.Ct. 1492 (1987).
14. *United States v. Jacobsen,* 466 U.S. 109, 104 S.Ct. 1652 (1984).
15. *United States v. Jacobsen,* 466 U.S. 109, 104 S.Ct. 1652 (1984).
16. *Jones v. United States,* 362 U.S. 257, 80 S.Ct. 725 (1960).
17. *Wong Sun v. United States,* 371 U.S. 471, 83 S.Ct. 407 (1963).
18. *Taylor v. Alabama,* 457 U.S. 687, 102 S.Ct. 2664 (1982).
19. *United States v. Ceccolini,* 435 U.S. 268, 98 S.Ct. 1054 (1978).
20. *Brown v. Illinois,* 422 U.S. 590, 95 S.Ct. 2254 (1975).
21. *United States v. Sprinkle,* 106 F.3d 613 (4th Cir. 1997).
22. *Wong Sun v. United States,* 371 U.S. 471, 83 S.Ct. 407 (1963).
23. *Nix v. Williams,* 467 U.S. 431, 104 S.Ct. 2501 (1984).
24. *United States v. Calandra,* 414 U.S. 338, 94 S.Ct. 613 (1974).
25. *Giordenello v. United States,* 357 U.S. 480, 78 S.Ct. 1245 (1958).
26. 18 U.S.C.A. § 3146(f).
27. *United States v. Schipani,* 315 F.Supp. 253 (E.D.N.Y. 1970).
28. *Walder v. United States,* 347 U.S. 62, 74 S.Ct. 354 (1954).
29. *James v. Illinois,* 493 U.S. 307, 110 S.Ct. 648 (1990).
30. See, *Lo-Ji Sales, Inc. v. New York,* 442 U.S. 319, 99 S.Ct. 2319 (1979).
31. See, *Franks v. Delaware,* 438 U.S. 154, 98 S.Ct. 2674 (1978).

32. *Illinois v. Rodriguez,* 497 U.S. 177, 110 S.Ct. 2793 (1990).

33. *West Covina v. Perkins,* 525 U.S. 234, 119 S.Ct. 678 (1999).

34. See *Caplin & Drysdale, Chartered v. United States,* 491 U.S. 617, 109 S.Ct. 2646 (1989).

35. *Simon & Schuster, Inc. v. New York Crime Victim Board,* 502 U.S. 105, 112 S.Ct. 501 (1991).

INTERROGATION AND SELF-INCRIMINATION

Chapter 12

CHAPTER OUTLINE

CONFESSIONS

The Fifth Amendment to the U.S. Constitution provides that no persons shall be compelled to be witnesses against themselves in criminal proceedings. The later portion of this chapter discusses the amendment's applicability at trial. In pretrial settings, additional rules and standards apply to confessions obtained by government interrogation of suspects. Such confessions must be voluntary, obtained in compliance with the *Miranda* decision, corroborated by independent evidence, and must not have violated the suspect's Sixth Amendment right to counsel.

Interrogation law is controversial, in large part because of the conflict between the Crime Control and Due Process models of the criminal justice system. Advocates of the Crime Control Model emphasize the truth-seeking function of criminal investigation and maintain that confessions are generally reliable. As the Supreme Court suggested in *Ashcraft v. Tennessee,* "It probably is the normal instinct to deny and conceal any shameful or guilty act."[1] Therefore, when a suspect admits guilt, most people assume that the admission is true. Proponents of the Due Process Model question this assumption precisely because confessing runs contrary to normal instincts. Why would a person admit guilt unless coerced into confessing by overbearing police interrogators? Due Process advocates are thus more skeptical of the trustworthiness of confessions and more suspicious of police coercion. In *Escobedo v. Illinois,* the Supreme Court observed that:

> We have learned the lesson of history, ancient and modern, that a system of criminal law enforcement which comes to depend on the "confession" will, in the long run, be less reliable and more subject to abuses than a system which depends on extrinsic evidence independently secured through skillful investigation.[2]

Voluntariness of Confessions

Voluntary confession
a statement of guilt, which is "the product of an essentially free and unconstrained choice by its maker."

In early English common law, all confessions, even those obtained by torture, were admissible at trial. Today, a confession must be a **voluntary confession,** which means that the statement is "the product of an essentially free and unconstrained choice by its maker."[3] An alternative expression of this concept is whether a person's free will has been overborne and that person's capacity for self-determination critically impaired. The voluntariness requirement has its roots in common law, Due Process, and the Fifth Amendment itself. For example, an involuntary statement can be viewed as an invalid waiver of the Fifth Amendment privilege against self-incrimination. An involuntary statement also may be inherently untrustworthy under common law rules of evidence; or an involuntary statement may be obtained by government coercion that violates Due Process standards. Although these distinct rationales sometimes complement each other, at times they may conflict, as when a confession obtained by coercion is proven to be trustworthy because its disclosures are confirmed by independent evidence. For example, the police may "beat" the defendant into a confession that the defendant killed the victim and then buried the victim in the defendant's backyard. If the police dig up the body from the backyard, they have corroborated the trustworthiness of the confession, despite the use of coercion. The Supreme Court has noted, "The aim of the [voluntariness] requirement . . . is not to exclude presumptively false evidence, but to prevent fundamental unfairness in the use of evidence whether true or false."[4]

The voluntariness of a confession is determined by considering the totality of the circumstances, which can be grouped into categories relating to the physical and psychological condition of the suspect, and by police tactics used during interrogation.

Physical and Psychological Factors   The voluntariness of a confession is not determined by considering how a reasonably prudent person would react to interrogation. The appropriate question for the court is whether the particular individual freely and voluntarily made a decision to speak. Thus the court must consider all of the individual characteristics of the defendant, including (1) intelligence, (2) education, (3) prior experience with police, (4) use of drugs or alcohol prior to interrogation, (5) emotional or mental disability, and (6) whether the suspect was deprived of physical comforts such as sleep, food, or bathroom visits. The mere existence of any of the preceding factors does not render the confession involuntary, but the factors must be weighed in determining whether the suspect was capable of making, and did in fact make, a voluntarily decision to speak.

Police Interrogation Tactics   In addition to considering the suspect's physical or psychological condition, the courts must consider whether the police interrogators utilized (1) violence or threats of violence, (2) trickery and deceit, (3) psychological pressures, (4) threats, (5) promises of lenience, or (6) prolonged and intimidating interrogation. The use of these tactics or some other form of police "misconduct" does not automatically render the confession involuntary, but it does require the court to assess what impact these tactics had on the voluntariness of the confession. For example, in *Frazier v. Cupp,* although the police falsely informed a suspect that his cousin had implicated the suspect in the crime, the U.S. Supreme Court held that, standing alone, this lie did not render the confession inadmissible.[5]

Colorado v. Connelly established that the involuntary nature of a defendant's statement must be caused by some form of improper police conduct.

COLORADO v. CONNELLY
479 U.S. 157, 107 S.Ct. 515 (1986)

On August 18, 1983, Officer Anderson of the Denver Police Department was in uniform, working in an off-duty capacity in downtown Denver. Respondent Connelly approached Officer Anderson and, without any prompting, stated that he had murdered someone and wanted to talk about it. Anderson immediately advised respondent that he had the right to remain silent, that anything he said could be used against him in court, and that he had the right to an attorney prior to any police questioning. Respondent stated that he understood these rights but he still wanted to talk about the murder. Respondent was held overnight. The following morning, he began giving confused answers to questions, and for the first time, stated that "voices" had told him to come to Denver and that he had followed the directions of these voices in confessing. Respondent was sent to a state hospital for evaluation where a psychiatrist concluded that respondent was suffering from chronic schizophrenia and was in a psychotic state when he confessed. The doctor also testified that respondent was experiencing "command hallucinations" which interfered with his ability to make free and rational choices.

On the basis of this evidence the Colorado trial court decided that respondent's statements must be suppressed because they were "involuntary," and because Connelly's mental state vitiated his attempted waiver of the right to counsel and the privilege against compulsory self-incrimination. According to the Colorado court, "the absence of police coercion or duress does not foreclose a finding of involuntariness. One's capacity for rational judgment and free choice may be overborne as much by certain forms of severe mental illness as by external pressure."

CHIEF JUSTICE REHNQUIST delivered the opinion of the Court:
The Due Process Clause of the Fourteenth Amendment provides that no State shall "deprive any person of life, liberty, or property, without due process of law." Absent police conduct causally related to the confession, there is simply no basis for concluding that any state actor has deprived a criminal defendant of due process of law. We hold that coercive police activity is a necessary predicate to the finding that a confession is not "voluntary"

within the meaning of the Due Process Clause of the Fourteenth Amendment.

We also conclude that the taking of respondent's statements, and their admission into evidence, constitute no violation of *Miranda* or the Fifth Amendment privilege against self-incrimination. The sole concern of the Fifth Amendment, on which *Miranda* was based, is governmental coercion. Indeed, the Fifth Amendment privilege is not concerned with moral and psychological pressures to confess emanating from sources other than official coercion. The voluntariness of a waiver of this privilege has always depended on the absence of police overreaching, not on "free choice" in any broader sense of the word.

The judgment of the Supreme Court of Colorado is accordingly reversed.

JUSTICE BRENNAN, with whom JUSTICE MARSHALL joins, dissenting.
The Court's failure to recognize all forms of involuntariness or coercion as antithetical to due process reflects a refusal to acknowledge free will as a value of constitutional consequence. A true commitment of fundamental fairness requires that the inquiry be not whether the conduct of state officers in obtaining the confession is shocking, but whether the confession was free and voluntary.

All factors relating to police interrogation tactics and the suspect's condition must be considered by the trial judge in determining whether the prosecution has proved that the confession was voluntary. The question of voluntariness is initially a question of fact for the trial judge, but ultimately, voluntariness is a legal question subject to independent judicial determination upon appeal.[6]

If the trial judge determines that a confession is involuntary, the confession cannot be admitted on the merits of the case. If the trial court finds the confession to be voluntary, the confession is admitted into evidence for the jury's consideration. As with all evidence, however, the ultimate truth and persuasiveness of the confession are questions for the jury. Although the jury does not determine the issue of voluntariness (the **admissibility of a confession**), the same factors that the judge considered in determining voluntariness may be considered by the jury when determining the believability or the *weight* to be given to the confession. In effect, the defendant enjoys "two bites of the apple" and may argue to the judge that the confession is inadmissible due to factors such as police coercion. Should the judge rule the confession to be admissible in evidence, the defendant may argue to the jury that they should not believe a confession obtained by police coercion. Even though the trial judge has determined that the confession is voluntary and admissible evidence, the judge may not limit the defendant's right to challenge the confession's reliability during the course of the trial.[7]

Admissibility of a confession the voluntariness of the statement, determined by the trial judge; the jury determines the weight to be given a confession.

The *Miranda* Decision

Miranda v. Arizona remains the most controversial and most important case in the area of confessions.[8] In essence, *Miranda* held that

1. An individual subjected to custodial interrogation must be advised of certain rights.
2. Although no precise language is required, the substance of the *Miranda* warnings is that the suspect be informed
   a. of the right to remain silent,
   b. that any statements made may be used as evidence against her or him,
   c. that she or he has the right to the presence of an attorney, and
   d. that if she or he cannot afford an attorney, one will be appointed prior to any questioning.
3. The prescribed warnings must be given regardless of the defendant's possible familiarity with constitutional rights. (Even a Supreme Court Justice must be given *Miranda* warnings when interrogated by law enforcement officials.)

4. An individual is free to exercise the right to remain silent by indicating in any manner at any time prior to or during the questioning that the individual wishes to remain silent. If the person does so, questioning must cease immediately.
5. The prosecution bears a "heavy burden" of establishing that the defendant knowingly and intelligently waived the right to silence and chose to make a statement.
6. An accused may not be penalized for exercising the privilege against self-incrimination, thus no adverse inference may be drawn when the suspect chooses to remain silent. (At trial, the prosecution may not suggest to the jury that only guilty people hide behind their *Miranda* rights.)
7. Any statement obtained in violation of the *Miranda* decision is not admissible as part of the prosecution's case-in-chief.

In the pre-*Miranda* era defense lawyers were excluded from police interrogation rooms while the police questioned suspects in private. Perhaps because of the incommunicado nature of the interrogation process, the use of police brutality and the "third degree" were believed to be widespread practices. *Miranda* characterized interrogation practices as thrusting suspects into an "unfamiliar atmosphere and run through menacing police interrogation procedures" where suspects are "surrounded by antagonistic forces" and kept incommunicado in a "police-dominated atmosphere" where they are "deprived of every psychological advantage." The Court concluded that such interrogation "exacts a heavy toll on individual liberty and trades on the weakness of the individuals." The *Miranda* decision thus sought to balance the rights of suspects against the power of the police by invoking "one overriding thought," namely,

> the respect a government . . . must accord to the dignity and integrity of its citizens. To maintain a "fair state-individual balance," to require the government "to shoulder the entire load." . . . To respect the inviolability of the human personality, our accusatory system of justice demands that the government seeking to punish an individual produce the evidence against him by its own independent labors, rather than by the cruel, simple expedient of compelling it from his own mouth.

Because *Miranda* was designed to deter improper interrogation techniques used by U.S. law enforcement officials, *Miranda* warnings are not required when an independent interrogation is conducted by officials of a foreign government or by private security police. The voluntariness standard, however, may apply to interrogation by such officials because of the possible unreliability of coerced confessions.

Over the years the Supreme Court began to refer to the *Miranda* warnings as "prophylactic safeguards" that were "not themselves rights protected by the Constitution." In 1968 Congress enacted a statute providing that confessions are admissible if they are voluntarily given. In 1999 the federal Fourth Circuit Court of Appeals combined the congressional statute with the Supreme Court's statements about the nonconstitutional nature of *Miranda,* and ruled that *Miranda* had in fact been overruled by Congress. The Supreme Court, however, held that *Miranda* was a constitutional decision that could not be overturned by Congress. The Court noted that, "*Miranda* has become embedded in routine police practice to the point where the warnings have become part of our national culture. While we have overruled our precedents when subsequent cases have undermined their doctrinal underpinnings, we do not believe that this has happened to the *Miranda* decision."[9]

Custody for Purposes of *Miranda*

The necessity of giving the *Miranda* warnings exists only when an individual is questioned while in custody. According to the *Miranda* decision, **custodial interrogation** means "questioning initiated by law-enforcement officers after a person has been taken into custody or otherwise deprived of his freedom of action in any significant

Custodial interrogation "questioning initiated by law-enforcement officers after a person has been taken into custody or otherwise deprived of his freedom of action in any significant way."

way." Custodial interrogation may take place in a suspect's own home as in *Orozco v. Texas* when four police officers entered the suspect's bedroom and questioned him at 4:00 A.M.[10] But a suspect may not be in custody even though the suspect is at the police station. In *Oregon v. Mathiason,* the defendant was properly interrogated without *Miranda* warnings after he voluntarily came to the police station and after he was told that he was not under arrest.[11] "It is the custodial nature rather than the location of the interrogation that triggers the necessity of giving *Miranda* warnings."[12]

The U.S. Supreme Court has defined **custody** as "a formal arrest or restraint on freedom of movement associated with a formal arrest."[13] The question of custody is resolved by examining the following factors

1. Whether the suspect is questioned in familiar or neutral surroundings
2. The number of police officers present
3. The degree of physical restraint
4. The duration and character of the interrogation
5. Whether or when probable cause to arrest exists
6. If the suspect has become the focus of the investigation
7. The language used by the officer to summon the individual
8. The extent to which the suspect is confronted with evidence of guilt

In determining whether a suspect was in custody, the preceding factors must be viewed from the vantage point of "how a reasonable man in the suspect's position would have understood his situation."[14] Even a suspect in custody in a "technical sense" is not entitled to *Miranda* warnings if the suspect is unaware of being questioned by law enforcement officials. For example, placing an undercover agent in the suspect's prison cell did not necessitate *Miranda* warnings because "when a suspect considers himself in the company of cellmates and not officers, the coercive atmosphere is lacking."[15]

In *Berkemer v. McCarty,* the U.S. Supreme Court recognized that *Miranda* applies "regardless of the nature or severity of the offense of which [the defendant] is suspected or for which he was arrested."[16] Thus *Miranda* does not turn upon the nature of the offense—whether classified as a felony or misdemeanor. Instead, *Miranda* turns upon the nature of the custody imposed on a suspect; even arrests for minor traffic violations may necessitate *Miranda* warnings. However, custody for purposes of *Miranda* must be distinguished from seizures of a person for purposes of the Fourth Amendment. Roadside questioning of a motorist detained in a routine traffic stop is a seizure within the meaning of the Fourth Amendment because the motorist is "not free to leave." But routine traffic stops do not implicate *Miranda* rights unless "a traffic stop exerts upon a detained person pressures that sufficiently impair his privilege against self-incrimination to require that he be warned of his constitutional rights." Custody for purposes of *Miranda* thus requires a Fourth Amendment seizure "plus" a coercive atmosphere.

Interrogation Within the Meaning of *Miranda*

Contrary to portrayals on television "cop" shows, *Miranda* warnings are not required as soon as the suspect is apprehended. *Miranda* warnings are required only when **interrogation** is to take place, which *Miranda* defined as "questioning initiated by law enforcement officers." For example, when the police arrest a suspect, the suspect is transported to the police station, booked, and placed in a holding cell, but interrogation may be postponed until the detectives arrive. The suspect need not be given *Miranda* warnings until the detectives begin the actual interrogation.

If the defendant initiates a conversation with the police prior to interrogation, *Miranda* recognized that "there is no requirement that police stop a person who . . . states that he wishes to confess to a crime. . . . Volunteered statements

Custody
"a formal arrest or restraint on freedom of movement associated with a formal arrest."

Interrogation
express questioning and any words or actions on the part of the police that the police should know are reasonably likely to elicit an incriminating response from the suspect.

of any kind are not barred by the Fifth Amendment and their admissibility is not affected by our holding today." For example, no interrogation took place when the suspect volunteered to speak with his wife, knowing that a police officer was present and taping the conversation.[17] The officer did not question the defendant or otherwise participate in the conversation.

Rhode Island v. Innis expanded Miranda's definition of interrogation by recognizing that interrogation occurs "whenever a person in custody is subjected to either express questioning or its functional equivalent."

RHODE ISLAND v. INNIS
Supreme Court of the United States, 1980
446 U.S. 291, 100 S.Ct. 1682

At approximately 4:30 A.M., a patrolman arrested a defendant suspected of robbing a taxicab driver and murdering him with a shotgun blast to the back of the head. Defendant was advised of his rights and he asked to speak with a lawyer. The defendant was then placed in a police vehicle with three police officers. Although the record is somewhat unclear, it appears that Patrolman Gleckman initiated a conversation with Patrolman McKenna concerning the missing shotgun. As Patrolman Gleckman testified at trial:

"At this point, I was talking back and forth with Patrolman McKenna stating that I frequent this area while on patrol and [that because a school for handicapped children is located nearby] there's a lot of handicapped children running around in this area, and God forbid one of them might find a weapon with shells and they might hurt themselves."

Patrolman McKenna shared his fellow officer's concern: "I more or less concurred with him [Gleckman] that it was a safety factor and that we should, you know, continue to search for the weapon and try to find it."

The defendant then interrupted the conversation, stating that he would show the officers where the gun was located. The police vehicle returned to the scene of the arrest where a search for the shotgun was in progress. There, the police again advised defendant of his rights. He replied that he understood his rights, but "wanted to get the gun out of the way because of the kids in the area in the school." He then led the police to a nearby field, where he pointed out the shotgun under some rocks.

JUSTICE STEWART delivered the opinion of the Court: Because the parties agree that defendant was fully informed of his Miranda rights, that he asserted his right to counsel, and that he was in custody while being driven to the police station, the issue is whether he was "interrogated" in violation of Miranda.

The concern of the Court in Miranda was that the "interrogation environment" created by the interplay of interrogation and custody would "subjugate the individual to the will of his examiner" and thereby undermine the privilege against compulsory self-incrimination. . . . It is clear [that the Miranda warnings] are required not where a suspect is simply taken into custody, but rather where a suspect in custody is subjected to interrogation. "Interrogation," as conceptualized [in Miranda] must reflect a measure of compulsion above and beyond that inherent in custody itself.

We conclude that the Miranda safeguards come into play whenever a person in custody is subjected to either express questioning or its functional equivalent. That is to say, the term "interrogation" under Miranda refers not only to express questioning, but also to any words or actions on the part of the police (other than those normally attendant to arrest and custody) that the police should know are reasonably likely to elicit an incriminating response from the suspect. The latter portion of this definition focuses primarily upon the perceptions of the suspect, rather than the intent of the police. This focus reflects the fact that the Miranda safeguards were designed to vest a suspect in custody with an added measure of protection against coercive police practices, without regard to objective proof of the underlying intent of the police. A practice that the police should know is reasonably likely to evoke an incrimination response from a suspect thus amounts to interrogation. But since the police surely cannot be held accountable for the unforeseeable results of their words or actions, the definition of interrogation can extend only to words or actions on the part of police officers that they *should have known* were reasonably likely to elicit an incrimination response.

Turning to the facts of the present case, we conclude that the defendant was not "interrogated" within the meaning of *Miranda*. . . . [I]t cannot be fairly concluded that the respondent was subjected to the "functional equivalent" of questioning. It cannot be said, in short, that the officers should have known that their conversation was reasonably likely to elicit an incriminating response from the defendant. There is nothing in the record to suggest that the officers were aware that the defendant was peculiarly susceptible to an appeal to his conscience concerning the safety of handicapped children or that the police knew that the defendant was unusually disoriented or upset at the time of his arrest.

The case thus boils down to whether, in the context of a brief conversation, the officers should have known that the defendant would suddenly be moved to make a self-incriminating response. Given the fact that the entire conversation appears to have consisted of no more than a few off-hand remarks, we cannot say that the officers should have known that it was reasonably likely that Innis would so respond. This is not a case where the police carried on a lengthy harangue in the presence of the suspect. Nor does the record support the defendant's contention that under the circumstances, the officers' comments were particularly "evocative."

Booking question exception
police may ask questions that secure the "biographical data necessary to complete booking or pretrial services."

Public safety exception
the police may ask questions "reasonably prompted by a concern for the public safety."

Rhode Island v. Innis excluded from the definition of interrogation any words or actions on the part of the police "normally attendant to arrest and custody." *Pennsylvania v. Muniz* clarified this language by recognizing a routine **booking question exception** which exempts from *Miranda* coverage those questions which secure the "biographical data necessary to complete booking or pretrial services."[18] Booking procedures are primarily clerical in nature and consist of (1) completing the arrest report and preparing the arrestee's permanent police record, (2) fingerprinting and photographing the accused, (3) entry on the police "blotter" of the name of the arrestee and the personal effects in the arrestee's possession, and (4) the date, time, and place of the arrest.

In *New York v. Quarles,* the U.S. Supreme Court recognized another exception to *Miranda*—the **public safety exception.**[19] When police officers ask questions "reasonably prompted by a concern for the public safety," they may dispense with the *Miranda* warnings.

NEW YORK v. QUARLES
Supreme Court of the United States, 1984
467 U.S. 649, 104 S.Ct. 2626

[At approximately 12:30 A.M., police apprehended defendant in the rear of a supermarket. He matched the description of the man who had just raped a woman. The woman had told the police that the rapist had just entered the supermarket and that he was carrying a gun. The police frisked the defendant and discovered that he was wearing an empty shoulder holster. After handcuffing the defendant, the police asked where the gun was. The defendant nodded in the direction of some empty cartons and responded, "The gun is over there."]

CHIEF JUSTICE REHNQUIST delivered the opinion of the Court:
We hold that on these facts there is a "public safety" exception to the requirement that *Miranda* warnings be given before a suspect's answers may be admitted

into evidence, and that the availability of that exception does not depend upon the motivation of the individual officers involved. In a kaleidoscopic situation such as the one confronting these officers, where spontaneity rather than adherence to a police manual is necessarily the order of the day, the application of the exception which we recognize today should not be made to depend on post hoc findings at a suppression hearing concerning the subjective motivation of the arresting officer. Undoubtedly most police officers would act out of a host of different, instinctive, and largely unverifiable motives—their own safety, the safety of others, and perhaps as well the desire to obtain incriminating evidence from the suspect.

Whatever the motivation of individual officers in such a situation, we do not believe that the doctrinal underpinnings of *Miranda* require that it be applied in all its rigor to a situation in which police officers ask questions reasonably prompted by a concern for the public safety.

Quarles is an example of how "hard cases" raise fundamental questions about reconciling collective societal interests with individual constitutional rights. Perhaps the ultimate test for the Supreme Court would be a situation where police seek to use torture or some form of intrusion upon the personal autonomy of a terrorist in order to discover the location of a pirated atomic bomb threatening the lives of millions. Is such a dilemma to be resolved by adopting society's interest as paramount to individual rights, or by allowing individual rights to prevail over social concerns? In our constitutional democracy where neither individual autonomy nor collective security may utterly dominate the other, reconciling or accommodating the conflict between governmental and individual interests is a daunting task for the judiciary.

Waiver of *Miranda* Rights

A suspect may **waive the right to remain silent** and the right to counsel if such waiver is made voluntarily, knowingly, and intelligently. A voluntary waiver of rights, like the voluntariness of a confession, must be determined by the particular circumstances, including the physical and psychological condition of the suspect, and any trickery or deceit utilized by the police. Although the same factors bear upon voluntariness and waiver, the trial court must make separate and distinct findings regarding the voluntariness of the confession and the validity of any waiver. Waivers of *Miranda* rights "must not only be voluntary, but constitute a knowing and intelligent relinquishment or abandonment of a known right or privilege."[20]

The prosecution bears a "heavy burden" in demonstrating the requisite waiver, thus the police often have the suspect sign the "*Miranda* rights card" as shown in Exhibit 12–1 beside the statement, "Sign if you waive these rights." Such an express written waiver is "strong proof of the validity of waiver," but even in the absence of an explicit waiver, a waiver can be "inferred from the actions and words of the person interrogated." For example, in *North Carolina v. Butler,* the defendant refused to sign any waiver form but did agree to talk.[21] This willingness to talk was deemed to be an implied waiver of defendant's *Miranda* rights.

Waiver of the right to remain silent
a suspect "voluntarily, knowingly, and intelligently" gives up the right not to answer law enforcement officers' questions.

DATE:
TIME:
NAME OF ACCUSED:
　　I am Detective _____ of the _____ Bureau of Police.

1. You are being interviewed in connection with the alleged commission of the crime of _____ .
2. You have an absolute right to remain silent and make no statement to me and your silence will be guarded by the police.
3. Any statement you make without counsel can be used as evidence against you.
4. You have a right to the presence of an attorney during this or any future interview the police might have with you. The attorney may be one of your own choosing which you retain, or if you are without funds to employ counsel, the court will appoint one for you.

Do you understand the rights that have been explained to you?
　　If you voluntarily waive the above rights and desire to make a statement, sign below.

EXHIBIT 12–1
Miranda Waiver Form

When a waiver is declined and the suspect chooses to remain silent, this decision must be "scrupulously honored." However, certain circumstances permit the police to reapproach a defendant who has chosen to remain silent. In *Michigan v. Mosely,* the police sought to question the defendant about two robberies, but the defendant elected not to make a statement.[22] Several hours later the defendant was taken to another location, again given the *Miranda* warnings, and questioned by a different police officer about a third robbery. The U.S. Supreme Court held that a valid waiver occurred at the second interrogation because the police had "scrupulously honored" the defendant's decision to remain silent at the first interrogation.

Unlike the right to remain silent, the *Miranda* right to counsel precludes the police from reapproaching a defendant who requested a lawyer. A suspect who requests the assistance of counsel "is not subject to further interrogation by the authorities until counsel has been made available to him, unless the accused himself initiates further communication, exchanges or conversations with the police."[23] In *Oregon v. Bradshaw,* the U. S. Supreme Court explained that waiver of counsel requires two separate determinations: (1) Did the defendant or the police initiate further communication? (2) Even though the defendant initiates the conversation, the burden remains on the prosecution to show a knowing and intelligent waiver of her *Miranda* rights.[24] Unlike the rule of *Michigan v. Mosley* permitting the police to reapproach a defendant who elected to remain silent, *Oregon v. Bradshaw* held that

> as a matter of law, the presumption raised by a suspect's request for counsel—that he considers himself unable to deal with the pressures of custodial interrogation without legal assistance—does not disappear simply because the police have approached the suspect, still in custody, still without counsel, about a separate investigation.[25]

Although the police may not reapproach a suspect who requests counsel, the police need not inform the suspect that an attorney has requested to see the suspect. In *Moran v. Burbine,* the public defender telephoned the police department and stated that she would act as defendant's legal counsel for any lineup or interrogation.[26] She was informed that the police were through with the defendant for the night, and he would not be questioned or placed in a lineup. Less than an hour later, the police interrogated the defendant after obtaining a waiver of his *Miranda* rights. The Supreme Court stated:

> Whether intentional or inadvertent, the state of mind of the police is irrelevant to the question of the intelligence and voluntariness of respondent's election to abandon his rights. Although highly inappropriate, even deliberate deception of an attorney could not possibly affect a suspect's decision to waive his *Miranda* rights unless he were at least aware of the incident.

Sixth Amendment Right to Counsel

Miranda established the right to counsel at custodial interrogations, but the Sixth Amendment right to counsel also applies to certain interrogations not covered by *Miranda*. In *Massiah v. United States,* the police secretly interrogated an indicted individual by placing an electronic listening device in an automobile where the defendant spoke with a police informant.[27] Although this interrogation of a suspect free on bail could not be considered as "custodial" for *Miranda* purposes, the U.S. Supreme Court held that defendant's Sixth Amendment right to counsel prohibited such interrogation after the **commencement of judicial proceedings** (in this case, the defendant's indictment by a grand jury).

Commencement of judicial proceedings
triggers the Sixth Amendment right to counsel during interrogation.

The Sixth Amendment and *Miranda* versions of the right to counsel are necessarily treated separately because the triggering mechanism for *Miranda* rights is custody plus interrogation, while the triggering mechanism for the Sixth Amendment right to counsel is interrogation plus the commencement of judicial proceedings. The distinctions and the overlap between these two versions of a right to counsel becomes apparent when *Rhode Island v. Innis* is compared with *Brewer v. Williams*.

BREWER v. WILLIAMS
Supreme Court of the United States, 1977
430 U.S. 387, 97 S.Ct. 1232

On the afternoon of December 24, 1968, a 10-year-old girl failed to return from a trip to the washroom. A search for her was unsuccessful. On December 26, a Des Moines lawyer named Henry McKnight informed the Des Moines police that he had received a long distance call from the defendant Williams, and that he advised Williams to turn himself in to the Davenport police. When Williams surrendered to the Davenport police, he was arraigned before a judge, advised of his *Miranda* rights, and committed to jail. McKnight and Des Moines police officials agreed that Detective Learning and a fellow officer would drive to Davenport to pick up Williams, that they would bring him directly back to Des Moines, and that they would not question him during the trip.

The two detectives picked up Williams and began the 160-mile drive to Des Moines. At no time during the trip did Williams express a willingness to be interrogated in the absence of an attorney. Instead, he stated several times, "When I get to Des Moines and see Mr. McKnight, I am going to tell you the whole story." Detective Learning knew that Williams was a former mental patient and knew also that he was deeply religious. Not long after leaving Davenport, Detective Learning delivered what has been referred to as the "Christian burial speech." Addressing Williams as "Reverend," the Detective said:

"I want to give you something to think about while we're traveling down the road. . . . Number one, I want you to observe the weather conditions, it's raining, it's sleeting, it's freezing, driving is very treacherous, visibility is poor, it's going to be dark early this evening. They are predicting several inches of snow for tonight, and I feel that you yourself are the only person that knows where this little girl's body is, that you yourself have only been there once, and if you get a snow on top of it you yourself may be unable to find it. And, since we will be going right past the area on the way into Des Moines, I feel that we could stop and locate the body, that the parents of this little girl should be entitled to a Christian burial for the little girl who was snatched away from them on Christmas Eve and murdered. And I feel we

should stop and locate it on the way in rather than waiting until morning and trying to come back out after a snow storm and possibly not being able to find it at all."

The car continued towards Des Moines, and as it approached Mitchellville, Williams said that he would show the officers where the body was. He then directed the police to the body.

JUSTICE STEWART delivered the opinion of the Court: There is no need to review the *Miranda* doctrine for it is clear that the judgment before us [excluding Williams' statements in the police car] must in any event be affirmed upon the ground that Williams was deprived of a different constitutional right—the right to the assistance of counsel.

Whatever else it may mean, the right to counsel . . . means at least that a person is entitled to the help of a lawyer at or after the time that judicial proceedings have been initiated against him—"whether by way of formal charge, preliminary hearing, indictment, information, or arraignment."

There can be no doubt in the present case that judicial proceedings had been initiated against Williams before the start of the automobile ride from Davenport to Des Moines. A warrant had been issued for his arrest, he had been arraigned on that warrant before a judge in a Davenport courtroom, and he had been committed by the court to confinement in jail. There can be no serious doubt, either, that Detective Learning deliberately and designedly set out to elicit information from Williams just as surely as—and perhaps more effectively than—if he had formally interrogated him.

It is true that Williams had been informed of and appeared to understand his right to counsel. But waiver requires not merely comprehension but relinquishment, and Williams' consistent reliance upon the advice of counsel in dealing with the authorities refutes any suggestion that he waived that right. . . . His statements while in the car that he would tell the whole story **after** seeing McKnight in Des Moines were the clearest expression by Williams himself that he desired the presence of an attorney before any interrogation took place.

Despite Williams' express and implicit assertions of his right to counsel, Detective Learning proceeded to elicit incriminating statements from Williams. Learning did not preface this effort by telling Williams that he had a right to the presence of a lawyer, and made no effort at all to ascertain whether Williams wished to relinquish that right. We do not hold that under the circumstances of this case Williams *could not,* without notice to counsel, have waived his rights under the Sixth Amendment. We only hold that he did not.

Although we do not lightly affirm the issuance of a writ of habeas corpus in this case, so clear a violation of the Sixth Amendment as here occurred cannot be condoned.

Maine v. Moulton characterized *Brewer* as establishing that once the right to counsel has attached, the police may not interfere with the efforts of a defendant's attorney to act as a "medium" between the state and the accused.[28] *Moulton,* however, held that when police confront an indicted defendant as part of an investigation of a new and different offense, the incriminating statements relating to the new offense are admissible. (Statements relating to the pending charges are inadmissible.)

Moulton was distinguished in *Kuhlmann v. Wilson,* where the U.S. Supreme Court stated that its primary concern was with secret interrogation by investigative techniques that are "the equivalent of direct police interrogation."[29] Thus the Sixth Amendment does not forbid admission of a defendant's statements to a jailhouse informant who was "placed in close proximity but made no effort to stimulate conversations about the crime charged. Rather, the defendant must demonstrate that the police and their informant took some action, beyond merely listening, that was designed deliberately to elicit incriminating remarks."

Corroboration of Confessions

A voluntary confession obtained in compliance with *Miranda* and the Sixth Amendment right to counsel must still be corroborated by other evidence. At common law, corroboration usually consisted of independent proof of the *corpus delicti* (the body of the crime). The prosecution was required to establish, independent of the confession, that someone committed the offense, and only then could the confession be utilized to identify the offender. In *Opper v. United States,* however, the U.S. Supreme Court rejected the common law **corroboration requirement** that the prosecution must independently establish the corpus delicti.[30] Instead, the Court held that the prosecution must produce substantial independent evidence which establishes the trustworthiness of the confession and supports the essential facts admitted. For example, suppose the defendant confesses to using cocaine in the defendant's apartment, and a subsequent search of the apartment reveals drug paraphernalia, but no residue of cocaine. Under the common law standard, the corpus delicti of illegal drug use has not been established because no illegal drugs were actually found. But under the *Opper* standard, some independent evidence (the drug paraphernalia) corroborates the trustworthiness of the confession.

Corroboration requirement the prosecution must produce independent evidence that establishes the trustworthiness of a confession.

Suppression of Illegally Obtained Confessions

Basic concepts, such as standing to exclude evidence and the fruit of the poison tree doctrine, are common to all suppression motions and were discussed in the previous chapter. This section focuses upon the unique aspects of illegally obtained confessions.

An involuntary confession may be unreliable evidence and therefore inadmissible for any purpose. It cannot be used as part of the prosecution's case-in-chief, nor can it be used to impeach the testimony of the defendant. However, admission of an illegally obtained confession may be harmless error if the remaining evidence establishes guilt beyond a reasonable doubt.[31] If the defendant makes an involuntary confession, any subsequent confession is presumed to be caused by or derived from the first confession. For example, once the defendant let "the cat out of the bag" in a first confession, the defendant would then have little point in refusing to repeat the statement in a second confession. However, strong and clear evidence may establish that a subsequent confession was not induced by the initial confession.[32]

Any statement obtained in violation of *Miranda* taints all derivative evidence except guilty pleas and, perhaps, the identity of witnesses.[33] Although statements obtained in violation of *Miranda* cannot be introduced as part of the prosecution's case-in-chief, such statements can be used to impeach a defendant whose trial testimony is inconsistent with any pretrial statement. Such situations arise when the defendant "opens the door" to impeachment by testifying at trial. For example, when the defendant in *Harris v. New York* testified that he had not possessed heroin, the prosecution introduced an otherwise inadmissible confession (admitting possession of heroin) as an inconsistent statement which impeached the defendant's credibility as a witness.[34] The U.S. Supreme Court stated:

> The privilege to testify in one's defense cannot be construed to include the right to commit perjury. Having voluntarily taken the stand, petitioner was under an obligation to speak truthfully and accurately, and the prosecution here did no more than utilize the traditional truth-testing devices of the adversary process. The shield provided by *Miranda* cannot be perverted into a license to use perjury by way of a defense, free from the risk of confrontation with prior inconsistent utterances.

A number of cases have recognized situations in which the accused's silence may or may not be used to impeach trial testimony.

1. Silence after the *Miranda* warnings cannot be used to impeach the defendant or to establish the defendant's sanity.[35]
2. The defendant's pre-arrest silence may be used for impeachment.[36]
3. The defendant's silence in the interim between arrest and the giving of *Miranda* warnings also may be used for impeachment.[37]
4. When the defendant waives *Miranda* rights and makes a statement, the defendant can be impeached by cross-examination focusing on the failure to tell the arresting officers the same story now offered at trial.[38]

Third-Party Confessions

The preceding sections dealt with cases in which the prosecution attempted to introduce at trial the confession to the crime with which the defendant is charged. In other cases, the trial court must pass upon the admissibility of third-party confessions, that is, statements of a person admitting the commission of the crime with which the accused is charged. These situations arise in one of two ways: (1) the prosecution offers the confession of an accomplice who inculpates the defendant in the crime; or (2) the defendant offers the confession of a person who then admits to committing the crime. (The latter situation is a familiar conclusion to many Perry Mason stories.)

The U.S. Supreme Court recently affirmed that accomplices' confessions that inculpate a criminal defendant are "inherently unreliable," and that in a joint trial, the admission of a co-defendant't extrajudicial confession incriminating the defendant violates the defendant's Sixth Amendment right to confrontation unless the co-defendant testifies at trial. (When the co-defendant testifies, the co-defendant is subject to cross-examination and there is no lack of confrontation.)[39] Faced with a case where only one of the co-defendants has confessed, the prosecution has two alternatives. The first alternative is to sever the two defendants and give each a separate trial. For example, in *United States v. McVeigh*,[40] the trial court severed the Oklahoma City bombing defendants' trial because the prosecution intended to use several statements of one of the defendants against another defendant. The Court granted the severance after considering and rejecting all possible mechanisms for remedying the co-defendant confession problem.

An alternative to separate trials is a procedure called *redaction,* where all references to the nonconfessing defendant are deleted from the confession. This may be accomplished by removing parts of or retyping the offending confession or requiring the witness to paraphrase the confession in such a manner as to avoid any references that might directly implicate other defendants. To be effective, the deletion must not call attention to the fact that the statement implicates other persons who are obviously at trial. For example, it would not be permissible to amend the confession to say, "Me and _____ robbed the bank," because this suggests to the jurors that they are in the midst of a game called "Fill in the Blank." It is proper, however, to have the confession refer to the existence of another party through neutral pronouns, for example, "Me and a few guys beat up the victim."[41]

If the defense offers a third party's confession, the confession is admissible when the third party is unavailable to testify and the confession is reliable or trustworthy. The question of reliability is dependent upon the facts and circumstances of the case and turns upon a determination that "there is anything substantial other than the bare confession to connect the declarant with the crime."[42] As was true of the defendant's own confession, some corroboration must accompany the third party's confession.

SELF-INCRIMINATION

The Privilege Against Self-Incrimination

The Fifth Amendment to the United States Constitution provides that "no person . . . shall be compelled in any criminal case to be a witness against himself." The privilege applies to the states through the Fourteenth Amendment Due Process clause.

The privilege against self-incrimination has broader application than the *Miranda* decision, which is limited to "custodial interrogation." Thus, the privilege against self-incrimination, but not *Miranda* rights, can be invoked before a grand jury.[43] In general, the privilege against self-incrimination can be asserted "anywhere, before any tribunal, in any proceeding."[44] The privilege has been successfully asserted in civil actions, juvenile proceedings, grand jury proceedings, and psychiatric examinations. The privilege, however, is generally not applicable to the pretrial discovery process where the prosecution may have a right to compel the defendant to disclose certain evidence.[45] For example, many jurisdictions require defendants to disclose whether they intend to raise an insanity defense at trial.

Although the privilege against self-incrimination applies in proceedings in which *Miranda* is inapplicable, the privilege is narrower than *Miranda* because it does not recognize a right to remain silent. The Fifth Amendment protects only against compulsory self-incrimination brought about through the disclosure of evidence of a testimonial or communicative nature.

Compulsion

An individual may waive the privilege against self-incrimination and voluntarily choose to disclose incriminating information because the privilege only protects the individual against being compelled to incriminate oneself. Compulsion includes pressures directly applied to the individual, such as contempt of court for refusal to testify. Compulsion also encompasses more subtle pressures such as the loss of government employment if an employee asserts the privilege.[46] However, no compulsion has been used—within the meaning of the Fifth Amendment—if a defendant decides to testify at trial because of the strength of the prosecution's case.

If an individual voluntarily prepares written documents, the courts distinguish between the defendant's voluntary communication in creating the initial documents and a subsequent court order or subpoena that compels the defendant to physically deliver the documents to a court.[47] When a subpoena does not force the individual to restate, repeat, or affirm the truth of the substantive material contained within the documents, courts may compel the physical act of producing records within the person's possession. The act of producing documents is privileged only if the act of producing the documents would compel the defendant to admit that they exist, that they are in the defendant's possession, or that they are authentic. In such situations, the production of documents is no longer a mere physical act but becomes a form of testimony. Thus compliance with the subpoena cannot be enforced because it violates the privilege against self-incrimination.

In limited situations the government may compel individuals to report information which might be self-incriminating. Such reporting requirements violate the privilege against self-incrimination only if the government's primary purpose is to prosecute the individual submitting the information. For example, in *Marchetti v. United States,* the defendant's failure to register and to pay an occupational tax for engaging in the business of accepting wagers was protected by the Fifth Amendment because the government sought to use this information when prosecuting illegal gamblers.[48] If, however, the reporting requirement serves a valid nonprosecutorial purpose, the privilege against self-incrimination is not violated. For example, in *California v. Byers,* the defendant's failure to stop at the scene of an accident and to leave her name and address was not protected by the Fifth Amendment because the government required motorists to stop for purposes of safety, not for the purpose of criminal prosecution.[49]

Baltimore Dept. of Social Services v. Bouknight presents a dramatic context within which the courts must balance two conflicting interests: a criminal defendant's Fifth Amendment rights and society's interest in protecting juveniles from child abuse.

BALTIMORE DEPT. OF SOCIAL SERVICES v. BOUKNIGHT

Supreme Court of the United States, 1990
1493 U.S. 549, 110 S.Ct. 900

[The Department of Social Services obtained a court order declaring Maurice Bouknight to be a "child in need of assistance." Maurice was removed from the custody of his mother, and subsequently returned to her custody under extensive conditions imposed by a protective order. Ms. Bouknight did not comply with those conditions, and the Juvenile Court granted the Department's petition again to remove Maurice from his mother's control. Ms. Bouknight failed to produce Maurice, and Department officials feared that he might be dead. The case was referred to the police homicide division and the Juvenile Court directed that Ms. Bouknight be held in contempt for failing to produce Maurice.]

JUSTICE O'CONNOR delivered the opinion of the Court:

When the government demands that an item be produced, "the only thing compelled is the act of producing the item." The Fifth Amendment's protection may nonetheless be implicated because the act of complying with the government's demand testifies to the existence, possession, or authenticity of the things produced. But a person may not claim the Amendment's protections based upon the incrimination that may result from the contents or nature of the thing demanded. Bouknight therefore cannot claim the privilege based upon anything that examination of Maurice might reveal. Rather,

Bouknight claims the benefit of the privilege because the act of production would amount to testimony regarding her control over and possession of Maurice.

Bouknight may not invoke the privilege to resist the production order because she has assumed custodial duties related to production and because production is required as part of a noncriminal regulatory regime. The Court has on several occasions recognized that the Fifth Amendment privilege may not be invoked to resist compliance with a regulatory regime constructed to effect the State's public purposes unrelated to the enforcement of its criminal laws.

By accepting care of Maurice subject to the custodial order's conditions, Bouknight submitted to the routine operation of the regulatory system and agreed to hold Maurice in a manner consonant with the State's regulatory interests and subject to inspection. Ms. Bouknight may not invoke the Fifth Amendment privilege to resist compliance with the custodial order's conditions.

We are not called upon to define the precise limitation that may exist upon the State's ability to use the testimonial aspects of Bouknight's act of production in subsequent criminal proceedings.

Incrimination

Incrimination
the Fifth Amendment privilege against self-incrimination applies when a "real danger" that the testimony will lead to the imposition of criminal sanctions is apparent.

Unlike *Miranda,* which recognizes a right to silence, the Fifth Amendment privilege against self-incrimination protects only those statements that would be incriminating. The privilege applies when a "real danger" that the testimony will lead to the imposition of criminal sanctions is apparent.[50] The privilege may not be invoked to save the witness mere social embarrassment.[51] The privilege can be asserted if the compelled testimony would reveal "a single remote link" that may expose the witness to criminal penalties. In order to decide whether a real danger of **incrimination** exists, the trial court must consider: (1) "how conceivably a prosecutor, building on the seemingly harmless answer, might proceed step by step to link the witness with some crime . . . and (2) that this suggested course and scheme of linkage not seem incredible in the circumstances of the particular case."[52]

Allen v. Illinois held that the Fifth Amendment applies when a person faces criminal sanctions, but the amendment does not encompass civil deprivations of a citizen's liberty.[53] The issue in the case was whether the defendant could be forced to testify and whether the testimony could be used to confine him as a "sexually dangerous person" under Illinois law. This potential confinement, however, was civil, not criminal, in nature. As long as the defendant's compelled statements could not be used in future criminal proceedings, the privilege could not be invoked in the civil proceeding to determine his status as a sexually dangerous person.

Testimonial Communications

The privilege against self-incrimination only protects against the disclosure of "evidence of a testimonial or communicative nature." Handwriting samples,[54] voice samples,[55] and blood samples,[56] are considered nontestimonial and not within the scope of the privilege. A suspect also can be compelled to participate in lineups, to submit to fingerprinting and photography, and to don distinctive clothing as part of an identification procedure.

The distinction between a physical act and a testimonial communication is not readily apparent in all cases. Can a suspect be questioned as to name, address, age, and other biographical information? If a suspect's answer is incoherent or slurred, is this evidence of intoxication? *Pennsylvania v. Muniz* characterizes slurred speech as a physical act not covered by the Fifth Amendment, while an incoherent answer may constitute a testimonial response protected by the Fifth Amendment.

PENNSYLVANIA v. MUNIZ
Supreme Court of the United States, 1990
496 U.S. 582, 110 S.Ct. 2638

[Defendant Muniz was arrested for driving while intoxicated. After failing several field sobriety tests, Muniz was taken to a booking center. Muniz was told that his action and voice were being videotaped, but he was not advised of his *Miranda* rights. Police asked Muniz his name, address, height, weight, eye color, date of birth, and current age. Both the delivery and content of his answers were incriminating. Next, the police asked Muniz what the court called "the sixth birthday question": "Do you know what the date was of your sixth birthday?" Muniz responded, "No, I don't."

The Court quickly disposed of any objections to the defendant's response to the "booking questions" on grounds that "any slurring of speech and other evidence of lack of muscular coordination revealed by Muniz's responses . . . constitute nontestimonial components of those responses."]

JUSTICE BRENNAN delivered the opinion of the Court: [The "sixth birthday question," however, violated the defendant's privilege against self-incrimination because it] required a testimonial response. When [police] asked Muniz if he knew the date of his sixth birthday and Muniz, for whatever reason, could not remember or calculate that date, he was placed in a predicament the self-incrimination clause was designed to prevent. By hypothesis, the inherently coercive interrogation precluded the option of remaining silent. Muniz was left with the choice of incriminating himself by admitting that he did not then know the date of his sixth birthday, or answering untruthfully by reporting a date that he did not then believe to be accurate (an incorrect guess would be incriminating as well as truthful). The incriminating inference of impaired mental facilities stemmed, not just from the fact that Muniz slurred his response, but also from a testimonial aspect of that response.

Invoking the Fifth Amendment Privilege

During pretrial depositions or at trial, the privilege against self-incrimination must be asserted before an incriminating response is made.[57] Unlike the *Miranda* rights applicable to custodial interrogation, witnesses cannot change their minds and assert the privilege after they have begun to testify about the relevant subject matter. Once a witness begins to testify about a particular subject matter, the witness must then submit to cross-examination on the full details of the subject matter.

At trial, the accused in a criminal case cannot be compelled to take the witness stand, thus the privilege is automatically asserted unless the defendant voluntarily chooses to testify. By taking the stand, the accused thereby waives the privilege and is subject to cross-examination like any other witness. Witnesses other than the criminal defendant, however, cannot avoid taking the stand by asserting the privilege. The witness must take the stand and assert the privilege in response to each question that calls for an incriminating answer. Although it is "a drastic remedy," a witness's entire testimony may be struck if the witness repeatedly refuses to answer additional questions.[58]

Waivers and Grants of Immunity

A defendant in a criminal trial may make a knowing and intelligent partial waiver in order to testify about collateral matters such as motions for a continuance, the admissibility of a confession, or the fruits of a search. Such a partial waiver does not subject the accused to cross-examination on the merits of the case. If the defendant testifies on the merits of the case, however, the defendant is then subject to cross-examination because a witness may not testify to favorable facts, while refusing to address unfavorable facts.[59] If any witness, including the defendant, testifies as to an event, the witness thereby waives the privilege and "opens the door" to cross-examination as to the details of that event. (New events that might lead to further self-incrimination are not within the scope of proper cross-examination.)

The privilege against self-incrimination exists only when the compelled testimony could lead to the imposition of criminal sanctions. Because a grant of immunity eliminates the possibility of criminal sanctions, it precludes invocation of the privilege. Two forms of immunity may set aside the privilege against self-incrimination:

Transactional immunity
prohibits the trial of an individual for any offense about which the individual testifies.

Testimonial immunity (use immunity)
does not prohibit subsequent prosecution, bars the use of compelled testimony or any evidence derived from the testimony.

1. **Transactional immunity** prohibits the trial of an individual for any offense about which the individual testifies. *Kastigar v. United States,* however, recognized that transactional immunity is not constitutionally required and that testimonial immunity is sufficient to eliminate the privilege against self-incrimination.[60]

2. **Testimonial immunity (use immunity)** does not prohibit a subsequent trial of the witness, but bars the use of the testimony or any evidence derived from the testimony in a subsequent prosecution.[61] If the government subsequently elects to prosecute the witness, the government must prove that its evidence of guilt is independent of, and not derived from, the testimony given under a grant of immunity.[62] For example, Oliver North was given testimonial immunity for his testimony before Congress on the Iran-Contra affair. He was subsequently prosecuted on the basis of evidence that the government claimed was independent of his Congressional testimony. (His conviction was reversed because the appellate court found that the government's evidence was derived from his Congressional testimony.)[63]

Exhibit 12–2 (below) shows a typical immunity agreement.

Consequences of Asserting the Privilege

Although the common perception may be that only guilty people hide behind the Fifth Amendment privilege against self-incrimination, the Supreme Court has held that no adverse inferences flow from an assertion of the privilege. Thus the prosecution may not comment on the defendant's failure to testify at trial.[64] The prosecution may comment, however, upon the strength of the government's case and point out that its evidence is not contradicted. Whether the prosecution's statement is a permissible comment on the weakness of the defense case, or an improper comment on the defendant's silence depends on whether "the language used was manifestly intended or was of such a character that the jury would naturally and necessarily take it to be a comment on the failure of the accused to testify."[65] For example, in *United States v. Hardy,* the defendants were apprehended after fleeing the scene of the

EXHIBIT 12–2
Immunity Agreement

In an ongoing effort to cooperate with the Government in investigation of narcotics violations within the United States of America, the Government agrees that the Defendant will receive use and transactional immunity for any and all information provided to any agent of the government concerning narcotics violations which the Defendant may have knowledge of. The government further agrees not to use the fruits of the Defendant's statements and/or further investigations thereof as evidence against the Defendant.

The Defendant agrees that if he knowingly misleads or lies to any government agent, he will be in violation of this agreement and the government may use his statements in prosecuting him.

_____   _____
Defendant   U.S. Attorney

crime.[66] During closing argument, the prosecutor sought to draw an analogy between the defendants' conduct on the night of their arrest and their defense at trial: "They're still running and hiding today. The time has come for them to stop running and stop hiding." In view of the fact that neither defendant testified at trial, and both were in custody and in court—not running and hiding—the "natural and necessary" implication to be drawn from the prosecutor's remark was "that the defendants were running from the evidence presented against them, and hiding behind their right to silence during trial." The court held that the prosecutor's comment violated the defendant's Fifth Amendment right to be free from comment on their failure to take the stand and testify during trial.

The invited error doctrine authorizes the prosecution to comment on the defendant's silence if the defense "opens the door" by raising the issue of the defendant's silence. For example, suppose that in closing argument the defense counsel told the jury, "We think so little of the prosecution's case that we wouldn't even dignify it by having the defendant take the stand and respond to such weak evidence." Suppose the prosecutor responds, "Maybe the defendant is not testifying because the defendant is guilty." The U.S. Supreme Court explained the invited response doctrine in this manner:

> Where the prosecutor on his own initiative asks the jury to draw an adverse inference from a defendant's silence . . . the privilege against compulsory self-incrimination is violated. But where . . . the prosecutor's reference to the defendant's opportunity to testify is a fair response to a claim made by defendant or his counsel . . . there is no violation of the privilege.[67]

When the defendant elects not to testify, the trial court may of its own volition, and must upon a defense request, instruct the jury that the defendant's failure to testify may not be considered in determining innocence or guilt. Because such an instruction may highlight the defendant's failure to testify, defense counsel often request that the instruction not be given. Although it is deemed "better practice" not to give the instruction over the defendant's objection, the final decision rests within the discretion of the trial court.[68]

SUMMARY

Before a confession is admissible in evidence it must satisfy multiple requirements. The voluntariness requirement turns upon the circumstances under which the confession was obtained and whether those circumstances overwhelmed the accused's ability to decide whether to speak or remain silent. If the confession was obtained during custodial interrogation, the prosecution must establish that *Miranda* warnings were given, and that the accused waived the right to silence and the right to representation by an attorney during the interrogation. If a confession was obtained after the commencement of adversary judicial proceedings, the Sixth Amendment right to counsel attaches, and the prosecution must again prove that the defendant waived this right and consented to be interrogated. Finally, the trustworthiness of the confession must be corroborated by independent evidence.

The Fifth Amendment privilege against self-incrimination is at times broader, at other times narrower, than the rights recognized in *Miranda*. The privilege against self-incrimination applies at any proceeding and is not limited to custodial interrogation settings. The privilege, however, does not encompass a right to remain silent, but only the right to refuse to answer those questions that call for self-incrimination. Even this aspect of the privilege can be removed by a valid grant of immunity. The privilege against self-incrimination only protects against the compulsory disclosure of what is testimonial or communicative in nature. The government is permitted to compel mere physical acts such as producing documents or other items, and the accused may be compelled to participate in lineups, submit to fingerprinting, or any other evidence-gathering technique that does not involve testimonial self-incrimination.

CONCEPT SUMMARY

Requirements for Admission of a Confession

Consult local law to determine what changes have been made in a particular jurisdiction.

Voluntariness	The confession must be "the product of an essentially free and unconstrained choice by its maker."
Miranda	*Miranda* warnings must be given if the suspect is faced with custodial interrogation.
Waiver of *Miranda*	Waiver must be made "voluntarily, knowingly, and intelligently."
Sixth Amendment Right to Counsel	Independent of *Miranda*, the right to counsel applies to interrogation after the commencement of judicial proceedings.
Corroboration	The prosecution must produce independent evidence that establishes the trustworthiness of the confession.

DISCUSSION QUESTIONS

1. Should all forms of police trickery or deceit render a confession inadmissible? Can you think of a situation where police lie to the suspect, but the suspect still gives a voluntary confession?
2. Why has the Supreme Court used different definitions for custody under *Miranda* and a seizure of the person for purposes of the Fourth Amendment? Why does the right to counsel under *Miranda* differ from the right to counsel under the Sixth Amendment?
3. If a witness claims the Fifth Amendment privilege against self-incrimination, how can a trial judge decide, without hearing the answer, whether the answer might incriminate the witness?
4. Has a violation of the privilege against self-incrimination occurred if the jury looks at the defendant while listening to a witness describe the person who committed the crime? May the prosecutor ask the jury to observe the defendant's demeanor at trial as an indication of guilt? See *Winston v. Commonwealth*, 404 S.E.2d 239 (Va. 1991).
5. Why is *Miranda* limited to custodial interrogation? Should police give *Miranda* warnings before questioning any citizen?

PRACTICE EXERCISES

1. Does your jurisdiction specify when transactional or testimonial immunity may be granted? Is immunity granted by the prosecutor, the judge, or both?
2. What form of corroboration of confessions is required in your jurisdiction? Must the prosecution establish the corpus delicti, or may the prosecution rely on some independent evidence that establishes the trustworthiness of the confession?
3. What should the police do when the suspect listens to the *Miranda* warnings and says, "Gee, I'm confused. Do you think I need a lawyer?" See *Davis v. United States*, 512 U.S. 452, 114 S.Ct. 2350 (1994).
4. How would you prepare a defendant to testify about a charge of burglary, while exercising the privilege to remain silent on a charge that the burglary led to a larceny inside the dwelling?

5. How does your jurisdiction deal with coerced confessions when the coercion comes from a private citizen who has no connection with the government?

For example, an irate father "beats a confession" out of his son, and the father gives the confession to the police.

WEB SITE

Bureau of Justice Assistance,
www.ojp.usdoj.gov.bja

KEY TERMS

Voluntary confession
Admissibility of a confession
Custodial interrogation
Custody
Interrogation

Booking question exception
Public safety exception
Waiver of the right to remain silent
Commencement of judicial
     proceedings

Corroboration requirement
Incrimination
Transactional immunity
Testimonial immunity (use
     immunity)

NOTES

1. *Ashcraft v. Tennessee,* 322 U.S. 143, 64 S.Ct. 921 (1944).
2. *Escobedo v. Illinois,* 378 U.S. 478, 84 S.Ct. 1758 (1964).
3. *Colorado v. Connelly,* 479 U.S. 157, 107 S.Ct. 515 (1986).
4. *Lisenba v. California,* 314 U.S. 219, 62 S.Ct. 280 (1941).
5. *Frazier v. Cupp,* 394 U.S. 731, 89 S.Ct. 1420 (1969).
6. *Miller v. Fenton,* 474 U.S. 104, 106 S.Ct. 445 (1985).
7. *Crane v. Kentucky,* 476 U.S. 683, 106 S.Ct. 2142 (1986).
8. *Miranda v. Arizona,* 384 U.S. 436, 86 S.Ct. 1602 (1966).
9. *Dickerson v. United States,* 530 U.S.,428, 120 S.Ct. 2326 (2000).
10. *Orozco v. Texas,* 394 U.S. 324, 89 S.Ct. 1095 (1969).
11. *Oregon v. Mathiason,* 429 U.S. 492, 97 S.Ct. 711 (1977).
12. *Coleman v. Commonwealth,* 226 Va. 31, 307 S.E.2d 864 (1983).
13. *California v. Beheler,* 463 U.S. 1121, 103 S.Ct. 3517 (1983).
14. *Berkemer v. McCarty,* 468 U.S. 420, 104 S.Ct. 3138 (1984).
15. *Illinois v. Perkins,* 496 U.S. 292, 110 S.Ct. 2394 (1990).
16. *Berkemer v. McCarty,* 468 U.S. 420, 104 S.Ct. 3138 (1984).
17. *Arizona v. Mauro,* 481 U.S. 520, 107 S.Ct. 1931 (1987).
18. *Pennsylvania v. Muniz,* 496 U.S. 582, 110 S.Ct. 2638 (1990).
19. *New York v. Quarles,* 467 U.S. 649, 104 S.Ct. 2626 (1984).

20. *Edwards v. Arizona,* 451 U.S. 477, 101 S.Ct. 1880 (1981). But see, *Colorado v. Connelly,* 479 U.S. 157, 107 S.Ct. 515 (1986).
21. *North Carolina v. Butler,* 441 U.S. 369, 99 S.Ct. 1755 (1979).
22. *Michigan v. Mosley,* 423 U.S. 96, 96 S.Ct. 321 (1975).
23. *Edwards v. Arizona,* 451 U.S. 477, 101 S.Ct. 1880 (1981).
24. *Oregon v. Bradshaw,* 462 U.S. 1039, 103 S.Ct. 2830 (1983).
25. *Arizona v. Roberson,* 486 U.S. 675, 108 S.Ct. 2093 (1988).
26. *Moran v. Burbine,* 475 U.S. 412, 106 S.Ct. 1135 (1986).
27. *Massiah v. United States,* 377 U.S. 201, 84 S.Ct. 1199 (1964).
28. *Maine v. Moulton,* 474 U.S. 159, 106 S.Ct. 477 (1985).
29. *Kuhlmann v. Wilson,* 477 U.S. 436, 106 S.Ct. 2616 (1986).
30. *Opper v. United States,* 348 U.S. 84, 75 S.Ct. 158 (1954).
31. *Fulminante v. Arizona,* 494 U.S. 1058, 110 S.Ct. 1528 (1991).
32. *Mathews v. Commonwealth,* 207 Va. 915, 153 S.E.2d 238 (1967).
33. *McMann v. Richardson,* 397 U.S. 759, 90 S.Ct. 1441 (1970); *Michigan v. Tucker,* 417 U.S. 433, 94 S.Ct. 2357 (1974).
34. *Harris v. New York,* 401 U.S. 222, 91 S.Ct. 643 (1971).
35. *Doyle v. Ohio,* 426 U.S. 610, 96 S.Ct. 2240 (1976); *Wainwright v. Greenfield,* 474 U.S. 284, 106 S.Ct. 634 (1986).
36. *Jenkins v. Anderson,* 447 U.S. 231, 100 S.Ct. 2124 (1980).

37. *Fletcher v. Weir,* 455 U.S. 603, 102 S.Ct. 1309 (1982).

38. *Anderson v. Charles,* 447 U.S. 404, 100 S.Ct. 2180 (1980).

39. *Lilly v. Virginia,* 527 U.S. 116, 119 S.Ct. 1899 (1999).

40. *United States v. McVeigh,* 169 F.R.D. 362 (D.Colo. 1996).

41. *United States v. Akinkoye,* 185 F.3d 192, 198 (4th Cir. 1999).

42. *Ellison v. Commonwealth,* 219 Va. 404, 247 S.E.2d 685 (1978).

43. *United States v. Mandujano,* 425 U.S. 564, 96 S.Ct. 1768 (1976).

44. *Allen v. Illinois,* 478 U.S. 364, 106 S.Ct. 2988 (1986).

45. *Williams v. Florida,* 399 U.S. 78, 90 S.Ct. 1893 (1970).

46. *Lefkowitz v. Turley,* 414 U.S. 70, 94 S.Ct. 316 (1973).

47. *United States v. Doe,* 465 U.S. 605, 104 S.Ct. 1237 (1984).

48. *Marchetti v. United States,* 390 U.S. 39, 88 S.Ct. 697 (1968).

49. *California v. Byers,* 402 U.S. 424, 91 S.Ct. 1535 (1971).

50. *Zicarelli v. New Jersey State Comm'n of Investigation,* 406 U.S. 472, 92 S.Ct. 1670 (1972).

51. *Ullmann v. United States,* 350 U.S. 422, 76 S.Ct. 497 (1956).

52. *North American Mortgage Investors v. Pomponio,* 219 Va. 914, 252 S.E.2d 345 (1979).

53. *Allen v. Illinois,* 478 U.S. 364, 106 S.Ct. 2988 (1986).

54. *United States v. Euge,* 444 U.S. 707, 100 S.Ct. 874 (1980).

55. *United States v. Dionisio,* 410 U.S. 1, 93 S.Ct. 764 (1973).

56. *Schmerber v. California,* 384 U.S. 757, 86 S.Ct. 1826 (1966).

57. *Minnesota v. Murphy,* 465 U.S. 420, 104 S.Ct. 1136 (1984).

58. *Lawson v. Murray,* 837 F.2d 653 (4th Cir. 1988).

59. *United States v. Rylander,* 460 U.S. 752, 103 S.Ct. 1548 (1983).

60. *Kastigar v. United States,* 406 U.S. 441, 92 S.Ct. 1653 (1972).

61. *Murphy v. Waterfront Comm'n,* 378 U.S. 52, 84 S.Ct. 1594 (1964).

62. *New Jersey v. Portash,* 440 U.S. 450, 99 S.Ct. 1292 (1979).

63. *United States v. North,* 910 F.2d 843 (D.C. Cir. 1990), modified, 920 F.2d 940 (1990).

64. *Griffin v. California,* 380 U.S. 609, 85 S.Ct. 1229 (1965).

65. *Hines v. Commonwealth,* 217 Va. 905, 234 S.E.2d 262 (1977).

66. *United States v. Hardy,* 37 F.3d 753 (1st Cir. 1994).

67. *United States v. Robinson,* 485 U.S. 25, 108 S.Ct. 864 (1988).

68. *James v. Kentucky,* 466 U.S. 341, 104 S.Ct. 1830 (1984).

PRELIMINARY STAGES OF THE PROSECUTION

Chapter 13

PRETRIAL RELEASE AND BAIL

First appearance before a judicial officer
the initial opportunity for a determination of whether to grant the accused pretrial release, and if so, under what conditions.

Bail
money deposited or bond posted as a condition of an accused's pretrial release from custody.

Surety
one who posts bond on behalf of the accused.

After being arrested, "booked," and perhaps subjected to interrogation and identification procedures, a suspect's initial opportunity to be released from custody arises at the **first appearance before a judicial officer,** normally a magistrate or a lower court judge. This appearance must occur "without unnecessary delay," usually within twenty-four hours after arrest, except on weekends.[1] At the hearing, the judge or magistrate determines whether to release the arrestee, and if so, under what conditions.

Money deposited or bond posted as a condition of an accused's pretrial release from custody is called **bail.** Prior to the 1960s (and the emergence of the bail reform movement), an accused was often released only after depositing cash or property with the court. An accused might employ a professional bondsperson or prevail upon family or friends to act as **surety**—one who posts bond on behalf of the accused. An accused unable to post sufficient monetary funds with the court often remained in jail pending trial.

Although an individual placed in pretrial confinement is not subject to the type of punishment imposed on convicted persons, a pretrial detainee is subject to the restraints inherent in maintaining jail security.[2] Perhaps, more importantly, pretrial confinement can be emotionally and financially disruptive to the accused and the accused's family. An accused who is incarcerated pending trial may lose employment, which in turn causes the inability to provide support for the accused's family as well as the inability to earn the money necessary to pay for counsel of the accused's choice. Pretrial confinement also may hamper the defendant's ability to assist defense counsel in preparing for trial. For example, the defendant may be unable to locate witnesses and convince them to testify on the defendant's behalf.

The Eighth Amendment to the U.S. Constitution provides that "excessive bail shall not be required" and all states, by constitution or statute, have similar prohibitions against excessive bail. Requiring an accused to post a substantial monetary bond that the accused may be unable to secure raises questions about the equal administration of justice. Can an indigent be denied freedom in situations that a wealthy individual would not? Must the magistrate consider the accused's financial status as well as other factors unique to the particular defendant? The Supreme Court addressed some of these fundamental concerns in *Stack v. Boyle.*

STACK v. BOYLE
Supreme Court of the United States, 1951
342 U.S. 1, 72 S.Ct. 1

[Twelve individuals were indicted for conspiring to violate the Smith Act (which made it a crime to advocate the overthrow of the government by force or violence). Bail was fixed in the uniform amount of $50,000 for each defendant. The defendants moved to reduce bail on the grounds that the bail fixed was excessive, and in support of their motion submitted statements as to their financial resources, family relationships, prior criminal records, and other information. The government responded by showing that four persons previously convicted under the Smith Act had forfeited bail.]

CHIEF JUSTICE VINSON delivered the opinion of the Court:

From the passage of the Judiciary Act of 1789, to the present, federal law has unequivocally provided that a person arrested for a non-capital offense *shall* be admitted to bail. This traditional right to freedom before conviction permits the unhampered preparation of a defense, and serves to prevent the infliction of punishment prior to conviction. . . . Unless this right to bail before trial is preserved, the presumption of innocence, secured only after centuries of struggle, would lose its meaning.

The right to release before trial is conditioned upon the accused's giving adequate assurance that he will stand trial and submit to sentence if found guilty. . . . Bail set at a figure higher than an amount reasonably calculated to fulfill this purpose is "excessive" under the Eighth Amendment.

Since the function of bail is limited, the fixing of bail for any individual defendant must be based upon standards relevant to the purpose of assuring the presence of that defendant. . . . It is not denied that bail for each defendant in this case has been fixed in a sum much higher than that usually imposed for offenses with like penalties and yet there has been no factual showing to justify such action in this case. The Government asks the courts to depart from the norm by assuming, without the introduction of evidence, that each defendant is a pawn in a conspiracy and will, in obedience to a superior, flee the jurisdiction. To infer from the fact of indictment alone a need for bail in a unusually high amount is an arbitrary act. Such conduct would inject into our own system of government the very principles of totalitarianism which Congress was seeking to guard against in passing the statute under which defendants have been indicted.

If bail in a amount greater than that usually fixed for serious charges of crimes is required in the case of any of the defendants, that is a matter to which evidence should be directed in a hearing so that the constitutional rights of each defendant may be preserved. In the absence of such a showing, we are of the opinion that the fixing of bail before trial in these cases cannot be squared with the statutory and constitutional standards for admission to bail.

The prime deficiency of the bail determination in *Stack v. Boyle* was the magistrate's act of grouping together all Smith Act defendants as being a risk to "jump bail." The Supreme Court demanded that each accused be treated as a unique individual and that pretrial release be tailored to the particular circumstances of each defendant. When determining the conditions of pretrial release, a magistrate is required to consider (1) the nature and circumstances of the offense, (2) the weight of the evidence, (3) the defendant's financial ability to pay bail, and (4) the character of the defendant. This focus on the unique circumstances applicable to individual defendants became the prime thrust of the Bail Reform Movement of the 1960s.

Bail Reform

At the federal level, Congress enacted the Federal Bail Reform Act of 1966, which created a presumption in favor of the release of arrestees on their own recognizance. A **recognizance** is the accused's unsecured promise to appear as required at criminal proceedings leading up to and including trial. An accused who is released on his or her own recognizance is not required to post a bond with the court. In determining whether to release a defendant upon recognizance the magistrate must consider (1) the nature and circumstances of the offense charged, (2) the accused's family ties, (3) the accused's employment, (4) the accused's financial resources, (5) the length of the accused's residence in the community, (6) any record of convictions, (7) the accused's record of appearance at court proceedings or of flight to avoid prosecution, and (8) any other available information relevant to whether the accused is likely to appear at court proceedings. These factors reflect the insistence of federal **bail reform legislation** that the conditions of pretrial release be tailored to each individual accused.

Recognizance
the accused's unsecured promise to appear at proceedings leading up to and including trial.

If a magistrate concludes that the accused cannot be released on his or her own recognizance, the magistrate may impose such conditions as are reasonably calculated to ensure the presence of the accused at proceedings leading up to and including trial. In choosing the appropriate conditions of pretrial release, the magistrate must apply a "least restrictive condition" approach to pretrial release. In ascending order from least to most restrictive, the magistrate may impose one or any combination of the following conditions:

Bail reform legislation
pretrial release is determined by considering the nature and circumstances of the offense, the weight of the evidence, the defendant's financial ability to pay bail, and the character of the defendant.

1. Place the accused in the custody of a designated person or organization agreeing to supervise the accused.

2. Place restrictions on the travel, association, or place of abode of the accused.
3. Require the execution of a bail bond with solvent sureties or the deposit of cash in lieu of a bail bond.
4. Impose any other condition deemed reasonably necessary to assure the accused's appearance at, and good behavior pending, trial.

In addition to any specific conditions set by the magistrate, pretrial release automatically includes the following conditions: (1) that the accused appear before the court at the time and place designated; (2) that the accused not depart from the jurisdiction without permission of the court; and (3) that the accused shall keep the peace and be of good behavior until final disposition of the case. See Exhibit 13–1 for an example of a recognizance release.

The Federal Bail Reform Act of 1966 focused the magistrate's attention on one factor: assuring the defendant's appearance at trial. According to the Act, at least in theory if not in practice, federal magistrates could not deny bail and confine the accused in order to protect against future criminal conduct by the defendant. The Federal Bail Reform Act of 1984, however, authorized the magistrate to consider the extent to which the defendant's release "will endanger the safety of any other person or the community." This form of preventative detention raises a fundamental conflict between those who argue that society must exercise power to detain potentially dangerous individuals and those who maintain that it is wrong to jail persons on the basis of what society fears they will do in the future, rather than for what they have already done in the past. *United States v. Salerno* resolved this conflict in favor of the constitutionality of the 1984 Federal Bail Reform Act.

UNITED STATES v. SALERNO
Supreme Court of the United States, 1987
481 U.S. 739, 107 S.Ct. 2095

CHIEF JUSTICE REHNQUIST delivered the opinion of the Court:

The Bail Reform Act of 1984 allows a federal court to detain an arrestee pending trial if the government demonstrates by clear and convincing evidence after an adversary hearing that no release conditions "will reasonably assure . . . the safety of any other person and the community." The United States Court of Appeals for the Second Circuit struck down this provision of the Act as facially unconstitutional.

Respondents first argue that the Act violates substantive due process because the pretrial detention it authorizes constitutes impermissible punishment before trial. The Government, however, has never argued that pretrial detention could be upheld if it were "punishment." As an initial matter, the mere fact that a person is detained does not inexorably lead to the conclusion that the government has imposed punishment. To determine whether a restriction on liberty constitutes impermissible punishment or permissible regulation, we first look to legislative intent. Unless Congress expressly intended to impose punitive restrictions, the

punitive/regulatory distinction turns on "whether an alternative purpose to which [the restriction] may rationally be connected is assignable for it, and whether it appears excessive in relation to the alternative purpose assigned to it.

We conclude that the detention imposed by the Act falls on the regulatory side of the dichotomy. The legislative history of the Bail Reform Act clearly indicates that Congress did not formulate the pretrial detention provisions as punishment for dangerous individuals. Congress instead perceived pretrial detention as a potential solution to a pressing societal problem. There is no doubt that preventing danger to the community is a legitimate regulatory goal.

Respondents also contend that the Bail Reform Act violates the Excessive Bail Clause of the Eight Amendment. Respondents concede that the right to bail they have discovered in the Eight Amendment is not absolute. A court may, for example, refuse bail in capital cases. And, a court may refuse bail when the defendant presents a threat to the judicial process by intimidating witnesses. Respondent characterize these exceptions as

RECOGNIZANCE

VA. CODE ANN. §§ 19.2-123, 19.2-258

....
Hearing Date and Time

Case No. ....

....
Court — City or County .... Court — Street Address

☐ Commonwealth of Virginia   v. ....
☐ ....   Defendant–Name (last name first, then first name and initials)

....
Defendant — Residential Address and Telephone Number

Mailing address: ☐ Same as above ☐ ....

Offenses Charged: ....

....

I, THE DEFENDANT, by signing this form, promise to appear in court on the date and time noted above. If this date, time or place is changed for any reason by any court or judge, I also promise to appear as so directed. I understand that I ☐ may ☐ may not leave the Commonwealth of Virginia until my case, and any appeals in my case, are finished. I further agree to keep the peace and be of good behavior and agree to follow the conditions listed below ☐ and other conditions listed on the reverse.

....

....

I UNDERSTAND THAT: (1) If I fail to obey any of the above terms and conditions, I may be ARRESTED and, if a bond was posted, the court may forfeit (collect on) the bond; (2) if I fail to appear, the court may try and convict me in my absence; (3) if I fail to appear in Circuit Court on a misdemeanor charge, I give up my right to a jury trial; (4) failure to appear is a separate crime; (5) I must promptly notify the court of any change in my mailing address or where I live while this case is pending.

I certify that this document contains my current mailing address.   _____

Defendant

(☐ check if applicable) The defendant is released into the custody of the person/organization named below upon completion of this part: By signing this part, the custodian named below agrees to take custody of the defendant and see that the defendant obeys the conditions listed above. If the defendant disappears or does not obey every condition, the custodian promises to notify the court at once.

....
Custodian — Name and Address   Signature of Custodian

BOND AS CONDITION OF RECOGNIZANCE: By signing this Bond, the defendant and each person signing as surety agree that they and their heirs and assigns owe the sum of $ .... to ☐ the Commonwealth of Virginia ☐ Locality whose laws are alleged to have been violated. This debt is: ☐ UNSECURED ☐ SECURED BY ☐ Cash ☐ Corporate Surety ☐ Professional Bondsman (DC-332, attached) ☐ Other Solvent Surety(ies) whose ability to pay this debt is measured by the value of real or personal property which they own and who further swear or affirm that the value of such property (after subtracting debts that are liens against the property such as mortgages, unpaid judgments, and unpaid tax liens) equals or exceeds the amount of this bond, (DC-332, attached). Each person who signs this bond agrees to the bond terms on both sides of this form and the terms on the other side are incorporated by reference.

(Insert each surety's name, address and social security number below, also names of authorized agent(s)/attorney(s)-in-fact:

.... _____ (SEAL)
DEFENDANT

.... _____ (SEAL)
SURETY

.... _____ (SEAL)
SURETY

_____
CLERK'S RECEIPT NUMBER

ADMITTANCE TO BAIL: After I explained the conditions and warnings contained in this document, the defendant and each person signing as surety swore or affirmed to fulfill the recognizance and, if any, the bond. I order the defendant released on the conditions listed in this document.

_____
☐ CLERK ☐ MAGISTRATE ☐ JUDGE

....
JURISDICTION (IF DIFFERENT FROM COURT)

....
DATE AND TIME

FORM DC-330 11/93PC (114:3-021 12/94)

EXHIBIT 13–1
Conditions of Pretrial Release

ADDITIONAL CONDITIONS OF RECOGNIZANCE:

....

....

....

....

....

ADDITIONAL BOND PROVISIONS:

The defendant and each person who signed the bond as a surety give up any homestead exemption as to the debt of this bond and understand that the court may force the sale of ANY property owned by the defendant or any surety to pay the debt if the defendant fails to obey all of the terms and conditions of the recognizance. Each person who signed this bond promised to keep title and possession of all property used to measure the ability to pay the debt of this bond in his or her name and not use such property as collateral for any loan or debt or to allow liens against such property which would prevent the payment of the debt of the bond. The terms and conditions of the Recognizance are incorporated by reference, and each person who signed the forms agrees to obey all of the terms and conditions on both sides of this form. If the defendant obeys all of the conditions listed in the Recognizance, the debt of this bond is void. If the defendant fails to obey any of the conditions listed in the Recognizance, the people who signed the bond may be required to pay the amount of the bond.

BOND SECURED WITH CASH:

1. According to the provisions of § 58.1-535, if the person who posted the cash bond (which means the defendant or any other person who posted the cash bond for him/her), owes any debts to the court where the bond is posted, the cash bond or any balance remaining after payment of fines and costs, may be claimed by the court under the Virginia Setoff Debt Collection Act.

2. If the defendant appears and obeys all of the conditions of the Recognizance and is convicted, according to the provisions of § 19.2-121 of the Code of Virginia, the court may not take the fines and costs out of the cash bond posted unless the defendant, if he/she posted the cash bond, or the person who posted the cash bond for the defendant, agrees to let the court do so.

    I have posted the cash bond. I agree to let the court take the fines and costs out of the cash bond.

    _____   _____
             Surety   Defendant

3. If the defendant fails to come to court on the date and time listed in this document, or on any other dates, times or places which any court or judge may set, the defendant gives up any right to notice of any proceeding to forfeit (collect on) the bond, and the court may forfeit the bond without notifying the defendant. The defendant also agrees that any notice of a proceeding to forfeit the bond does not renew a right to such notice. If the court does contact the defendant about a hearing to forfeit the bond, the court does not have to notify the defendant again if the bond is forfeited at the first hearing.

4. If the defendant posted a cash bond and does not come to court and if convicted, the court must take the fines and costs out of the cash bond posted. The court also must forfeit any of the cash bond left over without notifying the defendant. If the court grants a rehearing and finds that good cause has been shown, the court may remit any amount of the cash bond not applied to fines or costs and order a refund by the State Treasurer. This means that if the court decides that there is a good reason to do so, the defendant may get back that part of a cash bond not used to pay fines and costs.

5. If the defendant posted a cash bond and does not come to court and the court does not try the defendant in his or her absence, the court must forfeit the entire bond at once and without notice. If the defendant appears in court within sixty (60) days after the court forfeits the bond, the court may order the State Treasurer to refund all or part of the cash bond.

RIGHT TO APPEAL

You have the right to appeal the amount of this bond. You also have the right to appeal any condition of release. If you want to appeal, contact a lawyer or the court listed on the other side of this form.

FORM DC-330 (REVERSE) 11/93

EXHIBIT 13–1
Conditions of Pretrial Release—
Continued

consistent with what they claim to be the sole purpose of bail—to ensure integrity of the judicial process.

While we agree that a primary function of bail is to safeguard the courts' role in adjudicating the guilt or innocence of defendants, we reject the proposition that the Eight Amendment categorically prohibits the government from pursuing other admittedly compelling interests through regulation of pretrial release.

In our society liberty is the norm, and detention prior to trial or without trial is the carefully limited exception. We hold that the provisions for pretrial detention in the Bail Reform Act of 1984 fall within that carefully lim-

ited exception. The Act authorizes the detention prior to trial of arrestees charged with serious felonies who are found after an adversary hearing to pose a threat to the safety of individuals or to the community which no condition of release can dispel. The numerous procedural safeguards detailed above must attend this adversary hearing. We are unwilling to say that this congressional determination, based as it is upon that primary concern of every government—a concern for the safety and indeed the lives of its citizens—on its face violates either the Due Process Clause of the Fifth Amendment or the Excessive Bail Clause of the Eight Amendment.

The most dramatic recent example of a threat so serious that no condition of release could assure safety was the denial of bail to Terry Nichols while awaiting trial for his role in the Oklahoma City bombing case. The court noted that "defendant has a history of possessing a large number of firearms, ammonium nitrate, ground ammonium nitrate, diesel fuel oil, a fuel meter, detonator cord and blasting caps, which can be used in constructing bombs. Defendant has admitted that he knows how to make a bomb by combining ammonium nitrate and fuel oil. . . The offense defendant is charged with committing is a crime of violence unparalleled in United States history in terms of the resulting loss of lives, injuries and property destruction. . . . No conditions of release will reasonably assure the safety of the community."[3]

Following the magistrate's initial determination of pretrial release, most jurisdictions allow the accused, and sometimes the state, to appeal any restrictions placed on the accused's liberty. Most often, the accused will ask a higher court to lessen the constraints on the accused's pretrial liberty. Less often, the state may ask a higher court to increase the pretrial restrictions placed on the accused. The accused in a state criminal proceeding also may seek review of the bail determination by filing a petition for a writ of habeas corpus in the federal courts. The federal courts, however, may not substitute their judgment for the state officials' determination of the appropriate conditions of pretrial release. A federal court may grant habeas corpus relief only upon a finding that the state court acted in an arbitrary or discriminatory manner.

Violation of Pretrial Release Conditions

A person who willfully fails to comply with the conditions of pretrial release is subject to various penalties:

1. The accused may be found to be in contempt of court.
2. Statutes may create a separate offense for disobeying the conditions of pretrial release (particularly the failure to appear for trial).
3. The accused's pretrial release may be revoked or the conditions of release made more severe.
4. Any security given or pledged for the defendant's release may be forfeited. The forfeiture of any bond, however, must be distinguished from the revocation of bail.

In a **bond forfeiture proceeding,** the bondsperson's or surety's money is subject to forfeiture because of the accused's violation of a condition of pretrial release. No punishment may be imposed on the accused at this proceeding because the sole

Bond forfeiture proceeding
a civil proceeding to determine whether the surety's bond should be forfeited to the court because the accused violated a condition of pretrial release.

Bail revocation
a hearing to consider changes to the conditions of the accused's pretrial release.

issue is whether the bond should be forfeited to the court. In contrast, a **bail revocation** hearing focuses on what if any changes should be made to the conditions of the accused's pretrial release. The accused's pretrial liberty, rather than the surety's bond, is at issue in a bail revocation hearing. Bail revocation and bond forfeiture remain separate issues, even though they may be resolved at a single proceeding.

PRELIMINARY HEARING

The accused's first appearance before a judicial officer determined what, if any, restrictions would be placed on the accused's pretrial liberty until such time as further proceedings could determine the validity of the charges. In the interim between the first appearance and the trial, some assessment is made as to whether sufficient evidence supports the charges and whether to proceed with trial. The prosecutor, of course, has decided to go forward with trial, or the prosecutor would have dropped the charges and the prosecution would end at that point. But standing alone, the prosecutor's commitment to bring criminal charges may not be constitutionally adequate. Like all government officials, prosecutors make mistakes or may be motivated by prejudice, political considerations, or other improper factors that lead them to select a particular defendant for prosecution. The U.S. Supreme Court has recognized that selectivity in the enforcement of criminal laws may not be "deliberately based upon an unjustifiable standard such as race, religion or other arbitrary classification."[4] As part of the American political system's checks and balances on government power, the factual basis of the prosecutor's decision to prosecute is often tested before disinterested parties. The two mechanisms employed to test the government's case are preliminary hearings and grand jury review.

Preliminary hearings
a determination of whether sufficient evidence exists to proceed further in the criminal justice process by bringing the defendant to trial.

Preliminary hearings and grand jury review are primarily designed to serve the same purpose: to determine whether sufficient evidence supports taking the additional step in the criminal justice process of bringing the defendant to trial. Because preliminary hearings and grand jury review can be redundant, most jurisdictions provide that the defendant is entitled to either a preliminary hearing or grand jury review, but not both. For example, Rule 5(c) of the Federal Rules of Criminal Procedure provides that a preliminary hearing will not be held if a grand jury indictment is returned before the scheduled time for the preliminary hearing. The U.S. Constitution provides no right to a preliminary hearing, thus federal prosecutors commonly manipulate Rule 5(c) to avoid preliminary hearings.[5] Many states, however, guarantee the accused's right to a preliminary hearing; a few states provide for both preliminary hearings and grand jury review.

Preliminary hearings are adversary proceedings. In practice they are a form of "mini-trial" at which the prosecution and the defense engage in the presentation of evidence. The preliminary hearing, however, is not a full trial because the quantum of proof required is less than the trial standard of proof beyond a reasonable doubt. The quantum of proof required at a preliminary hearing is most often expressed as either probable cause or a prima facie case. **Probable cause to bind the accused over for trial** is often equated with probable cause to arrest, while a **prima facie case** requires evidence that could lead to a conviction if the defense did not rebut it at trial. Other jurisdictions express the quantum of evidence in terms of "sufficient cause" for charging the accused or "reasonable grounds" to believe that the accused committed the crime. The courts have not been precise in defining these standards except to indicate that the required quantum of proof is far less than proof beyond a reasonable doubt.

Probable cause to bind the accused over for trial
the level of proof required at a preliminary hearing; often equated with probable cause to arrest.

Prima facie case
evidence that could lead to a conviction if the defense does not rebut it at trial.

Jurisdictions also vary greatly as to the type of evidence that is admissible at preliminary hearings. For example, Rule 5.1 of the Federal Rules of Criminal Procedure specifies that the finding of probable cause may be based upon hearsay evidence (which might not be admissible at trial) and that the defendant may not object to evidence on the ground that it was acquired by unlawful means. Thus the Fourth Amendment exclusionary rule does not apply to federal preliminary hearings. These relaxed rules of evidence coupled with the lowered standard of proof make it relatively easy for the prosecution to establish probable cause and prevail at the preliminary hearing. The question thus arises as to why a defendant would exercise the right to such a perfunctory hearing, rather than waive the preliminary hearing in order to save time and money. The answer lies in the secondary but useful byproducts of preliminary hearings: providing an opportunity for discovery, laying the groundwork for future impeachment of witnesses, and the preservation of testimony.

Discovery

Discovery is the process of exchanging information between the prosecution and defense in order to decrease the opportunities for surprise and gamesmanship at trial itself. Court-prescribed or statutory rules covering discovery outside the preliminary hearing are discussed in Chapter Fourteen. Although they are not part of the formal pretrial discovery process, preliminary hearings may provide the defense with the most valuable discovery technique available. At the preliminary hearing the defense will view and may cross-examine the prosecution witnesses, and may be able to inspect the prosecution's physical, documentary, or scientific evidence. In practice, defense counsel rarely present any defense at a preliminary hearing; instead they passively observe the prosecution's case in order to prepare to meet it at the trial itself. (Prosecutors who wish to limit the defendant's discovery will present the bare minimum of evidence required to establish a prima facie case.)

Future Impeachment of Witnesses

When defense counsel does take an active role at the preliminary hearing, it is most often to cross-examine prosecution witnesses in hopes of developing a basis for future impeachment of the witness at trial. (Impeachment of a witness is an attempt to discredit the witness's testimony.) Defense counsel rarely have any hope of convincing the preliminary hearing judge that a witness is so unreliable that probable cause for trial is lacking. But cross-examination at the preliminary hearing may lead the witness to make statements that can later be shown to be inconsistent with testimony offered at the trial itself. In practice, the more that witnesses say at the preliminary hearing, the greater the chances are that they will contradict themselves at the trial. However, defense counsel must strike a fine balance between cross-examination that leads to future impeachment, and excessive cross-examination that focuses on witnesses' weaknesses and thus educates the witnesses (and the prosecutor) about what weaknesses need to be strengthened during trial testimony.

Preservation of Testimony

Witnesses who testified at a preliminary hearing may be unable to testify at trial due to death, illness, or other factors that make them unavailable on the date of trial. At the actual trial, the rule against hearsay evidence generally bars the use of statements made outside the trial itself. But the prior testimony exception to the hearsay rule admits testimony taken under oath prior to trial, if witnesses are no longer available to testify. Thus testimony at preliminary hearings may fall within this exception to the hearsay rule if the accused was given a full and fair opportunity to cross-examine the witness at the preliminary hearing. While the defense often requests a preliminary hearing because of its potential for discovering the prosecution's case, the prosecution may favor convening a preliminary hearing as a means of preserving the testimony of witnesses.

   All jurisdictions that utilize preliminary hearings recognize that its primary function is to determine whether sufficient facts exist to warrant the continuation of the prosecution. Jurisdictions differ, however, in how they conduct preliminary hearings, how extensively they review the evidence, and what type of evidence is admissible. Thus, one must necessarily consult the local jurisdiction's specific provisions governing preliminary hearings.

GRAND JURY REVIEW

Both grand jury review and preliminary hearings test the government's case for the quantum of proof required to go to trial. They differ, however, in important respects. For example, preliminary hearings are public, while grand jury proceedings are secret. The defendant and defense counsel attend preliminary hearings, while most grand jury proceedings take place outside the presence of defendants and their counsel. Preliminary hearings are adversary proceedings in which the defense can challenge the prosecution's case, but grand juries normally hear only the prosecution's case. Judges preside over preliminary hearings, while grand jury proceedings occur without judicial participation. Finally, judges determine the sufficiency of the evidence in preliminary hearings, while grand jurors (citizens of the local community) make this determination in grand jury proceedings.

Grand jury
a panel of citizens who examine the available evidence and determine whether to indict the accused for a criminal offense.

The **grand jury** is an ancient common law institution that originated as a body of local residents who helped look into possible crimes. This investigative function of a grand jury has been characterized as a sword to root out crime. By the time of the American Revolution, however, the grand jury assumed another function as a shield to protect citizens against malicious and unfounded prosecutions. As the U.S. Supreme Court noted:

> Historically, [the grand jury] has been regarded as a primary security to the innocent against hasty, malicious and oppressive persecution; it serves the invaluable function in our society of standing between the accuser and the accused, whether the latter be an individual, minority group, or other, to determine whether a charge is founded upon reason or was dictated by an intimidating power or by malice and personal ill will.[6]

Information
a charge drawn up by the prosecutor and not submitted to a grand jury, although it may be screened by a judicial officer at a preliminary hearing.

In the federal system, the view that the grand jury acts as a "shield" or "screen" against improper prosecutions is recognized by the Fifth Amendment to the United States Constitution: "No person shall be held to answer for a capital, or otherwise infamous crime, unless on a presentment or indictment of a grand jury." The Supreme Court, however, has held that the states are not required to abide by the grand jury requirement imposed on the federal courts. About half the states have their own constitutional provisions or statutory requirements for grand jury indictment. The other half have either eliminated grand juries and permit prosecution by information, or allow the prosecutor to choose between grand jury indictment and information. An **information** is a charge drawn up by the prosecutor and not submitted to a grand jury, although it may or may not be screened by a judicial officer at a preliminary hearing.

The U.S. Supreme Court has often emphasized that screening charges before a grand jury creates a shield to protect innocent citizens against unfounded prosecutions. In practice, however, the grand jury's potential to "shield" innocent citizens is often subordinate to its functioning as part of the prosecutor's arsenal, that is, a "sword" to root out crime through use of its investigative authority.

The grand jury offers prosecutors many of the advantages that civil litigants obtain through discovery depositions. The grand jury has the power to compel testimony and documents from many sources, and the whole process occurs ex parte and in secret. In the typical grand jury proceeding the prosecutor determines what witnesses and evidence will be subpoenaed by the grand jury as part of their investigation. The prosecutor then proceeds unhampered by objections because the witness testifies without counsel at his side. Thus, rather than viewing grand jury indictment as an unnecessary burden, many prosecutors welcome the opportunity to use the grand jury's broad subpoena powers over witnesses and documents as a means of uncovering additional evidence. In the clash between Special Prosecutor Kenneth Starr and President Clinton, the grand jury was not convened for the purpose of shielding the President against unwarranted charges.

The clash between Special Prosecutor Kenneth Starr and President Clinton also raised questions about the potential abuse of the grand jury's extensive investigative powers. In 1919 the Supreme Court held that a witness called before the grand jury may not set limits to the investigation that the grand jury may conduct, nor challenge the authority of the grand jury, provided it has a de facto existence and organization.[7] On another occasion, however, the Supreme Court recognized that: "The investigatory powers of the grand jury are nevertheless not unlimited. Grand juries are not licensed to engage in arbitrary fishing expeditions, nor may they select targets of investigation out of malice or an intent to harass."[8]

Some observers suggested that Special Prosecutor Starr subpoenaed the President to testify before a grand jury suspecting that the President would give false testimony about his alleged sexual relations with Monica Lewinsky, and that this was a form of entrapment. In a case unrelated to the special grand jury, the Fourth Circuit Court of Appeals explained that: "Perjury entrapment occurs when a government agent coaxes a defendant to testify under oath for the sole purpose of eliciting perjury.[9] The Court held, however, that "when the government has a legitimate reason for asking a witness to testify before the grand jury and the witness is provided with adequate warnings, the mere fact that the government knows that the witness possibly may provide false testimony does not establish . . . the defense of perjury entrapment." Although it never surfaced in a court proceeding, there was considerable criticism of the grand jury's subpoena for the records of a Washington bookstore disclosing what books Monica Lewinsky had purchased. (Special Prosecutor Starr apparently had information that Ms. Lewinsky purchased a book dealing with telephone sex.)

Selection of the Grand Jury

Grand juries in individual jurisdictions differ greatly in their composition and selection processes. At common law, the grand jury was comprised of twenty-three persons, at least twelve of whom had to agree in order to hand down an indictment for a criminal offense. Today, federal grand juries consist of between sixteen and twenty-three jurors, twelve of whom must agree to indict the defendant for any charge. Other jurisdictions utilize much smaller grand juries, although all jurisdictions require that an indictment be based on the concurrence of at least a majority of the grand jurors empaneled to review the charges.

The process of selecting grand jurors begins with the court's summoning of a number of persons qualified to serve as grand jurors. The qualifications for grand jury service are set out in the jurisdiction's statutes and normally include requirements that the prospective grand juror be (1) a citizen of the jurisdiction, (2) reside in the jurisdiction, (3) be over eighteen years of age, (4) have no felony convictions, and (5) be a person of honesty, intelligence, and good demeanor. **Purging the grand jury** is the process of narrowing down the number of qualified grand jurors to the number of jurors who will actually serve. The process eliminates otherwise qualified grand jurors who have legitimate excuses for not serving, such as health problems, family obligations, or other similar reasons.

Defense counsel does not participate in the selection of the grand jury, thus any objection to the composition of the grand jury must be made when the defendant is brought to trial. A timely pretrial objection allows the trial court to void the indictment and send the prosecutor back to a lawfully constituted grand jury. Objections

Purging the grand jury
the process of narrowing down the number of qualified grand jurors to the number of jurors who will actually serve.

Motion to quash the indictment
raises objections to the composition of the grand jury or the form of the indictment.

to the composition of the grand jury are made by a motion to dismiss or a **motion to quash the indictment** returned by the grand jury. Such objections must be made prior to the defendant's plea on the merits and cannot be raised for the first time on appeal. Generally, the courts have recognized only two proper grounds for objecting to the composition of the grand jury: (1) one or more of the grand jurors failed to meet the statutory qualifications for service; or (2) the process for selecting grand jurors violated constitutional standards. Although the states are not required to utilize grand juries, if they choose to do so, the Due Process Clause of the U.S. Constitution requires that a grand jury be representative of a cross-section of the community. No State may deliberately and systematically exclude citizens because of race, class, gender, or national origin.[10]

The Constitution does not provide the right to have a cross-section of the community on each and every grand jury, thus a defendant challenging the composition of a grand jury must establish a pattern of systematic discrimination over an extended period of time. For example, a significant disparity must be demonstrated between the number of qualified individuals within the excluded group and their proportion on the grand jury.[11] Systematic discrimination is most often proved by statistical evidence as in *Alexander v. Louisiana* where African-Americans composed 21 percent of the population but only 5–7 percent were included on the grand jury list.[12] The defendant is permitted to establish systematic discrimination even though the defendant is not a member of the group discriminated against. Thus a Caucasian defendant may challenge the lack of African-American representation on juries.[13] Likewise, a male defendant may challenge exclusion of females.[14]

Scope of Grand Jury Investigations

Once the grand jury is selected and impanelled, the judge will charge the grand jury. This charge may range from the judge's statements about the general state of the Union, to suggestions about particular matters that will come before the grand jury. All judges, however, will caution the grand jury to maintain the secrecy of its proceedings. Once the judge has charged the grand jury, the grand jury independently conducts its investigation of alleged criminal offenses. Unlike preliminary hearings, the judge usually does not preside over grand jury proceedings.

Indictment
a written accusation of crime prepared by the prosecutor and submitted to a grand jury.

In the absence of the judge, the prosecutor will focus the grand jury's attention on the task at hand by (1) submitting an **indictment**, which is a written accusation of crime prepared by the prosecutor, and (2) suggesting which witnesses and evidence the grand jury should consider. If the grand jury agrees that the evidence indicates that a crime has occurred, they will return a "true bill" of indictment upon which the accused will face trial. If the grand jury concludes that the evidence does not warrant a trial they will return "no bill." The grand jury's refusal to return a true bill does not preclude the prosecutor from resubmitting the indictment to another grand jury. Until the actual trial begins, double jeopardy does not protect the accused from undergoing successive grand jury investigations (see Chapter Fourteen).

Runaway grand jury
a grand jury that launches its own investigation and returns charges not requested by the prosecutor.

Presentments
an accusation of crime drawn up at the grand jury's initiative.

Although the prosecutor may direct the grand jury's attention to the charges prepared by the prosecutor, no prosecutor may limit the scope of the grand jury's investigation of other crimes, because grand juries are often charged to inquire into and present all felonies, misdemeanors, and violations of penal laws committed within its jurisdiction. A grand jury that goes beyond the indictments prepared by the prosecutor and launches its own investigation is often referred to as a **runaway grand jury.** The charges returned by such a grand jury are referred to as presentments rather than indictments. (Indictments are submitted to the grand jury by a prosecutor; **presentments** are drawn up at the grand jury's initiative.) The information necessary to return a presentment can be obtained from additional witnesses called by the grand jury or from the personal knowledge of the grand jurors. Unlike trial jurors, grand jurors need not stand impartial in the case.

The investigative power of grand juries is broad and includes the authority to compel the attendance and testimony of witnesses. The grand jury also may issue a **subpoena duces tecum,** which is a command to a person to produce writings or objects described in the subpoena. The only constitutional limitations on subpoenas duces tecum or other grand jury investigative powers are the constitutional rights of individual witnesses. The accused named in the indictment is not yet a "defendant," and thus enjoys no rights or protections beyond that afforded any witness called before the grand jury.

Subpoena duces tecum
a command to a person to produce writings or objects described in the subpoena.

Witnesses' Rights Before a Grand Jury

The Fourth Amendment provides only limited protection to witnesses called before a grand jury. A subpoena to appear before the grand jury as a witness is not an arrest or a seizure of the person within the meaning of the Fourth Amendment (see Chapter Nine). Thus, a subpoena for the person need not comply with the constitutional standards required for the arrest of a suspect. The Fourth Amendment exclusionary rule is inapplicable at a grand jury proceeding, which allows the grand jury to question witnesses based on evidence derived from illegal searches and seizures.[15]

Any witness appearing before a grand jury may assert the Fifth Amendment privilege against self-incrimination, but the witness has no right to receive *Miranda* warnings.[16] Unlike suspects or witnesses who are questioned by the police, an individual subpoenaed to appear before the grand jury has no general right to remain silent or to refuse to cooperate. Any grand jury witness who refuses to testify without adequate cause may be found in contempt of court.[17] The contempt sanction makes the grand jury subpoena particularly useful in obtaining statements from persons who will not voluntarily furnish information to the police. Even when a witness validly invokes the privilege against self-incrimination, the grand jury may, if so empowered by local statute, grant the witness immunity and thus force an answer to its question.

A dramatic example of forcing a witness to reveal intimate secrets arose when Marcia Lewis, Monica Lewinsky's mother, was called before the grand jury to relate everything her daughter had told her about Monica's sexual relationship with President Clinton. Ms. Lewis was given use immunity and compelled to testify before the grand jury for six hours over a two-day period. Newspaper accounts related that she broke down on the witness stand and a doctor was called to attend to her. Lewis's lawyer told the press: "No mother should ever be forced by federal prosecutors to testify against her child."

In the absence of a grant of immunity, the witness may refuse to answer questions that call for self-incrimination or to produce books or papers that would incriminate the witness.[18]

A witness before a jury has no Sixth Amendment right to be represented by counsel.[19] Consultation between a witness and counsel may be necessary, however, in order that the witness may determine whether to invoke the Fifth Amendment privilege against self-incrimination in response to a particular question. In such situations, the witness has a right to consult with an attorney outside the grand jury room. This right to consult with, but not have counsel present, often leads to almost farcical scenes where the grand jurors pose a question to a witness who then asks to be excused in order to consult with an attorney in the hallway. The witness will repeat the question to the attorney who will advise whether the question calls for self-incrimination. The witness will return to the grand jury room where the scenario may be repeated after each question is posed.

Grand Jury Secrecy

Unlike most stages of a criminal prosecution, grand jury proceedings are conducted in secret. The U.S. Supreme Court has explained that the secrecy requirement is designed to serve five important objectives:

> (1) to prevent the escape of those whose indictment may be contemplated; (2) to insure the utmost freedom to the grand jury in its deliberations, and to prevent persons subject to indictment or their friends from importuning the grand jurors; (3) to prevent subornation of perjury or tampering with the witnesses who may testify before the grand jury and later appear at the trial of those indicted by it; (4) to encourage free and untrammeled disclosures by persons who have information with respect to the commission of crimes; (5) to protect the innocent accused who is exonerated from disclosure of the fact that he has been under investigation, and from the expense of standing trial where there was no probability of guilt.[20]

Grand jury secrecy requirements vary among jurisdictions, but all jurisdictions prohibit the prosecutor and the grand jurors from disclosing grand jury testimony except when authorized by court order. Most jurisdictions do not impose an obligation of secrecy upon grand jury witnesses; the U.S. Supreme Court has held that a state may not prohibit grand jury witnesses from disclosing their own testimony after the term of the grand jury has ended.[21]

Despite strict rules on grand jury secrecy, leaks in prominent cases are common. For example, following a complaint filed by White House lawyers, a federal judge ordered an investigation into whether Special Prosecutor Starr's office leaked to reporters parts of the seven-month probe of Monica Lewinsky's sexual affair with President Clinton. When the tape of President Clinton's grand jury testimony was given to the House Judiciary Committee considering impeachment charges, the Committee released the tapes for broadcast on television networks.

PERFECTING THE CHARGE

During the early stages of the criminal process the prosecutor may still be investigating and considering the possible crimes committed by the accused. One function of the grand jury or a preliminary hearing is to "screen" the possible charges and identify those that are adequately supported by evidence. At the point that the preliminary hearing judge certifies a charge for trial, or the grand jury returns a true bill of indictment, the possible crimes have crystallized sufficiently to satisfy the Due Process requirement that an accused be given clear notification of the offense with which the accused is charged, also known as **perfecting the charge**.[22] Every formal charge must plainly and concisely (1) name the accused, (2) describe the offense charged, (3) identify the county, city, or town in which the accused committed the offense, and (4) recite that the accused committed the offense on or about a certain date. Failure to state the charge plainly or sufficiently will result in a defense motion to dismiss the indictment as shown in Exhibit 13–2.

Perfecting the charge
the charge must plainly and concisely name the accused, describe the offense charged, identify the place where the accused committed the offense, and recite that the accused committed the offense on or about a certain date.

Identifying the Accused

Although every formal charge must correctly name the accused, courts will not deem a charge invalid for minor omissions or mistakes in the accused's name. For example, omitting "Jr." from the accused's name is not a fatal defect. When no true question arises concerning the accused's identity, the trial court may at any time amend the charge to accurately reflect the accused's name. But when the entire name is

The defendant moves his Honorable Court to dismiss the Indictment filed in this case, and as grounds shows as follows:

1. The indictment fails to contain allegations stating as definitely as possible the time and place of the commission of the alleged offense.
2. No overt act is alleged in the indictment and therefore it is defective.
3. The indictment is vague and ambiguous and does not apprise the defendant of the charge with sufficient specificity to permit an adequate preparation of defenses, and to plead any judgment in the instant case as a bar to any later proceedings against the defendant based on this same alleged offense in contravention to the double jeopardy clause of the Fifth Amendment to the United States Constitution.
4. The indictment is based upon a unconstitutional statute, or in the alternative, said statute is unconstitutional as applied to the facts of this case. The constitutional provisions violated are the Fourth, Fifth, Sixth, and Fourteenth Amendments.
5. The allegations of the indictment fail to state facts sufficient to constitute a crime and said facts do not constitute the violation of any statute.
6. There may have been presented before the Grand Jury considering the indictment in this case intercepted wire and oral communications and evidence derived therefrom which were obtained unlawfully, and accordingly, the indictment must be dismissed.

EXHIBIT 13–2
Motion to Dismiss Indictment

wrong, the charge cannot be amended by striking out the wrong name and inserting the name of the person intended. To do so would subject the "substituted" accused to trial without having had the charge approved by a grand jury or a preliminary hearing. Following the dismissal of this defective indictment, the prosecutor must return to the grand jury to obtain a new indictment against the correctly named defendant.

Describing the Offense Charged

When describing the offense for which the accused must stand trial, the charge need not track the identical words of the statute defining the crime. The offense, however, must be sufficiently stated to give the accused notice of the nature and character of the crime so that the accused can mount an adequate defense. The indictment need not allege every fact in the chain of circumstances comprising the offense charged, nor need it disclose the prosecution's particular theory of the case. For example, in *Simpson v. Commonwealth*, the indictment alleged that the accused "feloniously did kill and murder the victim during the commission of robbery."[23] The Court held that the allegation—"feloniously did kill and murder"—adequately informed the accused of the charge of first degree murder. The fact that the indictment went on to allege that the murder occurred during the commission of a robbery did not limit the prosecution to proving felony-murder. The Court reasoned that felony-murder and premeditated murder are merely alternative methods of committing first degree murder, the sole offense with which the accused was charged.

Identifying the Place the Offense Was Committed

The indictment must identify the site of the offense in order to establish the court's jurisdiction and the appropriate venue (the physical location of the trial). In order for a state to have jurisdiction over an offense, some part of the criminal transaction must have occurred within its geographical boundaries. The offense may occur within a state although the defendant never sets foot within the state. For example, although the Uni-bomber rarely left his isolated mountain cabin, he committed a crime in every state where he shipped a bomb—"It has long been a commonplace of criminal liability that a person may be charged in the place where evil results, though he is beyond the jurisdiction when he starts the train of events of which the evil is the fruit."[24]

Once the court has jurisdiction over the crime, the trial must take place at the appropriate physical location. For example, Article III Section 2 of the U.S. Constitution establishes the defendant's right to a jury of "the state and district wherein the crime shall have been committed." State Constitutions often provide that the appropriate venue for the trial is in the county where the crime was committed.

In most cases the failure to allege jurisdiction or venue in the indictment is not grounds for quashing the indictment. The trial court may amend the indictment upon proof that the offense occurred within the jurisdiction and venue of the court.

Stating the Time of the Offense

The indictment's failure to state the date and time of the offense is also subject to amendment by the trial court unless the time factor affects the accused's substantive rights. For example, time may be of the essence if (1) time is an essential element of the offense (e.g., nighttime burglary); (2) the statute of limitations for the offense may have run; or (3) statutory changes have altered the definition of the offense or the punishment that may be imposed.

DUPLICITY, JOINDER, AND CHARGING IN THE ALTERNATIVE

Duplicity
more than one offense is alleged in a single count of an indictment.

Duplicity occurs when more than one offense is alleged in a single count of an indictment. For example, count one of the indictment may not allege that the defendant "did rape, rob, and murder the victim" because each count of an indictment must allege a distinct offense. The remedy for alleging multiple offenses in a single count is not a motion to quash the indictment, but a motion to compel the prosecutor to elect which particular offense to prosecute. This election must be made at the conclusion of the prosecution case and before the defendant offers evidence, so that the defendant knows which charge to rebut when making a defense. No duplicity occurs, however, if the same count charges that a single offense may have been committed in different ways. For example, if a statute makes it unlawful to play or bet on a game, the indictment may allege that the defendant did play *and* bet on a game. Such a charge is not duplicitous because the defendant has been charged "really but for one offense."[25]

Joinder
multiple offenses may be charged in a single indictment if the offenses are based on the same act or transaction, or on two or more acts or transactions that are connected or constitute parts of a common scheme or plan.

Although distinct offenses cannot be joined in a single count, an indictment often includes multiple counts for offenses of the same general nature. Most jurisdictions recognize that **joinder** of multiple offenses in a single indictment is proper if the offenses are based on the same act or transaction, or on two or more acts or transactions that are connected or constitute parts of a common scheme or plan. For example, count one of the indictment charges burglary, while count two charges a larceny committed after the breaking and entry. Joinder of related offenses is generally appropriate unless it would unduly confuse the defendant or the trial jury. Even improper joinder does not constitute reversible error unless the substantive rights of the defendant have been affected.

Charging in the alternative
the indictment contains separate counts charging alternative ways of committing a single offense.

Charging in the alternative is a common practice that permits an indictment to contain any number of counts charging the commission of a single offense stated in different ways so as to meet the contingencies of proof. For example, in *Bryant v. Commonwealth* the indictment contained three counts pertaining to the single offense of mayhem.[26] The only difference between the counts was that one count charged both defendants as perpetrators, while the other two counts charged one of the defendants as the perpetrator and the other defendant as an aider and abettor.

The indictment was not quashed, nor could the prosecution be forced to an election in the absence of proof that the defendant would be prejudiced or the jury unduly confused. As one court noted, "The [prosecution] is free to indict an individual for as many separate crimes as the [prosecution], in good faith, thinks it can prove. Further, the [prosecution] is free to charge the commission of a single offense in several different ways in order to meet the contingencies of proof."[27]

AMENDING THE INDICTMENT

A prosecutor who anticipates contingencies of proof will ask the grand jury to indict in the alternative. A prosecutor who is surprised at trial by variance between the facts and the charged offense will ask the judge to amend the indictment to coincide with the evidence produced at trial. Indictments may be amended at any time before verdict provided the amendment does not change the nature or character of the offense charged. Amendments that correct minor defects in the indictment are liberally allowed, but amendments cannot save an indictment that fails to state an offense, nor can the amendment change a misdemeanor to a felony. The general rule that allegations and proof must correspond is based upon the following requirements:

> that the accused shall be definitely informed as to the charges against him, so that he may be enabled to present his defense and not be taken by surprise by the evidence offered at the trial; and that he may be protected against another prosecution for the offense.[28]

At trial, defense counsel may oppose an amendment and move to quash a defective indictment. However, because a motion to quash must be made before the commencement of trial, double jeopardy will not prevent the prosecution from obtaining another valid indictment. Therefore, the benefits of opposing amendment (for example, gaining additional time to prepare for trial while another grand jury considers the proper charge) must be balanced against the cost of subjecting the defendant to another arrest, bonding procedure, and grand jury proceeding.

BILL OF PARTICULARS

A **bill of particulars** is what it sounds like, that is, more particular information than what is set out in an indictment. The purpose of a bill of particulars is to make overly general indictments and charges more specific by providing the defendant with information about the details of the charge. For example, the indictment need only describe the offense of murder by charging that the defendant "did feloniously kill" the victim. In preparing for trial, however, defense counsel needs to know whether the defendant supposedly killed by using a firearm, ice pick, or chainsaw. Whenever the indictment is comprehensive enough to identify the offense charged but not specific enough to give the information necessary to enable the accused to prepare a defense, the court may order the prosecution to furnish the defense with a bill of particulars. The decision as to whether a bill of particulars should be given is within the discretion of the trial court because the accused is not entitled to a bill of particulars when the indictment is sufficiently clear and detailed. (See Exhibit 13–3 for an example of a motion that defense counsel may file to obtain a bill of particulars.) Many of the purposes served by a bill of particulars can be accomplished when defense counsel files motions for pretrial discovery.

Bill of particulars provides more specific information than what is set out in an indictment.

EXHIBIT 13–3
Motion for Bill of Particulars

State;

v.   INDICTMENT NO.

_____

Defendant

The Defendant, by and through counsel, moves this Court for entry of an Order directing the prosecution to particularize the indictment as requested below:

1. the precise date, time, location, and address at which the charged conspiracy is alleged to have occurred;
2. the means by which the conspiracy is alleged to have been planned and/or effectuated;
3. the relationship within the conspiracy that each alleged conspirator is alleged to have had with each other alleged conspirator;
4. the date, location and manner by which each alleged conspirator is alleged to have joined the said conspiracy as well as the like information regarding any alleged withdrawals from the said conspiracy;
5. each and every overt act that was committed in the conspiracy;
6. the names and addresses of each conspirator (indicted or unindicted) that are known to the prosecution.

As grounds for the foregoing, Defendant states the following:

1. that the indictment does not contain the requested information;
2. that the information requested is necessary to avoid double jeopardy and prepare an adequate defense.

WHEREFORE, Defendant requests this Honorable Court to grant this motion and such other relief as may be deemed just.

Summary

The purpose of bail is to enable defendants to stay out of jail until a trial has found them guilty. Any restrictions on the accused's pretrial liberty must be related to assuring the defendant's appearance at trial or to protecting the community from future criminal conduct by the accused.

As part of the American political system's checks and balances on government power, the prosecutor's decision to bring charges is often tested before disinterested parties such as preliminary hearing examiners or grand juries. The preliminary hearing examiner reviews the prosecution and defense evidence in order to determine whether sufficient evidence warrants proceeding to trial. Preliminary hearings also may provide opportunities for discovery, preservation of testimony, and a basis for impeaching trial testimony. Grand juries review the prosecution's evidence in order to ascertain whether to indict for the alleged crime, but unlike preliminary hearings, grand jury proceedings are conducted in secret. Thus the defendant has no right to be present before the grand jury or to present defense evidence. All witnesses (including the accused) who appear before the grand jury have limited Fourth and Fifth Amendment rights that may protect them from overly intrusive grand jury investigations.

Whether the charging process includes a preliminary hearing, a grand jury proceeding, both, or neither, the final charge upon which the accused stands trial must clearly name the accused, describe the offense charged, and identify the site of the offense and the time of its commission. Although the charging instrument may meet the above requirements, the trial court has discretion to order the prosecution to provide a bill of particulars that provides additional details of the charged offense.

DISCUSSION QUESTIONS

1. If pretrial liberty can be restricted because of an accused's potential for committing future crimes, can the government impose restraints on others who are not charged with a crime but who pose the same potential for committing future crimes? For example, can the government restrain the freedom of a person whom experts identify as a psychotic "time bomb" just waiting to explode and hurt someone?

2. An arrest, a preliminary hearing, and grand jury indictment all focus on determining whether some form of probable cause indicates that the accused committed a crime and should be brought to trial. Are these proceedings overly repetitive or do they serve different purposes?

3. Why should the prosecution be able to charge alternative theories of how and what crime was committed? If the prosecution is unable to settle on one clear theory of the case, isn't it apparent that the prosecution cannot prove the crime beyond a reasonable doubt?

4. By what means may a court control a runaway grand jury? May the court dismiss the grand jury? refuse to extend its term? refuse to issue subpoenas requested by the grand jury?

5. Consider the following situation: In the course of an alleged robbery of an inner-city grocery store, the grocer shot and killed the fleeing robber, a member of a racial minority. Local merchant groups are insisting that no charges be brought, while various civil rights groups are demanding prosecution of the grocer. You are the prosecutor, an elected official, how will you proceed? If you opt to submit the matter to a grand jury, will you allow the local merchants' association and/or the civil rights groups to address the grand jury? How would you respond to the grand jury's request that you furnish them with statistical evidence of interracial violence in the city?

PRACTICE EXERCISES

1. Has your jurisdiction enacted any form of bail reform legislation? What factors govern pretrial release in your state?

2. How are charges brought to trial (preliminary hearing, information, or grand jury indictment) in your jurisdiction?

3. Does your jurisdiction have specific rules governing the secrecy of grand jury proceedings?

4. Do any rules limit the type of evidence or subject matter that may be considered by a grand jury in your state?

WEB SITE

Federal Law Homepage, Legal.gs/.gov

KEY TERMS

First appearance before a judicial officer
Bail
Surety
Recognizance
Bail reform legislation
Bond forfeiture proceeding
Bail revocation
Preliminary hearings

Probable cause to bind the accused over for trial
Prima facie case
Grand jury
Information
Purging the grand jury
Motion to quash the indictment
Indictment
Runaway grand jury

Presentments
Subpoena duces tecum
Perfecting the charge
Duplicity
Joinder
Charging in the alternative
Bill of particulars

NOTES

1. Federal Rules of Criminal Procedure 5(a).
2. *Bell v. Wolfish*, 441 U.S. 520, 99 S.Ct. 1861 (1979). Pretrial detainees have no constitutional right to contact visits, nor do they have any due process right to observe jail officials' random shakedown searches of their cells. *Block v. Rutherford*, 468 U.S. 576, 104 S.Ct. 3227 (1984).
3. *United States v. Nichols*, 897 F.Supp. 542 (W.D. Okla. 1995).
4. *Bordenkircher v. Hayes*, 434 U.S. 357, 98 S.Ct. 663 (1978).
5. *Lem Woon v. Oregon*, 229 U.S. 586, 33 S.Ct. 783 (1913).
6. *Wood v. Georgia*, 370 U.S. 375, 82 S.Ct. 1364 (1962).
7. *Blair v. United States*, 250 U.S. 273, 39 S.Ct. 469 (1919).
8. *United States v. R. Enterprises*, 498 U.S. 292, 111 S.Ct. 722 (1991).
9. *United States v. Sarihigard*, 155 F.3d 301 (4th Cir. 1998).
10. *Taylor v. Louisiana*, 419 U.S. 522, 95 S.Ct. 692 (1975).
11. *Apodaca v. Oregon*, 406 U.S. 404, 92 S.Ct. 1628 (1972).
12. *Alexander v. Louisiana*, 405 U.S. 625, 92 S.Ct. 1221 (1972).
13. *Peters v. Kiff*, 407 U.S. 493, 92 S.Ct. 2163 (1972).
14. *Taylor v. Louisiana*, 419 U.S. 522, 95 S.Ct. 692 (1975).
15. *United States v. Calandra*, 414 U.S. 338, 94 S.Ct. 613 (1974).
16. *United States v. Mandujano*, 425 U.S. 564, 96 S.Ct. 1768 (1976).
17. *Branzburg v. Hayes*, 408 U.S. 665, 92 S.Ct. 2646 (1972).
18. *United States v. Doe*, 465 U.S. 605, 104 S.Ct. 1237 (1984).
19. *Anonymous v. Baker*, 360 U.S. 287, 79 S.Ct. 1157 (1959).
20. *United States v. Procter & Gamble Co.*, 356 U.S. 677, 78 S.Ct. 983 (1958).
21. *Butterworth v. Smith*, 494 U.S. 624, 110 S.Ct. 1376 (1990).
22. *Russell v. United States*, 369 U.S. 749, 82 S.Ct. 1038 (1962).
23. *Simpson v. Commonwealth*, 221 Va. 109, 267 S.E.2d 134 (1980).
24. *Gregory v. Commonwealth*, 360 S.E.2d 719 (Va. 1988)
25. *Mitchell v. Commonwealth*, 141 Va. 541, 127 S.E. 368 (1925).
26. *Bryant v. Commonwealth*, 189 Va. 310, 53 S.E.2d 54 (1949).
27. *Buchanan v. Commonwealth*, 238 Va. 389, 384 S.E.2d 757 (1989).
28. *Berger v. United States*, 295 U.S. 78, 55 S.Ct. 629 (1935).

PRETRIAL MOTIONS

Chapter 14

CHAPTER OUTLINE

OVERVIEW OF PRETRIAL MOTIONS

After an indictment fixed the specific charges, the common law required the accused to appear in court to plead to, or answer the charges. In addition to pleading simply guilty or not guilty the accused could enter other "technical" pleas. For example, a plea in abatement could challenge the sufficiency of the indictment; a plea in bar might raise defenses such as double jeopardy; or the defendant might file a demurrer challenging the prosecution's failure to state a recognized offense. Today, most if not all jurisdictions have abolished these formalistic and often confusing special forms of pleas. For example, the Federal Rules of Criminal Procedure provide:

> Rule 12(a) *Pleadings and Motions.* Pleadings in criminal proceedings shall be the indictment and information, and the pleas of not guilty, guilty, and nolo contendere. All other pleas, and demurrers and motions to quash are abolished, and defenses and objections raised before trial which heretofore could have been raised by one or more of them shall be raised only by motions to dismiss or grant appropriate relief, as provided in these rules.
>
> Rule 12(b) *Pretrial Motions.* Any defense, objection, or request which is capable of determination without the trial of the general issue may be raised before trial by motion. Motions may be written or oral at the discretion of the judge. The following must be raised prior to trial:
>
> 1. Defenses and objections based on defects in the institution of prosecution, or
> 2. Defenses and objections based on defects in the indictment or information (other than that it fails to show jurisdiction in the court or to charge an offense which objections shall be noticed by the court at any time during the pendency of the proceedings); or
> 3. Motions to suppress evidence; or
> 4. Requests for discovery; or
> 5. Requests for a severance of charges or defendants.

Pretrial motions
requests made to a court asking the court to take some action such as dismissing a defective indictment or ordering the parties to disclose certain information.

Pretrial motions are requests made to a court asking the court to take some action such as dismissing a defective indictment or ordering the parties to disclose certain information. Although counsel must specify the grounds on which the motion is based and the particular relief sought from the court, counsel no longer need distinguish between pleas in abatement, pleas in bar, demurrers, motions to quash, and other antiquated pleas. In current practice, counsel need only distinguish between motions that must be raised before trial begins and motions that may be raised any time before a verdict is returned. Failure to file a pretrial motion at the appropriate time constitutes waiver.

Chapter Eleven discussed pretrial motions to suppress evidence under the exclusionary rule. This chapter addresses pretrial motions dealing with discovery, statutes of limitations, speedy trial, double jeopardy, severance of parties or offenses, and change of venue.

DISCOVERY

Pretrial discovery
the process of exchanging information between the prosecution and the defense.

Pretrial discovery is the process of exchanging information between the prosecution and the defense. Prior to filing a pretrial motion for court-ordered discovery, the prosecution and defense may utilize other formal and informal methods for obtaining information. Prosecutors primarily look to police departments and grand jury investigations to uncover relevant facts. The grand jury offers prosecutors many of the advantages that civil litigants obtain through discovery depositions. The grand jury has the power to compel testimony and documents from many sources, and, unlike a civil deposition, the whole process occurs ex parte and in secret. The prosecutor proceeds unhampered by objections. The witness testifies without counsel at his or her side.

Defendants, on the other hand, have no control over the grand jury process and in many cases are unaware of the grand jury's investigation until it is over. Once the investigation is complete, as a general rule defendants are not even entitled to the transcribed record of grand jury proceedings unless and until a grand jury witness later testifies for the government at trial. Defendants, however, have many other avenues for discovery. As discussed in Chapter Thirteen, the indictment, a Bill of Particulars, and the Preliminary Hearing often yield important information about the nature of the prosecution's case. Outside the confines of judicial proceedings, discovery may occur as part of the give and take of plea bargaining between defense counsel and the prosecution. "When a prosecutor enters into an informal discovery agreement he must abide by its spirit as well as its letter."[1] Finally, some prosecutors subscribe to an "open office" philosophy where the prosecutor voluntarily discusses the nature of the government's case and makes documentary and real evidence available for inspection by the defense. In the absence of voluntary disclosure, the parties must ask the court to order pretrial discovery.

When granting a motion for discovery the court will specify the time, place, and manner of making the discovery, and may prescribe such additional terms and conditions as are required to prevent confusion or misunderstandings between defense counsel and the prosecutor. The party requesting discovery is entitled to a reasonable opportunity to examine the discovery material and prepare for its use at trial. If counsel fails to provide adequate discovery, the court may order counsel to permit further discovery, grant a continuance of the trial to allow for additional discovery, or prohibit counsel from introducing evidence not disclosed.

Scope of Discovery

At early common law, courts lacked any inherent authority to require pretrial discovery. During the 1940s, however, discovery in civil cases was dramatically expanded to give each side pretrial access to almost all relevant information possessed by the other side. The success of this liberalized civil discovery led to proposals to similarly expand pretrial discovery in criminal cases. Proponents of expanded discovery conceded that surprising the opponent at trial created exciting Perry Mason—style drama, but insisted that a criminal trial should emphasize the quest for truth rather than the gamesmanship of opposing counsel. As one commentator suggested, "The truth is more likely to emerge when each side seeks to take the other by reason rather than by surprise."[2]

Opponents of expansive discovery contended that liberal discovery in criminal cases would give an unfair advantage to the defense, because the defendant's privilege against self-incrimination would prohibit the prosecution from discovering defense evidence. The issues raised in the discovery debate have been resolved in each jurisdiction by court rules or statutes that detail what discovery must or may be granted to each side. Although their specific rules vary, most jurisdictions require the government to disclose (1) all prior statements of the defendant that are in the possession of the prosecution or other government agencies such as the police department, (2) a copy of the defendant's prior criminal record, (3) documents and tangible objects the prosecution intends to use at trial, and (4) scientific reports and tests such as autopsy reports and fingerprint analysis. In return, many jurisdictions require the defense to inform the prosecution of the defendant's intent to raise certain defenses such as alibi, insanity, self-defense, or entrapment.

The only United States constitutional limitation on a state's discovery rules is that the state must be evenhanded in its treatment of the prosecution and the defense. In *Wardius v. Oregon*,[3] the state required the defendant to disclose his intent to present an alibi defense, but the defendant had no right of discovery against the prosecution. The Supreme Court stated:

> Although the Due Process Clause has little to say regarding the amount of discovery which the parties must be afforded, it does speak to the balance of forces between the accused and his accuser. . . . In the absence of a strong showing of state interests to the contrary, discovery must be a two-way street. The State may not insist that trials be run as a 'search for truth' so far as defense witnesses are concerned, while maintaining 'poker game' secrecy for its own witnesses. It is fundamentally unfair to require a defendant to divulge the details of his own case while at the same time subjecting him to the hazard of surprise covering refutation of the very pieces of evidence which he disclosed to the State.

Given the limited holding of *Wardius,* it is not surprising to find a great deal of variation among the states' discovery provisions. While some jurisdictions provide for broad discovery, others place severe limitations on the government's obligation to disclose portions of its case. Rule 16 of the Federal Rules of Criminal Procedure serves as a model for discovery rules in many jurisdictions and generally addresses:

1. *Items within the control or possession of the prosecution.* Federal Rule 16(a)(1) refers to material "within . . . the control of the government, the existence of which is known, or by the exercise of due diligence may become known, to the attorney for the government." The due diligence requirement may impose on the prosecution the responsibility to interview all government personnel involved in a case in order to comply with its discovery obligations.
2. *The defendant's written or recorded statements.* Only the defendant's own statements are covered by the rule. Even though statements of coconspirators are imputed to the defendant for purposes of admissibility at trial, such statements are not discoverable under Federal Rule 16(a)(A).[4]
3. *The defendant's oral statements.* Federal Rule 16 requires disclosure only when the defendant's oral statement was made "in response to interrogation" to a person "then known to the defendant to be a government agent." A confession made to a private citizen who then repeats the confession to the police is a statement of the citizen, not a statement of the defendant for discovery purposes.
4. *The defendant's criminal record.* Federal Rule 16 and most states provide for disclosure of the defendant's criminal record. On the surface there seems to be little need to disclose to the defendant information of which he is already aware. Aside from the possibility that the client has forgotten or misled defense counsel about any prior convictions, the prime benefit of such disclosure is the opportunity to resolve *pretrial* any disputes as to the correctness or scope of the prior convictions. (The federal rules and most states do not address disclosure of prior misconduct not resulting in a criminal conviction. Such evidence may be admissible at trial to prove motive, modus operandi, or other recognized exceptions to evidence rules prohibiting the use of the defendant's uncharged misconduct. In the absence of specific discovery provisions, the trial court retains discretion to permit or deny disclosure of uncharged misconduct.)
5. *Documents and tangible objects.* Discovery generally applies to items that the prosecution intends to use at trial or that were obtained from the defendant. Other than forgoing the opportunity to surprise the defendant with these items at trial, the prosecution has little legitimate interest in objecting to disclosure of documents and objects. The prosecution's understandable desire to shield internal memorandum and other documents deemed to be the prosecutor's "work product" is recognized in (a)(2) of Rule 16.

6. *Scientific reports.* Scientific evidence is practically impossible for the defense to contest or rebut at trial without an opportunity to examine it pretrial. In most cases defense experts must be given an adequate opportunity to study the government's scientific reports and to conduct their own tests. The most commonly utilized scientific reports are autopsy findings, testing of drugs, blood, urine, and breath, analysis of semen, fingerprints, ballistics, handwriting or voice, and physical or mental examination of the accused or the alleged victim.

7. *Prosecution witnesses.* Many states require the prosecution to provide the defense with the names and addresses of persons whom the prosecution intends to call as witnesses. Other jurisdictions specifically prohibit pretrial disclosure of the witnesses' identity because of concerns that the defense may harass, intimidate, or suborn perjury on the part of the witness. (The defendant has no constitutional right to receive notice that a witness will identify him in court.)[5]

In the federal system, the rules of discovery are limited and supplemented by the Jencks Act, which strikes an accommodation between protecting witnesses from possible pretrial harassment, and providing the defense with an opportunity to impeach witnesses who have made statements inconsistent with their trial testimony. In *Jencks v. United States*,[6] the Court exercised its supervisory power over federal courts to require disclosure of prior statements by witnesses *after* they testify. Congress then enacted the Jencks Act,[7] which provides:

> In any criminal prosecution brought by the United States, no statement or report in the possession of the United States which was made by a Government witness or prospective Government witness (other than the defendant) shall be the subject of subpoena, discovery, or inspection until said witness has testified on direct examination in the trial of the case. . . . After a witness other than the defendant has testified on direct examination, the court, on motion of a party who did not call the witness, shall order the attorney for the government or the defendant and the defendant's attorney, as the case may be, to produce, for the examination and use of the moving party, any statement of the witness that is in their possession and that relates to the subject matter concerning which the witness has testified.

Constitutional Discovery

Although most discovery occurs under the authority of local statutes and court rules, the U.S. Constitution requires disclosure of certain information possessed by the government. *United States v. Bagley* identified constitutionally discoverable evidence as any evidence that undermines the reliability of the trial court's verdict.

UNITED STATES v. BAGLEY
Supreme Court of the United States, 1985
473 U.S. 667, 105 S.Ct. 3375

JUSTICE BLACKMUN delivered the opinion of the Court:

In *Brady v. Maryland*, 373 U.S. 83 (1963), this Court held that "the suppression by the prosecution of evidence favorable to an accused upon request violates due process where the evidence is material either to guilt or punishment." The issue in the present case concerns the standard of materiality to be applied in determining whether a conviction should be reversed because the prosecutor failed to disclose requested evidence that could have been used to impeach Government witnesses.

The *Brady* rule is based on the requirement of due process. Its purpose is not to displace the adversary system as the primary means by which truth is uncovered, but to ensure that a miscarriage of justice does not occur. Thus, the prosecutor is not required to deliver his entire file to defense counsel, but only to disclose evidence favorable to the accused that, if suppressed, would deprive the defendant of a fair trial.

In *Brady* and *United States v. Agurs*, 427 U.S. 97 (1976), the prosecutor failed to disclose exculpatory evidence. In the present case, the prosecutor failed to disclose evidence that the defense might have used to impeach the Government's witnesses by showing bias or interest. Impeachment evidence, however, as well as exculpatory evidence, falls within the *Brady* rule. Such evidence is "evidence favorable to an accused, so that, if disclosed and used effectively, it may make the difference between conviction and acquittal."

It remains to determine the standard of materiality applicable to the nondisclosed evidence at issue in this case. Our starting point is the framework for evaluating the materiality of *Brady* evidence established in *Agurs*. The Court in *Agurs* distinguished three situations involving the discovery, after trial, of information favorable to the accused that had been known to the prosecution but unknown to the defense. The first situation was the prosecutor's knowing use of perjured testimony or, equivalently, the prosecutor's knowing failure to disclose that testimony used to convict the defendant was false. At the other extreme is the situation in *Agurs* itself, where the defendant does not make a *Brady* request and the prosecutor fails to disclose certain evidence favorable to the accused. The third situation is where the defense makes a specific request and the prosecutor fails to disclose responsive evidence.

[In all three situations] the "no request," "general request," and "specific request" cases of prosecutorial failure to disclose evidence favorable to the accused, reversal of the conviction is required if there is a reasonable probability that, had the evidence been disclosed to the defense, the result of the proceeding would have been different. A "reasonable probability" is a probability sufficient to undermine confidence in the outcome.

As the Court noted in *Bagley,* a discovery motion may be so general as to be meaningless ("We request all exculpatory evidence,"), or the discovery request may be quite protracted. Exhibit 14–1 is a lengthy, but not untypical motion for discovery.

The right to discover potentially exculpatory evidence is not unlimited, nor will discovery be ordered upon pure speculation as to the possibly exculpatory nature of the requested materials. The defendant is entitled to inspect material only upon a "plausible" showing that the material might have exculpatory relevance.[8] Even if discovery is ordered, the defendant has no constitutional right to search through the government's files free of court supervision. In *Pennsylvania v. Ritchie,* the Supreme Court held that the defendant's right to discovery could be fully protected by requiring that discoverable child abuse files be submitted to the trial court for in camera review.[9] (In camera review consists of the trial judge privately inspecting a document before ruling on its possible use at trial.) The trial court could determine whether the file contains information that probably would change the outcome of the trial, which must then be disclosed to the defendant.

Finally, the constitutional right to discovery of exculpatory evidence does not require the state to preserve all potentially exculpatory evidence for possible discovery by defendants: for example, other "leads" the police pursued before arresting the suspect. Evidence must be preserved when its exculpatory value was apparent before the evidence was destroyed and when the evidence was of such a nature that the defendant would be unable to obtain comparable evidence by other reasonably available means.[10] "Unless a criminal defendant can show bad faith on the part of the police, failure to preserve potentially useful evidence does not constitute a denial of due process of law."[11]

Discovery Orders Against the Victims or Third Parties

The criminal defendant's right to pretrial discovery may come in conflict with the privacy rights of victims or other third parties. For example, in *Clark v. Common-*

The Defendant moves the Court, for an Order permitting discovery and inspection and for obtaining exculpatory evidence. The prosecution is requested to provide the following information:

1. Any and all exculpatory information or materials.
2. The names and addresses of any other suspects in the case.
3. Any physical evidence, information, statements, or notes which are evidence or may lead to evidence that the accused may have a defense to the crime alleged or may have committed an offense lesser than that with which the accused is charged, or that someone else may have committed the alleged crime.
4. Any anonymous notes received by the Commonwealth or its agents, or tapes made by the Commonwealth or its agents of any anonymous telephone calls received with regard to this case.
5. A complete inspection and option to copy the Commonwealth's entire file in the above case.
6. Written or recorded statements, admissions, or confessions made by the Defendant.
7. Any relevant statements made by the Defendant to any law enforcement officer of this Commonwealth or agent, or any copies of the same.
8. The substance of any oral declarations of the Defendant of which a written or other tangible recording has been made and which were made by the Defendant, whether before or after arrest, in response to interrogatories by any person then known to the Defendant to be a law enforcement officer or agent, or a prosecuting authority or agent.
9. All relevant statements, admissions, confessions, or declarations made by the Defendant, whether written, signed or unsigned, oral or electronically recorded, or obtained by eavesdropping.
10. When, where, and in whose presence any statements, admissions, confessions, or declarations of the Defendant were made.
11. Who, if the Defendant made any admission, statement, or confession, advised the Defendant of his constitutional rights at any time, and if so, then where, when, and how was the defendant so advised.
12. Copies of any waivers signed by the Defendant, if any.
13. Copies of the Defendant's prior criminal record, if any, which are within the possession, custody, or control of the Commonwealth, the existence of which is known, or by the exercise of due diligence may become known, to the prosecuting authority.
14. A specific listing of the felony and misdemeanor convictions, if any, which the Commonwealth intends to introduce against the Defendant.
15. The nature, date, and place of any criminal offenses or acts of misconduct, other than those charged in the present indictment and those offered for impeachment purposes, which the Commonwealth will attempt to prove at the trial against the Defendant.
16. Copies of records or reports of physical or mental examinations of the Defendant which are within the possession, custody, or control of any Commonwealth agency, the existence of which is known, or by the exercise of due diligence may become known to the Commonwealth's Attorney and which are obtainable with the permission of the Defendant.
17. By what means was the Defendant identified as the alleged perpetrator of the crimes charged.
18. **(a)** If said identification was by real, demonstrative, or tangible evidence such as, but not limited to, blood, hair, fingerprints, clothing, etc., where, when, and by whom was said evidence obtained.
    (b) If said identification was by said real, tangible, or demonstrative evidence, then the Defendant hereby respectfully requests the Court to permit the defendant to inspect and/or copy, or photograph said items or objects.
19. If said identification was by means of a photograph, then:
    (a) What person or persons identified the Defendant?

EXHIBIT 14–1
Motion for Discovery

EXHIBIT 14–1
Motion for Discovery—Continued

(b) Where, when, and under what circumstances was the identification made, and who presented said photographs?

(c) On how many occasions was the person or persons requested to view photographs for purposes of identification, and what were the dates and times?

(d) How many photographs and what photographs were shown on each of such occasions?

20. If said identification was by means of a photograph, then the Defendant respectfully requests the Court to order the Commonwealth and/or its agents to specify and produce, in the sequence shown, all photographs shown so that the Defendant can inspect and/or copy all photographs of the Defendant and/or anyone else.

21. The names and addresses of all other persons arrested for the same alleged incident and a report on the status of their cases.

22. The names, ages, and addresses of all witnesses to be called by the Commonwealth.

23. The name or names of any person other than informants, who were not informants with knowledge that they were acting as such at the time of the alleged offenses, who participated directly or indirectly in the alleged criminal acts which are the subject of the pending proceeding in the knowledge or possession of the Commonwealth, or were present at the time of commission of the acts.

24. The name or names and addresses of any other informants involved.

25. The criminal, youthful offender, and juvenile records of any informant, including matters pending.

26. The dates, times, places, and the kinds and amounts involved of any financial or other compensation paid or made to any informant.

27. The number of, dates of, and statute involved of any convictions which were initiated by information supplied by any informant.

28. The name or names and addresses of those persons who witnessed the alleged crime, if said information is known to any Commonwealth agent.

29. The name or names of any persons who provided the police with information leading to the arrest in the above matters.

30. The names and addresses of any persons interviewed regarding this case by the Commonwealth or its agents or employees whom the Commonwealth does not intend to call as a witness.

31. The list of names and addresses of anyone who might give favorable testimony on behalf of the Defendant if those persons are known to any Commonwealth agent.

32. A list of the names of the arresting police officers.

33. A list of the names of those officers involved in the investigation of the case.

34. All police reports in the case.

35. Any statement, before a grand jury or otherwise, by any witness who is to be called to testify, said statement being within the possession, custody, or control of the Commonwealth or any governmental agency.

36. All relevant oral statements made by the Commonwealth's witnesses and which are known to any agent of the Commonwealth.

37. **(a)** The juvenile record, including any charges pending of all witnesses to be called by the Commonwealth.

(b) Any current juvenile probation or parole and any pending juvenile matter of a criminal nature of any Commonwealth witness.

38. All uncharged criminal misconduct of any Commonwealth witness, which is known to any agents of the Commonwealth.

39. The criminal record, including any charges pending, of all witnesses to be called by the Commonwealth.

40. All information relating to any understanding or agreement between any Commonwealth witness and the Commonwealth, including the Commonwealth's Attorney, any Prosecutor, State Police, or any Police Department, probation officers, or any of their agents regarding prosecutions of said witness for past, present, or future crim-

EXHIBIT 14–1
Motion for Discovery—Continued

inal conduct and regarding sentencing or sentencing recommendations as to any such witness.

41. The nature of any other promise or consideration given by any agent of the Commonwealth to any person in return for information, assistance, or testimony of that person.

42. The nature of any threat of unfavorable treatment given by any agent of the Commonwealth to any person in order to obtain information, assistance, or testim1 which that witness is to testify, and if so, then what was the amount and type of the alcohol and/or drug.

44. Any mental, psychological, or physical problem that any Commonwealth witness has, including but not limited to alcoholism or mental illness or defect, and reports of same.

45. The identity and location of buildings, places, or portions thereof, which are in the possession, custody, or control of any governmental agency and which are material to the defense or which the prosecuting authority intends to introduce as evidence in chief at the trial.

46. Books, photographs, papers, documents, or tangible objects obtained from or belonging to the Defendant and/or obtained from others involved in the case by seizure or process.

47. All books, tangible objects, papers, photographs, or documents which are within the possession, custody, or control of any Commonwealth agency and which are material to the preparation of the Defendant's defense or are intended for use by the prosecuting authority as evidence in chief at the trial.

48. Whether or not a knife or gun or other dangerous or deadly instrument or dangerous or deadly weapon, or any instrument was used during the commission of the alleged offenses, and if so, the kind and description of such weapon, dangerous instrument, knife, gun, or instrument.

49. An inspection or examination of any weapon or any instrument which is alleged to have been used in the alleged crimes.

50. Any objects, if any, taken in the alleged crime.

51. Clothing worn by the Defendant when arrested and a description of it.

52. Copies of results or reports of scientific tests, experiments, or comparisons made in connection with the particular case which are known to the prosecuting authority and within the possession, custody, or control of any governmental agency and which are material to the preparation of the defense or are intended for use by the prosecuting authority as evidence in chief at the trial.

53. Copies of results or reports of scientific tests, experiments, or comparisons made in connection with the particular case which are known to the prosecuting authority and within the possession, custody, or control of any governmental agency made in connection with this case and which will not be used by the prosecuting authority as evidence in chief at the trial.

54. What, if any, fingerprints of the Defendant and/or anyone else were lifted at or near the scene of the alleged offenses, and/or from any other places or objects related to the incident; and the Defendant requests an inspection and examination of said fingerprints and a listing of the names and addresses of those whose fingerprints were lifted.

55. Copies of the search and arrest warrants issued, if any, and if so, copies of the affidavit in support thereof, the application, and the return of the warrant.

56. The date, time, and place of the initial arrest of the Defendant and any co-defendant or co-conspirator.

WHEREFORE, the Defendant respectfully prays that this Motion for Discovery and Inspection and for Exculpatory Evidence be granted.

wealth,[12] the defendant was charged with sodomy and statutory rape. Defense counsel discovered that the alleged victim had made prior false claims of rape, and counsel was particularly skeptical of the physical findings of the sexual assault nurse examiner. Defense counsel then moved for disclosure of the complaining witness's prior medical records and an independent medical examination of the complaining witness. The Court of Appeals held that the trial count had discretion:

> to require a complaining witness to submit to an independent physical examination, provided the defendant makes a threshold showing of a compelling need or reason. . . . In addition, after a defendant demonstrates a compelling need or reason, the trial court is then required to balance the defendant's due process and Sixth Amendment rights to present evidence in his or her favor against the complaining witness' welfare. . . . When considering the effects that a required examination may have upon the complaining witness, the trial court must be mindful of the due process rights of the complaining witness. Accordingly, the complaining witness should receive notice and have an opportunity to be heard before a decision is rendered involving his or her rights.

All jurisdictions empower the court to protect third-party privacy by issuing protective orders or limiting the scope and terms of discovery, subject to constitutional limitations. For example, the Federal Rules of Criminal Procedure provide that upon a sufficient showing the court may at any time order that the discovery or inspection be denied, restricted, or deferred, or make such other order as is appropriate.

Prosecution's Right to Discovery

Many jurisdictions give the prosecution an unconditional right to be notified prior to trial that the defendant intends to raise the defense of insanity and to present expert testimony to support this claim. Such provisions allow the prosecution the time to prepare its own expert witnesses to rebut the claim of insanity. Other than notice of an insanity defense, the prosecution's right to discovery is often made contingent upon whether the defense has been granted discovery. If the defendant files no motion to discover the prosecution's evidence, the prosecution may have no right to discover defense evidence. If, however, the defendant has been granted discovery, the prosecution may be granted a reciprocal right to discovery. For example, a defendant who intends to raise an alibi defense may be ordered to reveal that intention as well as the place at which the defendant claims to have been at the time of the alleged crime.

Does requiring a criminal defendant to disclose information violate the privilege against self-incrimination? *Williams v. Florida* considered this issue and upheld the constitutionality of rules that require the defendant to disclose certain information.

WILLIAMS v. FLORIDA
Supreme Court of the United States, 1970
399 U.S. 78, 90 S.Ct. 1893

JUSTICE WHITE delivered the opinion of the Court:
Prior to his trial for robbery in the State of Florida, petitioner filed a "Motion for a Protective Order," seeking to be excused from the Florida Rules of Criminal Procedure requirement that a defendant give notice in advance of trial if the defendant intends to claim an alibi, and to furnish the prosecuting attorney with information as to the place he claims to have been and with the

names and addresses of the alibi witnesses he intends to use. The defendant contends that the Florida Rule "compels the defendant in a criminal case to be a witness against himself" in violation of his Fifth and Fourteenth Amendment rights.

We need not linger over the suggestion that the discovery permitted the State against petitioner in this case deprived him of "due process" or a "fair trial." Florida law provides for liberal discovery by the defendant against the State, and the notice-of-alibi rule is itself carefully hedged with reciprocal duties requiring state disclosure to the defendant. Given the ease with which an alibi can be fabricated, the State's interest in protecting itself against an eleventh hour defense is both obvious and legitimate. Reflecting this interest, notice-of-alibi provisions, dating at least from 1927, are now in existence in a substantial number of States.

Defendant's major contention is that he was "compelled to be a witness against himself" contrary to the commands of the Fifth and Fourteenth Amendments because the notice-of-alibi rule required him to give the State the name and address of alibi witnesses in advance of trial and thus to furnish the State with information useful in convicting him. Also, requiring him to reveal the elements of his defense is claimed to have interfered with his right to wait until after the State had presented its case to decide how to defend against it. We conclude, however, as has apparently every other court which has considered the issue, that the privilege against self-incrimination is not violated by a requirement that the defendant give notice of an alibi defense and disclose his alibi witnesses.

The defendant in a criminal trial is frequently forced to testify himself and to call other witnesses in an effort to reduce the risk of conviction. When he presents his witnesses, he must reveal their identity and submit them to cross-examination which in itself may prove incriminating or which may furnish the State with leads to incriminating rebuttal evidence. That the defendant faces such a dilemma demanding a choice between complete silence and presenting a defense has never been thought an invasion of the privilege against compelled self-incrimination.

In the case before us, the notice-of-alibi rule by itself in no way affected defendant's crucial decision to call alibi witnesses or added to the legitimate pressures leading to that course of action. At most, the rule only compelled defendant to accelerate the timing of his disclosure, forcing him to divulge at an earlier date information which the defendant from the beginning planned to divulge at trial. Nothing in the Fifth Amendment privilege entitles a defendant as a matter of constitutional right to await the end of the State's case before announcing the nature of his defense, any more that it entitles him to await the jury's verdict on the State's case-in-chief before deciding whether or not to take the stand himself.

Remedies for Violation of Discovery Orders

If either party fails to comply with the court's discovery orders the court generally has a number of options for dealing with the violation. For example, the federal rules provide: If at any time during the course of the proceedings it is brought to the attention of the court that a party has failed to comply with this rule, the court may order such party to permit the discovery or inspection, grant a continuance, or prohibit the party from introducing evidence not disclosed, or it may enter such other order as it deems just under the circumstances. The least drastic and preferred remedy for violations of discovery orders is to order immediate disclosure and offer a continuance for the party to examine the material. Other possible sanctions authorized in various states include instructing the jury to assume the accuracy of certain facts that might have been established through the nondisclosed material; holding the offending party in contempt of court; declaring a mistrial; or in the case of a violation by the government, dismissing the prosecution.

Discovery violations by the defense may occur when defense counsel are conflicted about their dual roles as advocates for the defendant and as members of the bar charged with responsibilities to the legal profession. For example, standards of professional responsibility and statutory prohibitions against concealing evidence require defense counsel to turn over certain items (i.e., the fruits and instrumentalities of the crime) to the police. Surrendering such evidence to the police, however, may assist in the conviction of counsel's client. Defense counsel usually avoid such dilemmas by refusing to accept tainted evidence from their clients. The rule of thumb for defense counsel is look don't touch.

In addition to statutes or court rules governing discovery, Codes of Professional Responsibility establish ethical duties with respect to disclosure of evidence. For example, counsel is prohibited from advising or causing a person to secrete himself or to leave the jurisdiction of a tribunal for the purpose of making him unavailable as a witness therein. The *American Bar Association Standards for Criminal Justice* provide that a prosecutor "should not" and "it is unprofessional conduct" for defense counsel to advise any person, other than defense counsel's client, to decline to give to counsel for the other side information which such person has the right to give. Either counsel, however, may *inform* witnesses of their right to decide whether to grant or refuse an interview with opposing counsel. The distinction between *informing* and *advising* witnesses regarding interviews with the opposing counsel may test counsel's commitment to the letter or spirit of the ABA Standards.

STATUTES OF LIMITATIONS

Statutes of limitations
specify the length of time
permitted between the
commission of a crime and
the initiation of prosecution.

Statutes of limitations specify the length of time permitted between the commission of a crime and the initiation of prosecution. At common law there were no time limitations, thus statutes of limitations are legislative creations that vary according to the will of the jurisdiction's legislative body. Generally, the more serious the crime the longer the statute of limitations. Major felonies like murder usually have no limitations on the time within which the prosecution may bring charges. With less serious offenses, the legislature may favor short statutes of limitations in order to help ensure that prosecutions will be based upon reasonably fresh evidence. With the passage of time, memories fade, witnesses die or leave the area, and physical evidence becomes more difficult to obtain, identify, or preserve. In short, the possibility of erroneous conviction is minimized when prosecution is prompt. In *United States v. Marion,*[13] the Court stated that

> the purpose of a statute of limitations is to limit exposure to prosecution to a fixed period of time [and] to protect individuals from having to defend themselves against charges when the basic facts may have become obscured by the passage of time. Such a time limit may also have the salutary effect of encouraging law enforcement officials promptly to investigate suspected criminal activity.

Tolling the statute of limitations
the statute ceases to run under certain conditions, most commonly while the accused is fleeing from justice.

Statutes of limitations begin running when the crime occurs, however, the time period may be *tolled* (cease to run) under certain conditions. **Tolling the statute of limitations** most commonly occurs while the accused is fleeing from justice or in hiding within or without the state in order to avoid arrest. The statute of limitations ceases to run upon the commencement of the prosecution, which is generally defined as the issuance of an indictment or arrest warrant. A claim that the statute of limitations bars prosecution is one of the issues that must be raised before verdict or it is deemed to be waived. If the defendant successfully establishes that the statute of limitations has run, the appropriate remedy is dismissal of the charge.

SPEEDY TRIAL

Like the statute of limitations, a claim that the defendant was denied a speedy trial must be raised before verdict, and if the claim is established, the charges must be dismissed. All jurisdictions have a number of constitutional and statutory provisions that govern the time period within which a criminal prosecution must begin and conclude. The initiation of prosecutions is governed by statutes of limitations, while the termination of the criminal justice process is often governed by statutes or court rules that fix the time periods within which any final appeals must be filed. The sequential stages of prosecution between filing of charges and filing of appeals is also regulated by local rules or statutes. For example, some states recognize a right to a "speedy indictment" by providing that an accused in pretrial confinement must be discharged from confinement unless a presentment, indictment, or information is filed against the defendant within a certain time period. Constitutional Due Process considerations also may apply to delays prior to arrest or indictment if such delays cause prejudice to the defendant.[14]

The above provisions relating to the overall timing of criminal prosecutions must be distinguished from the right to a speedy trial guaranteed by the Sixth Amendment to the U.S. Constitution. In *United States v. MacDonald*, the Supreme Court held that the right to a speedy trial does not apply to the period before a defendant is indicted, arrested, or otherwise officially accused.[15] In the *MacDonald* case (the basis of a book and film entitled *Fatal Vision*), an army doctor was charged in 1970 with three counts of murder. The charges were subsequently dismissed before the court martial began, but the defendant was indicted for the same offenses by a civilian grand jury in 1975. The defendant argued that the speedy trial "clock" began to run on the date of the original charge, thus his trial had been delayed for almost five years. The Court held that when the original charges were dismissed the speedy trial guarantee was no longer applicable. The Court explained:

> The speedy trial guarantee is designed to minimize the possibility of lengthy incarceration prior to trial, to reduce the lesser, but nevertheless substantial, impairment of liberty imposed on an accused while released on bail, and to shorten the disruption of life caused by arrest and the presence of unresolved criminal charges.

The *MacDonald* court held that when formal charges are dismissed, the defendant is no longer subject to pretrial confinement and no longer faces unresolved criminal charges. Thus the constitutional right to a speedy trial attaches only at the time a person is accused of a crime by way of arrest or indictment.

Once an arrest or indictment begins the running of the speedy trial clock, no precise formula determines when the constitutional right to a speedy trial has been abridged. In place of a rigid time limitation, *Barker v. Wingo* adopted a case-by-case balancing of four factors: (1) the length of the delay, (2) the reasons for the delay, (3) whether the defendant asserted the right to a speedy trial, and (4) prejudice to the defendant.

BARKER v. WINGO
Supreme Court of the United States, 1972
407 U.S. 514, 92 S.Ct. 2182

[Barker was tried for murder more than five years after his arrest, during which time the prosecution secured numerous continuances. Barker did not object to the continuances until some three years after his arrest. The lower court held that Barker had waived his right to speedy trial. The Supreme Court rejected the waiver rationale, but upheld the lower court's ruling after balancing the relative factors in what the Court referred to as a close case.]

JUSTICE POWELL delivered the opinion of the Court: The right to a speedy trial is generically different from any of the other rights enshrined in the Constitution for the protection of the accused. In addition to the general concern that all accused persons be treated according to decent and fair procedures, there is a societal interest in providing a speedy trial which exists separate from, and at times in opposition to, the interests of the accused. The inability of courts to provide a prompt trial has contributed to a large backlog of cases in urban courts which, among other things, enables defendants to negotiate more effectively for pleas of guilty to lesser offenses, and otherwise manipulate the system. In addition, persons released on bond for lengthy periods awaiting trial have an opportunity to commit other crimes. Moreover, the longer an accused is free awaiting trial, the more tempting becomes his opportunity to jump bail and escape. Finally, delay between arrest and punishment may have a detrimental effect on rehabilitation.

[T]he right to speedy trial is a more vague concept than other procedural rights. It is, for example, impossible to determine with precision when the right has been denied. We cannot definitely say how long is too long in a system where justice is supposed to be swift but deliberate.

The approach we accept is a balancing test, in which the conduct of both the prosecution and the defendant are weighed. A balancing test necessarily compels courts to approach speedy trial cases on an ad hoc basis. We can do little more than identify some of the factors which courts should assess in determining whether a particular defendant has been deprived of his right. Though some might express them in different ways, we identify four such factors: length of delay, the reason for the delay, the defendant's assertion of his right, and prejudice to the defendant.

The length of delay is to some extent a triggering mechanism. Closely related to length of delay is the reason the government assigns to justify the delay. A deliberate attempt to delay the trial in order to hamper the defense should be weighted heavily against the government. A more neutral reason such as negligence or overcrowded courts should be weighted less heavily but nevertheless should be considered since the ultimate responsibility for such circumstances must rest with the government rather than with the defendant. Finally, a valid reason, such as a missing witness, should serve to justify appropriate delay.

Whether and how a defendant asserts his right is closely related to the other factors we have mentioned. The strength of his efforts will be affected by the length of the delay, to some extent by the reason for the delay, and most particularly by the personal prejudice, which is not always readily identifiable, that he experiences.

A fourth factor is prejudice to the defendant. Prejudice, of course, should be assessed in the light of the interests of defendant which the speedy trial right was designed to protect. The Court has identified three such interests: (i) to prevent oppressive pretrial incarceration; (ii) to minimize anxiety and concern of the accused; and (iii) to limit the possibility that the defense will be impaired.

We regard none of the four factors identified above as either a necessary or sufficient condition to the finding of a deprivation of the right of speedy trial. Rather, they are related factors and must be considered together with such other circumstances as may be relevant. In sum, these factors have no talismanic qualities; courts must still engage in a difficult and sensitive balancing process.

Barker v. Wingo referred to the length of delay as a "triggering mechanism" that established the need for further inquiry, but on balance the Court upheld the reasonableness of the five-year delay. *Doggett v. United States,* however, condemned an eight-and-a-half-year delay caused by "inexcusable oversights" on the government's part as "far in excess of the threshold needed to state a speedy trial claim."[16] The burden is on the prosecution to justify any delay in bringing the accused to trial, and simple negligence is not an adequate excuse. The defendant's failure to demand a speedy trial does not constitute a waiver, but the defendant's assertion or failure to assert the right to a speedy trial is one of the factors to be considered. Although any actual prejudice to the defendant weighs heavily in the balancing approach, the failure to establish specific prejudice is not fatal to the defendant's claim.[17]

The balancing approach to the constitutional right to a speedy trial lacks the precise time periods established by speedy trial provisions of individual jurisdictions. Unlike the constitutional standard, which makes the passage of time a "triggering mechanism," speedy trial statutes make the passage of time dispositive of whether there is a violation. Most speedy trial statutes do not require a defendant to show either that he or she demanded a speedy trial or that the effect of the delay was prejudicial. For example, at the federal level, the Speedy Trial Act of 1974 requires that individuals be formally charged within thirty days from the date of arrest and tried within seventy days of the date of the filling of charges, or from the date of the defendant's initial appearance before a judicial officer, whichever is later.[18] The statute excludes delay caused by factors such as the accused's flight from justice or necessary mental examinations of the defendant. Most states have similar statutory provisions governing speedy trial, although the specific time periods vary greatly.

DOUBLE JEOPARDY

The double jeopardy clause of the Fifth Amendment provides: "nor shall any person be subject for the same offense to be twice put in jeopardy of life or limb." The concept of **double jeopardy** prohibits the retrial of a defendant who has been convicted or acquitted of the same offense at a previous trial. It also protects against multiple punishments for the same offense.

The rationale behind the double jeopardy clause was identified by Justice Black:

> The underlying idea, one that is deeply ingrained in at least the Anglo-American system of jurisprudence, is that the State with all its resources and power should not be allowed to make repeated attempts to convict an individual for an alleged offense, thereby subjecting him to embarrassment, expense and ordeal and compelling him to live in a continuing state of anxiety and insecurity, as well as enhancing the possibility that even though innocent he may be found guilty.[19]

Historically, double jeopardy was an affirmative defense that was waived if not raised by the defendant prior to verdict. However, the requirement that the defendant formally plead the defense of double jeopardy may no longer be valid in all circumstances in light of *Menna v. New York.*[20] In *Menna,* the U.S. Supreme Court held that "a plea of guilty to a charge does not waive a claim that—judged on its face— the charge is one which the State may not constitutionally prosecute." On the other hand, *United States v. Broce* held that a collateral attack based on double jeopardy grounds was barred because the defendant entered a voluntary plea of guilty and failed to raise the double jeopardy issue at trial.[21] In the absence of further clarification from the courts, the only "safe" course for the defendant is to raise a double jeopardy claim prior to the judge or jury returning a verdict.

Jeopardy does not attach, and the constitutional prohibition against double jeopardy does not apply, until a defendant is put to trial before a jury or judge.[22] Pretrial proceedings, such as preliminary hearings or indictments by the grand jury are irrelevant for purposes of double jeopardy. In a jury trial, jeopardy attaches when the jury is impanelled and sworn, while in a bench trial, jeopardy attaches when the prosecution begins to introduce evidence.

If the trial court dismisses an indictment before the jury is sworn or before the court hears evidence, jeopardy has not attached, and the defendant may again be indicted and tried for the same offense. Depending on the local rules, the prosecutor may be entitled to dismiss the case (enter a *nolle prosequi*) before trial commences. Once the defendant is placed in jeopardy, however, the defendant is entitled to have the trial proceed to a final verdict unless "manifest necessity" warrants a mistrial.[23]

The trial judge exercises broad discretion in identifying situations in which a mistrial is appropriate.[24] However, the appellate courts have recognized several forms of manifest necessity:

1. If a mistrial is declared because of a deadlocked jury, double jeopardy does not bar a second trial.[25]
2. Misconduct by the defendant or defense counsel, which necessitates a mistrial, will not bar a second trial.[26]
3. A defense motion for a mistrial constitutes a deliberate election to forego a claim of double jeopardy at a subsequent prosecution.[27] (Retrial is barred, however, if the defendant's motion for a mistrial was motivated by prosecutorial or judicial conduct intended to provoke the mistrial motion.)[28]

Double jeopardy prohibits the retrial of a defendant who has been convicted or acquitted of the same offense at a previous trial; also protects against multiple punishments for the same offense.

If the trial concludes in a conviction that is reversed on appeal, the defendant normally can be retried for the same offense.[29] However, double jeopardy imposes two limitations upon a second prosecution.

1. A reversal of the initial conviction because of the insufficiency of the evidence amounts to a directed verdict of acquittal, which bars further prosecution. In *Tibbs v. Florida,* U.S. Supreme Court treated reversal because of insufficiency of the evidence as distinct from reversal on the weight of the evidence.[30] A decision that the verdict was against the weight of the evidence is similar to a mistrial because of a deadlocked jury, and a retrial is permissible. Only a decision that the evidence was legally insufficient to support the verdict will shield the defendant from retrial.

2. The second limitation upon retrial is that the defendant cannot be charged with a greater offense than that for which the defendant was convicted at the first trial. A conviction of a lesser included offense (e.g., second degree murder) at the first trial constitutes an implied acquittal of the greater offense (first degree murder). Thus, the defendant cannot be charged with the greater offense on retrial.[31] The prohibition of double jeopardy does not bar imposition of a harsher sentence at a second trial, but the due process clause places some limitations upon increased sentences (see Chapter Sixteen).

Double jeopardy may bar successive prosecutions for the same offense, but it also may preclude multiple punishment for convictions obtained in a single trial. The standard for determining whether the defendant can receive multiple punishments is commonly referred to as the **Blockburger test for double jeopardy.** *Blockburger v. United States* established that if the defendant's conduct violates two or more criminal statutes, the double jeopardy clause prohibits multiple punishments unless each offense requires proof of an element which the other does not.[32] For example, common law burglary requires proof of the breaking and entry of a dwelling, while a larceny committed in the dwelling requires proof of the separate element of taking and carrying away personal property. The two offenses are thus distinct for purposes of double jeopardy, and the defendant may be convicted and punished for two separate offenses even though they arose during a single continuous course of conduct. If, however, proof of one offense requires proof of all of the elements of the other offense, then the crimes merge into one (the lesser offense is included within the greater offense). For example, because robbery is larceny from a person by force or intimidation, the elements of larceny are a lesser part of the greater offense of robbery. The offenses are thus the same under the Blockburger test, and the court may not punish the defendant both for robbery and the necessarily included lessor offense of larceny.

For three exceptions, the Blockburger test does not apply: (1) when the legislature clearly intends to impose multiple punishments for a single offense; (2) when multiple offenses arise from separate transactions; and (3) when a single transaction violates the laws of two or more jurisdictions.

Legislative Intent

The U.S. Supreme Court has recognized that for double jeopardy purposes "the question of what punishments are constitutionally permissible is not different from the question of what punishments the legislative branch intended to be imposed."[33] If the legislature clearly indicates its desire to impose multiple punishments, it is immaterial whether the punishments are based on a single offense or separate offenses. Thus, the Blockburger test for defining separate offenses is inapplicable. For example, many jurisdictions create an offense and then recognize an additional crime if the offense is committed while armed with a dangerous weapon. Although the use of a weapon and the commission of a crime may be parts of a single course of con-

Blockburger test for double jeopardy
determines whether a defendant's conduct constitutes one crime or separate crimes for purposes of punishment; multiple punishment is permitted if each offense requires proof of an element which the other does not.

duct, the legislature often imposes multiple punishments for the underlying crime and the use of a weapon.

Separate Transactions

The second exception to the Blockburger test applies when multiple offenses arise from separate acts. In *Jones v. Commonwealth,* the defendant robbed a clerk of the money in the hotel safe, and then fled in the hotel courtesy car, which was located some 200 yards from the hotel.[34] The defendant contended only one offense of robbery resulted in the taking of cash *and* an automobile, thus Blockburger should preclude punishment for both robbery of the money and larceny of the automobile. The court, however, held that Blockburger was applicable only when multiple articles are stolen "at one and the same time." According to the court, the facts in *Jones* revealed that "in terms of time and situs, the two thefts involved separate and distinct acts of caption, and two different sets of asportation." The dissent in *Jones* maintained that the court was splitting hairs by artificially subdividing a defendant's conduct into separate acts, and *Brown v. Ohio* suggested that "the double jeopardy clause is not such a fragile guarantee that prosecutors can avoid its limitations by the simple expedient of dividing a single crime into a series of temporal or spatial units."[35]

Separate Sovereigns

The final exception to the Blockburger test is known as the **separate sovereigns** doctrine. Double jeopardy does not prevent second punishments for the same offense if the punishments are imposed by different jurisdictions. For example, a person who robs a federally insured bank may be prosecuted by both the state where the bank is located and by the United States. The separate sovereigns doctrine also applies to two states, thus "successive prosecutions by two states for the same conduct are not barred by the Double Jeopardy Clause."[36] Cities and counties, however, are not separate sovereigns but are subordinate political subdivisions of the state, thus double jeopardy prevents a state and city from punishing for the same offense.[37] The separate sovereigns doctrine was invoked during the controversy surrounding the Rodney King incident. Although the arresting police officers were acquitted of all charges in the state prosecution, several officers were convicted of the federal offense of violating Mr. King's civil rights.

Separate sovereigns exception to the prohibition against double jeopardy; different jurisdictions may impose punishment for the same offense.

Collateral Estoppel

Unlike double jeopardy, the doctrine of **collateral estoppel** does not prohibit successive prosecutions, but the doctrine does bar relitigation of facts that were decided in the defendant's favor at a previous trial. The leading case on collateral estoppel is *Ash v. Swenson* in which the defendant was initially acquitted of robbing one of six participants in a poker game.[38] The defendant, however, was subsequently convicted at a second trial for robbing another participant in the poker game. The U.S. Supreme Court recognized that double jeopardy did not bar the second trial because robbery is a crime of violence against a person, and there are as many separate crimes as there are victims of the crime. The Court, however, distinguished double jeopardy from collateral estoppel by noting that

Collateral estoppel bars the prosecution from relitigating an issue of fact previously resolved in the defendant's favor at a prior trial.

> Collateral estoppel is an awkward phrase, but it stands for an extremely important principle in our adversary system of justice. It means simply that when an issue of ultimate fact has once been determined by a valid and final judgment, that issue cannot again be litigated between the same parties in any future lawsuit.
>
> The question is not whether Missouri could validly charge the defendant with six separate offenses for the robbery of the six poker players. It is not whether he

could have received a total of six punishments if he had been convicted in a single trial of robbing the six victims. It is simply whether, after a jury determined by its verdict that the defendant was not one of the robbers, the State could constitutionally hale him before a new jury to litigate that issue again.

Collateral estoppel is applicable only when a prior acquittal necessarily and clearly resolved the issue that is in litigation at the second trial. Since criminal verdicts are general verdicts and normally do not specify the reasons for the verdict, whether the precise factual issue was decided in the defendant's favor is often difficult to determine. A reviewing court must examine the record of the prior proceeding, taking into account the pleadings, evidence, charge, and other relevant matters, and conclude "whether a rational jury could have granted its verdict upon an issue other than that which the defendant seeks to foreclose from consideration."[39] For example, if the first jury in *Ash v. Swenson* had acquitted the defendant because the alleged victim was not in fact a victim of robbery, the state would be permitted a second prosecution charging that there was another person who was actually a victim of the defendant's robbery. The defendant in *Ash v. Swenson* prevailed upon the claim of collateral estoppel because he established that the precise issue of his identity as the robber was clearly decided in his favor at the first trial.

SEVERANCE OF OFFENSES AND/OR PARTIES

Trying multiple offenses and multiple defendants at a single trial generates obvious economies. According to Justice Scalia:

> Joint trials play a vital role in the criminal justice system, accounting for almost one-third of federal criminal trials in the past five years. . . . It would impair both the efficiency and the fairness of the criminal justice system to require that prosecutors bring separate proceedings, presenting the same evidence again and again, requiring victims and witnesses to repeat the inconvenience (and sometimes trauma) of testifying, and randomly favoring the last tried defendants who have the advantage of knowing the prosecution's case beforehand. Joint trials generally serve the interests of justice by avoiding inconsistent verdicts and enabling more accurate assessment of relative culpability—advantages which sometimes operate to the defendant's benefit. Even apart from these tactical considerations, joint trials generally serve the interests of justice by avoiding the scandal and inequity of inconsistent verdicts.[40]

Joinder and Severance of Offenses

Joinder of offenses
the defendant faces multiple charges at a single trial.

Motion to sever offenses
asks the court to schedule separate trials for separate offenses.

Most jurisdictions recognize that the trial court may direct that a defendant be tried at one time for all offenses then pending against the defendant if (1) the offenses are based on the same act or transaction; (2) the offenses are based on two or more acts or transactions that are connected or constitute parts of a common scheme or plan; or (3) the defendant and the prosecution consent to a trial for all offenses. The defendant may favor a single trial of all charges in order to save time, money, and the trauma of undergoing successive prosecutions. On the other hand, a defendant who wishes to testify regarding one offense while exercising the right to remain silent on the other charge may oppose **joinder of offenses.** If the defendant opposes the prosecution's scheduling of a single trial on all pending charges, the defendant must file a pretrial **motion to sever the offenses** and ask the court to schedule separate trials. The courts have recognized that the defendant should not face multiple charges at a single trial when the offenses "are so separated by time and circumstance that it would confuse and disconcert him in preparation for the trial, or the jury in the consideration of the case."[41]

Courts are most likely to sever charges when shown how joinder works to the defendant's prejudice. Following are some examples:

1. The jury may consider the defendant a "bad person" or infer a criminal propensity by the defendant simply because he is charged with so many offenses.
2. The proof on one charge may "spill over" and assist in conviction on another charge.
3. The defendant may wish to testify about one offense, but not about another.
4. The defendant may wish to assert inconsistent or antagonistic defenses to the joinable charges. In such situations, one defense may diminish the credibility of the other.

Although the prosecution usually favors joinder of offenses, in some instances the prosecution schedules separate trials, even when the defendant seeks joinder, in hopes of wearing down the defense or to increase the odds of winning at least one case. In such situations, the defendant may file a motion to join or consolidate all pending charges. *Ciucci v. Illinois* raised the issue of whether the prosecutor acted conscientiously or unethically by scheduling multiple trials.

CIUCCI v. ILLINOIS
Supreme Court of the United States, 1958
356 U.S. 571, 78 S.Ct. 839

Per Curiam Opinion:
The defendant was charged in four separate indictments with murdering his wife and three children, all of whom were found dead in a burning building. In three successive trials, defendant was found guilty of the first degree murder of his wife, and two of his children. At each trial the prosecution introduced into evidence details of all four deaths. At the first two trials, the jury fixed the penalty at 20 and 45 years imprisonment respectively. At the third trial, involving the death of a second child, the penalty was fixed at death.

It is conceded that under Illinois law each of the murders, although apparently taking place at the same time, constitute a separate crime and it is undisputed that evidence of the entire occurrence was relevant in each of the three prosecutions.

The five members of the Court who join in this opinion are in agreement that upon the record as it stands no violation of due process has been shown. The State was constitutionally entitled to prosecute these individual offenses singly at separate trials, and to utilize therein all relevant evidence, in the absence of proof establishing that such a course of action entailed fundamental unfairness.

JUSTICE DOUGLAS dissenting:
This case presents an instance of the prosecution being allowed to harass the accused with repeated trials and convictions on the same evidence, until it achieves its desired result of a capital verdict.

Each trial was in effect a trial for the murder of all four victims for the gruesome details of each of the four deaths were introduced into evidence. After obtaining two convictions, but no death penalty, the prosecutor was still not satisfied with the result. And so a third trial was held, the one involved here. Once more the accused was tried in form for one murder, in substance for four.

In my view the Due Process Clause of the Fourteenth Amendment prevents this effort by a State to obtain the death penalty. This is an unseemly and oppressive use of a criminal trial that violates the concept of due process.

Joinder and Severance of Defendants

Prosecutors exercise broad discretion in deciding whether to prosecute multiple defendants separately or jointly. For example, Federal Rule of Criminal Procedure 8(b) provides that "two or more defendants may be charged in the same indictment or information if they are alleged to have participated in the same act or transaction or if the same series of acts or transactions constitutes an offense or offenses." The most common **joinder of defendants** situation is one in which several defendants are part of a conspiracy.

Joinder of defendants
one trial of two or more defendants who participated in the same act.

If a defendant objects to a joint trial with other defendants, the defendant must file a pretrial motion asking the court to sever the defendants and schedule separate trials. The trial court has great discretion in ruling upon the motion and must consider whether the offenses charged against the defendants are based on the same act or transaction, or on two or more acts or transactions that are connected or constitute parts of a common scheme or plan. The court also must consider the special problems that arise in joint trials where one defendant's confession refers to a co-defendant's participation in the crime. In such situations the use of one defendant's confession may violate other defendants' rights to confront the witnesses against them.[42] Another factor for the court's consideration is whether the defendants have defenses that are antagonistic or irreconcilable, such that the acceptance of one party's defense will preclude the acquittal of the other party.[43] For example, defendant X admits to committing the crime, but claims to have done so under duress created by defendant Y. If the jury accepts the duress defense, they must logically conclude that defendant Y committed the crime. In an interesting recent case a court held that in the absence of evidence that the witnesses or the jury confused the two defendants, there is no per se rule entitling identical twins to separate trials.[44]

Joint trials have constitutional implications when the prosecution seeks to introduce in evidence an extrajudicial confession made by only one of the co-defendants, but the confession incriminates both defendants. If the confessing defendant does not testify, the admission of this confession incriminating the co-defendant violates the co-defendant's Sixth Amendment right to confront the witnesses against him. (Where the co-defendant does testify, there is no confrontation issue because the co-defendant is subject to cross-examination.) The prosecutor's range of alternatives is discussed in Chapter Twelve but the easiest solution is to grant a severance to the nonconfessing defendant. In this way, the co-defendant's confession will not be used against the defendant. For example, in *United States v. McVeigh*,[45] the Court severed the Oklahoma City bombing defendants' trial because the prosecution intended to use several statements of one of the defendants against another defendant.

A motion to sever the trials of the defendants must be made pretrial. Once jeopardy attaches at a joint trial, a defendant can be severed from the proceedings only upon a finding of manifest necessity. However, once such necessity exists, the trial court, within its discretion, may choose which defendant shall continue the trial and which defendant shall be severed for a subsequent retrial.[46]

MOTION TO CHANGE VENUE

The Sixth Amendment to the United States Constitution guarantees that "in all criminal prosecutions, the accused shall enjoy the right to a public trial, by an impartial jury of the State and district wherein the crime shall have been committed." In the federal system only the defendant may request a change of **venue**—the place where the trial is held—but some states allow either the defense or the prosecution to re-

Venue
the place where the trial is held.

quest a change of venue. Although venue may be changed in civil proceedings for the convenience of the parties or witnesses, in many jurisdictions the sole ground for a change of venue in criminal proceedings is that the accused cannot obtain a fair and impartial trial in the location at which the crime was committed.

Courts generally presume that a fair trial can be conducted in the locality where the offense occurred, thus the burden to overcome this presumption rests upon the party moving for a change of venue. The defense often attempts to meet this burden by establishing that prejudicial news coverage prior to trial prevents the empaneling of an impartial jury. In *Sheppard v. Maxwell,* the U.S. Supreme Court condemned the "carnival atmosphere" created by inflammatory publicity and held that "where there is a reasonable likelihood that the prejudicial news prior to trial will prevent a fair trial, the judge should continue the case until the threat abates, or transfer it to another county not so permeated with publicity."[47]

As the *Sheppard* case suggests, a change of venue is merely one of the options a court must consider when dealing with extensive pretrial publicity. Chapter Fifteen addresses alternative methods of counteracting extensive publicity: for example, (1) granting a continuance until such publicity abates; (2) issuing "gag" orders limiting any further publicity; (3) exercising great care in selecting jurors who have not been exposed to the publicity; (4) sequestrating the jurors to shield them from continuing publicity; or (5) summoning jurors from another county or city exposed to less publicity surrounding the case.

Pretrial motions to change venue are normally disfavored by the courts because moving the trial to another locality impedes administrative efficiency and adds to the financial costs of prosecution. Perhaps more importantly, a change of venue frustrates the local community's interest in seeing the law enforced against wrongdoers. The accused's right to a fair trial, however, may override these interests and necessitate a change of venue.

UNITED STATES v. MCVEIGH
918 F.Supp. 1467 (W.D. Okla. 1996)

This criminal proceeding arises from an explosion in Oklahoma City on April 19, 1995. The measurable effects of that event include the deaths of 168 identified men, women and children, injuries to hundreds of other people, the complete destruction of the Federal Office Building. A damage assessment estimated the total incident cost at $651,594,000.

The character of the crimes charged is so contrary to the public expectation of human behavior that there is a prevailing belief that some action must be taken to make things right again. There is a fair inference that only a guilty verdict with a death sentence could be considered a just result in the minds of many.

Upon all of the evidence presented, this court finds and concludes that there is so great a prejudice against these two defendants in the State of Oklahoma that they cannot obtain a fair and impartial trial at any place fixed by law for holding court in that state. The court also finds that an appropriate alternative venue is in the U.S. District Court for the District of Colorado. In reaching this ruling, the court is acutely aware of the wishes of the victims of the Oklahoma city explosion to attend this trial and that it will be a hardship for those victims to travel to Denver. The interests of the victims in being able to attend this trial in Oklahoma are outweighed by the court's obligation to assure that the trial be conducted with fundamental fairness and with due regard for all constitutional requirements. Upon the foregoing, it is ORDERED that this criminal proceeding is transferred to the District of Colorado.

SUMMARY

Certain motions must be raised pretrial, or they are waived forever. For example, motions for discovery, motions to change venue, and motions dealing with joinder or severance of charges and/or defendants must be raised pretrial. Jurisdictions often specify a precise number of days before trial when these motions must be filed with the trial court. Other motions addressing statutes of limitations, speedy trial, or double jeopardy can be raised anytime before the trial court returns a verdict.

The scope of mandatory or permissive discovery is generally covered by statute or rule of court. However, a criminal defendant has a constitutional right to the discovery of exculpatory evidence. Constitutional issues also arise when the prosecution is given a right to pretrial discovery, but the U.S. Supreme Court has upheld provisions mandating that the defendant notify the prosecution of alibi and insanity defenses.

Statutes of limitations are creations of legislatures and generally lack any constitutional dimensions. The right to a speedy trial, however, involves both constitutional considerations and statutory enactments. The Sixth Amendment right to a speedy trial requires a balancing of four factors: the length of any delay, the reasons for the delay, whether the defendant requested a speedy trial, and any prejudice to the defendant caused by the delay. At the federal and state levels, statutory speedy trial provisions often specify exact time periods within which a criminal prosecution must begin.

Double jeopardy is a constitutional concept that prohibits successive prosecutions for the same charge and multiple punishment for a single offense. Collateral estoppel is a related concept that bars a prosecutor from relitigating a fact decided in the defendant's favor at a previous trial.

Motions to change venue raise constitutional issues because the accused has a right to be tried in the place where the crime was committed. The defendant's right to a fair trial, however, may override considerations of venue. Motions to join or sever parties or offenses may raise issues of due process, but for the most part these matters are governed by statutes or rules of court.

DISCUSSION QUESTIONS

1. Why do courts require that certain motions be filed pretrial or prior to verdict? For example, if an appellate court determines that the statute of limitations ran prior to trial, why shouldn't the appellate court reverse the conviction on its own motion?

2. Do statutes of limitations or the right to a speedy trial serve any societal purpose, or are they "mere technicalities" that stand in the way of convicting those who are guilty of crime?

3. Does pretrial discovery enhance the truth-seeking function of a trial? Does discovery inherently favor the defense? Why would any prosecutor oppose an "open office" policy in which all documentary and real evidence is available for inspection by the defense?

4. Could the prosecution invoke collateral estoppel to bar a defendant from litigating an issue previously resolved against the defendant? For example, during prosecution for robbery the defendant raised an alibi defense, but the jury convicted the defendant. If the defendant is subsequently tried for murdering the victim of the robbery, may (must) the second jury again consider the alibi defense rejected by the first jury?

5. Do you agree with the Court's opinion or the dissenting opinion in *Ciucci v. Illinois?* Would your opinion change if the prosecutor had told the media that he would continue to bring as many charges as it took to get the death penalty for this defendant?

6. Suppose you are defense counsel for a defendant charged with purchasing cocaine. What do you do if the defendant brings you a white powder and says, "If you get this stuff tested, I'll bet it isn't cocaine." If you refuse to accept the powder, how do you respond when the client asks, "Well, what am I supposed to do with this stuff?" Suppose you send the powder to a testing laboratory that reports the substance is cocaine. What action do you take now? Suppose the prosecutor files a discovery motion requesting that you produce "any and all monies, weapons, or narcotics paid or delivered into your care, custody, or control by the defendant." What is the result?

7. As a prosecutor, how would you respond to a call from the victim asking you whether she should/must talk to defense counsel? What if the victim indicates that she will not talk to defense counsel unless you are present?

PRACTICE EXERCISES

1. In your jurisdiction, what is subject to pretrial discovery? Is anything excluded from pretrial discovery (e.g., the identity of witnesses)?

2. What, if any, statutes of limitations exist in your jurisdiction?

3. Does your state have a statute specifying a particular time within which a speedy trial must occur?

4. Does your jurisdiction provide guidance for, or restrictions upon, a trial court's discretionary decision to join or sever offenses and parties?

5. How does your state determine proper venue when the commission of a crime cuts across county or city lines?

6. Your client was in the home of Clay Snow drinking moonshine whiskey with Snow and James Crawford. They sat in a small living room with no more than five feet separating the three men. Around 5 P.M. some petty arguments and disagreements occurred between your client and Crawford. One person called the other a "damn liar," then your client and Crawford stood up and moved toward each other. Snow got between the two men and wrapped his arms around your client's waist to prevent violence. Snow felt Crawford behind him, and all three men started moving sideways toward the bed. Snow then heard gunfire and turned to see Crawford take three to four steps toward the dining room door before going down to his knees and collapsing on the floor. Your client admits shooting Crawford but claims he did so in self-defense. He maintains that Crawford jumped on top of him and choked him. When he saw Crawford reach into his pocket, he thought Crawford was reaching for a gun.

Before trial, the prosecutor furnished you with all the photographs of the crime scene in the prosecutor's possession. You conclude, however, that the photos do not afford you an adequate means of understanding the crime scene and determining the location and relationship between the objects of furniture in Snow's house. You feel that you need to know the actual size of the room in order to understand the explanation of events given to you by your client, since it would be difficult to examine and cross-examine witnesses about the details of events that occurred at a location with which you are unfamiliar. Snow denied your request to view the crime scene and you would like the court to order Snow to permit your inspection of the crime scene. Draft a motion that will give you access to the crime scene.

Precisely what are you requesting from the court, and what is the court's authority to order such an inspection? Will you request:
    a. Discovery from the state?
    b. Some variation on a subpoena duces tecum to Mr. Snow?
    c. A search warrant to inspect the crime scene?
    d. Enforcement of a constitutional guarantee of compulsory process that establishes the defendant's right to call for evidence in his behalf?

WEB SITE

The American Bar Association Homepage
www.abanet.org

KEY TERMS

Pretrial motions
Pretrial discovery
Statutes of limitations
Tolling the statute of limitations
Double jeopardy

Blockburger test for double jeopardy
Separate sovereigns
Collateral estoppel

Joinder of offenses
Motion to sever offenses
Joinder of defendants
Venue

NOTES

1. *United States v. Cole,* 857 F.2d 971 (4th Cir. 1988).
2. Traynor, "Ground Lost and Found in Criminal Discovery," 39 New York University Law Review 228, 249 (1964).
3. *Wardius v. Oregon,* 412 U.S. 470, 93 S.Ct. 2208 (1973).
4. *United States v. Roberts,* 811 F.2d 257 (4th Cir. 1986) (en banc).
5. *United States v. Peoples,* 748 F.2d. 934 (4th Cir. 1984).
6. *Jencks v. United States,* 353 U.S. 657, 77 S.Ct. 1007 (1957).
7. 18 U.S.C.A. § 3500.
8. *United States v. Alexander,* 748 F. 2d 185 (4th Cir. 1984).
9. *Pennsylvania v. Ritchie,* 480 U.S. 39, 107 S.Ct. 989 (1987).
10. *California v. Trombetta,* 467 U.S. 479, 104 S.Ct. 2528 (1984).
11. *Arizona v. Youngblood,* 488 U.S. 51, 109 S.Ct. 333 (1988).
12. *Clark v. Commonwealth,* 521 S.E.2d 313 (Va. 1999).
13. *United States v. Marion,* 404 U.S. 307, 92 S.Ct. 455 (1971).
14. *United States v. Lovasco,* 431 U.S. 783, 97 S.Ct. 2044 (1977).
15. *United States v. MacDonald,* 456 U.S. 1, 102 S.Ct. 1497 (1982).
16. *Doggett v. United States,* 505 U.S. 647, 112 S.Ct. 2686 (1992).
17. *Moore v. Arizona,* 414 U.S. 25, 94 S.Ct. 188 (1973).
18. 18 U.S.C.A. § 3161.
19. *Green v. United States,* 355 U.S. 184, 78 S.Ct. 221 (1957).
20. *Menna v. New York,* 423 U.S. 61, 96 S.Ct. 241 (1975).
21. *United States v. Broce,* 488 U.S. 563, 109 S.Ct. 757 (1989).
22. *Serfass v. United States,* 420 U.S. 377, 95 S.Ct. 1055 (1975).
23. *Arizona v. Washington,* 434 U.S. 497, 98 S.Ct. 824 (1978).
24. *Illinois v. Somerville,* 410 U.S. 458, 93 S.Ct. 1066 (1973).
25. *Richardson v. United States,* 468 U.S. 317, 104 S.Ct. 3081 (1984).
26. *United States v. Dinitz,* 424 U.S. 600, 96 S.Ct. 1075 (1976).
27. *United States v. Scott,* 437 U.S. 82, 98 S.Ct. 2187 (1978).
28. *Oregon v. Kennedy,* 456 U.S. 667, 102 S.Ct. 2083 (1982).
29. *Green v. United States,* 355 U.S. 184, 78 S.Ct. 221 (1957).
30. *Tibbs v. Florida,* 457 U.S. 31, 102 S.Ct. 2211 (1982).
31. *Benton v. Maryland,* 395 U.S. 784, 89 S.Ct. 2056 (1969).
32. *Blockburger v. United States,* 284 U.S. 299, 52 S.Ct. 180 (1932).
33. *Missouri v. Hunter,* 459 U.S. 359, 103 S.Ct. 673 (1983).
34. *Jones v. Commonwealth,* 218 Va. 18, 235 S.E.2d 313 (1977).
35. *Brown v. Ohio,* 432 U.S. 161, 97 S.Ct. 2221 (1977).
36. *Heath v. Alabama,* 474 U.S. 82, 106 S.Ct. 433 (1985).
37. *Waller v. Florida,* 397 U.S. 387, 90 S.Ct. 1184 (1970).
38. *Ashe v. Swenson,* 397 U.S. 436, 90 S.Ct. 1189 (1970).
39. *Ashe v. Swenson,* 397 U.S. 436, 90 S.Ct. 1189 (1970).
40. *Richardson v. Marsh,* 481 U.S. 200, 107 S.Ct. 1702 (1987).
41. *Pine v. Commonwealth,* 121 Va. 812, 93 S.E. 652 (1917).
42. See *Burton v. United States,* 391 U.S. 123, 88 S.Ct. 1620 (1968).
43. See *United States v. Walters,* 913 F. 2d 388 (7th Cir. 1990).
44. *United States v. Johnson,* 219 F.3d 349 (4th Cir. 2000).
45. *United States v. McVeigh,* 169 F.R.D. 362 (D.Colo. 1996).
46. *United States v. Odom,* 888 F. 2d 1014 (4th Cir. 1989).
47. *Sheppard v. Maxwell,* 384 U.S. 333, 86 S.Ct. 1507 (1966).

TRIAL

Chapter 15

CHAPTER OUTLINE

any European nations use an inquisitorial or investigative process by which judges and prosecutors actively investigate the case in a joint effort to determine the truth. The U.S. criminal justice system, however, is an adversarial process that assigns each participant in the trial a more limited role. The judge is a disinterested manager and arbiter, concerned primarily with following procedural rules in order to dispense justice. The prosecutor pursues an accusatory role, but is also interested in discovery of truth and the delivery of justice. The defendant has no obligation to present any evidence, but may rely on the presumption of innocence. The defense attorney, an advocate for the accused, is primarily responsible for winning the case without violating the law. The jury hears the evidence without bias and then decides whether the accused is guilty of the charged offense.

The adversary process rests on the belief that a clash between the adversaries (prosecution and defense) will best produce the information upon which a neutral decision maker can resolve the case. This clash takes the form of a trial, which can be seen as a contest between equal participants, regulated by neutral rules evenhandedly enforced, giving to each side an equal opportunity to emerge victorious upon presentation of the best case. Although some critics assail the adversary system as a sporting contest that has lost sight of the objective of achieving a "just result," advocates of the adversary system maintain that

> the criminal trial overshadows all other ceremonies as a dramatization of [our] values . . . , representing the dignity of the State as an enforcer of the law, and at the same time the dignity of the individual when he is an avowed opponent of the state, a dissenter, a radical, or even a criminal.[1]

Whether seen as a mere sporting contest or a dramatic symbol of our form of government, a criminal trial is heavily regulated by procedural rules—the subject matter of this chapter.

RIGHT TO A FAIR AND PUBLIC TRIAL

The U.S. Constitution gives each defendant the right to trial before a disinterested and impartial judge.[2] When the trial judge has some extrajudicial connection with the defendant or the victim, or is so situated as to render it improper to preside at trial, the judge must be excused from the case. "Canons of Judicial Conduct" go even further by suggesting that "A judge shall disqualify himself in any proceeding in which his impartiality might reasonably be questioned." A formal request that the judge step down from the case is known as a **motion to recuse** (see Exhibit 15–1).

Motion to recuse
a request that the judge step down from the case.

A defendant also may be deprived of a fair trial if the prosecutor engages in misconduct that prejudices the defendant's substantial rights. Whether the defendant suffered prejudice depends on the circumstances of each case as well as three generally relevant factors: (1) the strength of the properly admitted evidence against the defendant, (2) whether the prosecutor's misconduct was pronounced and persistent, creating a likelihood that the misconduct would mislead the jury, and (3) the action taken by the trial court to correct the prosecutor's misconduct. Most trial judges take prompt and decisive action to cure errors that arise from improper conduct of counsel, usually in the form of an instruction to the jury to disregard the misconduct. However, when the prosecutor's conduct is so impressive that it probably remains on the minds of the jury and influences their verdict, the prejudicial effect of the impropriety cannot be removed by the instructions of the trial court. In these cases, the defendant is entitled to a new trial before a jury that has not been influenced by the prosecutor's misconduct.

Another aspect of the right to a fair trial is the prohibition against using the conditions of the defendant's pretrial custody to influence the jury's determination of

EXHIBIT 15–1
Motion to Rescue

The defendant respectfully moves that the Honorable _____ voluntarily disqualify herself from sitting on the trial of this case. In support of this motion the Defendant states as follows:

1. That on or about _____ , 20____ , the above trial judge accepted a plea of guilty on behalf of the defendant for two counts of _____ .
2. Pursuant to this plea of guilty, said trial judge sentenced defendant to _____ years.
3. The defendant, after imprisonment, corresponded with said trial judge via the U. S. Mail requesting a review of the sentence and/or relocation from current place of imprisonment.
4. The trial judge responded to defendant's request on _____ , 20_____ , stating that upon review the court should have given a stronger sentence.
5. Defendant is now before the same judge charged with a different indictment (involving a crime of similar nature), and it is defendant's fear that the judge, having expressed herself as aforesaid after a reconsideration of the previous sentence, will not impose an unbiased, nonprejudiced sentence based on facts and circumstances herein charged.

Accordingly, the defendant respectfully requests that the judge disqualify herself and transfer this case to another judge for trial.

guilt or innocence. For instance, forcing the defendant to wear prison clothes when appearing before the jury is unconstitutional, because no "essential state policy" is served by compelling a defendant to dress in this manner.[3] Legitimate government interests in security, however, may justify measures taken to control the defendant. For example, boisterous and disruptive defendants may be bound and gagged.[4] Additional security guards may also be present in the courtroom to maintain control over particularly dangerous defendants.[5]

The right to a fair trial also encompasses the right to have the factfinder determine the case from the evidence presented at trial and not from any extraneous source. Judges routinely caution jurors against discussing the case with anyone or viewing media reports of the proceedings. When prejudicial publicity threatens the defendant's right to a fair trial, the judge may consider a number of options:

1. Sequester the jury to shield them from any outside influence
2. Remind the jurors that they are not to read or view any media coverage of the proceedings
3. Close portions of the proceedings to the public
4. Issue restraining orders (gag orders) limiting media coverage of the proceedings
5. Grant a continuance until the publicity abates
6. Order a change of venue.

The court's authority to close the proceedings or issue restraining orders may conflict with the dual concepts of a public trial: the defendant's Sixth Amendment right to a public trial, and the First Amendment right of the public and the press to observe criminal proceedings. A **public trial** is "a trial which is not limited or restricted to any particular class of the community, but is open to free observation of all."[6] While courts have historically closed portions of a trial (for example, during testimony by a juvenile victim of a sex crime), a blanket exclusion of all spectators is improper in the absence of extraordinary circumstances.[7]

At times the defendant may seek to close the proceedings by waiving the Sixth Amendment right to a public trial.[8] The defendant's consent, however, cannot set aside the public interest in having criminal trials open to the general public and the media. The U.S. Supreme Court has recognized that "the right to attend criminal trials is

Public trial
a trial open to observation by all members of the public.

implicit in the guarantees of the First Amendment."[9] The right of access extends not only to trials, but to pretrial proceedings such as preliminary hearings, hearings on pretrial motions, and jury selection. First Amendment considerations also greatly restrict the court's authority to issue restraining orders. Prior restraint on the news media cannot be justified unless all alternatives to prior restraint (for example, sequestering the jury) have proven insufficient to protect the defendant's right to a fair trial.[10] In highly publicized trials, like the O. J. Simpson case, the court must find a proper compromise between the defendant's right to a fair trial and the public's right of access to the workings of the criminal justice system.

The right of access to trials does not encompass any freedom for the media to use a particular technology to cover such proceedings. Cameras in the courtroom have become a staple in state courts, but have been disallowed at the federal level. The issue rests largely within the discretion of the judiciary because the Supreme Court has held that there is no constitutional bar to cameras in the courtroom.[11]

ARRAIGNMENT

Arraignment
identifies the defendant as the person named in the indictment, informs the defendant of the charges, and asks the defendant to plead to the charges.

Arraignment usually consists of identifying the defendant as the person named in the indictment, informing the defendant of the charges against him, and asking the defendant to enter a plea to the charges. Technically, the arraignment is complete when the accused is asked to plead, because the arraignment and the entry of a plea are separate stages of the proceeding. The arraignment is the act of the court, while the entry of a plea is the act of the accused.

Arraignment marks the commencement of trial for some, but not all, purposes. For example, trial does not begin for double jeopardy purposes until the jury is sworn or evidence is introduced in a bench trial. However, arraignment of the defendant may signal the beginning of trial for purposes of determining whether the accused has been afforded the right to a speedy trial. Whether arraignment constitutes the beginning of the trial depends upon the timing of the arraignment, which varies greatly from jurisdiction to jurisdiction. In some states the arraignment may take place weeks or even months in advance of the actual trial; other states hold arraignment on the day the trial is scheduled to begin.

Trial in absentia
a trial that proceeds without the defendant being present.

The point at which the trial commences is important in determining whether trial may proceed without the defendant being present (**trial in absentia**). Trial judges often advise the defendant that failure to appear after arraignment may be deemed a forfeiture of the right to be present during the trial and that the trial will continue in the defendant's absence. Trial in absentia, however, is not an automatic consequence of all absences. When deciding whether to conduct a trial in absentia, the judge must consider (1) the likelihood that the trial could soon take place with the defendant present, (2) the difficulty of rescheduling the trial, (3) the burden on the prosecution to secure the attendance of witnesses on another date, and (4) any factors given to explain the defendant's absence.

ENTRY OF THE PLEA AND PLEA AGREEMENTS

Nolo contendere
a plea by which the defendant does not admit guilt but will not contest the prosecution's case.

The arraignment is completed by asking the accused, "How do you plead?" The accused has three possible responses: guilty, not guilty, or nolo contendere. (Many jurisdictions allow special pleas such as not guilty by reason of insanity or guilty but mentally ill.) If an accused refuses to enter a plea, the court enters a plea of not guilty. A plea of **nolo contendere** ("I do not contest it") means that the defendant does not admit guilt but will not contest the prosecution's case. Such a plea is functionally equivalent to a plea of guilty for purposes of the criminal trial, but a plea of nolo contendere cannot be used in any collateral civil proceedings. For example, if the victim of an assault files a civil suit against the defendant, the defendant's plea of guilty to criminal assault would be admissible evidence (a confession) in the civil assault case. But a plea of nolo contendere is not admissible in the civil proceeding, thus the victim must offer independent evidence of the assault. The concern over potential civil suit is the prime reason many criminal defendants plead nolo contendere rather than guilty. Some states give the defendant the right to enter a plea of nolo contendere to all charges, while other jurisdictions, including the federal system, permit such pleas only with the consent of the court.

Special rules and considerations apply to a plea of guilty, because such a plea waives many important constitutional rights:

1. The privilege against self-incrimination
2. The right to trial by jury
3. The right to confront witnesses
4. The right to demand that the prosecution prove its case beyond a reasonable doubt
5. The right to object to illegally obtained evidence, such as the fruits of an illegal search or an illegally obtained confession.

In most situations, the defendant's plea of guilty reduces the grounds for appeal to issues of jurisdiction and the voluntariness of the guilty plea.[12] Some states, however, permit a conditional guilty plea that allows the accused to accept the imposition of conviction and punishment, while reserving the right to appeal any adverse determination on a pretrial motion to suppress evidence. A defendant who prevails on appeal will be allowed to withdraw a conditional guilty plea and enter a new plea at any retrial.

Because important constitutional rights are waived by a plea of guilty, the plea must be made voluntarily and knowingly. The *American Bar Association Standards for Criminal Justice* mandate that defense counsel ensure that "the decision whether to enter a plea of guilty or nolo contendere is ultimately made by the defendant."[13] The accused's awareness of the constitutional rights waived, the accused's understanding of the nature of the charge, and the consequences of the plea must appear on the trial record.[14] Many jurisdictions have formalized the trial court's acceptance of a guilty plea by requiring the trial judge to put certain questions to an accused who pleads guilty. These questions determine the accused's awareness of the nature of the charge and the possible punishment, inquire as to any pressures brought upon the accused, ascertain the existence and nature of any plea agreement, and attempt to ensure that the plea of guilty is a voluntary and knowing decision of the accused.

If the trial court is satisfied that the guilty plea is voluntarily entered, the court may be required by local law to question the defendant or examine a stipulation of facts to establish an adequate factual basis for the plea of guilty. Special problems arise, however, when the defendant pleads guilty but persistantly proclaims innocence. This type of situation is known as an *Alford* **plea.**

Alford **plea**
the defendant pleads guilty
but proclaims innocence.

NORTH CAROLINA v. ALFORD
Supreme Court of the United States, 1970
400 U.S. 25, 91 S.Ct. 160

Alford was indicted for first-degree murder, a capital offense. His appointed counsel recommended a plea of guilty, but left the final decision to Alford. Alford pleaded guilty to second-degree murder, following which the trial court received a summary of the state's case. Alford then took the stand and testified that he had not committed the murder but that he was pleading guilty because he faced the threat of the death penalty if he did not do so. Alford testified:

"I pleaded guilty on second degree murder because they said there is too much evidence, but I ain't shot no man, but I take the fault for the other man. We never had an argument in our life and I just pleaded guilty because they said if I didn't they would gas me for it, and that is all."

JUSTICE WHITE delivered the opinion of the Court: State and lower federal courts are divided upon whether a guilty plea can be accepted when it is accompanied by protestations of innocence and hence contains only a waiver of trial but no admission of guilt. Some courts, giving expression to the principle that "our law only authorizes a conviction where guilt is shown," require that trial judges reject such pleas. But others have concluded that they should not "force any defense on a defendant in a criminal case," particularly when advancement of the defense might end in disaster. They have argued that, since guilt, or the degree of guilt, is at times uncertain and elusive . . . an accused, though believing his inno-

cence, might reasonably conclude a jury would be convinced of his guilt and that he would fare better in the sentence by pleading guilty.

Implicit in the nolo contendere cases is a recognition that the Constitution does not bar imposition of a prison sentence upon an accused who is unwilling expressly to admit his guilt but who, faced with firm alternatives, is willing to waive his trial and accept the sentence.

These cases would be directly in point if Alford had simply insisted on his plea but refused to admit the crime. The fact that his plea was denominated a plea of guilty rather than a plea of nolo contendere is of no constitutional significance with respect to the issue now before us, for the Constitution is concerned with the practical consequences, not the formal categorizations of state law. Thus, while most pleas of guilty consist of both a waiver of trial and an express admission of guilt, the latter element is not a constitutional requisite to the imposition of criminal penalty. An individual accused of crime may voluntarily, knowingly, and understandingly consent to the imposition of a prison sentence even if he is unwilling or unable to admit his participation in the acts constituting the crime.

Plea Bargaining

Plea agreement
the prosecution and defense agree on the defendant's guilt and the sentence to be recommended by the prosecutor or imposed by the court.

In the majority of cases (some studies suggest 90 percent of felony cases) the defendant's guilt and the applicable range of sentences are determined by a **plea agreement** struck between the prosecutor and defense counsel. In contrast to the public nature of a trial, plea bargaining is often viewed as a clandestine practice. The U.S. Supreme Court, however, has upheld both the practical necessity for, and the beneficial nature of plea bargains:

The disposition of criminal charges by agreement between the prosecutor and the accused, sometimes loosely called "plea bargaining," is an essential component of the administration of justice. Properly administered, it is to be encouraged. If every criminal charge were subjected to a full-scale trial, the States and the Federal Government would need to multiply by many times the number of judges and court facilities.

Disposition of charges after plea discussions is not only an essential part of the process but a highly desirable part for many reasons. It leads to prompt and largely final disposition of most criminal cases; it avoids much of the corrosive impact of enforced idleness during pretrial confinement for those who are denied release pending trial; it protects the public from those accused persons who are prone to continue criminal conduct even while on pretrial release; and, by shortening the time between charge and disposition, it enhances whatever may be the rehabilitative prospects of the guilty when they are ultimately imprisoned.[15]

In most plea agreements, such as the one shown in Exhibit 15–2, the defendant agrees to plead guilty to a charge in exchange for the prosecutor's promise to drop other charges or to recommend a reduced sentence. Historically, most plea bargains were struck without any participation by the judge, and at trial the judge was not even informed that a plea bargain existed. As the U.S. Supreme Court noted in 1977,

EXHIBIT 15–2
Plea Agreement

1. The Defendant stands indicted in this Court for manufacturing marijuana not for his own use.
2. The Defendant acknowledges that he has (a) a right to plead not guilty, (b) a right to trial by a jury, (c) a right to confront and cross-examine all witnesses against him, and (d) a right to compel the attendance of witnesses to testify on his behalf.

    The Defendant hereby further acknowledges that the foregoing rights are waived by him as to each charge to which he pleads guilty as is his right to a direct appeal from a conviction predicated on a plea of guilty.
3. The Defendant further acknowledges that his counsel has fully explained to him all of the elements of the crime with which he stands charged and the respective punishment therefor. He also acknowledges that he has fully discussed with his counsel any possible defenses he may have to this crime and that his counsel has capably represented him as such.
4. In exchange for a plea of guilty to the crime as charged, the State's Attorney agrees that the following specific sentence is the appropriate disposition of this case, to-wit: (a) a term of imprisonment in the State Penitentiary of eight (8) years, with all time suspended on the condition that the Defendant be of good behavior, and follow all the laws of the State, her sister states, and the United States of America, said suspension to continue for a period of seven (7) years; (b) the Defendant to apply for acceptance into the Community Diversion Incentive Program and, if accepted, to abide by all rules, regulations, and requirements as set forth by said program.
5. The defendant acknowledges that this plea agreement is the total agreement between the parties and there have been no other inducements, promises, threats, or coercion of any kind imposed upon the defendant or suggested to the defendant by the Attorney for the State or any agent of the State.

"only recently has plea bargaining become a visible practice accepted as a legitimate component in the administration of criminal justice. For decades it was a *sub rosa* process shrouded in secrecy and deliberately concealed by participating defendants, defense lawyers, prosecutors, and even judges."[16] The extrajudicial nature of plea bargaining contributed to the public perception that the process was a disreputable practice that the legal profession kept hidden from judicial and public scrutiny. In order to counteract such perceptions, many jurisdictions require that the plea agreement be presented to the judge in open court. The court's disposition of the plea agreement depends upon the nature of the agreement.

1. **Recommendation plea agreements.** If the prosecution has agreed to recommend a particular sentence, the trial court must advise the defendant that the recommendation is not binding on the court and that the defendant has no right to withdraw the guilty plea if the actual sentence imposed exceeds the recommendation. In essence, the defendant must be aware that the bargain includes only a recommendation from the prosecutor, not for the actual sentence to be imposed by the judge. The defendant has a right to hold the prosecution to its promised recommendation.[17] However, the defendant has no legitimate claim upon the action of the court in determining sentence.

2. **Disposition plea agreements.** When the prosecution has agreed that a specific sentence is appropriate, the court may accept or reject the agreement, or the court may defer its decision until after consideration of a presentence report. If the court accepts the plea agreement the court will impose the sentence provided for in the agreement. Thus the accused will know in advance the extent of the sentence. If, however, the court rejects the plea agreement, neither party is bound by the agreement and the defendant has the right to withdraw a plea

Recommendation plea agreements
provide for a sentencing recommendation from the prosecution, but are not binding on the judge.

Disposition plea agreements
set specific sentences, which are binding if accepted by the trial judge.

of guilty. If the defendant persists in a guilty plea, the defendant must be advised that the final disposition of the case may be less favorable than that contemplated by the plea agreement.

Prior to the court's acceptance of the plea agreement, the prosecution's withdrawal from an unexecuted plea agreement is "without constitutional significance."[18] Prosecutors sometimes threaten that the proposed plea agreement is a "one-day-only" offer, and the defendant cannot force the prosecution to reinstate a previous offer. The defendant's plea of guilty with knowledge of the prosecution's withdrawal constitutes a voluntary and intelligent plea.

JURY TRIAL

In *Duncan v. Louisiana,* the U.S. Supreme Court concluded that "trial by jury in criminal cases is fundamental to the American scheme of justice" because:

> The guarantees of jury trial in the Federal and State Constitutions reflect a profound judgment about the way in which law should be enforced and justice administered. . . . Those who wrote our constitutions knew from history and experience that it was necessary to protect against unfounded criminal charges brought to eliminate enemies and against judges too responsive to the voice of higher authority. The framers of the constitutions strove to create an independent judiciary but insisted upon further protection against arbitrary action. Providing an accused with the right to be tried by a jury of his peers gave him an inestimable safeguard against the corrupt or overzealous prosecutor and against the compliant, biased, or eccentric judge. If the defendant preferred the common-sense judgment of a jury to the more tutored but perhaps less sympathetic reaction of the single judge, he was to have it. Beyond this, the jury trial provisions in the Federal and State Constitutions reflect a fundamental decision about the exercise of official power—a reluctance to entrust plenary powers over the life and liberty of the citizen to one judge or to a group of judges. Fear of unchecked power, so typical of our State and Federal Governments in other respects, found expression in the criminal law in this insistence upon community participation in the determination of guilt or innocence.[19]

The U.S. Constitution guarantees the right to trial by jury in all criminal cases in which the defendant is charged with a "serious" crime, which includes all cases of a defendant facing potential imprisonment of more than six months.[20] *Lewis v. United States,*[21] held that the federal jury trial right "does not change where a defendant faces a potential aggregate prison term in excess of six months for petty offenses charged. The fact that Lewis was charged with two counts of a petty offense does not transform the petty offense into a serious one." Trial by jury is necessarily waived when a defendant pleads guilty. But if a defendant pleads not guilty and desires to waive a jury, the waiver must be voluntarily and intelligently given. In many jurisdictions, the right to a jury trial belongs to the state as well as to the accused. Thus, the prosecution or the judge may insist upon a jury trial even when the accused wishes to waive trial by jury.[22]

In state court, the defendant does not have a federal constitutional right to a jury of twelve persons, nor to have the jury return a unanimous verdict. In *Williams v. Florida,*[23] the Supreme Court stated that a jury of 12 persons is "a historical accident, unnecessary to effect the purposes of the jury system." In *Ballew v. Georgia,* however, the Supreme Court set the number of six as the minimum for a constitutional jury trial:

The purpose of the jury trial, is to prevent oppression by the Government. This purpose is attained by the participation of the community in determinations of guilt and by the application of the common sense of laymen who, as jurors, consider the case. Rather than requiring 12 members, then, the Sixth Amendment mandated a jury only of sufficient size to promote group deliberation, to insulate members from outside intimidation, and to provide a representative cross-section of the community.

[We] conclude that the purpose and functioning of the jury in a criminal trial is seriously impaired, and to a constitutional degree, by a reduction in size to below six members.[24]

If a jurisdiction utilizes a six-person jury, their verdict must be unanimous.[25] If, however, the jurisdiction employs a twelve-person jury, *Apodaca v. Oregon* held that the defendant has no federal constitutional right to a unanimous verdict:

[W]e perceive no difference between juries required to act unanimously and those permitted to convict or acquit by votes of 10 to two or 11 to one. Requiring unanimity would obviously produce hung juries in some situations where nonunanimous juries will convict or acquit. But in either case, the interest of the defendant in having the judgment of his peers interposed between himself and the officers of the state who prosecute and judge him is equally well served.[26]

The Supreme Court's struggles with identifying a precise number of jurors, or the precise percentage of votes required for a valid verdict have been criticized as arbitrary decisions. But the Court has conceded "that lines must be drawn somewhere if the substance of the jury trial right is to be preserved."

In federal cases, unanimous jury verdicts are required by Rule 31 of the Federal Rules of Criminal Procedure unless the parties stipulate otherwise. A defendant who wishes to avoid a retrial may agree to a less than unanimous verdict in order to resolve cases where the jury reports that it is deadlocked.

JURY SELECTION

Jury selection begins with the creation of a panel of citizens who meet the statutory qualifications for jury service, such as age requisites and residency requirements. Most jurisdictions select jurors at random from the local census, tax rolls, telephone books, or driver's license lists. Each person drawn for jury service may be served with a summons directing him or her to report at a specified time and place and to be available for jury service for a period of time. Often the summons is accompanied by a jury qualification form that must be completed and returned. The form may seek information about the person's address, date of birth, level of education, employer, and members of the immediate family. The form may also seek information that would disqualify the person from serving as a juror, for example, physical or mental disabilities, which prevent effective jury service, past felony conviction, or recent jury service. Unless the court determines that the information contained on the form must be kept confidential or its use restricted in the interest of justice, the form is made available to the lawyers.

In addition, the Equal Protection clause of the Fourteenth Amendment requires that the jury panel be selected in such a way as to represent a cross-section of the community. The systematic exclusion of prospective jurors because of race, color, religion, gender, age, national origin, or economic status is prohibited by the Constitution and by federal statute.[27] A defendant challenging the jury selection process must establish a prima facie case of purposeful and systematic exclusion of certain groups from jury service. (See Chapter Thirteen's discussion of the challenges to the selection of grand juries.)

Voir Dire

Voir dire
the process in which defense and prosecution examine the panel of prospective jurors and select the jurors who will actually serve at trial.

Voir dire is the process in which defense and prosecution examine the panel of prospective jurors and select the ones who will actually serve at trial. The defendant has a right to be tried by an impartial jury, and voir dire examination serves to determine whether a prospective juror is free from partiality and prejudice. The voir dire examination begins with the court inquiring whether any juror is related to one of the parties, has an interest in the case, has acquired pretrial information that would affect the juror's impartiality, has formed an opinion as to guilt or innocence, or has any bias or prejudice against any of the parties (see Exhibit 15–3).

Challenge for cause
may be made against any prospective juror who does not stand impartial in the case.

After the judge has concluded the first portion of the voir dire, counsel may question the prospective jurors. Based upon the answers to these questions and any other evidence submitted to the court, counsel may **challenge for cause** any prospective juror who does not stand impartial in the case. If the judge agrees that a juror's impartiality is in doubt, the judge will grant the challenge and excuse the juror. The right to an impartial jury extends both to impartiality upon the issue of guilt or innocence and impartiality on the question of punishment. For example, in a trial where capital punishment is possible, prospective jurors may be excluded if they are irrevocably committed to voting against the death penalty.[28] The same applies to prospective jurors biased in favor of the death penalty.[29]

The U.S. Supreme Court also has recognized that capital cases may require a more searching inquiry into a prospective juror's feelings about interracial violence. *Turner v. Murray,* established three general principles: (1) the "wiser course" is to propound appropriate questions designed to identify racial prejudice, but refusal to do so is not constitutionally objectionable in the absence of "special circumstances," (2) the fact of interracial violence alone is not a special circumstance; (3) a capital defendant accused of an interracial crime is entitled to have prospective jurors informed of the race of the victim and questioned on the issue of racial bias.[30]

Impaneling an impartial jury becomes increasingly difficult in notorious cases that generate extensive national publicity, for example, the O. J. Simpson case; the Oklahoma City bombing case; or the Uni-bomber prosecution, had it not been resolved by a guilty plea. The Supreme Court has recognized that:

> It is not required, however, that the jurors be totally ignorant of the facts and issues involved. In these days of swift, widespread and diverse methods of

EXHIBIT 15–3
Voir Dire by a Judge

After the prospective jurors are sworn, the court shall question them individually or collectively to determine whether anyone:

1. Is related by blood or marriage to the accused or to a person against whom the alleged offense was committed.
2. Is an officer, director, agent, or employee of the accused.
3. Has any interest in the trial or the outcome of the case.
4. Has acquired any information about the alleged offense or the accused from the news media or other sources and, if so, whether such information would affect impartiality in the case.
5. Has expressed or formed any opinion as to the guilt or innocence of the accused.
6. Has a bias or prejudice against the prosecution or the accused.
7. Is, for any reason, unable to give a fair and impartial trial to the state and the accused based solely on the law and the evidence.

communication, an important case can be expected to arouse the interest of the public in the vicinity, and scarcely any of those best qualified to serve as jurors will not have formed some impression or opinion as to the merits of the case. This is particularly true in criminal cases. To hold that the mere existence of any preconceived notion as to the guilt or innocence of an accused, without more, is sufficient to rebut the presumption of a prospective juror's impartiality would be to establish an impossible standard. It is sufficient if the juror can lay aside his impression or opinion and render a verdict based on the evidence presented in court.[31]

Peremptory Challenges

In addition to challenges for cause, a juror may be eliminated from serving on the jury by either prosecution or defense exercising a **peremptory challenge**—striking any potential juror without stating a reason. Both prosecution and defense are given a specific number of peremptory challenges.

Peremptory challenge
may be used to strike any potential juror without stating a reason.

A peremptory challenge, however, may not be based on race or gender considerations. Although discrimination in selecting a grand jury or the trial jury panel must be established by a "systematic pattern" of discrimination, the Equal Protection clause protects against even a single peremptory challenge exercised on the basis of racial or gender discrimination.[32] If counsel's exercise of a peremptory challenge is questioned, counsel may be required to offer a nondiscriminatory basis for the challenge. The absence of discrimination cannot be established merely by counsel's assurances of acting in good faith when selecting qualified jurors. Although counsel's explanation need not rise to the level justifying a challenge for cause, counsel must offer a neutral explanation related to the facts of the particular case.

PRESENTATION OF EVIDENCE

Opening Statements

Prior to the presentation of evidence, the prosecution and defense are entitled to make opening statements to the jury. **Opening statements of counsel** may not be used to argue law, but may identify what the attorney expects the evidence to be and how that evidence will prove the case. Counsel must refrain from making remarks that cannot be proven, but may state fully the matters counsel expects to prove by admissible evidence.

Opening statements of counsel
alert the jury to what the attorney expects the evidence to be and how that evidence proves the case.

Although the prosecution and defense may argue as forcefully and ably as their abilities permit, they may not inflame the passions of the jury or appeal to jury prejudice. This restraint is particularly applicable to the prosecutor's opening argument, because "whatever liberties are permitted to counsel for persons who are guilty of crime to appeal for mercy for their clients, . . . and to refer to those near and dear to them who will vicariously suffer under such circumstances, the prosecutor has no corresponding liberty. The [state] does not rely upon prejudice or sympathy for the enforcement of its laws."[33]

In the heat of trial, attorneys sometimes overstep the bounds of proper argument as in *Darden v. Wainwright,* when the prosecutor argued that

[the crime was] the work of an animal, there's no doubt about it. . . . [The defendant] shouldn't be out of his cell unless he has a leash on him and a prison guard at the other end of that leash. . . . I wish [the victim] had had a shotgun in his hand when he walked in the back door and blown [the defendant's] face off. I wish that I could see him sitting here with no face, blown away by a shotgun.[34]

While noting that this "argument deserves the condemnation it has received from every court to review it," the U.S. Supreme Court held that the prosecutor's comments had not "so infected the trial with unfairness as to make the resulting conviction a denial of due process."

Proving Venue and Jurisdiction

Venue
the location of the trial.

Proper **venue** (the location of the trial) must be alleged in the indictment, and at trial the prosecution must prove venue by either direct or circumstantial evidence. Factual disputes as to venue may be submitted to the jury, provided that the facts can be properly interpreted to fulfill the legal requirements for venue. Proof of venue is not a major consideration at most trials because unless the defense raises the issue, the venue charged in the indictment is accepted as true and accurate. In appropriate circumstances, the court may take judicial notice of the location of the crime.

Extradition
one state surrenders custody of a fugitive who is then transported to another state to face pending charges.

Arrests (see Chapter Nine) terminate a person's existing liberty and bring the person within the court's jurisdiction. Extradition warrants and detainers are devices used to transfer persons from one form of government custody to another. In **extradition,** one state surrenders custody of a fugitive who is then transported to another state to face pending charges. Most states have adopted the Uniform Criminal Extradition Act, which sets forth procedures for the extradition of fugitives from justice. An accused facing extradition may either file a written waiver of extradition proceedings and agree to return to the demanding state, or the accused may challenge the extradition by writ of habeas corpus. In *Michigan v. Doran*, U.S. Supreme Court explained that a habeas corpus hearing may examine: "(a) whether the extradition documents on their face are in order; (b) whether the petitioner has been charged with a crime in the demanding state; (c) whether the petitioner is the person named in the request for extradition; and (d) whether the petitioner is a fugitive."[35]

Detainer
a request that a penal institution continue to hold a prisoner for the requesting agency or notify the agency when release of the prisoner is imminent.

The defendant also may be brought before the court by use of a **detainer,** a request filed by a criminal justice agency with a penal institution in which a prisoner is incarcerated. The detainer requests that the holding institution continue to hold the prisoner for the requesting agency or notify the agency when release of the prisoner is imminent.[36] In the typical situation, the accused is serving a prison sentence in State X while State Y has outstanding charges to bring against the accused. If State Y fails to file a detainer, the prisoner might be granted an early release without State Y's knowledge, or the wait to complete a lengthy sentence in State X might violate the accused right to a speedy trial in State Y.

Most states have adopted the Interstate Agreement on Detainers, which mandates that upon the filing of a detainer, the holding state must inform the prisoner that a detainer has been lodged against the prisoner. At this point, either the prisoner or the state filing the detainer may seek a trial of the charge upon which the detainer is based. The Interstate Agreement on Detainers contains separate time limitations that govern each situation. If the prisoner requests immediate trial on the pending charge, the state must bring the prisoner to trial within 180 days, absent good cause, or the court must dismiss the charge, and the detainer will cease to be of any force or effect. If, on the other hand, the receiving state requests the prisoner's presence for immediate trial, the prosecution must begin within 120 days from the day the prisoner arrives in the receiving state.[37]

Witnesses

Although the criminal defendant has the right to compel the attendance of witnesses on the defendant's behalf, the Sixth Amendment does not guarantee an accused the right to compel the attendance of any and all witnesses.[38] The defendant must make a plausible showing that the testimony sought would be both material and favorable to the defense.[39] The trial court also may limit the number of witnesses whose testimony is merely repetitive.

Witnesses are normally notified of their expected court appearance by means of a summons or subpoena, issued by the judge, the clerk of court, or the prosecutor. A subpoena is (1) directed to an appropriate official, such as a sheriff or police officer, (2) names the witness to be summoned, (3) states the name of the court and the title of the proceeding, (4) commands the witness to appear at the time and place specified in the subpoena, and (5) states on whose application the subpoena was issued. A recognizance to appear at trial may be used to insure the presence of material witnesses who seem unlikely to honor a subpoena; while a writ of habeas corpus ad testificandum compels the appearance of witnesses in the custody of the law at the time of trial. Failure to obey a subpoena may be deemed contempt of the court to which the subpoena is returnable.

The defendant's right to call for favorable evidence includes the right to prepare for trial, which, in turn, includes the right to interview material witnesses prior to trial. Although every witness holds the personal privilege to decline to talk with counsel, attorneys may not discourage a witness from giving relevant information to opposing counsel. Thus a defendant's Due Process right to present witnesses is violated by "substantial government interference with a defense witness's free and unhampered choice to testify."[40] Causing a potential witness to move beyond the reach of the defense is not prosecutorial misconduct, however, if the government has a legitimate reason for such action. For example, in *United States v. Valenzuela-Bernal* authorities acted properly in carrying out legislative policy by promptly deporting illegal aliens, one of whom was a defense witness.[41]

Upon motion of any party or upon its own motion, the trial court may exclude prospective witnesses from the courtroom and separate the witnesses so excluded. The exclusion of witnesses is designed to prevent a later witness from shaping testimony to correspond to earlier evidence. A witness who violates an exclusion order is not automatically disqualified from testifying, but the witness's misconduct may be used to impeach witness credibility. The misconduct also may subject the witness to punishment for contempt of court.

A witness's **competency to testify** is normally assumed, but if the witness's competency is challenged, all witnesses must be shown to have the ability to (1) observe the events about which the testimony is offered, (2) remember such events, (3) understand questions propounded and make intelligent answers, and (4) possess a sense of moral responsibility to tell the truth. Most questions of competency arise with respect to minors and mentally deficient witnesses. The competency of such witnesses must be determined on an individual basis and is often based upon questioning of the witness by the judge or upon psychiatric evaluations.

Expert witnesses may testify in criminal cases when the jury is confronted with issues that require scientific or specialized knowledge in order to be properly understood. If, however, the jury is as competent as the expert to form an accurate opinion on the subject matter, expert testimony is not needed. Depending upon local rules, an expert witness may render an opinion based upon facts in evidence, facts assumed in a hypothetical question, or facts made known to the expert before the trial.

Real and Scientific Evidence

Any **real evidence** (physical objects) discovered at the scene of the crime, which bears upon the defendant's guilt or innocence is admissible at trial: for example, bloodstained clothing, a plaster cast of a footprint, or a section of the ceiling showing the angle of a gunshot. Real evidence is admissible if proof can be offered that it is substantially in the same condition at trial as at the time of the offense. A jury view of the scene of the crime is another form of receiving real evidence. (Instead of bringing the real evidence to court, the jury is taken to the crime scene.) Because a jury view of the crime scene is a form of receiving evidence, it is a stage of the trial where the defendant has the right to be present, although such right can be waived.

Competency to testify
the witness has the ability to observe the events about which the testimony is offered, remember such events, understand questions propounded and make intelligent answers, and possess a sense of moral responsibility to tell the truth.

Real evidence
physical objects, most often those discovered at the scene of the crime.

Photographs of physical objects, places, or persons are admissible within the discretion of the trial court. For example, in murder cases the prosecution often presents photographs of the victim's body. These photographs are sometimes gruesome, but "if a photograph accurately portrays the scene created by a criminal in the commission of the offense on trial, it is not rendered inadmissible because it is 'gruesome' or 'shocking.'"[42] With the court's permission, counsel also may use visual aids (e.g., a toy pistol) to illustrate and explain testimony.

Relevant scientific evidence is admissible if the device, technique, or theory upon which the results are based have gained general acceptance in the scientific community. Jurisdictions commonly accept breath and blood alcohol analysis, drug analysis, radar speed tests, fingerprint evidence, and tracking by bloodhounds. Most states reject evidence derived from polygraphs, truth serum, or hypnosis.

The law is unsettled as to the extent to which the U.S. Constitution imposes a duty upon a state to preserve scientific evidence for inspection by the defense. For example, does a defendant charged with driving while intoxicated have a right to have defense experts examine a blood sample taken by the arresting officer? In *California v. Trombetta* the Court noted three factors that affect the duty to preserve evidence: (1) the evidence might be expected to play a significant role in the suspect's defense; (2) the exculpatory value of the evidence must be apparent before the evidence is destroyed; and (3) the evidence must be of such a nature that the defendant would be unable to obtain comparable evidence by other reasonably available means.[43]

Objections and Offers of Proof

Failure to object promptly to an item of evidence may constitute a waiver of any objection that could have been raised. In order to be timely, an objection must be made at the time the evidence is offered. Counsel also may waive an objection by explicitly or implicitly assenting to the trial court's ruling. For example, in *Spruill v. Commonwealth*, the trial judge indicated that a clinical psychologist had not been qualified as an expert witness.[44] Defense counsel responded: "I won't pursue it and I will put on the psychiatrist." The appellate court held that the defense counsel had acquiesced to the trial court's ruling on the psychologist's lack of qualification as an expert. In light of this acquiescence and in the absence of an objection, the trial court's ruling could not be challenged on appeal.

Proffer of evidence
a stipulation or testimony as to what the offered evidence would have been if the trial judge had ruled it admissible.

The grounds of objection must be stated with specificity so that opposing counsel may have an opportunity to remedy any defect, and so that the trial judge may understand the precise question to be decided. When the trial court overrules an objection and admits the evidence, counsel's initial objection is assumed to be a continuing objection that need not be repeated each time the evidence is referred to by opposing counsel. When the trial court sustains an objection, counsel offering the evidence must make a **proffer of evidence,** or an offer of proof in the form of a stipulation or testimony as to what the offered evidence would have been if the trial judge had ruled it admissible. Failure to make a proffer of evidence deprives the appellate court of the information necessary to review the trial court's ruling, and thus constitutes a waiver of any challenge to the trial court's decision on the admissibility of evidence. For example, the defense counsel in *Spruill* must first object to the judge's ruling disqualifying the witness, and then proffer the substance of what the witness's testimony would have been.

DEFENDANT'S CHARACTER

Character Evidence

Like any other witness, a defendant who chooses to testify thereby places personal character for truth and veracity at issue, subject to impeachment. (Impeachment of a witness is an attempt to discredit the witness's testimony.) Impeachment of the defendant's truthfulness as a witness must not be confused with use of the defendant's character as circumstantial evidence of innocence. A criminal defendant places personal truth and veracity at issue by testifying, but a defendant places personal character at issue only by introducing independent evidence of the defendant's good character.

Whether the defendant's character becomes an issue in any criminal case depends wholly upon the defendant's decision to raise the issue. (A defendant must "open the door" to character evidence.) The prosecution is not permitted to introduce evidence of the accused's bad character unless and until the accused has put the pertinent traits of character at issue by offering evidence of good character. "The price a defendant must pay for attempting to prove his good name is to throw open the entire subject which the law has kept closed for his benefit and to make himself vulnerable where the law otherwise shields him."[45]

At common law the only proper method of proving character was to call witnesses to testify to the defendant's reputation in the community. Today, most jurisdictions also allow witnesses to express personal opinions as to the defendant's character. After the criminal defendant places personal character at issue, the prosecution may offer evidence to rebut the defense of good character. The prosecution's rebuttal is limited to the same methods of proof that the defendant could use when proving good character, that is, reputation and/or opinion witnesses, depending on the jurisdiction.

As a general rule the prosecution may not offer evidence of the good character of the victim, subject to certain exceptions. For example, the prosecution may offer evidence of a victim's peacefulness in order to rebut the defendant's claim of self-defense against an attack by the victim.

Evidence of Other Crimes

Unlike reputation or opinion testimony as to character, evidence of specific acts of conduct (other criminal offenses) is generally inadmissible to prove the defendant's bad character or to prove commission of the offense charged at the current trial (see Exhibit 15–4). Although seemingly counterintuitive, the law holds that a defendant's previous conviction of a crime (e.g., rape) is inadmissible to prove commission of a similar crime (e.g., the current charge of rape).

The general prohibition against introducing evidence of the defendant's prior convictions is subject to certain exceptions. The most commonly arising situations where evidence of other crimes may be relevant include:

1. Proving motive to commit the crime charged
2. Establishing guilty knowledge or negating good faith
3. Negating the possibility of mistake or accident
4. Showing the conduct and feeling of the accused toward the victim or to establish their prior relations
5. Proving an opportunity to commit the crime
6. Proving the accused's modus operandi when committing certain crimes
7. Demonstrating a common scheme or plan involving multiple crimes.

Even if evidence of another crime falls within one of the above exceptions, it is only admissible when its legitimate probative value outweighs the possible prejudice to the accused. When evidence of other crimes is likely to produce passion and prejudice out of proportion to its probative value, such evidence will not be presented to the jury. For example, if the jury were to learn that the defendant previously sold drugs to young children, the jury may be inclined to convict of any current charge of drug dealing, even if it is unrelated to the earlier sale of drugs.

EXHIBIT 15–4
Motion To Prohibit Reference to
Defendant's Prior Conduct

The defendant moves the Court for an order instructing the prosecutor to refrain from making any reference to the evidence or testimony hereinafter described:

The defendant believes that at trial the prosecution will attempt to introduce evidence that the defendant has been convicted in previous cases charging crimes similar to the current charge.

It is immaterial and unnecessary to the disposition of this case and contrary to the rules of evidence recognized by law in this state to permit such evidence. These past activities of the defendant are too unrelated and too removed in time to have any evidentiary value in the case at bar.

An ordinary objection during the course of trial even if sustained with proper instructions to the jury will not remove the effect of such evidence from the minds of the jurors.

WHEREFORE, the defendant prays this Court to exercise its discretion and order the prosecution to make no reference to the defendant's prior convictions.

Limiting instruction
the trial judge informs the jury that they may consider an item of evidence for only a limited, proper purpose, and not for an improper purpose.

If the judge allows the jury to hear evidence of other crimes, the judge must diminish any prejudicial effect by giving the jury a limiting instruction. A **limiting instruction** informs the jury that they may consider an item of evidence for only a limited, proper purpose, and not for an improper purpose: for example, "Ladies and gentlemen of the jury, evidence that the defendant, **D**, previously sold drugs to **X** may indicate that **D** planned to sell drugs to **Y**, the current charge against **D**. You must, however, focus your attention on the current charge, and you may not punish **D** for any prior misconduct." Although there is no way to guarantee that the jury will be able or willing to utilize evidence for a limited purpose, limiting instructions rest on the assumption that juries will make a good faith effort to follow the judge's instructions.

MOTION FOR MISTRIAL

Unless a mistrial is declared because of a manifest necessity, a criminal defendant has a constitutional right to a trial that concludes in a final verdict (see Chapter Fourteen). Although the trial judge exercises broad discretion in identifying situations in which a mistrial is appropriate, the most common grounds for mistrial are the introduction of prejudicial evidence, improper comment of counsel during opening or closing argument, and jury misconduct. In such situations, the trial judge is in the best position to determine whether a mistrial is necessary or whether the error can be corrected by an instruction to disregard the potentially prejudicial occurrence.

The general rule is that an error arising from admission of evidence or improper conduct of counsel may be cured by prompt action of the trial court in instructing the jury to disregard the prejudicial material. If, however, the inadmissible evidence is likely to remain on the minds of the jury and influence its verdict, the effect of this evidence cannot be negated by instructions from the trial court. In this situation, a mistrial must be declared.

Jury misconduct as grounds for a mistrial may arise when the jury disregards the judge's instructions, most commonly, the court's admonitions to avoid media accounts of the trial and to refrain from discussing the case with anyone. In the absence of prejudice to the defendant, technical violations of the judge's instructions will not necessitate a mistrial. For example, in one case the jury disregarded the judge's instructions that they remain together when several jurors separated themselves from the others to smoke cigarettes before returning from a recess. This minor form of jury "misconduct" did not necessitate declaring a mistrial.

A motion for a mistrial must be made at the time the objectionable element is injected into the trial of a case. It is too late to move for a mistrial after the prosecution and defense have rested or after the jury has retired for deliberations on the verdict.

When considering whether to declare a mistrial, the judge must take into account the defendant's right, under the double jeopardy clause, to have trial proceed to a final verdict unless manifest necessity warrants a mistrial. However, a defense motion for a mistrial constitutes a deliberate election to forgo a claim of double jeopardy at a subsequent prosecution. Other examples of manifest necessity are discussed in Chapter Fourteen.

Motion for acquittal

In a jury trial, the judge may not direct a verdict of guilty, no matter how conclusive the evidence may be. However, the accused may move for a directed verdict of acquittal (also called a motion to strike the evidence or a motion for a directed verdict) after the prosecution has rested its case or at the conclusion of all the evidence. The proper grounds for a directed acquittal is that the evidence is insufficient, as a matter of law, to sustain a conviction. A defendant may not use a motion for acquittal to raise a question of admissibility of evidence, because the sole purpose of a motion for acquittal is to challenge the sufficiency, not the admissibility, of evidence.

If the court denies the motion for acquittal at the conclusion of the prosecution's case, defense counsel must make a tactical decision to either stand on the motion or proceed with the defense case. Such situations present a dilemma that is familiar to criminal defense attorneys. An experienced defense counsel may sometimes discern when the prosecution has failed to prove its case beyond a reasonable doubt; in such instances, defense evidence serves no constructive purpose. Should defense witnesses be caught in inconsistencies or reveal previously undisclosed facts, the prosecution might prove the criminal charge based on evidence offered by the defense. On the other hand, waiving the presentation of defense evidence is suicidal if the judge and jury ultimately conclude that the prosecution has proved the criminal charge. While absolute certainty in reading a judge's mind is impossible, defense counsel sometimes waive the presentation of defense evidence and gamble on their ability to anticipate the judge's view of the sufficiency of the evidence.

Summary

The right to a fair trial guarantees the accused an impartial judge and a government prosecutor who does not engage in misconduct prejudicing the accused's substantial rights. The right to a public trial requires that the proceeding be open to observation by the general public and the media.

The arraignment of a defendant often marks the commencement of trial for purposes of terminating the statute of limitations and for determining compliance with speedy trial provisions. After arraignment the accused may forfeit the right to be present, and the court may conduct a trial in absentia. The arraignment stage identifies the accused as the person named in the indictment, and asks that the defendant plead to the charges. Depending upon the jurisdiction, the accused may plead guilty, not guilty, or nolo contendere. A plea of guilty waives important constitutional rights, thus the trial judge must ascertain whether the accused has made a voluntary and informed decision to waive these rights and plead guilty. The two most common forms of plea agreements, recommendation and disposition agreements, are normally submitted to the trial judge for approval.

The accused has a constitutional right to a jury trial in serious cases, but no federal constitutional right provides a jury of twelve persons or a unanimous verdict from the jury in a state court. Local statutes and rules govern the selection of impartial jurors, but the Equal Protection clause of the Fourteenth Amendment prohibits any state from systematically excluding prospective jurors because of race, color, religion, gender, age, or national origin. Peremptory challenges to individual jurors may be exercised at the discretion of counsel, so long as the challenge is not based on the race or gender of the prospective juror.

The presentation of evidence at trial begins with counsel's opening statements, which alert the jury to the evidence that will be introduced. Both the prosecution and the defense have the right to offer witnesses with relevant knowledge of the case; reluctant witnesses may be subpoenaed to appear at the trial. Except for young children, a witness's competency to testify is assumed, but may be challenged by any party to the proceeding. Expert witnesses assist the jury in areas requiring specialized knowledge, while real and scientific evidence, documents, photographs, and visual aids also may be utilized to assist the jury in understanding the case. The prosecution may not offer evidence of the accused's bad character, but a criminal defendant has the option to introduce evidence of good character as a defense to the charge. An accused who exercises this option thereby "opens the door" for the prosecution to rebut with evidence of bad character.

Motions for a mistrial may be made whenever an error or misconduct at trial is likely to influence the jury's verdict. Motions for a directed acquittal are appropriate when the evidence is insufficient, as a matter of law, to sustain a conviction.

CONCEPT SUMMARY

Character Evidence

Consult local law to determine what changes have been made in a particular jurisdiction.

	CHARACTER OF DEFENDANT	IMPEACHMENT OF DEFENDANT	EVIDENCE OF OTHER CRIMES
Significance of Defendant Testifying	Defendant need not testify, but offers evidence of good character	Defendant testifies	Defendant need not testify
Type of Proof	Reputation or opinion witness	Methods of impeachment used against any witness	Factual evidence of commission of other crimes
Relevance of Character	Defendant may offer good character as a defense; prosecution may rebut with evidence of bad character	Character for truth and veracity affects weight to be given to defendant's testimony	Other crime(s) may prove that the defendant committed the charged offense
Court's Instruction	Good character is evidence of innocence; bad character is not affirmative evidence of guilt, but rebuts defense of good character	Impeaching evidence is not evidence of guilt, it merely affects the believability of defendant's testimony	Evidence may be considered as bearing upon the defendant's guilt

DISCUSSION QUESTIONS

1. If the media seem obsessed with a notorious trial (e.g., the prosecution of O. J. Simpson), what can a trial judge do to protect the accused's right to a fair trial?
2. If a defendant cannot be made to appear before the jury in prison clothes, can a defendant be prohibited from appearing in a military uniform? See *Johnson v. Commonwealth*, 19 Va.App. 163, 449 S.E.2d 819 (1994).
3. If a plea agreement providing for reduced charges or sentence explicitly "rewards" the defendant for admitting guilt, doesn't this reward inherently "punish" defendants who exercise their constitutional rights to plead not guilty and request a jury trial?
4. Can a peremptory challenge be based on a juror's religious beliefs, economic status, or educational level?
5. Why must the prosecution wait for the defendant to "open the door" to character evidence? Is evidence of the defendant's bad character and past crimes relevant to establish that the defendant committed the crime charged?
6. What purpose is served by allowing the trial judge to direct a verdict of acquittal, while prohibiting a directed verdict of guilty?
7. Should American courts adopt an English procedure where the jury is instructed to return a unanimous verdict, but if they have not returned a verdict after two hours, they are brought back into court and instructed that they may reach a verdict by vote of 10 to 2? (When a nine-person jury is used, there must be unanimity.)

PRACTICE EXERCISES

1. Does your jurisdiction have rules governing plea agreements? Do those rules demand that agreements be in writing or submitted in open court?
2. Under what circumstances and to what crimes does your jurisdiction permit pleas of nolo contendere? Does your jurisdiction accept an *Alford* plea?
3. Does your jurisdiction recognize any grounds upon which the governor can refuse to extradict a fugitive? For example, if your state has abolished the death penalty, can the governor refuse to extradite a fugitive to a jurisdiction that utilizes the death penalty?
4. Does your jurisdiction permit the trial judge to comment on the weight of the evidence in a jury trial, or does this constitute misconduct, perhaps justifying a mistrial?
5. What forms of scientific evidence (for example, polygraph examinations, statements made under hypnosis, sniffing by trained canines, radar speed tests, breathalyzer tests) are admissible in your jurisdiction?
6. What does your jurisdiction permit the prosecution to tell the jury about prior convictions used to impeach a defendant's testimony? May the prosecution refer to the prior conviction as a felony? identify the specific felony? elaborate on the circumstances underlying the felony? or inform the jury of the punishment awarded at the prior conviction?

WEB SITE

The Federal Judiciary Homepage
www.uscourts.gov

KEY TERMS

Motion to recuse
Public trial
Arraignment
Trial in absentia
Nolo contendere
Alford plea
Plea agreement

Recommendation plea agreements
Disposition plea agreements
Voir dire
Challenge for cause
Peremptory challenge
Opening statements of counsel
Venue

Extradition
Detainer
Competency to testify
Real evidence
Proffer of evidence
Limiting instruction

NOTES

1. Thurmond Arnold, "The Symbols of Government" (1935).
2. *Ward v. Village of Monroeville*, 409 U.S. 57, 93 S.Ct. 80 (1972).
3. *Estelle v. Williams*, 425 U.S. 501, 96 S.Ct. 1691 (1976).
4. *Illinois v. Allen*, 397 U.S. 337, 90 S.Ct. 1057 (1970).
5. *Holbrook v. Flynn*, 475 U.S. 560, 106 S.Ct. 1340 (1986).
6. *Jones v. Peyton*, 208 Va. 378, 158 S.E.2d 179 (1967).
7. *Globe Newspaper Co. v. Superior Court*, 457 U.S. 596, 102 S.Ct. 2613 (1982).
8. *Estes v. Texas*, 381 U.S. 532, 85 S.Ct. 1628 (1965).
9. *Richmond Newspapers, Inc. v. Virginia*, 448 U.S. 555, 100 S.Ct. 2814 (1980).
10. *Nebraska Press Ass'n v. Stuart*, 427 U.S. 539, 96 S.Ct. 2791 (1976).
11. *Chandler v. Florida*, 449 U.S. 560, 101 S.Ct. 802 (1981).
12. *Boykin v. Alabama*, 395 U.S. 238, 89 S.Ct. 1709 (1969).
13. III American Bar Association Standards for Criminal Justice, Standard 14-3.2 (2d ed. 1986 Supp.).
14. *Boykin v. Alabama*, 395 U.S. 238, 89 S.Ct. 1709 (1969).
15. *Santobello v. New York*, 404 U.S. 257, 92 S.Ct. 495 (1971).
16. *Blackledge v. Allison*, 431 U.S. 63, 97 S.Ct. 1621 (1977).
17. *Santobello v. New York*, 404 U.S. 257, 92 S.Ct. 495 (1971).
18. *Mabry v. Johnson*, 467 U.S. 504, 104 S.Ct. 2543 (1984).
19. *Duncan v. Louisiana*, 391 U.S. 145, 88 S.Ct. 1444 (1968).
20. *Baldwin v. New York*, 399 U.S. 66, 90 S.Ct. 1886 (1970).
21. *Lewis v. United States*, 518 U.S. 322, 116 S.Ct. 2163 (1996).
22. The Sixth Amendment does not afford a defendant the right to be tried before a judge without a jury. *Singer v. United States*, 380 U.S. 24, 85 S.Ct. 783 (1965).
23. *Williams v. Florida*, 399 U.S. 78, 90 S.Ct. 1893 (1970).
24. *Ballew v. Georgia*, 435 U.S. 223, 98 S.Ct. 1029 (1978).
25. *Burch v. Louisiana*, 441 U.S. 130, 99 S.Ct. 1623 (1979).
26. *Apodaca v. Oregon*, 406 U.S. 404, 92 S.Ct. 1628 (1972).
27. See, generally, *McCree v. Lockhart*, 460 U.S. 1088, 103 S.Ct. 1782 (1983); Federal Jury Selection and Service Act, 28 U.S.C.A. §§ 1861, 1862.
28. *Whitherspoon v. Illinois*, 391 U.S. 510, 88 S.Ct. 1770 (1968).
29. *Morgan v. Illinois*, 504 U.S. 719, 112 S.Ct. 2222 (1992).
30. *Turner v. Murray*, 476 U.S. 28, 106 S.Ct. 1683 (1986).
31. *Irwin v. Dowd*, 366 U.S. 717, 81 S.Ct. 1639 (1961).
32. *Batson v. Kentucky*, 476 U.S. 79, 106 S.Ct. 1712 (1986); *J.E.B. v. Alabama*, 511 U.S. 127, 114 S.Ct. 1419 (1994).
33. *Dingus v. Commonwealth*, 153 Va. 846, 149 S.E. 414 (1930).
34. *Darden v. Wainwright*, 477 U.S. 168, 106 S.Ct. 2464 (1986).
35. *Michigan v. Doran*, 439 U.S. 282, 99 S.Ct. 530 (1978).
36. *Carchman v. Nash*, 473 U.S. 716, 105 S.Ct. 3401 (1985).
37. *Fex v. Michigan*, 507 U.S. 43, 113 S.Ct. 1085 (1993).
38. *Pennsylvania v. Ritchie*, 480 U.S. 39, 107 S.Ct. 989 (1987).
39. *United States v. Valenzuela-Bernal*, 458 U.S. 858, 102 S.Ct. 3440 (1982).
40. *United States v. Saunders*, 943 F.2d 388 (4th Cir. 1991).
41. *United States v. Valenzuela-Bernal*, 458 U.S. 858, 102 S.Ct. 3440 (1982).
42. *Washington v. Commonwealth*, 228 Va. 535, 323 S.E.2d 577 (1984).
43. *California v. Trombetta*, 467 U.S. 479, 104 S.Ct. 2528 (1984).
44. *Spruill v. Commonwealth*, 221 Va. 475, 271 S.E.2d 419 (1980).
45. *Michelson v. United States*, 335 U.S. 469, 69 S.Ct. 213 (1948).

VERDICT, PUNISHMENT, AND JUDICIAL REVIEW

Chapter 16

Verdict and punishment

After the presentation of evidence, the case is submitted to the jury. In order to assist the jury in their deliberations, prosecution and defense present their closing arguments, and the judge instructs the jury on the applicable law. Jurisdictions vary as to whether closing arguments come before or after the judge's instructions of law. Local law normally specifies the form of the verdict and also governs procedures for polling the jury and impeaching the jury's verdict. Although a few states authorize the jury to fix an appropriate sentence, in the majority of states the judge has sole responsibility to impose sentence.

Judicial review of the conviction and sentence takes the form of direct appeal and collateral review. The most common form of collateral review is habeas corpus petitions, which can be filed in both state and federal court. As a supplement to judicial review, all jurisdictions grant a defendant an opportunity to appeal to executive authority for a pardon or grant of clemency.

Closing Arguments and Summations

Closing arguments
Counsels' summations of the evidence and how that evidence points toward conviction or acquittal.

Closing arguments begin with the prosecution's summary of the case, followed by the closing argument of defense counsel, followed in turn by the prosecution's rebuttal. The time allowed counsel for argument is within the sound discretion of the trial court. **Closing arguments** focus on (1) summation of the evidence, (2) review of reasonable inferences deducible from the evidence, (3) a response to argument of opposing counsel, and (4) a plea for mercy or justice. In theory, counsel may not express personal opinions as to the credibility of a witness or the weight of the evidence, although this principle is often violated in practice. For example, counsel should not suggest, "In all my years in practice, I have never seen a witness lie the way that witness **X** did"; or "I've never seen a more brutal crime." Counsel also acts improperly if a closing argument is based on facts not introduced into evidence. As was true of opening statements (discussed in Chapter Fifteen), counsel may not inflame the passions of the jury or appeal to their prejudice against the defendant.

During closing argument, the prosecution may not comment on the defendant's failure to testify because no inference of guilt can be drawn from the defendant's choice to exercise the Fifth Amendment right to avoid self-incrimination.[1] The prosecution, however, is permitted to comment upon the strength of the government's case and point out that its evidence is not contradicted. Separating a permissible comment on the weakness of the defense case from an improper comment on the defendant's silence is not always easy. The distinction depends on whether "the language used was manifestly intended or was of such a character that the jury would naturally and necessarily take it to be a comment on the failure of the accused to testify."[2] The invited response doctrine authorizes the prosecution, during rebuttal, to comment on the defendant's silence if the defense raises the issue of the defendant's silence.[3] For example, defense counsel argued to the jury, "We felt the prosecution's case was so weak we wouldn't dignify it by having the defendant testify." In rebuttal, the prosecution suggested to the jury, "Did you ever think that maybe the reason the defendant didn't testify is because the defendant is guilty?" Although such comment on the defendant's silence is an "invited response," the U.S. Supreme Court suggested that the "better remedy" is for the trial judge to strike the defense's statements and thus blunt the need for the prosecutor to respond.[4]

Arguments of counsel are often made extemporaneously at the conclusions of trials that may be protracted and hotly contested, thus counsel customarily accord the opposing attorney reasonable latitude during summation. But counsel may have to interrupt the opponent's argument with a timely objection or run the risk that the judge deems counsel's silence to be a waiver of any objection. When objecting to an improper argument counsel must decide whether to move for a mistrial or request that the judge instruct the jury to disregard the improper statement. Highly prejudicial and inflammatory statements may necessitate a mistrial so that the defendant may start over with a new jury. In the absence of highly prejudicial material, an instruction to the jury to disregard the statement normally cures any error arising from closing arguments.

Instructions to the Jury

The trial court must give **instructions** that guide the jury on all principles of law applicable to the charged offense and the evidence presented at trial. Although the jury makes the ultimate determination of the facts of the case, the jury must accept the applicable law as stated by the judge. Judges often caution the jury that they must abide by the law as given by the court even if the jurors do not agree with the law.

In theory, the jury must follow the judge's legal instructions, but in practice, the jury exercises absolute power to disregard or nullify the law by returning a verdict of not guilty. **Jury nullification** of law occurs when the jury returns an acquittal because it sympathizes with the defendant or disagrees with the law. Because jury acquittals are final and not subject to review by the trial judge or appellate courts, the judiciary has no power over a jury that chooses to ignore the law and return an acquittal. Although judges have suggested that the jury's sole function is to determine "Who done it," acquittal rates for prosecutions under the Fugitive Slave Act and Prohibition laws demonstrate that jurors sometimes expand their reach beyond factual questions and address the fairness of the law itself. Even in the absence of dramatic political or moral issues, juries sometimes acquit the defendant in protest against a police or prosecution practice that the jury considers improper. For example, some observers believe that the acquittal of O. J. Simpson was based, not on the jurors' view of factual guilt or innocence, but on the jurors' reaction to the possible misuse of evidence by the allegedly "racist" Los Angeles Police Department. The O. J. Simpson trial also illustrated one of the most intriguing aspects of jury nullification—its clandestine nature. Although the jury possesses the absolute power to acquit on any basis including its dislike for the prosecutor or the law, defense counsel are not permitted to alert the jury to this nullification power or to ask the jury to invoke the power. Thus the law has accepted a compromise where nullification power exists, but no one is allowed to talk about it openly in court. That compromise was brought into question during closing arguments in the Simpson trial when defense counsel argued to the jury, "in our society who polices the police. You do. You can send a message to the police." Some critics feel that defense counsel stepped over the line and improperly argued nullification to the jury; others feel that his argument was brilliant lawyering that complied with the letter of the law, but nonetheless managed to communicate an important message to the jury. A California model jury instruction attempts to discourage jury nullification by providing:

> The integrity of a trial requires that jurors, at all times during their deliberations, conduct themselves as required by these instructions. Accordingly, should it occur that any juror refuses to deliberate or expresses an intention to disregard the law or to decode the case based on . . . any improper bases, it is the obligation of the other jurors to immediately advise the Court of the situation.

The judge's responsibility to instruct the jury requires the presentation of certain mandatory instructions as well as the consideration of all instructions requested by counsel.

Mandatory Instructions

1. *Defining the essential elements of the offense:* The prosecution must prove every essential element of the charged offense, which the judge must define for the jury. The duty to define the offense cannot be discharged by simply

Instructions
the trial judge's explanations of the law applicable to the charged offense and the evidence presented at trial.

Jury nullification
a jury disregards the judge's instructions and returns an acquittal because it sympathizes with the defendant or disagrees with the law.

reading the indictment to the jury. If the judge defines one offense (e.g., larceny), the prosecution cannot urge the jury to convict of another crime (e.g., robbery) upon which the jury was not instructed.

2. *Defining the burden of proof:* The jury must be instructed that the prosecution has the burden to prove its case beyond a reasonable doubt, but "trial courts should refrain from charging the jury on reasonable doubt unless such guidance is made unavoidable by a specific request from a confused jury."[5] The courts have noted that any attempts to define the phrase *beyond a reasonable doubt* are often less illuminating than the expression itself.

3. *The presumption of innocence:* The accused in every case is entitled to an instruction on the presumption of innocence. Except in rare cases, a conviction must be reversed if the judge refused to instruct the jury on the presumption of innocence. Although instructing the jury that the defendant is presumed to be innocent *and* that the prosecution must prove guilt beyond a reasonable doubt may seem redundant, the defendant is entitled to both instructions.

4. *The defendant's failure to testify:* When the defendant elects not to testify, the court may of its own volition, and must upon a defense request, instruct the jury that the defendant's failure to testify is not an indication of guilt.[6] Some experienced defense counsel regard such an instruction as a mixed blessing because the instruction may highlight the defendant's failure to testify. Accordingly, defense counsel may request that the instruction not be given. Although generally deemed a "better practice" not to give the instruction over defendant's objection, the final decision is left to the discretion of the trial court.[7]

5. *Lesser included offenses:* A lesser included offense is one composed entirely of elements that are also elements of the greater offense charged. For example, a charge of first degree murder necessarily includes lesser forms of homicide like second degree murder or manslaughter. If the evidence at trial would support a conviction of a lesser included offense, the court must, upon request of counsel, instruct the jury as to the lesser included offense. The defendant, however, is not entitled to an instruction on a lesser included offense when none of the evidence supports a conviction of the lesser offense. For example, the facts of a particular case may suggest that the killing of the deceased was either murder or self-defense, because no evidence supports the middle ground of manslaughter. In this case, the judge will not instruct the jury on the elements of manslaughter.

6. *Defenses:* "As a general proposition a defendant is entitled to an instruction as to any recognized defense for which there exists evidence sufficient for a reasonable jury to find in his favor."[8] If, however, the judge can rule as a matter of law that the defense is not valid, the judge need not instruct the jury on the defense.

Instructions Proposed by Counsel   The court may direct counsel to submit proposed instructions at any time during trial, but counsel must be given a final opportunity to submit proposed instructions at the conclusion of all evidence. Counsel may submit instructions that cover omissions in the court's proposed instructions and may request the court to give more definite or explicit instructions. Any objection to an instruction proposed by opposing counsel or the court must be made when the instruction is tendered.

Allen **charge**
may be given when a jury informs the judge that they are unable to agree on a verdict.

The *Allen* **charge**, also known as the "dynamite charge" or "hung jury charge," may be given when a jury informs the judge that they are unable to agree on a verdict. The instruction derives its name from the case of *Allen v. United States* in which the Supreme Court held that the jury could be informed that in a large proportion of cases, absolute certainty could not be expected; that although the verdict must be the verdict of each individual juror, and not a mere acquiescence in the conclusion of his fellows, yet they should examine the question submitted with candor and with a proper regard and deference to the opinions of each other; that it was their duty to decide the case if they could conscientiously do so; that they should listen, with a disposition to be convinced, to each other's arguments; that, if much the larger number were for conviction, a dissenting juror should consider whether his doubt was a reasonable one which made no impression upon the minds of so many men, equally honest, equally intelligent with himself. If, upon the other hand, the majority was for acquittal, the minority ought to ask themselves whether they might not reasonably doubt the correctness of a judgment which was not concurred in by the majority.[9]

The *Allen* charge has been criticized, but most jurisdictions approve variations of this type of instruction to a hung jury. The *Allen* charge also may be used in the sentencing phase of a capital murder trial when the jury is deadlocked over imposition of the death penalty.[10]

Verdicts, Polling the Jury, and Impeaching the Verdict

A jury verdict must be in writing, signed by the foreman, and returned in open court. Technical form is not required in the verdict, and any extraneous language can be disregarded without affecting the verdict. A verdict is proper if "the real finding of the jury may be determined, though it may not be accurately couched in the technical language of the law."[11] A verdict, however, must be set aside if the court cannot determine the crime of which the jury intended to find the accused guilty.[12] For example, the jury's verdict appears to convict the defendant of a misdemeanor, but the jury recommends a sentence appropriate only for a felony conviction. Objections to the form of the verdict must be made before the jury is discharged. After discharge, a jury cannot be reassembled to correct a substantive defect in its verdict, nor can objections to the form of the verdict be raised for the first time on appeal.

A defendant convicted by a jury on one charge may not challenge that conviction on grounds that it is inconsistent with the jury's verdict of acquittal on another charge. **Inconsistent verdicts** occur when the jury convicts of some charges while acquitting of charges that appear to be interrelated. For example, the jury convicts for felony-murder, but acquits the defendant of the underlying felony that gave rise to the murder. "It is the court's function to determine solely whether the verdict represents the juror's position; the court should not inquire into the reasoning process or motivation behind the verdict."[13] Consistency of jury verdicts is not required because the jury may have acquitted of one count and convicted of another based on a compromise or an act of mercy.[14]

Inconsistent verdicts
the jury convicts the defendant of some charges while acquitting of charges that appear to be interrelated.

Polling the Jury When a verdict is returned, the jury may be polled individually at the request of any party or upon the court's own motion. **Polling the jury** consists of the clerk of court inquiring of each juror: "Is this your verdict?" Each juror must reply in the affirmative or negative. Although the better practice is to ask each juror to respond individually, some trial judges merely ask for a show of hands. Polling the jury may seem like a mere formality, but the polling process sometimes produces surprises. In one case, when asked "Is this your verdict?" the juror responded, "I support the group decision." The trial judge refused to accept this answer and required the juror to respond yes or no to the question. The juror then answered, "No."[15] In jurisdictions that require a unanimous verdict, even one juror's statement contrary to the verdict rendered negates the unanimity of the verdict. In such cases the judge must either direct the jury to retire for further deliberations or discharge the jury and schedule a retrial.

Polling the jury
inquiring of each juror in open court, "Is this your verdict?" Each juror must reply in the affirmative or negative.

The jury is polled merely to ascertain if each juror assents to the verdict as rendered. The polling process cannot be used to inquire how or why a juror arrived at the verdict. The deliberations of the jury and the motives behind them in arriving at a verdict are secret. Even jurors themselves are not allowed to impeach their verdict during the polling process or by subsequent affidavit.

Impeaching the Verdict The major exception to the rule against impeaching verdicts involves situations in which some "outside" influence on the jury affects the defendant's constitutional right to an impartial jury. The physical or mental incompetence of a juror is an "internal" matter, thus allegations of juror intoxication do not warrant a postverdict evidentiary hearing into the juror's competency.[16] The prime instances of outside influence occur when matters not in evidence have been considered by one or more of the jurors. For example, a juror might view media accounts of the trial or make an unauthorized visit to the crime scene. A jury's examination of evidence not received in open court may be harmless error, but only slight evidence of influence or prejudice is required to warrant the granting of a new trial. The Due Process clause requires that a verdict of guilty be set aside if it might rest on a legally inadequate basis.

Sentencing

After conviction, sentence is imposed by either the judge or jury. A few states authorize the jury to fix or recommend an appropriate sentence, but in most jurisdictions the judge has sole responsibility to impose sentence. Juries figure most prominently in capital cases in which they often determine or recommend whether the defendant should be sentenced to death. However, no constitutional provision mandates that only a jury may impose the death penalty.[17]

Capital Cases *Furman v. Georgia* held that the then existing capital punishment procedures in America resulted in the infliction of cruel and unusual punishment in violation of the Eighth and Fourteenth Amendments.[18] Although the Supreme Court justices could not agree on a common rationale for their holding, a number of justices pointed to the arbitrariness with which the death penalty had been imposed. For example, Justice Stewart likened the imposition of capital punishment to the capriciousness of being struck by a "bolt of lightning."

FURMAN v. GEORGIA
Supreme Court of the United States, 1972
408 U.S. 238, 92 S.Ct. 2726

JUSTICE DOUGLAS concurring:
The generality of a law inflicting capital punishment is one thing. What may be said of the validity of a law on the books and what may be done with the law in the application do, or may, lead to quite different conclusions. It would seem to be incontestable that the death penalty inflicted on one defendant is "unusual" if it discriminates against him by reason of his race, religion, wealth, social position, or class, or if it is imposed under a procedure that gives room for the play of such prejudices.

In these three cases the death penalty was imposed, one of them for murder, and two for rape. In each the determination of whether the penalty should be death or a lighter punishment was left by the State to the discretion of the judge or of the jury. In each of the three cases the trial was by a jury. In each of the three cases the defendant was black.

We cannot say from the facts disclosed in these records that these defendants were sentenced to death because they were black. Yet our task is not restricted to an effort to define what motives impelled these death penalties. Rather, we deal with a system of law and of justice that leaves to the uncontrolled discretion of judges or juries the determination whether defendants committing these crimes should die or be imprisoned. Under these laws no standards govern the selection of the penalty. People live or die, dependent on the whim of one man or of 12.

Thus, these discretionary statutes are unconstitutional in their operation. They are pregnant with discrimination and discrimination is an ingredient not compatible with the idea of equal protection of the laws that is implicit in the ban on "cruel and unusual" punishments.

JUSTICE STEWART concurring:

The penalty of death differs from all other forms of criminal punishment, not in degree but in kind. It is unique in its total irrevocability. It is unique in its rejection of rehabilitation of the convict as a basic purpose of criminal justice. And it is unique, finally in its absolute renunciation of all that is embodied in our concept of humanity.

These death sentences are cruel and unusual in the same way that being struck by lightning is cruel and unusual. For, of all the people convicted of rapes and murders in 1967 and 1968, many just as reprehensible as these, the petitioners are among a capriciously selected random handful upon whom the sentence of death has in fact been imposed. I simply conclude that the Eighth and Fourteenth Amendments cannot tolerate the infliction of a sentence of death under legal systems that permit this unique penalty to be so wantonly and freakishly imposed.

JUSTICE BLACKMUN dissenting:

Were I a legislator, I would vote against the death penalty. . . . Although personally I may rejoice at the Court's result, I find it difficult to accept or to justify as a matter of history, of law, or of constitutional pronouncement. I fear the court has overstepped. It has sought and has achieved an end.

JUSTICE REHNQUIST dissenting:

Whatever its precise rationale, today's holding necessarily brings into sharp relief the fundamental question of the role of judicial review in a democratic society. How can government by the elected representatives of the people co-exist with the power of the federal judiciary, whose members are constitutionally insulated from responsiveness to the popular will, to declare invalid laws duly enacted by the popular branches of government?

Rigorous attention to the limits of this Court's authority is likewise enjoined because of the natural desire that beguiles judges along with other human beings into imposing their own views of goodness, truth, and justice upon others. . . . The most expansive reading of the leading constitutional cases does not remotely suggest that this Court has been granted a roving commission, either by the Founding Fathers or by the framers of the Fourteenth Amendment, to strike down laws that are based upon notions of policy or morality suddenly found unacceptable by a majority of this Court.

Four years later in *Gregg v. Georgia,* the Supreme Court revisited the issue and upheld the constitutionality of death sentences when the sentencing authority (judge or jury) is guided by statutory standards.[19] These standards require the judge or jury to consider specific aggravating circumstances and any mitigating evidence.

GREGG v. GEORGIA
Supreme Court of the United States, 1976
428 U.S. 153, 96 S.Ct. 2909

JUSTICE STEWART delivered the opinion of the Court:
The defendants in the cases before the Court today renew the arguments in *Furman v. Georgia* but developments during the four years since *Furman* have undercut substantially the assumptions upon which their argument rested. Despite the continuing debate, dating back to the 19th century, over the morality and utility of cap-

ital punishment, it is now evident that a large proportion of American society continues to regard it as an appropriate and necessary criminal sanction.

The most marked indication of society's endorsement of the death penalty for murder is the legislative response to *Furman.* The legislatures of at least 35 States have enacted new statutes that provide for the death penalty for at least some crimes that result in the death of another person. And the Congress of the United States, in 1974, enacted a statute providing the death penalty for aircraft piracy that results in death. These recently adopted statutes have attempted to address the concerns expressed by the Court in *Furman* primarily (i) by specifying the factors to be weighed and the procedures to be followed in deciding when to impose a capital sentence, or (ii) by making the death penalty mandatory for specified crimes. But all of the post-*Furman* statutes make clear that capital punishment itself has not been rejected by the elected representatives of the people.

The value of capital punishment as a deterrent of crime is a complex factual issue the resolution of which properly rests with the legislatures, which can evaluate the results of statistical studies in terms of their own local conditions and with a flexibility of approach that is not available to the courts. Indeed, many of the post-*Furman* statutes reflect just such a responsible effort to define those crimes and those criminals for which capital punishment is most probably an effective deterrent.

In sum, we cannot say that the judgment of the Georgia legislature that capital punishment may be necessary in some cases is clearly wrong. Considerations of federalism, as well as respect for the ability of a legislature to evaluate, in terms of its particular state the moral consensus concerning the death penalty and its social utility as a sanction, require us to conclude, in the absence of more convincing evidence, that the infliction of death as a punishment for murder is not without justification and thus is not unconstitutionally severe.

Statistical studies continue to suggest that racial considerations enter into capital sentencing determinations.[20] Most jurisdictions have sought to minimize the risk of arbitrary and capricious sentencing by requiring that the death penalty be imposed only when the prosecution establishes certain aggravating circumstances such as the probability that the defendant is likely to commit criminal acts of violence that would constitute a continuing threat to society, or the defendant's conduct in committing the offense for which the defendant was convicted was outrageously or wantonly vile, horrible, or inhuman because it involved torture, depravity of mind, or an aggravated battery to the victim. "The Constitution does not require a State to adopt specific standards for instructing the jury in its consideration of aggravating and mitigating circumstances."[21] However, general references to an offense as "especially heinous, atrocious or cruel" may be unconstitutionally vague.[22] Accordingly, most statutes provide guidance as to what factors make an offense especially heinous: for example, torture, mutilation, and multiple killings.

A court imposing the death penalty also must consider specific mitigating circumstances such as (1) the defendant's lack of prior criminal activity, (2) the defendant's extreme mental or emotional disturbance at the time of the offense, or (3) the defendant's age at the time of the offense.[23] A statutory list of mitigating circumstances is merely illustrative, however, and the sentencing body may not be precluded from considering any aspect of a defendant's character or prior record, or any of the circumstances of the offense that the defendant proffers as a basis for a sentence less than death.[24] The jury, however, may be instructed that it should not be swayed by mere sympathy or sentiment for the defendant.[25] The jury also may consider the impact of the murder on the victim's family.[26]

Finally, "it is constitutionally impermissible to rest a death sentence on a determination made by a sentencer who has been led to believe that the responsibility for determining the appropriateness of the defendant's death rests elsewhere."[27] Thus the prosecution may not argue to the jury that their verdict is merely the first step in a long process of appellate review of all death sentences.

Noncapital Cases A defendant who is convicted of a misdemeanor is usually sentenced immediately. For most felonies, however, sentencing is postponed to allow the defense, prosecution, and the probation officer an opportunity to complete an investigation that will be presented to the court as a presentence report. A **presentence report** typically includes a victim impact statement, an interview with the defendant, and such additional information as the court or the probation officer deems helpful

Presentence report prepared statements that inform the sentencing body of the defendant's background and the circumstances of the offense.

in imposing sentence. At the interview of the defendant, the convicted defendant is permitted to give a personal version of the facts surrounding the offense and may provide information on background, employment history, and psychological status. A presentence interview of the defendant is not a critical stage of the proceedings, thus the defendant has no Sixth Amendment right to counsel, nor does the defendant have a right to *Miranda* warnings.[28]

A copy of the presentence report must be furnished to defense counsel prior to its presentation in open court. Defense counsel is usually given the right to cross-examine the probation officer or preparer of the presentence report. The defendant may also comment on the presentence report and present any additional facts relevant to sentencing. Closely akin to, but legally distinct from, the presentence report is the defendant's right to allocution before sentence is imposed.[29] **Allocution** is the defendant's right to speak in her or his own behalf after the factfinder determines guilt but before the judge pronounces sentence. Failure to provide the right of allocution is normally harmless.

Probation or Suspension of Sentence

The sentencing court has discretion to (1) suspend imposition of sentence, (2) pronounce sentence but suspend it in whole or part, or (3) place the accused on probation. **Probation** releases the defendant from custody subject to the condition that the defendant follows an approved manner of conduct. From the defendant's standpoint, suspension of sentence without probation is the most desirable option. Suspension of sentence may be conditioned merely upon the defendant's future good behavior, but probation usually places the defendant under the supervision of a probation officer and includes the responsibility to report to such officer.

Placing the defendant on probation or suspending sentence automatically imposes the condition that the defendant be of good behavior. The court may impose additional conditions, such as requiring the defendant to pay fines or court costs, perform community service, or make restitution to the victim. Although sentencing courts have broad discretion when imposing conditions of probation, there is uncertainty and controversy as to whether a court's insistence on "moral" training runs afoul of prohibitions against the establishment of religion.

Allocution
the defendant's right to speak in her or his own behalf after the factfinder determines guilt but before the judge pronounces sentence.

Probation
releases the defendant from custody subject to the condition that the defendant behave in an approved manner, and subject to any other specific conditions imposed by the court.

M.C.L. v. STATE
682 So.2d 1209 (Fla. 1996)

The minor M.C.L. (ML) in exchange for the State's agreement to drop three counts of burglary, pleaded guilty to eight counts of burglary and one count of cruelty to animals.

ML's crime against the animal involved forcefully holding a bag over the head of a small household pet, breathing marijuana smoke into the bag, and then tossing the pet back and forth between juvenile codefendants. ML's burglaries included destruction of walls, windows, and plumbing fixtures in a number of homes, and resulted in $52,085.71 in damages.

The trial judge adjudicated ML delinquent; committed ML to high-risk juvenile detention for a term not to

exceed ML's nineteenth birthday; and imposed the following immediate condition:

The child and mother shall attend an organized moral and spiritual training program (chosen by his mother) for at least 2 hours each week, and he shall spend at least 30 minutes each day in some form of moral and spiritual training, and shall keep a daily journal categorizing what he has read and reflected upon. This shall be available for the counselors or the Court to inspect. During the next 9 months, he shall have covered in this personal spiritual training at least the lives of Moses, Kings David and Solomon of Israel, Jesus of Nazareth, Mohammed, Buddha, Confucius, George

Washington, Abraham Lincoln, and Martin Luther King. This daily journal requirement and reading shall begin to be required immediately and shall be required if possible during any commitment program.

This probation condition has a valid secular purpose— ML's rehabilitation; it primarily advances ML's rehabilitation, not religion; and it leads not at all to entanglement of church and state, for no church is involved. The judge's order avoids mandating the study of any religious practices; it merely orders the juvenile to study the lives of individuals who have made significant contributions to the code of civilized conduct upon which societies exist. The study of these lives presented as intellectual history neither necessitates the study of religion nor is unconstitutional.

The instant trial judge, by requiring ML to study historically renowned moral leaders, exercised reasonable discretion to foster ML's rehabilitation. We note however that some uncertainty exists as to the meaning of "spiritual," as opposed to "moral," training. The State at oral argument conceded, and we agree, that "spiritual" training, to the extent that it means religious training, is unconstitutional. We therefore strike the words "and spiritual" from the judge's order.

In contrast to *M.C.L., Griffin v. Coughlin,*[30] held that the Alcohol Anonymous 12-steps protocol is sufficiently imbued with a religious message that requiring an atheist or agnostic to participate in AA violates the First Amendment's Establishment Clause. In a similar vein, *Kerr v. Farrey,*[31] held that prison officials may not require an inmate to attend a substance abuse counseling program with explicit religious content, such as Narcotics Anonymous or Alcoholics Anonymous.

If the defendant violates the conditions of probation, the court may revoke probation and order the defendant to serve the full sentence originally imposed. The court has wide discretion when determining the sufficiency of the cause for revoking probation, but the most common grounds include substantial misconduct, commission of a subsequent criminal offense, failure to pay fines or costs, failure to make restitution to the victim, or violation of any of the specific conditions of probation.

A proceeding to revoke probation is not a prosecution for a criminal offense and the right to jury trial does not apply.[32] In *Gagnon v. Scarpelli,* however, the Supreme Court held that due process requires a judicial hearing at which the probationer has the right, (1) to receive written notice of the claimed violations of probation, (2) to have disclosure of the evidence, (3) to be heard in person and to present witnesses and documentary evidence, (4) to confront and cross-examine adverse witnesses (unless the court specifically finds good cause for not allowing confrontation), and (5) to receive a written statement from the court as to the evidence relied on and the reasons for revoking probation.[33]

Resentencing

Special problems arise when the court overturns a convicted defendant's initial conviction on appeal, then the defendant subsequently is retried and again convicted of the same offense. The Due Process clause prohibits increased punishment that is intended to penalize the defendant for successfully appealing the original conviction. The Supreme Court has applied this due process consideration to resentencing in three separate instances: (1) sentencing by a judge, (2) sentencing by a jury, and (3) sentencing at a trial de novo.[34]

1. *Resentencing by a judge:* The judge at the second trial may have been the judge at the first trial or may be aware of the first trial, thus the judge may possibly hold a vindictiveness against a defendant for successfully attacking the initial conviction. *North Carolina v. Pierce* recognized a "presumption of vindictiveness" that may be overcome only by objective evidence.[35] A judge may impose more severe punishment on resentencing, but the judge's reasons for doing so must be based upon objective information concerning identifiable conduct on the part of the defendant. Such conduct may occur after the time

of the original sentencing, or the judge may receive new evidence regarding the defendant's past "life, conduct and mental and moral propensities."[36]

2. *Jury sentencing:* In those jurisdictions where the jury imposes sentence, the possibility of vindictiveness does not exist because the jury is unlikely to be aware of the first conviction and is generally unconcerned with deterring appeals. In *Chaffin v. Stynchcombe,* the Supreme Court held that the jury may impose a harsher penalty on resentencing as long as the jury was not informed of the prior sentence.[37]

3. *Trial de novo:* No presumption of vindictiveness pertains in resentencing in a trial de novo in a higher court following conviction in a lower court. A **trial de novo** is a new trial in which the prosecution and defense "start over" and relitigate the charged offense as if no previous trial had taken place (see the section on judicial review). In *Colten v. Kentucky,* the U.S. Supreme Court found that when a jurisdiction grants the defendant an absolute right to a trial de novo, the jurisdiction's courts are unlikely to attempt to discourage such trials by increasing the sentence beyond that awarded by a lower court.[38] "The Due Process clause is not offended by all possibilities of increased punishment upon retrial after appeal, but only by those that pose a realistic likelihood of 'vindictiveness.'"[39]

Trial de novo
a new trial, not an appeal of the lower court's conviction.

Sentencing for Contempt of Court

All courts are invested with power to punish for contempt, both by the inherent nature of the court and by legislation. Contempt of court is divided into four categories: (1) **civil contempt,** in which the court imposes punishment to coerce compliance with an order of the court, (2) **criminal contempt,** in which punishment is imposed to preserve the power and vindicate the dignity of the court, (3) **direct contempt,** in which the court may summarily punish without conducting a hearing, (4) **indirect (constructive) contempt,** in which the contempt is not committed in the presence of the court, and for which a hearing must be held before the imposition of punishment.

Civil contempt is not limited to civil cases, nor is criminal contempt limited to criminal proceedings. A court may utilize civil contempt in a criminal proceeding to force compliance with a subpoena or to compel a witness to testify. Such contempt is civil in nature because the offender is not punished for past disobedience of the court. Instead, punishment is conditional and can be terminated by complying with the court order. For example, a witness sent to jail for refusal to testify must be released from custody as soon as the witness agrees to testify.

Civil contempt seeks to coerce "tomorrow's compliance," while criminal contempt penalizes "yesterday's defiance." Criminal contempt arises in a civil or criminal proceeding when the defendant defies the court, most often by threatening or insulting the judge. Both criminal and civil sanctions may be imposed as a result of the same conduct. For example, a witness sent to jail for failure to obey a court order to testify (i.e., civil contempt) must be released when the witness agrees to testify. The court, however, may subsequently impose additional confinement (i.e., criminal contempt) for the defiance inherent in the witness's past refusal to testify. Although confined twice, the witness was "punished" only once. The double jeopardy clause bars the imposition of two separate contempt penalties only if both are intended as punishment.[40]

Aside from distinguishing criminal and civil contempt, the important consideration in contempt proceedings is whether punishment may be imposed summarily or whether the defendant is entitled to certain procedural safeguards, such as the right to a hearing and trial by jury. The right to a hearing depends on whether the alleged contempt is classified as direct or indirect contempt. Direct contempt is committed in the presence of the court, for instance, the defendant insults the judge. In such situations the court may proceed upon its own knowledge of the facts

Civil contempt
the court imposes punishment to coerce compliance with an order of the court.

Criminal contempt
punishment is imposed to preserve the power and vindicate the dignity of the court.

Direct contempt
the court summarily punishes without conducting a hearing.

Indirect (constructive) contempt
not committed in the presence of the court; a hearing must be held before the imposition of punishment.

"without further proof, and without issue or trial in any form." In contrast, indirect contempt is not committed in the presence of the court, such as someone who makes a disparaging remark about the judge to the news media. In these cases the offender must be given notice of the charge and notice that a hearing will be held to show cause why the offender should not be adjudged in contempt of court. The accused must be given a reasonable opportunity to prepare for the hearing and to offer evidence in defense. The rules of evidence apply at the hearing, and the guilt of the offender must be established beyond a reasonable doubt.

In all criminal cases, including criminal contempt proceedings, the U.S. Constitution guarantees the right to trial by jury when the defendant faces potential imprisonment of more than six months.[41] If, however, the trial judge convicts and punishes summarily upon the occurrence of each contemptuous act, the aggregate sentences may exceed six months. For example, consider a courtroom scene in the movie *My Cousin Vinny.*

> Judge: *One more word and you are in contempt.*
> Counsel: *What?*
> Judge: *Thirty days for contempt.*
> Counsel: *Did you just hold me in contempt?*
> Judge: *That's another thirty days, and there'll be another thirty days for every word you utter.*
> Counsel: *You want me to be quiet?*
> Judge: *That's six words and another 180 days.*

In theory, this scenario could result in punishment far in excess of six months as long as the judge imposed punishment of less than six months at the time of each act of contempt. The judge, however, may not conduct a postverdict adjudication of contempt in a single proceeding and attempt to identify numerous "separate" instances of contempt. Even if each instance warrants a separate sentence of less than six months, the aggregate sentences may not total in excess of six months.[42] Thus if the judge postpones the contempt proceeding and seeks to impose a total of more than six months confinement, the offender is entitled to a jury trial on the issue of the contemptuous conduct.

JUDICIAL REVIEW

The Supreme Court has recognized that there are significant differences between the trial and appellate stages of a criminal proceeding. The purpose of the trial stage from the state's point of view is to convert a criminal defendant from a person presumed innocent to one found guilty beyond a reasonable doubt. By contrast, it is ordinarily the defendant, rather than the state, who initiates the appellate process, seeking not to fend off the efforts of the state's prosecutor but rather to overturn a finding of guilt made by a judge or a jury below. At trial, the Due Process clause requires the prosecution to prove, beyond a reasonable doubt, every fact necessary to constitute the charged crime. The beyond a reasonable doubt standard is not applicable on appellate review, instead "the relevant question is whether, after viewing the evidence in the light most favorable to the prosecution, *any* rational trier of fact could have found the essential elements of the crime beyond a reasonable doubt. [An appellate court thus] impinges upon jury discretion only to the extent necessary to guarantee the fundamental protection of due process of law."[43]

In recent years, criticism of the seemingly inexhaustible routes of appellate review, has increased, particularly in death penalty cases. The public sometimes perceives that justice is neither swift nor sure when death row inmates delay their execution for years while the courts consider yet another challenge to their conviction or sentence. The scope of appellate review is another instance in which the Crime Control and Due Process models of criminal justice present a stark contrast.

Proponents of the Crime Control Model emphasize the need for finality of court decisions and point out that, at least in theory, a defendant may have a single conviction reviewed ten separate times. The possible avenues of judicial review are illustrated in the chart in Exhibit 16–1.

Although many people might agree that ten instances of review are excessive, many would also agree that

> We would not send two astronauts to the moon without providing them with at least three or four backup systems. Should we send literally thousands of men to prison with even less reserves? . . . [W]ith knowledge of our fallibility and a realization of past errors, we can hardly insure our confidence by creating an irrevocable end to the guilt-determining process.[44]

Following conviction, the defendant has access to a number of forums in which the defendant may obtain various types of judicial review of a conviction. The remainder of this chapter addresses the forms of judicial review in the order in which they would normally arise.

1. Trials de novo may be granted following convictions for a misdemeanor in a lower court.

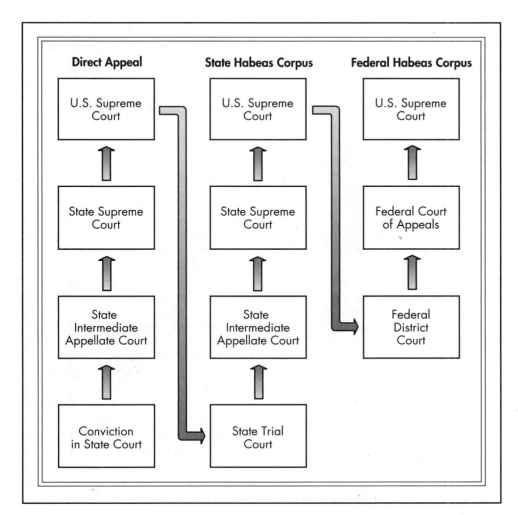

EXHIBIT 16–1
Appellate Review

2. Motions to set aside the verdict and motions for a new trial are addressed to the trial court.
3. Direct appeals are heard by appellate courts.
4. Collateral review, principally habeas corpus petitions, can be filed in both state and federal court.

Substantive differences distinguish each form of judicial review. Each also carries its own distinct procedural requirements relating to the filing of motions for postconviction remedies. The U.S. Constitution does not confer a right to appeal, but by statute or state constitution, every jurisdiction has established an appellate process.[45] Local statutes and rules have detailed provisions governing the length, content, and format of petitions for judicial review.

Trial de Novo

In most appeals, a higher court is asked to scrutinize the trial record for errors that would require reversal of the conviction. Many misdemeanor cases, however, are tried in lower courts, such as police courts or magistrate's courts, from which no record or transcript of the proceedings is available for review by a higher court. (These courts are sometimes referred to as courts-not-of-record.) Should the defendant object to a conviction in the lower court, many jurisdictions grant the defendant an absolute right to a trial de novo in a superior court (sometimes called a court-of-record).

A trial de novo is a new trial, not an appeal of the lower court's conviction. The defendant need not point to any errors occurring at the trial in the lower court because a trial de novo is often granted at the defendant's request, even though the defendant pled guilty in the lower court. Neither the defendant's plea nor the lower court's judgment are admissible evidence at the trial de novo, but the defendant's prior testimony is admissible at the trial in the higher court. In most situations, the Due Process clause prohibits prosecutorial vindictiveness in increasing the charges at the trial de novo. However, the punishment imposed at the trial de novo may be harsher than that imposed by the lower court.[46]

Motions to Set Aside the Verdict

Motion to set aside the verdict
directed to the trial court and based on the insufficiency of the evidence, error committed during trial, or newly discovered evidence.

Prior to appeal to an appellate court, the defense may ask the trial court to set aside the verdict. In some jurisdictions a **motion to set aside the verdict** is referred to as a judgment NOV (judgment not withstanding the verdict). This motion is similar to, but not identical with, a motion to strike the evidence or a motion for a directed verdict of acquittal (see Chapter Fifteen). A motion for a directed verdict of acquittal must be made prior to the return of a verdict, either after the prosecution has rested its case or at the conclusion of all the evidence. The only grounds for a directed verdict is that the evidence is insufficient as a matter of law to sustain a conviction. A motion to set aside the verdict, however, can be made after the verdict is returned, and the motion can be based on (1) the insufficiency of the evidence, (2) error committed during trial, or (3) newly discovered evidence.

If the trial court sets aside the verdict because of insufficiency of the evidence, the court must enter a judgment of acquittal. Double jeopardy bars a second trial when the prosecution had its day in court but failed to prove guilt beyond a reasonable doubt. However, if the court sets aside the verdict because of error committed during trial, the appropriate remedy is to grant a new trial. By asking the court to set aside the verdict because of error, the defendant requests a new trial and thus waives any double jeopardy claim. Motions to set aside the verdict because of insufficiency of the evidence or error occurring at trial require the trial judge to review the case, the evidence submitted, and any errors in dealing with the introduction of evidence. Regardless of what occurred at the actual trial, however, the defendant also may move to set aside the verdict and grant a new trial because of newly discovered evidence.

Motions for new trials because of newly discovered evidence are not looked upon with favor. The courts generally require that defense counsel prove the following issues:

1. The evidence was discovered after the trial concluded.
2. The evidence could not, by the exercise of diligence, have been discovered before the trial terminated.
3. The evidence is material and likely to produce a different verdict at the new trial.
4. The evidence is not merely cumulative, corroborative, or collateral.

These four requirements are not as harsh as they might seem because the defense can present newly discovered evidence to a state governor in a petition for a pardon, or to the parole board in an effort to obtain the defendant's immediate release from custody.

Preserving an Issue for Appeal

If the trial court refuses all motions to set aside a conviction, a defendant may appeal her case to a higher court. Although all jurisdictions have unique rules applicable to various stages of the appellate process, several common themes run throughout the review process.

The **contemporaneous objection rule** provides that no ruling of the trial court will be considered as a basis for reversal unless an objection was stated together with the ground therefor at the time of the ruling, except for good cause shown. This requirement is designed to preclude trial counsel from "sandbagging" the trial court by not calling possible errors to its attention. Objections must be raised at trial in order to afford opposing counsel an opportunity to respond to the objection and to allow the trial court to rule in the first instance as to the propriety of the objection. Appellate courts, however, are authorized to grant relief from this rule, and may conduct a full review of the conviction when necessary to attain the ends of justice. For example, Federal Rule of Criminal Procedure 52(b) provides that "plain errors or defects affecting substantial rights may be noticed although they were not brought to the attention of the court." (However, a more stringent standard for reversal is applied when the defendant fails to object at trial, and on appeal cites plain error by the trial court.)

Curative admissibility retroactively corrects a trial court's initial error in admitting evidence. For example, when a defendant unsuccessfully objects to evidence that she considers improper, and then on her own behalf introduces evidence of the same character, she thereby waives her objection and forfeits her right to contest the trial court's ruling on appeal. (Waiver is not made by the mere cross-examination of a witness or the introduction of rebuttal evidence.)

Proffers of evidence are required when the trial court sustains an objection and excludes evidence. At that point, counsel offering the evidence must ensure that the trial record reflects what the evidence would have been. The offer of proof may be in the form of a stipulation of testimony, or a witness may testify for the record in the absence of the jury. Failure to make a proffer of evidence deprives the appellate court of the information necessary to assess the propriety of the trial judge's ruling, thus the ruling will be upheld on appeal.

Harmless Error   Another universal rule which applies to postconviction review is the harmless error doctrine. A **harmless error** does not affect the defendant's right to a fair trial, nor does it call into question the accuracy of the finding of guilt. The defendant is entitled to a fair trial, not a perfect trial free from all minor or technical

Contemporaneous objection rule
provides that no ruling of the trial court will be reviewed on appeal unless an objection was made at the time of the ruling.

Curative admissibility
occurs when a party introduces the same type of evidence to which she previously objected.

Proffer of evidence
states for the trial record the evidence that would have been presented if the trial court had not sustained an objection to the evidence.

Harmless error
does not affect the defendant's right to a fair trial, nor does it call into question the accuracy of the finding of guilt.

defects. "A rule that would immunize a defendant from punishment when his trial contained *any error* sufficient to require a reversal would exact too high a price from law enforcement efforts because the complexity of courtroom procedure must inevitably lead to some errors, even when attorneys and judges are at their best."[47] If the reviewing court finds error in the record, reversal of the conviction is not warranted if the outcome of the trial would have remained the same in the absence of the error. A trial error that is not of constitutional dimension (for example, the trial judge erred in admitting some minor item of evidence) is harmless when it plainly appears from the facts and circumstances of the case that the error did not affect the verdict.

Constitutional error, however, is treated differently. The U.S. Supreme Court has recognized three distinct types of constitutional errors and four standards for determining harmless constitutional error.

1. Fourth Amendment errors are treated in a unique fashion. They may not be raised in a petition for federal habeas corpus review as long as the defendant was given an opportunity to litigate the Fourth Amendment issue in the state courts.[48] The rationale for this unique treatment of the Fourth Amendment lies in the amendment's exclusionary rule, which is "truth defeating"; thus Fourth Amendment errors rarely if ever affect the factual accuracy of the trial court's verdict.

2. "Structural defects in the constitution of the trial mechanism" (for example, violation of the right to counsel) require automatic reversal and are not subject to harmless error analysis.[49] The justification for this strict rule of automatic reversal is counsel's ability to raise issues that could alter the verdict if the defendant is accorded the assistance of counsel.

3. "Trial errors [occur] during the presentation of the case to the jury" and often involve questions of the admissibility of evidence. They are treated differently depending on whether they are raised on direct appeal or collateral review.

   a. On direct appeal, trial errors require reversal of the conviction unless the reviewing court finds such errors to be harmless "beyond a reasonable doubt."[50]

   b. On collateral review (e.g., habeas corpus petitions), trial errors require reversal of the conviction only if the defendant proves "actual prejudice" (i.e., the error had a "substantial and injurious effect or influence in determining the jury's verdict").[51]

Direct Appeal in the State Courts

Most jurisdictions have created a two-tiered appellate structure in which the convicted defendant has a right of appeal to an intermediate appellate court, but any further appeal to a higher court—usually the State Supreme Court—is discretionary. The distinction between a right of appeal and a discretionary review by an appellate court is important, because the U.S. Supreme Court has held that in felony cases, counsel must be provided to indigent persons exercising their right to appeal.[52] However, counsel need not be provided to indigent defendants seeking discretionary review.[53]

Notice or petition of appeal begins the appellate process by informing the parties, the trial judge, and the appellate court that the case is being appealed.

The appellate process begins with the defendant's filing of a **notice or petition of appeal.** Such notice informs the parties, the trial judge, and the appellate court that the case is being appealed. All jurisdictions require that the notice of appeal be filed within a specified period of time. For example, in the federal system the notice of appeal must be filed within ten days of the date of judgment.

At the time the notice of appeal is filed or at a subsequent specified date, the parties must designate portions of the trial record that will be sent to the appellate court. The appellate court bases its review of the case on the trial record, which commonly includes

1. Jury instructions either given or refused by the trial judge
2. Exhibits offered in evidence
3. Any orders entered by the trial court
4. Any opinion or memorandum decision rendered by the trial judge
5. Any pretrial discovery material requested
6. Portions of the trial transcript in which the judge ruled upon objections to the introduction of evidence.

Counsel also must alert the appellate court to the basis of appeal by filing a statement of issues that the appellate court is asked to resolve. Details of the issues are offered in counsels' written briefs, which summarize the factual background of the case and set forth relevant legal arguments. The appellate court, at its discretion, may hear oral arguments on the issues raised. The appellate court must then make an independent assessment of the legal rulings made by the trial judge, but the appellate court may not substitute its factual determinations for those of the trial court, as long as the evidence supports the trial court's findings. Many of the issues that arise in the course of a trial are to be resolved according to the broad discretion of the trial court. For example, trial judges have great leeway when scheduling recesses or granting continuances. On appeal, such rulings will not be disturbed in the absence of an abuse of discretion.

As noted earlier, the contemporaneous objection rule requires counsel to state the nature and basis of any objection. Many appellate courts also require opposing counsel to state the basis for opposing the objection, and require the trial judge to "state on the record" the grounds on which the court's ruling was based. The requirement that trial judges specify the grounds for their rulings sometimes conflicts with another appellate rule, which allows the reviewing court to sustain the trial court's ruling for reasons other than the reasons offered by the trial court. Thus "an appellate court may affirm the judgment of a trial court when it has reached the right result for the wrong reason." For example, in *Harris v. Commonwealth*,[54] the trial court upheld an arrest for attempted prostitution. The appellate court found this holding to be erroneous because there was no overt act that could constitute an attempted crime. However, the appellate court upheld the arrest as legal, because it could have been made for another offense—solicitation of a sexual act.

The appellate court may issue an opinion announcing and often explaining its decision. A **per curiam opinion** is not attributed to an individual judge but represents the court as a whole. Most opinions are signed by one judge, and when joined by a majority of the judges, this opinion constitutes the judgment of the court. Judges who agree with the decision but wish to address other considerations may write separate **concurring opinions**. Judges who disagree with the court's decision may write **dissenting opinions**. Most appellate court opinions are published and serve as the basis for decisions in future cases.

The Right to Appeal

There was no right to appeal in criminal cases at common law, and appellate review in the United States was rarely allowed until the latter part of the nineteenth century. At least in dicta, the U.S. Supreme Court has suggested that "there is no constitutional right to appeal," and "a State could, as far as the federal Constitution is concerned, subject its trial-court determinations to no review whatever. . . ."[55] A case challenging this dicta is unlikely to arise because by statute or state constitution, a right of appeal is now universal for all significant convictions.

Once a state provides for appellate review, the review process must not violate equal protection or due process rights. For example, *Douglas v. California*,[56] held that indigent defendants are constitutionally entitled to assistance of counsel on a first appeal granted as a matter of right. In a similar vein, *North Carolina v. Pearce*,[57]

Per curiam opinion
court decision not attributed to an individual judge, but represents the court as a whole.

Concurring opinions
written by a judge who agrees with the appellate court's disposition of the case but wishes to address other considerations.

Dissenting opinions
written by a judge who disagrees with the appellate court's decision.

stated that "it can hardly be doubted that it would be a flagrant violation of the Fourteenth Amendment for a state trial court to follow an announced practice of imposing a heavier sentence upon every reconvicted defendant for the explicit purpose of punishing the defendant for his having succeeded in getting his original conviction set aside."

Whatever the nature and scope of a right to appellate review, the right can be forfeited or waived. *Ortega-Rodriguez v. United States,*[58] recognized the fugitive dismissal rule, which denies a convicted defendant the right to appeal his conviction while he is a fugitive from justice. Questions of waiver have arisen when death row inmates request a prompt execution and order their attorneys not to appeal. On many such occasions, a family member or organization opposed to the death penalty intervenes as a friend of the court and attempts to appeal the defendant's scheduled execution. *State v. Robbins,*[59] held that a defendant sentenced to death can choose not to appeal the sentence as long as he has the capacity to understand the difference between life and death and to knowingly and voluntarily waive his right to appeal. Intervening third parties cannot override the defendant's choice to waive appeal, however, statutes often require the appellate court to review all death penalty cases for prejudicial error, regardless of the defendant's refusal to pursue an appeal.

In contrast to defendants who waive their right to appeal, other defendants raise frivolous issues that waste the appellate court's time. The U.S. Supreme Court recently observed that "no one has a right to a wholly frivolous appeal, against which the judicial system's first line of defense is its lawyers. Being officers of the court, members of the bar are bound 'not to clog the courts with frivolous motions or appeals.'"[60] In such cases defense counsel may be torn between an ethical duty as an officer of the court (which requires her not to present frivolous arguments) and counsel's duty to further her client's interests (which might not permit counsel to characterize her client's claims as frivolous). In such situations, the Supreme Court suggested that the attorney should: (1) advise the court and request permission to withdraw; (2) submit a brief referring to anything in the record that might arguably support the appeal; (3) furnish a copy of the brief to the defendant in time to allow him to raise any points that he chooses; and (4) request the court to conduct a full examination and decide whether the case is wholly frivolous.[61]

Prosecution Appeals

Although the double jeopardy clause precludes the prosecution's appeal of an acquittal, many jurisdictions authorize limited appeals by the prosecution of pretrial suppression orders or post-verdict dismissals based on some ground unrelated to factual innocence. For example, in the federal system the government may appeal the dismissal of an indictment or a decision "suppressing or excluding evidence . . . not made after the defendant has been put in jeopardy." The proper scope of the prosecution's appeal must be tested against the double jeopardy clause and against the precise wording of the enabling statute. Double jeopardy is also inapplicable where the defendant moves for a mistrial or otherwise "seeks to have the trial terminated without any submission to either judge or jury as to his guilt or innocence."[62]

Habeas Corpus

Habeas corpus petition
not a continuation of the criminal process, but a civil suit brought to challenge the legality of the restraint under which a person is held.

A defendant who fails on direct appeal may file a collateral attack on the conviction. The most common form of collateral attack is a **habeas corpus petition.** Habeas corpus is a Latin term meaning "you have the body." A habeas corpus action is a collateral attack because it is not a continuation of the criminal process, but rather a civil suit brought to challenge the legality of the restraint under which a person is held. The petitioner in this civil suit, having lost the presumption of innocence upon conviction, has the burden to prove by a preponderance of evidence that his confinement is illegal. The respondent in a habeas corpus action is the prisoner's custodian—the warden or other prison official.

At common law, people who believed that their detention was illegal could use the writ of habeas corpus to gain freedom. The writ of habeas corpus has been called "the most celebrated writ in the English law," and the U.S. Supreme Court has paid homage to this "Great Writ of Liberty."

FAY v. NOIA
Supreme Court of the United States, 1963
372 U.S. 391, 83 S.Ct. 822

JUSTICE BRENNAN delivered the opinion of the Court:

We do well to bear in mind the extraordinary prestige of the Great Writ . . . in Anglo-American jurisprudence. Received into our own law in the colonial period, given explicit recognition in the Federal Constitution, Art. I, section 9, cl. 2, incorporated in the first grant of federal court jurisdiction, habeas corpus was early confirmed by Chief Justice Marshall to be a "great constitutional privilege."

Although in form the Great Writ is simply a mode of procedure, its history is inextricably intertwined with the growth of fundamental rights of personal liberty. For its function has been to provide a prompt and efficacious remedy for whatever society deems to be intolerable restraints. Its root principle is that in a civilized society, government must always be accountable to the judiciary for a man's imprisonment: if the imprisonment cannot be shown to conform with fundamental requirements of law, the individual is entitled to his immediate release. Thus, there is nothing novel in the fact that to-day habeas corpus in the federal courts provides a mode for the redress of denials of due process of law. Vindication of due process is precisely its historic office.

The decision in *Fay v. Noia* was rendered by the Warren Court, whose critics maintained that federal habeas review of state court convictions had become excessive because of the Court's attempts to "constitutionalize" too many aspects of criminal procedure. The Warren Court's approach to federal habeas corpus was partially premised on a belief that the state courts could not be trusted to protect the constitutional rights of criminal defendants. For example, in the landmark case of *Gideon v. Wainwright*,[63] Justice Harlan expressed dissatisfaction with many state courts' discharge of their "front-line responsibility for the enforcement of constitutional rights." The Burger and Rehnquist Courts, however, embraced the concept of a "new federalism" by resurrecting faith in the state courts as protectors of individual freedom.

In the Antiterrorism and Effective Death Penalty Act of 1996 (AEDPA), Congress expressed its views on the Court's fluctuations between expansive and narrow review of state court decisions. For the most part, the AEDPA imposes legislative restraints on federal habeas corpus review. For example, however great the historic scope and focus of the writ, merely filing a habeas corpus petition does not ensure that a federal court will review the merits of the petitioner's claim. If the habeas corpus petition is patently frivolous, or if the court can determine the merits of the allegations by reference to records of previous state or federal judicial proceedings, the AEDPA mandates that the petition be denied without a full evidentiary hearing. If a federal district court grants a hearing on the habeas petition, both the petitioner and the government must be given the opportunity to present evidence. Upon denial of the petition, the petitioner will be remanded to custody. If the court grants the petition, the petitioner shall be discharged from custody, but the court may suspend execution of its order to allow the government to appeal or to institute a new trial within a specified period of time.

Most states have habeas corpus-like proceedings that closely follow the federal habeas corpus proceedings discussed in the remainder of this section (see Exhibit 16–2). Federal habeas corpus may be used to challenge state court convictions obtained in violation of the defendant's federal constitutional rights. However, before a state prisoner can seek habeas corpus review in a federal court, the prisoner must meet certain requirements.

EXHIBIT 16–2
Habeas Corpus Petition

PETITION FOR WRIT OF HABEAS CORPUS
Instructions—Read Carefully

In order for this petition to receive consideration by the Court, it must be legibly handwritten or typewritten, signed by the petitioner and verified before a notary or other officer authorized to administer oaths. It must set forth in concise form the answers to each applicable question. If necessary, petitioner may finish his answer to a particular question on an additional page. Petitioner must make it clear to which question any such continued answer refers. The petitioner may also submit exhibits.

Since every petition for habeas corpus must be sworn to under oath, any false statement of a material fact therein may serve as the basis of prosecution and conviction for perjury. Petitioners should, therefore, exercise care to assure that all answers are true and correct.

When the petition is completed, the original and two copies (total of three) should be mailed to the clerk of the court. The petitioner shall keep one copy.

Place of detention: _____

Criminal Trial

1. Name and location of court which imposed the sentence from which you seek relief:

2. The offense or offenses for which sentence was imposed (include indictment number or numbers if known):

3. The date upon which sentence was imposed and the terms of the sentence:

4. Check which plea you made and whether trial by jury:
   Plea of guilty: _____ ;
   Plea of not guilty: _____ ;
   Trial by jury: _____ ;
   Trial by judge without jury: _____ .

5. The name and address of each attorney, if any, who represented you at your criminal trial:

6. Did you appeal the conviction?

7. If you answered "yes" to 6, state:
   The result and the date in your appeal or petition for certiorari:
   Citations of the appellate court opinions or orders:

8. List the name and address of each attorney, if any, who represented you on your appeal:

EXHIBIT 16–2
Habeas Corpus Petition—Continued

Habeas Corpus

9. Before this petition, did you file with respect to this conviction any other petition for habeas corpus in either a state or federal court?

10. If you answered "yes" to 9, list with respect to each petition:
The name and location of the court in which each was filed:
The disposition and the date:
The name and address of each attorney, if any, who who represented you on your habeas corpus:

11. Did you appeal from the disposition of your petition for habeas corpus?

12. If you answered "yes" to 11, state:
The result and the date of each petition:
Citations of court opinions or orders on your habeas corpus petition:
The name and address of each attorney, if any, who represented you on your habeas corpus:

Other Petitions, Motions or Applications

13. List all other petitions, motions or applications filed with any court following a final order of conviction and not set out in A or B. Include the nature of the motion, the name and location of the court, the result, the date, and citations to opinions or orders. Give the name and address of each attorney, if any, who represented you.

Present Position

14. State the grounds which make your detention unlawful, including the facts on which you intend to rely:

15. List each ground set forth in 14, which has been presented in any other proceeding:

List the proceedings in which each ground was raised:

16. If any ground set forth in 14 has not been presented to a court, list each ground and the reason why it was not:

Signature of Petitioner
Address of Petitioner

The petitioner being first duly sworn, says:
1. He signed the foregoing petition;
2. The facts stated in the petition are true to the best of his information and belief.

Signature of Petitioner

The petition will not be filed without payment of court costs unless the petitioner is entitled to proceed in forma pauperis and has executed the affidavit in forma pauperis.

The petitioner who proceeds in forma pauperis shall be furnished, without cost, certified copies of the arrest warrants, indictment, and order of his conviction at his criminal trial in order to comply with the instructions of this petition.

1. *One-year limitation:* In order to promote speedy punishment and the finality of criminal justice proceedings, the Antiterrorism and Effective Death Penalty Act of 1996 created a rigid one-year limitation for filing a petition for habeas corpus relief.

2. *Custody:* The writ of habeas corpus is available only to a person who is in custody in violation of the Constitution. A person is in custody when presently serving sentence for the conviction challenged by the writ or following release from confinement but subject to the control of the parole board, probation officer, or the court that imposed a suspended sentence. The writ may not be used to attack a sentence that has been fully served, or to attack a conviction that merely imposed a fine or collateral civil disability not resulting in incarceration.

As a remedy of last resort, a convicted person no longer subject to confinement may file the common law writ of *coram nobis* to challenge his prior conviction. For example, in *Korematsu v. United States,*[64] the Supreme Court upheld the conviction of an American citizen of Japanese ancestry for being in a location designated as off limits to all persons of Japanese ancestry. Forty years later, *Korematsu v. United States,*[65] vacated the conviction on grounds that the government had misled the courts as to the military necessity of wartime relocation and internment of civilians in 1944.

3. *Constitutional violations:* A federal habeas corpus petition can be filed only on the ground that the petitioner is in custody in violation of the Constitution or laws of the United States. "Federal habeas corpus relief does not lie for errors of state law."[66]

4. *Exhaustion of remedies:* "Exhaustion generally requires that before a federal court will review a constitutional claim in habeas, the claim must first be fairly presented to the state court system."[67] The prisoner must use all means available in the state system to correct the alleged error because the federal courts will not permit a state prisoner to bypass the state courts and initiate the first review of the case in the federal courts.

If the petitioner fails to exhaust his state remedies, the federal court may dismiss the petition until such time as the petitioner has exhausted the available state remedies. The only exceptions to the exhaustion of remedies requirement are when there is an absence of available state remedies or special circumstances render such remedies ineffective to protect the rights of the petitioner. The exhaustion of state remedies doctrine is based on comity and is not a jurisdictional requirement, thus the government may waive the requirement.[68]

5. *Abuse of the writ by successive petitions:* The exhaustion requirement does not preclude habeas review; it merely delays such review. Following dismissal of the habeas petition, the petitioner must return to state court to present the unexhausted claims before resubmitting the claims to a federal court. The Antiterrorism and Effective Death Penalty Act of 1996 provides that when a petitioner resubmits a second or successive habeas corpus petition, the petitioner must obtain an order from the court of appeals authorizing the district court to consider the second petition. A motion in the court of appeals for an order authorizing the district court to consider a second or successive application shall be determined by a three-judge panel of the court of appeals.

6. *Procedural default:* "The doctrine of exhaustion and the procedural default rule are two different things. Exhaustion generally requires that before a federal court will review a constitutional claim in habeas, the claim must first be fairly presented to the state court system. . . . The procedural default rule requires that if a state court rejects a habeas petitioner's federal constitutional

challenge on the adequate and independent state ground that the claim is defaulted under a state procedural rule, a federal habeas court is ordinarily precluded from reviewing that claim unless the petitioner can show cause for the default and prejudice resulting from it."[69]

The most common form of procedural default is the defendant's failure to present a federal constitutional claim to the trial court and thus preserve the issue for appellate review. The consequence of a procedural default is that the petitioner may be barred from judicial review of the forfeited claim in both state and federal courts. Unlike the exhaustion doctrine, which may merely postpone federal habeas review, if there is a procedural bar there is no hearing on the constitutional challenge in any state or federal court.

Claims of Innocence

A common misconception is that federal courts, and ultimately the U.S. Supreme Court, sit as courts of last resort to correct any and all injustice done to American citizens. Justice Scalia, a frequent critic of expansive federal habeas review, recently explained that:

> It would be marvelously inspiring to be able to boast that we have a criminal-justice system in which a claim of "actual innocence" will always be heard, no matter how late it is brought forward, and no matter how much the failure to bring it forward at the proper time is the defendant's own fault. But of course we do not have such a system, and no society unwilling to devote unlimited resources to repetitive criminal litigation ever could.[70]

In *Herrera v. Collins*,[71] the Court refused to recognize that a claim of factual innocence constitutes an independent constitutional issue subject to review on federal habeas corpus. The Court suggested that executive clemency has provided the "fail safe" in our criminal justice system and is the traditional remedy for claims of innocence based on newly discovered evidence of innocence. "Over the past century clemency has been exercised frequently in capital cases in which demonstrations of actual innocence have been made."

Nonjudicial Review of Convictions

As a supplement to judicial review, all jurisdictions grant a convicted defendant an opportunity to appeal to executive authority for a **pardon or grant of clemency**. For example, Article II, Section 2, Clause 1 of the U.S. Constitution gives the president "Power to grant Reprieves and Pardons for Offenses against the United States, except in Cases of Impeachment." President Gerald Ford pardoned, prior to trial, former President Richard Nixon for his role in the Watergate scandal. Former President Nixon was given a "full pardon," but the president has the power to "forgive the convicted person in part or entirely, to reduce a penalty in terms of a specified number of years, or to alter it with conditions which are in themselves constitutionally unobjectionable."[72]

In all states the governor is given broad power to pardon and commute sentences of persons convicted of violating state criminal laws. Administrative procedures for considering pardons or clemency vary greatly among the fifty states.

Pardon or grant of clemency forgiveness of a conviction granted by an official of the executive branch—normally, the governor at the state level and the president at the federal level.

SUMMARY

A criminal trial concludes with counsel's closing arguments and the judge's instructions on the applicable law. Mandatory instructions must be given in each case (e.g., defining the elements of the crime), and the judge must consider any instruction requested by counsel.

If a jury returns a verdict of guilty, the jury may be polled in open court to assure that the verdict represents the decision of all jurors. If a jury is unable to agree on a verdict, a mistrial will be declared and the defendant may be retried. Jurors may not impeach their own verdict, but verdicts can be set aside if some outside source has improperly influenced the jury.

In most jurisdictions, sentence is imposed by the judge, but some jurisdictions permit the jury to determine the sentence. Particularly in capital cases, the sentencing body must consider both aggravating and mitigating circumstances that may affect the sentence. Special problems arise when a defendant's initial conviction is overturned on appeal, but then the defendant subsequently is retried and convicted of the same offense. The Due Process clause prohibits increased punishment that is intended to penalize a defendant for appealing an original conviction.

Judicial review of a conviction takes many forms, but all reviewing courts insist that no ruling of the trial court will be considered as a basis for reversal unless an objection to the ruling was made at the time of the ruling. All reviewing courts also apply some form of the harmless error rule: an error is harmless if it did not affect the fairness of the trial, nor did it undermine confidence in the accuracy of the verdict.

Motions to set aside the verdict are addressed to the trial court. The motion can be based on insufficiency of the evidence, error committed during trial, or newly discovered evidence. Direct appeal of the conviction lies to an intermediate appellate court, and/or the state supreme court. Habeas corpus petitions can be filed in state or federal court, but federal habeas corpus must be based on a U.S. constitutional law rather than state law. All jurisdictions authorize a convicted person to petition the governor for a pardon or grant of clemency.

DISCUSSION QUESTIONS _____

1. Is jury nullification of law merely a form of juror misconduct that the judiciary is powerless to control? Is the independent nature of jury deliberations a right of the accused or a limitation on the potential abuse of judicial power? Is such a limitation necessary in light of the many avenues of appellate review available to a convicted defendant?

2. Should defense counsel be permitted to question jurors about their deliberations and how they arrived at their verdict?

3. Suppose a majority of the states authorize castration as the appropriate punishment for male "sexual predators" who have been convicted of three violent sexual assaults. Can the U.S. Supreme Court find such punishment to be cruel and unusual?

4. Are the conditions of probation imposed by a court subject to any limitations? May the judge specify that the defendant must attend religious services once a week?

5. Why does the justice system permit federal court review of a conviction obtained in a state court? Can't the state courts be trusted to correctly apply the U.S. Constitution?

PRACTICE EXERCISES _____

1. Who fixes the sentence in your state, judge or jury? Must they follow sentencing guidelines when determining punishment?

2. What aggravating circumstances must exist before capital punishment can be imposed in your state?

3. What information does your jurisdiction include in presentence reports? Does your state require or permit victim impact statements?

4. What avenues of judicial review are available in your state?

5. Does your state permit appeals by the prosecution? If so, what issues may the prosecutor appeal?

WEB SITE

National Criminal Justice Reference Service
www.ncjrs.org

KEY TERMS

Closing arguments
Instructions
Jury nullification
Allen charge
Inconsistent verdicts
Polling the jury
Presentence reports
Allocution
Probation

Trial de novo
Civil contempt
Criminal contempt
Direct contempt
Indirect (constructive) contempt
Motion to set aside the verdict
Contemporaneous objection rule
Curative admissibility

Proffer of evidence
Harmless error
Notice or petition of appeal
Per curiam opinion
Concurring opinions
Dissenting opinions
Habeas corpus petitions
Pardon or grant of clemency

NOTES

1. *Griffin v. California,* 380 U.S. 609, 85 S.Ct. 1229 (1965).
2. *Hines v. Commonwealth,* 217 Va. 905, 234 S.E.2d 262 (1977).
3. See *United States v. Robinson,* 485 U.S. 25, 108 S.Ct. 864 (1988).
4. *United States v. Young,* 470 U.S. 1, 105 S.Ct. 1038 (1985).
5. *Murphy v. Holland,* 776 F. 2d 470 (4th Cir. 1985).
6. See *James v. Kentucky,* 466 U.S. 341, 104 S.Ct. 1830 (1984).
7. See *Lakeside v. Oregon,* 435 U.S. 333, 98 S.Ct. 1091 (1978).
8. *Mathews v. United States,* 487 U.S. 1240, 108 S.Ct. 2913 (1988).
9. *Allen v. United States,* 164 U.S. 492, 17 S.Ct. 154 (1896).
10. *Lowenfield v. Phelps,* 484 U.S. 231, 108 S.Ct. 546 (1988).
11. *Williams v. Commonwealth,* 153 Va. 987, 151 S.E. 151 (1930).
12. *United States v. Alexander,* 748 F. 2d 185 (4th Cir. 1984).
13. *United States v. Blankenship,* 707 F. 2d 807 (4th Cir. 1983).
14. *United States v. Powell,* 469 U.S. 57, 105 S.Ct. 471 (1984).
15. *Gardner v. Commonwealth,* 3 Va. App. 418, 350 S.E.2d 229 (1986).
16. *Tanner v. United States,* 483 U.S. 107, 107 S.Ct. 2739 (1987).
17. *Walton v. Arizona,* 497 U.S. 639, 110 S.Ct. 3047 (1990).
18. *Furman v. Georgia,* 408 U.S. 238, 92 S.Ct. 2726 (1972).
19. *Gregg v. Georgia,* 428 U.S. 153, 96 S.Ct. 2909 (1976).
20. *McCleskey v. Kemp,* 481 U.S. 279, 107 S.Ct. 1756 (1987) held that such statistical studies did not establish racial discrimination in violation of the Eighth or Fourteenth Amendments.
21. *Zant v. Stephens,* 462 U.S. 862, 103 S.Ct. 2733 (1983).
22. *Maynard v. Cartwright,* 486 U.S. 356, 108 S.Ct. 1853 (1988).
23. The law is unclear as to the special status of juvenile offenders sentenced to death. *Thompson v. Oklahoma,* 487 U.S. 815, 108 S.Ct. 2687 (1988).
24. *Skipper v. South Carolina,* 476 U.S. 1, 106 S.Ct. 1669 (1986).
25. *California v. Brown,* 479 U.S. 538, 107 S.Ct. 837 (1987).
26. *Payne v. Tennessee,* 501 U.S. 1277, 112 S.Ct. 28 (1991).
27. *Caldwell v. Mississippi,* 472 U.S. 320, 105 S.Ct. 2633 (1985).
28. *United States v. Hicks,* 948 F. 2d 877 (4th Cir. 1991).
29. See *Green v. United States,* 365 U.S. 301, 81 S.Ct. 653 (1961).
30. *Griffin v. Coughlin,* 673 N.E.2d 98 (N.Y. 1996).
31. *Kerr v. Farrey,* 95 F.3d 472 (7th Cir. 1996).
32. *Moody v. Daggett,* 429 U.S. 78, 97 S.Ct. 274 (1976).
33. *Gagnon v. Scarpelli,* 411 U.S. 778, 93 S.Ct. 1756 (1973). See also *Board of Pardons v. Allen,* 482 U.S. 369, 107 S.Ct. 2415 (1987).
34. The Supreme Court has also recognized that due process prohibits prosecutorial vindictiveness in increasing the charges on retrial. *Blackledge v. Perry,* 417 U.S. 21, 94 S.Ct. 2098 (1974).

35. *North Carolina v. Pierce*, 395 U.S. 711, 89 S.Ct. 2072 (1969).
36. *Texas v. McCullough*, 475 U.S. 134, 106 S.Ct. 976 (1986).
37. *Chaffin v. Stynchcombe*, 412 U.S. 17, 93 S.Ct. 1977 (1973).
38. *Colten v. Kentucky*, 407 U.S. 104, 92 S.Ct. 1953 (1972).
39. *United States v. Goodwin*, 457 U.S. 368, 102 S.Ct. 2485 (1982).
40. *United States v. Halper*, 490 U.S. 435, 109 S.Ct. 1892 (1989).
41. *Taylor v. Hayes*, 418 U.S. 488, 94 S.Ct. 2697 (1974).
42. *Codispoti v. Pennsylvania*, 418 U.S. 506, 94 S.Ct. 2687 (1974).
43. *Jackson v. Virginia*, 443 U.S. 307, 99 S.Ct. 2781 (1979).
44. Lay, Modern Administrative Proposals for Federal Habeas, 21 DePaul Law Review 701, 709-10 (1972).
45. *McKane v. Durston*, 153 U.S. 684, 14 S.Ct. 913 (1894).
46. *Colten v. Kentucky*, 407 U.S. 104, 92 S.Ct. 1953 (1972).
47. *United States v. Akpi*, 26 F. 3d 24 (4th Cir. 1994).
48. *Stone v. Powell*, 428 U.S. 465, 96 S.Ct. 3037 (1976). Compare *Withrow v. WQilliams*, 507 U.S. 608, 113 S.Ct. 1745 (1993). (*Miranda* violations are subject to collateral review.)1
49. See *Sullivan v. Louisiana*, 508 U.S. 275, 113 S.Ct. 2078 (1993). (Constitutionally inadequate definitions of "reasonable doubt" can never be harmless error.)
50. *Chapman v. California*, 386 U.S. 18, 87 S.Ct. 824 (1967).
51. *Brecht v. Abrahamson*, 507 U.S. 619, 113 S.Ct. 1710 (1993).
52. *Douglas v. California*, 372 U.S. 353, 83 S.Ct. 814 (1963).
53. *Ross v. Moffitt*, 417 U.S. 600, 94 S.Ct. 2437 (1974).
54. *Harris v. Commonwealth*, 533 S.E.2d 18 (Va. 2000).
55. *Martinez v. Court of Appeal*, 528 U.S. 152, 120 S.Ct. 684 (2000).
56. *Douglas v. California*, 372 U.S. 353, 83 S.Ct. 814 (1963).
57. *North Carolina v. Pearce*, 395 U.S. 711, 89 S.Ct. 2072 (1969).
58. *Ortega-Rodriguez v. United States*, 507 U.S. 234, 113 S.Ct. 1199 (1993).
59. *State v. Robbins*, 5 S.W.3d 51 (Alaska 1999).
60. *Smith v. Robbins*, 528 U.S. 259, 120 S.Ct. 746 (2000).
61. *Anders v. California*, 386 U.S. 738, 87 S.Ct. 1396 (1967).
62. *United States v. Scott*, 437 U.S. 82, 98 S.Ct. 2187 (1978).
63. *Gideon v. Wainwright*, 372 U.S. 335, 83 S.Ct. 792 (1963).
64. *Korematsu v. United States*, 323 U.S. 214, 65 S.Ct. 193 (1944).
65. *Korematsu v. United States*, 584 F.Supp. 1406 (N.D.Cal. 1984).
66. *Lewis v. Jeffers*, 497 U.S. 764, 110 S.Ct. 3092 (1990).
67. *Justus v. Murray*, 897 F.2d 709 (4th Cir. 1990).
68. *Strickland v. Washington*, 466 U.S. 668, 104 S.Ct. 2052 (1984).
69. *Justus v. Murray*, 897 F.2d 709 (4th Cir. 1990).
70. *Bousley v. United States*, 523 U.S. 614, 118 S.Ct. 1604 (1998).
71. *Herrera v. Collins*, 506 U.S. 390, 113 S.Ct. 853 (1993).
72. *Schick v. Reed*, 419 U.S. 256, 95 S.Ct. 379 (1974).

GLOSSARY

A

Abandonment discontinuance of a plan to commit a crime; sometimes recognized as a valid defense to charges of attempting to commit a crime.

Accessory after the fact one who impedes the apprehension, trial, or punishment of a felon.

Accessory before the fact one who is not present when the crime is committed, but who previously solicited, counseled, or advised another on how to commit the crime.

Accommodation defense the defendant intended to provide the illegal drug to others without making a profit from the sale of drugs.

Actual possession physical contact with or control over the drug, and knowledge that the substance is an illegal drug.

Actus res an act by the defendant, which results in a prohibited harm to society.

Adequate provocation circumstances that "would naturally tend to arouse the passion of an ordinarily reasonable person."

Adjudicatory stage formal judicial proceedings such as bail hearings, pretrial hearings, and trial itself.

Admissibility of a confession the voluntariness of the statement, determined by the trial judge; the jury determines the weight to be given a confession.

Adversary judicial proceedings signal that the government has commitmed itself to prosecution of the defendant and that the adverse positions of government and defendant have solidified.

Affirmative defense the defendant admits committing the acts charged, but seeks to justify or excuse the defendant's conduct by establishing additional facts.

Aider and abettor (principal in the second degree) person who assists the perpetrator in the commission of the crime while being actually or constructively present at the scene of the crime.

Alford **plea** the defendant pleads guilty but persists in proclaiming innocence.

Alibi a claim that the defendant was not in a position to commit the crime charged.

Allen **charge** may be given when a jury informs the judge that they are unable to agree on a verdict; also known as the "hung jury" charge.

Allocution the defendant's right to speak in her or his own behalf after the factfinder determines guilt but before the judge pronounces sentence.

Alter-ego theory a defendant acts to protect a person who has a lawful right of self-defense.

Arraignment identifies the defendant as the person named in the indictment or information, informs the defendant of the charges, and asks the defendant to plead to the charges.

Arrest in a suspect's dwelling taking a suspect into custody requires either an arrest warrant or exigent circumstances that permit a warrantless entry.

Arson malicious burning of another's dwelling house.

Asportation any physical movement of property taken from another's possession.

Assault may be either an attempted battery form of assault which requires that the defendant specifically intend to, and come close to, touching another; or an offer type of assault which places another in fear of an imminent battery.

Attempted battery from assault act in which the defendant specifically intends to, and comes close to, touching another.

Attempted crime the defendant intends to commit a specific offense and performs an act that constitutes a substantial step toward completing that offense.

B

Bail money deposited or bond posted as a condition of an accused's pretrial release from custody.

Bail reform legislation pretrial release is determined by considering the nature and circumstances of the offense, the weight of the evidence, the defendant's financial ability to pay bail, and the character of the defendant.

Bail revocation hearing a hearing to determine if any changes should be made to the conditions of the accused's pretrial release.

Battery the unlawful application of force to the person of another.

Bills of attainder legislative act convicting an individual of a crime.

Bill of particulars provides more specific information than what is set out in an indictment.

Blockburger test for double jeopardy determines whether a defendant's conduct constitutes one crime or separate crimes for purposes of punishment; multiple punishment is permitted if each offense requires proof of an element which the other does not.

Bond forfeiture proceeding a proceeding to determine whether the surety's bond should be forfeited to the court because the accused violated a condition of pretrial release.

Booking process the primarily clerical function of recording information relating to the arrestee's identity.

Booking question exception police may ask questions that secure the "biographical data necessary to complete booking or pretrial services."

Breach of the peace conduct that disturbs the tranquility or order of the community.

Breaking and entering setting aside some portion of the structure that would prevent intrusion.

Burden of proof the task of presenting evidence to a factfinder, normally a jury, who then weighs the cumulative evidence and decides whether it "constitutes the crime charged."

Burglary breaking and entering of another's dwelling at night with intent to commit a felony once inside.

C

Capital murder killing characterized by the existence of a statutorily defined aggravating circumstance in addition to the other requirements for murder.

Case-in-chief defense challenges the prosecution's version of the facts, but does not introduce an independent legal claim into the case.

Challenge for cause may be made against any prospective juror who does not stand impartial in the case.

Charging in the alternative the indictment contains separate counts charging alternative ways of committing a single offense.

Civil contempt of court the court imposes punishment to coerce compliance with an order of the court.

Clear and convincing evidence is a higher standard than preponderance but lower than beyond a reasonable doubt.

Closing arguments counsels' summations of the evidence and how that evidence points toward conviction or acquittal.

Collateral estoppel bars the prosecution from relitigating an issue of fact previously resolved in the defendant's favor at a prior trial.

Collateral stages proceedings that do not directly relate to the defendant's ultimate guilt or innocence in which the exclusionary rule is normally inapplicable.

Commencement of judicial proceedings triggers the Sixth Amendment right to counsel during interrogation.

Common law judge-made law defining crimes and establishing the rules of criminal responsibility according to custom and tradition.

Common law rape sexual intercourse with a woman other than the defendant's wife by force and without the victim's consent.

Common nuisance conduct that disturbs the tranquility or order of the community.

Communication of a threat words conveying the intent to inflict harm; unlike the crime of assault, it does not require a menacing gesture.

Competency to stand trial the defendant must be rational, possess the ability to testify coherently, and be able to meaningfully discuss the case with defense counsel.

Competency to testify the witness is able to observe the events about which the testimony is offered, remember such events, understand questions propounded and make intelligent answers, and possess a sense of moral responsibility to tell the truth.

Complaint a sworn statement of facts establishing probable cause that a person has committed a crime.

Compounding a felony accepting a benefit in return for concealing a known crime.

Concurring opinion written by a judge who agrees with the appellate court's disposition of the case but wishes to address other considerations.

Conflict of interests occurs when representation of one client jeopardizes the adequate representation of another; may prevent a single attorney from representing multiple clients.

Consensual search the defendant's permission to search must be freely and voluntarily given.

Conspiracy an agreement by two or more persons to commit an unlawful act. (An overt act in furtherance of a conspiracy is required in many jurisdictions.)

Constructive possession of an illegal drug occurs when a controlled substance is in a place accessible to the defendant and subject to the defendant's control.

Contemporaneous objection rule provides that no ruling of the trial court will be reviewed on appeal unless an objection was made at the time of the ruling.

Conversion use of another's property in a way that is inconsistent with the other's right of possession.

Corpus delicti the body of the crime—the fact of its having been committed.

Corroboration requirement the prosecution must produce independent evidence that establishes the trustworthiness of a confession and supports the essential facts admitted in a confession.

Crime Control Model focuses on determining factual guilt or innocence; favors only those procedures that help ensure the accuracy of the fact-finding process.

Criminal contempt of court punishment is imposed to preserve the power and vindicate the dignity of the court.

Criminal homicide taking another's life in a manner proscribed by law; a killing in the absence of justification or excuse.

Curative admissibility occurs when a party introduces the same type of evidence to which she previously objected.

Curtilage the area within which lie structures closely associated with a dwelling.

Custodial interrogation "questioning initiated by law enforcement officers after a person has been taken into custody or otherwise deprived of his freedom of action in any significant way."

Custody "a formal arrest or restraint on freedom of movement associated with a formal arrest."

Custody (of property) physical control of personal property, but use of the property is limited by another's lawful possession of the property.

D

DUI (driving under the influence); DWI (driving while intoxicated) the illegal operation of a motor vehicle while under the influence of alcohol or other drugs.

Defense of others the act of protecting another from harm, which may excuse or justify the defendant's use of force.

Deliberate bodily movement an affirmative action consciously taken by the defendant, distinguished from an unconscious or reflective act.

Derivative evidence evidentiary obtained by the police as the result of an illegal arrest.

Detainer a request that a penal institution continue to hold a prisoner for the requesting agency or notify the agency when release of the prisoner is imminent.

Diminished capacity test for insanity recognizes that defendants may lack "substantial" but not total mental capacity.

Direct contempt the court summarily punishes without conducting a hearing.

Directed verdict of acquittal a device used to remove the case from the jury's consideration. The trial judge will enter an acquittal whenever a rational jury must conclude that the prosecution failed to prove guilt beyond a reasonable doubt.

Disorderly conduct; breach of peace; common nuisance acts that disturb the tranquility or order of the community.

Disposition plea agreement sets a specific sentence, which is binding if accepted by the trial judge.

Dissenting opinion written by a judge who disagrees with the appellate court's decision.

Dominion (of property) carrying away from another's possession into the defendant's control.

Double jeopardy prohibits the retrial of a defendant who has been convicted or acquitted of the same offense at a previous trial; also protects against multiple punishments for the same offense.

Due Process Model recognizes that determination of factual guilt may be subordinated to other goals, such as controlling and correcting misconduct by government officials.

Duplicity more than one offense is alleged in a single count of an indictment.

Duress an unlawful threat of imminent death or serious bodily injury, which induces a person to commit a crime; may be used as a defense (except in the case of murder).

Dwelling a structure in which people normally slept at night.

E

Electronic tracking devices often some form of "beeper" that emits an electronic signal indicating the position of the beeper placed on a moving person or object.

Embezzlement the defendant who was entrusted with possession of the property of another, and then fraudulently converted the property with the intent to deprive another of the property permanently.

Entry an intrusion by any portion of the burglar's body or an instrumentality for purposes of consummating a felony within the dwelling.

Exclusionary rule bars the prosecution from introducing evidence seized in the course of an illegal search or seizure.

Exigent circumstance a situation in which a law enforcement officer confronts "an immediate major crisis in the performance of duty which affords neither time nor opportunity to apply to a magistrate."

Ex post facto laws laws that retroactively make innocent conduct illegal; increase the punishment for a criminal act; or decrease the standard of proof required for a conviction.

Extortion or blackmail threats to injure a person's reputation or to expose a person to shame and ridicule.

Extradition one state surrenders custody of a fugitive who is then transported to another state to face pending charges.

F

Factual cause a prohibited harm would not have occurred when it did in the absence of the defendant's conduct.

Factual guilt a showing that in all probability the defendant committed the alleged crime.

Factual impossibility a claim of defense because the defendant's conduct could not succeed in bringing about the intended offense.

False imprisonment confining a person against the person's will.

False pretenses a false representation of a material fact made with knowledge that the fact is false and with the intent to defraud the victim, thereby causing the victim to pass title to property.

Federal test for insanity uses the *M'Naghten* right-from-wrong standard, but requires that the defendant prove insanity by clear and convincing evidence.

Felony-murder rule applies a first degree murder charge for killing a person intentionally, recklessly, or even accidentally while committing a dangerous felony.

Field sobriety tests physical coordination or mental clarity tasks administered by a police officer to determine whether a person is drunk; includes such tests as touching finger to nose or walking a straight line.

Fighting words words that inflict injury, tend to create a breach of the peace, and are not primarily an expression of ideas protected by free speech.

First appearance before a judicial officer the initial opportunity for a determination of whether to grant the accused pretrial release, and if so, under what conditions.

First degree murder killing often characterized by premeditation.

Freeze the status quo an act to prevent the destruction of evidence until a search warrant can be obtained, which is permitted when the police encounter exigent circumstances.

G

Good faith exception the prosecution may introduce the results of an illegal search, if the police relied in good faith upon a search warrant.

Grand jury a panel of citizens who examine the available evidence and determine whether to indict the accused for a criminal offense.

Grand larceny distinguished from petit larceny by the value of the stolen property.

Guilty but mentally ill verdicts confines the defendant for treatment until such time as the defendant is healthy and able to serve a normal sentence in a penitentiary.

H

Habeas corpus petition not a continuation of the criminal process, but a civil suit brought to challenge the legality of the restraint under which a person is held.

Habitual offenders a person who has been adjudged guilty of drunk driving on a specified number of occasions (more than one).

Harmless error trial error that does not affect the defendant's right to a fair trial, nor does it call into question the accuracy of the finding of guilt.

I

Impeachment of a witness an attempt to discredit the witness's testimony.

Impermissibly suggestive a situation in which the identification procedure gives rise to a substantial likelihood of irreparable misidentification.

Implied consent laws possession of a driver's license mandates voluntary submission to blood, breath, or urine tests; refusal to submit results in a suspension of the defendant's driver's license.

Incest sex between closely related family members.

Inchoate crime an incomplete or imperfect offense.

Inconsistent verdicts the jury convicts the defendant of some charges while acquitting of charges that appear to be interrelated.

Incrimination the Fifth Amendment privilege against self-incrimination applies when a "real danger" that the testimony will lead to the imposition of criminal sanctions is apparent.

Independent discovery the exclusionary rule does not bar evidence obtained by means unrelated to any illegal search.

Indictment a written accusation of crime prepared by the prosecutor and submitted to a grand jury.

Indigent an accused facing prosecution who lacks funds to employ a defense attorney.

Indirect (constructive) contempt not committed in the presence of the court; a hearing must be held before the imposition of punishment.

Ineffective assistance of counsel deficiency of counsel's performance was so serious as to deprive the defendant of a trial with a reliable result.

Inevitable discovery the exclusionary rule does not bar evidence that "ultimately or inevitably would have been discovered by lawful means."

Informant a person who does not appear before a magistrate, but who provides information for the issuance of a search or arrest warrant.

Information a charge drawn up by the prosecutor and not submitted to a grand jury, although it may be screened by a judicial officer at a preliminary hearing.

Innocent human agent one who commits the physical acts constituting a crime, but who is innocent of the crime because of a legitimate defense.

Instantaneous premeditation a view of forethought to the crime that recognizes that "no time is too short for a wicked man to frame in his mind the scheme of murder."

Instructions the trial judge's explanations of the law applicable to the charged offense and the evidence presented at trial.

Instrumentality use of an inanimate object, an animal, or an innocent human being to commit a crime.

Interrogation express questioning and any words or actions on the part of the police that the police should know are reasonably likely to elicit an incriminating response from the suspect.

Investigatory process includes temporary detentions, arrests, searches and seizures, interrogation, and identification procedures as conducted by law enforcement officials.

Involuntary intoxication may be a defense if the defendant did not know of the ingested substance's intoxicating effect, or if someone forced or tricked the defendant into ingesting the intoxicating substance.

Involuntary manslaughter a homicide that results from the defendant's reckless or criminally negligent conduct or the defendant's commission of an unlawful act.

Irresistible impulse test for insanity determines whether the defendant acted from an uncontrollable impulse.

J

Joinder multiple offenses may be charged in a single indictment if the offenses are based on the same act or transaction, or on two or more acts or transactions that are connected or constitute parts of a common scheme or plan.

Joinder of defendants one trial of two or more defendants who participated in related acts.

Joinder of offenses the defendant faces multiple charges at a single trial.

Judicial activism interpretation of the law by judges to achieve broad social goals.

Judicial restraint practiced by judges who view judicial power as strictly limited by the separation of powers doctrine and by earlier case decisions.

Jury nullification occurs when a jury disregards the judge's instructions and returns an acquittal because it sympathizes with the defendant or disagrees with the law.

K

Kidnapping seizing and carrying away another person by force, threat of force, fraud, or deception.

Knock and notice police must announce their presence, identify themselves, and state their purpose ("no knock" warrants dispense with this requirement).

L

Larceny at common law, the trespassory taking and carrying away of the personal property of another with intent to deprive the other of permanent possession.

Legal causation one of the factual causes as the legally significant act that warrants conviction and punishment.

Legal guilt requires that the factual determination of guilt be made in a procedurally correct fashion.

Legal impossibility a claim of defense because the defendant's state of mind precludes commission of a recognized crime.

Legislative intent the purpose for which the legislators enacted a particular statute.

Limiting instruction the trial judge informs the jury that they may consider an item of evidence for only a limited, proper purpose, and not for an improper purpose.

Lineup a suspect is exhibited to a witness in the company of others similar in appearance to the suspect.

M

Malice aforethought distinguishes murder from manslaughter.

Malicious wounding the shooting, stabbing, cutting, or wounding of any person with the intent to maim, disfigure, disable, or kill.

Mayhem a common law in which the victim was dismembered or disfigured in such a way that the victim was less able to engage in self-defense.

Mens rea wrongful state of mind.

Mere preparation portion of an attempted crime prior to the point at which consumation of the offense begins.

Merger a previously distinct offense is subsumed within a greater offense; the defendant can be convicted of either, but not both, offenses.

Misdemeanor committed in the arresting officer's presence the officer has direct personal knowledge, through sight, hearing, or other senses, that a misdemanor is then and there being committed.

Misdemeanor-manslaughter rule applies a manslaughter charge to a homicide that results from the defendant's commission of an unlawful act.

Misprison of a felony failure to report a known crime.

Mistake of law or fact a lack of knowledge of a particular piece of information; which may be a defense if it negates a material element of the offense.

M'Naghten test for insanity determines whether the defendant is able to distinguish right from wrong.

Model Penal Code a suggested guide for enactment and interpretation of criminal law; the Code is not law unless adopted and enacted by a legislature.

Motion to quash the indictment raises objections to the composition of the grand jury or the form of the indictment.

Motion to recuse a request that the judge step down from the case.

Motion to set aside the verdict directed to the trial court and based on the insufficiency of the evidence, error committed during trial, or newly discovered evidence.

Motion to sever offenses asks the court to schedule separate trials for separate offenses.

N

Necessity excuses a violation of criminal law if (1) the defendant reasonably believes the threat of harm is imminent; (2) the only way to prevent the threatened harm is to violate the law; and (3) the harm that will be caused by violating the law is less serious than the harm the defendant seeks to avoid.

Negligence occurs when a person fails to act as a reasonably prudent person under the circumstances.

No knock warrant dispenses with the requirement that police announce their presence before entering a dwelling.

Nolo contendere a plea by which the defendant does not admit guilt but will not contest the prosecution's case.

Notice or petition of appeal begins the appellate process by informing the parties, the trial judge, and the appellate court that the case is being appealed.

O

Objective approach to entrapment focuses on whether the government's conduct in inducing the crime was beyond judicial toleration.

Offer type of assault places another in fear of an imminent battery.

Omission the failure to act when the law imposes a duty to act.

Omnibus Crime Control and Safe Streets Act a regulatory scheme aimed at wiretapping and eavesdropping.

Open fields not protected by the Fourth Amendment because a person has no reasonable expectation of privacy in areas open to public view.

Opening statements of counsel alert the jury to what the attorney expects the evidence to be and how that evidence proves the case.

Overt act for an attempted crime a substantial step toward commission of the intended offense.

Overt act for a conspiracy an act committed in furtherance of a conspiracy.

P

Pardon or grant of clemency forgiveness of a conviction granted by an official of the executive branch—normally, the governor at the state level and the president at the federal level.

Pen register records the numbers dialed on a telephone by monitoring electrical impulses, but does not overhear conversations.

Per curiam opinion court decision not attributed to an individual judge, but represents the court as a whole.

Peremptory challenge may be used to strike any potential juror without stating a reason.

Perfecting the charge the charge must plainly and concisely name the accused, describe the offense charged, identify the place where the accused committed the offense, and recite that the accused committed the offense on or about a certain date.

Permissive inference a possible conclusion that may be drawn but is not exclusively required if certain predicate facts are proved.

Perpetrator (principal in the first degree) one who performs the physical acts that constitute the offense or commits the offense by use of an instrumentality.

Photographic array photographs of several potential suspects are shown to a witness.

Photographic showup a picture of a single suspect is shown to a witness.

Pinkerton doctrine each member of a conspiracy is criminally responsible for any crime committed by another party to the agreement as long as the committed crime was the object of the conspiracy or a natural consequence of the unlawful agreement.

Plain view doctrine the police may seize items not specified in a search warrant if they discover such items while conducting a valid search.

Plea agreement the prosecution and the defense agree on the defendant's guilt and the sentence to be recommended by the prosecutor or imposed by the court.

Police power the government's broad authority to advance public health, safety, morality, and welfare.

Polling the jury inquiring of each juror in open court, "Is this your verdict?" Each juror must reply in the affirmative or negative.

Possession (of property) the right to use personal property in a reasonably unrestricted manner.

Possession with intent to distribute a purposeful plan to sell or provide the drug to others.

Preliminary hearing a determination of whether sufficient evidence exists to proceed further in the criminal justice process by bringing the defendant to trial.

Premeditation careful, prior deliberation of an act committed in cold blood.

Preponderance of the evidence the standard of proof often required to establish an affirmative defense; asks the jury to determine whether an accused has established the reasonable likelihood of the defense.

Presentence reports prepared statements that inform the sentencing body of the defendant's background and the circumstances of the offense.

Presentment an acquisition of crime drawn up at the grand jury's initiative.

Presumption a fact that must be inferred (presumed) on the basis of certain predicate facts that have been proved.

Pretrial discovery the process of exchanging information between the prosecution and the defense.

Pretrial motions requests made to a court asking the court to take some action such as dismissing a defective indictment or ordering the parties to disclose certain information.

Prima facie case evidence that could lead to a conviction if the defense does not rebut it at trial.

Prima facie evidence requires that the defendant offer some plausible evidence of the defendant's claim.

Principal in the first degree (perpetrator) the person who performs the physical acts that constitute the offense or commits the offense by use of an instrumentality.

Principal in the second degree (aider and abettor) one who assists the perpetrator in the commission of the crime while being actually or constructively present at the scene of the crime.

Privilege for attorney–client communications protects the confidentiality of counsel's discussions with a defendant.

Probable cause to arrest a reasonable belief that the suspect committed a crime.

Probable cause to bind the accused over for trial the level of proof required at a preliminary hearing; often equated with probable cause to arrest.

Probable cause to search a reasonable belief that seizable items will be found in a particular place at the time that the search is to be conducted; a flexible standard identified by balancing the degree of intrusion upon individual privacy against the importance of the government purpose to be served by the intrusion.

Probation releases the defendant from custody subject to the condition that the defendant behave in an approved manner, and subject to any other specific conditions imposed by the court.

Proceed pro se a criminal defendant waives counsel and chooses self-representation.

Proffer of evidence a stipulation or testimony as to what the offered evidence would have been if the trial judge had ruled it admissible.

Proof beyond a reasonable doubt often defined as proof that excludes every reasonable hypothesis except guilt; proof that excludes every reasonable possibility of innocence; or proof to a moral certainty.

Protective sweep a cursory and limited search for weapons within the area under the suspect's immediate control.

Public intoxication presence in a public place in a drunken state, which may be a form of disorderly conduct or covered by a specific statute.

Public safety exception the police may ask questions "reasonably prompted by a concern for the public safety."

Public trial a trial open to observation by all members of the public.

Purging the grand jury the process of narrowing down the number of qualified grand jurors to the number of jurors who will actually serve.

R

Rape at common law, sexual intercourse with a woman other than the defendant's wife by force and without the victim's consent.

Rape shield laws prohibit use of evidence of victim's prior sexual conduct, except for prior consensual sexual relations with the defendant.

Real evidence physical objects introduced at trial, most often those discovered at the scene of the crime.

Reasonable perception theory the defendant acts upon a perception that the aided person has a right to use defensive force, even when the perception is erroneous.

Reasonable suspicion the required basis for a temporary detention; the suspect has committed or is committing a crime.

Reasonableness clause "the right of the people to be secure in their persons, houses, papers, and effects, against unreasonable searches and seizures."

Reasonably prudent person standard measures the defendant's actual conduct against that of a reasonably prudent person under the same or similar circumstances.

Receiving stolen property exercising control over property that has been stolen with knowledge of its stolen nature and with intent to deprive the owner of the property.

Recklessness (criminal negligence) the defendant's deviation from reasonable conduct is excessive or more than simple (noncriminal) negligence.

Recognizance the accused's unsecured promise to appear at proceedings leading up to and including trial.

Recommendation plea agreement provides for a sentencing recommendation from the prosecution, but is not binding on the judge.

Retreat an avenue of safe escape; a prerequisite to self-defense in some jurisdictions.

Right to a speedy trial guaranteed by the Sixth Amendment to the U.S. Constitution. (Statutes often specify exact time periods within which a criminal prosecution must begin.)

Riot at least one member of an unlawful assembly threatens or commits an act of violence.

Robbery larceny from the victim's person or presence by use of either force or threats of force.

Runaway grand jury a grand jury that launches its own investigation and returns charges not requested by the prosecutor.

S

Search a government official's intrusion upon a defendant's subjective expectation of privacy; and the expectation is one that society is prepared to recognize as reasonable.

Search incident to arrest must be substantially contemporaneous with a lawful arrest.

Second degree murder killing with a state of mind characterized as a wanton or an extremely reckless disregard for the risk to human life.

Self-defense actions in a situation in which (1) the defendant was not the aggressor; (2) the defendant reasonably perceived an immediate threat of bodily harm; (3) the defendant reasonably believed that defensive force was necessary to avoid the harm; and (4) the amount of defensive force used was reasonable.

Separate sovereigns an exception to the prohibition against double jeopardy; different jurisdictions may impose punishment for the same offense.

Showup a single suspect is exhibited to a witness.

Simple negligence occurs when a person fails to act as a reasonably prudent person under the circumstances.

Sodomy "a crime against nature"; "any sexual intercourse held to be abnormal, especially bestiality or anal intercourse."

Solicitation occurs when a person invites or requests another to commit a crime.

Specific intent the defendant subjectively intends or desires to bring about the prohibited social harm.

Standing the defendant must be "a victim of the search or seizure"; the defendant's personal right to privacy was violated.

Statutes of limitations specify the length of time permitted between the commission of a crime and the initiation of prosecution.

Stop and frisk (temporary detention) police briefly detain the suspect and pat down the suspect's outer clothing to determine if the suspect possesses a weapon.

Strict liability crime the defendant commits an act that causes a prohibited harm, regardless of the defendant's state of mind or reasonableness of actions.

Subjective approach to entrapment prohibits police officers from instigating criminal acts by people not predisposed to commit the crime.

Subpoena duces tecum a command to a person to produce writings or objects described in the subpoena.

Summons commands the accused to appear at a stated time and place before a court of appropriate jurisdiction.

Surety one who posts bond on behalf of the accused.

T

Temporary detention the suspect is detained briefly, at which time an officer may pat down the suspect's clothing to determine whether the suspect possesses a weapon.

Testimonial immunity (use immunity) does not prohibit a subsequent prosecution, but bars the use of the compelled testimony or any evidence derived from the testimony.

Third-party consent to search permission to search given by one who shares use, access, or control of the defendant's property or premises.

Title III of the Omnibus Crime Control and Safe Streets Act a regulatory scheme governing wiretapping and eavesdropping.

Tolling the statute of limitations the statute ceases to run under certain conditions, most commonly while the accused is fleeing from justice.

Totality of circumstances facts that establish a fair probability that seizable items will be found in a particular place.

Transactional immunity prohibits the trial of an individual for any offense about which the individual testifies.

Transferred intent the act of killing a person while intending to kill someone else.

Trespass taking possession of another's personal property without consent or legal justification.

Trial de novo a new trial, not an appeal of the lower court's conviction.

Trial in absentia a trial that proceeds without the defendant being present.

U

Unlawful assembly a gathering of a designated number of persons (three at common law) for any purpose or under circumstances endangering the public peace.

Ultimate issue the question of whether the defendant is guilty or not guilty of the charge.

Unlawful assembly a gathering of a designated number of persons (three at common law) for any unlawful purpose or under circumstances endangering the public peace.

V

Vagueness doctrine holds any statute unconstitutional when citizens "must necessarily guess at its meaning and differ as to its application."

Venue the place where the trial is held.

Voir dire the process in which defense and prosecution examine the panel of prospective jurors and select the jurors who will actually serve at trial.

Voluntary confession a statement of guilt, which is "the product of an essentially free and unconstrained choice by its maker."

Voluntary intoxication may be a defense if it produces clouded mental faculties that negate the mental state required for a particular crime.

Voluntary manslaughter killing while in a state of passion, which was caused by adequate provocation, and without a reasonable opportunity to cool off before killing.

W

Waiver of the right to remain silent a suspect "voluntarily, knowingly, and intelligently" gives up the right not to answer law enforcement officers' questions.

Wanton state of mind extremely reckless disregard of the safety of others, or of other prohibited consequences.

Warrant clause "no warrant shall issue, but upon probable cause, supported by oath or affirmation, and particularly describing the place to be searched, and the person or things to be seized."

Warrantless felony arrest taking a suspected felon into custody, which may take place in a public place even though the police had adequate opportunity to procure an arrest warrant.

Wharton's rule states that no conspiracy has occured in an agreement between only the parties necessary for the commission of a substantive offense.

Willful state of mind actual knowledge of the threat to another's safety, or of other prohibited consequences.

Index